RUSSIA
PEOPLE AND EMPIRE

RUSSIA

PEOPLE AND EMPIRE
1552–1917

Geoffrey Hosking

HarperCollinsPublishers

HarperCollins*Publishers*
77–85 Fulham Palace Road,
Hammersmith, London w6 8jb

Published by HarperCollins*Publishers* 1997
3 5 7 9 8 6 4 2

A catalogue record for this book is
available from the British Library

ISBN 0 00 255536-0

Maps by John Gilkes

Set in Postscript Linotype Janson
Rowland Phototypesetting Ltd,
Bury St Edmunds, Suffolk

Printed and bound in Great Britain by
Caledonian International Book Manufacturing Ltd, Glasgow

Contents

PART 4 *Imperial Russia under pressure*

MAPS

The Expansion of Muscovy in the 16th and 17th centuries

North Sea

NORWAY

DENMARK

SWEDEN

Barents Sea

Novaya Zemlya

Kara Sea

Stockholm

Baltic Sea

Riga
PRUSSIA
LIVONIA

Warsaw

W. Dvina

Vistula

POLAND-
LITHUANIA

Smolensk

BELORUSSIA

Kiev

UKRAINE

Dnepr

Dnestr

L. Ladoga

L. Onega

Archangel

N. Dvina

Volga

Moscow

Yaroslavl

RUSSIA

Oka

Voronezh

Kazan

Kama

Ural Mountains

Ob

Don

Saratov

Volga

Ufa

Tobolsk
Sibir

Azov

Tsaritsyn

Tobol

Tara

Tomsk

Black
Sea

Astrakhan

Kuzhetsk

Irtysh

OTTOMAN
EMPIRE

Aral Sea

Caspian
Sea

PERSIA

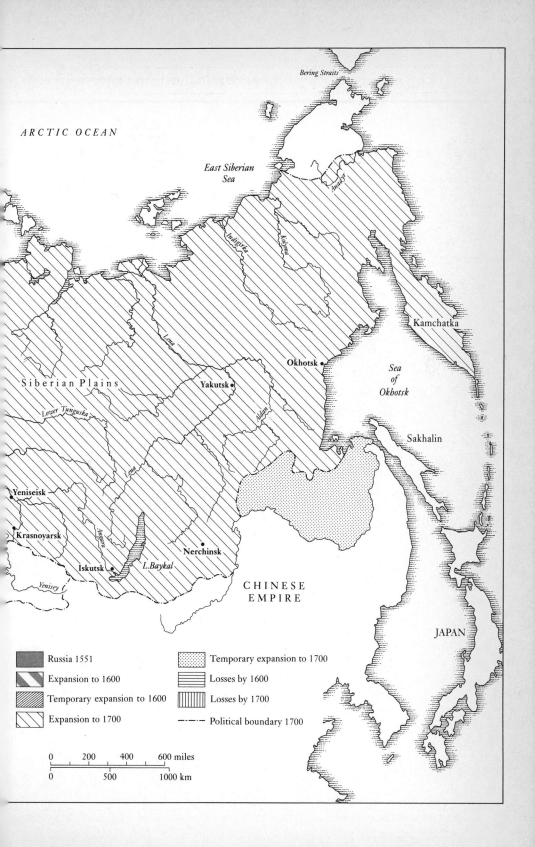

ARCTIC OCEAN

Bering Straits

East Siberian Sea

Anadyr

Indigirka

Kolyma

Kamchatka

Lena

Okhotsk

Yakutsk

Sea of Okhotsk

Siberian Plains

Lower Tunguska

Aldan

Sakhalin

Yeniseisk

Lena

Krasnoyarsk

Angara

Nerchinsk

Iskutsk

L.Baykal

CHINESE EMPIRE

Yenisey

JAPAN

Russia 1551	Temporary expansion to 1700
Expansion to 1600	Losses by 1600
Temporary expansion to 1600	Losses by 1700
Expansion to 1700	Political boundary 1700

0   200   400   600 miles

0   500   1000 km

SWEDEN

FINLAND

Baltic Sea

ESTONIA

LIVONIA

Mittau • • Riga

COURLAND

L. Onega

L. Ladoga

St.Petersburg

Ustyug •

PRUSSIA

Vistula

Warsaw •

LITHUANIA

W. Dvina

• Pskov

• Novgorod

• Minsk

• Smolensk

Volga

Yaroslavl •

Perm •

Kama

POLAND

Pripet

• Moscow

Nizhniy

Novgorod

Kazan •

AUSTRIA

VOLHYNIA

Dniester

• Kiev

UKRAINE

Ryazan •

R U S S I A N E M P I R E

Ufa •

• Samara

• Kharkov

Saratov •

Don

Volga

Odessa • • Ochakov

• Zaporozhye

Orenburg •

Lletskaya

Zaschita

Taganrog •

• Cherkassk

CRIMEA

Sevastopol •

Sea of Azov

• Azov

Tsaritsyn •

Ural (Yaik)

Black Sea

• Constantinople

Astrakhan •

Terek

O T T O M A N   E M P I R E

Caucasus Mountains

GEORGIA

• Derbent

• Baku

Caspian Sea

PERSIA

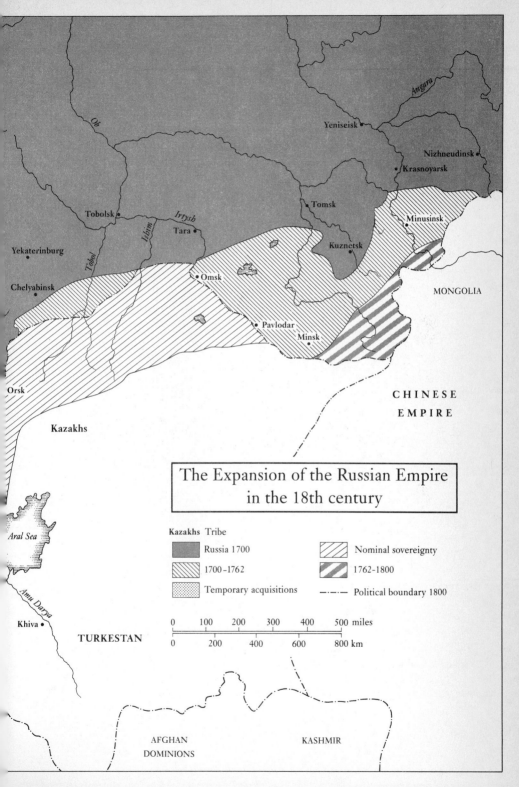

The Expansion of the Russian Empire
in the 18th century

Kazakhs Tribe

Russia 1700

1700–1762

Temporary acquisitions

Nominal sovereignty

1762–1800

—·—·— Political boundary 1800

| 0 | 100 | 200 | 300 | 400 | 500 miles |
| 0 | 200 | 400 | 600 | 800 km |

Yeniseisk

Nizhneudinsk
Krasnoyarsk

Ob

Tomsk

Tobolsk
Irtysh
Tara

Minusinsk

Yekaterinburg
Ishim
Kuznetsk

Chelyabinsk
Tobol

Omsk

MONGOLIA

Orsk

Pavlodar
Minsk

CHINESE
EMPIRE

Kazakhs

Aral Sea

Amu Darya

Khiva

TURKESTAN

AFGHAN
DOMINIONS

KASHMIR

Russian Expansion under Catherine the Great

The Provinces of Russia 1750

Territory annexed by Russia in 1762-1796, giving Russia an outlet on the Black Sea, and a common frontier with Prussia and Austria

FINLAND

Archangel

ARCHANGEL

Helsingfors

ST. PETERSBURG

ESTONIA

LIVONIA

Pskov

NOVGOROD

Novgorod

Vologda

Viatka

Perm

KAZAN

KURLAND

Niemen

Vilna

Tver

MOSCOW

NIZHNI NOVGOROD

Kazan

Ufa

UFA

PRUSSIA

LITHUANIA

Minsk

SMOLENSK

Moscow

Warsaw

WHITE RUSSIA

Pinsk

Stavropol

Samara

AUSTRIA

PODLESIA

Lutsk

KIEV

Orel

BELGOROD

VORONEZH

Jassy

Kiev

Dnieper

Belgorod

ASTRAKHAN

PODOLIA

ZAPOROZHE

Dniester

Odessa

Taganrog

Astrakhan

Kutchuk
Kainardji

CRIMEA

Sebastopol

KUBAN

KABARDA

Tarki

Caspian
Sea

Black Sea

THE

Constantinople

Kars

OTTOMAN

EMPIRE

PERSIA

| 0 | 100 | 200 | 300 miles |
| 0 | 250 | 500 km |

Russia at its Greatest Extent

North
Sea

NORWAY

SWEDEN

Stockholm

Berlin •

Baltic Sea

Barents
Sea

Novaya
Zemlya

Kara
Sea

Riga •

W.Dvina

L.Ladoga *L.Onega*

N.Dvina

Archangel

Ob

Ural Mountains

Vienna •

Warsaw •

Vistula

Budapest •

Smolensk •

Moscow •

Yaroslavl •

Volga

Oka

Kiev •

Dnieper

Dniester

Kazan •

Kama

Voronezh •

Bucharest •

Odessa •

Saratov •

Volga

Ufa •

Tobolsk •
Sibir •

Tobol

Tara •

Constantinople •

Don

Azov •

Tsaritsyn •

Irtish

Black
Sea

Astrakhan •

KAZAKHSTAN

OTTOMAN EMPIRE

Aral Sea

Caspian
Sea

TURKESTAN

Tehran •

PERSIA

AFGHANISTAN

Kabul
•

INDIA

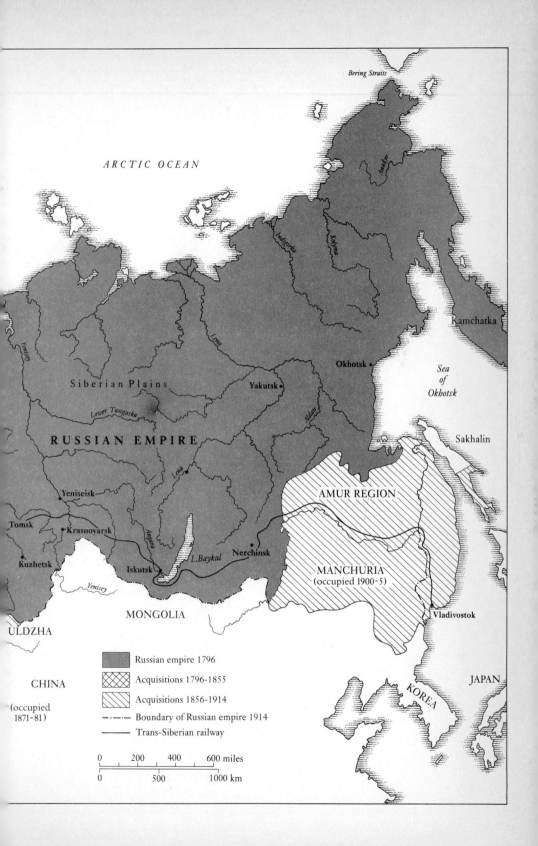

ARCTIC OCEAN

Bering Straits

Kamchatka

Indigirka

Kolyma

Anadir

Okhotsk •

Sea
of
Okhotsk

Siberian Plains

Yakutsk •

Lower Tunguska

Lena

Aldan

RUSSIAN EMPIRE

Sakhalin

Yeniseisk •

Lena

AMUR REGION

Tomsk •

• Krasnoyarsk

Angara

Kuzhetsk •

Iskutsk •

L.Baykal

Nerchinsk •

MANCHURIA
(occupied 1900-5)

Yenisey

MONGOLIA

Vladivostok •

ULDZHA

CHINA

KOREA

JAPAN

(occupied
1871-81)

	Russian empire 1796
	Acquisitions 1796-1855
	Acquisitions 1856-1914
–·–·–	Boundary of Russian empire 1914
——	Trans-Siberian railway

0   200   400   600 miles

0   500   1000 km

Acknowledgements

In writing such a long and ambitious work, one inevitably contracts more debts than can possibly be acknowledged. The History Department of Baylor University, Waco, Texas, encouraged me to set down my preliminary hypotheses and to deliver them in the form of the Charles Edmondson Memorial Lectures in 1992. The School of Slavonic & East European Studies of London University allowed me two periods of study leave, in 1992 and 1994, during which much of the actual writing was done; and colleagues in the History Department offered me constant support and interest, in the form of a 'work in progress' seminar and in other ways. The following read all or part of an earlier draft: Edward Acton, Roger Bartlett, Pete Duncan, Mark von Hagen, Lindsey Hughes, Dominic Lieven, David Morton, Bob Service. I am most grateful to them for saving me from a good many errors and misconceptions: those which remain are my responsibility. I have also benefited greatly from conversations with the late Ernest Gellner, Simon Dixon, Leopold Haimson and Andreas Kappeler.

Lena Nemirovskaia and Yurii Senokosov offered generous hospitality and a continual flow of ideas whenever I was in Moscow. Stuart Proffitt, of HarperCollins, and Murray Pollinger, my literary agent, continued to support me during long periods when it looked as if this book would never be written. My wife, Anne, and my daughters, Katya and Janet, had even more cause to think the same, but managed to keep me going.

GEOFFREY HOSKING
School of Slavonic & East European Studies
University of London

April 1996

Introduction

Rus' was the victim of *Rossiia*
Georgii Gachev

If this book were in Russian, the title would contain two distinct epithets: *russkii* for the people and *rossiiskii* for the empire. The first derives from *Rus'*, the word customarily employed to denote the Kievan state and the Muscovite one in its early years. The second comes from *Rossiia*, a Latinized version probably first used in Poland, which penetrated to Muscovy in the sixteenth century and became common currency in the seventeenth – precisely during the time when the empire was being founded and extended.[1]

In that way the Russian language reflects the fact that there are two kinds of Russianness, one connected with the people, the language and the pre-imperial principalities, the other with the territory, the multi-national empire, the European great power. Usage is not absolutely consistent, but any Russian will acknowledge that there is a considerable difference in tonality and association between the two words. *Rus'* is humble, homely, sacred and definitely feminine (the poet Alexander Blok called her 'my mother'); *Rossiia* grandiose, cosmopolitan, secular and, *pace* grammarians, masculine. The culturologist Georgii Gachev has dramatized the distinction: '*Rossiia* is the fate of *Rus'*. *Rossiia* is attraction, ideal and service – but also abyss and perdition. *Rossiia* uprooted the Russian people, enticed them away from *Rus'*, transformed the peasant into a soldier, an organiser, a boss, but no longer a husbandman.'[2]

The theme of this book is how *Rossiia* obstructed the flowering of *Rus'*, or if you prefer it, how the building of an empire impeded the formation of a nation. So my story concerns above all the Russians. There have been many books in recent years about the non-Russian peoples of the empire, and the problems of their national development.[3] It is time to redress the balance in favour of the Russians, whose nationhood has probably been even more blighted by the empire which bore their name.

Russians, especially in the nineteenth century, have always believed that their distinctiveness – some saw it as their curse – derived from an underlying problem of national identity, but few western historians have taken the notion seriously, preferring to dismiss the Russian obsession with the national problem as an excuse for imperial domination or reactionary politics. I believe the Russians are right, and that a fractured and underdeveloped nationhood has been their principal historical burden in the last two centuries or so, continuing throughout the period of the Soviet Union and persisting beyond its fall. Such an assertion may surprise Russia's neighbours, who are accustomed to regard Russian nationalism as overdeveloped and domineering. This is an understandable optical illusion, but an illusion nevertheless, as I shall try to demonstrate.

Social scientists have been reluctant to define the term 'nation', and indeed, whenever the attempt is made, there invariably turn out to be one or two anomalous 'nations' which do not fit the definition. I shall nevertheless try to pin the notion down. A nation, it seems to me, is a large, territorially extended and socially differentiated aggregate of people who share a sense of a common fate or of belonging together, which we call nationhood.

Nationhood has two main aspects. One is civic: a nation is a participating citizenry, participating in the sense of being involved in law-making, law-adjudication and government, through elected central and local assemblies, through courts and tribunals, and also as members of political parties, interest groups, voluntary associations and other institutions of civil society. The second aspect of nationhood is ethnic: a nation is a community bound together by sharing a common language, culture, traditions, history, economy and territory. In some nations, for historical reasons, one aspect predominates over the other: the French, Swiss and American nations are primarily 'civic', while the German and East European nations have tended to emphasize ethnicity.[4] I believe that both aspects of Russians' nationhood have been gravely impaired by the way in which their empire evolved.

Would it have been better for Russians if they had been able to form a nation? I believe it would have made their evolution less unstable, polarized and violent, especially during the nineteenth and twentieth centuries. The nation-state has proved to be the most effective political unit during that time, not only in Europe but throughout the world, because it is the largest one compatible with creating and sustaining a feeling of community and solidarity, such as induces loyalty and reduces the need for coercion. National identity plays an important compensatory role in a period when the operations of the market have tended to break down older, smaller and simpler forms of social solidarity. In an era of large-scale warfare it is even more crucial, as Charles Tilly has commented:

> Because of their advantages in translating national resources into success in international war, large national states super-seded tribute-taking empires, federations, city-states and all their other competitors as the predominant European politi-cal entities and as the models for state formation. Those states finally defined the character of the European state system and spearheaded its extension to the entire world.[5]

Empires, by contrast, proved to be too large, unwieldy and above all too diverse to generate an equivalent sense of community. That proved to be true of the Hapsburg and Ottoman as well as the Russian Empires.

There is, however, such a thing as compound national identity. Britain in the eighteenth–twentieth century is a good example, rest-ing as it does on four ethnic components: the English, Welsh, Scot-tish and Irish. The Irish, being the least well integrated of the four, have provoked easily the most serious internal crises of the British political system during that time. The great question for Russian leaders during the nineteenth and twentieth centuries might be for-mulated as whether they could inculcate an analogous compound national identity in their empire's more diverse ethnic elements. The attempt was made, both by the Tsars and more systematically by the Soviet leaders, and at one time it looked close to success, but at present it seems ultimately to have failed.

There has been much debate among historians, sociologists and anthropologists over the origins of modern nationhood. Today many theorists would assert that nations are not very old, that they emerged only from the late eighteenth century onwards. In this view what distinguishes them from earlier forms of human community are that:

1. Nations are larger, more socially and economically diverse, offering a framework for the capitalist market, with its complex division of labour and its need for more extensive units than were afforded by regional and kinship boundaries.

2. They embody the Enlightenment vision of the rational and self-governing human being: the nation-state is a community of such people.

3. They are bound together by the printed language, which is needed so that the skills of a high culture can be widely disseminated. The bearers and purveyors of this language, writers, journalists, teachers and the professional strata in general, are those who are likely to identify most closely with the nation-state.

4. They are based on the principle that ethnic and political boundaries coincide. Lower-level entities, duchies, principalities, city-states, and so on, have been amalgamated, while higher-level ones, multi-ethnic empires, have been broken up. This has proved the most contentious and destructive of the characteristics of nations, yet also the hardest to dispense with in practice.[6]

In this view, nations evolved only with the growth of widespread education, mass media, a diversified economy and social structure, a penetrative urban culture and a civil society. This is when, in the terminology of Karl Deutsch, 'assimilation' (to a dominant urban language and culture) and 'mobilization' (into a multiplicity of contacts with others) became possible for the mass of the people. The extreme version of this position has been expounded by Ernest Gellner who denies that nationalism is simply the political manifestation of age-old national communities, and asserts roundly; 'It is nationalism which engenders nations, and not the other way round.' He adds, 'Nationalism is *not* the awakening of an old, latent, dormant force, though that is indeed how it presents itself. It is in reality the consequence of a new form of social organisation, based on deeply internalised, education-dependent high cultures, each protected by its own state.'[7]

It is possible to accept that nations as we know them are products of the modern era, and yet to assert that, in a simpler and cruder form, an ethnic or proto-national awareness straddling different social strata existed much earlier in history. Such awareness can crystallize around a tribe, a royal court, an aristocracy, an armed fraternity or a religious sect. It can be stimulated by various factors, of which probably the most potent is prolonged warfare against powerful neighbours. One theorist, John Armstrong, has specifically taken as an example the national identity of *Rus'* during and after the Tatar overlordship.[8]

If nations do indeed have a pre-history, then the crucial question is why and when they emerge from the chrysalis. Benedict Anderson has hypothesized that the stage is set with the 'convergence of capitalism and print technology' and the emergence of monarchical bureaucracies: these 'create unified fields of exchange and communication below Latin and above the spoken vernaculars' and 'give a new fixity to language', helping to 'build that image of antiquity so central to the subjective idea of the nation'.[9]

In this reading, the central issue is language and the culture and information carried by language, which enable courtiers, intellectuals and bureaucrats to synthesize and project their concept of what binds the nation together. Eric Hobsbawm and Terence Ranger called this process, or a later version of it, the 'invention of tradition', the tactic by which elites, faced with the crises of social change, overcome them by invoking values and rituals associated with the past, adapting them to suit contemporary means of communication. Thus British royal pageantry was recreated to suit the needs first of newspapers, then of radio, then of television. These values and rituals need not of course be national ones, but experience has taught modern politicians that appeals to nationhood have the broadest and strongest allure.[10] They perform the function of binding elites and masses in a common identity.

Actually, traditions cannot be simply invented: they must have existed in some form in which they can be authenticated. They then have to be rediscovered and synthesized in a form suitable for the contemporary world. The process by which this is done has been examined by Miroslav Hroch. He posits three stages through which all nations pass, though they are chronologically different for each nation. The first, which he calls phase A, is the period of scholarly interest, when linguists, ethnographers and historians investigate the lore and traditions of the people and assemble from them a cultural package suitable for wider distribution. Phase B is the stage when politicians take from this package what they find useful and deploy it for patriotic agitation among the people, and it leads on to Phase C, which is the rise of mass national movements. In each case Hroch finds a particular social group – again different from nation to nation – which plays a central role in the mobilization of national sentiment.[11] Strictly speaking, his theory applies only to nations mobilizing *against* the state in which they find themselves, but I shall maintain that it is relevant to Russia, since there too nationhood had to be generated partly in opposition to the empire bearing its name.

This 'nation-building' is quite distinct from 'state-building', though the tantology processes are easier to accomplish when they accompany each other. State-building is concerned with defending, controlling and administering a given territory and the population living on it, and entails devising and operating a system for recruiting troops and raising taxes to pay for them, as well as matters like conflict regulation, the imposition and adjudication of law, the establishment of a reliable coinage, and so on. Nation-building is more intangible, but has to do with eliciting the loyalty and commitment of the population, which is usually achieved by fostering the sense of belonging, often by manipulation of culture, history and symbolism.[12]

The thesis of this book is that in Russia state-building obstructed nation-building. The effort required to mobilize revenues and raise armies for the needs of the empire entailed the subjection of virtually the whole population, but especially the Russians, to the demands of state service, and thus enfeebled the creation of the community associations which commonly provide the basis for the civic sense of nationhood. As the nineteenth-century Russian historian Vasily Kliuchevskii once remarked, 'The state swelled up, the people languished.'[13]

State-building also necessitated the borrowing of a foreign culture and ethos, which displaced the native inheritance. A potential national identity had already been created for Russia by the 'invention of tradition' in the sixteenth century, and it served as impetus and justification for the first stages of empire-building; but it was suddenly repudiated by the imperial state itself in the mid-seventeenth century in circumstances which I examine in Part 2, Chapter 1. This repudiation generated a rift within Russia's ethnic community whose consequences have not been entirely eradicated even today.

In his recent study of national identity, Anthony Smith distinguishes between two types of nation-building. The first is accomplished by what he calls 'aristocratic' ethnies ('ethnie' is his term for a proto-nation). They command the mechanism of the state, and so are able to carry out nation-building by using its resources, as well as by economic and cultural patronage. In this way, they assimilate lower social classes and outlying ethnic groups to their heritage. This was the historical path to the nation-state taken by England, France, Spain, Sweden and, up to the eighteenth century, Poland.

The second type of nation-building, which Smith terms 'demotic', proceeds from non-aristocratic, localized, often subject communities. Lacking their own state, they have to build the elements of one from below, in opposition to some existing state: to accomplish this they need strongly held views of law, religion, culture and community. Examples of this kind are the Irish, Czechs, Finns, Jews, Armenians and the Poles in the nineteenth and twentieth centuries.[14]

In the case of Russia, we may hypothesize that both types of nation-building were at work concurrently, with the conflict between them reaching special intensity in the late nineteenth and early twentieth century. There were two poles round which Russian national feeling could crystallize. One was the imperial court, army and bureaucracy, with its attendant nobility and increasingly Europeanized culture. The other was the peasant community. Peasants cannot lead a nationalist movement, but they can provide a model for it and, given leadership from outside, they can become its numerical strength. The values of village communities have inspired many politicians in the assertion of their nation's identity against alien domination: one has only to think of Gandhi, Mao Zedong and many East European politicians after the first world war. In Russia it was the intelligentsia, drawing on imperial culture but trying to break away from it, which provided this leadership.

During the eighteenth and nineteenth centuries, the notions of authority, culture and community held by the imperial nobility and by the peasantry were diametrically opposed on cardinal points. We may lay out the dichotomy roughly as follows:

NOBILITY	PEASANTRY
Hierarchical	Egalitarian
Held together by subordination	Held together by mutual responsibility
Cosmopolitan	Parochial
Oriented to state service	Oriented to survival
Land seen as private property	Land seen as communal resource

The contrast between these views of community was not absolute. Both sides, for example, shared the feeling of reverence for the Tsar and, on the whole, for the Orthodox Church. At times of supreme crisis, like the Napoleonic invasion, the two sides could work together. Nevertheless, the gap between them was very wide and, what was more important, getting wider during the eighteenth and most of the nineteenth century, as the crisis of nation-building approached its apogee.

The result was that the two Russias weakened each other. The political, economic and cultural institutions of what might have become the Russian nation were destroyed or emasculated for the needs of the empire, while the state was enfeebled by the hollowness of its ethnic substance, its inability at most times to attract the deep loyalty of even its Russian, let alone its non-Russian subjects. The intelligentsia, trying to mediate between them, to create an 'imagined community' as a synthesis of imperial culture and ethnic community, was crushed between them. The culmination of this process was the revolution and civil war of 1917–21.

This book has been written in the belief that we need a new interpretive approach to the history of Russia. Most western accounts of Russia's evolution revolve around the concepts of 'autocracy' and 'backwardness'. In my view, neither of them is a fundamental or ineluctable factor. Autocracy, I shall argue, was generated by the needs of empire, and had to be reinforced as that empire came increasingly into conflict with nation-building.

The same is true of backwardness. What is striking is not that Russia was economically backward in either the sixteenth, eighteenth or early twentieth century, but rather that every attempt at reform and modernization tended in the long run to reproduce that backwardness. As the history of Germany, Japan and modern south-east Asia shows, backwardness can be not only escaped from but triumphantly overcome and turned to competitive advantage. Russia did not do this: the economic policies deemed necessary to sustain the empire systematically held back the entrepreneurial and productive potentialities of the mass of the people.

In my view, then, autocracy and backwardness were symptoms and not causes: both were generated by the way in which the building and maintaining of empire obstructed the formation of a nation. I deploy the evidence for this assertion in what follows.

If I am right, the implications for contemporary Russia are profound. If she can find a new identity for herself, as a nation-state among other nation-states, autocracy and backwardness will fade out. It may perhaps be objected that the nation-state is not the be-all and end-all of history, and that we are moving into a post-national era.[15] In particular, in the case of Russia, it may be argued that the relatively low level of virulent nationalism has spared the collapsing Soviet empire the spasms of violence which accompanied, for example, the departure of the French *pieds noirs* from Algeria. (There has been considerable violence, but most of it has been directed by non-Russians against other non-Russians.)

There is something to be said for these arguments, but I believe the nation-state is likely to be with us for a long time yet as the foundation of the international order, and that in Russia the sense of solidarity associated with nationhood would do much to diminish the criminality and the bitter political conflicts which still disfigure its internal order. I do not pretend, of course, that the process of strengthening national identity in Russia can be wholly reassuring either for her neighbours or for the international community at large. But I believe it is preferable to any attempt at rebuilding empire, which I take to be the only serious alternative.

A word about the structure of this book. I decided at an early stage that a purely chronological exposition would obscure permanent or long-lasting features of Russian society – what one might call its 'deep structures' – to such an extent as to undermine the presentation of my overall thesis. I have therefore made Parts 1 and 3 structural, and Parts 2 and 4 chronological. Part 1 examines why a Russian Empire arose at all and what were its abiding features, Part 3 its effects on the major social strata and institutions of Russian society. Parts 2 and 4 adopt a more familiar kind of historical narrative. I hope that the accompanying Chronology (pp. 487–492), Index and occasional cross-references will make it easier to understand the way the sections relate to each other.

For the present, I have ended my study in 1917. After that year the problem of the relationship between Russians and their empire certainly remained crucial, but its terms changed radically, as is symbolized by the bare fact that the empire was no longer named after them. If life and energy persist, perhaps I shall one day try to trace that story too. For the moment, I have confined myself to a few preliminary thoughts on the way my story has affected the Soviet and post-Soviet experience.

GEOFFREY HOSKING,
School of Slavonic & East European Studies,
University of London.

April 1996

PART ONE

The Russian Empire: How and Why?

The Russian Empire:
How and Why?

A. The Theory of Empire

'With the aid of our Almighty Lord Jesus Christ and the prayers of the Mother of God ... our pious Tsar and Grand Prince Ivan Vasilievich, crowned by God, Autocrat of all *Rus'*, fought against the infidels, defeated them finally and captured the Tsar of Kazan' Edigei-Mahmet. And the pious Tsar and Grand Prince ordered his regiment to sing an anthem under his banner, to give thanks to God for the victory; and at the same time ordered a life-giving cross to be placed and a church to be built, with the uncreated image of our Lord Jesus Christ, where the Tsar's colours had stood during the battle.'[1]

Thus the official chronicle recorded the moment in October 1552 when Muscovy set out on its career of empire by conquering and annexing for the first time a non-Russian sovereign state, the Khanate of Kazan'. Muscovite Rus' was already a multi-national state, since it included within its borders some Tatars, as well as Finno-Ugrian tribes, but the conquest of Kazan' signified a new approach to relations with its neighbours. Rus' had embarked on a course of conquest and expansion which was to last for more than three centuries and create the largest and most diverse territorial empire the world has ever seen.[2]

The chronicle emphasizes the religious motives for the Kazan' campaign. But there were many others. One of them was quite simply the longing for security, a terrible problem for an agricultural realm whose eastern and southern frontiers lay open and exposed to the steppes which stretched thousands of miles without major barrier all the way into Central Asia. The Golden Horde, which had dominated

3

those steppes since the thirteenth century, had broken up into a patchwork of successor khanates which fought among themselves for the territories north of the Black and Caspian Seas: the Nogai Horde, the Khanates of Crimea, Astrakhan', Kazan' and [West] Siberia.

The openness and extent of this terrain generated a shifting pattern of temporary alliances and enmities, a constant and restless jostling for power, for the domination over or elimination of one's neighbour. Security was sought but never attained, since, however far hegemony might be extended, there was always a farther border beyond, and with it a further neighbour and a further potential enemy. On this hazardous terrain Muscovy learned its diplomatic and military skills. Like a cumbersome and nervous amoeba, it expanded to fill the space it was able to dominate, and was impelled into a perpetual dynamic of conquest, reversing the thrust of the Mongols of three centuries earlier.

It is not enough, however, to say that Moscow was one of the contestants in the struggle for the steppes, for in many ways it was the odd man out amongst them. It was an agricultural realm, and its population was sedentary, whereas the other protagonists were all nomadic principalities, at least in their origins and in many of their abiding characteristics. The rulers of Muscovy regarded their dominions as a patrimony, to be ruled over in undivided sovereignty, whereas its adversaries lived by nomadic rules: homage to an ultimate ruling dynasty (the Chingisids) underpinned a pattern of shifting clan allegiances, which changed according to circumstance and need. Tatar nobles might swear homage to the Grand Prince of Muscovy, but they regarded their obligation as a treaty relationship which could be revoked without dishonour to either side. The Muscovite ruler, by contrast, deemed that they had permanently entered his service and acknowledged his sovereignty, so that a subsequent break was nothing less than an act of treason. The chronicle records that Ivan IV, having occupied Kazan', 'had all the armed people put to death as traitors'.[3]

In some ways, then, what Moscow had undertaken in invading the Khanate of Kazan' was an act of retribution for oathbreaking, of vengeance for violated sovereignty. But also underlying it was a combined sense of religious and national mission which had assumed greater prominence as Muscovy became the strongest among the principalities of *Rus'* after the Battle of Kulikovo in 1380, in which the Grand Prince of Moscow, Dmitrii Donskoi, defeated the Mongols. In the earliest chronicles, *Rus'* was identified with the 'Russian land', with the Orthodox Church, and with the patrimony of the princes of the Riurik dynasty. During the fourteenth century these concepts had begun to coalesce around Moscow. In 1328 what had been the Metropolitanate of Kiev, the principal Orthodox juris-diction in *Rus'*, moved its seat there.

Under Ivan III in the late fifteenth century the first steps had been taken towards harnessing to Moscow's growing dominance a new and more grandiose concept of statehood than that associated with a dynastic patrimony. Not long before Moscow finally repudiated the sovereignty of Mongols in 1480, Ivan married Sofia Paleologue, niece of the last Byzantine Emperor. He established a sumptuous court, attended with magnificent ceremonial, on the Byzantine pat-tern. Ivan put about the story that Constantine Monomakh (Byzan-tine Emperor 1042–1055) had conferred the insignia and imperial crown on Vladimir Monomakh of Kiev, so that Kiev was retrospec-tively promoted to imperial status, and through Kiev Moscow claimed itself the heir to an imperial succession which went right back to Augustus. This post-factum creation of a glorious genealogy reached its culmination in the coronation of the young Ivan IV as Tsar (Caesar) in 1547. The 'invention of tradition' implied that Muscovy had a natural right to reclaim all the territories which had at any time been ruled over by any of the princes of *Rus'*.

The fall of Byzantium to the Ottomans in 1453 lent these imperial pretensions a religious colouring – again in retrospect. Not long before, in 1439, at the Council of Florence, the Greek Orthodox Church had consented to reunion with Rome, a move which had been rejected as heretical in Muscovy. The infidel conquest of Byzan-tium could thereafter be construed as God's punishment for its church's apostasy. This interpretation was not put forward immedi-ately in Muscovy, but, once it was, it implied an awesome role for the church of *Rus'*, as the one Orthodox Church free from the thrall of Islam, a distinction which could plausibly be seen as a reward for faithfulness, and as a pledge of God's special favour.

These secular and religious heritages amalgamated to generate the legend of 'Moscow the Third Rome', expounded with the greatest fervour in the epistles of the monk Filofei of Pskov. He wrote to Ivan III in 1500 or 1501: 'This present church of the third, new Rome, of Thy sovereign Empire: the Holy Catholic [*sobornaia*] Apostolic Church . . . shines in the whole universe more resplendent than the sun. And let it be known to thy Lordship, o pious Tsar, that all the empires of the Orthodox Christian faith have converged into Thine one Empire. Thou art the sole Emperor of all the Christians in the whole universe . . . For two Romes have fallen, the Third stands, and there shall be no fourth.'[4]

In the early years of Ivan IV's reign these various myths of origin were collated and systematized by his leading prelate, Metropolitan Makarii, in such a way as to combine the themes of church, dynasty and land, and to tie them to an imperial heritage. He compiled two great books of readings, in some ways like the collections of legitimizing documents put together by Chinese Emperors: they were the Great Almanach (*Velikie Chet'i-Minei*), and the Book of Degrees of the Imperial Genealogy (*Stepennaia kniga tsarskogo rodosloviia*). The first one included lives of the saints, resolutions of church councils, sermons, epistles (among them those of Filofei) and historical documents, laid out so that they could be read each day of the year. They were selected and arranged to demonstrate how God's purpose, from the Creation onwards, had been to found a truly Christian empire on earth, and how the land of *Rus'* was now called upon to fulfil this purpose. Its ruler was 'everywhere under the vault of heaven the one Christian Tsar, mounted on the holy throne of God of the holy apostolic church, in place of the Roman and Constantinopolitan [thrones] in the God-saved city of Moscow.' In two church councils, of 1547 and 1549, these texts were confirmed and a large number of local saints were canonized, to attest both to the unity of the Muscovite church and to its divinely ordained sanctity. One historian has called Makarii the 'gatherer of the Russian church'.[5]

The Book of Degrees evoked a secular tradition to reinforce the religious one: it was an account of the 'enlightened God-ordained sceptre-holders who ruled in piety the Russian land'. It was a highly selective list: it ignored the claims of rival successors to Kiev, like Lithuania and Novgorod, as well as the junior lines of the Riurik dynasty, and also the Golden Horde, but it emphasized the heritage of Byzantium, as befitted an imperial mission which rested on Orthodox Christianity.[6]

By the time that he embarked on his Kazan' campaign, then, and on that against the Khanate of Astrakhan' (1556), Ivan IV was fortified by an exalted vision of his earthly mission, which he employed to complement the humbler claims of steppe diplomacy. Though he never explicitly endorsed the 'Third Rome' theory to justify his aggression, Ivan deployed an eclectic bundle of arguments: that Kazan' had acknowledged the sovereignty of Moscow and in effect Moscow's right to claim the succession of the Golden Horde, that Kazan' was a long-standing patrimony of the Riurik dynasty and part of the land of *Rus'* 'since antiquity', that there was a need to maintain peace and end disorder, and that it was his duty as a Christian monarch to extirpate the rule of the infidel.[7]

The trouble was that the various aspects of this imperial ideology were scarcely compatible with one another. It is difficult to see what a Christian Emperor was doing claiming the heritage of an infidel ruler. As Michael Cherniavsky has commented, the two images, the *basileus* and the *khan*, were never really synthesized, but 'existed separately . . . in a state of tension'. 'If the image of the *basileus* stood for the Orthodox and pious ruler, leading his Christian people towards salvation, then the image of the *khan* was perhaps preserved in the idea of the Russian ruler as the conqueror of Russia and of its people, responsible to no one. If the *basileus* signified the holy tsar, the "most gentle" (*tishaishii*) tsar in spiritual union with his flock, then the *khan*, perhaps, stood for the absolutist secularised state, arbitrary through its separation from its subjects.'[8] This ambivalence was vividly exemplified in the personality of Ivan the Terrible, and was to persist for centuries thereafter.

There were other contradictions too. Did the ecumenical leadership Moscow proclaimed embrace the entire world of Orthodox Christianity, including the Balkans and Constantinople itself, or was it confined to the lands of *Rus'*? As we shall see, when in the seventeenth century an energetic prelate championed the former view against the latter, he unleashed a destructive schism. And if Moscow pretended to be a universal empire, then how could it be so closely identified with one people, the Russians, however broadly one might define their nationhood? That ambiguity too was never to be fully resolved. Finally, in an empire both spiritual and secular, could a perfect partnership between church and state be achieved, or, if not, which was to be the dominant partner? The Tsars, perhaps nervous of conceding too much to the church, never deployed the 'Third Rome' argument as part of their diplomatic armoury: it remained a powerful cultural and religious motif latent in their claims to imperial domination.

B. The Practice of Empire

Whatever was the theory of the Russian empire, many of its practical difficulties were to result from its huge size and diversity, and from its hybrid position as Asiatic empire and European great power. The appearance of such a realm was far from being unprecedented historically. Some of the world's greatest empires have been created by a peripheral power on the edge of an ecumene: one thinks of Macedonia and later Rome at the edge of the Hellenic world, of the Mongols in Eastern Asia, or of the Ottomans in the Middle East. Such states borrow techniques and customs from their more advanced neighbours, and then employ their own relatively primitive and warlike social structure to achieve dominance. This is how Russia proceeded too. However, despite its considerable successes from the sixteenth to the eighteenth centuries, it never quite achieved dominance, even over Central and Eastern Europe. And it found itself facing a European civilization which was continuing to make swift progress, partly in response to the Russian challenge.

Asiatic empires were used to exercising suzerainty over myriad ethnic groups, dominating them through a multi-ethnic imperial aristocracy, taxing them by exploiting the 'mutual responsibility' of local communities, offering them an imperial high culture and language to integrate their elites, but otherwise leaving them largely to their own devices on condition of obedience. John Kautsky has called such empires 'collections of agrarian societies which, remaining independent of one another, are linked to another society, the aristocracy, through being exploited by it . . . Aristocrats and peasants are generally separated from each other by far-reaching cultural distinctions involving difference of language and religion and sometimes of race.

They are, far more than the nineteenth-century British upper and lower classes to whom Disraeli applied the term, "two nations", though the word "nation" with its modern connotations is not really applicable to them.[9] In most respects, Russia remained an empire of this type right up to the early twentieth century.

The Asiatic imperial style implied a huge gap between the elites and the masses. In Europe, by contrast, states were moving between the sixteenth and nineteenth centuries towards the integration of the masses into nationhood, often crystallized around royal courts, as their armies became larger and better equipped, their economies developed, and their vernacular languages took shape out of myriads of local dialects.

Russia was straddled awkwardly between these two different political milieux, its bureaucratic sinews still largely Asiatic, while its culture became European. If it wished to remain an empire, it had no choice but to become a European great power, for there were no natural barriers to protect it from its western neighbours. But becoming a European great power carried a high cost: from the seventeenth century onwards, the high culture it offered its various peoples was not, like that of, for example, China, generated internally but was borrowed from outside, from a culture and way of life which Russia had to imitate in order to compete with the European powers. That meant that its imperial traditions were at odds with the people after whom the empire was named, and with its own previous state traditions. The tensions thus generated became especially acute in the late nineteenth century, when Russia's Europeanization was becoming most advanced, and other European states were becoming nations.

THE STEPPES   In the Asian part of the empire, the assimilation of new territories was fairly simple. Expansion began with the fomenting of disunity in the target society and the seduction of discontented elites, not too difficult a task when, like Kazan' and Astrakhan', they were confederacies of clans with a nomadic history. Shifting allegiances were part of the texture of steppe diplomacy and warfare. Once the conquest had been completed there would be a phase of the ruthless suppression of indigenous resistance, in order to leave no doubt about who was now master. Thus, within the former Khanate of Kazan', revolts of the Cheremisy in 1570–2 and of the Tatars in 1581–4 were put down with exemplary firmness. Kazan' was transformed into a Russian city, with an Orthodox cathedral dominating its skyline, while Russian servitors were awarded land in the area and Russian peasants (often former soldiers) were encouraged to resettle there. Russian merchants came in to take advantage of the new opportunities for trade opened by possession of the whole length of the River Volga. The indigenous peoples were forbidden to bear weapons. A system of fortresses was erected to prevent them allying with nomads further afield, and to provide protection against further raids by the Crimean and Nogai Tatars from south and east. The whole newly assimilated region was placed under the rule of military governors (*voevody*).

Once the immediate danger of rebellion and renewal of war had passed, Muscovite rulers took care to exercise their authority so as not to disturb unduly the customs, laws and religion of the conquered peoples. The ultimate aim was always the secure integration of the new territories and populations inside the empire, but the means employed to achieve this goal were varied and pragmatic.

Elites were co-opted where this was practical: thus the Muslim Tatar landowners were assimilated into the Russian nobility, but the tribal leaders of the animist Cheremis, Chuvash, Votiak and Mordvin peoples were not, since their status, beliefs and way of life were too alien. The Tatar nobles were encouraged to convert to Orthodoxy, which some did, but at least initially they were not required to. Since some of them in time acquired Russian peasants on their land, this tolerance led to the paradoxical result that in a supposedly Christian empire Orthodox Russians were being enserfed to Muslim non-Russians. At the same time the indigenous peoples were protected against serfdom: they were guaranteed the status of '*iasak* folk', that is tribute-payers, whose property and way of life were left unmolested provided they discharged their dues. There can be no clearer indication of the way in which the needs of empire (in this case for taxes and peaceful assimilation) overrode both religious and national allegiance, even though Muscovy rested its extravagant imperial claims on both religion and nationhood. By the seventeenth century, the Volga basin had what might be called an 'onion-shaped' demography, with relatively few Russians in the highest and lowest social layers, and large numbers of indigenous peoples in the middle.

Thereafter the authorities gradually assimilated the territory and the peoples into the structure of the empire, drawing back whenever integratory measures provoked disproportionate resistance. In the early eighteenth century Tatar nobles were required to convert to Orthodoxy or lose their status, while the *iasak* peoples became subject to military recruitment and had to pay the poll-tax, like their Russian neighbours. After the Pugachev rebellion (which showed that Russians and non-Russians resisted the empire in the same way and for more or less the same reasons) the whole region was assimilated into the newly-created imperial structure of *gubernii* (an administrative unit of some 200,000–300,000 population) and *uezdy* (a similar unit of 20,000–30,000 population), each with its own nobles' association as the nucleus of the local ruling class. From time to time, campaigns were launched to convert the indigenous peoples to Orthodoxy, but they were dropped whenever they seemed likely to cause widespread trouble. The Volga region offered a prototype: the methods first tried out here – administrative and economic followed by cultural and religious integration – were later to be applied elsewhere in the empire too.[10]

The conquest of the Volga-Kama basin, of great importance in itself, proved also to be the starting-point for the most spectacular feat of expansion of all: the penetration and settlement of Siberia and the Far East, all the way to the Pacific Ocean. This process, though it had the support of the government, was accomplished without its direct intervention. The impulse came from hunters, trappers and traders, interested in expanding the fur trade, and from that semi-nomadic breed of Russians, the Cossacks.

Cossacks were hunters and brigands, horsemen and stock-raisers who roamed the no man's land – the so-called 'wild country' – between Muscovy, Poland-Lithuania, the Ottoman Empire and the successor khanates of the Golden Horde. They had learned to cope with the harsh and risky life of the steppe by forming themselves into military fraternities and mastering the skills which had reaped the Tatars such success in earlier centuries, including those of raiding and pillaging. Their very name was Tatar, and signified 'free men'. Settled agriculture they disdained as beneath their dignity, and in any case futile in such vulnerable terrain. But they were prepared to hire themselves out to any overlord ready to offer them favourable terms to act as patrols and frontier defence troops.

Cossacks practised the mixture of ruthless authoritarianism and primitive democracy of those who inhabit a hazardous environment and are utterly dependent on each other for survival. Each unit of a hundred or so men held periodic meetings of its *krug* or warriors' assembly, where they allocated hunting and fishing rights, and decided about campaigning, the distribution of booty and service to sovereign powers. When necessary an *ataman* or 'headman' (*hetman* among the Zaporozhian Cossacks of the Dnieper) would be elected to lead them: once he was chosen, his word was law during combat.

Both for imperial expansion and frontier defence the Cossacks were indispensable, but they were double-edged allies, liable to turn against paymasters who dissatisfied them and to raid and plunder peaceful populations, while their way of life, their prized *vol'nost'* (freedom) offered an alluring alternative model for the serfs and tributaries of the Tsar. In a sense they were an alternative Russian ethnos, the embryo of a potential Russian nation with a quite differ-ent social structure. Significantly, criminal bands often adopted Cossack customs, organizing themselves in *arteli*, who would take decisions in common, share out their booty and observe a strict code of conduct – which, however, in their case excluded any collaboration with the state. This has made the criminal world in Russia remarkably tenacious and durable, through numerous changes of regime, right into the late twentieth century.[11]

During its great period of expansion, in the late sixteenth and early seventeenth centuries, the Muscovite/Russian Empire had much in common with the Spanish one. In bath cases a militant Christian country had conquered Muslims on what it considered to be its primordial territory, and continued the impetus of conquest to take over a huge and distant empire. The prime agents of expansion, the Cossacks and the conquistadores, were not unlike one another in spirit. The mixture of autocracy with intrepid, self-willed freebooting troops, and an intolerant, crusading faith characterized both coun-tries. But of course there were also crucial differences: Russia's empire, being an overland one, was closer at hand and easier to reach, but also more vulnerable to invasion by hostile neighbours. Even more important, perhaps, the Russians had no Pyrenees at their back to protect them from the ambitions of other European powers. These circumstances imparted to Russian imperialism a degree of caution and pragmatism which the Spanish did not practise.

SIBERIA   As in Spain, the government gave its general approval for the expansion of empire, but the pioneers on the frontier provided the impetus and took the crucial decisions, often turning defensive dispositions into campaigns of conquest. In the case of Siberia, a single entrepreneurial family took the initiative which brought together traders, administrators and warriors for a concerted effort of territorial and economic expansion. The Stroganovs, who for decades had enjoyed an official monopoly in the highly lucrative businesses of furs and salt-mining, engaged a Don Cossack army, under Ataman Ermak, to protect its operations against raids by the Khan of [Western] Siberia. Turning defence into attack, in 1581–2 Ermak succeeding in conquering the Khan's capital on the lower River Irtysh.

Thereafter the way lay open, through taiga and tundra, right across Siberia. The peoples who populated this immense territory were primitive and loosely ordered, without state structures: they sometimes offered bitter resistance to the invaders from the west, but were overcome with comparative ease even when superior in numbers, since their military equipment and organization were rudimentary.

Leaving fortresses (*ostrogi*) behind them at major river crossings to consolidate their advance, the Cossack pioneers reached the Pacific Ocean by 1639 and founded there the harbour of Okhotsk in 1648. Thereby the advancing Russians gave substance to their claim on the heritage of the Golden Horde, adding it to their existing ethnic and imperial claims in Europe. Their actual domination of the territory was, however, fragmentary. Freebooters, hunters and traders came first, drawn by the fabled wealth of the region, while the government subsequently improvised a thin web of colonization, sending soldiers, clergy, officials and a few resettled peasants. Spontaneous peasant settlement played a minor role, since the distances and dangers were sufficient to deter all but the boldest.[12]

The occupation of Siberia offers the first example of a characteristic feature of Russian imperialism: its tendency to forestall possible danger by expanding to fill the space it is able to dominate. This has meant that for Russians the sense of border is vague and protean, shaped by the constellation of power on its frontiers at any given moment. Expansion comes to an end only when Russia fetches up against another power capable of offering effective resistance and of affording a stable and predictable frontier, so that future relations can be conducted on a diplomatic rather than a military footing. Such frontiers Russia has normally respected, challenging them only when it appears that the power on the other side can no longer guarantee them. These tendencies have lent Russian imperialism a paradoxical air of aggression combined with caution.

In the Far East, China was both an obstacle to further advance and a stabilizing influence. After a period of indecisive conflict, the Russians signed with them the Treaty of Nerchinsk (1689), which settled the mutual border for nearly two centuries. Further north, where no such power existed to restrain and mould the forward impetus, even the Pacific did not pose an insurmountable barrier: Russian expansion continued across Alaska and down the west coast of North America. It was followed, however, by only the sparsest of settlement, and never put down firm roots.

Mindful of the vast distances and the perilous situation of the thinly scattered Russian settlers in Siberia, the Muscovite government pursued towards the natives a pragmatic policy similar to the one tried out on the Volga. Having first established undisputed control, where necessary by harsh and violent methods, it left the local peoples as far as possible to continue their traditional way of life, on condition of paying a regular tribute in furs (*iasak*). *Voevody* were exhorted to treat them 'with leniency and benevolence, and not to levy the *iasak* by brute force'.[13] Siberian clan and tribal leaders were confirmed in their powers, though, unlike the Tatars, none of them was assimilated into the Russian nobility, since their way of life was felt to be too alien.

In practice, such intended forbearance was difficult to sustain. Disputes often broke out between Russians and natives. Sometimes Russian officials took hostages to ensure payment of the *iasak*; sometimes, knowingly or not, they infringed native hunting rights, or new peasant settlements blocked traditional pastoral routes. On any of these grounds, conflict might flare up, whereupon the Russians would exploit their superior weaponry to restore order as they conceived it.[14]

Siberia gave Russians a reassuring sense of space. Its immense expanses formed a kind of geo-political confirmation of the notion of universal empire. At the same time its huge material resources were never properly exploited. Siberia is a prime example of the way in which the empire was run for considerations of great power status, not for economic ones. Its first and most obvious source of wealth, furs, was mercilessly exploited in the interests of traders and the exchequer, with no thought for restocking, so that by the early eighteenth century it was starting to decline from sheer misuse. The agricultural potential of the south and west lay almost completely fallow until the late nineteenth century. The mineral wealth, despite numerous geological expeditions, was grossly underexploited right into the twentieth century.

Admittedly there were major difficulties with transport, but that did not prevent the regime using Siberia as a dumping ground for the empire's undesirables, its criminals and its persecuted, who were conveyed in their thousands over its wastes to their confinement in convict camp or administrative exile. Some of them worked in saltworks and silver mines, but ironically the more educated sometimes found employment in official posts: at that distance it was considered safe for them to serve the Tsar they were allegedly trying to undermine! Siberia thus became a means of bolstering internal security rather than a great resource for economic growth.

STEPPES OF EAST AND SOUTH   The straddling of northern Eurasia left the Russians with an immensely long, indeterminate and exposed flank to the south, where the steppes were flat and vulnerable to invasion. They applied to it the techniques they had first tried out in the Volga region, building a loose line of fortifications from the southern Urals to the Altai, manned by Cossack patrols or armed peasants to protect their communications from raiders.[15] In practice peasants and soldiers were hard to distinguish, since perforce they acquired each other's characteristics in this harsh environment where the arts of war and agriculture were needed in equal measure for survival.

Given the immensely greater scale of the problem than on the

Volga, security was not to be attained in this way, and eventually the Russians sought it by the only available alternative: to envelop and stifle conflict by expanding south and east across the desert to the khanates of the Central Asian oases, building loose chains of fortresses and redoubts as they went. In the course of this progress, they encountered by turn the semi-sedentary, semi-nomadic Bashkirs, then the nomadic Nogais and Kalmyks, then the Kazakhs. At each stage the Russians would begin by applying the technique which had served them well against Kazan', exploiting feuds within tribal confederations and drawing some tribes into a vassalage which was then interpreted as long-term subjection. There would follow a campaign of retribution against violated sovereignty, after which the indigenous peoples would be drawn into the permanent service of the Tsar, sometimes as special regiments within the Russian army, just as the British did with the Gurkhas. Russia would alternately threaten them and offer them trade privileges to fix them in service.[16]

Russia's most persistent and redoubtable opponents in this steppe confrontation were the Crimean Tatars in the south. They were so formidable because they had the mobility and ferocity of any nomadic host, but also a relatively high level of civilization, and the backing of a great power, the Ottoman Empire. Since the slave trade was a mainstay of their economy, they mounted frequent raids northwards towards Moscow: in 1571 they even sacked the city itself.[17] The Russians, confined to the forests, marshes and poor soils of the north, had to stand by and see the fertile expanses of the Pontic steppes, to the north of the Black Sea, remain under-inhabited and scarcely cultivated because of the blight the Tatars cast over them from their fastness in the Crimea.

Until the late seventeenth century, no Russian government felt strong enough to challenge the Crimean Tatars militarily. When at length they did so, they found the obstacles formidable. The hundreds of miles of open steppe which afforded such ideal hunting ground for Nogai and Tatar cavalry were a nightmare for infantry and artillery to traverse. Unable to rely on foraging in the sun-baked plains, the Russian army had to take with it a huge supply train, whose burdens were further swollen by the fodder needed for the draught animals pulling it. A whole series of Russian campaigns failed because of these difficulties, sometimes after initial encouraging success. In 1689 Prince Vasilii Golitsyn's troops reached the isthmus fortress of Perekop, but had to abandon the siege because they had already consumed most of their supplies. In 1696 Peter I captured the fort of Azov, but had to relinquish it some years later for similar reasons. In 1736 General Münnich actually breached the walls of Perekop but had to retire without capturing it because he had run out of food and water: the Tatars had providently burnt their granaries and poisoned their wells.[18]

Right up to the late eighteenth century, Russia continued to rely for its security on extended chains of forts in the steppe, connected by an elaborate system of signalling linked to reserves situated near Kiev. About a quarter of the army was stationed on or behind these fortifications to prevent cavalry raids, which it could barely manage to do even with such profligate use of manpower. The power of the service nobility over their serfs was justified mainly by the need to staff these defences.[19]

Eventually the Russians were able to overcome the Crimean Tatars by employing their time-honoured steppe strategy, using diplomacy and military pressure to weaken their ties with the Ottoman Empire and to entice some of their vassals, the Nogai clans. With their help the Russian army was able to break into the Crimea in 1771. It declared the khanate a Russian protectorate, and then abolished it twelve years later, incorporating the territory directly into the empire and replacing the Khan with a Russian Governor. The Tatar *murzy* (nobles) were absorbed into the imperial nobility, if they could furnish proof of legitimate title, while the peasants were confirmed in their landholdings and their free status. The Muslim religious authorities were permitted to retain their endowments (*waqf*) and their traditional status.[20]

From the Russians' viewpoint this policy was wholly successful: there was no major Tatar rising against their rule. But there was a heavy price to be paid – by the Tatars: many of them emigrated to the Ottoman Empire, leaving behind land which was occupied by incoming Russian peasants and other colonists. Gradually the Tatars became a minority in what had been their own realm. It transpired, then, that large numbers of Muslims would emigrate if they had the chance to do so rather than endure an alien Christian domination. This was to happen again later in the Caucasus, leaving a legacy of hatred and bitterness which was to render Russia's frontier in that region a permanent source of potential weakness.

Victory in the Crimea cleared the way for the Russian armies to consolidate their growing superiority over the Ottoman Empire on the whole northern coast of the Black Sea, which they gradually asserted in a series of wars fought between the 1760s and 1790s. These conquests were of cardinal strategic and economic significance. Russia was at last able to break out of her meagre woodland and exploit in security the rich steppe lands which had so long tantalized her people. Agriculturalists were able to make incomparably more productive use of them than slave-traders, and during the nineteenth century the grain grown there became the commercial mainstay of the empire. [See Part 2, Chapter 3]

CAUCASUS Domination of the Volga basin and of the Pontic steppes inevitably involved Russia in the politics of the Trans-Caucasus, for reasons which General Rostislav Fadeev outlined in the 1850s.

> Domination on the Black and Caspian Seas, or in extremity the neutrality of those seas, is a vital interest for the whole southern half of Russia, from the Oka to the Crimea, the area where the principal strength of the empire, material and personal, is more and more concentrated ... If Russia's horizons ended on the snowy summits of the Caucasus range, then the whole western half of the Asian continent would be outside our sphere of influence and, given the present impotence of Turkey and Persia, would not long wait for another master.[21]

The Caucasus mountain range and its hinterland constituted very different terrain from the steppes but posed analogous problems of turbulence and power vacuum on Russia's borders, aggravated in this case by the presence of Persia and the Ottoman Empire, and behind them Britain, hovering in the background, always ready to intervene. The region was a bewildering patchwork of tiny ethnic groups, often confined to single valleys or clusters of valleys, divided from each other by high mountain walls. The indigenous peoples were staunch in the Islamic faith, jealous of their tribal independence and their pastoral way of life.

Beyond the Caucasus range, in the basins of the Rion and Kura/Araxes rivers and the hills around them, lived two of the oldest Christian peoples in the world, the Georgians and the Armenians. The Georgians were largely a people of peasants and landed nobles, Orthodox by religion, organized till the late eighteenth century in a kingdom which was a loose confederation of principalities, wedged between the Persian and Ottoman Empires. The Armenians, by contrast, were traders, artisans and professional people of the Gregorian monophysite faith; they had had their own kingdom in the middle ages, but by the eighteenth century most lived in the Ottoman Empire, where they enjoyed a tolerably secure, if subordinate status as a recognized *millet* (a self-governing ethnic or religious community). Some were subjects of the various khans of the Persian Empire. Intermingled among them in the lower Kura basin and along the Caspian Sea were also Azeris, Shia Muslims whose religion inclined them towards Persia while their language was close to Turkish.

With their territories the object of contention between two Muslim empires, it was natural that the Georgians and Armenians should both look to Orthodox Russia as a potential protector. As early as 1556, when Muscovy was first established on the borders of the Caspian Sea, the east Georgian kingdom of Kakhetia sent envoys to consult about the possibility of becoming a protectorate.[22]

However, it was not for more than two centuries that Russia, at last controlling the north coast of the Black Sea and the Kuban' steppes, was able to intervene decisively in Transcaucasian affairs. It was motivated to do so by the fear, later articulated by Fadeev, that otherwise the region, already unstable, would become the base of operation for another power, Asiatic or conceivably even European, to threaten the newly acquired steppes. Every time there was war with the Ottoman Empire, the Caucasus became an additional front, and even in peacetime the raids of the hill tribesmen constantly endangered the productive agricultural settlements establishing themselves on the Kuban' plains to the north. Well before the end of the eighteenth century Russia constructed a line of forts along the Terek river, which annoyed the neighbouring Kabardinian chiefs.

This was the motive which impelled Russia in 1783 to offer protection of Georgia's sovereignty and territorial integrity in return for acknowledgement of overlordship. Georgia got a bad bargain, for within two decades its separate kingdom had been abolished, and its royal family banished, yet effective Russian protection had not been forthcoming when its capital city, Tbilisi, was sacked by the Persians in 1795.

All the same, the Georgian people survived, and were able during the nineteenth century to develop a sense of nationhood in reasonably stable circumstances – something which might not have been possible had Russia never intervened. For the Russian masters themselves, the experience of dealing with Siberian and steppe peoples was largely misleading when handling a long-established and cultured people like the Georgians. Proud of their distinctive traditions, they were not content gradually to lose their identity in an Asian-style empire.

Administrative assimilation actually proceeded much faster than it had done in the steppes. Georgian principalities were amalgamated to form the Russian gubernii of Tiflis and Kutaisi. The elaborate, multi-layered hierarchy of the Georgian nobility was reduced to the simpler model of the Russian *dvorianstvo*, while the Georgian custom of entail was replaced by the Russian one of dividing estates among all heirs. The city of Tiflis was rebuilt on European lines, and the palace of the viceroy became the centre of a brilliant social and cultural life.[23]

Under the Russians, the Georgian kingdom, though subordinate, was more united than it had been for centuries. This factor, together with the provision of stability, the construction of communications, the offering of commercial opportunity and the inculcation of a European-style culture furnished the conditions in which it proved possible during the nineteenth century for Georgian nobles to find a sense of common identity with their own people, and to take the first steps towards nationhood in the modern sense.[24] This is a paradox we shall see several times: the Russian empire providing the pre-conditions for the creation of a nation, which cannot flower fully within the empire and turns against it.

As for the Armenians, their hopes were roused by the Russian incursion into their territories, and especially by the victories over the Persians in 1828 and the Ottomans in 1829. For a time Russia held the strategically vital areas of Kars and Erzerum, but returned them to Turkey by the Treaty of Adrianople (1829). However, Armenians living there were allowed to emigrate to Russia, and did so in large numbers: this contingent included many peasants, who mostly settled in the hill country of Nagornyi Karabakh. Armenian traders, artisans and professional people became a significant element in all the Transcaucasian cities, in Tiflis and Baku as much as in Erivan. By a Statute of 1836 the Armenian Gregorian Church was recognized as self-governing.[25]

These population movements certainly provided new hope for thousands of Armenians. Yet they also had the effect of arousing the suspicion and enmity of the Azeris who had previously dominated the territories where they settled. The new Armenians were thus potentially insecure: basically, they remained, as before, a people divided among different empires, with no land they could securely call their own.

Paradoxically the Russians established themselves in Transcaucasia without having gained mastery of the Caucasus itself. The new Russian dominions depended on a tenuous line of communication, the Georgian Military Highway, running through the heart of the mountains. While the chieftains of the Ossetian people, who lived along it, were favourable to Russia, it was tolerably secure, nor did Russians need to fear permanent disruption so long as the diverse peoples of the mountains, the Chechens, Kabardinians, Circassians, Kumyks and so on, were held back from mutual cooperation by ethnic and princely feuds.

However, even before the end of the eighteenth century, there were signs that this disunity might not last for ever. In 1785, after an earthquake, a Sufi leader, Sheikh Mansur, called on his fellow Chechens to join with other tribes in resisting further encroachments by the infidel. The Sufi brotherhoods provided an ideal focus for the emergence of a new democratic Islamic resistance, often repudiating the chieftains and their compromises with imperial authority. In this case, therefore, by endeavouring as usual to co-opt local elites, Russia did not gain the docility of the mass of the population, but on the contrary provoked them to rebellion.

Sufism might seem an odd focus for such rebellion: originally it was a mystical movement of contemplation, self-denial and with-drawal from the world. But the intense relationship which existed between mentor (*murshid* or *sheikh*) and his disciples could, in circum-stances of danger and instability, readily generate a collective com-mitment to militant action. By the early nineteenth century, the call for *jihad*, or 'exertion in defence of the faith' was becoming popular among ordinary people, overriding local feuds and cementing armed resistance under Sufi leadership. Egalitarianism, self-sacrifice and devotion to the prophet supplanted hierarchy and obedience to the tribal *beg*.[26]

In the 1820s Ghazi Muhammad taught that 'He who is a Muslim must be a free man, and there must be equality among all Muslims'. To promote this freedom and equality it was the duty of all the faithful to cast out the infidel though *qazawat* or 'holy war'. 'He who holds to the Shariat must arm no matter what the cost, must abandon his family, his house, his land and not spare his very life.'[27]

Ghazi's successor, the Imam Shamil', led the resistance movement for quarter of a century (1834–59), exploiting all the advantages the terrain afforded him. Small bands of lightly armed men could descend at any moment on a Russian outpost or convoy, exploiting surprise and mobility to inflict the maximum damage and loss of life, before vanishing into the mountains and forests. This was a kind of warfare to which the Russians, with their long experience of the steppes, were not at all accustomed, and it was very difficult for them, despite their considerable superiority in numbers and technology, to overcome their nimble foe. Deploying more troops simply generated more casualties. The Russians' attempts to divide their opponents and gain allies would call forth swift and ferocious retaliation from Shamil'.[28]

The Crimean War (1853–6) revealed what a threat this endless Caucasian fighting could be to the empire: two hundred thousand troops had to be stationed there throughout the war to keep an eye on both Shamil'' and the Turks and were thus unable to intervene in the decisive theatre of war. In the end only a systematic campaign of forest-felling, crop-burning, road-building and destruction of vil-lages enabled the Russians to gain a permanent grip on the Caucasus range.[29]

In a word, they were able to attain their ends only by genocide.

Following the pacification, the Russian authorities resettled many mountaineers on the plains. Many more chose instead to leave, seeking a new home in the Ottoman Empire. At least 300,000 Circassians departed, nearly their entire population; so too did many Abkhaz, Chechens, Kabardinians and Nogai Tatars.[30] This outcome, very different from what had been experienced on the steppes and anticipating the massive deportations of the twentieth century, displayed dramatically the costs of empire: in this case a lasting legacy of hatred, bitterness and desire for vengeance which has made the Caucasian frontier a permanent source of weakness for Russia.

UKRAINE The flat, open region to the south and south-west of Muscovy was geographically part of the steppes, and presented Russia with the problems characteristic of steppe terrain. Here, however, there was a vital additional element: national identity was directly at stake, since the area had been for centuries part of the patrimony of the princes of *Rus'*, and its principal city, Kiev, had been the seat of the first East Slav state from the ninth to the thirteenth centuries. At that time a thriving trading centre and agricultural region, it had suffered grievously from the Mongol invasion, and later from the collapse of Byzantium and the establishment of the Ottoman Empire. It became an insecure hinterland, defenceless before the Crimean Tatars' slave raids, traversed by Cossacks, nomads and by the marauding robber bands which flourished where there was no fixed civil authority.[31]

During the fourteenth century Lithuania became the dominant power in the region, and it repulsed the Mongols a century before Muscovy was able to do so. Lithuania in turn fell under the influence of Poland, with which the Grand Prince of Lithuania concluded a dynastic union in 1385, later converted into a joint Commonwealth. The Catholic and Latinate culture of Poland took hold among the elites of the region, though profession of the Orthodox faith continued to be tolerated. The stage was set for a centuries-long national and religious struggle between Poland and Russia, Roman Catholicism and Orthodoxy.

During the fifteenth and sixteenth centuries, with the greater physical security afforded by the Polish-Lithuanian state, Ukraine became its grain belt. The landed nobility gained in both privilege

23

and material wealth, while imposing an ever more debilitating serf-dom on the peasants. The Lithuanian Statute of 1529, together with the Magdeburg Law in the cities, provided some guarantees of citizenship for all non-serfs and, although often in practice ignored, it inculcated a stronger legal awareness in Ukraine than was prevalent in Muscovy.

Polish culture proved highly attractive to many Ukrainian land-owners, especially since those who converted to Catholicism received the full rights of the *szlachta* (Polish nobility) to enserf the peasants and to participate as citizens in the political life of the Common-wealth. With the coming of the counter-reformation, the Polish king encouraged the expansion of a network of Jesuit colleges, which brought with them the latest in European culture and thinking, while a new Greek Catholic (or Uniate) Church was created, Orthodox in ritual, but administratively in union with Rome, which took over all Orthodox parishes. Originally conceived as an attempt to begin the reunification of Catholicism and Orthodoxy, the Uniate Church became in effect an instrument of Polonization.[32]

Where the ill-defined borders of the joint Commonwealth faded into the steppe, however, Catholicism and high culture made but few and feeble inroads. There the Cossack community of the lower Dnieper continued its steppe way of life, hunting, fishing, raiding across the sea into the Ottoman Empire, and striking up temporary alliances with Muscovy or Poland for the defence of its frontiers. The Cossacks' headquarters, the Sech', on an island below the Dnieper rapids, was almost impregnable and guaranteed their dogged self-rule as well as their privileges, notably their exemption from taxation, which were registered by the Polish crown.

By the mid-seventeenth century the Polish king and *szlachta*, tiring of the anarchy on their borders and jealous of the Cossacks' privi-leges, attempted forcefully to subjugate the Dnieper community and incorporate it fully into the Commonwealth. The attempt provoked a rebellion in defence of Cossack self-rule: its leader, Hetman Bohdan Khmel'nyts'kyi, sought the protection of the Muscovite Tsar.

The resultant Treaty of Pereiaslavl' (1654) was a *locus classicus* of the discrepancy between steppe diplomacy and that of Muscovy. Khmel'nyts'kyi expected the Tsar's envoy, Vasilii Buturlin, to join him in taking an oath to observe the terms of the treaty. When

Buturlin refused, declaring that it was unthinkable for the Tsar to bind himself by oath to a subject, Khmel'nyts'kyi walked out of the negotiations. So pressing was his military need, however, that he subsequently changed his mind and consented to accept Buturlin's assurances of the Tsar's good faith instead of an explicit oath. The Cossacks pledged the Tsar 'eternal loyalty', while he in turn confirmed the Cossack Host in its privileges, including its own law and administration, the right to elect its own Hetman and to receive foreign envoys not hostile to the Tsar. He also guaranteed the Ukrainian nobility, church and cities their traditional rights. Under these arrangements the alliance was concluded and Poland was driven out of left-bank Ukraine and Kiev.[33]

Left-bank Ukraine became the site of a new state, the Ukrainian Hetmanate, which preserved a degree of autonomy, as well as its own culture, well into the eighteenth century. The representatives of nobles, clergymen and burghers were given their place alongside Cossacks in the General Council which elected the Hetman. An institutional foundation was thus laid for the Cossacks to create the framework of a Ukrainian nation-state in alliance with Russia.

Moscow, however, regarded the Treaty of Pereiaslavl' as the first step in the permanent incorporation – or reincorporation – of the territories of what it called 'Little Russia' into the empire, as part of the 'gathering of the Russian lands'. It began a process of creeping integration, sowing and exploiting dissensions within Ukrainian society. Muscovite voevodas listened to the grievances of peasants and rank-and-file Cossacks against their elites, and sometimes passed them on to Moscow to settle. In 1686, after long negotiations with the Patriarch of Constantinople, the Kievan metropolitanate, symbol of the autocephaly of the Orthodox Church in Ukraine, was subordinated to Moscow.[34]

The turning-point in relations came during Peter I's war against Sweden. The Hetman, Ivan Mazepa, discovered that the Russian army was so preoccupied with defending the road to Moscow against Charles XII that it had no troops to spare to come to the aid of the Ukrainians. This unwelcome discovery raised the question whether the Treaty of Pereiaslavl' was still valid: both in feudal and in steppe diplomacy, an overlord who was no longer willing or able to provide protection for a vassal forfeited any claim on his continuing loyalty.

Mazepa decided to throw in his lot with the Swedes and the Poles, in the expectation that Ukraine would eventually become a partner in the Polish-Lithuanian Commonwealth. Peter reacted swiftly and ruthlessly to his defection. He accused him of treason, and sent an army under Prince Menshikov to his headquarters town of Baturyn, which was taken with the slaughter of all its inhabitants. Elsewhere too Russian commanders sought out Mazepa's supporters, interrogated them and sent them to execution or exile. They turned out to be fewer than expected, perhaps because of Peter's demonstrative ruthlessness, or perhaps because many Cossacks did not want to resubmit themselves to a Catholic realm.[35]

Thereafter the way was open for the complete integration of Ukraine into the Russian Empire. Ukrainian affairs were transferred from the College for Foreign Affairs to the Senate, implying that Ukraine was an integral part of Russia. The Hetmanate was first suspended and then abolished in 1763. Its institutions were in decline anyway, since Cossacks had to bear full military duties without serfs to cultivate their lands. Growing polarization among the Cossacks also weakened their sense of a common political destiny: poorer Cossacks and townsfolk looked to the Russian administration and law courts to protect them against exploitation by their superiors.

Besides, there were benefits for Ukrainian nobles in being fully assimilated into the imperial *dvorianstvo*. For one thing, it converted their peasants into serfs, over whom they had full rights. Besides, thanks to their relatively high level of culture and education, they were often at an advantage when competing with their Muscovite counterparts for official positions, especially since they were ethnically close and able to speak good Russian. Incorporation offered them scope for their talents, rather as the Union of England and Scotland offered attractive career opportunities to Scots far outside their ancestral homeland.

By the 1780s the Hetmanate had been abolished and divided up into gubernii identical with those elsewhere in the empire. Cossack regiments were absorbed into the Russian army, though with their own distinctive names, uniforms and ranks as a relic of their separate status. The Sech' was not only closed down but razed, now that it was no longer needed for defence against the Turks.[36]

Ukraine's loss of its distinct identity was more complete than that of any other region of the empire. During the late eighteenth and nineteenth centuries, the Ukrainian rural elites became to all intents and purposes Russian, while the larger towns were cosmopolitan, with Russians, Jews, Poles, Germans, Greeks and others living side by side. The peasants spoke a variety of Ukrainian dialects, but were far from any sense of identity with their landowners or of belonging to a Ukrainian nation. In so far as a separate Ukrainian identity lingered, it was among scholars and professional people interested in literature, folklore and antiquities.

BESSARABIA Bessarabia was really an extension of the southern part of Ukraine, and had a similarly mixed urban population; only here the peasantry was Romanian. It was a thin sliver of land between the rivers Dniester and the Prut, conquered by Russia in 1812. It formed the north-eastern half of the province of Moldavia, itself one of the two Romanian principalities which had been in dispute between the Russian and Ottoman empires since the early eighteenth century. Traditionally ruled over by Romanian boyars under Greek Phanariot *hospodars*, it had been subjected to an especially rapacious system of tax-farming which had left its peasants, despite a fertile soil, among the most poverty-stricken in Europe. After the Crimean War and the declaration of Romanian independence in 1861, it became for a time part of Romania, and even after its return at the Congress of Berlin it remained the only part of Russia's European territory directly threatened by potential national irredentism, that is, claimed by a nation-state across the border.

After its initial annexation in 1812, Bessarabia enjoyed a period of autonomy on the Finnish model, but this was ended in 1828. Thereafter both the poverty of the region and its exposed situation led the imperial authorities to do everything possible to weaken the indigenous elites and to import Russian officials and landowners. By the late nineteenth century Bessarabia had thus become home to a peculiarly raw and brash immigrant Russian ruling class; it was a soil in which monarchist and anti-Semitic movements found abundant nourishment.[37]

POLAND In the second half of the eighteenth century Russia embarked on perhaps its most fateful episode of imperial expansion when it destroyed the Polish state and annexed a large part of its territory. To understand why this happened, and why Russia displayed such cynicism and brutality, we have to remember that Poland had itself once been a rival great power, contesting the same territories and claiming the same right to absorb all East Slavs into its realm, for a time with considerable success. It is as if, during the British Civil War of the seventeenth century, an Irish Catholic king had invaded England, captured London, and for a time occupied the throne.

This was not just great power rivalry, but also a bitter family quarrel. The territories which formed the eastern half of the Commonwealth of Poland-Lithuania had belonged in pre-Mongol days to the patrimony of the princes of *Rus'*: they were thus part of the agenda of the 'gathering of the lands of *Rus'*. The Poles, being Slavs, and having inherited part of the legacy of Kievan *Rus'*, could put forward perfectly plausible rival claims to the loyalty of the Ukrainians and Belorussians. The fact that they were also Catholics made their pretensions doubly repugnant in the eyes of Orthodox Russians. Their culture, conspicuously aristocratic and westernized, completed the picture of family perfidy.

Poland was moreover strategically vital to Russia. It commanded the flat, open approaches from the west, across which European powers over the centuries repeatedly invaded Russia. Applying the logic of steppe diplomacy by which Russia was accustomed to regulate its dealings with its neighbours, Poland must either be strong enough to offer both resistance and a stable frontier, like China, or else, if weak, it must be under Russia's thumb.

As it became obvious during the late seventeenth and early eighteenth centuries that Poland was in fact growing dangerously weak, Russia began to deploy the techniques which had served it well in overcoming adversaries of the steppe: promoting internal splits in order to achieve domination and if necessary destruction. It was Poland's misfortune that these devices were singularly effective when applied to her. Her monarchy was elective, not hereditary, allowing ample scope for the free play of faction. Her libertarian constitution permitted a single member of the Diet to thwart a resolution – a right reputedly not exercised lightly, but nevertheless one which enfeebled the state's capacity to act – and also envisaged the right of 'confederation', which entitled groups of citizens to uphold what they believed to be the law by means of joint armed action.[38]

Peter I and his successors exploited these defects to keep Poland weak and to maintain a Russian hegemony over it, backing aristocratic factions, impeding attempts to reform the constitution and interfering in royal elections. When necessary, Russian troops were sent in, on one occasion breaking into the Diet when it was in session and arresting deputies unfavourable to the Russian cause.

Unlike the steppe khanates, however, Poland was a power among other European powers, who therefore had a legitimate interest in what happened to her. Without provoking a general European war, which was clearly not in her interests, Russia could not carry out the destruction of Poland without considering the susceptibilities of at least Austria and Prussia. Hence the eventual dismemberment of the Polish state could take place only by agreement among all three powers. It happened in three stages, in 1772, 1793 and 1795. In conception, however, this was an act of traditional Russian empire-building: in announcing the second partition, Catherine II claimed that Russia was resuming sovereignty over 'lands and citizens which once belonged to the Russian Empire, which are inhabited by their fellow-countrymen and are illuminated by the Orthodox faith'.[39]

The population Russia absorbed during the partitions was very diverse: it included some 40% Ruthenians (Ukrainians or Belorussians), 26% Poles, 20% Lithuanians, 10% Jews and 4% Russians; 38% were Catholics, 40% Uniate, 10% of the Jewish faith and 6.5% Orthodox.[40] But it was not the diversity which caused Russia difficulties: after all, she had coped with plenty of that already. More fateful was the fact that in the Poles and the Jews she had taken in the two nations who were to prove the most irreconcilable to Russian imperial rule, a permanent source of bitterness and conflict.

The Poles were Roman Catholic, and most of them identified with the Latin West of the Counter-Reformation. Culturally and economically they were more advanced than the Russians. Their concept of citizenship ran counter to the whole theory and practice of political authority in Russia. In Poland, as in England, political rights proceeded from a broadening of feudal aristocratic privilege – the 'golden liberty', as it was known – to embrace the whole population. This process had begun belatedly but unmistakably in the last years of the Commonwealth, in the constitution of 3 May 1791. Both in its traditional aristocratic and in its new democratic forms, the Polish ideal was incompatible with Russian autocracy. Unfortunately for the Poles, and probably for the Russians too, the continuing split in their society, between the nobility (*szlachta*) and the rest, made it impossible for them to mount a united movement of national resistance after incorporation into Russia. Unable either to throw off Russian domination or to submit meekly to it, Poland became a permanent festering sore on the body politic of Russia. It demonstrated vividly the problem of an Asiatic empire trying to dominate a European nation.

The old *szlachta* feeling for liberty was never altogether lost: under Russian rule it revived in the guise of romanticism. With the aid of its misty evocations Poles could dream of a nation – a Christ-like nation Mickiewicz called it – without the imperfections which reality perforce imposes, and each Polish patriot could indulge his own vision of a perfect community without sacrificing one jot of his individuality for the sake of it. In this way the Poles somehow elided the centuries which most peoples passed through between medieval chivalry and the modern nation-state. The poet Kazimierz Brodzinski put it simply:

> *Hail, O Christ, Thou Lord of Men!*
> *Poland in Thy footsteps treading*
> *Like Thee suffers, at Thy bidding;*
> *Like Thee, too, shall rise again.*[41]

The Tsars were not wholly insensitive to the peculiar problem they faced in Poland, and they made some attempt, as they had in other parts of the empire, to find ways of working peacefully with the Polish elite. Alexander I appointed a leading Polish nobleman, Prince Adam Czartoryski, who was also his close friend, as his Foreign Minister, and for a time took seriously his proposal for a 'Europe of nations', in which Poland would be independent under Russian protectorate.[42] Even after the defeat of Napoleon, when he turned his Holy Alliance *against* nations rather than in favour of them, the Tsar still granted Poland a constitution which gave it home rule in personal union with Russia.

From 1815, the Congress Kingdom of Poland, which included Warsaw, the old capital city, had its own government, its own elected legislative assembly (the Sejm), its own army, passports, currency and citizenship. Civil liberties were guaranteed; Polish was the official language, and the Catholic Church was accorded a recognized status as that of the majority of the people. Similar arrangements were being made for Finland at the time [see below, p. 37], and many educated Russians hoped that they might prove to be prototypes of a future Russian constitution. In a speech to the Sejm in 1818, Alexander himself expressed the hope that the Polish constitution would 'extend a beneficial influence over all the countries which Providence has committed to my care'.[43]

On the other hand, many other Russians never ceased to be suspicious that granting Poland real nationhood would enable it to filch the old principality of Lithuania, which was largely populated by Ukrainian, Belorussian and Lithuanian peasants, whom they considered natural subjects of Russia. Besides, Alexander was not accustomed to a real parliament and tended to equate serious opposition with sedition. When members of the Sejm spoke out against censorship and claimed the right to impeach ministers, he suspended it for four years and revoked the mandates of some of the deputies. Growing increasingly suspicious of the numerous patriotic and masonic societies which flourished in Poland, he closed them down (as in Russia) and instituted a purge of Wilno University.[44]

After the Decembrist rebellion of 1825, Nicholas I was even more suspicious of the Poles, and was not satisfied that Polish courts dealt firmly enough with those he believed to have been involved in treason. Matters came to a head when in November 1830 one of the patriotic societies tried to assassinate the Viceroy, Grand Duke Konstantin, and to disarm the Russian garrison. They failed in their immediate aim, but did seize control of the city of Warsaw, turning discontent into an armed insurrection and polarizing the situation. Every Pole had to decide for or against participation in the revolt, and Czartoryski reluctantly sponsored it, becoming head of an independent Polish government at war with Russia.

As before, however, Poland remained divided, both between moderates and radicals in the capital, and more generally between the *szlachta* and the peasants. A land reform was urgent if the insurrection was to gain the support of the peasants, and without that support it had no chance of success against the much larger Russian army. But the Polish government temporized until it was too late. In spite of the sterling fighting qualities which the Polish army displayed then, the Russians were able to restore complete control by the autumn of 1831.[45]

The result was the destruction of Poland's distinctive institutions. Nicholas I warned in 1835: 'If you persist in nursing your dreams of a distinct nationality, of an independent Poland . . . you can only bring the greatest of misfortunes upon yourselves.' The Sejm and the separate army were abolished, and most of Poland's affairs brought under Russian ministries. The ruble replaced the zloty. The University of Warsaw was closed, and all schools subjected to direct Russian control. The Russian language became officially acceptable alongside Polish in administration and justice, and the Russian criminal code replaced the Polish one. The Uniate Church in former Lithuania was assimilated into the Orthodox Church.[46]

In short, Poland, a proud and independent European nation, was treated as if it were less than a steppe khanate. Officers who had served in the rebellious army were cashiered and deported to Siberia, and nobles lost their estates. Many forestalled this fate by emigrating, mostly to France, which became the home of an alternative Poland. At the Hotel Lambert Czartoryski became a kind of king in exile. The Polish Democratic Society in Paris mocked Europe's diplomatic arrangements by talking of a 'Holy Alliance of Peoples'. Naturally the Russians were cast in the role of principal enemy of this 'Alliance', and the Polish emigration, with its brilliant poets, musicians, soldiers and elder statesmen aroused lively anti-Russian sentiment over most of Europe. The 'saviour of Europe' in 1812–15, Russia now became the 'gendarme of Europe', a reputation which was to hamper her diplomatic efforts greatly for the rest of the nineteenth century.

Even worse, when the Russian government resumed the path of reform in Poland, in the 1860s, the result was more or less a repetition of the 1830 rebellion. By making concessions to the church, permitting the re-opening of part of Warsaw University and encouraging serious discussion of reforms, including the abolition of serfdom, Alexander II aroused exaggerated hopes and also provoked bitter disagreements. The result was an armed insurrection in 1863–4, which aimed to restore Polish independence. It proved very tenacious: for a time it succeeded in driving the Russian army almost out of Poland and in establishing an alternative administration, effective at least in the rural areas. But as before the rising was undermined by its own internal divisions and by the failure to attract support from any European power. By the end of 1864 the Russian army regained complete control, and this time Poland lost the last vestiges of its separate status: what had been the 'Congress Kingdom' became merely 'the Vistula region'.[47] The debacle was not only disastrous for Poland, but led to a decisive souring of the reform efforts of Alexander II [see Part 4, Chapter 1].

THE JEWS   The partitions of Poland brought some 400,000 Jews into the empire.[48] They confronted their new masters with problems analogous to those of the Poles, yet also different. They were yet another 'awkward nationality' as far as Russian administrators were concerned, resistant to assimilation and difficult to fit into the empire's categories of population. They had an ancient religion and culture, a level of literacy and communal cohesion far higher than those of the Russians. They usually excelled at any trade, manufacture or profession they practised, so that they were dangerous competitors for others. They were widely resented among the population, partly for this reason, and partly because of religion: talk of the 'murderers of Christ' found a sympathetic echo among some believers, both Catholic and Orthodox.

Yet, in spite of their remarkable culture and talents, the Jews were nearly all poor, partly owing to discrimination long practised against them, partly because of the economic decline of eighteenth-century Poland. Their poverty, together with the economic functions they usually filled – as shopkeepers, traders, artisans, stewards, innkeepers and moneylenders – made it out of the question that any of them should be assimilated into the Russian nobility. They thus remained condemned to a conjunction of high achievement and low status: an unstable and explosive mixture.

From the outset the Russian government was concerned not only to integrate them, but also to protect other nationalities against them. When Moscow merchants petitioned in 1791 to be shielded from their competition, the government responded with a decree forbidding them to settle in the capital cities: this became the basis for the creation of the Pale of Settlement, which confined them, with few exceptions, to the former territories of Poland, plus the rest of Ukraine and New Russia.

For much of the nineteenth century, however, the Russian authorities did attempt to find some way of integrating Jews into society. The Jewish Statute of 1804 in some respects exemplified European enlightenment thinking about how this might best be accomplished. Jews were, for example, to be admitted without restriction to education at all levels, or, if they wished, to their own schools, where, however, they would be obliged to learn Russian, Polish or German. Their right of self-government in the *kahal* was confirmed in so far as it was separate from the rabbinate. They were allowed to set up and own factories, and to buy or lease land in New Russia and certain other provinces. On the other hand, even here there were restrictions: Jews were forbidden to engage in the liquor trade, which had been a major source of income for them in Poland. They were barred from military service, and required instead to pay a special tax. Above all, the Pale of Settlement was confirmed.[49]

In practice, the assimilatory aspects of the Statute remained a dead letter, while the restrictive ones were applied in full. Russian schools at all levels were so sparse that the Jews were scarcely able to take advantage of them. Even those who did could find it difficult to obtain appropriate employment afterwards: when one Simon Vul'f graduated in law at Dorpat University in 1816, he was briefly hired by the Ministry of Justice, but soon dismissed on the grounds that he could not handle cases involving ecclesiastical law.[50] As for the prospect of agricultural settlement in New Russia, the government never backed it up with funds. In local government, it proved impossible to separate the secular functions of the *kahal* from the religious function of the rabbinate: Russians made the distinction without difficulty, but it was quite alien to Jewish tradition. In 1844 the *kahal* was officially abolished, but in practice continued to exist, since the authorities were unable to replace it with anything effective. Henceforth, however, it had no acknowledgement or protection at law.

Overall, the Jews suffered from the Russian government's endemic tendency to promise well-tailored reforms which it was unable to deliver: only for the Jews this tendency was to prove especially damaging. Under Nicholas I assimilation was viewed not as an ultimate goal to be achieved, but as an immediate bureaucratic criterion, to be manipulated in 'carrot and stick' fashion. Conversion to Orthodoxy became a pre-condition for Jews' enjoyment of the normal rights of Russian subjects; for the vast majority who remained loyal to their ancestral faith discrimination intensified. In 1827 the exemption from military service was abolished. This did not merely mean that Jews henceforth bore the same obligations as Russians: many Jewish boys were picked out at the age of twelve for compulsory military training, after which they remained in the army for the customary twenty-five years.

Up to the mid-nineteenth century, the Jews suffered from their anomalous position within the empire, from popular prejudice and from the government's inability to match aspirations with practical measures. There was as yet, however, no concerted ethnic or racial doctrine directed against them: that was to be a product of a more nationally conscious era, when publicists wanted to explain away the continuing rift between Russian people and Russian empire.

THE BALTIC   At the opposite extremity from the Poles and the Jews were the German landed nobles of the Baltic provinces which Peter I conquered from the Swedes in the early eighteenth century. They entered the Tsar's service with conviction and remained perhaps of all ethnic groups the most loyal to him right up to the end of the empire, even in the period when national identity became the cardinal question in European politics.

There were good reasons for this. Of all the empire's elites, the Baltic German barons were alone in having nobody with whom they might potentially form a nation. On the lands they owned the peasants were Estonian and Latvian-speaking, fairly labile as regards ethnic identity, but certainly not identifying with Germany.[51] Furthermore, from the time of their incorporation, the Baltic barons possessed privileges which no other social or ethnic group managed to gain under the autocracy. Peter I confirmed the *Ritterschaften* of Estland and Livland in all the corporate rights and privileges which they had enjoyed under the Swedish crown, but had been in danger of losing: these included the right to run local government in the countryside, preservation of the Lutheran church, of German law and the German court system, and use of the German language for all official business. They were not absorbed into the Russian nobility, but kept their distinct identity and institutions.[52] Succeeding monarchs confirmed these arrangements: indeed, they later provided some of the principles on which Catherine II reformed the imperial nobility in 1785. (It is true that in carrying out this reform, Catherine also abolished the Baltic nobles' self-governing institutions, but they were restored by Paul a couple of decades later, and not interfered with again till the later nineteenth century.)

Peter took this unusual line with the Baltic barons because he recognized in them the ideal servitors he needed to carry through the kind of reforms he had in mind. They had long experience of corporate self-government on western models. They had easy access to German universities, where public administration in the spirit of cameralism was taught better than anywhere else in the world. Their Lutheran faith, with its emphasis on personal probity and loyalty to the state, was also an asset. In effect, Peter offered them a deal: confirmation of their privileges in return for loyal service to the Russian Empire.

This was a deal which had much to commend it from their viewpoint as well, and not merely in order to preserve their privileges. Young Germans imbued with ideals of good government picked up at Jena or Göttingen found that the petty principalities of their motherland could offer scant scope for their talents. Even relatively large and enlightened Prussia yielded to Russia in the opportunities it afforded for the deployment of their skills. Russia was a huge and backward empire, whose ruler was determined to develop its resources and mobilize its people: there, if anywhere, was the chance of achievement and promotion. The Tsars entrusted them with high positions of command, both in the armed forces and the civil service. During the eighteenth and nineteenth centuries, of the 2,867 senior officials mentioned by Erik Amburger in his detailed study of the imperial bureaucracy, 498 (17.4%) were of German origin, and 355 of those from the Baltic provinces alone. In the second quarter of the nineteenth century, when this German influence reached its height, the figures were even higher.[53]

Like the English aristocracy of the nineteenth century, the Baltic

German nobles combined ancient institutions with a modern understanding of statecraft and usually a ruthless exploitation of the rural population working on their estates. Uniquely among the nobilities of the Russian Empire, they practised entail rather than dividing their estates on the death of the owner. They combined a close interest in agriculture on their domains with an urban and cosmopolitan lifestyle: Riga and Reval, both centres of international trade, ensured contact with Germany and with a wider world and gave them regular intercourse with professional and commercial people, who were often German too, or at least spoke the language.

FINLAND Finland was an unusual success story for Russian imperial policy in the nineteenth century, at least until the final decade. That relative success was due partly to the singular circumstances in which Finland was received into the Empire. A province of Sweden at the beginning of the nineteenth century, it was conquered by the Russians during the war against Sweden in 1808–9.

The defeat of the Swedish army did not automatically entail the willing acquiescence of the Finnish people: guerrilla armies were formed and became troublesome to the new Russian administration. In an attempt to win over the Finns, Alexander I promised to uphold all the liberties they had enjoyed under the Swedish crown, and he summoned a meeting of the Finnish Diet at Poorvoo in March 1809. Under the arrangements worked out then, Finland kept its own laws and institutions, and had its own ruling council, or Senate, quite separate from the Russian government, and reporting personally to the Tsar in his capacity as Grand Duke of Finland. The Grand Duchy was even permitted to have its own small army. This kind of concession went further than the normal Russian imperial practice of respecting local traditions and conciliating local elites: it left Finland with unmistakable home rule.

Alexander's policy was almost completely successful in gaining the Finns' allegiance, and in this way a unique situation arose: the Russian Empire became home to a small European state, with its traditional laws and liberties inherited from the past. It is true that the Tsars did not see fit to convene the Diet for more than half a century, but in other respects they honoured the engagements they had entered into. The Finns reciprocated: in 1830 they remained quiescent, and some of their army units actually took part in the repression of the Polish rebellion. Finns did quite well out of the settlement with Russia: their high-flyers could take service in the Russian army and civil service, while the reverse road was closed to Russians.

More than that, the Finnish national movement, once it began to take hold during the mid-nineteenth century, initially received the support of the Russian government, as a counter-weight to the cultural and linguistic influence of the Swedes, which had hitherto been dominant. As late as the 1880s, one might have pointed to Finland as an example of successful Russian imperial integration.[54]

CENTRAL ASIA   Turkestan and the oases of Central Asia were not brought into the Russian Empire till the second half of the nineteenth century. They were conquered partly for traditional reasons of security: to protect the open southern border of steppe and desert. As Foreign Minister Gorchakov argued in a classic defence of Russian imperialism sent to other European powers in 1864: 'The situation of Russia in Central Asia is similar to that of all civilised states which come into contact with half-savage nomadic tribes without a firm social organisation. In such cases, the interests of border security and trade relations always require that the more civilised state have a certain authority over its neighbours, whose wild and unruly customs render them very troublesome. It begins first by curbing raids and pillaging. To put an end to these, it is often compelled to reduce the neighbouring tribes to some degree of close subordination.'[55]

There were also economic motives in play: the need for a secure supply of cotton at a time when the American Civil War threatened supplies from across the Atlantic, and in general the opportunities opened up by Central Asian raw materials and markets. Above all, the Russian need to shore up its European great power status by means of military successes after the humiliation of the Crimean War, and the ambition of local generals ensured that military solutions were sought for problems which might otherwise have been settled by diplomatic means.[56]

More than any other Russian imperial territories, Turkestan resembled right up to 1917 a colony of the normal European type, in that it was an area of economic exploitation, distant from the metropolis and recognized as being quite distinct from it. Its native peoples were classified as *inorodtsy* (aliens) and no attempt was made to Russify them or convert them to Christianity. Their elites, unlike those of the Caucasus, were not incorporated into the Russian nobility, though they were allowed to continue exercising most of their pre-existing powers under a Russian military Governor-General. The Islamic law courts were left undisturbed to exercise their prerogatives, at least in local affairs.

Probably with time, this attitude would have changed, and Russia would have begun the long, patient integration of the territory and its peoples into the imperial structure, as it had done over three centuries with the initially no less distinct Muslim peoples of the Volga basin. But their conquest came too late for this process to be seriously launched before the Tsarist empire itself collapsed.

C. Russia as empire – conclusions[57]

In the light of modern European imperial experience, mostly overseas and commercial, Russia looks decidedly odd. But that oddness largely fades if one examines it in the light of Asiatic or indeed pre-modern European experience, say that of Rome. Like an Asiatic empire, the Russian one created a supra-national elite with a strongly military ethos to integrate and rule the various subordinate peoples in their charge. It operated by gradually incorporating all those peoples more closely in the structure of the empire. Local tribute-gathering was integrated into the imperial fiscal system; tribal leaders were subordinated to the army command or to St Petersburg ministries; imperial law was given precedence over indigenous custom; Russian peasants or Cossacks were encouraged to move in and settle. All this took place without any presumption that ordinary Russians were superior to other peoples of the empire. Rather the reverse: Russians bore all the burdens of serfdom, from which some other peoples were exempted. All peoples, Russians included, were the raw material of empire, to be manipulated or dominated as seemed expedient to its unity and strength.

Let us sum up the main distinctive features of this empire.

1. It was an overland military empire, not only at the stage of

conquest and defence of a new territory, but usually in its long-term administrative provisions, especially in areas considered vulnerable to insurrection or to outside incursion, like Poland or the Caucasus. This did not mean that trade was non-existent, but it was certainly not paramount, and it was often closely associated with the military. This gave military leaders the chance of power and profit in the localities where they exercised their command. In this respect, the Russian empire resembled the Roman, though it lacked traditions of citizenship, and the dynasty remained strong enough to prevent any military leader making a bid for supreme authority.

2. The authorities' economic and fiscal policies gave priority to maintaining the armed forces and the administration. They tended to work in such a manner as to impede the mobilization of the economic potential of the empire, its population and resources.

3. The church played a relatively minor role. This is at first sight surprising, since at certain crucial phases the expansion of Russia took on the form of an anti-Islamic crusade, as in Spain. But in Asiatic empires there is no place for an independent church: ideology is part of the state's armoury, and the ruler rules with the 'mandate of heaven'.

4. There was usually no distinction between metropolis and colonies. Annexed territories became full components of the empire as soon as practicable. The stability of the empire was maintained over time by co-opting local elites and integrating them into the Russian nobility and bureaucracy. This co-option had the effect both of making the empire multi-national in principle and of widening the gap between elites and masses of all ethnic groups, including the Russians themselves. On the other hand, relations between the diverse peoples were markedly less racist than in, say, the British Empire. On the mass level, the worst relationships were between nomadic and sedentary peoples, with the sedentary ones steadily gaining ground, and between the Islamic and Christian peoples of the Caucasus.

5. The Russian culture and language were tangible integrating fac-

tors for most ethnic groups, but did not succeed, as they did in China, in obliterating and replacing other cultures. Whereas in China high culture was endogenous and worked along with the official ideology in maintaining order and social integration, in Russia high culture was to a large extent borrowed from outside and became subversive of official values. China was the heartland of Asia, while Russia was on the periphery of Europe, with all the advantages and disadvantages which that position entailed.

6. The empire was permanently open to the surrounding world, to both trade and invasion. Isolationism was not an option: Russia could not become 'the middle kingdom' in proud detachment, like China. Foreign and military policy were always crucial. Even when stability and security were attained on the Asian frontiers, they were never complete in the direction of Europe, from where the most dangerous and destructive invasions came, since the European states were technically and culturally on the whole more advanced. That is why the major crises came from there too.

7. At all times the survival of the empire and the maintenance of its territorial integrity were the paramount priorities for Russia's rulers, before which national, religious, economic and other priorities invariably yielded. The Russian imperial sense of identity was powerful: it rested on pride in the size and diversity of the empire, as well as on military victories. As Karamzin put it in his *History of the Russian State*, 'If we look at the expanse of this unique state, our minds are stunned: Rome in its greatness never equalled it ... One need not be a Russian, only a thinking individual, to read with admiration accounts of the history of a nation which, through its courage and fortitude, won dominion over one-ninth of the world, opened up countries hitherto unknown, brought them into the universal system of geography and history, and enlightened them in the Divine Faith.'[58] Thus Russian national identity tended to be subsumed in that of the empire, whose values were in principle multi-national. That worked well enough until the other European powers, Russia's bitter rivals, started to become nation-states.

PART TWO

State-building

1

The First Crises of Empire

At its origins in the sixteenth century, this new empire with its grandiose claims was built on very fragile political foundations. Muscovy had inherited a system of rule based on kinship, which provided that on the death of a senior member of the ruling dynasty, his patrimony, i.e. the land he both owned and ruled over, would descend not to his eldest son but to all his surviving sons. As a result Kievan *Rus'* and its successor principalities (known as *udely* or 'appanages') were constantly fragmenting and being fought over. To counter this tendency a principle of 'seniority' was introduced, which was supposed to regulate the relations between male members of the dynastic family and ensure harmony between them. It does not appear that it ever worked properly. Feuding within princely families was a constant problem, while retainers, both boyars and peasants, were able to transfer their allegiance from one to another. The whole system seems more suited to a pastoral way of life, where control over flocks and rights of pasture is at issue, rather than to settled agricultural and urban life: perhaps it originated through interaction with nomadic tribes.

The southern territories of *Rus'*, both because of their geographical vulnerability and because of the persistence of the kinship system, succumbed especially easily to the Mongol incursion in the thirteenth century, and later to domination by the Grand Duchy of Lithuania. The northern, more wooded territories, however, provided a better environment for the emergence of strong princely authority. Finding the terrain less congenial to them there, the Mongols were content to exercise a loose suzerainty, insisting on the timely rendering of dues and tributes, but leaving administration and the collecting of them to the local princes and their retainers. The cunning and

45

prudent exercise of this delegated authority, a kind of tax-farming, enabled Muscovy to augment and consolidate its power to the point where it was eventually able to challenge the Mongols' sovereignty outright.[1]

Already for a century before the conquest of Kazan' the Grand Duchy of Moscow had been reorganizing itself to meet the challenge of absorbing new territories and assuming a more significant historical mission. It was not the only power which could lay claim to the inheritance of Kievan *Rus'*. The loosely organized aristocratic Grand Duchy of Lithuania was also a realistic contender, as was the oligarchic urban republic of Novgorod, with its ruling city council (*veche*) and its immense northern hinterland.

Ivan III, however, decisively defeated the Novgorodian army in 1471 and thereafter took advantage of the city's extensive territories to introduce a new system of both administration and army recruitment. He confiscated many of the lands belonging to Novgorod's boyars and awarded them to his own servitors on condition that they raised troops to make available to him. This was the first widespread application of the *pomest'e* system: the rewarding of civil and military officials with 'service estates' which provided them with a living while they served the Grand Duke in the chancery or on the battlefield. Ivan III used it to raise troops to fight under his banner, and also to attract boyars from the other duchies of *Rus'*.

The system was continued by his son, Vasilii III, and extended each time Muscovy absorbed new territories, for example, from Tver', Riazan' or Pskov. However, there were limits to the system: the Grand Duke did not wish to uproot his own followers who held their patrimonial estates within his own Grand Duchy. Furthermore, the church held huge landholdings which it was not prepared to surrender to the secular power. Ivan and Vasilii also started the process of converting their administration from one run by word of mouth for household management to one conducted in writing for the governance of a whole realm; in other words they created an embryonic bureaucracy.[2]

Ivan III and Vasilii III bolstered their augmented power by beginning to adopt the external show of sovereignty – asserting their independence of the Mongols – and of imperial dignity. Ivan married the niece of the last Byzantine Emperor, Sofia Paleologue, and he and his son intermittently employed the title *Tsar'* (Caesar or Emperor), when they felt they could get it acknowledged. This symbolic acquisition of authority culminated in the coronation of Ivan IV as Tsar in 1547.

To some extent, however, these quasi-imperial pretensions were an illusion, concealing the reality that, given primitive technology and communications, power still rested with boyar clans, which used the autocratic façade to lend some stability and decorum to a power constellation which would otherwise have fallen apart in perpetual feuding. Court ceremonial, the Tsar's religious processions, his public almsgivings and pilgrimages to distant monasteries all gave substance to an ideal of God-ordained rule which veiled the sordid brutality of internecine boyar rivalry. Boyars might fight each other for influence, but not for the throne itself, for that would plunge the entire realm into chaos. Ivan IV had ample opportunity to convince himself of this underlying reality during his minority, when boyars squabbled violently over the regency and his own favourites were murdered before his eyes, but he himself was left unharmed. He assumed full royal power convinced of the need to tame the boyars and make the reality more like the image.[3]

Soon after his coronation Ivan and his advisers made a start towards equipping Moscow for the role it was gradually but ostentatiously assuming, that of a sovereign and integrated Eurasian great power with extensive imperial responsibilities. The theorist who inspired this brief and imperfect but fruitful period of state-building was Ivan Semenovich Peresvetov, a minor nobleman from Lithuania who had seen service in a number of countries, including the Ottoman Empire, before coming to Moscow. When Ivan was crowned, Peresvetov presented him with a most unusual *chelobitnaia* (humble petition) in the form of two treatises, *The Legend of the Fall of Tsar'grad* and *The Legend of Sultan Mehmet*, which recounted the conquest of Constantinople in 1453 by the Ottomans.[4]

The theme was well chosen. The fate of Byzantium was a constant preoccupation of the Muscovites, both because by now they were claiming its heritage, and also because its eclipse at the hands of the Ottomans was a precedent whose repetition they wished to avoid. The persistent raids from the south were a constant reminder of the danger. Peresvetov charged that Byzantium had fallen because of the irresponsible lifestyle of its aristocrats: their idleness, their greed, their feuding, their rapacious exploitation of the common people. The parallel with the Muscovite boyars was inescapable, especially to Ivan after his childhood experiences. Peresvetov contrasted the laxity of the Byzantine Emperors in tolerating this kind of behaviour with the wise statesmanship of the victorious Sultan Mehmet II, who drew his advisers and military leaders from all social classes according to merit, and did not allow kinship and precedence to enfeeble the sinews of the state.

Peresvetov was almost certainly right. The Ottomans owed the creation of their empire at least in large part to reforms which weakened the native Turkish nobles who had previously formed the backbone of its tribal confederacies. Those nobles had been supplanted at the Ottoman court by Christian youths recruited from the Balkans and converted to Islam under the *devshirme* system. They furnished both the Janissaries, the elite corps of the army, and the principal civilian advisers. The Sultan required all his military and governmental leaders, whatever their provenance, to accept the status of his personal slaves, in order to separate them forcibly from their kinship loyalties. The conquered city of Constantinople was used for the same purpose: to give his new elite a power base remote from the native grazing lands of the Turkish nobles.

Such a system had obvious attractions for a Muscovite ruler also building an empire on vulnerable territories on the frontier between Christianity and Islam, and also struggling to free himself from aristocratic clans. Peresvetov did not go as far as his Ottoman model, and refrained from recommending slavery; but he did propose that the army should be recruited and trained by the state and paid for directly out of the treasury. This would ensure that individual regiments could not become instruments of baronial feuding. He favoured a service nobility promoted on the basis of merit and achievement, but he did not envisage serfdom as a means of providing them with their livelihood: in so far as he considered the matter at all, he assumed they would be salaried out of tax revenues.

Peresvetov's importance was that he offered a vision of a state able to mobilize the resources of its peoples and lands equitably and efficiently. He was one of the first European theorists of monarchical absolutism resting on the rule of law. He believed that a consistent law code should be published, and that its provisions should be guided by the concept of *pravda* (which in Russian means both truth and justice): it would be the task of the 'wise and severe monarch' to discern and uphold this principle, according no favour to the privileged and powerful.

In the early years of his reign we can see Ivan endeavouring to implement, in his own way, some of Peresvetov's ideas, especially where they would enhance the strength and efficiency of the monarchy. At the same time he was trying to reach out beyond the fractious boyars and courtiers to make contact with the local elites of town and countryside and bind them into a more cohesive system of rule. Together with his Chosen Council, an ad hoc grouping of boyars, clergymen and service nobles personally chosen by him, he tried to make a start towards removing the 'sovereign's affairs' (*gosudarevo delo*) from the private whims of the boyars and their agents, and bringing them under the control of himself in alliance with the 'land' (*zemlia*). The word *zemlia* is crucial to an understanding of Muscovite politics. It referred to local communities as contrasted with the sovereign or the central government – what in English we often call the 'grass roots'.

Hitherto taxation, local government and justice had been 'privatized' under a system known as *kormlenie* or 'feeding', that is, handled by the prince's appointed officials as part of their patrimony. In return for their services they kept a part of the income raised. In theory the amount they were entitled to was agreed in advance, but in practice it was difficult to monitor. Ivan wanted greater control over both the revenues and the 'feeders', so he now replaced *kormlenie* with a system under which these functions were exercised by elected local assemblies, known as *zemstva* (or in the case of criminal justice, *guby*). In doing this, Ivan was giving official status to elected village and urban assemblies (usually denoted by the word *mir*) which already existed informally in many places. Their *starosty*, or 'elders', now took over most of the functions of the prince's appointees.

This reform was very imperfect. It did not apply in territories where there was direct military danger, like the south, or the western border with Lithuania and Livonia. Furthermore, it created very tiny local government units, often just one village or group of villages, not linked with one another or with the central government. The members of the *mir* assemblies were bound by 'mutual responsibility' for their tax revenues and for the conduct of their elected officials, which meant they had to make up shortfalls and damages out of their own pockets. All this generated a reluctant and ineffective local administrative, judicial and fiscal system, which in practice soon had to be supplemented once more by appointed officials.[5]

Nevertheless Ivan made some attempt to draw the people of the *zemlia* into consultation with himself. In 1549 he convened a so-called 'Council of Reconciliation' (*sobor primireniia*) to deal with the conflicts which had flared up during his minority and had provoked rioting in Moscow after his coronation. There were consultations with lay people over a law code in 1550 and with clergymen, service nobles, merchants and government officials in 1566 over whether to continue the war he was waging in Livonia [see the p. 52] and how to pay for it.[6] Often referred to in historical literature as *zemskie sobory* or 'assemblies of the land', these were not representative assemblies in the sense in which that term was understood in the medieval West: they were more like consultations of the Tsar with such local agents as could be conveniently assembled. But they do indicate a desire to spread the responsibility for state authority wider than the court.[7]

To gain a tighter grip over the army Ivan tried to extend the system of 'service estates' (*pomest'ia*) introduced by his grandfather. In 1550 he published a so-called 'Thousand Book', a list of one thousand leading servitors whom he wished to summon to state service, endowing them with cultivated land in the neighbourhood of Moscow. He was unable, however, to implement his plan in full because the church refused to surrender any of the immense acreage in the hands of its bishops and monasteries. All the same, he issued a decree in 1556 laying down in principle the military duties of all those who held landed estates, whether hereditary patrimonies (*votchiny*) or *pomest'ia*. Their obligations varied somewhat from region to region, but broadly speaking 150 desiatiny of arable land obliged a servitor to furnish one fully equipped armed man for the Tsar's service. These requirements meant that for the first time, at least in theory, there were now limits to the rights of holders of patrimonial estates. Ivan also restricted the right of boyars to serve in the army according to the seniority of their family.[8]

Ivan tried to incorporate these measures in the religious world view to which he subscribed personally and which, as we have seen, was the legitimization of his burgeoning empire. He began his reign and his marriage with a pilgrimage to the monastery of the Trinity and St Sergii, which had been at the centre of Moscow's religious life in the middle ages. He launched his work of reform, as we have seen, by summoning a special so-called 'Council of Reconciliation', at which he reproached the boyars with their disloyal behaviour towards him, but also confessed his own sins and called for general repentance.

Since his imperial claims rested on religious as much as on secular grounds, Ivan tried to bring order and discipline to the church as much as to the state. If the priests were drunken and the monks corrupt, and if the scriptures were mistranslated, then what price talk of the Third Rome? In 1551 he summoned a Church Council and submitted to it a long series of questions, a hundred in number – hence the Council's generally accepted name, *Stoglav*, or 'a hundred headings'. He himself participated in the debates, as the Byzantine Emperor had done at the early ecumenical councils. The Councils of 1547 and 1549 had consolidated the church's claim to a 'great tradition' of its own. Now Ivan wanted both to discipline the church internally to make it more worthy of its great mission, and to persuade it to yield some of its landholdings to award to his military servitors.

The Council decreed a large number of measures raising standards and tightening discipline within both parishes and monasteries. It also considered the question whether the scriptures and liturgical practices needed reforming to bring them into line with Greek models. It explicitly upheld existing texts and liturgical practices – such as making the sign of the cross with two fingers raised, rather than with three as was the practice elsewhere in the Orthodox world, including Novgorod. The Council resisted Ivan's wish to pursue a widespread secularization of church lands, but accepted a degree of limitation on them.[9]

The problem with the *Stoglav* resolutions was that in the turbulence of the coming decades there was no way of ensuring that they were carried out, and in the seventeenth century most of the reforming work had to be carried out again from the beginning. The question of the scriptures and liturgy would also be raised again then.

Ivan was a pious, learned and intense young man. His view of the world and of his own duties was imbued with a kind of monastic spirit, as if he took wholly seriously the notion of the 'Third Rome' becoming God's kingdom on earth.[10] At the same time, his ideals were patently too grandiose, ascetic and demanding. As a result, at times he would veer from heartfelt contrition and self-denial into orgies of sensuality and sadism. The tension was present in his personality, as a result probably of his strange upbringing, but it was exacerbated by the circumstances in which he had to rule, as head of an empire proclaiming an exalted religious and secular mission on the basis of inadequate resources and a still insecure tradition.

It is not surprising, then, that before long his reform programme ran into the ground and both Ivan and his realm were plunged into a divisive and destructive crisis. In 1558 he launched a third military campaign, to follow those of Kazan' and Astrakhan', this time against the Livonian Knights, in order to secure an outlet to the Baltic Sea and thus to easier contact with other European powers. Early successes gave way to setbacks as Lithuania intervened against Muscovy and the war became more general and costly. In 1560, moreover, Ivan's beloved wife, Anastasia, died, removing a restraining element on his unstable personality, and he fell out with several leading members of his Chosen Council.

One of them, Prince Andrei Kurbskii, actually abandoned his military command and went over to Lithuania. From the safety of his new home he wrote a series of devastating epistles designed to discredit Ivan. They raise issues of fundamental importance in understanding the new style of monarchy, not least because Kurbskii accepted its basic validity as a model. He was not a proponent of appanage princely freedoms, nor was he a western liberal humanist of the renaissance type. He believed in the religious mission of *Rus'* and in absolute monarchy as the means to fulfil it, but he felt that to be true to that mission, the monarchy must observe its own laws and those of God. He referred to *Rus'* as 'the holy Russian land', and he accused Ivan of defiling her by his gross and sinful behaviour. The Muscovite armies he called 'the strong in Israel', and berated Ivan for beating and killing his own commanders. Ivan rejected many of the charges and hurled others back in Kurbskii's face, but the main burden of his response was that his authority had been granted to him by God, and that Kurbskii's flight was therefore treachery and apostasy. Both parties to the correspondence believed in *Rus*'s mission and in autocracy, but differed over the moral and legal obligations incumbent on the autocrat.[11]

Ivan was convinced that harsh and even cruel means were justified when sovereignty had to be demonstratively exercised. He was determined to put an end to the kinship appanage principle, under which a member of a princely family could choose for himself under which liege lord to serve: this was doubly dangerous to him when he was waging war with Lithuania, which had a rival claim as 'gatherer of the Russian lands'. He feared particularly the claims to the throne of his cousin, Prince Vladimir Staritskii, the most powerful of the surviving appanage lords. At the same time he wanted to have at his disposal more land which he could award to his military servitors: the simplest way to obtain it was to confiscate it from those same free-wheeling boyars.

In autumn 1564, a Lithuanian offensive, supported by Kurbskii, coincided with one mounted from the south by the Crimean Khan, Devlet-Girei. Muscovite forces managed to repel the double danger, but it nevertheless dramatized the country's vulnerability, and Ivan reacted to it in an abrupt and histrionic manner. In December 1564 he suddenly withdrew from Moscow along with his court and resettled in Aleksandrovskaia Sloboda, a minor princely residence to the north-east. From there he sent the bewildered boyars, prelates and officials a missive accusing them of treason and of plundering the treasury for their own selfish interests. If they wished him to return to the throne, he demanded that they must give him the right to set up his own separate and special realm (*oprichnina*), which would guarantee him the income he needed for his court and army, and they must leave him free to proceed against peculators, traitors and heretics as he saw fit.

Ivan's expedition was an act of pure theatre, externalizing his crushing sense of lonely responsibility, isolation and rejection (more or less as British royals nowadays resort to the press to conduct their own psychological and familial struggles), but also dramatizing the country's helplessness without a strong ruler. As he had anticipated, the boyars begged him to return and conceded to him what he was demanding. There followed another set-piece scene of mutual repentance and simulated forgiveness, after which Ivan put his design into effect.

He divided his territory into two realms, in one of which, the *oprichnina*, he had complete and unrestricted power, while the other, the *zemshchina*, was governed by the boyar council (the Boyar Duma) according to existing customs. The *oprichnina* included extensive lands in the north and east which had originally belonged to Novgorod, as well as some towns and regions within the appanage principality of Moscow. Boyars living on it were expropriated and assigned territory in the *zemshchina*, while their former lands were offered to Ivan's newly promoted servitors. This exchange of land uprooted many, though not all, of the leading boyar clans, including the Staritskiis, from their ancestral domains and their local power bases, and eliminated the restraints on endowing the 'chosen thousand' servitors with land and peasants. Some of the boyars were executed on charges of heresy or treason, others were exiled or awarded land in remote regions. The process was not a tidy one: Ivan rewarded individuals not for their social origin but for their loyalty and devotion to him. The general tendency was to strengthen the service nobility at the expense of the boyars, but the process was far from completed, and the boyars remained a considerable force in the land.

Meanwhile the *oprichnina* lands provided the finances for a wholly new army and police force, charged both with defending the frontiers and with extirpating treason and heresy. The *oprichnina* was also a kind of grotesque monastic court: Ivan referred to his *oprichniki* as 'brothers'. Their humble unadorned clothes and ascetic existence were intended to serve as a model of the Christian life Ivan intended his subjects to lead. The *oprichniki* were given special powers of investigation, arrest and emergency judicial procedure. Dressed in long black cloaks, resembling a monk's habit, they rode on black horses, each carrying a dog's head and a broom mounted on a long stick. 'This means that first of all they bite like dogs, and then they sweep away everything superfluous out of the land.'[12]

Within a short time, their arbitrary, violent and sadistic procedures had inspired fear in every subject and horrified incredulity among foreign observers. Far from exemplifying the Christian life, the 'brothers' seemed only to demonstrate what monstrous atrocities can befall a people whose ruler tramples underfoot not only human laws but those of God as well. This was precisely what Kurbskii had alleged. The leading churchman, Metropolitan Filipp, not in the safety of Lithuania, protested courageously in the same terms. Once, in the cathedral, he asked in the presence of clergy and boyars, 'How long will you go on spilling the innocent blood of faithful people and Christians ... ? Tatars and heathens and the whole world can say that all peoples have justice and laws, but only in Russia do they not exist.' Ivan tolerated Filipp for a while, so anxious was he to preserve his alliance with the church, but eventually had him arrested in the middle of a sermon and confined in a monastery where he was later strangled.[13]

Ivan got rid of his most dangerous rival in 1569, when he accused Vladimir Staritskii publicly of plotting to assassinate him and compelled him to drink poison. This murder was followed by an inquisitorial visit to the ancient city of Novgorod, which he suspected of supporting Staritskii and seeking a rapprochement with Lithuania. In January 1570 he took his revenge, unleashing his *oprichniki* on the townsfolk in a frenzy of vindictiveness. In the course of a few weeks, thousands of people were tortured and killed: a once prosperous city, model for an alternative *Rus'*, was left devastated, a mere shadow of its former self.

The Novgorod excesses revealed that the *oprichnyi* army had become a travesty of Peresvetov's vision of soldiers selected for their courage and achievement. Corrupted and enfeebled by their own impunity, they proved incapable in 1571 of repelling Khan Devlet-Girei, who attacked and sacked the city of Moscow, capturing thousands of its inhabitants for slaves. After this debacle, Ivan executed the *oprichnyi* commanders and reunited the army with its *zemskii* counterpart. Together, they succeeded in repelling Devlet-Girei the following year.

The episode of the *oprichnina* suggests the extraordinary vulnerability of the Muscovite state at the time when it had just taken on itself extensive new claims and responsibilities both religious and secular. It was poorly adapted to an assertion of imperial and ecumenical power which required internal unity and the efficient use of resources. The inherited kinship principle obstructed both these ideals. Ivan had set out to create the framework of what might have become a national government, but, stumbling at the first hurdle, he changed course convulsively in completely the opposite direction.

Paradoxically, in order to overcome the appanage mentality, Ivan himself set up what was in effect a vastly bloated appanage territory, where in the name of a higher state principle he attempted to exercise an authority even more complete than that of any patrimonial ruler. To add to the hubris, he tried to combine church and state in one monopolistic dispensation: to promote a Christian ideal, he unleashed a frenzy of debauchery and cruelty. He succeeded in almost none of his aims, and he exposed the population of Muscovy to such privations and excesses as seriously to weaken their economic and military potential for the following decades. The Livonian Wars, which he fought on and off for quarter of a century, ended with Muscovy not only failing to gain territory, but also losing the foothold on the eastern Baltic which she had inherited from Novgorod. As a founder of empire, Ivan had made a promising start, but had then jeopardized all his gains through his external over-ambition and his unbalanced internal policy.

Time of Troubles

Ivan IV's endless wars, his ruthless and haphazard remodelling of Muscovy's political and social structure, his campaigns of unrestrained terror against his own people – all these upheavals left a country traumatized. Every stratum of society was affected. Many of the boyars had been evicted from their ancestral domains and shorn of the power they had previously taken for granted, the service nobility was still insecure, the clergy was torn apart by the heresy hunts, while the merchants and peasants were being fixed to their abode by 'mutual responsibility' and heavy taxation. More and more peasants were becoming enserfed by debt or by the dues they owed to the holders of service estates. Not a few decided to flee these new or increased burdens and seek a new life somewhere in the distant forests or among the Cossacks of the frontiers.

The late sixteenth century was thus a time of deep crisis, the central Russian lands becoming depopulated by peasant flight, the towns troubled by poverty and disorder. Ivan himself added a vital new element to the crisis when he killed his eldest son in a fit of fury. He of all people should have known what a disaster to Muscovy was the weakening of the succession to the throne. Of his two surviving sons, one, Fedor, ruled from 1584–98, but was always in poor health and died young, while the other, Dmitrii, was the offspring of his fifth wife and thus not acknowledged as heir by the Orthodox Church, in any case he died in mysterious circumstances in the provincial town of Uglich in 1591.

At this time, when the dynasty seemed to be faltering, Moscow took one final step to buttress its claims to be the 'Third Rome'. By a mixture of cajolery and pressure, the eastern Patriarchs were persuaded in 1589 to consent to the elevation of the title of Metropolitan of Moscow to that of Patriarch. This was a step of little practical importance, since the Muscovite church had long been self-governing, but its symbolic significance was considerable, since this was the first patriarchal title to be created since the age of the ecumenical councils ten centuries earlier. The Muscovite church joined the ranks of the most ancient and dignified Orthodox jurisdictions.[14]

The end of the Riurik dynasty in 1598 posed for the Muscovite state questions it had never faced before. Hitherto the state had been inseparable from the person of the Grand Prince/Tsar: indeed the word 'state' is a misnomer if applied to most people's contemporary understanding of the authority under which they lived. But now for the first time those active in politics – those holding a *chin*, or official status – had to learn to look at monarchical authority in a more abstract way, to ask themselves what qualities they expected of the person who would exercise it, and under what conditions he would do so. This was a mental leap which was extraordinarily difficult to make.

The problem was that Ivan IV's brief attempt to institutionalize and frame in law the demands the Tsar could make on the various strata of society had collapsed as a result of his wars and the grotesque machinations of the *oprichnina*. No service noble, merchant or peasant could know for certain in advance what obligations he would have to discharge from one year to the next, nor could he apply to a court if he felt they had been exceeded. The whole concept of sovereignty remained that of the appanage principality, whose lands and people were completely at the disposal of its ruler, while he answered only to God for his treatment of them. Muscovy had not outgrown this mentality before it became a proto-national state, claiming to speak for all Russians, and on top of that an incipient and fast-growing empire.

The patrimonial outlook had implications for the subjects as well as the ruler. They too could treat the realm as a master's estate which they were at liberty to quit if they preferred to seek employment elsewhere. The impenetrable forests and immense open plains gave them the geographical means to escape the most importunate ruler. This very fluidity of social relations made the creation of either legality or intermediate institutions extremely difficult. As we have seen, Ivan abandoned the attempt at an early stage. It also meant that subjects who wished to oppose authority rather than merely flee it had no accepted channels for doing so other than by sponsoring an alternative ruler, that is, a pretender.

The only shadowy institutions which did exist to represent the various strata of society were the *zemskie sobory*. The new importance of the Patriarchate was underlined when Patriarch Job convened a *sobor* to solve the crisis created by the abrupt end of the dynasty. It unanimously offered the throne to Boris Godunov, who, though not from one of the most senior boyar families, had been Fedor's brother-in-law and regent, and was thus a natural candidate.

The circumstances of his election are of interest, for they represent a moment when the beginnings of a covenant between Tsar and people might have been worked out. Godunov several times declined the throne when it was offered to him. According to the historian Kliuchevskii, the boyar members of the *sobor* were expecting that he would accept a charter (*gramota*) defining the limits of his power. By playing a 'comedy of silence', refusing the crown but also refusing to sign any kind of limitation on the authority of the crown, Godunov put the *sobor* in the position where they had either to offer him traditional unrestrained patrimonial authority or open the way to a potentially very damaging struggle for the succession. Not surprisingly, the delegates put stability first, and Godunov became Tsar without any restraints to his power. Kliuchevskii feels that Godunov's behaviour was misguided: 'Boris was not the hereditary patrimonial ruler of the Muscovite state, but the people's choice. He began a new succession of Tsars with a new political significance, In order not to be absurd or detested, he should have behaved in a different way, and not aped the defunct dynasty with its appanage customs and prejudices.'[15]

Most of the boyar clans were thus discontented with Godunov from the outset. The service nobles formed the bulk of his support, but many of them were worried that the peasants on whom they relied for their livelihood were being enticed away from them by wealthier landowners or monasteries, who could offer better conditions. Boris reacted to their complaints by limiting the peasants' right to move and facilitating procedures for reclaiming those who had done so. He combined this with trying to impose greater control over the Cossacks and small landowners of the vulnerable southern frontier regions.

As factionalism mounted, Boris set his minions to spy on his rivals and enemies: he imprisoned or murdered some, and exiled others to remote regions. Deportations, confiscations and executions multiplied, recalling sinister memories of Ivan the Terrible. These afflictions might have been tolerated in a Tsar who had come to the throne by heredity. But Boris had been chosen, and it followed that alternatives could be contemplated. The last straw was a series of bad harvests in 1601–3.

Before long a pretender appeared, claiming to be Ivan IV's son Dmitrii, escaped from his reported death in Uglich. He immediately attracted a large and diverse following: boyars jealous of Godunov, service nobles desirous of larger estates and a firmer grip on their peasants, Cossacks anxious to reassert their ancient freedoms, peasants calling for an easing of serfdom. Although representatives of all these classes flocked to his banner, their aspirations contradicted each other, and there was no way any ruler, no matter how skilful, could have reconciled them. However, Boris's sudden death in April 1605 opened the capital to them, without their mutual differences having been resolved.[16]

The chaos was compounded by international intervention: Poland-Lithuania and Sweden, eager to take advantage of the weakening of their threatening eastern neighbour, sent their troops in to enforce their own territorial, religious and dynastic interests. Over the next few years, Muscovy was torn apart by boyar feuds, social revolution and international warfare. Sovereignty over it was claimed or temporarily exercised by three pretenders, a leading boyar, a boyar council, a Polish prince and a triumvirate of service nobles. This was the epoch which Russians refer to as the 'Time of Troubles' (*smutnoe vremia*).

Yet in the end Muscovy did not disintegrate, and in 1613 the motley and disreputable parade of pretenders came to an end when a *zemskii sobor* elected a new Tsar, Mikhail Romanov, from a boyar family which had been a principal rival of the Godunovs. However one explains it, some sense of shared identity and destiny impelled the various warring groups to find sufficient common ground to cooperate in expelling the foreigners from their capital city and in restoring the authority of the state. The way in which the 'land' recovered in the absence of a legitimate Tsar suggested that Muscovy had the potential to outgrow the dynastic patrimonial framework, that a potentially state-bearing people existed.

Precisely because the state was falling apart and had to be reconstituted, the Time of Troubles was quite fruitful in political programmes, some of which indicate the way a Russian civic nation might have evolved had the relentless pressure of empire and great power status been eased. The founding document of a civic nation is often an agreement reached during a conflict between a ruler and his elites: witness the Magna Carta of 1215 in England and the Golden Bull of 1222 in Hungary. An analogous agreement was mooted in February 1610 when protagonists of the second pretender switched their support to the Polish crown. They presented King Sigismund with a set of conditions on which they were prepared to elect his son Wladyslaw as Tsar. The first was that the Orthodox faith should remain inviolate. Then came stipulations on the rights of individual estates, for example, not to be punished or to have property confiscated without trial before a properly constituted court, not to be demoted from high *chin* without clear and demonstrable fault. The document implied a state structure in which supreme authority would be shared with a combined boyar assembly and *zemskii sobor* (*duma boiar i vseia zemli*), in agreement with which questions of taxes, salaries of service people and the bestowal of patrimonial and service estates would be decided.[17] Such a document might have laid the basis for a constitutional Muscovite monarchy in personal union with Poland.

However, it never took effect, since Wladyslaw did not come to claim his throne. Instead, Sigismund declared his intention of doing so himself. This prompted the Patriarch, Hermogen, to issue a stern injunction that the Russian people were not to 'kiss the cross before a Catholic king'. This assertion of Orthodox fundamentalism seems to have struck a chord, and the death of the second pretender at about the same time removed an obstacle to combined national action. At any rate, within a few months an ad hoc alliance of service nobles and Cossacks had formed a militia and a provisional government and issued a statement recognizing as the supreme authority 'the whole land'. As we have seen, this term signified the power of local communities, separate from but allied with the supreme power. For the moment, the army council reserved to itself the exercise of this authority, but promised not to take certain steps, such as imposing the death penalty, without consulting the whole army. They indicated that lands wrongfully appropriated by boyars were to be returned to the state land fund, from which they would be awarded to servitors strictly in accordance with the duties they had discharged. Serving Cossacks were to be offered the choice of a *pomest'e* to settle down on or a salary for continuing military service on the borders. Peasants were to be forbidden to leave the estates on which they worked, and provisions were made for their recapture and return if they did so.[18]

This declaration represented a compromise between the interests of the Cossacks and those of the service nobility. It did not fully satisfy either: Cossacks in particular were suspicious that it would breach their ancient freedom. Moreover, it offered nothing to the towns or to the ordinary peasant soldiers. Relations between the different social groups broke down, and Prokopii Liapunov, a service noble from Riazan' who commanded the militia, was murdered. The first attempt to unite the nation behind a programme of expelling infidels and foreigners had failed because of the incompatible social interests of those involved.

The second and more successful attempt originated in the towns of the north and east. It began with a traditional *skhod*, or assembly, of the zemstvo elders in Nizhnii Novgorod, the principal city of the middle Volga. A merchant, Kuz'ma Minin, made an eloquent appeal to his colleagues to reject the rule of Cossacks and aliens as divisive and offensive to the true faith, and to take the initiative themselves in setting up a voluntary militia to march on Moscow, free it and enthrone a new Tsar 'whom God shall send us'. The assembly approved the idea and composed appeals to other towns for money and recruits: 'Let us be together of one accord ... Orthodox Christians in love and unity, and let us not tolerate the recent disorders, but let us fight untiringly to the death to purge the state of Muscovy from our enemies, the Poles and Lithuanians.'[19] Towns in the north and east, and on the Volga one by one joined the movement, sending contributions and troops, while subsidies were also received from the Stroganovs and from some monasteries.

The way the movement was built up demonstrates the importance of the wealth Moscow was by now receiving from the Volga basin and from its new northern and eastern territories, and also the potential of the elective *mir* assemblies which Ivan had tried to institutionalize at the start of his reign. As the historian Platonov put it, this was a movement of 'zemskaia Rus', of church, land and traditional local gatherings against disunity and foreign domination'.[20] The militia was placed under the command of a service noble and *voevoda*, Dmitrii Pozharskii, who had earlier distinguished himself in fighting against the Poles.

Pozharskii took up position in Iaroslavl', as a large town on the Volga much closer to Moscow, and established there a provisional government headed by Minin, with the title of 'The Man Chosen by the Entire People'. From there the militia advanced on Moscow and drove out the Poles. Then the military council issued invitations to all towns and districts to send their 'best, most sensible and trustworthy people', each equipped with a mandate, to a 'council of the land' (*sovet vseia zemli*) which would elect the new Tsar.

Some five hundred delegates came from everywhere between the White Sea and the Don, representing boyars, service nobles, clergy, merchants, Cossacks, *posad* people (townsfolk), and 'black' (non-enserfed) peasants. The bitter divisions which had plunged Russia into anarchy for so long were not fully stilled by the common victory: service nobles and Cossacks were at loggerheads, boyar clans continued to feud and insist on their pedigree, while some supported foreign candidates. The latter, however, were rejected by the assembly as a whole 'for their many injustices'. It was decided that the new monarch must be Russian and Orthodox.

On 7 February 1613 the *sobor* elected the sixteen-year-old Mikhail Romanov as the new Tsar. This choice illustrates the prevailing yearning for stability, the desire to restore a state of affairs as close as possible to what might be called 'normality'. Mikhail was the eldest son of a family closely related to the Riurik dynasty, and hence the nearest thing to a hereditary monarch that the assembly could find. To legitimate his choice, a story was assiduously put around that Fedor Ivanovich, the last Riurik Tsar, had entrusted his sceptre and crown to Mikhail's uncle. No explicit conditions were imposed or even requested: the dynastic sense triumphed over the aspiration to set a limit to the monarch's power, for which this would have been the ideal moment. The delegates, it turned out, had come to the meeting not with binding conditions to put to candidates in the course of the election, but with petitions to submit to him once he *was* elected.

In its greatest test hitherto, then, the people of Muscovy showed that they felt their vulnerability, from within and without, sufficiently to wish a dynastic, hereditary and autocratic ruler. The forces seeking unity – service nobles, townsfolk, clergy, 'black' peasants – triumphed over those – boyars, Cossacks, serfs – better able to profit from discord. The whole movement drew its inspiration, organization and financial support from the areas in the north and east which had been least affected by the *oprichnina* and by the encroachments of serfdom.

The whole protracted affair suggested that, in moments of supreme crisis, the Russians could and would eventually work together, temporarily putting aside their conflicts, their clannish and socio-economic interests and reconstituting themselves as a potential nation. The Nizhnii Novgorod militia was extremely suspicious of both boyars and Cossacks, but nevertheless cooperated with individuals from both categories when that seemed necessary for the common good. The outcome also suggested that Russians identified themselves with strong authority, backed by the Orthodox Church and unrestrained by any charter or covenant, such as might prove divisive and set one social group against another. Maureen Perrie has shown how, during the Time of Troubles, tales circulated among the common people of a 'good' or 'just' monarch, who would protect them against their oppressors.[21]

All the same, the election of a new autocrat did not just mean a return to old Muscovite ways. For one thing, the Time of Troubles had succeeded far better than Ivan IV in weakening the boyars. Individual boyars and their families continued to play a role in politics, but now through their presence at court and through the Tsar's service, rather than through their patrimonies and retainers. By contrast, the service nobles had gained in influence, and used it during the next half-century to put the final clamps on serfdom, which they achieved in the new Law Code (*Ulozhenie*) of 1649.

At the same time, the first serious breach had been created in the patrimonial state. In the Time of Troubles Muscovy had been like an estate whose master had died intestate: relatives, servants and labourers had fought among themselves to seize it, and a few neighbouring owners had joined in the fray. But then the *zemlia* had for the first time constituted itself as a reality, based on elective local government institutions, and had chosen a new master: they had demonstrated that the state was not just a patrimony. Platonov goes so far as to assert that 'the old patrimonial state had yielded to a new and more complex type, the national state'.[22] That was still far from being the case, as the next three centuries would show, but a movement had been made in that direction.

The Church Schism

The outcome of the Time of Troubles also enormously enhanced the standing of the Orthodox Church, which had shown that at a time of national breakdown it was capable of rousing people to a united effort and of helping to finance that revival. Besides, the first Romanov Tsar, Mikhail, being very young when he came to power, relied a great deal on his father, Metropolitan Filaret, who became Patriarch in 1619 and remained in effect co-ruler, using the title 'Great Sovereign' till his death in 1633. For a time it looked as if Tsardom and Patriarchate were a partnership in which the Patriarch was the senior.

However, the church itself was undergoing a period of upheaval caused by the import of new religious ideas from the West, and fuelled by memories of the horrors foreign intervention could inflict. The influence which appeared most threatening was the Counter-Reformation Catholicism of Poland, mediated through the Uniate Church. By the middle of the seventeenth century a reform movement had taken shape which aimed to outbid the intellectual sophistication of the Catholics by purifying the Orthodox Church and spreading its message to ordinary Russian people.

The Zealots of Piety (*Revniteli blagochestiia*) were a group of parish priests, mainly from the Volga region, who in the 1630s began to agitate for a programme of thorough-going church reform. They were concerned by drunkenness, debauchery and the persistence of pagan practices among the common people, and attributed these deficiencies to the low educational and spiritual level of the clergy, and to the negligent conduct of the liturgy, which they claimed hindered ordinary parishioners from obtaining a real understanding of the faith. In particular they criticized the custom of *mnogoglasie*, conducting different portions of the divine service simultaneously, so that it was impossible to follow any of them properly (this was done because parish churches had taken over the full monastic liturgy, under which each service would otherwise have lasted several hours). The Zealots recommended heightened discipline, regular fasting, confession and communion, and the frequent preaching of sermons.[23]

This was a reform programme not unlike that of the Cluniacs in eleventh-century France, and it had something in common with sixteenth-century Protestantism in much of Europe. At the same time it was firmly rooted in the tradition of Metropolitan Makarii and took a pride in Muscovy's religious mission. Clerics of this tendency drew attention to themselves by their fiery preaching, notably one Archpriest Avvakum, originally a peasant from beyond the Volga, a vehement protagonist of the simple Russian virtues in contra-distinction to western *khitrost'* (cunning or sophistry): he sometimes aroused the resentment of his Moscow parishioners by castigating their worldly vices. The Zealots became influential both in the Patriarchate and at court, especially following the accession of Tsar Alexei Mikhailovich in 1645. His personal confessor, Stefan

Vonifat'ev, was a sympathizer, as were two of his leading advisers, Boris Morozov and Fedor Rtishchev.

Another peasant from beyond the Volga who rose up through the Zealots' movement was the Mordovian monk Nikon, a tall and dominating figure who became one of Alexei's most trusted friends and Metropolitan of Novgorod, before being elevated in 1652 to the Patriarchate. In this position Nikon assumed the title of 'Great Sovereign' and exercised real secular as well as spiritual authority whenever Alexei was absent, as for example during the Polish war which began in 1654.

If the Zealots of Piety thought that through Nikon they would win a decisive influence over church policy, they were to be rudely disabused. True, he implemented certain aspects of their programme, for example by banning *mnogoglasie* and prohibiting the sale of vodka on holy days. But his priorities were different and much more ambitious. If they were the Cluniac reformers, he was Pope Gregory VII. The Zealots' vision was limited to Muscovy and their aim was to bring about an educated and morally pure church close to the people. Nikon by contrast wanted to create a theocracy in which the church would dominate the state and would take the lead in an imperial and ecumenical mission of expansion and salvation. Whereas Ivan Neronov, one of the leading Zealots, advised against war with Poland in 1648, because he feared the moral consequences of war, as well as further incursion of heresy, Nikon welcomed it as an opportunity to enhance the standing of both church and state, and actually encouraged Bohdan Khmel'nyts'kyi to rebel against Poland in the name of Orthodoxy. Nikon was in close touch with the Eastern Patriarchs, and was eager for the Russian church to play the leading role in Orthodoxy they could no longer fulfil because of their subjection to Ottoman rule.[24] In a word, Nikon took absolutely seriously the notion of Moscow as the Third Rome and believed that it meant the creation of a universal Christian empire.

His contact with Greek and Ukrainian churchmen had made him aware of the many discrepancies between Russian and Byzantine liturgical practice which had been discussed at the *Stoglav* Council. He hastened the work of studying and correcting the printed service books, so that the Russian church would be ready for the ecumenical role he intended it should play in Ukraine and perhaps beyond that in the Balkans. As early as the spring of 1653, he issued a new psalter and a set of instructions requiring congregations to introduce a number of ritual changes, including making the sign of the cross with three fingers instead of the traditional two. From the outset there were protests from priests who disliked the alterations and who objected that they had been introduced uncanonically, without a church council. Nikon plunged ahead regardless, with assurance of the Tsar's support, and during the next years added further amendments, none of them of dogmatic significance, but nevertheless repugnant to believers who held that ritual and faith were indissolubly connected.

In 1655 Nikon convened a church council and, with the help of his Greek supporters, pushed his liturgical reforms through. With the approval of the secular power, he set about dismissing his opponents and exiling them. By now, however, Alexei was beginning to be alarmed by the threat to his own authority represented by the Patriarchate, especially when occupied by an overweening character like Nikon. On his appointment, Nikon had made him swear to obey him in everything which concerned the church and God's law – an exceedingly broad concept in the seventeenth century. As Metropolitan of Novogorod, he had resisted the subordination of monasteries in his diocese to the new *Monastyrskii Prikaz*, the state monastic administration, and had fought the encroachment of secular courts on what he considered ecclesiastic jurisdiction. As Patriarch he continued to fight these battles.

At first Alexei had acquiesced in ecclesiastical hegemony, but as he gained in experience and self-confidence he grew to resent the domineering tone of his erstwhile 'bosom friend', and to worry that if the church acquired too much power, it might seriously obstruct the efforts of the secular state to mobilize the country's resources by taxation or by the assignment of land to nobles. The high-handedness which Nikon displayed in implementing his liturgical reforms confirmed Alexei's fears and eventually undermined his relationship with the Tsar.

Affronted by Alexei's increasingly conspicuous coolness towards him, Nikon in July 1658 suddenly and dramatically renounced the Patriarchate in the middle of a service. Declaring that he felt unworthy of the office, he took off his patriarchal robes and assumed the simple habit of a monk. This gesture of simulated humility was certainly calculated to compel concessions from Alexei, but it had the opposite effect. Alexei after much hesitation and heart-searching accepted his resignation.[25]

Whatever this rift was, it emphatically did not arise from a dispute over Nikon's reforms. Alexei was as keen on them as Nikon himself, since he thought they would raise the standing of the state *in alliance with* the church. He therefore took over the sponsorship of the reforms, while removing their originator. In this way the innovations became as closely identified with the state as they were with the church: a fateful development.

A church council of 1666–7, again attended by the Eastern Patriarchs, not only approved all the textual amendments and liturgical innovations, but went on to pronounce anathema on those who refused to accept them. It also reversed the decision of the *Stoglav* Council of 1551, which had upheld existing practices in the face of Greek questioning. This was a radical turning-point in more than ecclesiastical policy, since the 1551 Council had consolidated the whole Muscovite ideology propounded by Metropolitan Makarii. Its repudiation implied a rejection of the entire outlook. Symbolically the Council of 1666 explicitly condemned the legend of the 'white *klobuk*' (monk's cap): this was a story which enjoyed wide currency among ordinary people, telling how, after the Byzantine church had sold out to the Catholics at the Council of Florence, it had been punished by the fall of its capital city to the Turks, and the mission of defending true Christianity had devolved on the Russians. Condemnation of this tale implied rejection of the whole notion of Moscow the Third Rome.[26] The Tsars had never explicitly invoked the Third Rome, but all the same to repudiate it undermined much of the justification for their authority.

The Council of 1666–7 thus converted the Russians' existing national myth into a heritage of those who opposed the state and its increasingly cosmopolitan outlook. It thereby opened up a rift in Russians' national consciousness which has never been fully healed. The Old Believers pointed out, with impeccable logic, that all the Tsars and bishops had hitherto lived by practices now deemed so heinous that they merited anathema. 'If we are schismatics,' they argued, 'then the Holy Fathers, Tsars and Patriarchs were also schismatics.' Quoting from the church's own *Book of Faith* of 1648, they charged Nikon with 'destroying the ancient native piety' and 'introducing the alien Roman abomination'.[27] 'To make the sign of the cross with three fingers', they protested, 'is a Latin tradition and the mark of the Antichrist.' Archpriest Avvakum, the most articulate and consistent of Nikon's opponents, wrote from his prison cell to Tsar Alexei: 'Say in good Russian "Lord have mercy on me". Leave all those Kyrie Eleisons to the Greeks: that's their language, spit on them! You are Russian, Alexei, not Greek. Speak your mother tongue and be not ashamed of it, either in church or at home!'[28]

The anathema supported by the secular power blew up minor liturgical problems not just into major theological issues but into criteria of a person's whole attitude to church and state. As Robert Crummey has remarked, 'Once opposition to the liturgical reform and all its implications carried the Old Believers into opposition to the Russian state, their movement became a rallying point for the discontented and dispossessed of Muscovite society.'[29] That included those who objected to the fixation of serfdom, Cossacks defending their ancient liberty, local communities losing their self-governing powers to voevodas and their agents, townsfolk fixed to their communes by 'mutual responsibility' and heavy taxation, as well as parishes who found that the Council of 1666 had also curtailed their power to choose their own priest.[30]

The combining of religious and secular motifs fanned the flames of an apocalyptic mood which was already abroad in Muscovite society, exemplified in the preachings of the hermit Kapiton, which were popular in the Volga basin and the north of the country. For if the piety of the Third Rome had indeed been disavowed by both church and state, then what could one conclude but that the reign of Antichrist had arrived and the end of the world was at hand? After all, according to prophecy, there was to be no Fourth Rome.

The final decades of the seventeenth century saw the culmination of this mood in a series of rebellions and mass suicides. The suicides started among communities of people who were determined not to defile themselves before the Judgement Day by contact with the forces of Antichrist, but rather, at the approach of government agents or troops, would shut themselves inside their wooden churches and set fire to them.

The rebellions began in 1668 in the island monastery of Solovki, the great centre both of piety and of economic life in the mouth of the White Sea. Its monks refused to accept the new prayer books. stopped praying for the Tsar and deposed their abbot when he seemed disposed to compromise. They told Alexei: 'We all wish to die in the old faith, in which your lordship's father, the true-believing lord, Tsar and Grand Prince Mikhail Fedorovich of all Russia and the other true-believing Tsars and Grand Princes lived out their days.'[31] Alexei sent an army to enforce his will, but the monks refused them access to their island. With the support of much of the local population, who helped them with supplies, they were able to withstand a siege of eight years, before finally succumbing in January 1676. Nearly all the inmates were summarily put to death by the victorious besiegers.

Many Old Believers fled to the south, to the region of the Don, which had been in upheaval in 1670–71, when the Cossack leader Sten'ka Razin led a campaign up the Volga, calling on serfs and non-Russians to murder the boyars, estate-owners and voevodas. Few if any Old Believers were involved in that insurrection, but they found the region still in turmoil, and they added to the discontent that survived from its defeat. The symbiosis of Cossackdom and Old Belief in the south and east, merging at times with the discontent of Tatars and Bashkirs, created a latent threat to the imperial state for the next century.

In 1682 Old Believers joined with discontented *strel'tsy* (musketeers) in Moscow to spark off a mutiny. The death of Tsar Fedor Alexeevich had left a disputed succession, which gave the *strel'tsy* a chance to press their own demands for the redress of grievances, for better pay and for the restoration of the Old Belief. The Regent Sofia, who had at first supported their revolt, turned against them when it became clear what a threat they represented to law and order: she had their chief spokesman, the Old Believer Nikita Dobrynin, arrested and beheaded, and thereafter persecuted his fellow-believers with ferocious determination.

For the most part, though, the Old Belief was a not a rebellious movement: it was more a desperate assertion of principle in the face of what seemed like overwhelming force. Old Believers would flee places where the official church and government could readily find them, and take themselves off to the borderlands – some, for example, to the Polish frontier, others as mentioned to the Don, while yet others sought out or created tiny settlements in the forests and lakes of the far north. This was an area which had seen little of landlords or serfdom, and where local self-governing *mir* communities had retained a rugged independence elsewhere diminished by the depredations of authority. Here religious refugees found a landscape ideal both for eluding officials and for cultivating an ascetic way of life. Thousands of square miles of forest, lake and marsh, crossed only by the occasional muddy track, guaranteed both isolation and a minimum of human comforts. Fishing, gathering and logging provided the bare necessities, which could also be used to trade with, where communications permitted. Usually without a priest, or seldom visited by one, Old Believers improvised services in hastily erected chapels or even ordinary peasant huts, with the help of an icon and an unamended prayer book.

Here in the far north during the 1670s and 80s refugees from the Solovki monastery set up their own hermitages, constructing flimsy shelters from available timber and grubbing up plots of land to grow a little food. Sometimes they would gather a few disciples around them, or allow peasants to visit them, and thus a new Old Believer settlement would come into existence. Lacking a priest, these communities had willy-nilly to devise their own forms of service, with lay people performing sacraments such as baptism and confessions being made mutually to one another. In this way Russia's most conservative believers were driven to undertake experiments which elsewhere in Europe were the province of the extreme religious radicals.

The most settled and successful of these communities was one set up on the River Vyg, which flows out to the White Sea. Its leaders, the brothers Andrei and Semen Denisov, were good organizers, with a practical sense of economics. They were also able polemicists. At a time when the official church began trying to counter the Old Belief by persuasion rather than persecution, Andrei composed a systematic exposition of its tenets laid out as answers to the accusations of the Nikonians. This *Pomorskie otvety* became thereafter the guide which all Old Believers accepted on dogmatic questions.

71

Semen, who succeeded him as abbot, wrote a treatise, *Vinograd rossiiskii* (The Russian Vineyard), in which he set out his view of the Holy Russia they had lost. According to him, *Rus'* had been the finest example of a people ruled by the divine will, the one truly Christian realm in a world threatened by Satan in the form of Catholicism, Protestantism and Western rationalism. Now however the Russians too had been corrupted, first by the 'papist Latin heresy' at the Council of Florence, then by the impious reforms of Nikon, which touched the very heart of Russia's sacred mission.

Nevertheless, in Semen Denisov's view, something had been preserved among the ordinary people. 'In Russia,' he wrote, 'there is not one single city which is not permeated with the radiance of faith, not one town which does not shine with piety, nor a village which does not abound with the true belief.' True, all this was overlaid by an apostate state bearing the mark of the apocalyptic beast, but staunch cultivation of the faith, together with courageous resistance to persecution would enable Russia one day to revive and return to the true path. Denisov evoked at length the memory of the saints of *Rus'*, who 'by their piety, faith and virtue unite the Russian nation with Christ in one single flock at pasture in the meadows of Heaven'.[32]

In reformulating the faith of Makarii for the needs of his own time, Denisov stumbled into a fateful novelty, the implications of which he certainly did not realize. He was unable to follow Makarii in seeing the essence of Russian nationhood as residing in the Tsar and the church, since both had departed from the true faith. Both might one day return to it, but until then the only possible bearer of ideal Russian nationhood was the people itself in their 'towns shining with piety' and their 'villages abounding with the true belief'. As Sergei Zen'kovskii has put it, Denisov 'transformed the old doctrine of an autocratic Christian state into a concept of a democratic Christian nation'.[33]

That was the real strength of the Old Belief. For all its shortcomings, its narrow-mindedness and parochialism, it offered a religious explanation for a perceived reality, the increasing alienation of the mass of the people from a cosmopolitan and secular state, which intensified during and after the reign of Peter I. The Old Belief not only withstood official persecution and discrimination throughout the eighteenth and nineteenth centuries, but in numerical terms actually flourished. By the early twentieth century, 250 years or so after the schism which gave it birth, it probably claimed some ten to twelve million adherents, or between a fifth and a quarter of adult Great Russians.[34]

Even that did not mark the full extent of its influence, for it exerted a partial hold on the consciences even of many who acknowledged the official church. Frederick Conybeare, an American anthropologist who investigated popular religion in the 1910s, commented that 'Its strength lies less in its overt adepts than in the masses who mutely sympathise with it . . . [as] a product no less than a glorification of popular customs and ideas . . . In many regions, among the *petit peuple* we meet with the singular opinion that official orthodoxy is only good for the lukewarm, that it is a worldly religion through which it is barely possible to attain salvation, and that the true and holy religion is that of the Old Believers.'[35]

An investigator of the Old Belief in the 1860s, V.I. Kel'siev, went even further. He asserted that 'The people continue to believe today that Moscow is the Third Rome and that there will be no fourth. So Russia is the new Israel, a chosen people, a prophetic land, in which shall be fulfilled all the prophecies of the Old and New Testaments, and in which even the Antichrist will appear, as Christ appeared in the previous Holy Land. The representative of Orthodoxy, the Russian Tsar, is the most legitimate emperor on earth, for he occupies the throne of Constantine.'[36]

Even allowing for an element of exaggeration here, it is clear that the schism had long ago ceased to be about making the sign of the cross with two fingers. It marked the opening of a radical split in Russian consciousness, when large numbers of conservative and patriotic Russians became alienated from the imperial state and took the decision to conduct their spiritual and even their community life outside the framework it offered. As Miliukov has remarked, 'Russian popular piety disengaged itself from the piety of the ruling church. The unhealthy and fateful rift between intelligentsia and people, for which the Slavophiles reproached Peter the Great, took place half a century earlier.'[37]

Already by the end of the seventeenth century, then, enserfment, recruitment and the pressures of the service state had combined with the ecumenical ambitions of the church to exhaust and embitter the population and to engender a schism which sapped popular loyalty to both state and church and undermined the sense of national unity.

2

The Secular State of Peter the Great

In the early eighteenth century the strains and rifts imposed on Russian society by the pursuit of empire during the previous century and a half were intensified by the active importation of foreign technological, social and cultural models designed to transform Russia into a fully European power. This alien inflow was necessary: if Russia was to protect her newly acquired imperial territories, she had to be able to match the military potential of the strongest European powers; but it was nonetheless extremely damaging to her social and ethnic cohesion.

By the end of the seventeenth century, Muscovy ruled a huge realm in northern Asia, but it had not yet succeeded in making its strategic situation secure, either from the raiders of the steppe or from the European powers to its west. True, it had won impressive victories against Poland, and with them a good deal of territory, but only after a long and exhausting war. In the north and west it was still blocked off from the Baltic and vulnerable to Swedish imperial designs, while in the south the danger of destructive Tatar raids had not been banned. If it was to remain an empire, it had to be able to defend its own territories, not only in the south and east but now especially in the west, from where the greatest dangers threatened.

In addition, the economic resources of its territories, potentially greater than those of any other power in the world, lay still almost wholly unmobilized. The vast distances, the primitive transport, the often infertile soil and the economic backwardness of the population made it difficult to develop mining, manufacture and trade, while Russia's land-locked situation, hemmed round by ice-bound ports and straits controlled by potential enemies, obstructed foreign commerce. The truth was that a long-term imperial future could not be secured without a marked improvement in the standard of Russia's armed forces and an activation of the resources of land and population.

In the early years of his reign, Peter I succeeded, though with great difficulty, in capturing the Turkish fortress of Azov, at the mouth of the Don, and thus gaining a precarious outlet to the Black Sea. But the uncertain nature of Russian military power was demonstrated by the failure of the first attempt for more than a hundred years to obtain a foothold on the Baltic: his large army, attempting to capture the port city of Narva, suffered a crushing defeat at the hands of a much smaller force of Swedes (1700).

Narva, however, proved to be a turning-point. Peter was deeply affected by the humiliation, and drew lessons from the experience – lessons which did not change his policies in their essentials, but imparted to them a new radicalism and a new sense of determination. He was already by character and upbringing disposed to make Russia more European, not just by bringing the country into the interplay of military and diplomatic forces which constituted European great power politics, but also by assimilating the new technology and the new ways of thinking which had transformed the life of the leading European states during the seventeenth century.

In his teenage years, when he was joint Tsar, foreigners were still isolated in a special suburb just outside Moscow, the so-called *nemetskaia sloboda*, or 'German suburb', to prevent them corrupting the morals of honest Russians. Their segregation attested to the suspicion with which Muscovites regarded the outside world, and especially the 'crafty ways' of the West. Peter had violated the taboos surrounding the *sloboda* by not only visiting the disreputable place, but striking up friendships there and engaging in long conversations with the traders, craftsmen and mercenaries. From his youth he went clean-shaven and in Western clothes, to the consternation of most of his contemporaries, and he ate meat during fast days, in contravention of Orthodox practice.

Inspired by an astrolabe which Prince Dolgorukii brought back from France, he began eagerly to study arithmetic, geometry, navigation, ballistics and fortification under the Dutchman Franz Timmerman. He took to wearing a Dutch sailor's uniform and calling himself a 'bombardier'. He listened with fascination to his tutor, Nikita Zotov, recounting the military campaigns of his father, Tsar Alexei, and, anxious to try out his own ideas, he formed 'play regiments' among the young noblemen of the court. He dressed them in dark green uniform, equipped them with weapons from the court arsenal, and led them out on manoeuvres which were far from being 'play' in the normal sense of the word: some of them involved thousands of people and led to injuries and deaths.[1]

When he was able to occupy the throne on his own, he violated Muscovite taboos on an even grander scale, by visiting the macrocosm from which the little world of the *nemetskaia sloboda* derived: Europe, and especially the maritime Protestant countries of northern Europe. During 1697–8, he travelled through the Swedish Baltic provinces, Poland, Prussia, Holland, England and Austria, under the assumed name of Petr Mikhailov, non-commissioned officer of the Preobrazhenskii Regiment (on solemn occasions he expected all the same to be received with the honours due to him).

This expedition was a kind of precursor of the 'industrial espionage' of our own days, with the Tsar officially (but not actually) incognito as the principal intelligence agent. In Königsberg he took a short course in artillery, in Amsterdam he worked as a carpenter in the shipbuilding yards, in London he visited factories, workshops, the observatory, the arsenal and the Royal Mint, and he attended a meeting of the Royal Society, which inspired him with ideas about how the state should patronize science and technology.[2] Most of this was about as far from royal dignity, especially in its Muscovite variant, as could be imagined, but he picked up in a haphazard way what he wanted from the journey, and he returned with the conviction that Russia must become more like the countries he had visited, not just in its military technology, but in social, cultural and intellectual life too.

He had to break off his journey and return prematurely to deal with a rebellion of the *strel'tsy*. Set up by Ivan IV to provide an infantry force with firearms, they had long been rendered superfluous by the advance of military science. Their way of life was a prime example of the marriage of privilege with obsolete technology which Peter was determined to eliminate, and he proceeded against them with vindictive ferocity, executing several hundred of their leaders, and then disbanding all their regiments. At the same time, he instituted his programme of introducing Western customs by issuing a decree forbidding the wearing of beards in polite society, and taking the shears personally to reluctant courtiers. It is difficult to imagine a grosser insult to inherited notions of male dignity and piety: Orthodox considered that beards were essential for God-fearing men, and it was popularly held that the clean-shaven could not gain admittance to heaven.

MILITARY REFORM AND INDUSTRY   The humiliating defeat at Narva occurred the following year, and it sharpened Peter's sense of urgency about change. The lesson he drew was one which his foreign journey had already disposed him to accept: that his army, though large, was insufficiently trained and inadequately equipped to fight open battles against the finest European armies, of which the Swedish was one. Methods which had served well in the 'wild field' against swift but lightly armed horsemen, weapons which had sufficed – though barely – against the Polish and Ottoman forces, revealed their deficiencies when pitted against the full might of Charles XII's troops.

Peter now had to lead Russia through what many European armies had undergone in the sixteenth and seventeenth centuries, the process which historians, if hesitantly, refer to as the 'military revolution'.[3] The key elements in this revolution were: (i) the deployment of large masses of well-disciplined infantry equipped with firearms; (ii) the use of highly mobile light cavalry able to fight when necessary as infantry (dragoons); (iii) an increase in the size and penetrative power of artillery; (iv) a strengthening of fortifications designed to withstand this artillery.

These innovations enormously increased the cost of warfare, compelling all European states to devise more effective means of mobilizing the human and natural resources at their disposal, with far-reaching and durable consequences for their forms of government.[4] In some respects, for all its backwardness, Russia was at a distinct advantage compared with its rivals in carrying through this process. The society was already structured for service to the state, and the privileges and immunities enjoyed by social groups were much weaker than almost anywhere else in Europe, which meant that taxation and recruitment were in principle easier for its rulers to achieve.

Especially under Tsar Alexei, Muscovy had made a start to its military revolution during the seventeenth century, but in a piecemeal manner which failed to deliver maximum benefit. Since its service nobles stuck firmly to the cavalry style of warfare they had learned on the steppes, 'new-style' formations had to be commanded and partly manned by foreigners. Like the traditional levies, they disbanded every autumn to other pursuits, so that the government would not have the expense of supporting them till the next campaigning season opened in the spring. By the 1680s the new-style formations outnumbered the traditional forces, and a reform of the army's whole structure had become overdue, so that it could adopt the latest strategies and technologies consistently.[5]

One of the main problems was that warfare was still essentially state-supported private enterprise. Even the new-style soldiers were still raised, clothed and equipped by individual *pomeshchiki* out of the income from their estates. Now originally, in the fifteenth and sixteenth centuries, the *pomest'e* had been a service estate, like the Ottoman *timar*, distinct from the *votchina*, or patrimonial estate, in that it was held on condition of state service being duly discharged. By the late seventeenth century, however, the distinction had been almost completely eroded: the *pomest'e* had become heritable property, with the result that *pomeshchiki* no longer had a strong material interest in their military service – though they might render it out of family pride.

Peter decided that the burden of recruiting, training and equipping the troops must henceforth fall directly on the state, which could be done by reinstating the service principle of landholding theoretically still in force. Rather than an army of semi-feudal levies, he aimed to create a regular standing army, and one, moreover, which would be permanently on war footing and not disbanded every winter. From 1705 he imposed the *rekrutchina*: the system whereby new troops were drawn directly from the village, selected by the landlord, or in the case of 'black' peasants by the communal assembly, and were sent to an assembly point with minimal supplies and clothing, thereafter to be taken care of by the state. The provision of recruits was to be covered by 'mutual responsibility': that is, if one recruit failed to report for duty or deserted, then the other households of his village had to provide a replacement for him.

Although other European countries had effected mass levies before in an emergency, Russia was the first country to institute conscription as a permanent method of raising its armed forces. From the military point of view conscription had considerable advantages. It enabled Peter to win a great victory over Charles XII at Poltava in 1709, and to follow it up by a sustained and ultimately successful military and naval campaign which ended in the capitulation of Sweden in 1721. [Further on the army, see Part 3, Chapter 2] But its effect on Russian society was to impose new obligations and to impart a new rigidity to the system of state service.

To create swiftly the industrial might which Russia needed to maintain and equip such an army, Peter proceeded in similar fashion. The empire already had a metallurgical and ordnance industry, but Peter used the power of the state to expand it tenfold, and added new branches, such as textiles to provide uniforms for his soldiers, and canvas, ropemaking and shipbuilding to create a navy from scratch. Whole new industrial districts sprang up, notably around the new capital city of St Petersburg, and in the ore-rich regions of the Urals. At first the new factories were run by the official Manufacturing College, but later they were usually sold or leased out to merchants or nobles, often provided with a monopoly.

Shortage of labour was always a great problem. Peter initially wanted to encourage the hiring of free wage labour, which he considered would promote the dignity of manufacture. But his underpopulated raw new industrial areas were uninviting, and in the end he permitted factory-owners, even when non-noble, to buy serfs. He also assigned whole villages to nearby factories to carry out the unskilled labour, while he sought foreigners to staff the administration and perform the skilled tasks. Work in the new plants was usually onerous, unpleasant and conducted in atrocious conditions; worst of all, it was protracted and regulated according to the clock, to which Russian peasants were unaccustomed. For indiscipline, factory-owners were authorized to apply all kinds of corporal punishment, confinement in irons or imprisonment. Factory serfs often complained about their conditions, and not infrequently whole villages would suddenly uproot themselves and flee in order to evade the intolerable transformation of their lives.[6]

Peter's industrialization achieved its aims, and it laid the basis for an economic development which endured for a century or so before its drawbacks became crippling. But it did so in a way which, through heavy taxation and forced labour, actually depressed the purchasing power of much of the population, as well as debasing their civil existence and increasing their alienation from the authorities.

THE NEW STATE MACHINERY   To defray the huge costs for which the state was now responsible, Peter drastically simplified the taxation system, introducing a poll tax because that was the easiest variety of tax to assess and collect from the mass of the people. In order to ensure that everyone paid their share, he pruned down the various complicated categories into which society had hitherto been divided. Everyone became a member of either a service (*sluzhiloe*) estate or a tax-paying (*tiagloe*) one. In the former category were the nobles (boyars and service nobles amalgamated to form one estate, called the *shliakhetstvo* and later known as the *dvorianstvo*), the merchants and the clergy: they provided state service directly and hence were not liable for the poll tax. In the latter category were the other townsfolk (*meshchane*) and the two classes of peasants: 'black' ones and serfs. The tax census (*podushnaia perepis'* or 'soul census' in Russian) took a long time to draw up, but once it was ready it provided the most detailed account of the population Russia had ever had and by its mere existence fixed each estate more firmly to its dwelling place and function. In particular, it became easier for landlords to prove their right to reclaim fugitive serfs.

The onerous and complicated new functions assumed by the state required a tighter and better-lubricated bureaucratic machinery than Russia had ever known before. It cannot be said that Peter succeeded fully in creating what was needed, but even so his innovations laid the foundations for structures that were to persist till 1917. By nature a technocrat, he delighted in things that worked, and his ambition for the Russian polity was that it should fulfil its God-given function to mobilize the resources of people and land to ensure the defence and prosperity of the realm. He viewed the state as a mechanism which, like a watch or a hydraulic pump, should be designed so that it could do its job with maximum efficiency and minimum expenditure.

This meant first of all reformulating the concept of divine right so that it would sanctify an active, interventionist state. He adopted the title of *Russorum Imperator*, using Latin to evoke the military glory of the First Rome, while the commonly used epithets 'pious and gentle' dropped out of currency. Religious processions were replaced by splendid entries through triumphal arches, with Peter cast in the personae of Mars or Hercules, pagan gods who owed their victories to their own strength and valour. After the final victory over Sweden he took the additional title of *Otets otechestva*, equivalent of the Latin *pater patriae*. The heritage of the Second Rome, Byzantium was downgraded, and the Russian saint whom Peter chose for special reverence was Aleksandr Nevskii, whose military victories had laid the basis for Russia's claims to the Baltic coast: his remains were transferred to a monastery in the new capital city.[7]

His emphasis on worldly greatness and achievement did not mean that Peter was not a believer, but it did decouple the secular power from its partnership with the church. He abolished the Patriarchate and subordinated the church to himself by creating the Holy Synod with his own appointed Over-Procurator as head of it. He appropriated to himself part of the dignity previously accorded to the Patriarch: at the Poltava entry he was greeted with the words formerly reserved for the Patriarch: 'Blessed be He who cometh in the name of the Lord!'[8]

In his concept, the state stood above selfish or partial interests, above ethnic or religious distinctions, above even the person of the monarch himself. Peter was the first Russian monarch to attempt to draw a distinction between the state on the one hand and the person and property of the ruler on the other. This distinction was implicit in the new oath recruits had to take when entering the army, to 'the Sovereign and the State' (*gosudariu i gosudarstvu*). He did not always observe the distinction himself, still less did his subordinates, but all the same the first move had been made away from the patrimonial system of rule towards a functional or bureaucratic one, where the public and private spheres are demarcated from one another and each branch of government has a function independent of the personal interests of those discharging the office. Peter even tried to eliminate biology and kinship from the monarchy by challenging the customary order of succession, and stipulating that each ruler should nominate his or her own successor.

Establishing the principles of functionalism and impartiality was the motive for the introduction of 'colleges' in 1718 in place of *prikazy* or 'offices'. Colleges were functional rather than personal or territorial: each college had its own defined sphere of jurisdiction, be it the army, justice or tax-collecting. Furthermore, each one was headed not by a single individual, but by an administrative board of several persons, to underline the principle that its authority was not to be used to further the interests of any individual or family. As Peter explained in his ukaz of 19 December 1718: 'The colleges have been instituted because they are an assembly of many persons, in which the presidents do not have so much power as the old magistrates (heads of the *prikazy*), who did as they liked. In the colleges the president may not undertake anything without the consent of his colleagues.'[9]

But of course colleges can generate their own inbred loyalties, of the kind evoked by the Russian proverb 'one hand washes another': bodies of men as well as individuals are capable of generating their own interests and defending them so stubbornly as to clog the best-designed mechanism. For that reason, the colleges had to accept another of Peter's principles, that the eye of the sovereign should be everywhere. If the state was a mechanism, then it required an operator, who would have a comprehensive overview of its working, and intervene to correct any malfunctioning. So he placed in each college a personal representative, the *fiskal*, 'who should watch that all business is conducted zealously and equitably; and should anyone fail to do so, then the *fiskal* should report on all this to the College, as the instruction commands him'.[10] Since Peter desired vigilance at all costs, he absolved *fiskaly* in advance of the charge of making false accusations, and in practice often awarded them part of the property of those they denounced. In this way he opened the road to a cult of exhaustive paperwork and malicious denunciations which was to become part of the texture of Russian bureaucratic life.

Peter's governmental reforms thus betrayed a fateful ambivalence. On the one hand they were imbued with a spirit of thrusting confidence in the capacity of human beings to accomplish far-reaching and beneficial change through rational organization. On the other hand, this confidence was clouded by the perpetual suspicion that, left to themselves, human beings would not actually behave in a rational fashion, but would obstruct the most perfectly designed mechanism through idleness, clumsiness, ignorance, egoism or the pursuit of clannish and partial interests. Peter's letters and instructions are replete with the anxious desire to impose his will on everyone at all times, even in the most trivial of matters, as if he were dimly conscious that reprobate human nature would frustrate his impeccably conceived schemes. He even forbade spitting and swearing by officials in colleges, and laid down punishments for persistent transgressors: 'as violators of good order and general peace, and as adversaries and enemies of His Majesty's will and institutions, they are to be punished on the body and by deprivation of estates and honour'.[11]

At bottom, this was his tacit recognition that the principles of secular, active government, based on strict subordination, impersonality, division of functions and formal regulations, were quite alien to the principles pertaining in kinship systems such as had hitherto pervaded Russian society from the village community right up to the court: informality, personalization, mutual responsibility, 'one hand washes the other'.[12]

The social class which was to be the bearer of his new ideals of state was the nobility (*shliakhetstvo*), amalgamated for the purpose out of the previous courtly and service estates. Peter wanted the *shliakhetstvo* to be a social category defined not by birth and inherited hierarchy, but by personal merit and distinction in the service of the state: 'We will allow no rank to anyone until they have rendered service to us and the fatherland'.[13] He put the concept into practice by requiring that young nobles should be trained in a skill useful to the state, should present themselves for examination in it, and should then enter service at the lowest rank. In the case of the army, this meant sons of aristocratic pedigree signing on as privates, though to soften the blow to family pride they were permitted to do so in one of the prestigious new Guards regiments, evolved from Peter's 'play' troops. At the height of his reforming zeal, Peter even tried to insist that no nobleman without a certificate of competence in mathematics and geometry could even be allowed to marry – a draconian stipulation he later had to drop.[14]

The ideal of promotion through personal service was formalized in the Table of Ranks, instituted in 1722. It supplanted the system of *mestnichestvo*, abolished thirty years earlier but never replaced, under which official posts had been distributed according to the inherited family standing of the aspirant. The new Table was based on the military hierarchy, but applied not only to the army and navy, but also to the civil service and the court. It contained fourteen parallel ranks: by working up from the fourteenth to the eighth, a non-noble could win noble status, not just for himself but for his descendants, who were 'to be considered equal in dignity and benefits to the best ancient *dvorianstvo*, even though they be of base lineage and were never previously promoted by the Crown to the noble status or furnished with a coat of arms.'[15]

There was of course a tacit contradiction here, reflecting Peter's chronic dualism over whether to coerce his subordinates or awaken their pride in service. In principle, a commoner became a noble only by merit, but, having once made the grade, he transmitted his standing to his heirs, who consequently did not have to jump through the same hoops. While Peter reigned, the sheer force of his personality ensured that nobles did what was required of them, but his successors were less punctilious and allowed the element of compulsion to wane. The long-term effect of Peter's reform, therefore, was to create a new hereditary privileged social estate.

He accepted the logic of this implication from the outset, and tried to buttress nobles' material capacity to perform state service hereditarily by introducing the system of 'entail', as practised in Britain, under which a landed estate would pass in its entirety to one heir, usually male. The intention was to prevent landed properties becoming subdivided until they were no longer able to provide a sufficient living for a nobleman, and also to compel non-inheritors to earn both their livelihood and noble status by entering the civil or military service.[16] In this matter, however, he was unable to overcome the deeply rooted kinship obligation to provide for all one's heirs. After his death the law on entail was repealed: nobles continued, like peasants, to subdivide their holdings.

THE NEW CAPITAL CITY   What Peter intended for his servitors was not just a revamped framework for service, but a whole new way of life and culture, of the kind he had observed during his travels. He laid out an exemplar of it in his new city of St Petersburg, constructed on marshy terrain freshly conquered from the Swedes at the easternmost extremity of the Baltic Sea. The city began life as a fortress and a base for the newly created Baltic Fleet, and it remained a demonstration that Russia was now a great naval power, more than a match for Sweden. But from the outset Peter cherished even more exalted ambitions for it. St Petersburg was to be a proto-type of the 'regular' Russia with which he wished to replace chaotic, rambling and nepotistic Muscovy. He referred to it as his *paradis* – using a Latinate word rather than the Russian *rai*.

This was no 'Third Rome', but a 'New Amsterdam'. Foreign architects were invited to submit plans for public buildings and stan-dard designs to be used for the homes of his courtiers. Gradually it became a real capital city, constructed in stone and laid out on a generous scale, affording spacious views of sky and water. Or, as an inhabitant of more than two centuries later, Joseph Brodsky, put it, 'Untouched till then by European styles, Russia opened the sluices, and baroque and classicism gushed into and inundated the streets and embankments of St Petersburg. Organ-like forests of columns sprang high and lined up on the palatial facades ad infinitum in their miles-long Euclidean triumph.'[17]

All this could not be accomplished without terrible cost. For years St Petersburg was nothing but a vast building site in a swamp. Con-script labourers were brought in from all over the country to flounder in the mud with their shovels and wheelbarrows and often to lose their lives in it as well, through negligence, overwork or as a result of one of the floods which regularly swept through the location until the River Neva could be contained in embankments of stone. A century later, the historian Nikolai Karamzin, an admirer of Peter and his works, nevertheless conceded that the city was 'built on tears and corpses'.[18]

By 1713, however, St Petersburg had taken shape sufficiently for Peter to move the court and the principal government buildings to it, and he began to insist that within a certain time nobles who wished to present themselves at court must build themselves a resi-dence there, employing one of the standard architectural designs he had commissioned. To economize on scarce stone, he stipulated that aristocratic town houses should be erected contiguous to one another, in terraces along the embankments of the rivers and canals. New residents, as they moved in, were presented with small sailing boats for their use, and were commanded on pain of fines to parade in them on the water every Sunday afternoon to perform exercises and demonstrate their navigational skill.[19]

One major symbolic change compared with Moscow: foreigners were no longer confined to the outskirts, but were allowed, indeed encouraged, to live within the city. Merchants dealing in foreign trade were required to re-route their business away from (usually) Arkhangel'sk and the White Sea to St Petersburg and the Baltic. The new capital was to become a 'window on Europe' in the commercial sense too.

St Petersburg, by its location and its appearance, was living proof that a new Russia, a European great power, had a palpable existence, and one moreover oriented towards future achievements. A century later an acute French observer, the Marquis de Custine, observed that 'the magnificence and immensity of St Petersburg are tokens set up by the Russians to honour their future power, and the hope that inspired such efforts strikes me as sublime'.[20]

But it was so different from any other Russian city, such an affront to their easygoing, semi-rural rambling streets and dwellings, that it has always retained an aura of unreality. Dostoevskii called it 'an invented city' and loved to evoke it in the ghostly light of the northern summer as a dreamlike setting in which his characters play out their spiritual dramas.

Prince Odoevskii, assiduous collector of folktales, cited a Finnish legend which well captured St Petersburg's origins and its insubstantial quality. The workmen building the city found that whenever they laid a stone it was sucked into the marsh. They piled stone on stone, rock on rock, timber on timber, but it made no difference: the swamp swallowed them all up, and only the mud remained. At length Peter, who was absorbed in building a ship, looked round and saw that there was no city. 'You don't know how to do anything,' he said to his people, and thereupon began to lift rock after rock, shaping each one in the air. When in this manner the whole city was built, he let it gently down on to the ground, and this time it stood without disappearing into the mud.[21]

Whether or not de Custine knew of this legend, he tempered his admiration for the city with analogous apprehensions: 'Should this capital, rooted neither in history nor in the soil, be forgotten by the sovereign for a single day; or should some change in policy carry the master's thoughts elsewhere, the granite hidden beneath the water would crumble, the flooded lowlands return to their natural state and the rightful owners of this solitude would regain possession of their home.'[22]

The new capital city became the forum for a new elite secular culture. Flowing Russian robes were replaced by the tight-fitting jackets and breeches current in most of Europe. A 'decree on assemblies' required nobles to gather regularly at soirées, balls and salons where they could meet each other, discuss business, learn what was going on in the world, and generally cultivate the social graces expounded in Peter's primer on etiquette, *An Honourable Mirror to Youth, or an Instruction for Social Intercourse, drawn from Divers Authors*. This manual, translated from the German, and much of it drawn originally from Erasmus, enjoined its readers 'not to snuffle at table', 'not to blow one's nose like a trumpet' and 'not to slobber over one's food or to scratch one's head'.[23] Women were expected to take a full part in these 'assemblies', in contrast to the seclusion imposed upon them previously. An official newspaper was issued, to announce and record the main social occasions, and to keep the public up to date with diplomatic, commercial and other news.

EDUCATION AND CULTURE   In his attitude to education and culture, Peter was at first strictly utilitarian: he set up schools which could train his young nobles in the skills required by the state. Hence the so-called 'cipher schools', which taught mathematics, navigation and other arts useful to future civil servants, army and naval officers. They were not always successful at attracting and holding their pupils, even when backed by Peter's compulsion, and towards the end of his life, he felt the need to integrate them into a more general educational framework, which would give science and technology a secure place in Russian society. At this time the only higher educational institutions were the Slav-Greek-Latin Academies in Moscow and Kiev, which provided for the needs of the church, their curriculum based partly on Byzantine tradition and partly on the

Jesuit Counter-Reformation learning of the seventeenth century.

Peter's aspiration to give science and technology a special place in Russian society originated in his correspondence with Leibniz, which began in 1697. Leibniz, who had grand schemes for the spread of civilization, learning and technology throughout the world, was delighted to number the Emperor of Russia among his adherents. He recommended that Peter should appoint foreigners able to disseminate good learning in Russia, and at the same time should establish schools, libraries, museums, botanical and zoological gardens able to collect knowledge in all its forms and make it available to Russians. He also advised that Russia should have its own research institutes, to investigate the country's immense and largely uncharted resources and to propose ways of improving and developing the national economy.

Peter implemented much of this programme. He opened Russia's first museum (the Kunstkamera in St Petersburg), directed the purchasing of books for the first public library, sponsored expeditions to little-known regions to look for minerals, survey natural resources and make maps. In his later years he laid the foundation for a national Academy of Sciences on the model of the Royal Society in London and the Académie des Sciences in Paris, both of which he had visited. To set up such an institution in Russia was not an easy task, for there were no native scholars with whom to staff it. Several advisers, including Christian Wolff, from the University of Halle, warned him that to found an Academy without a supporting network of lower educational institutions was to put the cart before the horse in no uncertain fashion.

Peter, who had already, as it were, built a capital city in mid-air and then lowered it to the ground, was not likely to falter before such advice. He was dissatisfied with his earlier schemes for introducing Western learning in Russia, and he decided, as so often in his career, to break the logjam from the very top. The draft plan which he approved in 1724 made provision for the Academy to be combined with a university, to teach the new knowledge generated therein, and even for a Gymnasium, to prepare suitable students for the university. It duly opened in this form shortly after his death.

The result of his efforts was that Russia did indeed receive science and learning at the highest international levels, as something sponsored by the state and connected with the empire's ambition to be in all ways a leading player among the powers of Europe. Science and learning from the outset had the highest prestige and priority in state expenditure.[24]

But there was a price to be paid for vaulting most of the normal stages in building up a scientific community. Nearly all Russia's early scientists were foreign – a good many of them German – and the suspicion came to be widely entertained that science was something alien to the life of the ordinary people. Since moreover it had been launched at the same time as the church was being restricted, learning had the air of being godless, perhaps even the work of the Antichrist.

A biography in the spirit of Peter was that of Mikhail Lomonosov (1711–1765), perhaps the first outstanding native Russian scholar. He came from the far northern Arkhangel'sk region, where serfdom was absent and where the Old Belief lent an independent air to spiritual life. Enchanted by Russian versions of the Psalms, the young Lomonosov managed to make his way to Moscow to study prosody by joining a caravan of salted fish. He contrived to enrol in the Slav-Greek-Latin Academy by declaring himself to be a nobleman: only through deception could he leap from the tax-paying to the service estates. Thanks to his evident abilities he was invited to become a student at the newly established Academy of Sciences, which was desperately short of home-grown talent, and he was sent to study in Germany.

On his return he was appointed at different stages to teach chemistry, mineralogy, rhetoric, versification and Russian language at the Academy, in all of which fields he made significant contributions. He also led a campaign to free higher education of German influence by establishing a Russian university in Moscow, which opened in 1755. His theory of the three levels of the Russian language did much to establish a consistent written language out of the confusion of Church Slavonic, bureaucratic and spoken Russian. Like Peter, however, he supplemented his work of enlightenment with episodes of coarse abuse, when he would make obscene gestures at German colleagues and call them *Hundsfotter* and *Spitzbuben*.[25]

THE TENSIONS OF PETER'S HERITAGE   Rousseau wrote in his *Social Contract* that in certain circumstances the ruler has no choice but 'to force men to be free'. One cannot help recalling the phrase when considering Peter's measures. He was artificially implanting enterprise, probity, discipline and the spirit of enquiry because such qualities had only the thinnest of soil in Russia in which to take root. For that reason the artifical implant gave rise to unwelcome side-effects: superficial knowledge, backsliding, insincerity and hypocrisy.

Peter's solution, as in administrative matters, was supervision by the state, or at least by officials appointed and trusted by him. They were policemen, for whom Peter had a special regard, as the regulation he composed for them in 1724 testifies: 'The police has its special calling: which is to intervene to protect justice and rights, to generate good order and morals, to guarantee safety from thieves, robbers, rapists and extortioners, to extirpate disordered and loose living. It binds everyone to labour and an honest profession ... It defends widows, orphans and foreigners in accordance with God's law, educates the young in chaste purity and honest learning; in short, for all of these, the police is the soul of citizenship and of all good order.[26]

The police as 'the soul of citizenship': a conception which seemed less strange, perhaps, in the age of enlightened absolutism than it does now, but one which nevertheless betrays the disjointed nature of Peter's enterprise. Freedom backed by compulsion; enlightenment bolstered by the convict camp. That was the shadow which hung over not just Peter's reign, but over Russian civilization throughout most of the next two centuries.

Peter's own character betrayed this dualism. The most authoritarian of Tsars, he was capable nevertheless of abandoning all the accoutrements of majesty and plunging into an ordinary tavern or workshop, to drink, talk and listen to the gossip and arguments of the common people. An apostle of the latest technology, he also valued popular culture, and would enjoy a folksong and a dance to simple melodies with the meanest of his subjects.

Strangest of all is the element of self-parody and of ritual renunciation in his personality. From time to time, he would solemnly install one of his nobles, Prince Fedor Iurevich Romadanovskii, as Tsar, take an oath of loyalty to him and promise to obey all his orders. One is reminded of Ivan IV renouncing his throne in favour of a

Tatar prince. Again, during *sviatki*, the period between Christmas and New Year, with some of his highest officials, he would enact 'the most foolish and drunken Synod'. The person chosen as Patriarch would parade with a naked Bacchus on his mitre, 'his eyes provoking licentiousness', while all present chanted a mock liturgy: 'Let Bacchic intoxication be upon you, bring darkness all around you, and let it cause you to tumble and roll, rob you of your reason every day of your life.'[27]

These and other burlesque entertainments suggest a striking degree of conflict inside Peter's own personality. His rationalist view of the deity and of his own sovereignty contrasted strongly with the beliefs inculcated in him as a child, and still almost universally held in the society around him. Evidently these contradictions generated within him tensions which he felt able to master only by such paradoxical and at first sight puzzling behaviour.

To change the culture even of an elite is of course more than one ruler can accomplish in his own lifetime. But, however haphazardly, Peter had succeeded in fundamentally redirecting the manners and outlook of what under his shaping had become Russia's ruling class. At first reluctant converts, they gradually warmed to the new cosmopolitan culture, and even embraced it enthusiastically as a mark of their social status.

In doing so, they distanced themselves from the mass of people, the peasants, townsfolk (except for a very few wealthy merchants) and clergy. In so far as they were not recruited into the army or the construction brigades of St Petersburg, ordinary people were spectators rather than participants in the 'revolution from above', and their feelings about it were mixed and often critical. Especially hostile were the Old Believers, already alienated by what they had seen of the secular state under Peter's more moderate predecessors. Most of his innovations could readily be construed as insults to religion or national tradition or both: the shaving of beards, the instruction to wear 'German' or 'Hungarian' clothes, the introduction of a new calendar, the encouragement of foreign learning, the admittance of women into social life, the introduction of the 'soul tax', the abolition of the Patriarchate, the requirement that priests violate the secrecy of the confessional. His blasphemous orgies seemed to confirm the worst fears. Even his policy of religious toleration, which ostensibly benefited the Old Belief, demonstrated that he was intent on undermining the true faith. The apocalyptically minded decided that he was the Antichrist. Popular woodcuts circulated depicting him with the double-head eagle, the official state insignia, as two horns protruding from his head.[28]

This was not just popular grumbling and irreverence. As under Ivan IV, many peasants fled from the new burdens. In the summer of 1707, when an armed detachment went under Prince Iu.V. Dolgorukii to look for absconded peasants on the Don, they were waylaid and massacred by some two hundred Cossacks, under their ataman, Kondratii Bulavin. This was the signal for a general campaign against official search parties, in the course of which Bulavin was elected head of all the Don Cossacks and concluded a treaty with the Zaporozhian Cossacks. Claiming the heritage of Sten'ka Razin, he advanced with his troops through the districts of Voronezh, Tambov and Borisoglebsk, gaining support from peasants for his appeal to come to the defence of 'the house of the Holy Mother of God and the Orthodox Church against the infidel and Greek teachings which the boyars and the Germans wish to impose upon us'.[29] At its height the Bulavin insurrection threatened the fortresses of Azov and Taganrog, and thus the whole precarious Russian position on the Black Sea. Peter had to divert dragoons he could ill afford from the Swedish front in order to put down the revolt.

Confirmation of Peter's diabolic status seemed to be delivered by his treatment of his son and heir Alexei. A physically frail and pious youth, Alexei was about as unlike his father as could be imagined. His mother, Evdokia, had been suspected of complicity in the *strel'tsy* revolt of 1698 and banned to a nunnery, something which Alexei never forgave. At the height of his personal conflict with Peter, Alexei fled abroad. He was induced to return by false promises, investigated in the *Preobrazhenskii Prikaz* (special investigatory chamber), and died under torture. In essence, his father murdered him, leaving the empire without an heir. Peter subsequently compounded this crime with his decree of 1722 stipulating that each ruler should appoint his own successor – something he signally failed to do himself before his sudden death in 1725.

It is no wonder that historians, Russian historians in particular, have been so divided in their opinions of Peter I. On the one hand, he did what was urgently needed if Russia was to remain an empire, which necessarily entailed becoming a European great power. At the same time, the institutions he created brought profound discord into Russian society, or perhaps it would be truer to say, enormously intensified discord which already existed. The cameralist state, imported from Germany and Sweden, with its impersonality, its functionalism, meritocratic hierarchy and strict regulation, differed fundamentally from the inherited kinship structures of Muscovy, with their personalism, informality, patriarchal hierarchy and absence of functional differentiation. His reforms took the first step towards creating a privileged ruling class, based on private landed wealth, and with a culture alien to that of the common people and of the clergy. At a time when, in other European countries, the distance between popular and elite culture was beginning to be reduced, in Russia it was immeasurably widened.

Of course, the revolution which he aimed at was far from complete at his death. Old attitudes persisted for many decades to come, and under his weaker successors aristocratic (the word 'boyar' now at last seems inappropriate) clans feuded for domination of the ship of state. All the same, there were enough highly-placed people who had internalized Peter's attitudes to ensure that his reforms outlasted him. Unlike after the reign of Ivan IV, there was no disintegration, no Time of Troubles. But by the same token, there was no reaching across the great social divide. On the contrary the chasm continued to widen during the eighteenth and first half of the nineteenth century. Peter had set Russia on the road to what the Marquis de Custine a century later prophesied would be 'the revolt of the bearded against the shaven'.[30]

3

Assimilating Peter's Heritage

In spite of the radicalism of Peter the Great's reforms and the wide-spread opposition to them in the church and among the common people, there was never any serious question of going back on them, even during the succeeding decades (1725–1762) of relatively weak rulers, disputed successions and attempted coups. Fundamentally, that was because they proved successful at promoting Russia's great power status, by making it possible to raise, equip and finance an army and navy.

They were also in the interests of the ruling class, the newly consolidated *dvorianstvo*, which, after some initial foot-dragging, was well aware of the fact. Many of the families which dominated Russia before Peter's reign continued to do so afterwards, and continued to exploit the influence of their kith and kin. The early stages of meritocratic reform often prove to be in the interests of existing elites, since their wealth and connections secure them access to the best education and to the vital early stages of a high-flying career (the Northcote-Trevelyan reforms in the nineteenth-century British civil service had the same effect).

Those elite families were sorely needed, owing to the ambivalence of Peter's reforms. On the one hand, impersonal *raison d'état* was proclaimed, on the other personal intervention was constantly needed to ensure its application in practice. Rational rule had to be implemented by personal authority, or nothing would work as intended. So the 'state', if it existed at all in this period, consisted of changing but not wholly unstable constellations of powerful clans, given legitimacy by promotion on merit, and held together by kin-ship, by symbolic devotion to the autocrat, by military uniforms, a new semi-Germanic administrative terminology and an increasingly exclusive culture borrowed from the royal courts of Europe.[1]

It would be wrong, however, to overestimate the effectiveness of Russian state authority in the mid-eighteenth century. In most respects the 'state' (to use what may be too pretentious a word) was still like a rickety framework in a howling gale, subject to all the chance cross-winds of court intrigue and kinship feuding. It was a mere skeleton whose flesh and sinews consisted of the clannish interests of the great families who provided its continuity and its motive power. As for local government, it was notional only, feeble to the point of being non-existent: for lack of suitable personnel to staff its offices, it lapsed back into the hands of the arbitrary and venal military governors from whom Peter had tried to rescue it.

Nor was there a consistent code of laws, only the chancery records of a succession of hasty, sometimes contradictory and often ill-worded decrees. In these circumstances law was, in the words of a popular saying, 'like the shafts of a cart: wherever the horse pulls, that's where it goes' – the horse being anyone in authority. To make matters worse, Peter himself had neglected to apply the elementary adhesive of a binding law of succession. In the absence of stable laws or institutions, not only peasants, but nobles as well could not feel fully secure in their persons or properties unless they had protection from a powerful patron, a member of one of the leading families, with access to the court.

That is why the forty years after Peter's death were so insecure and turbulent, with a succession of monarchs dependent on the fortuitous constellation of power in the capital's Guards regiments. The Guards regiments were the kernel of Imperial Russia in the eighteenth century. Stationed in the capital, with unbroken access to the court even for junior officers, they constituted for much of the century a police force as well as a personal bodyguard and a crack military formation. They were the nurseries of the power and patronage which not only decided crucial questions of domestic and foreign policy, but which made and broke rulers themselves. Controlling the disposition of physical force in the capital city, they took a decisive part in every monarchical succession from the death of Peter the Great in 1725 to the assassination of Paul I in 1801. They were the mechanism by which the leading families ensured that autocracy worked on the whole in their interests and not against it.

The one serious attempt to challenge the autocratic superstructure came in 1730, on the sudden death of the adolescent Peter II. Members of the Supreme Privy Council (which had been set up in 1727, in the absence of a dominating monarch, to coordinate the executive) offered the crown to Peter the Great's niece, Anna, Duchess of Kurland, on certain *konditsii* (conditions): the monarch must not marry or appoint her own heir, and in future must obtain the consent of the Council before deciding questions of war and peace, raising taxes, spending revenue, making high appointments in government or court, and making land grants. Members of the nobility were not to be deprived of life, honour or property without trial.

In the longer term, these *konditsii* might have formed the basis on which a constitutional monarchy could have evolved: analogous charters had had this effect in several European countries from the late middle ages onwards. Their immediate effect, however, would have been to subject Russia to oligarchic rule, with the monarch dependent on the few well-placed families which dominated the Supreme Privy Council, currently the Golitsyns and Dolgorukiis. Most of the service nobility was opposed to the idea, not only because they did not want to have to crawl to the Golitsyns and Dolgorukiis, but also because they were mindful of Russia's vulnerability when plagued by the feuds of boyar clans. With their support Anna demonstratively tore up the *konditsii* and assumed the throne as an autocrat.[2]

There was no other attempt in the eighteenth century to limit the monarchy nor till after 1762 to reform the institutions of state. Even during the relatively protracted reign of Empress Elizabeth (1741–62) power remained in the hands of aristocratic clans and their associated Guards regiments, unrestrained by the rule of law or powerful social institution.

The first ruler who tried to continue Peter the Great's work and to provide Russia with institutions more able to bear the weight of a huge empire was Catherine II – who, however, came to the throne in time-honoured fashion as beneficiary of a coup directed against her husband, Peter III. She saw the weaknesses of the Russian polity clearly enough. The voracious if indiscriminate reading which filled the vacant evenings of a loveless marriage had taught her that the remedy lay in promulgating good laws and founding good institutions. It is true that these laws and institutions took on a subtly different purpose in her mind from the one she found in her texts. The French and Italian Enlightenment theorists she studied – Montesquieu, Beccaria, Diderot – were thinking in terms of countries with old established institutions whose legal rights needed to be reaffirmed and buttressed about by liberal theory against the threat of an increasingly assertive monarchy. In Russia, however, law and intermediate institutions were so weak that, far from resisting the monarchy, they scarcely had backbone enough even to act as a passive transmitter of the ruler's will. To strengthen law and institutions was above all else to strengthen the monarchy, and this was Catherine's purpose.

For her this was doubly important because of her parlous individual situation. She occupied a throne to which she had no legitimate claim and so she urgently needed to broaden the circle of her supporters beyond the coterie of Guards officers who had acted on her behalf, beyond even the social class of which they were members. The best way to do this was to create institutions which would outlast the designs of even the most tenacious court clique, and laws which would be widely acceptable and might become permanent.

It so happened that P.I. Shuvalov, principal adviser to Empress Elizabeth, had convened a Law Codification Commission in 1754 to try and bring order to Peter I's peremptory and improvised lawmaking and coordinate it with the preceding Law Code (*Ulozhenie*) of 1649. Shuvalov's commission had been intended to examine the state of the law and make recommendations in four areas: (i) the rights of subjects according to their estate; (ii) court structures and procedures; (iii) property and contract law; (iv) punishments and penalties. The commission completed its work on the last three subjects and reported to Elizabeth, but its recommendations were not followed up, for reasons which are unclear, and the commission was abolished shortly after Catherine came to the throne.[3]

It is not clear that Catherine even read the materials of the commission, yet when she began her own work of codification in 1767, the principles she enunciated were very similar to its findings, and she herself called an analogous commission, with the same name and same remit. She composed for its consideration a *Nakaz*, an Instruction, really a set of principles, which reflected her own opinions on the political and legal structure desirable for Russia, though she did not release the final draft till she had had time to consult her advisers about the text.

Citing the Christian principle of doing 'all the Good we possibly can to each other', she declared it 'the Wish of every worthy Member of Society to see his Native Country raised to the highest degree of Prosperity, Glory, Happiness and Peace', and 'to see every Individual of his fellow-Citizens protected by Laws, which so far from injuring him, will shield him from every Attempt against his Welfare, and opposite to this Christian Precept'.[4]

Her version of law was a restricted and étatiste one compared with that of her Enlightenment mentors. In her eyes law was not an impersonal force adjudicating between autonomous and sometimes competing social institutions, but an instrument through which the ruler exercises his or her authority and through which moral precepts are put into practice. 'In a State, that is in a Collection of People living in Society where Laws are established, Liberty can consist only in the Ability of doing what everyone ought to desire, and in not being forced to do what should not be desired.'[5] This was the version of law and statehood propounded not by the French *philosophes*, but by the German cameralists, especially by Leibniz and Wolff. In this vision, the aim of law was to enable the authorities to provide for the well-being and security of their subjects. For the same purpose, subjects were to have their own functions, and would belong to social institutions which would enable them the better to fulfil those functions and to partake of the general well-being. There was no notion here of natural law, of inherent freedom or of a social contract.[6]

The members of Catherine's Law Code Commission were elected in local gatherings of the relevant estates: the nobility, townsfolk, state peasants, Cossacks, *odnodvortsy* (descendants of the militarized peasants who had manned the frontier lines) and non-Russians. Conspicuous by their absence were the serfs and the clergy. One might argue that the serfs were represented by their landlords, but the absence of the clergy can only mean that Catherine did not regard them as members of secular society, an astonishing lapse in view of the fact that she had just deprived them of the means – their landed wealth – of maintaining a separate, spiritual arm of government. [See chapter on church, p. 231]

Catherine's agenda was to draw up a law code along the lines indicated in her *Nakaz*. Now the deputies brought with them their own *nakazy* or 'cahiers', requests and statements of grievance originating from their electors. When the Commission first met in July 1767 to discuss them, it soon transpired that there was little meeting of minds. Each social estate concentrated in its presentation on its own narrowly conceived interests, insensitive to the broad vision of creative statesmanship laid before them by their monarch. The nobility wanted to restrict entry to its own estate, strengthen its property rights, secure its monopoly of higher civil and military posts and be freed from corporal punishment. Merchants requested a monopoly of trade in the towns and the right to own serfs. The peasants asked for relief from taxation and other burdens. Few deputies displayed an awareness of the overall structure of the state, which in any case most of them clearly expected to remain unchanged: their efforts were thus directed at obtaining what they could within the existing system rather than recommending fundamental reform.[7] The contrast is striking with the French Estates-General, which, meeting only some twenty years later, came up with radical programmes of reform, while the 'third estate' projected a vision of itself as the bearer of popular sovereignty, as 'the nation'.

For most of its sessions the Commission was divided into sub-committees, one of which was specifically charged to look into how a 'third estate' or 'middle sort of people' might be created. These sub-committees carried out some useful work in assimilating existing laws and drafting new ones. But the General Assembly ceased its sessions late in 1768, with the outbreak of war against Turkey: since many of the deputies belonged to the army, they had to report for service. Many of the sub-committees continued their work for a year or two longer, and some of them completed drafts on their sphere of legislation. Although there was now no General Assembly to refer these drafts to, they were not necessarily wasted, since Catherine later made use of them in elaborating laws. Furthermore, their materials were employed in a 'Description of the Russian Empire and its Internal Administration and Legal Enactments', drawn up by the Procurator-General and published in 1783: this was the closest thing Russia had to a law code for the next fifty years.[8]

Although the Turkish war genuinely precipitated the suspension of the Commission, it did not necessarily entail its abolition. Catherine let it fade away because she was disappointed by its work, especially perhaps by the fact that its members showed so little awareness of the needs of society as a whole and so little readiness to exercise self-restraint for the general good. She decided, probably rightly, that, before positing common interests which did not exist, she should put more backbone into a fragmented society by creating institutions which would enable citizens to work together at least within their own estates and orders. In a sense she was endeavouring actually to create social institutions which had hitherto been embryonic or non-existent.

With that in mind, during the rest of her reign she did much to impart substance to what had been an atomized society and polity, laying the foundation for what she herself called a 'civil society'. Like Peter, she believed that the monarch should make laws, but unlike him that the monarch should also be bound by laws once made, supervising the general process of administration, but not interfering with it at every step, and intervening only if urgency or the complexity of the issues demanded it. She did something to stimulate a science of jurisprudence in Russia, so that law and administrative practice could become regular and stable, a permanent factor which citizens could rely on in their daily activity, especially in economic affairs where predictability is so important. She read and annotated Blackstone's 'Commentary on the Laws': he saw the guarantee of legality as lying not so much in representative institutions as in having rational laws backed up by strong and stable authorities.[9] She sent young nobles abroad, mainly to German universities, to study the theory and practice of jurisprudence there (among them, as it happened, was Alexander Radishchev, who derived from his studies much more than she bargained for – an indication of the ambiguous results of her initiative).

To the same end she strengthened the Senate's role as supervisor of the administration and the law, though without going so far as to make it a 'repository of law' on the model of the French *parlements*, as she had once contemplated. Even more important was her strengthening of local government. European Russia was divided into *gubernii* (provinces), with a population of 200,000–300,000 and *uezdy* (districts) of 20,000–30,000. Each guberniia was to be overseen by a governor responsible to the Senate and having the right of personal report to the Emperor; he would be assisted by a provincial administrative board to handle matters like tax-collection, policing and trade monopolies. The higher administrative staff of these institutions was to come from the nobility, a provision intended to guarantee their probity and professional competence. To fortify the nobles' pride and corporate identity she granted them a Charter freeing them from corporal punishment and giving them the right to organize in local associations at the provincial and district level: these associations would then elect key local government officials. [For other provisions of the Charter, see Part 3, Chapter 1.]

Catherine promulgated a similar City Charter [see Part 3, Chapter 5]. This was part of a complex of measures aimed at encouraging manufacture and trade, reducing their direct dependence on the state and facilitating their penetration throughout the empire. Before her accession internal tariffs had been abolished (in 1753), and Catherine followed this up by measures to improve the provision of credit through a law to introduce bills of exchange, improve roads and canals, ease passport restrictions and enable both nobles and peasants to trade more widely (a measure which was however much resented by the merchants, since it infringed their monopoly of urban trade).[10] Nobles were given more secure property rights not only to the topsoil of their land, but to mineral resources which might be found below. All these measures were an important contribution towards making the empire an economic unit, and towards giving all classes of the population access to trade and manufacture on the basis of secure property rights.

She also contemplated a Charter for the State Peasants, which would have given them corporate status through their village communities, as well as secure property rights and the possibility of defending them before law courts. The draft was completed and ready to be promulgated: why it was never issued remains uncertain, though it seems likely that Catherine was deterred by the thought that its promulgation was bound to awaken dangerous hopes among the private serfs.[11] It was potentially extremely important, for it would have been the first occasion on which a Russian monarch accorded full property rights to peasants. Taken together, Catherine's Charters constitute her version of a society ruled by law; but this makes the exclusion of the state peasants (not to mention the serfs) an even more glaring anomaly.

The disordered and unpredictable condition of the laws was matched by the state of the empire's finances, which proved a lasting obstacle to attempts to mobilize the resources of population and territory. The fundamental problem was that, at least until the late eighteenth century, Russia was straining itself to the utmost to sustain the role of European great power, and could do so only by exploiting the population in ways which prevented them from deploying their own economic enterprise.

Like most eighteenth-century European states, Russia had no unified state budget, merely a collection of estimates or recorded expenditures for various departments, which could be enlarged for the requirements of the court and imperial favourites, and were occasionally reduced by loans from them. From the information we have, at the time of Peter's death in 1725 military and naval expenditure made up about 70% of the treasury's outgoings (6.5 million rubles out of 9.1 million). Most of the new expenditure arose from the introduction of the recruitment system, the creation of large infantry regiments and the introduction of improved firearms, ammunition and artillery.[12]

The introduction of the poll tax had been essential to cope with these unprecedented expenditures. It both simplified the tax system and made it much more productive, increasing revenues appreciably. Local branches of the Kamer-Kollegiia were set up all over the country, and local landowners and army officers were mobilized for the task. Since landowners were now in effect agents for both taxation and recruitment, their practical powers over the serfs were greatly augmented. Army units were used to back them up with coercion, when that was needed, as was frequently the case.

This was a remarkably centralized fiscal system for a country with such tenuous communications, and it is scarcely surprising that it did not always function as planned. Arrears and late payments were normal. Peasants and *posad* people (townsfolk) quite often refused point-blank to pay the levies due from them and were sometimes prepared to bolster their cause by armed resistance. Alternatively, following a long tradition, they might abandon their holdings and flee to the frontiers of south and east, to fill the ranks of Cossacks, *odnodvortsy* (single householders) and Old Believer communities.[13] Thus heavy-handed tax-collecting undermined the very wealth it was supposed to tap.

By the middle of the century, when expenditure increased sharply, especially during the Seven Years' War, it was obvious that more money could not be raised through the poll tax, and the authorities decided instead to cover the chronic deficits by increasing indirect taxes, the most remunerative of which was on alcoholic liquor, and by issuing paper money. These two methods – debauching the people and debauching the currency, Keynes might have called them – proved addictive [!] and lasted in one case well into the nineteenth century, in the other right up to 1917.

Apart from brief and not very successful experiments at direct administration, the state liquor monopoly was farmed out, and was a source of enrichment to its agents – officials, landowners, merchants and publicans – right up to the 1860s, when it was replaced by an excise levy. Between 1724 and 1759, the revenue from the sale of liquor rose from 11% to 21% of the state's income, while by the 1850s it had reached about 40% of the total, declining to about a third in the 1880s.[14]

It would be an exaggeration, but not an absurd one, to say that the empire was kept financially afloat on the proceeds of the drunkenness of the people. It was naturally far easier to raise revenue from thirsty drinkers than by means of punitive expeditions from reluctant poll-tax payers. Russian popular custom demanded bouts of heavy drinking at times of celebration, whether christenings, weddings and funerals or public festivals. Not to consume huge quantities of alcohol on such occasions, often over several days, was to render oneself liable to ridicule or worse. With the growth of towns and of migratory work during the nineteenth century, a new and probably more pernicious drinking culture took hold, involving casual heavy consumption in taverns with workmates on pay day, without the relatively long periods of abstinence in between such as marked rural customs. The state deliberately took advantage of these habits to augment its income – which meant in turn that it came to have a stake in popular drunkenness and even alcoholism.

It also had a stake in the corruption of its own officials. The liquor farm was auctioned out every four years, on which occasions the prospective farmers (*otkupshchiki*), to win the franchise, would undertake to sell vodka at approved (low) prices while generating maximum revenues for the state. In practice it was impossible for them to keep these promises without resorting to illegal methods, for example, adulteration, shortweight or claiming to have only expensive liquors in stock when by law they were obliged to have ordinary ones always available for sale. Provincial officials often considered bribes from publicans for indulgence over unavoidable abuses a normal and regular part of their income, which in many cases roughly doubled their meagre official salaries. As one commentator put it, 'the police officials are themselves farmed out to the tax farmers'.[15]

The Ministry of Finance admitted as much in a circular of 1859, which instructed governors to turn a blind eye to abuses. 'A certain increase in the sale of improved beverages at higher prices does not breach the tax farm regulations and should not be regarded as an abuse on the part of the farmers, but is rather the consequence of the calculations necessary for the successful transfer to the Treasury of 366,745,056 silver rubles, which the farmers are obliged to surrender over the present four-year period.'[16] As Herzen remarked, 'Who can buy from the government a fixed quantity at a fixed price, sell it to the people without raising its price, and pay the government ten times as much? Of course, having made such deals with the tax farmers, the government not only cannot prosecute them for abuses, but is actually obliged to protect them ... The government is consciously robbing the people, and then dividing up the spoils with the tax farmers and others who have participated in the crime.'[17]

Corruption, then, was not just a side-effect of the liquor tax system. It was a necessary consequence of the state's desperate need to raise cash in a still largely natural economy. One should not regard these expedients as all that unusual: both ancient Rome and 17th–18th century France relied on tax-farming for much of their income. But in both cases this reliance was damaging, and in Russia too it obstructed both economic growth and the state's ability to mobilize real wealth in the interests of the population as a whole. In the words of Charles Tilly, Russia was a state being formed by means which were highly 'coercion-intensive', because the country was so poor in capital. The poll tax, paper money and the farming of the liquor monopoly were natural methods to adopt in the circumstances.[18] That does not alter its obstructive effects.

Paper money (*assignaty*) was introduced in 1769, and inevitably public confidence in it fell fairly rapidly: by 1801 a paper ruble was worth 66k in silver, by 1817 after the outlays of the Napoleonic war, only 25k. Between 1817 and 1823 the state tried to treat paper rubles frankly as state debt and to buy them back for metal and destroy them, but had not enough bullion to complete the exercise. Another more successful attempt was made between 1839 and 1843, this time issuing bills of credit against them. For a time, gold and silver were the basic means of exchange, but the huge debts of the Crimean War were again covered by the issue of *assignaty*. Another attempt at monetary reform in the early 1860s ran aground on the expense of suppressing the Polish rebellion.[19]

The inflated paper money, the excessive taxation, the reliance on heavy popular drinking, the absence of budgetary discipline: all these evils were symptoms of a state which was straining itself beyond what the resources of land and people would bear at the current level of technology. Its demands, moreover, were obstructing the development of an internal market and investment such as might have raised the level of that technology. There was no shortage of proposals about how those resources might be more efficiently and less damagingly mobilized, but the pressure of immediate needs and the dead hand of serfdom ensured that they were never properly followed up.

In some ways Catherine's most successful economic measures were connected with the colonization of newly opened or under-populated territories, in the Volga basin and the Urals, and especially along the coast of the Black Sea, in so-called *Novorossiia* or 'New Russia', annexed from Turkey between 1774 and 1792. Here, presented with a *tabula rasa*, the combination of cameralism and mercantilism came into its own, in the absence of competing privileged social groups or corporate organizations. In territories largely unpopulated Catherine was able to attract immigrants both from within Russia and from more crowded European countries, especially from Germany, by offering them land, guarantees of religious toleration, favourable loans and a period of relief from taxation.[20]

The conquest and successful colonization of this region freed

Russia from many of the chronic disadvantages it had suffered for centuries while hemmed in among the forests and on the poor soils of the north. It provided secure and fertile soil and reliable all-year communications with Europe and the Middle East. During the early nineteenth century the production of grain and other agricultural goods from these regions decisively ameliorated the economic situation of the whole empire: in effect they underwrote Russia's great power status for another century.

The success of the policy was due to the way in which the Russian authorities could easily combine military and civilian arms of government, subordinating both to a rational vision of political economy untrammelled by inherited custom or ethnic prejudice.[21] Here the absence of intermediate associations with their own interests and privileges was a positive advantage.

The military campaigns necessary to conquer these regions imposed, however, a grievous burden on the population, nobles as well as peasants. Catherine's Turkish wars entailed calling up many able-bodied male peasants, requisitioning horses and grain stores, raising taxes, inflating the currency and in other ways undermining the productive potential of both noble estates and peasant holdings. Perhaps the most dangerous opposition Catherine ever faced was from groups of courtiers and writers centred first around Nikita Panin and later A. R. Vorontsov, and including the heir to the throne: they contended that her aggressive southern policy (which tactfully they identified with court favourites rather than with her personally) was both ruinous to the economy and exposed the northern regions, including the capital city, to strategic dangers, especially from Sweden. While they never gained a predominant influence, these thinkers – who included writers like Shcherbatov, Fonvizin, Radishchev and Novikov – presented a more 'organic' alternative to the expansive military and imperial policies of Catherine.[22]

THE PUGACHEV REBELLION Rationalism and disdain for tradition were the very characteristics which rendered the imperial regime so alien to many of its peoples. The Pugachev rebellion was the last and most serious in a long series of risings which broke out on the south-eastern borders of the Russian state, in that open and ill-defined region where Old Believers and other fugitives from imperial authority rubbed shoulders with non-Russian tribesmen of the steppes, and where Cossacks mounted defence of the Tsar's fortresses and stockades, while continuing to dream of the brigands' licence which they had been accustomed to enjoy.

By the mid-eighteenth century the region was being slowly but surely brought under firm imperial control. In fact, one may regard the Pugachev rebellion as the last – but powerful – spasm of peoples whose untrammelled way of life was incompatible with distinct and definite state authority. Nobles were being awarded new estates along and beyond the Volga, and peasants who already lived there were becoming serfs, while new ones were being imported. *Obrok* (dues in money or kind) was being raised or converted into *barshchina* (labour dues) by landlords anxious to maximize their revenues and to take advantage of fresh and lucrative trading opportunities. A census and land survey undertaken soon after Catherine II came to power fixed and perpetuated these still relatively unfamiliar arrangements. Also new market opportunities were opening up along the Volga and in the south, putting pressure on more traditional and less productive enterprises.[23]

A special group in the area were the *odnodvortsy*, survivors of the peasant-soldiers sent to man the Volga frontier during the sixteenth and seventeenth centuries, and most of them Old Believers. Still in theory freemen, they suffered from the economic competition of the nobles, feared losing their independence and falling into the regular taxpaying estates as state peasants.

The rebellion began among the Yaik Cossacks, whose situation reflected the changes wrought by the ever more intrusive Tsarist state. They had long enjoyed the freedom to run their own affairs, to elect their own leaders and to hunt, fish and raid along the lower Yaik (Ural) River as they chose, in return for acknowledging the Tsar's ultimate suzerainty and rendering him service when required. A change in this status came in 1748, when the government decreed the establishment of a Yaik Army of seven regiments to man the Orenburg Line currently being built to keep out the Kazakhs and divide them from the Bashkirs. A few Yaik Cossacks among the *starshyna* (officer class) reacted favourably to this idea, hoping that it would give them secure status within the Table of Ranks; but most rank-and-file Cossacks opposed integration into the Russian army as an infringement of their freedom and of their elective democratic institutions. They also feared being enlisted as common soldiers. Their suspicions were deepened by the proposal in 1769 to form a 'Moscow legion' from the smaller Cossack hosts to fight against the Turks. This implied wearing regular uniform, undergoing parade-ground drilling, and worst of all having beards shaven, a prospect deeply repugnant to Old Believers.

Emel'ian Pugachev was discovered and put up as a front man by the disaffected Yaik Cossacks. A Don Cossack by origin, he had deserted from the Russian army and become a fugitive: several times captured, he had always contrived to escape. He assumed the title of the dead Emperor Peter III and espoused the Old Belief. This ruse may have been suggested to him by a Yaik Cossack, but he took on his invented roles with conviction and panache, and he became a figure far outstripping the Cossacks' ability to manipulate him.

Peter III had aroused hopes among peasants and religious dissidents by some of the measures he had adopted during his brief period as Tsar. He had expropriated church lands and thereby converted ecclesiastical and monastic serfs to the more favourable status of state peasants. He had prohibited the purchase of serfs by non-nobles and halted the ascription of serfs to factories and mines. He had eased the persecution of Old Believers and pardoned fugitive schismatics who voluntarily returned from abroad. His emancipation of the nobility from state service, though not itself of direct benefit to the serfs, seemed to hold out the hope that they too might soon be emancipated from equivalent obligations.

At any rate, the sudden dethronement of Peter III aroused the strongest suspicions among ordinary peasants, especially since his successor was a German, popularly held not to be truly an Orthodox believer. Pugachev was not the first to profit from his reputation by claiming to be the suffering and wandering deposed Peter, ready to lead his people to the restoration of the true faith and of their traditional freedoms. There were a dozen or so such figures between 1762 and 1774. But he was much the most successful, partly by luck, partly by personality and partly because of the breadth of support he received.

The epidemic of pretenders in those years invites reflection. A pretender was a symptom of a serious disorder in the body politic, a disorder which could not be corrected through any institutional procedures, or through the clash of corporate and representative bodies, for these did not exist. For most Russians, if the state was pursuing fundamentally misguided policies, then that was a sign that the Tsar was not really Tsar – that he was an impostor, who had usurped the throne, unordained by God. It followed that the logical mode of opposition was to find the 'real' Tsar, the one who carried God's seal of approval (often thought to be discernible as an actual mark on his body) and to support his claim to the throne. It will be remembered that Ivan IV, when faced with a fundamental challenge to his rule, himself played the comedy of abdicating his royal powers, and even handing them over to another, in order to prove that he *was* in fact entitled to exercise divinely-ordained authority.[24]

Pugachev augmented his popularity by projecting an image of a suffering Christ-like leader, who had meekly accepted his dethronement, and instead of resisting had left St Petersburg to wander sadly among his people, learning of their sufferings and grievances. He also claimed to have visited Constantinople and Jerusalem, buttressing his sanctity and authority by these contacts with the second Rome and with the site of Christ's crucifixion.

The circumstances in which Catherine came to power were calculated to provoke speculation about her legitimacy. She deepened resentment by revoking some of her ex-husband's most popular decrees, moving on to measures which curbed the freedom of the Cossacks and oppressed still further the already meagre rights of the serfs – for example by forbidding them to present petitions to the sovereign.

Pugachev's first manifesto, addressed to the Yaik Cossacks and to Tatar and Kalmyk tribesmen, situated his appeal to them within the Muscovite tradition of state service as a legitimate corollary of their freedoms and privileges. He invoked the blood their fathers and grandfathers had shed in the service of previous Tsars, and in return for equivalent service promised them 'Cossack glory ... forever', forgiveness of sins, and return of their material privileges: 'the river from the heights to the mouth, and the land and grasses, and money, and lead, and powder, and provision of grain'.[25]

The major cause of Pugachev's success was his capacity to appeal not just to any one social group, but to a wide variety of the empire's discontented, finding enough in common in their grievances and aspirations to forge a sense of common purpose, however temporary it proved to be. The central feature of this appeal was the promise to restore a simplified, just and personalized service state of the kind which since the time of Peter I was gradually being replaced by more distant, impersonal and bureaucratic procedures. He certainly did not renounce autocracy: indeed, his improvised state offices were headed by a War College, on the Petrine model, while he himself granted notional estates and even notional serfs to his favoured followers.[26] The key to his appeal was his rejection of secularism in church and state and his campaign of hatred against the nobility, with their Westernized ways.

The adoption of the Old Belief set the seal on this projected image of an older and better Russia, for it evoked the ancient myth of national unity which the imperial state had disavowed. In his manifesto of 31 July 1774 Pugachev set forth the ideal which he knew would have most appeal to the common people. 'By God's grace We, Peter III, Emperor and Autocrat of all the Russias ... with royal and fatherly charity grant by this our personal ukaz to all who were previously peasants and subjects of the pomeshchiks to be true and loyal servants of our throne, and we reward them with the ancient cross and prayer, with bearded heads, with liberty and freedom and to be for ever Cossacks, demanding neither recruit enlistment, poll tax or other money dues, and we award them the ownership of the land, of forests, hay meadows and fishing grounds, and with salt lakes, without purchase and without dues in money or in kind, and we free peasants and all the people from the taxes and burdens which were previously imposed by the wicked nobles and mercenary urban judges.' He further accused the landlords of 'violating and abusing the ancient tradition of the Christian law, and having with pernicious intent introduced an alien law taken from German traditions, and the impious practice of shaving and other blasphemies contrary to the Christian faith.'[27]

Pugachev's use of the symbols of the Old Belief is worth dwelling on, since recent research shows that few members of Old Believer communities actually participated in the rising.[28] His appeal was rather to the numerous Old Believers among the Cossacks and *odnodvortsy*, and to Russian peasants generally, who he knew would respond strongly to evocations of the ancient Russian myth. The synthesis of Old Believer and Cossack ideals provided an alternative model of Russian nationhood which was deeply attractive in those unsettled regions.

This common appeal overarched specific promises made to each social group that enrolled under his banners: to the Cossacks the restoration of their traditional freedom and their democratic procedures, to the Bashkïrs and Kalmyks the return of their tribal lands, to the possessional and ascribed serfs of the Urals factories either a release from their bonded manual labour or an improvement in their pay and conditions, to the state peasants the easing of burdens and to the private serfs the ousting (and murder) of their landowners.

The Bashkirs were a special case. Their grievances at this time were deep and persistent. They were gradually losing their grazing lands both as a result of peasant settlement, the establishment of factories and of government attempts to persuade or compel them to settle down and take to agriculture. Like the Cossacks, they were being pressed into military service on the frontier, under conditions which were not always congenial. These grievances had stimulated bitter and tenacious armed rebellions in the first half of the eighteenth century.

The diversity of his appeal meant that when Pugachev suffered a serious setback, as he did in the spring of 1774, with the failure to capture Orenburg, and in the summer with the loss of Kazan', he was able to move into a new area and raise large numbers of fresh supporters with a speed which took the authorities by surprise. His success in the final stages of his campaign, along the mid- and lower Volga, was especially remarkable, for here he managed to spark off a general peasant rising, a *jacquerie* of French 1789 proportions, merely by his general presence in the region. This was 'Pugachevshchina without Pugachev', as one historian has called it.[29]

In the towns, as Pugachev's host approached, the local clergy would come out with the principal townsmen to greet their new 'Tsar' with icons, bell-ringing, bread and salt. They would celebrate divine service in honour of their lord Peter Fedorovich, after which the rebels would plunder the state salt and liquor monopoly warehouses, handing out their contents to the citizens, and open up the jails, recruiting fresh troops, or 'Cossacks', from among the inmates.

In the villages, minor emissaries sufficed, calling themselves 'Cossacks of Peter III', or even the mere rumour that Pugachev was in the vicinity. Peasants would gather at the sound of the tocsin, seize whatever weapons they could lay their hands on – scythes, pitchforks, clubs, and perhaps a musket or two – and march on the local manor house or state *kabak*. Several thousand nobles and their families, as well as stewards, publicans, tax officials and sometimes clergymen, lost their lives, or would flee at the approach of trouble, only to have their property confiscated and their homes rendered uninhabitable. Pugachev's emissaries would pronounce the peasants freed from private serfdom and exempt from the poll tax and military recruitment for the next seven years. The *odnodvortsy* also took a lively part in this stage of the rebellion.

In spite of the destruction he caused, and the fear he inspired both in landowners and the government, Pugachev succeeded in capturing only two major cities (Kazan' and Saratov) and was unable to hold either for more than a few days. His army, at times numerically quite formidable – at least 10,000 during the siege of Orenburg[30] – was effective against small garrisons and against other disaffected Cossacks. But it proved unequal to the task of countering sizeable units of the regular army. Here the wisdom of the government's policy of recruiting peasants for life manifested itself fully. Soldiers in the regular army were almost totally immune to Pugachev's appeals: they did not identify themselves with the serfs' grievances, still less the Cossack ones, and they were constrained by a harsh and all-embracing discipline. Pugachev's lightning campaign along the lower Volga, for all its success in attracting peasant support, was in reality a headlong flight before a pursuing army which he knew he could not defeat.

What is perhaps more surprising is that the Don Cossacks also failed to back Pugachev when he approached their region at the end of his campaign. The explanation may be that, since Pugachev was by origin a Don Cossack, they knew very well that he was not Peter III. Furthermore, they had been in revolt themselves a few years earlier, so that their energy had expended itself, and they were under particularly attentive official supervision.

It is significant that, although the Don Cossacks mostly withheld their support from Pugachev, they subsequently celebrated his memory no less than other Cossacks and peasants in songs and folklore.[31] As Marc Raeff has commented: 'They exemplified the discontent and rebelliousness of a traditional group in the face of transformations wrought (or threatened) by a centralised absolute monarchy. Like the feudal revolts and rebellions in the name of regional particularism and traditional privileges in Western Europe, the Cossacks opposed the tide of rational modernisation and the institutionalisation of political authority. They regarded their relationship to the ruler as a special and personal one based on their voluntary service obligations; in return they expected the Tsar's protection of their religion, traditional social organisation, and administrative autonomy. They followed the promises of a pretender and raised the standard of revolt in the hope of recapturing their previous special relationship and of securing the government's respect for their social and religious traditions.[32]

The rebellion deeply troubled Catherine. She tried in her correspondence with foreign powers to belittle it by contemptuous references to 'le Marquis Pougatchev', but actually she feared that, if the movement found a leader from among Russia's elites, it might succeed in overthrowing her. From the way she had come to the throne she had good cause to know the fragility of her courtiers' loyalty. She followed the progress of the rebellion closely and took an alert interest in the capture and interrogation of its leaders. In her manifestoes to the population, she displayed a shrewd sense of their psychology by using the old pre-Petrine alphabet.[33] It is uncertain what effect the rebellion had on her later policies, since the reforms she carried out in the later 1770s and 1780s were already being planned before it erupted. It probably reinforced her determination to integrate the Cossacks thoroughly within army and administration, a process which she carried through systematically in the remaining years of her reign.

There can be not much doubt that the rebellion intensified her caution and her distrust of all possible sources of internal disaffection. It had the same effect on her successors too: fears of a possible *pugachevshchina* figured among the arguments advanced over a possible emancipation of the serfs right up to 1861, nearly a century later.

Perhaps unnecessarily: the evidence suggests that peasants cannot rebel without leaders from outside their ranks. With the Cossacks tamed, no other potential leaders offered themselves for nearly a century. Before Bakunin, no educated Russian, even those grimly opposed to the autocracy, advocated peasant revolution as a way of overthrowing it. Most would have concurred with Pushkin's sentiment: 'God preserve us from a Russian revolt, senseless and merciless.'

Yet in another sense, Russia's officials and nobles were right not to forget Pugachev. For he had revealed just how wafer-thin was the loyalty of some of the non-Russians, and above all of the Russian peasants, to the regime which ruled over them and to its agents, their own lords. The nobles would not lightly forget the image of burnt-out manor houses, with the corpses of their former occupants hanging from the gates. It was a sharp reminder of the gulf – now perhaps at its widest – which separated the ordinary people from their superiors.[34]

EDUCATION AND CULTURE   It was natural that a ruler so conscious of the need to change society should be passionately interested in education. It was indeed one of Catherine's constant preoccupations. She read a lot about it in the fashionable works of the time, but professed herself unimpressed with Rousseau's *Émile*: probably its emphasis on the free formation of the personality clashed with her own greater interest in social order. On the other hand, she had a broader conception of education than did Peter I, wanting it to penetrate beyond the elites to the whole of society. She did her best to make the court a nursery and propagator of culture. In this she was continuing and broadening the initiative already taken by Elizabeth, who had established an excellent tradition of court theatre, music and ballet.

Perhaps her most remarkable initiative was the founding of a society journal, on the model of the London *Spectator*. Entitled *This and That (Vsiakaia vsiachina)*, it was edited by Catherine's secretary, G. Kozitskii, but contained frequent editorial contributions by a certain *Babushka*, who was widely known to be Catherine herself. Perhaps she wanted in its pages to revive the debate she felt she had not achieved through the Legislative Commission; perhaps she aimed through satire and pleasant reading to disseminate good moral principles and modern European cultural examples.

She pursued the same aim in her demonstrative promotion of links with some of the leading European thinkers of the time. She founded a Society for the Translation of Foreign Books into Russian, which she endowed with two thousand rubles. She corresponded with Voltaire, who applauded her resolute action against the Catholic Church (in Poland). She offered Diderot a press and publishing facilities for the *Encyclopédie* in Riga when he was having difficulties with the authorities in France and she invited him to St Petersburg, where they had long conversations in private. For an ambitious and politically committed thinker like Diderot, Russia, unencumbered by ancient institutions and privileges, appeared to offer enticing scope for an enlighted reformism which was continually frustrated in France. At any rate, he urged Catherine to issue a proper law on the succession, to keep the Legislative Commission in being as a 'repository of the laws' and to institute a free and compulsory system of primary education.[35]

She would have known that the last suggestion was impracticable (though Prussia attempted it in 1763), but she concurred with the sentiment, and did want to make a start on making general education more widely available than merely to the nobility. In 1786, after a commission under her ex-favourite, P.V. Zavadovskii, had examined the subject, she issued a National Statute of Education, which provided for a two-tier network of schools: secondary at the guberniia, and primary at the uezd level, free of charge, co-educational, and open to all classes of the population except serfs.

Not the least significant feature of the proposed new network was that it did not build in any way on the existing church schools, the only ones which were at all widespread. The new schools were to be secular, free of charge and co-educational, with the government providing the initial capital expenditure, and local boards of social welfare meeting the running costs. They were intended to instil 'a clear and intelligent understanding of the Creator and His divine law, the basic rules of firm belief in the state, and true love for the fatherland and one's fellow citizens'. Pupils were to be issued with a guidebook outlining the 'Duties of Man and Citizen', whose tone was that of the authoritarian secular state, as in the injunction to obey one's superiors. 'Those who give orders know what is useful to the state, their subjects and all civil society in general, [and] they do not wish for anything but what is generally recognised as useful by society.[36]

In 1764 Catherine set up a Foundling Hospital in Moscow, under her personal supervision, the first of several. It was to take orphans – the children most dependent on the state – and fashion them according to the latest educational theories as good citizens. In a sense, this was another of Catherine's initiatives to create a 'third estate'. In the same year she established the Smol'nyi Institute for Noble Women, which emphasized socially useful attainments, such as music, dancing and French. The new Institute was a token of her conviction that a more broadly-based society and culture required an informed input from women. Both were intended to advance her purpose of creating a secular civil society as a support for the state.

Catherine's educational initiatives were undoubtedly ambitious, perhaps too much so: many of the new schools had few pupils and relied on poorly paid and poorly qualified foreigners to provide the bulk of their teaching staff. By the end of the century scarcely more than one in a thousand inhabitants was receiving any kind of schooling. All the same, a basic network had been created on which Catherine's successors were able to build, and the principle had been accepted that education was not the preserve of the privileged or of males, but should eventually be open to all, free of charge. This principle passed into the life-blood of Russia's educationalists, giving them a bias towards a democratic, open-access system which survived all nineteenth-century attempts to narrow it.[37]

Catherine also did something to continue the drive to provide Russia with a scientific and research base outside as well as inside the Academy. She lifted the state monopoly on printing, enabling private entrepreneurs to enter the field, provided only that they registered their presses with the police. She encouraged the foundation of the Free Economic Society, which aimed to investigate techniques and practices in the field of agriculture and industry and to disseminate them as widely as possible. It was not an official institution, but was run by aristocrats and academics, and it sponsored experiments and studies, as well as the regular reading and publication of reports. On Catherine's suggestion it investigated the relative productivity of free and serf labour, but it does not seem that she paid much attention to its verdict in favour of the former. Even if its influence was not always great, however, the Free Economic Society survived right through to 1917 as a learned society genuinely independent of the state.[38]

Its work was supplemented by some of the earliest scientific expeditions to investigate the minerals, flora and fauna of the empire's immense territories, as well as their human potential. These expeditions were organized by the Academy of Sciences, which was the only institution in a position to coordinate all the disciplines involved: geography, ethnography, medicine, geology, zoology, botany, mineralogy. The results were made available in huge publication projects deposited in the Academy library, a mine of information to the present about all aspects of Russian life. Such information was essential to the eventual exploitation of the empire's full potential – still a long distant goal.[39]

CONCLUSIONS At the end of Catherine's reign, Russia was undoubtedly stronger militarily, culturally and economically than when she acceded to the throne. Both the state and society had taken on more palpable sinews, and the influence of European manners and culture had both broadened and deepened among the elites. Russia had become not only a European great power, but a successful one. Senior soldiers and statesmen, and people of high culture, would later look back on her years in power with nostalgia.

All this had not been achieved without cost, however. Catherine had shown that social estates could be created from above as well as from below, but that the process was slow, painful and contradictory. In strengthening the corporate status of the strong, it further undermined the already feeble defences of the weak. As one of Fonvizin's characters remarks: 'What use is the freedom of the nobility if we are not free to whip our serfs?'[40] Probably that is why she hankered throughout her reign after a 'third estate', which would be educated and fit for official employment without the divisive privileges held by the nobility.

Perhaps also that is why Catherine never promulgated her Charter of the State Peasants: it might have underlined the utter legal helplessness of the private serfs. It would have been her most ambitious attempt to extend civil rights to large numbers of the population. At any rate, she drew back, leaving one with the suspicion that civil society could only be created at the expense of deepening the civic and ethnic rift within the Russian population, between the elites and the masses.

4

The Apogee of the Secular State

By the end of the eighteenth century the society created by Peter the Great had survived, but its culture and traditions had taken root only in one social estate, the nobility. To bridge the gap thus opened between the nobility and other strata, the ruler could now proceed in two alternative ways: either by confirming the freedoms (or privileges) of the nobility and letting them percolate gradually down the social scale, or by reining the nobility back and enforcing more equitably the universal principle of state service.

PAUL I (1796–1801)   Paul was an exemplar of the second approach. He heartily disliked his mother, and took a positive pleasure in declaring her practice of enhancing privilege misguided. Everywhere, and especially in the army, he promoted obedience, discipline and efficiency. Paul was an extreme adherent of the 'Prussomania' prevalent in many late eighteenth-century European courts: the fascination with precise formation and immaculate drill. In seventeenth-century France drill had originally been introduced to enhance the battle-readiness of the soldiers; but under Paul its purpose changed, and it became a means of glorifying the monarch as symbolic hero, an embodiment of the disciplined social order he liked to think he headed. Each day at 11 a.m. throughout his reign, in the brooding Mikhailovskii Palace which was his residence, he would review the troops of the watch in their new-style Prussian uniforms.

He insisted that nobles should play their due part in this parade ground display and dedicate themselves to service, especially military service, whatever their theoretical exemption from it. He lavished decorations and serfs on those who excelled, but humiliated and punished those who evaded their duties. The Guards suffered especially from his authoritarianism: having being gallant comrades-in-arms at the elegant court of the Empress, they became mere subalterns in Paul's grim parade lines.[1]

Paul stabilized the monarchy by issuing an unambiguous Law of Succession, providing for descent of the throne by way of the oldest male heir, and stipulating the precise provisions for a regency, should one be needed. He also assumed the role of religious ruler with greater panache than any monarch since the seventeenth century. He accepted the office of Grand Master of the Knights of Malta after the Knights' home island had fallen to Napoleon, and used the occasion to cultivate his image as doughty defender of Christianity against the aggressive atheism of the French revolution. What was involved was not just Orthodoxy but Christianity as a whole, the first sign that the Russian monarch aspired to a universal religious mission. He intended that the new order of the Knights of Malta should offer an example of chivalry and re-inspire in nobles the ideals of service: self-sacrifice, duty and discipline.[2]

To isolate Russia from the contagion of the French revolution, Paul forbade the import of books and journals and, in an extraordinary abrogation of previous practice, prohibited travel abroad – which had been the normal way for Russian nobles to round off their education. He also made abundant use of his intelligence service, the *tainaia ekspeditsiia* (inherited, ironically, from his mother) to spy on nobles whom he suspected of opposition to himself. Although he never repealed the Charter to the Nobility, he undid many of its provisions. Local assemblies of the nobility were abolished, together with their right to elect local officials, who were instead appointed by the government. Landed estates were subjected to taxation, and the gentry's emancipation from corporal punishment was ended: in certain circumstances, nobles could now be flogged.

On the peasant question Paul was inconsistent, since he awarded his favourites land populated by serfs no less bountifully than his mother; but at the same time he restored the right of serfs to petition the crown over mistreatment, he restricted the selling of serfs without land, and he limited the number of days of the week on which landlords could require their serfs to work for them.[3]

As a person, Paul was harsh and punctilious, and given to furious outbursts of rage which generated widespread rumours that he was mentally unbalanced. He was undoubtedly inconsistent, but his madness, if that is what it was, reflected the objective situation of the Russian monarchy, with its vast claims to power and its limited practical means of exercising that power.

The nobles in general, and especially the Guards officers, chafed at the symbolic and substantive humiliations he inflicted. In 1801 a group of them, headed by Count Petr Palen, Governor-General of St Petersburg, managed to obtain the consent of the heir, Grand Duke Alexander, to depose Paul. In the event, they not only did that, but also murdered him, something to which Alexander had not agreed, and which left him with an abiding burden on his conscience.

ALEXANDER I   Paul's reign had shown how fragile were the privileges and freedoms of the nobility, and that the minimal civil liberties which existed in Russia could be liquidated at a stroke. The accession of Alexander was therefore welcomed with great satisfaction and eager expectation. Like his grandmother a devotee of the European Enlightenment, Alexander had been brought up under the guidance of a tutor chosen by her, La Harpe, a Swiss republican, who inculcated in him a vivid impression of the evils of despotism and the benefits of the rule of law. These lessons were reinforced by the negative experience of his father's rule.

Alexander, however, was not merely repelled by his father. He had spent his youth in two courts, that of his grandmother and that of his father, and he had learned from both. He found the contrast between them extremely difficult to digest, and it marked his personality with a permanent ambivalence. He was never quite able to make a clear choice between the alternative paths open to him.

As heir to the throne, he gathered round himself a circle of young aristocratic friends with whom he would discuss ideas for a future freer and better government, yet he never ceased to be attracted by the military model of social order. At times he would give up trying to reconcile the warring aspects of his personality and would shrink back before the awful responsibility of governing Russia, dreaming instead of withdrawing to a cottage in the country somewhere in Germany. Sometimes he hoped that it might be possible to grant a constitution first, and then seek out his rural idyll, leaving the nation to govern itself. He told his tutor: 'Once ... my turn comes, then it will be necessary to work, gradually of course, to create a representative assembly of the nation which, thus directed, will establish a free constitution, after which my authority will cease absolutely; and, if Providence supports our work, I will retire to some spot where I will live contentedly and happily, observing and taking pleasure in the well-being of my country.' It was sentiments of this kind which led Berdiaev to call Alexander a 'Russian *intelligent* on the throne'.[4]

When he came to power, Alexander declared in a manifesto that he would return to the principles of Catherine. He undid many of his father's acts, declaring a general amnesty for political prisoners, abolishing the *tainaia ekspeditsiia*, restoring the Charters to the Nobles and the Towns, and the right of importing books from abroad, and inviting the Senate to make proposals regarding its own future functions.

On the other hand, the circumstances of his father's deposition and murder left Alexander with a sense of guilt and unease which lasted the whole of his life. The conspirators who assassinated Paul were senior aristocrats who had definite views on these matters. They belonged to the 'Senatorial party', adherents of the view that noble privilege should be bolstered. Responding to Alexander's invitation, they outlined their view that the Senate should be elected by the *dvorianstvo*, and should act as guarantor of the rule of law, by advising the Emperor to reject any proposed legislation which contradicted the existing legal framework, by ensuring that freedom of property and person was upheld, and by supervising administrative officials. Under this scheme the Senate would also have the right to propose taxes, nominate senior personnel, and submit to the Tsar 'the nation's needs'. Count Alexander Vorontsov, the leading figure in the group, composed a 'Charter to the Russian People', enshrining these principles, which it was hoped Alexander would proclaim at his coronation. Such a proclamation could have laid the basis for an English Whig approach to government, or for an aristocratically guaranteed *Rechtstaat*.[5]

However, Alexander was also susceptible to the other concept of liberty, extended to all social classes rather than guaranteed by the privileges of only one of them. This was the French Jacobin rather than the English Whig view, and it was the one held in his circle of young friends, one of whom, Pavel Stroganov, had actually been a member of the Club des Jacobins in Paris. On his accession he summoned them to regular consultations as his 'Secret Committee' (*Neglasnyi Komitet*), or his 'Committee of Public Safety', as he sometimes jokingly called it. Before he came to the throne, he declared to another of its members, the young Polish aristocrat, Prince Adam Czartoryski, his 'hatred of despotism, wherever and by whatever means it was exercised', and affirmed that he 'loved liberty and that liberty was owed equally to all men'.[6]

It was not, though, at all clear how such a concept of liberty could be adapted to a country a large number of whose inhabitants were serfs. It could only be done, if at all, by abolishing serfdom, that is by undermining the property and privileges of those who possessed the limited amount of civil liberty currently available in the Russian state. And that in turn could only be done, if at all, by a monarch who retained in his hands the fullness of autocratic authority. That was the fundamental dilemma which Alexander never resolved, throughout his reign: to carry out serious reform, he needed to retain his autocratic powers intact. Alexander's personality was equivocal and secretive, as a result of his long sojourn at the court of his father, where he combined his humane and liberal studies with a genuine enthusiasm for the military parades which so delighted Paul. But his ambivalence was intensified by the objective situation in which he found himself when he came to the throne, for it meant he could introduce liberty only through despotism.

· For that reason, his Secret Committee remained secret, and its deliberations were never published. All its members were aware that any public discussion of the possible abolition or even amelioration of serfdom would excite expectations among the peasants which could easily lead to massive public disorder. In the event, Alexander got nowhere even with his modest proposal to regulate the burdens which landowners could impose on their serfs. The only product of their deliberations was a law of 1803 which *permitted* (but certainly did not require) landowners to emancipate whole villages of serfs, with all the land they cultivated. Even that law was passed without consulting the Senate, which might well have objected to it.

In 1802, in deference to the Senatorial party, Alexander had granted the Senate the *droit de remontrance*, but he had then ignored their advice the first time they tried to exercise it, over a law governing the conditions for the retirement of army officers. In practice, it lapsed thereafter. In that way, Russia received neither a *Rechtstaat* nor the Jacobin style of civil liberty.[7]

Though his early reforming efforts came to nothing, and the Secret Committee broke up, Alexander never altogether abandoned the hope of bringing about a beneficial transformation of Russian society. He tried to approach the dilemma from the side, as it were, by trying out reforms in the more westernized non-Russian areas, with constitutions in Finland and Poland [see Part 1], and with an emancipation of the serfs in the Baltic provinces. He continued to commission proposals for a Russian constitution from his advisers, notably Speranskii in 1808–12, and Novosil'tsev in 1817.

EDUCATION   At the end of the eighteenth century the crucial aspects of official education policy were in place, largely as a result of the work of Catherine II. The main aim at secondary and higher levels was to prepare candidates for state service, while at primary level it was to teach practical skills and to inculcate religious and moral principles – in spite of which the state system was kept quite separate from the church one, and Catherine II's 'Duties of Man and Citizen' was prescribed as a basic text. All social estates, except private serfs, were to have access to education at all levels, and a 'ladder' was to exist to ensure that progress was possible from one level to another. Higher education followed a German model of corporate autonomy, with freedom of research as the motor of all scholarship and teaching.

In many ways these principles were remarkable, and they showed how serious Russia was in trying to live up to the standards of a European great power: self-governing institutions and the spirit of free intellectual enquiry were difficult to accommodate to an autocracy, while broad social entry was at odds with a thoroughly hierarchical society. But a closed elite educational system was not an option for Russia. A strong service nobility based on the Table of Ranks required a steady supply of young men rising from below and educated to the highest European standards. As Prince Karl Lieven, rector of Dorpat University, pointed out, 'Where the nobility extends from the foot of the throne at one end and nearly merges with the peasantry at the other, where every year many from the lower urban and rural estates enter the nobility by achieving the necessary rank in the military or civil service – in Russia it is very difficult to organise schools [on the basis of closed hereditary estate].'[8]

In spite of the difficulties, then, Alexander confirmed his grandmother's principles in his 'Preliminary Regulation for Public Education' of 24 January 1803, and even extended them by declaring the intention of establishing schools at village as well as uezd and guberniia level. His plans specifically aimed to consolidate Catherine's meritocratic view of education: they envisaged providing a ladder from each level of schooling to the next, so that disadvantaged children with talent could rise from the lower classes to serve the state. His Regulations for Educational Establishments stipulated that they should 'inspire in [pupils] the eagerness and devotion to learning which, upon their leaving school, will stimulate them to continue towards even further improvement of themselves.'[9]

Furthermore, the existing universities at Moscow, Vil'na and Dorpat were to be joined by new foundations at St Petersburg, Khar'kov and Kazan'. Each university was to be self-governing, with control over its own curriculum and the appointment of professors, though under the supervision of a state-appointed curator. It was expected to assist the expansion of education by taking charge of an educational district, training teachers for the schools in it and establishing and. supervising their curriculum.[10]

The new universities experienced great difficulties in their early years. There were not enough students: those who did present themselves were often poorly prepared, indisciplined and rowdy, and dropped out before acquiring a diploma. Most of the early professors were foreign, and lectured in German or Latin, to the dismay of their less educated listeners; in 1814 Count Kochubei argued that it would be better to bring in clergymen to do the teaching rather than subject students to German tuition. With school districts to inspect, the faculty was greatly overworked, and not all of them took their teaching duties seriously. Conflicts often broke out between Russian and foreign teachers, with the Russians complaining that the foreigners were indifferent towards the students, and the foreigners dismissing the Russians as boorish and unscholarly. An established university, like Moscow, or one backed by fierce local loyalties, like

Vil'na or Dorpat, could overcome these problems. But Khar'kov, Kazan' and even St Petersburg experienced very trying early years, when they were vulnerable to financial and official pressure. Some of them were under attack for fostering libertinism and atheism.[11]

By the end of Alexander's reign, it was clear that neither the legacy of the Enlightenment nor the zeal of the Bible Society could provide an adequate foundation for flourishing universities which would be genuinely Russian. His successor, Nicholas I, was deeply suspicious of them, and would have liked to subordinate them completely to the state. But his Minister of Education, Count S.S. Uvarov, resisted this tendency and evolved a compromise, embodied in the University Statute of 1835. It deprived universities of their function of supervising schools, and also eroded their immunities by abolishing the courts in which they maintained student discipline. Professors were in future to be appointed by the Minister of Education.

Yet in all other respects Alexander's principles were upheld: universities continued to elect their own rectors, to determine their curricula, run their examinations and award their own diplomas. Uvarov did not waver from the view that a general liberal-arts education, rather than cameralism or vocational training, was most appropriate for the upper levels of the civil service. He wanted to combine Europeanism – including a good grounding in the classics – with religious-moral instruction and Russian patriotism. His was a compromise which was very difficult to maintain, but he stuck to it for some fifteen years, until the European revolutions of 1848 sharply intensified Nicholas's fear of thin and hungry graduates.[12]

The hard-won success of the universities greatly improved the quality of recruits to the civil service, and laid the basis for the later reforms of Alexander II. At the same time that success opened wider the gulf which separated the educated elites from the mass of the population. The further down the educational system one went, the more halting was the expansion of schooling. Alexander's plans for village schools proved especially over-optimistic: neither the treasury nor local sources were ready to provide the means to make even a serious start to their provision. At a time when Prussia and Austria were beginning to expand primary education even in the small towns and villages, Russia's rural regions were serviced only by a meagre network of small parish schools.

NAPOLEON BONAPARTE   Alexander's reign was overshadowed by a figure who was an example both to emulate and to abhor: Napoleon Bonaparte. The continual presence and intermittent deadly threat of Napoleon dramatized the duality of Alexander's personality and of his situation. Napoleon's principles of government were rooted in Enlightenment thinking, and in exaggerated form they exemplified what Alexander would have liked to achieve: a meritocracy led by an authoritarian leader, mobilizing the resources of the population for military action, and able to rely on convinced patriotism among all social classes. Yet Napoleon appeared in such a form that he was a challenge not only to Alexander personally, but to Russia as a whole. His social and political ideals were a direct affront to the unearned privileges of the nobility, while his 1812 invasion threatened the very survival of Russia. The way in which he unsettled Europe, both by his military campaigns and more fundamentally by the challenge to create new nation states on the French model, faced Alexander with ever fresh quandaries to which he had to find his own answers.

Alexander reacted, as ever, ambivalently. In 1806, at his instigation the Orthodox Church anathematized Napoleon as the 'Antichrist', and then had to withdraw the anathema in 1807 after the Tilsit agreement, which inaugurated a period of alliance (albeit uneasy) between France and Russia. Accounts of the meeting of the two emperors at Tilsit itself, and then at Erfurt in 1808, suggest that they found much in common, and testify that they engaged in long and earnest conversations, whose content is not known. Yet Alexander never ceased to be suspicious of Napoleon as an upstart and usurper, while Napoleon would from time to time, when it seemed expedient, insult Alexander by hinting that he owed his throne to patricide.[13]

It was during the uneasy peace with France that Alexander came perhaps closest to taking seriously a Jacobin-style constitution. The adviser who proposed it to him was Mikhail Speranskii, the son of a priest who had proved his unusual abilities in the Ministries of Interior and Justice, and had been Alexander's personal aide at the

Erfurt meeting with Napoleon. Speranskii certainly admired many features of France's post-revolutionary polity, especially its ideal of 'a career open to talents', and he incorporated some of them into Russian practice. His decree of 1809, for instance, required officials to pass examinations before they could reach the higher grades of the civil service. This measure aroused great resentment among the nobility, some of whom remarked darkly that clearly now 'a Russian gentleman is good for nothing unless he knows Latin'.[14]

For a long time it was thought that Speranskii shared the cautious *Rechtstaat* approach to a constitution held by his master, but the publication of his papers in the Soviet Union in 1961 showed that his drafts were a good deal more radical than his final proposals and his published works, in which he veiled his ultimate aspirations, probably out of deference. From these papers it seems clear that he believed unlimited autocracy to be incompatible with the rule of law, and that he tried to bring Alexander round to this point of view. Given Alexander's equivocal personality, it is probable that at times he thought he had succeeded.[15]

What Speranskii proposed in the draft he laid before the Emperor in 1809 was that the functions of government be separated into three streams, the executive, legislative and judiciary, according to advanced European and American theory, but with the Emperor heading each of them. The ministries would manage the executive, organized on functional lines. A State Council, consisting of senior statesmen appointed by the Emperor, would draft laws and present them for the Emperor's consideration. Its work would be supplemented by a State Duma, an assembly elected indirectly (through lower-level Dumas) by property-owners of town and countryside: it would not initiate legislation itself but would combine budgetary powers and the right to question ministers with a broad consultative function, including the right to refer back a bill it thought to be in contradiction with the fundamental laws.[16]

This was the most ambitious blueprint for reforming Russia's governmental system until 1905. If implemented in full, it might not in theory have limited the autocrat's power, but in practice it would have ensured that that power was channelled through publicly elected institutions authorized to comment, petition and protest, if not actually to veto. If supplemented by codification of the laws – another initiative which Speranskii took charge of but was unable to complete – then it would have provided the essentials out of which the rule of law could have evolved and thus provided the framework for civic nationhood.

It was, however, implemented only in part. The Ministries and the State Council were established in the roles Speranskii intended. But the lower-level bodies all remained on paper, and no elective institutions of any kind were created. The ministries brought functional expertise into government and made incisive decision-making possible, but they had to operate without proper coordination. The Council of Ministers, or cabinet, envisaged by Speranskii was seldom convened in practice, since Alexander preferred to deal with each of his ministers individually and preserve his right to reach the ultimate decisions himself, or to delegate them to a favourite such as the Novgorod landowner and artillery specialist whom he had inherited from his father, Alexander Arakcheev.

For the rest of the nineteenth century, then, Russia was governed under a system which might be called 'truncated Speranskii'. The State Council and the ministries genuinely injected a new and welcome professionalism into the tasks of government, helped by the expansion of higher education and by the civil service examinations; but they also remained centres of patronage, where the personal inclinations of the minister flourished unabated because there were no public institutions to restrict his powers or to comment on his exercise of them. The gap was filled, as ever since Peter, by personal agents of the Tsar, *fiskaly* or *revizory*, sent in to investigate a government agency or a provincial office. Furthermore, again because there were no representative bodies to act as counterweight, the imperial court and the imperial family remained decisive sources of influence, muddying the functional exercise of authority with personal and family considerations.

When ministries were created in 1802 each of them was expected to present an annual budget estimate, but its contents were kept secret (even from the Senate) and they were confirmed by the Tsar privately till 1862. Naturally, in these circumstances, there could be nothing like a serious official audit of expenditure. The Emperor was at liberty to award extra funds to any minister or even favourite without consulting the Minister of Finance: this was the essence of autocracy. The distinction between state funds and those of the Tsar personally was still not fully established. In 1850, when there was a 33.5 million ruble deficit, Nicholas I hid this even from the State Council, sending them a false budget with the War Ministry estimate 38 million rubles lower than in reality.[17] He thus honoured in the breach the principle that a single orderly budget ought to exist. Only from 1862 was a consolidated state budget introduced and the Ministry of Finance given complete control over all outgoings, assigning funds to each department only in accordance with its estimates.[18] Only at that stage was a limit finally set to the financial irresponsibility of the court.

Speranskii also had plans for financial reorganization which were aimed to stabilize the money supply, encourage private enterprise and mobilize better for the state the wealth of the empire. The greatest problem Alexander inherited was the huge quantity of *assignaty* in circulation, paper money printed to meet successive crises, especially the recent wars, and unbacked by the creation of new wealth. The inevitable result was chronic inflation. Speranskii proposed that the government should honestly declare the *assignaty* to be what they were, a form of state debt, should announce that the entire national wealth was to be collateral for them, and should promise to redeem them over a period of time by withdrawing them from circulation, and replacing them with silver coins issued by a single State Bank. Meanwhile the government should raise new revenue by selling land to state peasants, and replacing both *obrok* and poll tax by a land tax, payable by the nobility; and by selling state monopolies – for example in salt and alcohol – to private traders who would then pay tax on their profits.[19]

Overall these proposals represented a blending of Physiocrat principles with those of Adam Smith. Their general effect should have been to raise confidence in the state's capacity and willingness to assume responsibility for its own currency. They would also – a most important principle – have awarded some peasants private property, to stimulate private trade and manufacture while reducing the state debt and would have made possible a more efficient siphoning of national resources for necessary state expenditures. They would have harmonized well with Speranskii's proposal for an elected legislative assembly, which could have guaranteed the debt, as in early eighteenth-century Britain, where a similar deal, guaranteeing property in return for tax payments, may be said to have laid the fiscal basis of the parliamentary monarchy.

There was fierce opposition to Speranskii's proposals, not only from landed nobles and from the Senatorial party, but from those who regarded him as in effect an accomplice of Napoleon. The court historian Nikolai Karamzin, for example, regarded Speranskii's State Council as a mere copy of the French revolutionary institution of the same name. His objections to Speranskii, however, went far deeper. He was concerned that the division of powers was dangerously inappropriate in Russia, whose diversity and immense size would cause it to fall apart unless it were ruled by a single unambiguous authority. In a memorandum on 'Ancient and Modern Russia', written during 1810, he adduced historical evidence for his assertions, showing how Kievan *Rus'* had disintegrated and early seventeenth-century Muscovy had nearly repeated its fate.

Karamzin believed that liberty was a positive virtue – indeed he sometimes referred to himself as a 'republican' – but that in Russia it was best protected by undivided sovereignty. His approach to government was similar to that of Catherine II. He had no sense of natural law, but regarded law as something made by monarchs. However, he also rejected the lawless despotism exemplified by Paul, believing that monarchs should rule through the law and respect the laws they had made. The nobles were needed to make monarchical rule effective, so they should have such powers and corporate organization as they needed to be the monarch's agents. Because they devoted themselves to the service of the state, they were entitled to the labour of the serfs in their charge. In any case serfs would be helpless and pauperized without the protection of the nobility and the land they received from it (the notion of freeing the serfs *with* land apparently never entered his head).[20]

As Russia's relations with France worsened during 1810–12, the pressure on Speranskii from his opponents intensified. In some circles it was whispered that he was a Freemason and therefore connected to subversive foreign organizations. In March 1812 Alexander dismissed him, after a long and tearful unterview lasting for two hours, whose contents are not known. Pressure from those hostile to Speranskii was undoubtedly partly responsible for his dismissal, but it is also true that Alexander had long decided that he was not prepared to implement Speranskii's vision in full. By the spring of 1812, partly in preparation for the inevitable war with France, he was beginning to contemplate other schemes for reforming Russia as well as for facilitating the financing of a huge army.

THE PATRIOTIC WAR OF 1812   The Napoleonic invasion was the paramount watershed of Alexander's reign, and one of the great defining moments in Russia's evolution as a whole. It generated myths, true, partly true and false, which helped to determine Russians' attitude to their own imperial and national identity for at least a century, and in some ways right up to the present day.

The dominant patriotic legend tells of a nation united in its resistance to the foe. The truth is slightly more complicated: Russian elites and Russian peasants both fought Napoleon with ferocious determination, but for different and sometimes incompatible reasons.

Napoleon discovered when he reached Moscow, if he did not realize it before, that this was a different kind of war from those he had previously fought, except in Spain. As fires took hold in the city, and spread to the Kremlin itself, he finally realized that there would be no decisive victory and no negotiated peace, and he is said to have exclaimed, 'This is a war of extermination, a terrible strategy which has no precedents in the history of civilisation ... To burn down their own cities! A demon has got into them! What ferocious determination! What a people! What a people!'[21]

Yet initially this strategy was far from being settled. Alexander and his generals were afraid to let Napoleon too far into the country, both because of the destruction he would cause, and because of the effect he might have on the serfs, whom at one stage he had promised to emancipate. As one landowner wrote, 'Our muzhiks, thanks to the craving planted in them by Pugachev and other hotheads, dream about some kind of vol'nost'.' At the outset of the war, Alexander intended to give battle to the French army at an early stage, and certainly not to let them get as far as Smolensk. This strategy was agreed by all the commanders, even by Barclay de Tolly, who was the most favourably disposed to the 'Scythian tactic' of retreating and letting space do its work.[22] It was the sheer size and reputation of the French army which dissuaded them from taking it on earlier than Borodino, already ninety per cent of the way to Moscow.

To provide for possible internal disorders, Alexander ordered that half a battalion, 300 men, should be stationed in each guberniia, to be reinforced from the neighbouring guberniia if things got out of hand. Sure enough, soon after the invasion the excitable Count Rostopchin reported to the Committee of Ministers that an 'Old Believer sect' in Smolensk guberniia had enrolled about 1,500 serfs by promising them freedom from the landowners when Napoleon arrived.[23] In the provinces of Lithuania and Belorussia the invasion sparked off widespread unrest: peasants, apparently under the impression that Napoleon would soon free them, refused to be called up for military service, sacked manor houses and drove out the *pomeshchiki*. In one village, as the French approached, the assembly took the decision to murder the local landowner, who was notorious for his cruelty, burn down his manor house, and divide up his property among themselves.[24]

In these regions, of course, most of the landowners were Polish, so that one might interpret the peasants' reaction as patriotic. But there were some similar disorders further east: for example in Smolensk, where in one uezd peasants proclaimed themselves French citizens, and a punitive detachment had to be sent to restore obedience.[25] Overall it seems clear that the hope of emancipation was the main motive for peasant unrest, and indeed the disorders died away as it became apparent that the French Emperor was reacting just as the Russian one would have done: by sending in punitive expeditions and restoring the landowners. By doing so, Napoleon converted the war into a simple issue of national survival. The feelings aroused in peasants by that fact can be summarized by a proclamation issued by a peasant partisan leader to his followers: 'You are people of the Russian faith, you are Orthodox (*pravoslavnye*) peasants! Take up arms for the faith and die for your Tsar!'[26]

The effect was intensified by a new feature of this war. Most of Napoleon's previous campaigns had succeeded in engaging and defeating the enemy's main army at an early stage: as a result they had been fairly brief and conducted along manageable lines of communication and supply. Now for the first time, with the exception of Spain, Napoleon found himself drawn into a campaign of indeterminate length, with his supply lines getting ever longer and more tenuous. It was inevitable that his troops should begin to forage from the surrounding countryside on an ever larger scale.

The peasants responded by defending their homes and crops. In time the appearance of partisan detachments made this easier to do. Sometimes they went further than defence, *destroying* their homes and crops in order to deny them to the French, and disappearing into the forests to form armed bands. The result was that, especially after the retreat from Moscow, a real *narodnaia voina* (people's war) was being fought all along the route. As Field Marshal Kutuzov explained in September to Napoleon's envoy, General Loriston, the peasants by that time regarded the French as they had the Tatar invaders of centuries before.[27]

The partisans consisted mostly of light cavalry and Cossacks, commanded by young volunteer officers, but they relied heavily on intelligence and local know-how provided by the peasants, and sometimes recruited peasants to fight among them. A few partisan bands were actually made up entirely of peasants, including a famous one led by a certain Chetvertakov, a peasant who had deserted from the army in 1804 and been whipped. Operating in the region of Gzhatsk, he defended villages from attack and would on occasion mount lightning raids on small units of the regular French army, capturing their weapons and equipment. In the end he had some four thousand men under his command, and became a local legend.[28]

The government did not always view such peasant initiative with favour. A certain Captain Naryshkin handed out spare weapons to peasants forming a partisan group, and encouraged them to seek out and kill parties of French soldiers looking for forage in the neighbourhood of Moscow. In this task they were proving effective, when Naryshkin suddenly received instructions from his superiors. 'As a result of false denunciations and base slander, I received an order to disarm the peasants and to shoot those who caused disorders. Astonished by an order which fitted so poorly the noble behaviour of the peasants, I replied that I could not disarm those whom I had armed and who were destroying the enemies of the fatherland, nor could I treat as rebels those who were sacrificing their lives to defend their independence, their wives and homes.' According to the historian Evgenii Tarle, there were many such cases, where the authorities tried to disarm peasant partisans for fear that their arms should later be turned against the landowners.[29]

All the same, the government did set up a militia (*opolchenie*) to reinforce the army, recruiting it from the sixteen gubernii most likely to be affected by enemy activity. Significantly, state peasants were not invited to join it. If Alexander had wanted to create a patriotic volunteer force from among the peasants, they would have been the natural ones to appeal to. Instead, it was private serfs who were called upon, which meant that the landlords took the decision about who went to fight. Genuine volunteers were not wanted: when one serf turned up of his own accord at the recruiting centre in Dorogobuzh, he was treated as an escapee and sent to the police 'to be proceeded with according to the law'.[30]

Because the nobles' response to the appeal to form militias was so variable, the government imposed a compulsory rate of no less than ten recruits per one hundred souls, soon reduced to two. Some nobles responded with patriotic devotion, while others took the opportunity to rid themselves of notorious drunkards and layabouts. As a result the medical qualifications for militia recruits had to be reduced. Many militiamen never got as far as the battlefield, because they were so unfit. However, those who did acquitted themselves well, even when inadequately equipped. The British military attaché Sir Robert Wilson, often scathing about the Russian army, reported that at Borodino they 'displayed great steadiness during the whole day, even though only armed with pikes'.[31]

Overall, peasants played a vital part in the defeat of Napoleon and fought with great courage and spirit in doing so. Russian and Soviet historians who claim that they displayed remarkable patriotism are quite right. But it was patriotism of a particular kind, a yearning to be free under church and Tsar. The war, like the Time of Troubles two centuries earlier, awakened in Russians aspirations they did not usually express. In the case of peasants it was the desire for freedom, and the feeling that, if they volunteered and fought well, then the Tsar, who was just and benevolent, would award it to them.

This perhaps explains why the most serious disorders among militiamen took place towards the end of the war, when the opportunity to fight was already receding. In December 1812, in the town of Insar', in Penza guberniia, new militia recruits refused to set out on the march towards the front without seeing the Tsar's command, properly sealed in red, and taking an oath before it. They feared that the nobles had deceived them, and that, if the proper formalities were not observed, they would not receive their freedom. When the officers arrested twelve men for insubordination, the remainder set them free and then ran amok in the small town, plundering property from the nobles and from the regimental office. At their subsequent trial before a military court, the peasant recruits explained that they had intended to kill all the officers, go to the front themselves and defeat the French, then return, beg forgiveness of the Tsar and request emancipation as a reward for their valour.[32]

There was great bitterness among peasants who returned from their militia service to find that there was no emancipation. Alexander, in his manifesto of 30 August 1814, thanking and rewarding all his subjects for their heroic deeds, said of the peasants simply that they would 'receive their reward from God'. Most of them had to return to performing the same tasks as before. Some nobles tried to persuade the authorities not to allow them back, but to leave them in the regular army as ordinary soldiers. The poet Gavriil Derzhavin was informed by his returnees that they had been 'temporarily released' and were now state peasants and not obliged to serve him. Rumours circulated that Alexander had intended to free them all, but had been invited to a special meeting of indignant nobles at night in the Senate, from which he had allegedly been rescued, pleading for his life, by his brother Grand Duke Konstantin Pavlovich.[33]

Overall, then, the war aroused in the peasants fears and expectations which one might describe as millennial: quite realistic fears of the destruction of their homeland, unrealistic expectations of being freed from their bondage and being able to take their places as full citizens.

MILITARY SETTLEMENTS Alongside his ideal of constitutional order, Alexander harboured two alternative visions of social cohesion, both of which derived from his father, and both of which were reinforced by the outcome of the Napoleonic War.

One was the idea that society could be regenerated by organizing peasants on military lines. His Minister of War, Aleksandr

Arakcheev, had planted the idea in his mind when he set up a model estate at Gruzino, in Novgorod guberniia. Arakcheev had torn down the dilapidated peasant huts he found there, and replaced them with neat houses of brick or stone, each divided down the middle by a corridor, so that one family could live in each half. These semi-detached sanitary blocks were not popular with the peasants, who preferred the traditional detached hut, with its rambling outhouses.

It was Alexander's hope that such neat houses might be adapted for use by the army as an alternative to quartering. If soldiers lived in dwellings like those on the Gruzino estate, they could have their families with them – and thus conceive more children – and they could practise agriculture with their military training, which would save the treasury a great deal of money on their maintenance. Soldiers would become small property-owners, with a stake in Russia's economic future. Beyond that, Alexander also intended that the settlements should take the lead in trying out and assimilating the latest agricultural techniques, as well as social welfare schemes, which could later be adopted elsewhere.[34]

Yet, for reasons examined in Part 3, Chapter 2, the settlements were intensely unpopular both with educated Russian society and among the soldiers who had to live in them. They outlasted Alexander's reign, but there were frequent outbursts of unrest in them, culminating in a serious riot in Novgorod in 1831. The temptation of mixing social reform and military discipline had proved to be a mirage.

THE BIBLE SOCIETY   Alexander's other vision of social cohesion was a religious one, and it was given considerable impetus by the victory over the atheist Napoleon. Alexander was inspired to believe that he was the bearer of a 'sacred idea', to rebuild Europe in the spirit of a truly Christian morality. The embodiment of this idea was the Holy Alliance, agreed between the principal monarchs of Europe at the Congress of Vienna in 1815. Alexander was the main protagonist of the Alliance: it was an association of monarchs for the defence of the legitimist order throughout Europe against the twin threats of atheism and revolution. As Alexander wrote to his ambassador in London, Count Lieven, the idea of the Alliance was 'to apply more efficaciously to the civil and political relations between states the principles of peace, concord and love which are the fruit of religion and Christian morality'.[35]

To advance his concept inside Russia, he ordered copies of the Alliance's founding document to be displayed on walls and in churches. He reorganized the Holy Synod to take under its wing not only the Orthodox Church, but also the other Christian denominations, and he amalgamated it with the Ministry of Education under his close friend, Prince Aleksandr Golitsyn, to create a new super-ministry, of 'Spiritual Affairs and Popular Enlightenment', or what the religious historian Georgii Florovskii has called the 'ministry of religious-utopian propaganda'.[36] His intention was to create a synthesis of the Christian faiths, a kind of 'inner' or 'universal' Christianity, as a basis for reconciling the numerous peoples of the empire, and with them the peoples of Europe as well. This over-arching faith was to be preached in all the schools and universities. It was a vast extension of the religious ideals of his father; or one could regard it as a mystical-utopian version of what Peter the Great had tried to achieve through his ecclesiastical reforms.

An integral part of Alexander's concept was the idea of making the scriptures available to all the peoples of the empire in their various languages. For this purpose he encouraged the establishment of the Imperial Russian Bible Society in December 1812, as a branch of the British and Foreign Bible Society, to undertake the work of translation, publication and distribution.

The steering committee of the Bible Society brought together representatives of different Christian churches, including a Roman Catholic bishop and a Lutheran pastor. To avoid inter-denominational conflict, they agreed to publish the various editions of the Bible without commentary. The extent and coverage of the Society's work is demonstrated by the fact that in its first year it published or bought and distributed 37,700 New Testaments and 22,500 complete Bibles in Church Slavonic, French, German, Finnish, Estonian, Latvian, Lithuanian, Polish, Armenian, Georgian, Kalmyk and Tatar. For the purpose it set up new printing presses and imaginatively used retail outlets, such as apothecaries' shops, which had never previously been used for selling books. By 1821 the New Testament and Prayer Book were starting to appear in modern Russian.[37]

Significantly, the language which aroused the greatest opposition when it came to translation was none other than Russian itself. The Bible existed in a Church Slavonic version, and many churchmen felt that only the Slavonic tongue, consecrated by ancient usage, possessed the dignity to convey adequately the meaning of the scriptures. The Society's view, on the contrary, was that the Slavonic text was readily understood only by those who had been brought up on it since childhood, and that it was therefore unsuitable for evangelism. At Alexander's express wish, work was started on a translation into modern Russian, in order 'to give Russians the means of reading the word of God in their native Russian tongue, which is more comprehensible to them than the Slavonic language in which the scriptures have hitherto been published'.[38]

From the outset, some Orthodox clergymen had opposed the Society's activities. They were alarmed by its tendency to take its tone from Golitsyn's 'super-ministry', with its eclectic 'universal' Christianity. Their fears were deepened when the Society began to bring out not only the scriptures, but also the work of Pietist and Freemasonic thinkers whose exalted and mystical style appealed to Alexander and Golitsyn, but was highly suspect to conventional Orthodox clerics.

The resistance reached its apogee in 1824 with a denunciation of the Society by the abbot of the Iur'ev Monastery in Moscow, Arkhimandrit Fotii. He was the voice of a church demoralized by more than a century of subjection to a secular state, lacking confidence in its own capacity to ward off the intellectual and spiritual challenge posed by religious movements from the more sophisticated West.

In a memorandum presented personally to the Emperor, Fotii warned of certain 'Illuminists' – Freemasons – who were plotting to install a new worldwide religion, having first destroyed 'all empires, churches, religions, civil laws and all order'. The Bible Society, he maintained, was preparing the way for this revolution by soothing the clergy, jumbling all religions indiscriminately together, and by disseminating pernicious books, using for the purpose printing presses available only to it. 'In order to degrade the word of God, which is read with reverence in the churches,' he complained, 'they are instructed to sell it even in the apothecaries' shops, along with tinctures and ampoules.' Fotii appealed to Alexander to dismiss Golitsyn, abolish the dual ministry and restore the Holy Synod to its accustomed role. 'God defeated the visible Napoleon, invader of Russia: let Him now in Your Person defeat the invisible Napoleon.'[39]

This memorandum was perhaps the first major example of what was to become a characteristic Russian genre: a denunciation evoking in melodramatic terms the apocalyptic dangers facing the country from a mixture of international godless conspiracy and subversion sown by irresponsible and evil-minded people at home. In the early nineteenth century the malevolent spirits thus conjured up were Freemasons, Voltairians and Pietists; later on the Freemasons were joined by the Jews in this role. In such denunciations the sense of external vulnerability was coupled with the feeling of internal weakness generated by the elite's alienation from its own peoples. The fear and venom aroused by such writings was heightened by secrecy and the lack of public discussion of difficult issues, an atmosphere in which even grotesque fabrications easily seemed plausible.

Alexander was certainly susceptible to Fotii's insinuations. All his life he had been torn between the desire to enlighten and emancipate his people and the fear that by attempting to do so he would foment sedition and weaken the political order. In the last years of his life, these fears were intensified by the growth of secret societies inside Russia. He naturally associated them with the societies in Germany, Italy and Spain which threatened European peace and stability as guaranteed by his cherished Holy Alliance. As the historian Aleksandr Pypin remarked, 'He was haunted by the spectre of a huge secret conspiracy which embraced the whole of Europe and had penetrated into Russia. Given his mystical propensity, this spectre assumed even more fearful proportions.'[40]

He had hoped that the Bible Society would arm the ordinary people against atheism and sedition. Now he was being warned that, on the contrary, the Bible Society was part of the conspiracy, and that its members were revolutionaries in disguise. He went through agonies of doubt before he could come to a decision. In the event, he drew back from actually closing down the Bible Society, but he dismissed Golitsyn as head of it, replacing him with the irreproachably Orthodox Metropolitan of Novgorod, Serafim. At the same time, he redivided the super-ministry, restoring the Holy Synod to its former function of being responsible for the Orthodox Church alone.

He also appointed to the Ministry of Education, the other half of the 'super-ministry', Admiral Shishkov, the principal protagonist of Church Slavonic. Shishkov lost no time in putting pressure on Serafim to stop the Russian publication of the Bible. 'What! Who among us does not understand the divine service? Only he who has broken with his fatherland and forgotten his own tongue ... And can this supposed necessity [of publishing the Bible in modern Russian] do other than degrade the Holy Scriptures and thus implant heresies and schisms?'[41]

Serafim did not take much persuading. Publication of the catechism and the scriptures in 'the vernacular' (*prostoe narechie*) was terminated. Therewith the heart went out of the Bible Society, at least as far as Russians were concerned. Remarkably but characteristically, the continued publication of the scriptures in other 'vernacular' languages did not bother the Orthodox hierarchy, but the Holy Synod ordered the burning of thousands of copies of the Pentateuch, which were already being printed in Russian.[42]

The halting of the Russian Bible was fateful. It delayed by a vital half-century the moment when ordinary Russians could have access to the scriptures in a language which they could read and study with ease. Peter the Great had carried through a kind of Protestant revolution in the church, but a dangerously incomplete one, since it had never been supplemented by mass reading of the scriptures among the population. Without that the domination of the state within the church always threatened to hollow out its spiritual life. The situation had been created where the postman hero of Leskov's story *Odnodum* (The One-Track Mind) could be seen as a laughable and possibly dangerous eccentric merely because he was in the habit of regularly reading the Bible for himself. [Further on this question see Part 3, Chapter 4].

REBELLION   Meanwhile, those nobles who had stuck by Alexander's earlier vision of constitutional order and the rule of law had been gradually marginalized. In the officers' messes of the Imperial Russian Army and in the masonic lodges of the capital cities a mood of indignation and despair gradually took hold, as it became clear that Alexander was devoted to military settlements and religious evangelism, that he had no early intention of improving the lot of the ordinary people and that, if he was awarding constitutions, then it was to Poles and Finns, not to Russians.

These nobles were relatively few in number, but they were young, some of them were highly placed, and they had some experience of life outside Russia, gained during their education or in the Napoleonic War. They began to set up secret societies on the masonic model and to elaborate plans for a more civilized and humane future Russia – plans which most of them hoped the Emperor would one day return to. Some of them, however, recognized at an early stage that they would have to act without official support, possibly through conspiratorial action to overthrow the existing system. For his part Alexander acknowledged privately that he was not without responsibility for their plotting. When he was informed in 1821 of the existence of secret societies with political aims, he is reported to have remarked ruefully: 'You know that I have shared and encouraged these illusions and errors. It is not for me to be harsh.'[43]

The rebellion sparked off by these nobles was to cast a stigma over the reign of his younger brother, but it was Alexander himself who had created the pre-conditions for it, through his own ambiguous and vacillating policies. [Further on the Decembrists' ideas and organization, see Part 3, Chapter 1.]

The sudden death of Alexander, on 19 November 1825, plunged the secret societies into crisis. Their members had been contemplating some kind of military rising in 1826, but preparations for it were far from complete. The sovereign's demise faced them unexpectedly with the kind of situation they had often airily discussed, a moment when they might intervene to force the successor to take an oath to a constitution, or else seize the reins of power themselves. It seemed especially auspicious that there was confusion over the succession, and while a messenger was sent to Warsaw, to the heir, Grand Duke Konstantin, to obtain confirmation that he really had renounced the throne, the conspirators used the time to try and persuade regiments in the capital city to join them. Their public relations exercise was less successful than they had hoped, but did serve, thanks to the inevitable security leaks, to warn Grand Duke Nicholas, the next in line, of what was afoot.

Finally, when it became known in St Petersburg that Konstantin had definitely stepped down, the reluctant conspirators had to act immediately or lose all credibility. On 14 December they drew up such regiments as they could muster on Senate Square, declaring for Konstantin, who they claimed – quite without foundation – had intended to introduce a constitution and had been prevented from doing so. In their own way they had fabricated another pretender legend, and drawn their soldiers into it by making out – again unwarrantedly – that Konstantin would improve their pay and shorten their term of service. Thereafter, the leaders' activity lacked all conviction or coordination. Prince Sergei Trubetskoi, appointed 'dictator' for the seizure of power and period of provisional rule, simply disappeared and later took refuge in the Austrian Embassy. One rebel shot and killed General Miloradovich, Governor-General of St Petersburg, whom Nicholas had sent to parley with them. No one made any further effort to win over more officers, soldiers or civilians. Eventually Nicholas, with deep reluctance, not wishing to open his reign by firing on his own subjects, ordered that the rebel units be dispersed by artillery. This was done, with much bloodshed.

The Decembrists suffered from much the same ambivalence as Alexander himself. Like him, they wanted to introduce enlightenment and the amenities of a civil society more broadly to Russia, but knew that they had no support from the common people for this endeavour. Hence the dissimulation and irresolution with which they acted. Their failure was yet another indication of the enormous gap which separated elite and people.

NICHOLAS   In one sense, the reign of Nicholas I was merely a protracted epilogue to the Decembrist rising. Untroubled by the ambivalent impulses of his older brother, Nicholas returned to the methods of his father, reviving the paradomania, the heavy police presence and the restrictive censorship which had made Paul so hated.

However, there was more to Nicholas than that. Indeed, it can be argued that he represents a belated apogee of 'enlightened absolutism', that he completed the construction of an enlightened absolutist state where his eighteenth-century predecessors had left the work at best half done – for example, by publishing a consistent code of laws and by broadening the network of elite schools intended to train state servants.

But at the same time Nicholas's statecraft lacked the breezy self-confidence of most eighteenth-century monarchs. It was deeply affected by the post-Napoleonic European situation. Nicholas saw the Decembrist rebellion, not as the despairing spasm of a stifled civil society, but as an outgrowth of a Europe-wide conspiracy aiming at the destruction of legitimate monarchy and all moral and religious principles. He was especially alarmed by the way in which disloyalty had taken root among the nobility, the very social estate on which the monarchy rested. He gave close attention to the investigation of the rebellion, taking part in the questioning himself, and studying the reports of the interrogators. He instructed the secretary of the investigating commission, A.D. Borovkov, to draw up a summary of the Decembrists' views on the contemporary condition of his empire – a document which he subsequently kept by him and referred to frequently. Although he did not share their political views, Nicholas was guided in his governmental programme by the Decembrists' perceptions of the defects of the existing system.[44]

Borovkov's report told him that, although 'the government itself had nourished the youth on free-thinking as on mother's milk', the fundamental cause of the recent troubles was to be found elsewhere, in the faults of the system, in laws which contradicted one another, courts which operated with agonizing delay and expense, an administrative system which encouraged senior officials to avoid responsibility by hiding behind the emperor, a tariff and taxation system which discouraged honest trade and ruined the merchants, an ecclesiastical system which made priests dependent on peasants for their income, a military system which provided a large and inflexible army with no reserves.

'It is necessary,' Borovkov concluded, 'to grant clear positive laws, to implant justice by introducing speedy legal procedures, to raise the moral education of the clergy, to strengthen the nobility, which has fallen into decay, ruined by loans in credit institutions, revive trade and industry by unshakable charters, improve the position of the cultivators of the soil, stop the humiliating sale of human beings, resurrect the fleet and encourage private people to take up sea-going . . . in a word to correct countless failings and abuses.'[45]

To combat these evils Nicholas established a system of what might be called 'anxious centralization', intensifying central supervision of local government, increasing the number of ministries, but also of secret inter-ministerial committees, and strengthening his own chancellery to give him the means to gain knowledge and intervene personally in the affairs of all his officials. What he created was actually the opposite of systematic authoritarianism: it was more like a gaggle of rivalries in which he would from time to time intervene to restore order. His chosen instrument for this intervention was the Third Department of his own Imperial Chancellery, a kind of personal security police, which continued and systematized the tradition of the *fiskaly*.

Not content with repression alone, Nicholas tentatively introduced his own brand of ideology, as a deliberate challenge to liberalism and nationalism. His proclamation of principles was first of all an attempt to revive the sense of confidence which had bolstered the regime after the victories of 1812–15: that Russia had succeeded where more advanced and liberal regimes had failed, that the union of throne, altar and people had enabled her to repel the assaults of republicanism and atheism, and to save Europe when the latter was threatened by its own advancing inner decay, caused by atheism, republicanism and mercenary materialism.

Nicholas's alternative ideology was formulated by Count S.S. Uvarov, who circulated officials on his assumption of office at the Ministry of Education in 1833, declaring that 'It is our common obligation to ensure that the education of the people be conducted, according to the Supreme intention of our August Monarch, in the joint spirit of Orthodoxy, Autocracy and Nationality (*Narodnost*). I am convinced that every professor and teacher, being permeated by one and the same feeling of devotion to throne and fatherland, will use all his resources to become a worthy tool of the government and to earn its complete confidence.'[46]

This was the first time since the sixteenth century that the Russian monarchy had attempted to propagate an explicit ideology of its own. The problem about the triad of Orthodoxy, Autocracy and Nationality was that one of its columns, the church, was impoverished, intellectually backward and dependent on the state to such an extent that it was incapable of playing any independent political role.

A second, nationality, created even greater difficulties. *Narodnost'*, as officially conceived, implied that the Russians were the principal people of the empire, devoted to both altar and throne and prepared to sacrifice themselves for either. Russians, in this version, were not divided by ethnic or class struggles, unlike the peoples of the West, and in 1812 had shown that this national unity could defeat the strongest enemy where other nations had failed.[47]

But the concept had implications unwelcome to the ruler of a multi-national empire. For example, if Russians were the state-bearing people, why were so many leading officials German? Besides, if one took the concept seriously, then it implied that the common people, like the church, had at least a partial role in legitimizing the monarchy, a notion which Nicholas I rejected out of hand. It was a muffled echo of the revolutionary ideas which had generated rebellion in so many European countries and were to do so again. Besides, as we shall see in Part 3, Chapter 3, the mass of the Russian people, for all that they revered the monarch, were far from being reconciled to a system which rested on serfdom, poll tax and recruitment. On the other hand, if one did not take *narodnost'* seriously, then why include it at all?

That left only the third pillar: autocracy. During the succeeding decades in practice autocracy alone became the defining feature of the Russian polity, to an extent which made it an unremitting obsession with statesmen of conservative bent.

For Nicholas the virtues of autocracy were best summed up in the army. 'Here there is order, there is a strict unconditional legality, no impertinent claims to know all the answers, no contradiction, all things flow logically from one another; no one commands before he himself has learnt to obey; no one steps in front of anyone else without lawful reason; everything is subordinated to one goal, everything has its purpose. That is why I feel so well among these people, and why I shall always hold in honour the calling of a soldier. I consider the whole of human life to be merely service, because everybody serves.'[48]

Using the army for self-reassurance, however, was disastrous for its military efficiency. The real lesson of the Napoleonic era was not learnt: that is, that modern armies, if they are based on a strong sense of national solidarity, can be small in peacetime but rapidly mobilized for war, they can be both large and flexible, agile in manoeuvre, leaving much initiative to the junior officer and even the common soldier. That was a doctrine which Catherine II's commander, Suvorov, had already taught. Nicholas preferred instead to return to the well-tried Prussian system of close formation march and punctilious drill. This had the advantage of producing a pleasing impression on the parade ground, but it led to unwieldiness and rigidity on the battlefield.

Nicholas did have some concept of the rule of law, if, like Catherine II, mainly as a means by which the monarchy could reinforce its own authority. He sponsored the codification of the laws, for which purpose he recalled Speranskii. In 1833 his work culminated in the publication of a 'Complete Collection of Laws of the Russian Empire', which systematized all the various laws, decrees and edicts issued since 1649. Nicholas also established a School of Jurisprudence, to train lawyers for state service: among its alumni were many of the young officials who carried out the reforms of his successor. He was concerned about professionalism and technical proficiency in general, and continued to send students abroad to study, even though they sometimes returned with ideas very repugnant to the Russian system.

Nicholas was opposed to serfdom, for he saw that its existence ran counter to the rule of law. As he said in the State Council in 1842, 'There is no doubt that serfdom, in its present form, is an evil obvious to all; but to touch it now would of course be an even more ruinous evil.'[49] He confined himself to trying to reform it gradually, by convening a series of secret inter-departmental committees.

He did however, as a possible trial run, sponsor a serious attempt to improve the way of life and agriculture of the state peasants, under his Minister of State Domains, Count P. D. Kiselev. The peasants were declared 'free inhabitants residing on crown lands', and their existing self-governing *mir* institutions were confirmed and strengthened. A start was made towards converting their poll-tax payments into a land tax. Plans were drawn up to ensure that each household had enough land for subsistence and the discharge of official obligations: in a few cases land was actually reclaimed from the gentry for this purpose. In some areas serious attempts were made towards

encouraging improved sanitation and medical care, and towards disseminating better agricultural practice.

In some ways, the motives behind this reform were similar to
those which underlay the military settlements. It suffered from some
of the same drawbacks, too: corruption and insensitive leadership
often vitiated the benefits which peasants could obtain. In 1840–43
a scheme was introduced for the compulsory growing of potatoes to
create a public food reserve in case of famine. Peasants objected to
the unfamiliar crop and rioted in a number of provinces. Thereupon the
original intention to spread the reform gradually to private serfs was
dropped, and for the latter Nicholas brought in no serious
improvements.[50]

The 1848 revolutions in Europe, with their renewed threat of
rampant nationalism and republicanism, reduced Nicholas to a state
of almost catatonic fear. He originally intended to send an army to
the Rhine, but was dissuaded by his ministers. He did intervene,
though, to put down rebellions in Hungary and the Danube Principalities. At home he resurrected the practices of Paul, tightening the
censorship, making foreign travel more difficult and prohibiting the
import of books. In universities law and philosophy were banned
altogether, while the tuition of logic and psychology was entrusted
to theologians. Entrance to universities was severely pruned, and on
graduation students were assigned immediately to state service to
prevent them entering 'the slippery career of journalism'.[51]

Nicholas's reign ended in 1855 with the basic dilemma which had
faced Paul more than half a century earlier still unresolved. Russia
had not found a way to remould its empire in order to respond to
the growing attraction of nationalism in post-1789 Europe. The
delay had placed the empire in real jeopardy, as the outcome of the
Crimean War was soon to show. Nothing effective had been done
to narrow the gaping rift in culture and outlook between the elites
and the people, while a new split had been allowed to grow between
the imperial authorities and those same elites. The regime, obsess-
ively clinging to the idea of autocracy as a talisman of national
distinctiveness, was retreating into a bunker where it could no longer
rely on the support of even those educated to serve it at the highest
level.

PART THREE

Social classes, religion and culture in Imperial Russia

1

The Nobility

STATE SERVICE For most of the eighteenth and nineteenth century the nobility were the principal bearers of empire, the one social stratum which embodied its spirit, and was responsible for its defence and administration. The nobility dominated at court and in the chanceries, in regimental messes, in salons and ballrooms, in theatres and lecture halls. They wore the clothes and spoke the language of empire. In a real sense the empire was their homeland: 'Our fatherland is Tsarskoe Selo', as Pushkin once wrote.

Yet at the same time the nobles were in an ambiguous situation, for Peter the Great's reforms had created two incompatible roles for them, as Asiatic satraps and leisured European gentlemen. Before his time, there had been no single noble estate, but a variety of categories of 'service people' (*sluzhilye liudi*), some of whom were descended from the old princely and boyar families of the middle ages, and some of whom had been promoted from humble origins by earlier Tsars. Peter amalgamated those categories, creating a single estate bound to state service, yet at the same time he also laid the basis for it to become a hereditary privileged corporation – the first in Russian history.

For most families, even ones of ancient princely lineage, state service had always been highly desirable, for it guaranteed continued status and access to power and influence, without which the prevalent custom of dividing landed property among all male heirs gradually led to the fragmentation and dissipation of inherited wealth. Up to the late seventeenth century, though, a system had existed to ensure that the status of ancient and well-born families was not completely eroded by meritocratic upstarts who fulfilled the demands of service.

Known as *mestnichestvo*, or 'precedence', it provided that members of a given family (*rod*) should, provided they offered themselves for service, be appointed only to posts whose status was not lower than those which previous heads of their family had held. It was an attempt to balance the prerogatives of the autocrat with the claims of ancient lineage.

This was a cumbersome and inflexible system, certainly not conducive to the optimum deployment of talent. The Tsar occasionally overrode it in the interests of appointing good people, but it was expected that he would not do so as a normal practice. By the mid-seventeenth century, however, it was regularly ignored in military appointments, especially in the 'new formation' regiments. In 1682 it was abolished altogether.[1]

The Table of Ranks, which Peter instituted in 1722, was designed to replace family status with merit, measured by education, achievement and experience, as the principal criterion of promotion. As a token of his new approach, Peter began to pay salaries to his officials. The Table had parallels in the civil service establishments of Europe at the time, but in no other country did it stretch across the whole civil, military and court hierarchy, nor did it elsewhere so completely determine social as well as official status. On reaching the eighth rank (out of fourteen) of 'collegiate assessor' or its equivalent, an official's family 'though they be of base lineage, should be considered as for ever attached to the finest ancient *dvorianstvo* in all its dignities and privileges'. One's rank determined one's style of dress, one's mode of transport, the number of one's servants, the manner in which one was addressed, and one's precedence on all official occasions. Someone who rode down the Nevskii Prospekt in too grand a coach or with too many footmen would have to answer to the Master of Heraldry for his effrontery.[2]

At the very highest level, the immediate effect of Peter's reforms was actually to strengthen the grip of the old and wealthy families on the top jobs, since they had the means to provide a good education for their sons, and also the connections to ensure that the qualifications gained were deployed to maximum advantage. Peter's aim was not to undermine existing elites, but to revitalize them by training, foreign example and experience on the job. Hence his requirement that their sons attend schools, take on apprenticeships, pass inspections and serve from the lowest ranks upwards. In practice they often evaded this requirement by enrolling in a regiment as children, with the help of an influential patron: thus Andrei Bolotov 'enrolled' in his future regiment at the age of ten, and became a corporal a month later, thanks to his father's friendship with a Field Marshal. This kind of enlistment in a Guards regiment ensured high status for life, since Guards stood two ranks higher than ordinary officers in any official appointment, but to obtain such advancement one needed an influential patron in the regiment or at court. The hero of Pushkin's *Kapitanskaia dochka* is actually said to have been inscribed in the Semenovskii regiment while still in the womb, and was able to 'retire' before completing his student years.[3]

At the lower end of the nobility Peter's reforms opened the way in principle to enlargement and dilution of the estate with entrants from humbler social origins. Yet the effect was initially quite limited. In 1755, in the central state agencies, out of 189 officials at rank eight or above, 157 were themselves of noble origin, and only below that point were they outnumbered by the descendants of non-nobles.[4] By a century later, however, the effect was much more marked: in the 1850s 540 out of 1408 officials above grade eight came from non-noble families. Probably for that reason, to prevent excessive dilution of noble status, the grade required to achieve it was raised to number five in 1845 and to number four in 1856.[5]

EDUCATION AND CULTURE   In determining social status for both higher and lower ranks, education was the crucial social variable. Peter's notion of education had initially been largely utilitarian: hence the special schools in navigation, artillery, medicine, engineering, mining and foreign languages, as well as the 'cipher schools', which provided literacy and elementary knowledge, with a leaning towards mathematics. High-ranking families at first disdained these menial institutions, in spite of some threatening ukazes from Peter.

It was not until the prototype of a new kind of school, the Cadet Corps, opened in 1732 that the nobles' resistance began to abate. These schools were intended to train army officers and state officials, and graduation from them entitled one automatically to begin service on the first rung of the Table of Ranks. But they did not confine themselves to military training. Their founding charter announced that they would provide their pupils with a general education, with the theoretical and practical knowledge needed for a civil or military service career, and with the etiquette and social graces appropriate to someone who might well have to mix with the European aristocracy. Alumni distinguished themselves in cultural as well as administrative and military pursuits: a group of students led by Aleksandr Sumarokov founded the first Russian theatre at the court of the Empress Elizabeth, performing Racine, Molière and Shakespeare.[6]

With time the nobles began to internalize Peter's educational reforms. They began to see in the acquisition of science, learning and social graces the decisive criterion which would distinguish them from non-nobles and from less worthy members of their own estate. Now, in eighteenth-century Russia, science and learning meant principally that of Germany, while social graces came from France, mediated either through tutors at aristocratic houses, or through the young noblemen studying at foreign universities. This meant that to enhance their own standing nobles had to acquire an alien culture, one moreover which was reviled by large numbers of their own fellow-countrymen as the work of the Antichrist.

By the late eighteenth century many noble families spoke French not only in polite society, but even at home, relegating Russian to communication with servants, serfs and very young children. It is true that Russian remained the language of state offices, of serious literature and (in its Slavonic variant) of church services, so it was never in danger of being wholly eliminated from high culture or polite usage, but the fact remains that the nobility in much of their social and private life had adopted ways of life and a language which distanced them from most other Russians.

From our west European perspective, we may take it for granted, but in actuality it is very strange for an elite to be taken over so comprehensively by a culture initially alien to it. In no other empire of modern Europe was the assimilation of a foreign culture as complete, not even in the Ottoman Empire, which in the nineteenth century underwent European-inspired reforms as radical as those introduced by Peter in Russia. Presumably there Islam was an effective barrier to deeper cultural communication. The Russian fascination with west European culture is comparable to the way in which nineteenth-century colonial elites, having been educated in the mother country, would on return home yearn for the sophisticated social and intellectual life they had known in their youth.

But Russia was no colony: it was itself one of the strongest European great powers. Hence the incongruity of the nobles' situation and of the resultant rift within Russian culture.

Perhaps this wholesale borrowing from the west can be explained best by the fact that Russia did share with Europe a Christian tradition, albeit one with very distinctive characteristics, and weakened by the seventeenth-century schism, as well as by Peter the Great's church reforms. Being a member of the European diplomatic network also socialized Russia's elites in the same direction. These factors were powerfully reinforced by the nobles' desire to mark off their social standing against competitors from below. At a time when the significance of lineage was diminishing, and there were new claimants to noble status thronging in from below, European education and culture offered the most secure way of doing this. It offered the ambitious the opportunity to shine in high society or at court and thus to gain the best chance of a prestigious marriage or the receipt of land and serfs.

NOBLE ASSOCIATIONS   In 1762 Peter III emancipated the nobles from the duty of state service, and this enabled them, whenever they wished, to retire to their estates. This was an important stage in the process of transforming themselves into a leisured and cultured elite. Catherine II's local government reform and the Charter to the Nobility completed the process of recasting them as a privileged estate by endowing them with their own corporations and with entrenched functions in local life.

The Charter defined nobility as 'a hereditary distinction derived from the quality and virtue of outstanding men of former times who distinguished themselves by their deeds and who, having thereby made their service worthy of honour, acquired the title of nobility for their descendants.'[7] Membership was to be inscribed in a Book of Nobility, compiled by the nobles' assocation of each guberniia. These associations did not fully control their own membership, since anyone with the necessary service rank, plus a minimum of land and serfs, had the right to be inscribed. However, noble status or land could only be withdrawn for a crime incompatible with the honour of a nobleman, and then only after trial by one's peers. The nobles thus possessed certain secure rights, including that of private property in land. This was an unprecedented situation in Russian society, and, in the absence of a similar charter for peasants, it consolidated in practice their right to buy and sell the serfs who occupied that land as if they too were private property.[8]

Catherine's reforms thus took the first step towards creating a civil society in Russia, but at the cost of deepening yet further the already considerable juridical, political and cultural gap between the nobles and the serfs among whom they lived. Serfs became mere chattels in the eyes of their masters, objects which could be moved around or disposed of at will, as part of a gambling debt, a marriage settlement or an economic improvement scheme. In practice, they could normally be sold as commodities, without the land to which they were theoretically attached, and without members of their own families.

Lords had judicial and police powers over their serfs, as well as economic ones, which meant that they could punish serfs in any way they saw fit: they could flog them, send them to the army or exile them to Siberia. Theoretically, they were not permitted to kill a serf, but if a harsh flogging or other ill-treatment caused a serf's death, there was very little his fellow peasants could do about it.[9] Not that the great majority of lords were remotely so brutal or careless. But the mentality induced by this impunity nevertheless blunted the lord's sense of responsibility for the consequences of his own actions. Peter the Great had 'played' with his practice regiments, and this spirit of 'play' with the fates of human beings transmitted itself to the social elite he fostered.

After Catherine's reforms noble associations began to set up their own educational institutions, *blagorodnye pansiony, blagorodnye zhenskie instituty* (noble boarding schools for boys and girls) and further Cadet Corps. The state also opened a few schools which, because of their high cost or exclusive admissions policies, catered only for the children of the aristocracy or of favourites chosen personally by the Emperor: the Corps of Pages, the School of Guards' Sub-Ensigns, the Alexander Lyceum at Tsarkoe Selo, the Imperial Law School. The alumni of these institutions enjoyed unique social advantages, as well as exemptions from rungs on the Table of Ranks.[10]

The spread of education and culture among the sons and daughters of well-placed families meant that by the early nineteenth century the Russian nobility, at least in its upper ranks, was on its way to becoming the most cultured social estate in the whole of Europe. Coming late to European civilization, it had seized on it avidly, partly for the social advantages it brought, but partly for its own sake. Whereas the gentry of other countries was more confined by the horizons of its own homeland, the Russian nobles drank in English, French, German and Italian culture with equal enthusiasm: they were 'pan-European' and considered all Europe part of their spiritually augmented homeland. And what other European nobility could boast a cultural output to match Pushkin, Lermontov, Tiutchev, Turgenev, Tolstoi, Glinka, Musorgskii and Rakhmaninov?[11]

Marc Raeff has suggested that the experience of European travel and education 'denationalised' Russian nobles and made them 'foreign to their own country'. This view seemed to confirm one expressed long ago by Kliuchevskii, when he wrote of nobles 'who tried to be at home among foreigners and only succeeded in being foreigners at home'.[12] Michael Confino has questioned it, however, pointing out that nobles did actually serve for long periods in Russian institutions, that they were able to retire to their estates and devote themselves to agriculture or local government, and that in any case many of them retained strong and affectionate memories of their village childhoods, often brought up by serf nurses among serf children.[13]

Confino is right. Russian nobles were far from unpatriotic: in fact, it could be argued that in the modern sense they were the first consciously patriotic Russians. But there is also a kernel of truth in what Raeff and Kliuchevskii asserted, for the nobles' Russianness was very different from that of the peasants, and for that matter of the great majority of merchants and clergy. It was definitely an imperial Russianness, centred on elite school, Guards regiment and imperial court. Even their landed estates were islands of European culture in what they themselves often regarded as an ocean of semi-barbarism. The Russianness of the village was important to them, especially since it was bathed in childhood memories, but they knew it was something different.

The distinction between the two kinds of Russia is evoked in the childhood memories of the anarchist, Prince Petr Kropotkin, who imparted to it a moral dimension that became crucial in the later genesis of Russian socialism. 'Brought up in a pomeshchik family I, like all young people of my time, entered life with the sincere convic- 'tion that one must command, give orders, rebuke, punish and so on. But as soon as I had to undertake responsible business and so to enter into relationships with people ... I realised the difference between behaving on the basis of discipline and on the basis of mutual understanding ... between an official approach to business and a social or *mir* approach.'[14]

One group of nobles embodied the principles of the secular imperial state more fully than any other: the Baltic Germans. When their territory was incorporated into Russia in the course of the Great Northern War, Peter guaranteed their privileges and corporations, restoring them where the Swedish crown had begun to curtail them. He preserved the Ritterschaften, the noble associations which ran local government in the Baltic, he guaranteed the continued right to worship in the Lutheran faith, to use the German language for official business and to live under German law.[15] Almost certainly he did this because he knew that the Baltic landowners could be very useful to him. Their long experience of corporate life and local government was unique inside the Russian Empire, and their Ger- man upbringing meant that they were far better able to put into practice his new administrative principles than all but a very few Russian nobles.

And that is what they did. As we have seen, during the eighteenth and early nineteenth centuries, the Baltic Germans occupied an altogether disproportionate number of senior official posts. They were especially prominent in the military and diplomatic service, which were full of Lievens, Pahlens, Benckendorfs, Kleinmichels, Meyendorfs, Neidhards, Wrangels and Rennenkampfs.[16] Perhaps the single most egregious figure among them was the Foreign Minister, Count K.V. Nessel'rode, who, though representing Russia's interests for thirty years, scarcely spoke Russian at all. In the mid-nineteenth century Nicholas I's Third Department, or secret police, was com- monly known as the 'German department'. It is said that, when General Ermolov, hero of the Caucasus and founder of the city of Groznyi, was offered a reward by Alexander I, he replied 'Sire, I request to be promoted to the rank of German'.[17]

The Baltic nobles responded with fervent loyalty to the empire, or at least to the person of the Emperor. This is understandable in view of their situation. Distrusted by the Estonian and Latvian peasantry among whom they lived, they would have found it difficult to preserve their privileges or perhaps even their estates under any other rule. Renunciation of any identification with Germany, personal devotion to the Tsar and selfless dedication to the multinational empire gave them security and a function. Not only that, but the empire actually attracted Germans to resettle in the Baltic from Germany itself, since it offered much more scope for those well trained in the skills of public administration than any petty German principality. In a sense the Russian empire became a kind of adventure playground for the Baltic barons. That at least is how many Russians saw it – and resented it.

Probably that is one reason why, when Russians try to define their national character, they do so in terms which are expressly counterposed to German characteristics. They feel themselves to be warm, humane, informal, chaotic but able to get things done by community spirit, in contrast to Germans whom they see as cool, impersonal, formal, orderly, and addicted to bureaucratic methods. Actually, as Kropotkin realized, this contrast is just as much one within Russians themselves, between the *mirskoi* and the *gosudarstvennyi* concepts of action and community, between the informal local assembly and the rationalist secular state.

An early instance of the reaction against Germans came at the end of Anna's reign. Research suggests that about thirty per cent of her senior officials were non-Russian, not entirely German but also including some Poles. Germans such as Ostermann, Münnich and Bühren (Biron) were undeniably especially prominent.[18] Their overthrow and exile in 1741, at the accession of the Empress Elizabeth, called forth a wave of national rejoicing. Archimandrite Kirill proclaimed, 'The Holy Ghost has restored the great Peter's spirit to us in his daughter; He has helped her to wrest her father's sceptre from foreign hands, and to free nobles and people from the iniquity which they have suffered at the hands of their German masters.'[19] Here we see an important moment in the reformulation of Russian national identity: Peter is being incorporated into a notion of Russian-ness which he did his best to undermine by importing those very same

Germans. In this sense, too, Elizabeth was his true daughter: she may have exiled the most objectionable Germans, but she continued to appoint non-Russians to advise her, because she did not believe there were enough competent natives.[20] This alternation between distaste for Germans and reliance on them continued at least until the mid-nineteenth century.

ECONOMIC POSITION   The economic position of the nobility reflected the ambiguity of their social situation. During the eighteenth century, many of them received gifts of land and serfs – some of them huge – from monarchs who needed both their support and their official service. The resources at their disposal should in theory have enabled many of them to become significant entrepreneurs and to begin the task of mobilizing Russia's natural resources. However, their official duties and their dependence on a backward peasant economy prevented them from taking advantage of their opportunities.

The second half of the eighteenth century was a time when the Russian economy was growing dynamically, thanks to the annexation of huge and fertile new territories in the south. There grain could be grown for export through the Black Sea, while the cultivation of tobacco and sugar beet also brought new opportunities. Much of this new land was put at the disposal of the nobility, with the chance of settling serfs; they also received unoccupied steppes and forests belonging to the state in a general land settlement of 1763–5. The abolition of internal tariffs in 1753 encouraged greater regional specialization, with the result that non-agricultural activities developed in the north, as well as trading in foodstuffs grown in the south. In the north, as a result, nobles tended to charge their peasants *obrok*, or quit-rent paid in cash or kind from the proceeds of trade and small-scale manufacture, while in the south they tended to impose *barshchina*, or forced labour, on the fields where they cultivated their grain or sugar beet.[21]

However, the economic structure of the landowning estate changed little to take advantage of these opportunities. The estate might be large, but the techniques by which it was cultivated were those of the peasant. The lord was usually a relatively recent intruder in the village, and his domain was commonly held in strips, interspersed among those of the peasants. Strip distribution reflected the variable quality of the land, so that if the lord tried to enclose a consolidated area for himself, he would have received either mainly poor land, to the detriment of his own interests or mainly good land, to the detriment of the peasants, on whom he depended for his subsistence.[22]

So the landlord conducted an essentially peasant agriculture, characterized by the same crop-rotations, the same pasturing cycle, the same tools and work practices as determined the peasants' own techniques. For the most part, if he received his dues in the form of *barshchina*, he did not even supply the tools and seeds, but relied on the peasants' own. He was thus in a weak position to initiate change or innovation. If he was to influence peasant techniques, he had to do it through the villagers' own elected authorities, the elder and the clerk, with whom he would conduct business through his own steward (*prikazchik* or *upravitel'*). Much depended on their relationship. Some landlords were able regularly to have their own nominees elected as village elders; but many village assemblies had their own favoured candidates, and a steward would normally advise against overruling them: 'Of course, one could replace them, but there would be no point in doing so.' Landowner and steward were so dependent on village officials' influence over the peasant that they normally preferred the election of someone who enjoyed the villagers' confidence.[23]

The peasants thus possessed a kind of veto on innovation. Besides, the landlord was typically handicapped by ignorance of accounting methods, which might have enabled him to distinguish between productive and unproductive expenditure or to identify those aspects of his estate which, if improved, might offer the best prospects of securing a profit. He was interested in increasing his revenue, but that was not necessarily the same as increasing his profits, and he was ill-equipped to devise a way of doing the latter. It was simpler to put extra pressure on the peasants by raising their dues, to sell or mortgage part of the estate, or to request loans from the state.[24]

The state, which did not want to see its servitors bankrupt, was only too ready to come forward with the required sums. In 1754 it established a Noble Bank for that very purpose, and subsequently devised a number of other ways of making credit available. As nobles increasingly coveted the luxury westernized commodities which marked out their status – food, wines, clothes, furniture, gardens, architecture and interior decoration, paintings – they had frequent recourse to officially sponsored loans.[25] The result was an accumulating mountain of debt. By 1820 one-fifth of all serfs were mortgaged to credit institutions – which accepted serfs in preference to land as collateral. By 1842 half of all serfs were pledged in this way, and by 1859 two-thirds.[26] Altogether, the superimposition of of state-serving nobles on a primitive and communal peasant economy had the effect of freezing both in an archaic and inflexible agrarian routine which seriously held back both economic productivity and civic development.

FREEMASONRY Peter the Great, as we have seen, tended to think in terms of mechanisms and their efficient functioning. The subjective and spiritual needs of the human beings staffing those mechanisms were of much less concern to him. The strange consequence was that, although in the course of a couple of generations nobles internalized the ethic of service at least as well as he can have anticipated, the results were certainly not what he would have wished. During the second half of the eighteenth century Russian nobles began to look around restlessly for a belief system which would satisfy them better than the hermetic and semi-defunct culture of the Orthodox Church.

What many of them lighted upon was Freemasonry. Its attraction was that it offered a framework of communal life and ritual for the ethic of service in the secular, mobilizing state. The kind of religious outlook which Peter the Great had espoused and which he had endeavoured to inculcate in his servitors – deism, the *vita activa*, the idea of human beings redeemed by the use they make of their talents – was better accommodated within Freemasonry than within the Orthodox Church. Besides, masonic lodges were another aspect of the borrowing of things European.

In its eighteenth-century form, Freemasonry first caught on in England, and spread all over Europe among social elites looking for a form of congregation, ritual and self-improvement compatible with rationalism and deism. It also became a channel by which young men aspiring to high office or good social standing could find acquaintances and protectors among their superiors: in the Russian milieu this meant an easier and pleasanter way of rising up the Table of Ranks, which, as we have seen, depended partly on one's connections. Freemasonry was well suited to a hierarchical society which depended on personal links.

The first Russian lodges came into being in the 1730s. By the 1750s there was one in St Petersburg consisting largely of officers who had graduated from the Cadet Corps there, together with Aleksandr Sumarokov and his theatre people. The grandmaster of the principal St Petersburg lodge was Ivan Elagin, director of the court theatre. By a decade later, though the figures are not certain, as many as a third of St Petersburg's highest civil and military officials (above grade eight) may have been masons.[27]

The kinds of Freemasonry which rooted themselves best in Russia were those with elaborate hierarchies and rituals, perhaps because of the way the state accustomed Russians to distinctions of rank, perhaps because of a residual hankering for the magnificent ceremonies of the Orthodox Church. Catherine II on the whole approved of Freemasonry, at least initially, for it promised to put into effect many of the government's own stated aims in the field of philanthropy, justice, education and culture. It was only gradually that she became suspicious of secret societies with aims which could easily be construed as heretical.

For some nobles Freemasonry was a path towards something not unlike the 'Protestant ethic'. The principal exemplar of this trend was Nikolai Novikov. Though himself a nobleman with an estate not far from Moscow, he became the pioneer of Russia's own distinctive 'middle class' or 'professional' ethos, based not on wealth, commerce or industry, but on culture, learning and the idea of service. As a young man he was selected by Catherine II to be secretary to the sub-committee of her Legislative Commission whose brief was the formation of a middle class. During his work there he had the opportunity to observe at close quarters members of all estates (except clergy and serfs) and to reflect with abundant information at his disposal on their needs and aspirations.

After Catherine suspended the Legislative Commission, she took another path towards the formation of 'public opinion': she began to publish a journal, *Vsiakaia vsiachina* (This and That), modelled on the moral-satirical society journals of England, and she invited members of the public to follow her example. No one took her at her word more full-heartedly than Novikov, who during the 1770s issued a series of journals animated by his moral earnestness, his conviction that the nobility in Russia should distinguish itself not by birth, wealth or rank alone, but by 'nobility' in the moral sense of the word, through service to the community and through spreading enlightenment. His first journal, *Truten'* (The Drone), featured as editorial *persona* a·poor young nobleman making his way in the world through honest effort and virtue. Rejecting service in a corrupt bureaucracy, and spurning the offer of a well-meaning uncle to ease the way for him into its higher ranks, he devotes himself to good works, using the opportunities offered by social abuses for good-hearted satire. In a word, he internalizes the values which Russia's rulers envisaged for the nobility, rendering the hovering presence of the *fiskaly* superfluous.

Novikov's editorials posit the existence of an independent social life, centred on salons and clubs, where ideas could be discussed and polite behaviour exemplified. In actual fact, such a social life scarcely existed in Russia outside court circles. The first people who attempted to create it were the Freemasons, and we may say that Novikov, in joining them, was attempting to bring into being the world he had already projected in his writings.

The oath which he took on his entry to the lodge of Ivan Elagin demonstrates what it was about Freemasonry that attracted him. 'I swear on my honour before the Most High Creator of the world that on entering through my sincere desire the virtuous society of masons, I shall always remain an honest and humble man, a good, obedient and peaceful member of it, an unshakable witness to the majesty and great wisdom of my Maker Most High, a loyal subject of my gracious Sovereign, a straightforward and worthy son of my dear Fatherland, a peaceful and good citizen. That I at this moment will extirpate from my heart not only vengeance but also my indignation against those who despise and insult me in my life, that through my authority and my own property I shall always endeavour to help the poor, comfort the unhappy, defend the oppressed, not only among the masonic brotherhood but among worthy men of any calling.'[28]

There was not a word of this oath that would not have been approved by Peter the Great as an expression of his ideal for state servitors, an ideal which he endeavoured to impose through his *fiskaly*. But, as his successors were to discover, to have those ideals espoused with inner sincerity by active, patriotic and self-conscious citizens was something quite different from what they had envisaged, and not at all conducive to the peace of mind of autocrats.

Novikov, at any rate, took them with complete seriousness. As a result of his masonic connections, he was able to assume the lease of the printing press of Moscow University, and use it to launch an ambitious programme of publishing and book distribution, including Russian historical studies and documents, translations from foreign thinkers and writers, text-books and grammars, religious tracts and masonic works of devotion. With the monarch's initial encouragement, he set himself almost single-handed to enlighten public opinion.

Not content with such an ambition, he devoted the income from his publishing ventures to launching charitable schools, in which children were to be 'trained in piety and prepared for further study for the sake of themselves and their Fatherland'. Later, during the poor harvest of 1787, he raised funds to distribute grain in a hundred or so hungry villages. In this way, he employed the masonic network to found the first voluntary charitable associations outside the aegis of the church.[29]

By the mid-1780s Catherine became suspicious of Novikov's activities, partly because, secular though she was in her outlook, she regarded the Orthodox faith as a pillar of public order, and had decided to restrict non-ecclesiastical publication of religious works.[30] Even more important, though, was that Novikov had become the principal figure among the Moscow Rosicrucians, who were known to have connections with the Prussian court – currently hostile to Russia – and were suspected of trying to recruit the Grand Duke Paul.

In all societies Freemasons arouse misgivings and resentment because of their secrecy, their elite character and the suspicion that they are really just a network for promoting cronies to good jobs. In Russia these motives for disapproval were accentuated by the odour of foreign connections, especially after 1789 those associated with the French revolution, and by Catherine's own lingering insecurity on a throne which she had gained by conspiracy and might lose by the same means. As a Russian saying has it, 'Fear has big eyes'.

Catherine suspected Paul of being the centre of a conspiracy inspired by the Prussian court to dethrone her, and her suspicions seemed confirmed by the discovery that he was involved with a well-funded secret society, with Prussian connections, dabbling in the occult. Novikov became the victim of her suspicions: he was accused of heresy and of treasonable relations with foreigners hostile to Russia, and without trial was sentenced to fifteen years in the Schlüsselburg fortress. Only the accession of Paul in 1796 rescued him from this fate.[31]

Novikov was a test case of the capacity of Imperial Russia to generate its own civil society. In his devotion to learning and culture, and to the welfare of the common people, he reflected the officially projected ethos of the Russian state. The satire of his journals, though undoubtedly wounding to some officials, reaffirmed Catherine's own desire to preside over an honest and effective administration. Even in his religious works it might be argued that he tried to reinterpret the teachings of Orthodoxy for a modern audience, brought up on the intellectual fare of the Enlightenment: certainly he spoke out with passionate conviction against the French atheists. But his endeavour to put official ideals into practice by unofficial means, through independent publishing and by using such social institutions as existed in Russia, in the end rendered him suspicious to both church and state. The *fiskaly* triumphed over the ideals they were supposed to promote.

Alexander Radishchev was another nobleman, brought up on the officially approved values, who took them too seriously for his own good. He was educated at the Corps of Pages, where he picked up courtly skills as well as some genuine learning. As a young man he was personally chosen by Catherine to study at the University of Leipzig where, according to her instructions, he was to learn 'Latin, German and if possible Slavic languages . . . moral philosophy, history and particularly natural and universal law and something of the law of the Roman Empire'.[32]

What he actually imbibed there was a German, Pietist form of the

European Enlightenment, which provided a theoretical and spiritual underpinning for the service ethic. The lesson that this ethic was not actually observed in the Russian state was rubbed in for him by the cynical and brutal behaviour of the overseer who accompanied their student group, peculating the funds intended for their maintenance and using his position to squash all their complaints. Radishchev thus received, as it were, a double education, positive and negative, in the ideals and reality of the Russian state.

It was reinforced by the work he was assigned on his return home, in the Senate, where he had to investigate alleged abuses of official power. (He also had a number of contacts in masonic lodges, though, as far as is known, he never became a mason himself.) He came to the conclusion that, although monarchical authority was justified, it needed to be tempered by a separation of powers and the rule of law. He outlined his vision of civil society and patriotism in an article published in 1789, entitled 'What is a son of the fatherland?' (echoing Peter I's assumed title, 'father of the fatherland'). Slaves, he roundly asserted, cannot be 'sons of the fatherland', and he also refused the title to those who abuse their position to feather their own nests and oppress their subordinates. The true patriot, he concluded, exemplified the aristocratic virtues of honour, nobility and ambition supplemented by the unaristocratic characteristics of virtue (*blagonravie*) and love of one's neighbours.[33]

Radishchev's most important work was *A Journey from St Petersburg to Moscow*, which he published anonymously in 1790, with additions made after it had passed a careless censor. In this book a 'sentimental journey' becomes a bill of indictment for the evils of Russian society: the recruitment system, corruption, drunkenness, prostitution, superstition and serfdom as a moral evil and as a brake on the economy. Autocracy is attacked only in the verse section 'Ode to Freedom', which is presented as coming from a hand not the author's, but which of course epitomizes Radishchev's own view. He lends his indictment emphasis by warning of the possibility both of tyrannicide and of peasant revolution, when 'the alarm bell rings' and 'the destructive force of bestiality breaks loose with terrifying speed'.

Radishchev's language makes it clear that he is not advocating peasant insurrection, merely warning of its probability – a warning only too plausible in the era of the French *jacqueries* and less than two decades after the Pugachev rebellion. His ideal was not revolution, but the rule of law, and his *Journey* was intended both as warning and as appeal. Where he differed from Catherine was in his view of the nature of law. As we have seen, she regarded law as emanating from the sovereign power, whereas for Radishchev it was inherent in the nature of things. He was within a natural law tradition which in the West went back beyond the Middle Ages to the Roman Empire, but which in Russia was still a puny child of recent learning.

This strange and original book became known throughout the capital city almost as soon as it was published. Catherine II, alarmed by the French revolution, was in no mood to react tolerantly to its appearance, and commanded that the anonymous author be discovered. Radishchev was arrested, taken to the Peter-Paul Fortress, stripped of his noble title, charged with fomenting sedition and disorder, and sentenced to death. Later his sentence was commuted to ten years' exile in Siberia, from which he was freed by the Emperor Paul.[34]

Novikov and Radishchev had been relatively isolated figures, but by the first two decades of the nineteenth century the educational and cultural initiatives of Elizabeth and Catherine II were beginning to feed through into the creation of a cultured and leisured ruling stratum, consisting not just of a few individuals in the capital cities, but extending to provincial centres and country estates.

The situation at Moscow University exemplified the new freedom. During the first half-century since its opening in 1755, it had won a reputation both as an institution of scholarship, and as a centre where learning legitimated social mixing and where young aristocrats could spend some years without disgrace and with possible profit. Alexander I granted it a new charter in 1804, giving it greater freedom to run its own affairs. More important than its new syllabuses, however, were the learned societies and student fraternities which burgeoned within its walls, such as the Society for History and Russian Antiquities, the Society of Scientists and the Society of Lovers of Russian Literature, offering testimony to the growing demand for the kind of interests Novikov had promoted.

Such associations brought together scions of the nobility with a few sons of merchants, priests and ordinary townsfolk, all of whom had in common that they were being trained for service in church or state. They formed a kind of classless community of intellectual apprentices. They would discuss Christianity, deism and atheism, the ideas of the Enlightenment and their outcome in the events of the French Revolution. The first thick monthly journal, *Vestnik Evropy* (The European Herald), started to appear at this time, with its medley of poetry, drama and fiction together with book reviews and serious articles on history, literature, philosophy, religion and science – all excellent food for communal debate. The student debaters would read and argue over the latest Russian and foreign literature, including forbidden works, which they would pass from hand to hand. Their knowledge of such works was partly due to personal links: the father of the young Nikolai Turgenev, for instance, was a close friend of Novikov, and through mutual acquaintances Nikolai also got to read a manuscript copy of Radishchev's *Journey from St Petersburg to Moscow*. The university authorities were either ignorant of these activities or tolerated them, in order not to invite the police on to the campus.[35]

THE DECEMBRISTS   The outlook of this younger generation was further transformed by the Napoleonic war. The triumph of their motherland, and their own personal experience in the countries they had traversed, added a crucial element to their education: it enormously sharpened their sense of what it meant to be Russian, and imparted to it the intense comradeship of those who have endured dangers and hardships together, 'relationships woven at the bivouac and on the battlefield in the sharing of equal labours and perils', as Sergei Trubetskoi put it.[36] These martial links were enlivened by a vivid apprehension of what both allies and enemies enjoyed but Russia lacked: popular patriotic movements and representative institutions. As Nikolai Bestuzhev later testified, 'My five month stay in Holland in 1815, when a constitutional administration was being introduced there, gave me my first concept of the benefit of laws and civil rights; then two visits to France and a voyage to England and Spain confirmed my attitude.'[37]

Perhaps even more important, the war broadened the potential social base of Russian patriotism. For the first time members of the nobility felt that they shared a common fate with their own serfs. Ivan

Iakushkin, a young Smolensk landowner who fought at Borodino as an ensign in the Semenovskii Guards, observed that the peasants were capable of displaying a patriotism independent of orders from above: 'The 1812 war awoke the Russian people to life ... All the instructions and efforts of the government would not have sufficed to expel the Gauls and the multitude of other tribes which had invaded Russia, if the people had remained as passive as was its wont. But it was not owing to instructions from the authorities that, on the approach of the French, they withdrew into the forests and marshes, leaving their homes to burn.'[38] Yet on the conclusion of peace, these same peasants, scourges of Napoleon and saviours of their motherland, were subjected once more to the deprivations and indignities of serfdom. Some of them had volunteered for the militia under the impression that free service offered to the motherland would bring them liberty from bondage. 'Soldiers returning home were the first to raise complaint among the mass of the people,' as Aleksandr Bestuzhev later told Nicholas I, during the investigation of the Decembrist uprising. '"We spilt our blood", they would say, "but once again we are forced to sweat at forced labour. We delivered our homeland from the tyrant, yet now the lords tyrannise us again."'[39]

The experience of war and of west European life not only intensified Russian patriotism, then, but also suggested a new and broader content for it in the shape of a nation of citizens liberated from bondage and contributing through their freely elected representatives to the making of the laws by which they were governed.

Young army officers who wanted to promote this kind of vision of the Russian nation had some grounds for believing that they enjoyed the support of the Emperor. After all, he had espoused similar proposals during his early years on the throne. A few wished openly to appeal for his support, but in the end the general consensus among them, influenced by Freemasonry and the anti-Napoleonic movements in Europe, was that a secret society was a more effective way of promoting their arms. Accordingly, highly-placed young officers set up the Union of Salvation, later renamed the Society of True and Loyal Sons of the Fatherland.

In this way the 'Decembrists' first came into being as a coherent organization. In a way it is unfortunate that they have gone down to history with that name, for it directs all our attention to their violent and inglorious end, as if all their activity was consciously directed towards it. That was far from being the case: indeed scarcely a trace of their later ignominy can be discerned in their unassuming, decorous and patriotic beginnings.

The purpose initially proposed for the Union of Salvation suggests a narrow and non-imperial concept of the nation: 'resistance to the Germans in the Russian state service', but the Union swiftly adopted the broader and vaguer aim of 'the welfare of Russia'.[40] At an early stage its members decided that the best way to achieve this 'welfare' was by abolishing serfdom and transforming the autocracy into a constitutional monarchy. How this was to be accomplished was never really settled, but it seems to have been generally anticipated that at the next change of throne members should refuse to take the oath of allegiance to the new monarch till he swore to grant a constitution. There were a number of Guards officers in the Union, and such a tactic was well within their century-old tradition of influencing the succession process – indeed it would be much more peaceful and orderly than most of their previous exploits.[41]

Masonic lodges offered an apt model for the organization of the Union. The careful choice of members, with particular regard to their moral qualities; the degrees of initiation through which each new recruit must pass, receiving more information about the society at each stage; the tactic of exploiting personal connections to obtain access to official posts, and the use of those posts to advance the society's aims; all these characteristics, derived from Freemasonry, were well adapted to peaceful conspiratorial politics aiming at far-reaching change. Some members of the Union were in fact also members of masonic lodges, though it seems that none of these was actually integrated into the secret society.

From the outset, the Union of Salvation was a self-consciously nationalist association. It debarred foreigners from its ranks, and endeavoured to weaken their influence within the Russian state. Its members became increasingly hostile to Alexander I, primarily because they felt he was turning against his own people. As Alexander Murav'ev commented acidly, 'Poland received a constitution, and Russia, as a reward for 1812, received – military settlements!'[42] Some half-suspected Alexander was measuring himself up to become

Emperor of Europe. As Murav'ev's remark implies, his award of a constitution to the Congress Kingdom of Poland was not welcomed as a first step towards a similar charter for the whole empire, but on the contrary aroused a mood of offended patriotism; while the rumour that he was intending to restore to Poland its eastern provinces, annexed by Russia during the eighteenth-century partitions, actually provoked first thoughts of regicide.[43]

Of course, secret societies have their inevitable limitations when it comes to affecting public opinion, and it did not take long for the members of the Union to feel that its *modus operandi* was depriving it of the broad influence to which it aspired. Besides, small and clandestine though it was, it was beginning to split along lines which were to prove fateful. 'Europe' was not a monolithic entity, and it offered more than one potential model of a nation-state and of the means to create it. A minority of members, led by Pavel Pestel', adjutant to the commander-in-chief of the Russian army, Count Wittgenstein, took a Jacobin view, envisaging a unitary state, with no ethnic divisions, to be reached by some kind of seizure of power (including, in some circumstances, regicide) and a dictatorial transitional regime. The majority took a more Anglo-American view, favouring a gradual and moderate strategy, with the emphasis on education and influence rather than rebellion, and aiming at a federal state headed by a constitutional monarchy.

The tension between these two views was one of the motives for the dissolution of the Union of Salvation in 1817, but was not resolved by it, and persisted through all the subsequent debates. Its successor, the Union of Welfare (*Soiuz blagodenstviia*), was set up as a two-tiered organization. To obviate the drawbacks of clandestinity, it had a public section, with a 'green book', devoted to promoting enlightenment and good works, while actual politics continued to be conducted in a secret section. The aims and strategy of the latter were apparently never fully worked out (certainly no record of them has survived) – a failure which was to haunt the whole organization.

The avowed aim of the Union of Welfare was to complement the activities of the government in disseminating enlightenment and morality. In this respect it continued the work of Catherine II, and the preamble to the Green Book quoted her appeal for public support in these tasks. Its membership ignored the estate classification of

Russian society save in one respect: serfs were excluded. Members were, however, required to be male, Russian and Christian. This stipulation prefigured the expected composition of a future Russian citizenry. Russian nationhood was to embrace 'those who were born in Russia and speak Russian', a definition which would include many Tatars, Georgians and Baltic Germans, among others. On the other hand, 'Foreigners who have left their native land to serve an alien state thereby incur distrust and cannot be considered Russian citizens. The Union deems worthy of that name only those foreigners who have rendered outstanding services to our fatherland and are ardently devoted to it.'[44] In this way the Union's concept of nationhood included elements which were ethnic, religious, political and even moral.

Most of the Green Book was taken up with expounding the civic qualities which members of the Union should display and the practical obligations flowing from them. Each member was to take a branch of social endeavour – philanthropy, education, justice or the economy – and devote himself to promoting therein the aims of the Union, through personal example, practical activity, spoken and written advocacy and the denunciation of official abuses. Philanthropy entailed helping to set up and run hospitals, orphanages, refuges for war veterans and the like. Members were urged not to evade elective posts in local government, as was common practice among nobles, but actively to seek them, in order to use them to promote equity and integrity in public affairs. In economic matters, the Green Book propounded what might be called a 'Protestant ethic', condemning idleness and luxury, but aiming to maximize all 'useful economic activity', including agriculture, industry and commerce, while demanding honest dealing.

Interestingly, in relation to the serfs, the Green Book refrained from recommending emancipation, even by taking advantage of the modest existing laws permitting it, but contented itself with exhorting members to make provision for the needy, to treat their serfs well, and not to buy or sell them, on the grounds that 'human beings are not wares, and only peoples unilluminated by the light of Christianity can be excused for regarding their fellow creatures as property to be arbitrarily disposed of'.[45]

Iakushkin did make the effort to free his serfs, but – revealingly

– he did so without awarding them land. He intended to rent half his land out to them and keep the other half for himself, to be cultivated, presumably, by their paid labour. The Ministry of the Interior refused him permission to do this, pointing out that such a precedent could be abused by others less public-spirited than himself. His peasants were no more enthusiastic. When he explained to them that they would be free to rent land from him for their own use, they replied, 'Well, in that case, *batiushka*, let's leave things as they are: we are yours, but the land is ours.'[46]

The importance of the Green Book was that it established a paradigm for proper civic activity and projected a model for citizenship in the future Russian state. Members of the Union tried to follow its precepts in their everyday behaviour. As Iurii Lotman has hypothesized, they were trying to overcome the duality which existed between the Enlightenment culture to which they had been brought up and the reality of life both at court and on their estates, where most relationships were hierarchical and unadornedly 'dominant-submissive'. They did not so much reject social etiquette as try to impart to it a sincerity which it lacked. In reaction against hierarchy and frivolity, they practised an intense cult of sincerity and friendship, often among former members of the same school or regiment, but sometimes arising simply out of shared convictions. These formed some of the dominant themes in the early poetry of Pushkin, who was close to the Decembrists.[47]

In 1821 the Union of Welfare went through a fictitious self-dissolution, partly because its members knew the authorities were on their tracks as a prohibited secret society, but partly also because of the growing influence in their midst of Pavel Pestel', whose radical programme and dominating, irreconcilable personality aroused lively misgivings in most of his colleagues. He was not informed of the meeting which decided the dissolution, and he subsequently refused to accept it. He continued the Union's work in Tul'chin, in Chernigov guberniia. In this way, the dissolution led to a split between two fragments, which took on the provisional names of Northern and Southern Societies, with different and partly conflicting aims and strategies. Pestel made several attempts to reunite the whole movement under his own leadership; he failed, but did succeed in inspiring some Northern Society members with his own radicalism.

The Northern Society, though organizationally loose and tactically irresolute, was renewing its membership during the years which
followed. The dominance of aristocratic and wealthy Guards officers
was diluted by newcomers from the lower ranks of the service nobility, among whom the key figure was Kondratii Ryleev, son of a
bankrupt landowner, a romantic poet who sang of the civic virtues
of ancient Slavic heroes (usually bending the historical evidence to
obtain an acceptable portrait). He gathered round himself a small
coterie of passionate rebels, inspired both by figures of the ancient
world and also by recent examples from Spain and Greece. One of
them kept a copy of Brutus's letters to Cicero by his bedside as a
reminder that, if all else failed, tyrants must be killed.[48]

The difference between the Northern and Southern Societies was
manifest in the two documents they produced outlining their concep-
tions of a future Russia. The Southern one was composed by Pestel',
who spent several years writing it in the form of a handbook to
serve as guide to a transitional government charged with putting its
principal tenets into practice. Although it was unfinished at the time
of his arrest, and combines elements of a constitution with a political
treatise, it tells us a great deal about his concept of the Russian
nation and its relationship to the state. He entitled it *Russkaia pravda*,
consciously recalling the law code thought to have been promulgated
by Iaroslav the Wise of Kievan *Rus'* in the eleventh century. He
intended it to be published, as a guarantee that the transitional
regime would fulfil its duties towards the people.

Pestel believed, like the framers of the American Constitution,
that the government existed to promote the welfare of its subjects.
Provided that it did so, it had the right to demand their total obedience. The present regime did not, and 'from this there follow two
principal needs for Russia: the first consists in a complete transformation of the order of government, and the second in the issuance of a
complete new Code or collection of laws that will preserve everything
useful and destroy all that is harmful'.[49]

If the American and French revolutions had created new nation-
states by such means, the imitation of their example in Russia was
far from unproblematic. In this multi-national empire which was to
be the nation in whose name the state should be recreated? Pestel
had no doubt that it should be what he called the 'great Russians'.

He acknowledged that there existed categories of Russians: Little Russians, White Russians, Ukrainians and Ruthenians, as he called them. But he considered that these were pre-national forms, tribes with their own dialects which would dissolve naturally once civic nationhood was established.[50]

As for the non-Russian peoples, they would have to yield to the paramount law of welfare, which was security. The state had to have borders which it could defend, and the smaller tribes and nationalities within those borders had to acknowledge the priority of what he called the 'right of convenience' (*blagoudobstvo*, which might almost be translated here 'raison d'état') over the 'right of nationality'. Thus the Finns, Letts, Georgians, Tatars and so on, must remain for ever within the Russian Empire. And that did not just mean cultivating their own national existence under an overall Russian canopy. 'The Supreme Provisional Administration must constantly aim at making them into *one* single nation and at dissolving all differences into one common mass, so that the inhabitants throughout the entire territory of the Russian state be *all Russians*.'[51] This should be accomplished by promulgating everywhere the same laws, abolishing the separate ethnic names and making the Russian language everywhere prevail.

Only for the Poles and Jews did Pestel' conceive of possible alternatives. He recognized that the 'incredibly close bonds' which cemented the Jewish people might make them impossible to Russify. If that proved to be the case, then Pestel's solution was brutal in the extreme, a kind of press-gang Zionism: all two million of them should be expelled into the Ottoman Empire. 'So many people in search of a country will have no difficulty in overcoming all the obstacles which the Turks may put up; and after traversing European Turkey, they could cross over into Asiatic Turkey where, upon seizing sufficient territory, they could establish a separate Jewish state . . .'[52]

Pestel' also acknowledged that Poland, as a historic sovereign state, might prove indigestible for Russia; in any case it was embarrassing for him to offer her less than Alexander I had already granted. He therefore proposed that she receive independence, provided that she also be ruled according to the precepts of *Russkaia pravda* – which would entail abolishing the *szlachta*, hitherto the mainstay of Polish statehood – acknowledge frontiers convenient to Russia, and remain permanently at peace with her. In other words, Poland was to become essentially a Russian dependency.[53]

Russia would be a unitary state, with the same laws and the same administration operating everywhere. Its new capital would be Nizhnii Novgorod, renamed Vladimir in honour of the prince who had introduced Christianity to *Rus'*. The choice was a revealing one: Nizhnii Novgorod was associated with trade and the development of Russia's resources along the Volga and further east. It was also the city from which the revival of Russia had begun during the Time of Troubles.[54]

Serfdom was to be abolished, as were all social hierarchies: all citizens were to enjoy the same rights and were to be represented in the popular legislative assembly, or *narodnoe veche*.[55] They would be guaranteed private property in the means of production, including land; but, in order to provide everyone with enough land to ensure subsistence without infringing these rights, Pestel divided the land in each volost into two categories: (i) that which was available for purchase and sale, and (ii) the social land fund, distributed by the authorities in such a way as to ensure that everyone had a certain minimum.[56]

I have dwelt at length on Pestel's project, since it is the most coherently expounded outline of an alternative Russian state structure, not just among the Decembrists, but among all nineteenth-century oppositionists. It demonstrates clearly what might well have been the consequences for the empire of trying to introduce the principle of the nation-state as that had been conceived in France. It swept away the compromises and anomalies the Tsars had permitted themselves in their ramshackle assemblage of the empire, and instead erected as a principle the straightforward identity of the ethnic and the civic. The implications anticipate the later writings of Katkov and the policies of Pleve.[57]

The project which Nikita Murav'ev wrote for the Northern Society is revealing in that, though it proclaimed the principle of federalism, it differed little in substance from Pestel's unitary model. It divided Russia into thirteen states (*derzhavy*) and made provision for two-chamber popular assemblies in each, but they were to be subordinated to the supreme *narodnoe veche*. His *derzhavy* in no way reflected the ethnic make-up of their population, indeed they were mostly to be named after rivers. Doubtless he was influenced by the nation-building experience of the USA (where, however, the various ethnic groups were nearly all immigrants): certainly his bi-cameral legislature strongly resembled the American Congress, as did the planned dominance of property. Murav'ev laid out a complicated scheme of property qualifications for election to public office, which would exclude nearly all peasants and most town-dwellers, but the main requirement for citizenship, and thus for voting, was speaking Russian. Like Pestel's, this project emancipated the serfs, but did not provide them with land, so that the newly freed peasants would be thrown back on wage-labour or renting for subsistence.[58]

Neither of these programmes was calculated to attract the soldiers who were involved in the rebellion of December 1825 [for an account of which, see Part 2, Chapter 4]. Interestingly, however, during the crisis itself the southerners did at least make an attempt to appeal in good faith to the men whose lives they were putting at risk. Sergei Murav'ev-Apostol, one of the officers stationed at Tul'chin, drew up an Orthodox Catechism, which linked the Decembrists' political aims with the faith of ordinary people. It is worth quoting at some length.

Question: For what purpose did God create man?
Answer: So that he should believe in Him, be free and happy.
Question: Why are the Russian army and people unhappy?
Answer: Because the Tsars have robbed them of freedom.
Question: Consequently the Tsars are acting against God's will?
Answer: Yes, of course. Our God has said: 'But he that is greatest among you shall be your servant, while the Tsars only tyrannize the people.'
Question: Should one obey Tsars when they act against God's will?
Answer: No. Christ has said 'You cannot serve God and Mammon'. The Russian people and the Russian army suffer because they submit to Tsars.
Question: What does our Holy Writ command the Russian people and army to do?

Answer: To repent of their long servility and, rising against tyranny and lawlessness, to swear 'Let there be one Tsar for all, Jesus Christ in Heaven and on Earth'.[59]

This attempt to find a common language with the soldiers reminds one of Roundhead pamphlets in the English Civil War of the seventeenth century: it suggests that the vision of the evil Tsar transgressing God's laws as well as men's carried some conviction with all social classes. At any rate, it was apparently successful in rousing the soldiers to action, though they encountered a detachment of government hussars and artillery and were easily dispersed.

The ambivalence and almost comic irresolution displayed especially in the north were characteristic of a movement which had never succeeded either in defining a clear strategy or in rooting itself among the common people. Those involved were from the empire's elites, its natural leaders: deprived of their natural role, they could neither realize their ideals nor renounce them. They behaved almost like adolescents playing with toy soldiers who suddenly find themselves thrust into the smoke and blood of a real battle. Some hesitated, some panicked, some reacted with exaggerated and thoughtless bravura. Long-discussed plans were ditched and headlong improvisation took over.

In this manner, what had begun as an attempt to introduce gradually and undemonstratively some of the institutions of civil society ended in a makeshift and abortive rebellion. In the attempt to render genuine service to the people, its instigators came into collision with the state which had demanded that service of them. This was a real tragedy, for in high society there was widespread acceptance of the kind of changes the more moderate Decembrists envisaged – but not at the cost of disloyalty and rebellion. This was the attitude of, for example, Pushkin. The prospect of violence caused many members to leave the Northern Society in its later years, and it fell into the hands of a chaotic but determined group round Ryleev. When it came to the crisis, this group could not muster the degree of support everyone had anticipated.

The fiasco of December 1825 was a decisive turning-point in the failure of civil society to evolve in Russia. Hovering in disembodied manner between empire and people, the Decembrists derived their vision largely from the culture disseminated by the empire, but were unable to create an audience for it either among the people or among the authorities.

It was at this moment that, having suffered such a debacle, the aristocratic vision of a Russian civil society lost its impetus. Instead, in the reign of Nicholas I, disaffected nobles joined forces with members of other social estates. Their joint offspring was the first generation of the intelligentsia, a stratum of a new kind which generated its own distinctive concept of Russian nationhood. The rift between elite and people was now compounded by a new and no less fateful rift: between the regime and a significant section of the elite.

2

The Army

In a novel by the contemporary Russian satirist Vladimir Voinovich, a clumsy and ungainly Red Army soldier, Private Ivan Chonkin, is despatched to a remote village just before the outbreak of the second world war to guard a plane which has crashed there. When the war starts the authorities forget all about him. In due course he takes up with one of the village women, digs her garden plot, mends her leaking roof, and gradually settles down and reverts to being a peasant. He gives up being a thoroughly unsatisfactory soldier, and becomes instead a model cultivator of the soil.[1]

The tale of Chonkin is a kind of parable for the situation of the Russian people in both the Tsarist and Soviet empires. The state tears them from the soil and thrusts them into imperial institutions which are alien to their nature. It then compounds the problem of adaptation by supplying them with insufficient resources to their job properly. The people react by attempting to reclaim those institutions, using their own weapons of kinship (adapted to circumstance), personalism, informality and mutual aid, doing their best to turn official structures into unofficial associations of a kind with which they feel comfortable and which enable them to get on with their lives, even in the incongruous circumstances imposed on them by the state. In that way, the ethnos constantly threatens in its rambling way to reabsorb the empire. Civil servants struggle against this tendency, but the weary, frustrated tone of their memoranda to each other suggests that they are conscious of fighting a losing battle.

Yet the imperial institutions have worked, in their own way. The army is a prime example. For all the maladminstration and under-resourcing it has been for quite long periods of the last three centuries the most effective army in Europe, and not merely because it was usually the largest. How can one explain this paradox?

Peter the Great's major innovation was to create an army directly recruited and financed by the state, in which the conscripts, in their overwhelming majority peasants, served for life, torn away from homes, families and villages. This brutal and permanent separation was imposed to wean the recruit away from the very unmilitary routines of rural life, and from the association with a local landowner which had characterized the old feudal levies. He was to become a professional soldier, dedicated to the service of Tsar and empire.

During Peter's reign some 53 levies were taken up, at rates ranging from one per 250 households to one per ten, and raising a total of some 300,000 men. Because of casualties and desertions, though, the army's total size probably did not much exceed 200,000.[2] This was a large army by the standards of the time, and it grew further during the eighteenth century. In the Seven Years' War (1756–63) more than 200,000 were called up during a five-year period alone. By this time the size of the army was about 300,000 – a little smaller than the French army, which was the largest in Europe – and by 1800 it reached 450,000, some 25% larger than any European rival.[3]

All the same, so great were the demands made upon it, that it had the utmost difficulty in meeting them, and usually only a small proportion of its effectives could be deployed against any one particular contingency. The frontiers it had to defend were several times longer than those of any other European power, and on the other side of some of those frontiers were potentially or actively hostile states: Sweden, Poland, the Ottoman Empire, Persia. Until the 1770s fully a quarter of Russia's military strength was deployed on the open southern steppes to guard against the possibility of Tatar raids from the Crimea. And for much of the time there was the danger of internal disaffection, from Cossacks, Bashkirs, Caucasian Muslim tribes or peasant revolt, to mention only the most obvious hazards. Deploying the army to meet all these threats adequately was impossible, which is why much of the skill of Russia's military men and diplomats was engaged in anticipating trouble, negotiating and pacifying to forestall danger.

For most of the eighteenth century the state's finances were so shaky that it was not possible to fulfil Peter's ideal of equipping the army fully from treasury funds. Under-provision was a permanent problem. For example, in 1729 an inspector found that the Kargopol' dragoons had not been issued with boots, stockings or shirts for three years, while units which had received supplies often found that they were defective: headgear which dripped glue after a shower of rain, or sword belts which fell apart after the first washing. Inadequate fodder meant that the cavalry was often operating with under-nourished horses, liable to break down in combat. In 1757 things were so bad that General Count Petr Shuvalov ordered in his instructions on the annual induction of recruits: 'In the event of an insufficient supply of real muskets, give them wooden ones.'[4]

This when Russia was actually at war! And incidentally, Chonkin was not just a parable: in 1788 three soldiers who had taken part in the siege of Ochakov were left behind to guard some stores and were simply forgotten. More than a year passed before they were discovered, 'suffering extreme need, and the state property rotting away owing to holes in the roof'.[5]

Non-receipt of pay and food shortages were a major cause of desertion, so that these shortcomings threatened not just the efficiency but also the size of the army. Cruel and inhumane treatment by officers also took their toll. Recruiting sergeants would sometimes place new recruits in irons on their way to the induction station, or would confine them in prison cells until their regiments could receive them. Desertion rates varied enormously from one year to another, but were very high in the early years after Peter's reforms, when sometimes a third or more of new batches would abscond.[6] To forestall such occurrences and to make the culprits easier to recapture, Peter at one stage ordered that all new recruits should be branded. Later it was decided that they should be shaved in the front of the head in an unmistakable manner.[7]

The most inhuman disciplinary infliction was 'running the gauntlet', a penalty seldom applied in other European armies but regularly encountered in Russia, and sometimes for comparatively trivial offences, like appearing late on parade for the third time or holding one's weapon incorrectly for the second time. This was a particularly ghoulish example of 'mutual responsibility', since the soldier was beaten by his own comrades, who could expect to be punished themselves if they were insufficiently zealous.[8]

A French count who served in the Russian army at the end of the eighteenth century remarked: 'Given its composition and the abuses which prevail in it, the Russian army ought to be the worst in Europe, but actually it is one of the best.'[9] Certainly it emerged victorious from most of its campaigns from the early eighteenth century through to the eve of the Crimean War, and it was the main mover of the expansion of empire during this period, including the conquest of the Baltic and Black Sea coasts, the invasion of the Caucasus region and the eventual victory over Napoleonic France. How can one explain these successes?

In a certain sense, they were achieved because the eighteenth-century Russian army was closer to being truly national than any other in Europe. Whereas most European armies contained large numbers of mercenaries, criminals and other misfits of society, the Russian one was recruited from among the Emperor's ordinary subjects, the peasants. Other European monarchs were beginning to rebuild their armies in the same fashion, but except for the Swedes had not advanced far by the end of the eighteenth century, mainly because of the resistance of intermediate elites who did not want the monarch to have unrivalled control of huge military forces.[10]

Even so, one could not call the Russian army a national one in the modern sense. Peasants might come from the ordinary people, but, once they were inducted into the army, the authorities totally severed them from their roots. Though regiments were often quartered on villages and small towns, they were usually a long way from home, their presence was borne grudgingly by the local inhabitants, and in general the circumstances of their sojourn did not conduce to good relations with the civilian population.

Service was for life, or from 1793 for twenty-five years, which came to the same thing: leave was almost unknown, and after a quarter of a century, a returning veteran was unlikely to encounter anyone who would recognize him, nor had he any residual property rights in his home village. This fact was acknowledged in the ceremony which customarily marked the departure of a recruit: he would be accompanied by his relatives and fellow villagers 'with tears, lamentations and songs, as if it were his funeral, the purport of which is that they shall never see him more'.[11] Those who did survive their military term often remained in service with their commanding officer, as a coachman or domestic servant, or would look for a similar job in a town. Some became schoolteachers, since the literacy rate was considerably higher in the army than elsewhere.

However, as William Fuller has put it, 'If induction was a kind of death, it was also a kind of rebirth, for the new recruit now found himself a member of a regimental family'.[12] The deprivations of army life more or less compelled him to reproduce village society in a different form under the colours. The regiment was not only a military entity, but also an economic one. For all Peter's efforts, as a result of underfunding it still embodied a partnership between the state and private enterprise, with the colonel as the entrepreneur. Much of the provisioning, clothing and arming of the men was contracted out to him, with the result that he played a role analogous to that of the *pomeshchik* in the village.

In peacetime the basic unit in the material life of the soldier was the *artel'*, a collective usually comprising a platoon of perhaps twenty or thirty men, run by a non-commissioned officer elected by them, the *artel'shchik*. It received revenue from the commanding officer and supplemented it with part of the soldiers' pay, the proceeds of plunder and other material assets belonging to the men, and it used these various resources to make up for the deficiencies of the state supply system by buying food, extra clothing and transport. As a contemporary observer remarked, 'The low pay of the ordinary soldiers makes it vital for them to stretch their imagination and make themselves self-sufficient in every respect. They become their own bakers, brewers, butchers, tailors, cobblers, perruquiers, locksmiths, wheelwrights, saddlers, blacksmiths, carpenters, masons, coppersmiths, musicians and painters – in other words, any occupation which comes to mind. Nowhere in the world are there people who are so resourceful.'[13]

This versatility went so far that in peacetime the *artel'shchik* would sometimes arrange for his charges to be hired out for remunerative labour at times when they were not required for parades or manoeuvres. In Saratov one enterprising colonel ran a funeral business, employing the men and horses in his unit. 'The regimental horses pulled the hearse; the pall-bearers were private soldiers dressed in mourning clothes, moving at a dignified, measured tread; and out in front marched a reserve corporal in braid, with baton aloft.' Even the prestigious Guards regiments sometimes had to stoop to such contrivances: in 1826 the Preobrazhenskii Regiment was reported to be operating three market gardens, three shops and a bath-house.[14]

Like the village commune, which it resembled in structure, the military *artel'* arose from the requirement to bear the excessive burdens which the state imposed on its subjects. It took over functions which in other armies are normally performed by NCOs or the quartermaster's office. Created out of necessity, it nevertheless generated its own internal cohesion and mutual solidarity among the men who made it up. Perhaps here we have a key to understanding the relative effectiveness of the Russian army. As John Keegan and Richard Holmes have shown, a vital factor in creating high morale in combat is a sense of being bound by strong ties to one's fellow soldiers, especially when it is backed by good leadership and strict discipline.[15] Improvisation in adversity is another valuable resource in wartime. The Russian army, inadvertently rather than deliberately, fostered both these assets.

However, there was more than small-group solidarity to the relatively high morale of the Russian army. Peter and his successors consciously promoted a strong sense of imperial corporate pride among the soldiers. His was the first European army in which all the men wore uniforms, even if they had to stitch them together themselves. Their regiments bore regional names, so that the identification of a soldier with his homeland would be maintained, even if he had permanently left it. After victorious battles or valorous feats of arms, whole regiments would receive silver medals in recognition of their achievement: Peter I began this custom at a time when the decoration of private soldiers was almost unknown in the rest of Europe.[16]

Service in the army, then, though terribly harsh, was at least one sphere where serfs might begin to feel themselves citizens, members of a kind of national community, with their own pride and dignity. For one thing, on induction they were automatically freed from serfdom (which was one reason why their later return to the village was unwanted). They had their own modest property rights in the *artel'*. Officers, unlike serf-owners, could not maltreat them wholly without restraint: military courts sometimes proceeded against gross abuses of power, and even occasionally offered redress to private soldiers, something of which no serf could dream.[17] Besides, there was always the hope of promotion, to NCO or even (though it seldom happened) officer status.

A good commander could make use of the distinctive features of the Russian army. Probably the best of them was Field Marshal Alexander Suvorov, who over a period of more than thirty years at the end of the eighteenth century is credited with never having lost a battle, whether against the Poles, the Turks or the French. He realized that, given clear leadership and strong discipline, the average regiment was more cohesive than most of its adversaries. He used this to initiate bolder manoeuvres than most of his contemporaries thought advisable: forced night marches, sudden and unexpected assaults. This is how he was able to storm two Ottoman fortresses, Ochakov (1788) and Izmail (1790), both considered virtually impregnable. He also let his troops live off the land, knowing that their artels would not permit them to desert or to drift into gross indiscipline. In some of these features he anticipated Bonaparte, who was able to exploit similar high morale in the post-revolutionary French armies.

Small, wiry and of eccentric behaviour, Suvorov did not get on well with his superiors, but he attributed great importance to maintaining close contact with his troops. To the horror of his officers, he would suddenly turn up uninvited at a regimental bivouac to share a meal and discuss how the battle had gone, and whether the men were satisfied with their food, clothing and equipment. He also knew how to use religious ceremonial to bridge the gap between officers and men. Despite being a stern disciplinarian (or perhaps because of it) he knew as few officers did how to awaken the trust of his men.

Successful officers, then, were the ones who recognized and fostered this potential for conscious solidarity among their men. Even those who inflicted brutal discipline might be able to arouse passionate loyalty among their men, though the social distance between officers and men remained considerable. Religious ritual was especially important for cultivating such loyalty, since it was an area where there was a meeting between the culture of the men and that of many officers, as well as a consolation for the terrifying and unpredictable contingencies of battle. One observer reported that after the battle of Zurich in 1799 'there was hardly one of the mortally wounded Russians who had not clutched at the image of the patron saint which he wore about his neck, and pressed it to his lips before drawing his last breath'.[18]

In effect, the army became the principal social base for an imperial Russian consciousness which was weak or absent in the village. That is undoubtedly why so many Tsars felt themselves at home in the army more than anywhere else in their realm, and why the army became an obsession with them.

In the nineteenth century the army faced new challenges, which it was less well equipped to meet. From Napoleon onwards, other European armies began to practise mass conscription, becoming *la nation en armes*, citizen armies, in a way which freed Russian serfs could not emulate. Technology was becoming more sophisticated, and other nations were developing their industries, their railway and steamship communications. By the Crimean War, Russian soldiers were still equipped with flintlock muskets which had a range of 200 yards, while British and French troops fired rifles which could hit at up to 1000 yards.[19]

With the new technology came the need for a higher level of education and training, not just for officers, but for NCOs and even men. In the eighteenth century it had hardly mattered that senior military appointments were decided by court patronage, but by the second half of the nineteenth century, commanders needed a high level of professionalism to cope with the complex demands of their job. With the more scattered deployment of modern infantry, even ordinary soldiers needed to take personal initiative and to have some vision of what was happening on the battlefield as a whole. Compact, well-drilled formations, loved by all the Tsars from Paul to Nicholas II, became more a reassuring display than a guarantee of battlefield efficiency.

Perhaps the greatest disadvantage of the army, though, was its enormous expense. Since serving men were not discharged till they were too old for further fighting, reserves were almost non-existent and had to be hurriedly improvised at times of emergency. Raising volunteers was dangerous, for it aroused expectations which could not be met, as we have seen in the Napoleonic war. Consequently the peacetime army had to be almost as large as that with which Russia needed to go to war. In the worst years of the eighteenth century, military needs consumed some 60–70% of the entire state expenditure (in so far as this can be accurately calculated in the absence of a consolidated budget), while during and after the Napoleonic war it was still in the region of 50–60%.[20]

To lessen the expense of this permanent military establishment and also to make the provisioning of the army easier, Alexander I experimented with a way of making part of the army self-supporting. He set up so-called 'military settlements' [see Part 2, Chapter 4], an idea which grew into a major project in social engineering. The first settlement was instituted in Mogilev guberniia shortly before the Napoleonic invasion, and the experiment was resumed on a much wider scale thereafter. Alexander's aim was 'to cover Russia with a veritable network of . . . villages which the army would make as neat, orderly and elegant as the estate of Arakcheev'. It was one of the visions of order through which he hoped to get a grip on the chaotic reality of Russia. But it was not only neatness which attracted him. More important, units stationed in the settlements would become mutually self-supporting, easing the burden on the treasury and relieving the population of the unpopular duty of quartering soldiers. This kind of mixed agricultural-military establishment was not new to Russia: it had been normal on the southern steppe frontier and in parts of Siberia for most of the seventeenth and eighteenth centuries.

However, the settlements Alexander had in mind were to be much more consciously innovatory, as befitted the active secular state. Regiments chosen for them were to be assigned personally to the Emperor, who placed them under the command of Arakcheev. All married soldiers with six or more years of service formed a 'settled battalion': they received land, livestock and tools in permanent tenure so that they could perform the agricultural labour necessary to feed and support the 'active battalions'. Soldiers in the latter would spend a good deal of time on manoeuvres, and they would be permanently ready for dispatch to the front if there was danger of war; otherwise they were to be quartered alongside the 'settled' men and help them with their work. Wives were allowed to live in the colonies, and it was intended that their male children, known as 'cantonists', should receive special military training and become soldiers themselves. This would relieve the ordinary peasant population of some of the burden of the *rekrutchina* and perhaps in time replace it altogether.

Alexander's aims went even further than military reform. He hoped that the settlements would take the lead in trying out and assimilating modern agricultural practices and social welfare schemes, which could later be disseminated elsewhere. He was trying in his own way to reintegrate the army into village society and the peasant into Imperial Russia by providing the basis both for a citizen army and a property-owning class of smallholders. As one historian has commented, 'if soldiers became farmers and farmers became soldiers, might not Russia's social and geopolitical problems be solved at a stroke?'[21]

Each settlement was laid out to a standard formula. It consisted of sixty-four square wooden buildings painted in identical colours and arranged in eight symmetrical rows, with the company office, the chapel and the fire station in the middle. New varieties of seed and crop rotation were introduced, to increase output. Social provisions were far in advance of their time. There were primary schools for all children, male and female, between the ages of seven and twelve, and for adult illiterates, hospitals with maternity wards, bathhouses and 'English latrines'. The administrative arrangements were also enlightened, at least on paper: each company had its own committee, with elected delegates of the soldiers, who were also represented on the disciplinary courts. Foreigners who visited the settlements were impressed by their external appearance and social arrangements.[22]

Yet the settlements were a disastrous failure. Fundamentally this was due to the incongruity of introducing the 'Protestant ethic' in rural Russia or, if you like, of mixing the 'imperial peasantry', the soldiers, with the ordinary peasants. As Barclay de Tolly warned as early as 1817, 'It is well known that farming can only be carried on successfully and will only produce results when peasants are given complete freedom to organise their farming as they think best.' As for soldiers: 'Maybe in time they will learn to ... turn their hands from the gun to the plough or the sickle; but then their martial spirit must be expected to disappear completely, and the good soldier will be transformed into an indifferent or poor farmer.'[23] The army functioned tolerably well as long as it was strictly segregated from village society, but the attempt to fuse the two generated an explosion.

Overbearing and unimaginative administration aggravated the situation. Roads and buildings had to be constructed by the settlers themselves, which meant that they began their experience of their new life as conscript labourers. The officers were not specially trained for the delicate combination of economic and military functions they were expected to supervise, and, knowing that their careers depended on demonstrable results, they tended to make excessive demands on their charges. Neither they nor Arakcheev had the managerial flexibility or respect for their men which would have been required to give the settlements some chance of settling down to their novel amalgam of roles. Discipline, as in the army proper, was petty, harsh and arbitrary.

From the first, soldiers found life in the settlements abhorrent. In 1817 on the Bug there was unrest among Cossacks who believed that their rights were being violated, while in Novgorod guberniia Old Believer conscripts refused to have their beards shaved. In 1819, near Khar'kov, soldiers from the 'settled battalion' refused to reap hay for their unit's horses when they needed to work on their own plots of land. In the subsequent disorders they burned down three buildings and murdered an NCO who declined to join them. Arakcheev came down personally to take charge of restoring order, and ordered that 52 men should run the gauntlet up to twelve times: 25 of them died from the ordeal.[24]

The worst unrest took place in Novgorod guberniia in 1831, during the cholera epidemic of that year. Special hygienic precautions were taken, including the fumigation of buildings and the purification of wells, but the men interpreted these operations as the *cause* of the disease, and went on the rampage, seizing doctors and officers. They hauled them before kangaroo courts, accused them of murder and then lynched them. They took nearly two hundred lives before a punitive expedition arrived to restore order, which it did by executing more than a hundred soldiers. Nikolai Turgenev compared this massacre with Peter I's bloodbath among the *strel'tsy* in 1698.[25] There could, at any rate, be no clearer example of the clash between the rational secular state and the superstitions of the mass of the people.

The military settlements were incapable of bringing about a meeting between imperial and popular Russia.

Up till the mid-nineteenth century it was still possible for the Russian army to function more or less adequately on the basis of what an agrarian society could produce when bolstered by good ordnance and textile factories. The Crimean War provided the first clear warning that this was ceasing to be the case. The army proved unable to defend a fortified base in its own homeland against troops despatched from thousands of miles away. It was huge, with 1.8 million regulars, plus 171,000 reserves and 370,000 militia, but the state could not afford to finance it, and as a result troops were poorly trained, equipped with out-of-date flintlock muskets, and inadequately provided with food, clothes and medical equipment.

Besides, only a small proportion of this immense host could be brought to bear on the crucial Crimean theatre, since so many soldiers were needed to man other regions of the empire, where external invasion or internal unrest was feared. Only 100,000 or so could be mustered for the defence of Sevastopol' itself, where the outcome of the war was decided. It became clear that defending an empire of such size, diversity and potential restlessness was not possible with the army in its present condition.[26]

The army's training and leadership were also revealed as deficient. The troops fought effectively where they were well led and had a simple and obvious function. The old advantages of group morale still paid off in these situations: the Russian infantry's massed bayonet charges were celebrated, as was their grim tenacity in defence. But in circumstances which were more complicated, which required initiative or flexibility, they were markedly weaker: the great failing here was among their junior officers and NCOs, who were of low quality, poorly educated and trained. Their senior commanders, too – like their leader for much of the campaign, Prince Aleksandr Menshikov – tended to value will-power, bravery and ostentatious display on the parade ground above detailed study of the strategic situation and consultation with their officers. Their mentality was the natural product of an appointment system which relied on court patronage more than professionalism, and in which General Staff officers were regarded with suspicion, after the Decembrist revolt, as too clever by half.[27]

After the Crimean War, the government tried to find a wholly different way of providing for a large army in times of emergency without being committed to a huge and expensive peacetime establishment. This was by creating a national army in the more modern sense current in Europe ever since the French revolution: by the universal conscription of young adult males, not for life, but for a relatively short period of service with the colours, followed by a longer period in the reserve. Under the law of 1874, introduced by the War Minister, Dmitrii Miliutin, all able-bodied young men were liable to active service for up to six years (four if they had completed primary education, two for secondary education, and a mere six months for higher education), followed by nine in the reserve.

By that time serfdom had been abolished, and there was therefore no question of freed peasants coming back from the army to settle among their enserfed colleagues. The way was open for a greater mingling of the different social classes, and the army was to become in that respect something of a melting pot. Miliutin would have liked to see it become the crucible for the formation of a Russian nationhood comparable to that of other European powers of the time, while Minister of the Interior Valuev remarked, under the influence of the Prussian victories of 1864–71, 'Military service is a form of national elementary education. The habit of military order, the concept of military discipline are not lost when active service ends.'[28]

Miliutin reorganized the system of military education so as to increase the professionalism of officers and to make it far easier for non-nobles to gain promotion to officer status. He abolished the Cadet Corps (though the Corps of Pages remained in being), replacing them with military colleges (*voennye uchilishcha*), offering a more general secondary education. He also introduced new 'iunker schools' specifically designed to offer the kind of education and training needed by non-noble aspirants to a commission. There was, then, still a two-track military education system, one for elite entrants and leading to the Guards, another for more humble entrants (many of them also nobles) and leading to ordinary regiments. But the overall level of education had been raised and the way smoothed for the gradual creation of a meritocratic officer corps.[29]

However, it did not prove so simple to dismantle the privileges of the higher landowning nobility, especially in the army, which they regarded as peculiarly their domain. The domination of the court over senior military appointments, though weakened by the increased powers of the Ministry of War, was also far from being ended. Grand Dukes joined Guards regiments as children, grew up in the company of their officers, and identified very closely with them. Under Alexander III the Cadet Corps were restored, and with them duelling and aristocratic 'courts of honour' were once again accepted.

The officer-corps became a multi-layered cake: at the top were senior officers often in their sixties or seventies, of little or no military training but beneficiaries of court patronage. In the middle there were the graduates of the Cadet Corps, of noble origin and reasonably well-trained, spiced with a dash of General Staff graduates, contemptuously known as 'pheasants'. Then, usually in the lower ranks, there were the non-nobles and landless nobles, graduates of the iunker schools, sometimes quite professional in outlook, but looked down upon by their social superiors.[30]

John Bushnell and Bruce Menning have shown how, despite better organization, the Russian army failed to do itself justice in the Turkish war of 1877–8, partly because of inadequacies in the senior command, and partly because of insufficient training still caused by underfunding which meant that men spent far too much time on economic activities. Much the same applied to the Japanese war of 1904–5.[31]

Despite a programme of barrack-building, by the end of the nineteenth century men were still inadequately housed, and the regimental economy still bore a penurious and makeshift character. In 1899, General Dragomirov, commander of the Kiev Military District, noted in his annual report that after the summer manoeuvres, 'the other ranks disperse to the meadows, forests, railway lines and building sites, they disfigure their uniforms, take on a wholly inappropriate external appearance, become unaccustomed to discipline and lose their military bearing'.[32] He at any rate was conscious of the 'Chonkin syndrome', of the danger of soldiers simply merging back into their peasant background.

That danger was real, as was shown by the events of 1905–6. In his excellent study of mutinies during this period, John Bushnell has shown how soldiers went through alternate bouts of suppressing urban unrest, joining it and then suppressing it again. In both kinds of behaviour, he hypothesizes, soldiers were behaving like peasants; suspicious of town-dwellers, but also of their own authorities, joining the revolution when the regime seemed mortally weakened but otherwise obeying orders. 'The soldiers' revolution of 1905–6', he concludes, 'was a special case of peasant rebellion.'[33]

As for 1917, the soldier-peasant alliance in that year was perhaps the vital force which brought down the Provisional Government and made possible a Bolshevik regime. Miliutin had already narrowed the chasm which separated soldiers and peasants, and the massive inductions of World War One eliminated it completely. An army which had long been partly run by artels took naturally to the elected 'soldiers' committees' mandated by the soviets. Peasant society, with its improvised *skhody*, invaded and reclaimed the army altogether.

3

The Peasantry

In the situation of the peasants, and especially of the Russian peasants, the paradox of this overbearing yet vulnerable empire was made manifest. The peasants were its mainstay: they provided its food, its troops and most of its taxes. It was to supply the service nobility with the means of existence, to furnish recruits for the army and to ensure the payment of taxes that peasants were attached to the soil and bound to each other by 'mutual responsibility'. As Prince Menshikov said in a report of 1727, 'The army is so necessary that without it the state cannot stand, and for its sake we must take care of the peasants; for the soldier is bound to the peasant, like the soul to the body, and if there is no peasant, then there will be no soldier.'[1]

For all that, the authorities were not generous in their 'care of the peasant'. For the most part peasants had to look after themselves as well as prop up the state. The self-governing communities in which they lived had their origin in Kievan *Rus'*, and the term *mir* was used to describe them in *Russkaia pravda*, its first law code. The custom of 'mutual responsibility' provided that the community as a whole was responsible for the discharge of dues and taxes: if one household fell short on its contribution, the others were expected to make up the difference. That usage was strengthened under Mongol overlordship, and became universal during the fifteenth to seventeenth centuries, when the Grand Princes were transferring previously 'black' lands – owned by the state or by nobody – to service nobles, and was juridically fixed in the Law Code (*Ulozhenie*) of 1649, as a convenient way for landlords and the state to ensure that dues were paid promptly and in full.[2]

The agrarian order based on serfdom and the village commune

was developing during the sixteenth century and was in place in its essentials by the mid-seventeenth century. Most of its features proved extremely durable and survived even the abolition of serfdom in 1861. The forests of the north and the open steppes of the south and east made flight relatively easy for the peasants, so that elaborate state regulation was needed to ensure that they would stay in one place, cultivate the soil and render their dues. In 1580 the practice of allowing a household to quit and move on elsewhere around St George's Day (in late November, when the annual agricultural cycle reached its natural close) was suspended and finally abolished in 1603. Land cadasters taken in 1581 and 1592 established where a peasant's legal residence was, and could be used for reclaiming and returning him if he moved on illegally. At first a statute of limitations operated, so that after a period of years, which varied, a fugitive became a free man. However, the Law Code of 1649 removed even this last fragile immunity: thereafter a peasant was fixed for life to a certain plot of land, and so were his descendants. In practice, too, if a private rather than a 'black' or state peasant, he was bound to the person of the landlord, who had full police and judicial powers over him, as well as answering for his payment of taxes and other dues. Since most of the Tsars readily used grants of land to reward favourites or servitors who had distinguished themselves, this personal bondage became the lot of an increasing number of peasants. By 1811 serfs constituted 58% of the total male population of Russia, though it fell back thereafter, reaching 45% by 1858, on the eve of emancipation.[3]

The greatest concentration of private serfs was in the heartlands of the old Muscovite principality, and to the west and south of it, areas where conquest had brought the Tsars land they could award to favoured servitors. By contrast, in the north and east private serfdom was much less common, and in Siberia it was unknown. Serfs paid their dues in two alternative forms, as we have seen: *barshchina* or *obrok*. The former was commoner in the southern black-earth and steppe regions, for here the fertility of the soil made arable cultivation or specialist agriculture, such as wine-growing, profitable, with the result that working hands were at a premium, especially when some lords began during the nineteenth century to introduce improved scientific farming methods. In the area around Moscow, on the other hand, and to the north and east of it, the soil was much poorer. Peasants there could often not rely wholly on agricultural income, but would practise some form of cottage industry or would go off, with permission of the lord, to work in factories, mines or river transport, handing over part of their income to the lord.

A visiting Englishman, William Richardson, wrote in 1784 that 'the peasants in Russia ... are in a state of abject slavery, and are reckoned the property of the nobles to whom they belong, as much as their horses or dogs'.[4] Indeed, by the mid-eighteenth century it was normal for serfs to be sold at market, sometimes separately from their families, for all the world like slaves, and the unpunished cruelty with which the lords sometimes treated them was reminiscent of Caribbean plantations at their worst.

All the same, the comparison is not completely apt, and the differences between serfdom and slavery remained crucial. Serfs were liable to taxation and military service: not benefits, to be sure, but not characteristic of slavery either. Above all, the serfs were profoundly convinced that, whatever landlord or government might do, the land belonged to them. If it ever came to a frank exchange of views on this subject, the standard peasant refrain was 'We are yours, but the land is ours' – or alternatively 'the land is God's'. Historically, of course, they were right: they had been there first. Even from the classical liberal point of view they had a strong case, having fulfilled in relation to the land Locke's essential condition for a property-owner: 'Whatsoever he removes out of the state that Nature hath provided and left it in, he hath mixed his labour with it, and joined to it something that is his own, and thereby makes it his property.'[5] As an embodiment of this basic conviction, the peasants had their own self-governing institutions, and ran their own economy: as we have seen, most landowners were not anxious to concern themselves directly with agricultural management, and were content to leave the matter to a steward who would usually try to reach a *modus vivendi* with the village commune and its elder.

The fact was that, historically speaking, the landlord was a new-comer, and it was most convenient for him to accommodate himself to the existing agrarian practices of the peasants. This he would usually do, unless he had strong ideas about agrarian improvement, and the determination to put them into practice. Besides, in spite of the obvious clashes of interest between lord and peasants, they had one overwhelming interest in common: the stability and prosperity of the village's life. Poverty and instability endangered the landlord, and ultimately the state, almost as much as they did the peasants.

Usually, then, it was possible for manor and village community to reach a working agreement about how to conduct affairs, and how to discharge dues. It was important to both sides that each household could grow enough produce or in other ways raise enough income to feed itself and to discharge its share of the community's obligations. This basic imperative underlay the complex network of customs and norms which evolved in the village, naturally with variants from region to region.

To ensure survival in a harsh climate and on infertile soils, the overall strategy of the peasant community was to minimize risk by spreading it as widely as possible. This was the rationale of the strip system of land tenure, together with the three-field system of crop rotation, which was very widely practised. They ensured that each household had a share in land of different types, near and far away, dry and marshy, fertile and less fertile, and access to different kinds of cultivation. 'Mutual responsibility' had the same function: it not only suited the landlord, but also ensured minimal subsistence for each household, even in times of difficulty. In fact, the habit of 'mutual responsibility' spread to all aspects of peasant life, colouring their outlook on law, property and authority: it rendered more or less imperative the practice of equality, mutual aid and the taking of decisions in common, which became the distinctive characteristics of peasant political and economic life.

These principles were embodied in the village assembly, the *skhod*, as it was usually known. It consisted of all heads of households, customarily the oldest male in each – though it might be a younger man if the oldest was infirm. Very seldom was the head of household a woman. The assembly was responsible for apportioning the burden of taxes and dues, regulating land tenure and managing common land (pasture, woods etc), deciding the crop rotation, maintaining communal facilities (roads, bridges, church buildings, stores and so on) and supervising law and order. For the day-to-day discharge of these duties the *skhod* would elect from among its own members an 'elder' (*starosta* or *burmistr*), who assumed the unenviable multiple role of representing the village to the outside world, working with the steward to ensure that the landlord's commands were carried out, and acting as the (unpaid or very poorly-paid) lowest-level official of the state in matters of law and order, taxation and recruitment.[6]

The *starosta* was also responsible for chairing the meetings of the assembly, which would usually be held in a large peasant hut, in the church porch, or even in the open air. Anything from a dozen to several hundred people might be present, and there was no set procedure, so that the conduct of affairs could be chaotic and decisions fortuitous. Often opinion would swing towards those who spoke loudest, or who were most adroit in catching the chairman's eye. In these circumstances, the older, wealthier or more experienced members inevitably tended to exercise a predominant influence. In principle, this was direct democracy, but in practice functioned as an oligarchy, in which tradition, seniority and wealth bore the decisive weight.[7]

Not surprisingly, many village elders were ambivalent about their tricky job. 'Some elders considered their post almost as a punishment, and would offer vodka to persuade people to leave them in peace [i.e. not to vote for them]. Others, on the contrary, would actively solicit the post, which would make them a boss of a sort, and they would celebrate their election with a round of vodka. Some villages would elect someone with tax arrears, so that his salary would cover the debt.'[8]

In many parts of Russia, though not all, the *skhod* would maintain the material equality of households through the periodic redistribution of the community's main resource, which in most regions was its arable land, though in the far north it might be fishing rights or the right to fell timber. The aim of this procedure was to ensure that each household had enough for subsistence and for the discharge of its obligations. Since all households went through cycles of growth and decline caused by births, marriages, deaths and prolonged sickness – old people would fall ill or die, daughters would marry out of the family, sons would demand their own plot – most people saw some benefit in repeating the process of redistribution every so often, whether as partial adjustments or wholesale rearrangements, to reflect these changes. The commonest criterion for allotting land was the amount of labour power at the disposal of each household, measured in a unit known as the *tiaglo*, which was usually reckoned to be that of an able-bodied married couple between the ages of eighteen and sixty. In some places, however, a consumption norm was applied, based on the number of 'eaters' (*edoki*), or mouths, that had to be fed. The amount of land held by a household then determined its share of the burden of dues borne by the whole village.[9]

Some degree of equality was also maintained within each household. At the death of its head, land was divided up equally among all the male heirs, while in the central Russian provinces a widow usually had a right to a portion of between 1/7 and 1/10 of the holding. This meant that there was a long-term tendency to the fragmentation of holdings and their consequent diminution, a process which led to bitter conflicts and recriminations within families.[10]

These arrangements did not prevent individual state peasants (or private ones after the emancipation) buying or leasing land in addition to their communal allotment and using it to build up a relative degree of wealth, either as agricultural producers, or as publicans, moneylenders or operators of the state liquor monopoly. Such peasants might be successful enough to become independent entrepreneurs, to all intents and purposes outside the commune's economic provisions. These were the *kulaki* (fists) or *miroedy* (commune-eaters) of village demonology.

Because of the relative infertility of the soil, peasants in some regions of Russia had to supplement their income by work outside the village. When they did so, they commonly formed associations analogous to the village commune. These went under a variety of names, though the most common by the nineteenth century 'was the *artel*'. The Populist Stepniak called the artel a 'free union of people, who combine for the mutual advantages of cooperation in labour, or consumption, or both', while the Brockhaus and Efron encyclopedia defines it more soberly as 'a contractual association of several equal persons, usually from the lower classes of the population, who together are pursuing economic aims, are joined by mutual responsibility, and who contribute to the common activity either labour, or labour and capital'.[11] The nineteenth-century German economist Georg Staehr, who investigated the phenomenon, came to the conclusion that the artel was 'modelled on the archaic family or family association' and that it 'consists of individuals who belong to various different families, and are temporarily separated from them, and it lasts for the duration of that separation'.[12] If one ignores the word 'temporary', that explanation helps one to understand the army artel (see previous chapter).

Artels generally fell into one of two types. Firstly, there were those in which workers hired themselves out together to an employer, who would furnish premises, raw materials, and perhaps tools and equipment, paying them a common wage, which they would divide among themselves. Secondly, there were those in which the artel itself provided these prerequisites of production and concluded a contract with a customer. Procedures in the latter case were naturally more complicated and fully developed.

The artel would be established by written or oral contract, with each member's initial contribution and his share in the revenues minutely stipulated, and a *starosta* would be elected. This arrangement was normally concluded in front of an icon, to emphasize the solemnity of the mutual undertakings. A similar procedure was followed in the reception of new members – a fateful occasion, since the artel was liable as a whole for the poor work or misdeeds of any of its members, and an ill-advised admission could spell disaster for the whole collective.

A typical artel would contain between half a dozen and twenty members. Its general assembly, like the village *skhod*, enjoyed ultimate sovereignty within the community, and would take fundamental decisions, such as those about new members. For everyday purposes, however, power was entrusted to the *starosta* (alternatively known as *artel'shchik*, *desiatnik* or *ataman* – the last an interesting usage, since it derives from Cossack terminology): he had responsibility for securing contracts, ensuring good work discipline and behaviour, planning the details of the work organization and assigning individuals to particular jobs. He also received the wages or revenues, and distributed them to the members, again usually before the icon. In some artels a weekly or even daily meeting of the members would help him with these tasks, and would confirm punishments.

The artels of *burlaki*, or barge-haulers, on the Volga have become well-known, since one of their songs descended to posterity. These would usually be formed and hired out at a 'burlak market' in one of the Volga port towns, to where individuals or groups would go in search of work. Thus, for example, in 1856, a burlak artel signed a contract with a Rybinsk *meshchanin* Ivan Fedorovich Shchapleevskii to take his sailing boat down to the village of Balakovo, load it up with grain, transport it back to Rybinsk and unload it. The work was to be accomplished as fast as possible, 'so that the boat does not stand idle or suffer delay through the laziness, lack of zeal or drunkenness of any of us, especially when there is a favourable wind'. For this service, the *burlaki* were to be paid according to a scale laid down in the local shipping office, plus fifteen silver kopecks a day for board. Detailed instructions were given in case the boat went aground. Each member of the artel was to watch that his colleagues did not shirk, simulate illness or abscond, for if they did, the owner was to have the right to leave them all unpaid and hire a new artel. The owner kept the passports of the members and returned them only with the final payment, once the job was completed.[13]

Other occupations where the artel form of organization was common were construction work, fishing, logging, stevedoring and any form of rural industry which could not be accommodated within the ordinary peasant hut but required outlay on special premises. When peasants went into town to seek industrial work, an artel often tided them over the early difficult period of looking for a dwelling and a job. They would club together to rent rooms, to buy food and fuel, and in some cases would pay a cook to prepare their meals. If they came from the same village or uezd such an artel would be known as a *zemliachestvo*, an 'association of the land': later immigrants from the same area could then join them. When the young Semen Kanatchikov was brought by his father from the Volokolamsk region to Moscow, he joined just such a group. 'We rented the apartment communally, an artel of about fifteen men. Some were bachelors, others had wives who lived in the village and ran their households ... Our food and the woman who prepared it were also paid for communally. The food was purchased on credit at a shop; our individual shares were assessed twice monthly.'[14]

The artel, then, had the same function as the *mir*: in the absence of a secure legal basis for contracts, to provide a framework for collective economic activity, and at the same time to spread the risks and share the difficulties of such activity. It could be a self-reliant and democratic group of workmen controlling their own economic lives for mutual benefit; but it might also be a subordinate and internally hierarchical unit in an authoritarian environment. It could even be both at the same time, in which it rather resembled the *mir*. It mixed economic and moral, democratic and authoritarian characteristics.

Now, communal arrangements of the *mir* and artel types had been common in many parts of western Europe in the middle ages, but were in decline by the fifteenth or sixteenth centuries, along with serfdom.[15] In Russia, however, the modernizing absolutist state perpetuated and strengthened both serfdom and the archaic, introverted village community. This paradox is a key to understanding Russia's failure to move very far towards nationhood in the eighteenth and nineteenth centuries. It radicalized the distinction between peasants and the rest of society, confining the majority of the population in what might be called the rural ghetto. In the heartlands of the empire, at least, nobles and peasants were both Russian, but they looked different, they dressed differently, talked a different language, belonged to different worlds of politics, custom and tradition.

In his *Gulag Archipelago*, Solzhenitsyn called the *zeki*, the inmates of the Soviet prisons and labour camps, a separate nation, with its own distinctive ethnic characteristics. The same could be said of the Russian peasants in the eighteenth and nineteenth centuries. Nobles lived in a world defined for them by a cosmopolitan culture, the habit of command, bureaucratic or military service, the hierarchical Table of Ranks and by competition for posts and honours. The peasants, on the contrary, inhabited an egalitarian universe, whose culture was parochial, whose decision-making was done in common, and where the paramount priority was survival. The mentalities generated by these very different life-situations were often not mutually comprehensible: hence the gulf of which most rural nobles were uneasily aware.

'Mutual responsibility' came into its own at times of emergency. If one household suffered a major misfortune – a fire, a serious illness, the death of an able-bodied member – then other households were expected to do what they could to help the victims. This custom, known as *pomochi* or *toloka*, should not necessarily be interpreted as altruism: a household would offer aid to a neighbour partly in order to minimize the payment of extra dues to cover arrears, partly in the hope of receiving reciprocal benefits one day in case of need. Who knew, for as peasants would say: 'The Lord giveth and the Lord taketh away'? The beneficiaries of *pomochi* would if possible offer vodka to those who had rallied round them, so that the work might be rounded off with a bout of celebration: drinking, singing and dancing. But if they were too poor to be able to offer hospitality, it was accepted that the help should be given anyway, free of obligation.[16]

Such arrangements might even include a favoured landowner. A.N. Engel'gardt, a professor of chemistry who gave up his chair to become a landlord in Smolensk guberniia in the 1870s, was actually offered *pomochi* by the peasants who had formerly been serfs on the estate. His dam had been breached in a sudden flood, and to his surprise the peasants offered to repair it free of charge. The rationale they put to him was exactly that which they applied to their own kind. The breach was 'an act of God, so of course one must help in a neighbourly fashion . . . If you hire repair workers for money, that means you don't want to live as a good neighbour (*po-sosedski*), but want to do everything for money, like the Germans. Today your dam needs mending, so you pay us. Tomorrow we need something, so we pay you. No – better to live as good neighbours.'[17]

Mutual aid, then, was motivated partly by good-neighbourliness, partly by the desire to get by with a minimum of cash in a still largely non-monetarized economy, where the use of money was felt to be a foreign (German) custom. For that reason *pomochi* was also quite widely practised to get through the difficult times of year, like haymaking and harvesting, when labour demands taxed the resources of most households to the utmost. Again, such common labour might well be celebrated with songs, dancing and drinking.

Mutual dependence was at its most marked in the lean time of year, the spring, when the previous year's harvest was exhausted and the poorer families had nothing to fall back on. Then they would wander round the huts of their more fortunate neighbours in a silent search for help. This kind of dependence aroused shame, but it was generally acknowledged that help must be offered when needed. 'A person begging for pieces of bread is embarrassed to ask for it directly. He will go into the hut, stand silently on the threshold, crossing himself and muttering, as if to himself, "Please, for the sake of Christ". No one takes any notice of the visitor: they all go about their business as usual, talking and laughing, as if no one had come in. But the housewife will go to the table, take a small piece of bread, between three and eight square inches, and hand it over. The visitor crosses himself and leaves.'[18]

Whether welcomed, shamefacedly acknowledged or resented, mutual responsibility had entered the peasants' blood. For many, it was a stifling form of intimacy, which probably explains why so many young men were anxious to get out of the village, and later looked back on it with repugnance. The affairs of each family, of each individual, were open to everyone to discuss, were in effect common property as much as the grazing land, and offered ample scope for gossip, benevolent or otherwise. Talented or unusual people, or simply eccentrics, could find the atmosphere claustrophobic. So too could young people, especially women, in a collective where the tone was set by older males. Permanently poor peasants were despised, while wealthy ones could easily become the object of suspicion and resentment, unless they made their devotion to the common good unmistakable. Those who transgressed the norms of village life could pay for it dearly, as we can see from the community's judicial practice.

Village law was customary law. Even after the judicial reforms of 1864 introduced western-style courts for all other social estates, the peasants retained their own segregated courts, governed by distinctive principles. The guardians of the law were the older men of the village, who would convene informal court sessions as required. These were sometimes known as the 'court of the elder and people of good conscience' (*sud starosty s dobrosovestnymi*). If necessary the verdicts of these rustic magistrates could be appealed to the landlord (before 1861), or, in the case of state peasants, to volost officials; but peasants were usually reluctant to take their disputes to higher authority, preferring to settle them within the village, among their own people. This was partly a matter of not washing dirty linen in public, or 'not carrying dirt out of the hut', as peasants put it. But in any case peasants drew a clear distinction between the authorities' law (*panskii zakon* or *barskii zakon*) and God's law (*bozhii zakon*).[19] Even after the 1864 law introduced elected peasant judges at volost level, many peasants would still try to keep cases within the village, to be settled by an improvised court there, rather than go higher up.[20]

Some contemporary jurists considered peasant customary law to be no better than lawlessness.[21] It is quite true that procedures were ill-defined, and the norms guiding village judges, though rooted in tradition, were to some extent arbitrary, open to influence by the standing of the litigants, bribery or drink. All the same, certain underlying principles can be discerned in the practice of peasant courts, and naturally enough they grew out of the sense of mutual responsibility for the economic well-being of the community.

With that in mind, judges would often aim to reconcile two conflicting parties rather than observe strict neutrality between them. Compromise was preferable to an outcome, however just, which drove one household to penury. Sometimes a court would even resort to drawing lots to settle a case, rather than let a conflict fester on, setting households against one another and perhaps dividing the whole community. In the case of a minor criminal offence, peasant judges would usually sentence the accused to a flogging, which would weaken him physically for a few days, rather than to a fine or imprisonment, which might cause long-term economic harm to his household. Or they would decide a case in favour of someone with a good reputation rather than someone who was regarded as a 'shirker' or 'drunkard'.[22]

Popular legal consciousness was displayed still more unadorned when villagers took the law into their own hands, disdaining any court procedure, even their own. This kind of *samosud* took place when they feared that a court would not take the alleged offence seriously enough, or might pass a sentence which would damage the interests of the community. This could be the case with petty theft: unpunished, it could encourage further theft, but a formal punishment would weaken the guilty party's household. For that reason, the thief would often simply undergo a ritual humiliation: perhaps he would be led along the main street naked, while bystanders threw dirt at him or hit him with a stick, and others would play 'harsh music', banging on pots and pans as he went by. After the ordeal was over, the victim might be expected to stand everyone a round of vodka, as a token of reconciliation and re-admission to the community. There the matter ended. This kind of procedure served as a warning to others, and at the same time reaffirmed the solidarity of the village, without causing serious physical or economic damage to anyone.[23]

In the case of repeated or more serious offences, however, the reaction of villagers could be far harsher than the expected sentence of an official court. Unrepentant and hardened criminals were a danger to everyone, and were treated as such, being driven out of the village or even killed. Horse thieves were especially abhorred. Not all peasants could aspire to a horse, and those who could relied on it as the mainstay of their husbandry. Since they were usually among the more affluent members of the community, the loss of their horse was a blow to everyone. If a horse thief was caught, he might be lynched, a process in which every member of the village was expected to take part. In that way, if the police got wind of the affair, they could not pin responsibility for the murder on anyone in particular. This is an especially striking example of 'mutual responsibility'.[24]

If one had asked a nineteenth-century peasant what nation he belonged to, he would probably have answered by referring to his religion, 'Orthodox' (*pravoslavnyi*) or by using the adjective *russkii*. The two concepts were closely connected in the peasants' mind, and what they knew of the history of their country usually focused on the victories of the Tsars over the enemies of their faith. Thus peasants, especially in localities directly affected, had preserved the memory of Tatar devastation (though the term 'Tatar' might be used for any nomadic raiders from east or south), and of 'Lithuanian' incursions (a 'Lithuanian' being any Catholic invader). They recalled Ivan IV's triumphant campaign against the Tatars at Kazan' and Peter I's victory over the Swedes at Poltava. Even their historical misconceptions tended to reflect the connection of religion and ethnos: Peter I was said by some peasants to have lost the battle of Narva because he had 'disobeyed the Patriarch', and only to have achieved ultimate victory when had 'celebrated divine service and received the Patriarch's blessing'.[25]

The other dominant feature of peasant historical consciousness was protest against oppression and exploitation suffered at the hands of the landowners. The richest vein of historical folksongs concerned

Sten'ka Razin, who exemplified both Cossack *vol'nitsa* and the restoration of justice by murdering landowners. The sentiment that 'Razin was not dead', i.e. that *volia* might still be gained, was widespread. In similar tone, many tales of Pugachev dwelt on the hanging of nobles: 'Many lords and princes have I hanged, and many unjust people throughout Russia.' Revealingly, some accounts of Ivan's Kazan' campaign showed him anachronistically in alliance with Yermak, the Tsar's power reinforced by the appeal of Cossack *vol'nitsa*.[26] In a sense this was the peasant's 'ideal Russia' steering his historical imagination.

It cannot be said, then, that peasants had no concept of 'Russia', but their awareness of it was bound by the immediate region, the small towns and villages they inhabited, and was strongly influenced by the guiding principles of military power, religious rectitude and social equality – a Russia both strong and holy. Only in the final decades of the nineteenth century were large numbers of peasants beginning to develop a broader geographical sense, as a result of work in more distant towns or military service.[27]

Of course many Russian peasants knew about other ethnic groups, since they lived intermingled among them, or at least in neighbouring villages, in various regions of the empire. They were aware of the differences between them, but formulated them mainly in religious terms. In that sense, they conceived of their national identity as 'Orthodox' (*pravoslavnyi*). Religious identity was what in their own eyes distinguished them from other peoples of the empire. and it was what, at least on the surface, they had in common with their own elites. Yet their Orthodoxy did not necessarily resemble that of the nobles – many of whom in any case were less than lukewarm in their adherence to the faith. Some observers denied that the peasants were Christian at all, seeing them as superstitious and semi-pagan. Nowadays the notion of *dvoeverie* or 'dual faith' (pagan and Christian) is widely used to describe the beliefs of European peasants, especially in the middle ages, and we need not feel embarrassed in applying it to Russians. Right through to the late nineteenth century, most peasants had not learnt to read and write – and even if they had, there was no modern Russian Bible for them to read – nor had they undergone the Reformation process of the authorities banning their pagan rituals. The authenticity of their Christianity manifested itself in many ways: they would regularly attend divine service, take holy communion when the church allowed, would observe fasts and celebrate the sacraments for birth, marriage and death. Most peasants would cross themselves on passing a crucifix or on hearing bad news. A good many would occasionally go on pilgrimage to shrines and monasteries, or would màke a visit for confession to a *starets* (holy man). Their sayings testified to the fact that Christianity had penetrated deep into their mentality: of an unscrupulous person they would say 'there is no cross on you' (*kresta na tebe net*), or of a gentle, honest person, 'he lives according to God's will' (*zhivet po-bozheski*).

Yet their Christianity was only partly connected to the official church. During the eighteenth century, the funds and personnel of the parish came under ever stronger control from the diocese, and by the nineteenth century were little influenced by decisions of the village assembly, though it is true that the assembly usually continued to appoint the churchwarden and to set aside sums for church repair.[28] For most purposes the parish had become the lowest rung of the ecclesiastical bureaucracy rather than a constituent element of village life. Since peasants were accustomed to take an active part in decisions concerning their community, their attitude to the parish tended to be rather remote.

Much of course would depend on the character of the parish priest. Those who were pious, open-minded and sympathetic to need could get on well with their parishioners and mitigate the growing alienation which peasants felt towards the church. But the situation of the clergy in the village was a very difficult one, and there is plenty of evidence of priests whose behaviour fell well below the ideal, who were arrogant, uncaring, miserly or even habitually drunk. External circumstances predisposed to such deficiencies. Priests were educated people, but with a scholastic Latin-based education which prepared them poorly for pastoral duties in the countryside. The priest received from the diocese either a minimal salary or none at all, so that he had to look to the indigent villagers for his principal source of income, by charging for any sacraments he performed for them. In addition, to make ends meet, he had to cultivate a small plot of land, with the help of his wife and family, so that in his lifestyle he both was and was not a peasant. Nor was there any prospect of promotion, since the episcopacy and the higher ranks of ecclesiastical administration were reserved for the 'black' or monastic clergy. Spiritually robust clergymen could endure these circumstances and even turn them to advantage, but not all of them were so resilient.[29]

It is scarcely to be wondered at, then, if the peasants conducted much of their religious life outside the framework of the official church. Many beliefs and rituals centred on the home and garden plot. Most peasants were convinced of the existence of a guardian-spirit of the home, the *domovoi*, whose benevolence was essential to a well-run household. It was said that if the *domovoi* was well-disposed, he would help the family by completing unfinished jobs, or by feeding and grooming the animals, but that if he was in a bad mood, he would tangle needlework, spread manure on the threshold or put tools where no one could find them. To appease him, peasants would hang old bast shoes out on the fence as a gift, or buy animals of a colour he was known to favour. When moving house, the head of the household would combine Christian and pagan motifs by crossing himself, then holding an icon in one hand and bread and salt in the other and formally inviting the *domovoi* to accompany them.[30]

The bath-house, usually a log hut set at some distance from the main hut, was the home of another spirit, the *bannik*, who could be extremely dangerous if offended: he might react by burning down the bath-house, and perhaps the main dwelling too. For fear of him, people did not bathe alone or at night, and they would leave soap, fir branches or a little water for him on leaving, saying a formal 'thank you'.[31]

Sorcery and folk magic were still widely practised in the nineteenth and early twentieth century. Some elderly women were suspected of possessing the power of 'spoiling' (*porcha*) or casting the evil eye, causing their victims to suffer crop failure, illness, infertility, family discord or the drying up of milch-cows. As protection against them, prayers and the sign of the cross were employed, but so also were certain potions or plants offered to their potential victims. Newly-wedded couples were considered especially vulnerable: they might be offered onions, garlic, amber or incense, or a cross could be sewn into the bride's head-dress. Alternatively, villagers could proceed as they did against persistent criminals, by driving witches out or murdering them.[32]

All these beliefs and practices coexisted with official Orthodoxy in a mixture which did not seem to the peasants incongruous. Nor was it: similar eclecticism can be found amongst most peasantries in the middle ages and even well after. In fact, one should probably regard it as 'popular Christianity' rather than 'dual faith'.[33]

What was peculiar about the Russian version of 'popular Christianity' was that it persisted so long, and moreover did not seem to be losing its strength during the late nineteenth century. This trend accompanied the survival and even growth in sectarian and schismatic forms of Christianity. Much the most popular of them were the various varieties of the Old Belief. As we have seen, the Old Belief contained encoded within it an older form of Russian national consciousness, an attachment to the idea of *Rus'* as a sacred land, 'Holy Russia', the only place where Christianity was professed and practised in its integrity, as Christ had intended. During the eighteenth and nineteenth century, the intensity of the Old Believers' apocalyptic fervour faded somewhat. The persistent failure of the Last Judgement to arrive compelled all but an implacable few to devise ways of compromising with this life and even with a state run by the Antichrist.

To sustain their independence, Old Believers studied the scriptures avidly and deliberately fostered a level of literacy much higher than that prevailing among the ordinary Orthodox peasantry. In the words of one historian, they were a 'textual community'. Their use of what they read, however, reflected the limitations of their culture: they would seize on scraps of text uncritically and without any awareness of context, interpreting them as ultimate revelations. Dostoevskii, who observed them in the Siberian convict camp, remarked that 'they were highly developed people, shrewd peasants, skilled in argument, who believed pedantically and uncritically in the literal truth of their old books'.[34]

Their attachment to the Muscovite view of 'Holy Russia' helps to explain their extreme tenacity: they represented a long-standing protest against the way in which the imperial state had lost touch with the older roots of Russian national identity. They were an extreme expression of the Russian peasants' alienation from the secular state: they thus had a constant reservoir of potential devotees from which to replenish their numbers.

Parallel to the Old Belief there were other sectarian movements also generated by the peasant need to create forms of religious life independent of the official church. Whereas in most countries religious experimentation takes place among the urban orders, in Russia it took root among the peasants because they were the social class most alienated both from the state and from the established church. Significantly, most sects had their origin in the late seventeenth and eighteenth centuries, when the crisis of popular religious consciousness caused by the schism and the rise of the secular state was at its deepest.

Congregations without an ecclesiastical framework have to base their devotion on some principle independent of the church. It may be the scriptures, but, since they were in an ancient language, Church Slavonic, they were difficult for peasants to study independently. Instead, some congregations deified their own spiritual experience, interpreting it in the light of the collectivism and 'mutual responsibility' with which we are familiar.

Such were the *Khristovovery*, (Believers in Christ), who held that the coming of the Holy Spirit to Christ after his baptism could be repeated in the life of contemporary humanity. Their congregations, known as 'ships' (*korabli*), each formed around their own 'Christ', who had undergone such an experience. Divine worship was begun by the 'Christ', who would read from the scriptures, and it would continue with hymn singing and then dancing, and conclude with the *radenie*, during which the dancing became frenzied – as with Muslim Dervishes or American Shakers – reaching ecstasy and exhaustion, in the course of which there would be uttering in tongues, which the believers held to be outpourings of the Holy Spirit. Evil tongues rumoured that at this stage sexual orgies would take place. There is no convincing confirmation or refutation of this allegation, but it is clear that their rituals at the very least generated an intense collective experience.[35]

The *Dukhobory* (Wrestlers of the Spirit) took a similar spiritual orientation. They appeared in the eighteenth century, though it is not clear by whom they were influenced. They rejected the priesthood and the sacraments, and downplayed the scriptures, teaching that the Holy Spirit was sufficient unto itself, and dwelt within each individual in the form of conscience. They denied the incarnation and the resurrection of the body, and believed in the transmigration of souls, which suggests an eastern influence, likely enough in a Eurasian empire. At their meetings they sang psalms and expound the word of God 'without books', relying on memory and spiritual inspiration. Their cardinal tenet was mutual love, and some of their settlements practised the communal ownership of all property and the pooling of financial resources. They were pacifists and refused military service, which brought them into conflict with the state on those grounds alone.[36]

The *Molokane* (milk-drinkers) broke away from the Dukhobors and became more numerous in the end. They modified the extreme spiritualism of the Dukhobors by returning to the scriptures and some of them to the sacraments of communion and marriage. But they rejected the church's fasting precepts and introduced Jewish dietary laws instead: their name derived from their drinking of milk on fast days, which was forbidden to the Orthodox. They enjoyed the reputation of being highly literate, extremely neat and clean in their dwellings, and prosperous in their agriculture and business dealings.[37]

Overall, the importance of the sects lies partly in their numbers, but partly in the alienation they embodied and the permanent challenge they represented to the official church. Sectarianism could also represent a direct political threat. In 1839, for example, the Third Department warned that serfdom was a 'powder keg threatening the state' and that the schismatics and sectarians were well positioned to exploit the grievances arising from it in their seditious agitation.[39] Count Buturlin, investigating unrest in Tambov guberniia in 1842–4, singled out the Molokane as an especially pernicious source of trouble. As a result of their preaching, he reported, 'the villagers in their ignorance regard the authorities and the community as two opposite and, as it were, competing and hostile principles ... They are therefore convinced that people persecuted by the authorities are victims who are perishing for their devotion to the community, and they believe that only concerted action by the whole community can preserve them from oppression by hostile authorities.'[40]

The imperial state remained so alien to the peasants in all its manifestations that, in so far as they understood what it was, they never really reconciled themselves to it. They acknowledged its strength and they personally revered the Tsar, so that most of the time they behaved in an orderly manner, but the intermediate agents of the state – landowners and their stewards, policemen, court officials, tax collectors, recruiting officers, even sometimes priests – they regarded with reserve, which might burst out into active malevolence and even resistance if some incident aroused their resentment. The imposition of serfdom, with its accompanying obligations, was a major grievance, though not the fundamental one, since disorder was almost as frequent among state peasants as among private serfs, and besides, as we shall see, peasants were not reconciled to the existing order by the abolition of serfdom in 1861. Nevertheless, it is indicative that the two most serious peasant rebellions of all took place (i) that of Sten'ka Razin in 1670–1, soon after the final codification of serfdom in the *Ulozhenie*, and (ii) that of Emel'ian Pugachev in 1773–5, soon after the roughly equivalent landlords' service duty was abolished in 1762, removing the last vestige of moral justification for the serfs' subjection. [See Part 2, Chapter 3]

Did the peasants have a social ideal to counterpose to the arrogant practices of the secular state? The collectivism, egalitarianism, mutual responsibility and participatory self-government of the *mir* did potentially offer an alternative ideology, but it was one which the peasants, for the most part, could not articulate themselves – although one summed it up not badly in a pamphlet he wrote in the 1830s: 'Freedom, the Tsar and one Christian law for all'. Many peasants used the word *pravda* to sum up that ideal, plus the notion that all who needed land and were prepared to work it should have access to it.[41]

In general, however, peasants needed outsiders to articulate their alternative social ideal in a persuasive statement, and to organize and lead unrest that went beyond the horizon of a few villages or a volost. In the sixteenth to eighteenth centuries those outside leaders were Cossacks, with their intoxicating and vividly projected ideal of *vol'nitsa*: the democratic, participatory frontier community with its elected leader, the ataman or hetman. In the case of Bulavin and Pugachev (see Part 2, Chapter 3), those rebel leaders were also Old Believers – or at least, what is just as important, they believed that to assume the mantle of the Old Belief would advance their cause. Thus Cossackdom and the Old Belief became the banners of peasant rebellion. The characteristic mixture can be seen in the proclamation issued by Pugachev on 31 July 1774.

We know from the extent and strength of Pugachev's rebellion just how attractive this manifesto proved to be. Of course, his ideas were completely unpractical as a basis for a state, but they probably represent a close approximation to what most peasants regarded as the ideal society: self-governing, without serfdom, taxes or recruitment, with the cultivators owning the land, and ruled over by a benevolent, patriarchal monarch professing the ancient Russian faith. As we have seen, few Old Believers actually took part in his movement: it was the old Russian ideal which counted rather than the precise confession.[42] On the other hand, many non-Russians, Bashkirs, Mordvins and others, were caught up in the movement: in this case, as in others, Russian peasants worked together with non-Russians against their own empire.

During the second half of the eighteenth century, Cossacks were becoming more and more integrated into the imperial system, and particularly the army (indeed the Pugachev rebellion began as a last desperate protest against that process). Thereafter the peasants were leaderless till the late nineteenth century when, as we shall see, the radical urban intelligentsia moved in to fill the gap. That does not mean that in the meantime peasant protest ceased: it merely became less coherent, more limited in spatial and political scope. During the first half of the nineteenth century, it seems that the frequency of incidents of unrest increased with each passing decade, to reach a climax in the years 1856–62, when emancipation was in the air and rumours intensified the peasants' excitability. It is difficult to be certain of the extent of this increase, because of the difficulty of defining exactly what is meant by 'unrest' (in Russian *volnenie*). But the general trend is clear, and seems to indicate that, even without outside leaders, peasant discontent was at the very least persistent and active.[43]

In general, it was times of turbulence, sudden changes or unusual happenings in the village or manor which would spark off rural unrest: anything which disturbed the uneasy equilibrium peasants had come to accept as justified by custom if by nothing else. It might be the death of a landlord, a raising of the dues, the behaviour of a new steward, a harsh punishment imposed by the lord, or many other contingencies. Whatever it was, the peasants would usually act collectively: individual protest was acknowledged to be futile and was strongly discouraged as likely to bring down retribution on the whole community.

Normally, the village assembly was the forum in which the major decisions were taken: first of all, very often, was the despatch of some kind of petition to the authorities requesting a rectification of the alleged abuse, and often citing other problems as well. Then, if this was not satisfied, there would come a resolution to refuse obedience to landlord, steward or police. Typically, though, peasants tried to avoid violence: they knew that their opponents commanded much greater resources in this respect. As a result, disputes could drag on for a long time. The landlord, steward or volost elder would send for the *ispravnik* (local magistrate and chief of police) who would come down and try to talk the peasants round, promising to investigate their grievances and threatening them with serious punishment if they should persist in their defiance. If that did not work, then 'gendarmes' (armed police) would have to be sent in to arrest 'ringleaders' – though these were often difficult to identify, in view of the peasants' normal strategy of joint responsibility. In a few cases the army had to be summoned to overcome stubborn resistance: then peasants would be flogged, exiled or sent to penal servitude. This, however, was an outcome both sides did their utmost to avoid, for it seriously damaged the village economy on which both depended.[44]

Let us take an individual case which exemplifies some of the issues involved. In November 1823 twenty-five peasants from the Vereia okrug of Moscow guberniia presented a petition to the Governor, speaking on behalf of colleagues from a number of surrounding villages and hamlets, all part of one large estate. They complained that after the death of their pomeshchitsa two years ago, her steward, one Lapyrev, had continued to demand *obrok* at the rate of 26 rubles 'per soul': 'and what that *obrok* gets used for we do not know, and the steward will not let us check up'. The ispravnik went down to inform the peasants that their estate was now owned by two under-age members of the Shuvalov family, and in the trusteeship of a senior relative. The peasants gathered in large numbers at the estate office and 'declared unanimously that without having personally seen the new pomeshchiki they would not obey the steward and the elder and would not pay *obrok*'.

Next morning about two thousand peasants gathered from all over the volost in front of the manor house 'and unanimously, with great shouting and boorishness, demanded that they be allowed to install a new *burmistr* in place of the steward and to elect new elders to replace the old ones, and that the new ones be let into the office containing the estate papers and finances'. In spite of the ispravnik's objections, they set about electing their new officials, and sent for two priests to administer the oath of office.

The ispravnik managed to persuade the priests not to do this, and to prevent the peasants breaking into the office. The next day, anticipating yet another big meeting, the ispravnik called in the army to forestall it, and later a whole battalion was quartered on the villages.

When the peasants gathered and declared they would not accept the quartering, the troops managed to surround them and arrest those suspected of being 'ringleaders', after which the rest dispersed. In the end, nine villagers were imprisoned for a year and then sent to Siberia.[45]

This case well illustrates how a change of situation, the death of the owner, made obligations earlier accepted now seem intolerable, how an absentee landlord aroused suspicions, and how the peasants acted collectively, trying to take control of the situation by electing new officials. It is also noteworthy that both sides several times tried to avoid pushing the conflict to irreversible extremes, which were in the interests of neither.

Events in the macrocosm of the empire could also generate turbulence in the microcosm of the village. In 1796, for example, the accession of the Emperor Paul gave rise to rumours that the serfs would be freed, and there was a wave of unrest. Comparable waves followed the Napoleonic invasion, the Decembrist rising and the year 1848, when there was a bad harvest, accompanied by news of revolutions in Europe and in particular of a peasant rebellion in neighbouring Galicia, in the Habsburg Monarchy.[46]

Examining peasant reactions of this kind, David Moon has come to the conclusion that their meaning was located on two levels. One was what might be termed 'utopian': behaving as if the world were arranged the way the peasants would like it to be. This was 'a safety-valve for pent-up feelings, or psychological wish-fulfilment', rather like the function of carnival in many societies. The other was more practical, 'taking advantage of the situations presented by legislation [and other acts of the authorities] to achieve those of their aims and aspirations which seemed attainable'. Sometimes they exercised what might be called 'creative misunderstanding' of laws or instructions: this could arise from loose wording, from the peasants' own poor education, or from deliberate misreading. Rumours were a frequent source of exaggeration and misinformation: they represented a distorting channel of communication which reflected peasant hopes and resentments as much as they did reality.[47]

In many areas the peasant reaction to emancipation in 1861 exemplified such 'creative misunderstanding'. It was clear that the emancipation edict did not embody *volia* as the peasants understood it. They learned that they were not to receive all the land they cultivated – which would have satisfied their understanding of economic justice – and that the portion of if they were allotted would be awarded to them only if they started a long programme of paying for it. [For an account of the emancipation terms, see below, p. 321]

To steer round the affront, some peasants exercised 'creative misunderstanding', claiming that the Tsar had granted them true *volia*, but that the landowners and bureaucrats had withheld the genuine emancipation charter and had substituted for it a bogus document upholding their own power. And so, according to a report from the Tsar's Adjutant General, A.S. Apraksin, 'when they saw that no one could extract from the Statute the *volia* they dreamed of – that is, *barshchina* is not abolished and the pomeshchiki are to retain control of the land – they began to distrust educated people and to seek readers among the literate peasants'.[48]

One such who presented himself in the village of Bezdna in Kazan' guberniia was a certain Anton Petrov, variously described as a schismatic or a sectarian. He claimed to speak in the name of the Tsar, who, he asserted, had indeed granted the peasants full *volia*: to those who knew how to read it, the Emancipation Statute contained the necessary provisions, encoded in the mysterious figures and percentages of the appendices and sealed with the 'cross of St Anne'. Peasants from villages around Bezdna flocked to hear the prophet interpret the document, and resolved that they would refuse all labour on the lords' land until 'the Tsar's will' was accepted.

Troops were sent in to arrest Petrov and quell the disorders, but Petrov persuaded the peasants that this was the Tsar testing their resolve: if they stood firm in the face of fire, then they would at last receive *volia*. To all attempts to persuade them to desist, the peasants would merely reply with shouts of '*volia!*' The troops then fired, but the peasants did not budge, although some of them were killed and wounded. Only after several volleys had been fired did they disperse.

It is not clear how far Petrov and the peasants really believed what they claimed. But one thing is certain: the peasants were utterly convinced of the justice of what they were demanding – so much so that they were prepared to stand firm for it in the face of bullets.[49] The emancipation edict did not satisfy them because it did not cede them the full right to control the land they cultivated and to run their own affairs in deference to a distant and benign Tsar.

These are the themes which run like a thread through the numerous, but sporadic episodes of peasant discontent of the decades following emancipation. They tended to put the blame for their disappointed hopes on the pomeshchik, whose broad acres were a permanent mockery of their own meagre strips. Often they turned to renting parts of those broad acres, either for cash or for labour, in a partial restoration of the dependent relationship of *obrok* and *barshchina*. When this relationship turned sour, peasants would sometimes express their feelings in more or less coercive or violent acts, which would vary according to season and circumstance: witholding labour, grazing cattle on the lord's pastures, stealing his grain or his tools, setting fire to his barns or even his manor house. Or they would obstruct officials come to survey the land prior to redrawing boundaries.

The epicentre of such disturbances was the Central Agricultural Region, where peasant dependence on agriculture was highest and urban markets and alternative employment most distant. It was not till 1905 that such outbursts became sufficiently widespread to constitute a threat to internal security, for reasons we shall examine later, but throughout the post-emancipation decades it was impossible to say that the Russian countryside was free of discontent.[50]

In emancipating the serfs, the government had taken the decision not only to preserve the village commune under the new name of 'rural society' (*sel'skoe obshchestvo*), but to give it increased powers as the basic unit of local administration in the countryside. Several 'rural societies' constituted a *volost'*, also headed by elected peasant officials. Yet, although they gained new powers, the commune and volost were not integrated into the new local government structure at uezd and guberniia level, nor were they given jurisdiction over non-peasants. Even government supervision over them was weak till the establishment of the office of 'land commandant' (*zemskii nachal'nik*) in 1889. They remained segregated peasant institutions outside the formal administrative and judicial structure, running their affairs in their own customary ways.

This reinforcement of archaic forms was intended to ensure that peasants would continue paying their taxes, and also to provide against the possibility of rural immiseration leading to mass vagrancy. But it stood in blatant contradiction to what was happening in the peasant economy. In recent decades there has been sharp controversy over whether peasants as a whole were becoming poorer or less poor between 1861 and 1905, but both sides of the argument would agree that peasants were becoming more involved in the imperial economy as a whole, whether as participants in a growing market, or as victims of rapacious exploitation.[51]

Here the evidence is overwhelming. The personal freedom bestowed by the emancipation edict plus an improving communications network far outweighed the institutional obstacles posed by the commune, and enabled peasants to travel widely round the country, seeking work in towns, in factories, on the railways and rivers. Even the village back at home did not remain unchanged: the money economy became generally accepted, retail trade spread and cottage industry expanded. Peasants bought and sold land, buying overall much more than they sold, and increasing inequalities within the village. The traditional artel began to yield as an economic association to the more market-oriented cooperative. Primary education gave young men (far more than young women) broader horizons and the chance of more varied employment. Military service gave some a period of encounter with other people and unfamiliar parts of the empire, perhaps even with a foreign land.

The effects of a change of scenery could be unsettling for

traditional authority patterns. Peasant-soldiers returning from the Turkish war of 1877–8, like their predecessors from the Crimean War, spread rumours that the Tsar would now at last redistribute the land in their favour.[52] In more general terms, literacy and travel began to reorient the peasant's conception of Russia from a fixation on the Orthodox Church and Tsar to a more complex and inclusive picture, of diverse peoples and landscapes, in which Russians as a people helped their less civilized brethren to progress and prosperity. It became possible to take a pride in Russianness.[53] How far this transformation of national identity towards geography and ethnicity had moved before 1914 is uncertain, but it seems clear that it had started.

Yet, in the midst of these economic and cultural changes, the peasants gained no new outlets for their political aspirations. Other than the zemstvos (which had limited functions and powers – see Part 4, Chapter 1), they had no institutions through which they could express their grievances and seek solutions to them. Even as they were beginning from below to bridge the gap between themselves and the empire's elites, there was no sign of a civic nation which they could join.

4

The Orthodox Church

In many European countries, especially the Protestant ones, the church played a vital role in creating and sustaining a sense of nationhood by mediating between high and low cultures. Its parish schools were the anteroom to a wider world for the children of peasants and workers. Its priests, trained in the high culture, ministered in the course of their daily work to the needs of ordinary folk of town and country, who spoke a dialect and might be illiterate. The scriptures, translated into the vernacular, were often the means by which those ordinary people first encountered their national language and the accompanying high culture; if they were literate, they could then explore further and work out their own personal beliefs. One thinks especially of the formative influence of the Lutheran Bible in Germany and of the Authorized Version in England, in fixing a national language and encouraging individuals to explore their personal feelings through the medium of that language.

From a knowledge of its early history, one might have expected that in Russia the church would be at the very centre of nationhood. Like the Spanish church, it had been the ideological leader in the crusade against the Muslims and had played a decisive role in justifying empire. The idea of 'Moscow the Third Rome' had legitimated its own position within that empire. Ivan IV had intended Orthodoxy to be the keystone of his united and centralized realm, and after his death the establishment of the Patriarchate in 1589 had confirmed Russia's independent position, even hegemony, among the various Orthodox churches. During the Time of Troubles the Patriarch had taken the initiative in recreating a unified and sovereign Muscovite state. Over the centuries, moreover, the church had become a huge owner of land and serfs.

CHURCH AND STATE   Perhaps it was the very dominance of the church which in the long run proved fatal to it. As we saw in Part 2, Chapter 1, Tsar Alexei was genuinely alarmed by the overweening ambition of Patriarch Nikon: he was convinced that sedition and disorder could not be avoided if the empire had two rival sovereigns.

Peter I perpetuated this suspicion: of all rulers, he was not one to tolerate competitors. He was determined to cut the church down to size and to bring it under his control. He regarded it as he did all other social institutions, as an instrument through which the sovereign could mobilize the resources of society and nip in the bud any tendency to disloyalty.

The means he employed to achieve this were suggested to him by the example of the Church of England. While visiting England in 1698, Peter spent many hours in the company of Dr Gilbert Burnet, Bishop of Salisbury, who subsequently recalled in a letter to a colleague that 'he hearkened to no part of what I told him more attentively than when I explained the authority that the Christian Emperours assumed in matters of religion and the supremacy of our Kings'.[1]

Now Burnet was the author of a tract entitled *Of the Rights of Princes in the Disposing of Ecclesiastical Benefices and Church Lands* (1682), in which he spoke of the monarch's duty to appoint bishops and generally to provide for the welfare and discipline of the church in such a way as to promote the good of the common people. As he put it in the Conclusion to his *History of My own Time*, 'The great and comprehensive rule of all is that a King should consider himself as exalted by Almighty God into that high dignity as into a capacity of doing much good and of being a great blessing to mankind, and in some sort a god on earth . . .'[2]

Peter, of course, was inclined to view himself in this light regardless of Burnet's homilies, but he must have been pleased to find his opinion confirmed by a prelate of one of the most successful realms in Europe. When Patriarch Adrian died shortly after his return from abroad, Peter declined to appoint a successor, and in the end never did so. Instead he revived the *Monastyrskii Prikaz* to take over the patriarchal domain, administer it and collect its revenues.[3] This gave him the power to divert some of the church's income for military and other secular purposes.

In 1721 he went much further and abolished the Patriarchate altogether. He replaced it with a new institution, known at first as the Spiritual College, which implied that it was just one of many branches of the state administration; later it was given supplementary dignity and independent standing as the 'Most Holy Synod'. The Emperor himself became head or 'supreme protector' of the church, and employed the Synod as the official channel for his authority, while its senior official, the Over-Procurator, acted as his representative. In practice, at least during the eighteenth century, the Over-Procurator was effectively counter-balanced by the combined expertise of the bishops who made up the majority of the Synod's collegiate board. By the nineteenth century, however, with the establishment of ministries at the head of the executive under Alexander I, the Procurator became more like any other minister in his authority.[4]

The new relationship of church and state as conceived by Peter was set forth and justified in a proclamation entitled *The Spiritual Regulation* (1721). Its title was an oxymoron which well captured the spirit of the document. The author, Feofan Prokopovich, was a Ukrainian prelate who had completed a full Jesuit education, including a spell at the College of St Athanasius in Rome, the principal training-ground for the Counter-Reformation in Eastern Europe. He had reacted against this upbringing to embrace a mixture of Erastian Protestantism and secular Enlightenment principles which endeared him to Peter.[5]

The tone of the *Spiritual Regulation* could have come straight out of Hobbes's *Leviathan*. It claimed that autocracy was necessary because human beings were naturally evil and would constantly make war on one another were they not restrained by an unambiguous and undivided authority, which was not the case when Patriarchal authority seemed to rival that of the Tsar. 'The fatherland need have no fear of revolts and disturbances from a conciliar administration such as proceeds from a single, independent ecclesiastical administrator. For the common people do not understand how the spiritual authority is distinguishable from the autocratic, but marvelling at the dignity and glory of the Highest Pastor, they imagine that such an administrator is a second sovereign, a power equal to that of the Autocrat, or even greater.'[6]

The *Regulation* prescribed in detail the duties of bishops, priests and monks. On ordination, priests had to take an oath pledging them to 'defend unsparingly all the powers, rights and prerogatives belonging to the High Autocracy of His Majesty'. They were required to keep a record of parishioners' fulfilment of their religious duties, their attendance at communion and confession. They also had to read decrees from the pulpit, administer oaths of loyalty to the state and to keep up to date the registers of births, marriages and deaths.[7] They were, in short, spiritual administrators and grass-roots agents of the autocratic state.

When a gathering of bishops requested Peter to allow them to elect another Patriarch, he replied by banging the *Spiritual Regulation* down on the table in front of them and barking out 'This is your spiritual Patriarch, and those who object to him will (taking a dagger from his pocket) get to know the Patriarch of the Sword! [*bulatnyi patriarkh*]'. He backed up his word by attaching to the Synod a staff of 'fiscals' to assist the Over-Procurator in his task of ensuring that it discharged business efficiently and according to the regulations. Characteristically they were known as 'inquisitors'.[8]

The inquisitorial function was not confined to them. Priests had to exercise it too. According to an ukaz of 17 May 1722, 'If during confession someone discloses to the spiritual father an uncommitted but still intended crime, especially treason or rebellion against the Sovereign or the State, or an evil design against the honour or health of the Sovereign and his Family, and in declaring such evil intent shows that he does not repent of it ... then the confessor must not only withhold absolution and remission from the sinner, but most promptly report him to the appropriate place.' The 'appropriate place' was the *Preobrazhenskii Prikaz* (see part 2, chapter 2). Priests who failed to discharge this duty were warned that 'as an accomplice in crime, they will be sentenced to condign punishment on the body and sent to the galleys, or, if the matter is serious, will be executed'.[9]

Priests were thus brusquely co-opted into the ranks of the *fiskaly*. The weakening of congregation which this step implied was reinforced by the fact that during the eighteenth century the ecclesiastical hierarchy was taking into its hands control over the appointment of parish priests. Previously incumbencies had usually either been hereditary or subject to election by the parishioners. The *Spiritual Regulation*, however, stipulated that a priest must have graduated from a seminary before taking responsibility for a parish. There were too few qualified candidates to meet this requirement immediately, but all the same it placed more power in the hands of the bishop, who supervised the seminaries in his diocese and was in a position to check candidates' credentials. Often in practice it proved most convenient to appoint the previous incumbent's son: priests' sons almost invariably attended seminaries themselves, since Peter had decreed that supernumerary clergy were to be deprived of their status and fall into the 'taxable' ranks of society. (From time to time Peter and his successors would conduct compulsory levies into the army for such unfortunates.)

The election of priests gradually atrophied, or would be conducted exclusively by the 'better parishioners' – selected by the consistory, the diocesan administrative board. Only in the western provinces were bishops instructed to encourage proper parish elections, as a means of keeping the faith strong in the face of the challenge from the Catholic and Uniate Churches. Elsewhere, the election of parish priests was finally abolished by the Holy Synod in 1797. By the same token, the churchwarden (*starosta*), who was in charge of the parish finances, came more and more to be appointed from above, leaving parishioners with far less control over their material resources. This diminution of the role of the parish was one of the most fateful results of Peter's ecclesiastical reforms, for it weakened the link between the village community and the church, and hence also between the village community and the state.[10] As Ivan Aksakov commented in 1868, 'There are parishioners, but there is no parish in the proper sense of the word; people are registered with the church, but these people do not constitute a church congregation in the proper and original meaning of that term.'[11]

Not surprisingly, Peter's active and restless nature was impatient with monks and their contemplative calling. Unlike his Anglican counterpart, Henry VIII, he did not close the monasteries down, but he did discipline them to try to ensure that they would act effectively as agents of social security. Their role was to offer a refuge to invalids, beggars and to retired and maimed army veterans. To enforce this task upon them, he expropriated their revenues, replacing them with a fixed allowance of money and provisions for each monk and nun, conditional on strict discipline and the accomplishment of prescribed charitable work. Admission to the novitiate was to be tightly regulated, men under thirty and women under fifty being barred. Though they were expected to be literate, monks were forbidden to do any writing without permission from their superior, or even to keep pen and paper in their cells, since 'nothing so ruins monastic tranquillity as vain and useless writing'. Those who violated this prohibition were to be expelled.[12]

Some scholars have called Peter's reform a 'Protestant reformation'.[13] In one sense this is obviously correct: Peter subordinated the church to the state, took over its finances and disciplined it to carry out educational, charitable and social work. But he was not King of England, nor a German *Landesherr* imposing a *Kirchenregiment*. Certain crucial conditions for a Protestant reformation were lacking. There was no intellectual tradition of covenant theology or natural law. Congregational and parish life were relatively underdeveloped, and were actually undermined by his reform. Above all, there were no scriptures in the vernacular language which ordinary people could read in order to form and develop their own personal piety. In so far as congregational and scriptural traditions were strong, it was among the Old Believers, who were the most opposed to Peter's innovations.

Consequently, a Protestant reform programme remained an alien imposition on the Russian church. Most of the clergy and laity continued to see the Tsar as God's Anointed, a Vasileus in the Byzantine sense, ruling in harmony or 'symphony' with it, even as Peter pursued a totally different agenda, with the church as an instrument for secular policies. This mismatch in the mutual relationship of church and state has been called by one ecclesiastical historian 'the cardinal falsehood of the Synodal period', while another has claimed that Peter inaugurated 'the real and profound schism . . . a schism not so much between the government and the people (as the Slavophiles thought), but between the authorities and the church'.[14]

In a state where the ruler claimed his supreme authority on the basis of divine right, that schism was also extremely dangerous. The imperial state's humiliation of the church which underpinned its legitimizing ideology was perhaps its gravest mistake and certainly a fundamental cause of the revolution of 1917.

Peter III and Catherine II completed the official expropriation and rationalization of the church's wealth. In 1762–4 they took over the running of all its remaining landholdings and replaced the income from them with an official endowment to dioceses and monasteries which amounted to only about a quarter of their previous value. These endowments were conditional on the church's carrying out educational and charitable work and observing 'establishment lists' (*shtaty*) for each individual parish and monastery. One bishop, Metropolitan Arsenii of Rostov, protested against these provisions, and further affronted Catherine by commenting that 'our present sovereign is not native, and is not firm in the faith'. But he found himself alone among his colleagues. He was tried for *lèse majesté*, defrocked and imprisoned for life.[15]

The cumulative effect of these changes was enormously damaging to the church in its relations with the state, with the elites of society and with the mass of the people. The clergy became a segregated and relatively impoverished estate. The segregation was symbolized by clergymen's style of dress: alone among the elites, they had been exempted from Peter I's injunction to wear western clothes, so that their appearance was distinctive and old-fashioned. Although the clergy was a service estate, its members held no *chin* or official rank, and so possessed neither the career openings nor the social status conferred by it. Characteristically, Catherine II failed to invite the clergy, along with the serfs, to the Legislative Commission which opened her reign.

EDUCATION The church's educational system, until the eighteenth century the only one available to the population, remained largely unchanged. It was still based on the Latinate learning of the Counter-Reformation which had penetrated to Russia, often mediated by the Jesuits, through the numerous Ukrainian prelates. This tradition was itself somewhat incongruous for a country whose religious roots lay in the Greek world of Byzantium.[16] As a system of secular schools developed, disseminating the ideals of the European Enlightenment, the church's educational offerings came to seem more and more archaic, and served to isolate the clergy culturally as well as socially from the empire's elites. Symptomatically, Russia was the only country in Europe whose universities had no theological faculties. Learned laymen and learned clerics lived in separate worlds.

At the grass roots, the *mir* and the parish began to drift apart during the eighteenth century, and not only because of the appointment of priests from above. Previously they had been more less identical, as the *prikhodskaia obshchina* (parish commune), the basic unit of both secular and ecclesiastical government. Peter I's provincial reform of 1718 ended the parish's role in secular government, however, so that it became a purely ecclesiastical institution at the very time when the parishioners were losing their influence within the church.

This was all part of the purification and 'de-magification' of the church, which the Zealots of Piety had begun, only to have their work rudely sidetracked by Nikon. The bishops wanted to remove unworthy secular accretions from church buildings: markets were banned from churchyards and taverns from their immediate vicinity, while all celebrations involving laughter, ribald conversation and drinking were transferred elsewhere. Priests were expected to eliminate pagan practices and popular superstition from worship, often to the disapproval of ordinary folk. In a notorious case, a Moscow crowd tracked down and lynch-murdered Metropolitan Amvrosii, who had ordered the removal of an unauthorized 'wonder-working icon' during the plague of 1771.[17]

Such prophylactic measures tended to weaken the church's function as the focus of the village's (or town's) cultural life. It was ceasing to be the educational centre too, as parish schools, available to all comers, yielded gradually to specialized clergy schools. These schools offered a good education, of a Central European Catholic kind, requiring proficiency in Latin and Church Slavonic, Biblical history, classical mythology and literature, rhetoric, philosophy and theology. Some fine scholars emerged from this curriculum, but ordinary clergymen found it a poor preparation for the pastoral and practical tasks they would have to perform in the village. Many of them in any case dropped out before completing the course because of poverty or ineptitude.[18]

Nor did most seminaries, the church's secondary schools, deliver the curriculum as promised: they were chronically under-resourced, and suffered from dilapidated buildings, inadequate libraries and equipment, under-qualified teachers and under-nourished pupils. Inspection of one seminary in 1840, for example, disclosed that the library had not one of the textbooks laid down in the syllabus, nor a New Testament in any language. In Perm' in 1829, pupils were sleeping on desks because of the shortage of dormitory accommodation. Everywhere buildings were damp, unhygienic and structurally unsound, generating a high level of disease and even mortality.[19]

The result was a haphazard and rather anorexic mode of education, oriented towards rote-learning and formal achievement rather than broad culture or spiritual nourishment. It tended to inspire in its alumni the narrow-minded philistine outlook which moved Turgenev to decry those with 'vulgar seminarian principles' and 'soiled collars' who seek to 'wipe poetry, fine arts and all aesthetic pleasure from the face of the earth'.[20]

The seminary reform of 1808–14, passed by Alexander I, reduced the emphasis on Latin and prescribed more practical and modern subjects, such as mathematics, geography and secular history, but it also ambitiously broadened the graduate's education by adding Greek, Hebrew, French and German to the curriculum. It created a hierarchy of clergy schools, enabling those who wished to leave early, or who had no choice, to do so without disgrace and with a more or less systematic education behind them.[21] It did not however, reduce the cultural distance between priesthood and flock.

THE SCRIPTURES We have seen in Part 2, Chapter 4 that in the early 1820s Alexander I tried but failed to bring about the publication of the scriptures in modern Russian. This failure also helped to preserve the cultural gap between priesthood and people. One prelate, however, fought a long campaign to reverse it. That was Metropolitan Filaret of Moscow, a brilliant scholar and former Rector of the St Petersburg Theological Academy, who had done more than anyone else to direct the translation process. He was convinced that the Orthodox Church could only survive against its rivals if the scriptures were made available to ordinary believers in the parishes in a language they could readily comprehend. 'Everything which is necessary to salvation,' he argued, 'is expounded in the Holy Scriptures with a clarity such that any reader moved by the sincere wish to be enlightened can understand it. Certainly, trained interpreters of the Scriptures are useful for less educated Christians. But to state as a principle that an authoritative interpreter is required to bring out the propositions of the faith, demeans the dignity of God's word and subjects the faith to human exposition.'[22]

When Filaret raised the matter in 1842, Metropolitan Serafim of St Petersburg objected that a modern Russian Bible would only 'provoke idle minds to controversy, polemic and other aberrations'; the impression would be given that 'the people can be judges in matters of faith'. Over-Procurator Protasov connected the issue with that of the new textual criticism coming in from Germany: 'Lutheran principles have crept into Biblical exegesis . . . Questions are raised which would have affronted our forefathers, on the authenticity, reliability and revelatory nature of the scriptures, all with the aim . . . of replacing faith with reason.' Even Filaret's attempt to publish a new catechism was long delayed because he had included in it the Credo, the Ten Commandments and the Lord's Prayer in modern Russian.[23]

Eventually, however, Filaret's patience was rewarded. In 1859 Alexander II finally authorized the Holy Synod to give permission for a full modern Russian translation of the Bible, to be carried out under the supervision of all four theological academies. Because so much of the work had already been done, the project was launched relatively speedily: the Gospels appeared in 1861, the New Testament in 1862, and the whole Bible in 1876. It immediately proved immensely popular, and new editions had to be printed forthwith. In St Petersburg a Society for the Dissemination of the Holy Scriptures sold or distributed nearly 1.25 million copies between 1863 and 1865.[24]

Ironically, the final appearance of the Bible in Russian took place just *after* the publication of Marx's *Das Kapital* in the same language. One might regard the succeeding century as a competition between the two doctrines for the allegiance of Russian working people.

THE PARISH CLERGY   After the Pugachev rebellion, Catherine II forbade the presentation of petitions by peasants. Since these petitions had often been drafted by priests, her decree discouraged contact between priest and villagers over political and social affairs. It certainly did not end it, however, and when the Emperor Paul rescinded the ban, priests sometimes explicitly supported their parishioners' protests. In Vladimir guberniia in 1796, a priest signed a village assembly resolution (*mirskoi prigovor*), forwarded to Paul, complaining that the local landlord had absorbed nearly all the village's arable and meadow land into his own domain, leaving them very little for subsistence. A similar petition, sent during a famine the following year, was signed by the parish deacon, and charged that the landlord was compelling serfs to work in his paper mill, so that they had no time to cultivate their fields.[25]

The parishes' loss of rights and influence did not mean that they ceased to be responsible for the upkeep of their clergymen and families. They were expected to provide a certain amount of glebe land, as well as payment for ritual services provided outside the normal weekly divine worship. The capacity of parishes to bear this burden varied enormously, according to such factors as the number and wealth of the parishioners, and whether or not nearby landowners contributed a generous share of the costs. A poverty-stricken village with a stingy or godless landlord could condemn a priest and his family to lifelong penury. Attempts to lay down a formal scale of charges seldom came to anything. The result was that clergymen not infrequently had to haggle with members of their flock before solemnizing a marriage or performing a burial – a process many of them found humiliating. As one mid-nineteenth century priest remarked, 'Oh, here is the height of dishonour and shame: even when he has reconciled a confessing sinner with God, he takes money; even when he has administered the sacrament of communion, he does not recoil in horror from payment . . . Is he not simply a hireling?'[26]

By the end of the eighteenth century the clergy had become more or less a closed social estate, that is to say, virtually a caste. This was the case even though there was no formal prohibition on entry to it or exit from it. There were very few recruits to the clergy from among the nobles, who had the wrong type of education and in any case had no wish to degrade their social standing, which is what becoming a clergyman would have meant. Ordinary peasants and townsfolk (*meshchane*) seldom had the means to afford the protracted education, and, even if they had, could rarely obtain permission from their own communities, who would have had to take over their tax payments. As for clergy children themselves, they had little choice but to become clergymen or the wives of clergymen. Their education unfitted them for higher social station, and the only alternative was to descend into the tax-paying estates, with the risk of being drafted into the army.[27]

As a result, by the late eighteenth century the clergy estate was swelling to a size far beyond what the available parish postings would support. This dearth engendered vicious and destructive conflicts among the clergy themselves, as families fought for scarce incumbencies which alone would enable their dependants to avoid penury or social degradation. An ageing priest in Vladimir diocese, having like all his colleagues no pension in prospect, wrote to his bishop with uncommon candour in 1781: 'To take care of me and my impoverished family and wife, order a student at the Suzdal' seminary to marry my daughter and then appoint this son-in-law to my position.'[28] Most clergymen were trying to achieve something similar, if less openly. The pressure on them was aggravated by the fact that married clergymen were not eligible to be promoted to a bishopric. Normally only monks could become bishops, which created another gulf: that between parish and monastic clergy.

Under this kind of pressure, the church had become not least an employment bureau-cum-social security agency for its staff and their dependants. This function thwarted all attempts at reform. Under Nicholas I, in 1829 and 1842, the Holy Synod twice attempted to reform parish structures, to reduce the number of clergy the parishioners had to support, and also to provide more reliable sources of income, in the form of glebe land, state subsidies or regulated fees for ritual services. Implementation of these measures was so patchy that they must be accounted a failure. Clergy resisted transfer or redundancy, and bishops were reluctant to put pressure on them. Parishioners and landowners were unwilling to stump up any more, and state subsidies remained inadequate and poorly directed. A further attempt under Alexander II in the 1860s and 1870s was not much more successful.[29]

THE THREAT OF SECTARIANISM   By the nineteenth century, then, the Russian Orthodox Church had become a kind of welfare office for its underpaid and insecure clerics. It was also a welfare office under siege, constantly threatened by neighbouring faiths which seemed to be more attractive and successful: the Old Belief, sectarian movements, Protestant denominations, Catholicism and the Uniate church. The historian Mikhail Pogodin once commented that, if the ban on apostasy were lifted, half the Russian peasants would join the *raskol*, while half the aristocrats would convert to Catholicism.[30]

The state tried a variety of approaches to the Old Believers, or, as they insisted on calling them, the 'schismatics' (*raskol'niki*). Peter I abandoned the outright persecution of Old Believers. He was always anxious to encourage commercial activity, and, finding some Old Believers to be reliable and successful businessmen, he allowed them to settle in towns, register with the authorities and use the opportunity to charge them a double tax. Many of them, however, were not willing to register – in their eyes, to be stamped with the 'mark of the beast' – and preferred to remain outlawed in remote regions.

The Empresses Anna and Elizabeth resumed persecution, but Peter III and Catherine II allowed registered Old Believers to settle in certain areas in Siberia, Belorussia and the north of Russia, and even to establish their own monasteries on the river Irgiz in the Urals. The urban charter of 1785 permitted them to be elected to municipal offices.[31] In Moscow they established a whole merchant community, with its own chapel and cemetery, the *Rogozhskoe kladbishche*.

In some dioceses bishops went so far as to allow congregations to celebrate the liturgy according to the old books and usages, a practice which was officially sanctioned by Metropolitan Platon of Moscow in 1800, with the approval of Emperor Paul. In this way the United Faith (*edinoverie*) was created, a movement which offered a real chance to overcome the pernicious schism in the Orthodox faith, or at any rate to attract all but the most fanatical schismatics back into the official church. But the latter refused to withdraw the anathema of 1667, as the Old Believers asked them to do, nor would they permit inter-communion between the two denominations, maybe fearing that, if it was allowed, many clandestine schismatics would 'come out' and profess their true faith openly.[32]

Nicholas I adopted precisely the opposite policy, resuming persecution of the schismatics. Many of their chapels and prayer houses were closed, and their bells confiscated, while Orthodox priests who officiated at their services were disciplined. The Irgiz monasteries were closed down and the monks dispersed. Old Believer marriages were declared invalid. A 'special committee' was set up to coordinate measures against schismatics and sectarians.[33] These measures were inspired by the view, widespread in the church, that the Old Belief was an especially dangerous enemy of the official church, since its origin was the same and its teachings therefore particularly seductive for the simple and uneducated.

All the same, by the final decades of the nineteenth century, both church and state had other enemies who were more obviously menacing and effective, and in 1883 some of the Old Believers' rights were restored to them, such as that of building new prayer houses. As before, they were forbidden to propagate their views or to make converts from the Orthodox Church.[34]

For much of the eighteenth and nineteenth century the church made a concerted effort to conduct a mission among the Old Believers, in an attempt to bring them back into the official church. A special chair for the study of the *raskol* was instituted at the St Petersburg Theological Academy, and departments to train missionaries were opened in several seminaries. The missionaries found the effort remarkably frustrating. This was partly because the schism had split up into so many currents (*tolki* or *soglasiia*) that it was difficult to keep track of their diverse beliefs. But it was also because the schismatics were on average better read and more versed in the faith than the Orthodox: their devotion to their old books, passed on from parent to child, made them formidable opponents in exegetical argument.

All the same, the attempt was made. Bishops were instructed to keep lists of Old Believers in their dioceses, and in those which were particularly 'infected', like Perm', Penza, Saratov, Chernigov, Irkutsk and Olonets, special committees were set up to coordinate the mission. In the 1870s the Bishop of Saratov, Ioannikii, founded a Brotherhood of the Holy Cross to combat the *raskol*, and this proved to be the first of a number of such communities.[35]

For all their efforts, church leaders remained at best uncertain whether they were making any headway. Pobedonostsev, one of the most vehement opponents of the Old Belief, complained in the 1880s that 'we print books and distribute them, and then it turns out that they merely moulder in the diocesan offices', while his friend N. I. Subbotin, professor at the Moscow Theological Academy, lamented that bishops and clergy showed 'not the slightest interest' in the anti-schismatic periodical he was editing.[36]

Their gloomy scepticism was almost certainly well-founded. As we have seen, by the late nineteenth century, there were probably some ten million Old Believers, and they enjoyed considerable respect among many ordinary Orthodox believers. Nor was the number of other sectarians getting any smaller: by the late nineteenth century the new Protestant sects, the Baptists, Stundists, Adventists and Jehovah's Witnesses were mushrooming, finding a ready audience among the uprooted and newly literate working class of the cities and industrial settlements. Against the sects which they considered 'especially dangerous', the government proceeded with administrative exile. Among them were the Stundists (a sect derived from the German Baptists), since they 'reject all ecclesiastical rituals and sacraments, recognise no authority, refuse all defence or military service, describing the defenders of throne and fatherland as "bandits", and preach socialist principles, such as equality and the redistribution of wealth'.[37]

THE 'HOLY MEN'   Externally, then, the church presented a sorry spectacle for much of the eighteenth and nineteenth centuries: impoverished, dependent on the state, defensive in the face of rivals, isolated from social and intellectual life. All the same, at this very time a revival movement was just beginning to germinate which would enable it to make its own distinctive and creative contribution to Russian national life.

To understand the roots of this growth, one must realize that the Orthodox churches have a different view from the Catholic and Protestant ones of the way in which 'grace' reaches the sinner. In the Western view, the conferring of 'grace' is an act of God, granted to individual human beings either because they merit it (Pelagius) or because God in His inscrutable wisdom has so ordained (Augustine). In the Eastern view, however, 'grace' is a permanent state, implied in the act of creation itself, and potentially available to any human being at any time merely by virtue of having been created.[38]

In this view, what the believer needs in order to approach closer to God is a kind of 'spiritual map', which enables him to know himself and to cope better with the snares and hazards that await him on his journey. The general contours of this map have been provided in the New Testament and further topographical indications were filled in by the church fathers. Its subsequent custodians were the monks, who transmitted over the centuries a tradition within which the insights of the 'map' could be cultivated and brought to fruition within the heart of the believer. Their role in doing this was the principal function of monasteries within Orthodox Christianity.

Their method was to achieve a state of spiritual concentration in which a person would be in close touch with the divine 'energies' (the emanation of God's essence, rather than the essence itself). The key figure in transmitting this method was the *starets* or 'holy man', without whose guidance and inspiration the believer was always in danger of losing his way. The aspiring novice would swear absolute obedience to him, and would reveal to him all the secrets of his mind and heart.[39]

The theology of this tradition, known as 'hesychasm', was expounded in its most intense form by the fourteenth-century Byzantine saint, Gregory of Palamas, who was also writing at a time of religious crisis in a crumbling Empire. He proposed that through concentration on a simple prayer, addressed to Jesus and repeated many times in rhythm with breathing, the believer could attain a higher realm of knowledge and make contact with the 'energies' of God. In its extreme form, this teaching was contested by some within the Byzantine church, perhaps because it seemed to be connected with eastern religions, but it was never condemned as heretical.[40] It was cultivated and passed on after the fall of Byzantium in the great complex of monasteries on Mount Athos, which managed to survive the vicissitudes of Ottoman rule.

The first Russian flowering of this doctrine came with St Nil Sorskii (1433–1508), who spent some time on Mount Athos and studied the writings of the church fathers and the Byzantine contemplatives. He recommended practising a life of poverty and asceticism together with regular repetition of the 'Jesus prayer' as the best path to spiritual concentration. St Nil's doctrine of poverty and asceticism did not find favour in the Muscovite church in the centuries after his death, when it was cultivating a close relationship with the state and was a large-scale owner of land and serfs. It is probably no accident that it re-emerged in the second half of the eighteenth century, when the church had been forced to abandon both roles, and had to adjust to a life of relative humility and poverty in the modest space left for it by the secular Russian imperial state.

The man who did most to revive hesychasm was the *starets* Father Paisii Velichkovskii (1722–1794). Dissatisfied with the Latinate learning of the Kiev Academy, and unable to find the spiritual direction he needed in the monasteries of his homeland, he undertook in his youth a pilgrimage to Mount Athos, and there studied the patristic texts 'like a sacred treasure sent to us by God Himself'. He went on to collate, edit and translate them for Russian readers. With a number of disciples he founded a monastery at Niamets in Moldavia, where the ascetic contemplative techniques of the 'hesychasts' were consciously fostered, and from where followers subsequently spread all over Russia.[41]

The most celebrated centre of the contemplative 'holy men' was Optyna Pustyn', a hermitage (*skit*) near the town of Kozel'sk in Kaluga province, revived in the early nineteenth century by disciples of Paisii. A *skit* had little or no communal life: the hermits would spend the great majority of their time in their individual cells in private meditation, prayer, the reading of the scriptures and Holy Fathers, or in some form of handicraft. One or two divine services would be performed in common each week, and in addition each hermit was required to confess regularly to a *starets*, giving a full description of thoughts and wishes, as a kind of spiritual accounting. Three successive 'holy men' of Optyna Pustyn', Leonid, Makarii, and Amvrosii, maintained the hesychast tradition for nearly a century (1828–1911), and achieved widespread renown among both the common people and intellectuals for their spiritual wisdom and for their generosity in dispensing counsel.[42] It would scarcely be exaggerating to say that these three men achieved a kind of informal reintegration of Russian culture, in both its high and low variants, in a way which neither the imperial state nor the intellectuals were able to emulate.

This was happening at the very time when Russian literature, on a parallel but initially separate path, was moving towards minute psychological analysis and concern with moral questions as they manifest themselves within society. It is indicative that many of

Russia's major nineteenth-century thinkers and writers visited Optyna Pustyn' at times of distress or in the hope of finding spiritual illumination. Ivan Kireevskii went there frequently in the later years of his life, to help with the translation of the church fathers, and to take advice of the elders. At the time of his religious crisis Gogol visited it at least twice, and derived considerable consolation from the experience.[43]

Similarly Dostoevskii spent three days there in 1878 in the company of Vladimir Solov'ev after the death of his infant son. According to his wife, he returned thence 'much reassured and at peace with himself . . . He saw the famous *starets* Father Amvrosii three times, once among a crowd of people and twice alone, and felt the most deep and penetrating influence from conversation with him.'[44]

He described Amvrosii in the figure of Father Zosima in *The Brothers Karamazov*. 'All sorts of people, the simplest and the most aristocratic, would flock to see the *startsy* of our monastery, to fall at their feet and confess to them their doubts, their sins and sufferings and to ask for advice and instruction . . . The *starets* would come out to the crowd of simple pilgrims awaiting him at the gates of the hermitage . . . They would fall before him, weep, cry out, kiss his feet, kiss the ground on which he stood; women would hold out to him their children and lead up to him those possessed by hysteria. The elder would talk to them, say a short prayer, bless them and let them go.'[45]

For Lev Tolstoi things were not so simple. He was in rebellion against the church, proposing as an alternative his own rationalist and moralist doctrine based on the Gospels as he understood them. Yet the *startsy* fascinated him. He visited Optina Pustyn' five times, and he was bound for it yet again in 1910, during his final spiritual crisis, when he died. He was not able to receive simple comfort from his sojourns there: by his own admission, he felt the holiness of Amvrosii, his spiritual purity and wisdom, but was unable to achieve a dialogue with him. Amvrosii thought him 'arrogant'. Tolstoy remarked to his sister; 'How I would love to live there, carrying out the most humble and difficult tasks: but I would make it a condition that they should not compel me to go to church.'[46]

THE FAILURE OF REFORM   By the early twentieth century it was generally agreed that the church was not realizing its potential because of the way in which it was run. In April 1905 a manifesto was issued promising religious tolerance, and it brought matters to a head, since it removed the barrier to apostasy of which Pogodin had spoken as the only saviour of the church. From now on it was legal to leave the Orthodox Church and convert to another denomination.

During the spring of 1905 all bishops were asked to give their views on the possibility of reform. It transpired that almost none of them was satisfied with the current state of affairs. There was general agreement that the absolute power of the Holy Synod was uncanonical, since it breached the principle of *sobornost'* and subordinated the spiritual to the secular power – one bishop called it 'Protestant Caesaropapism'. To conform to its own stated principles and to exercise its proper influence in society, most bishops felt that the church should be governed by an elected Local Council (*Pomestnyi sobor*), of which the Synod would be merely the executive office. They recommended too that the office of Over-Procurator, as the bearer of secular dominance, should be abolished. As a whole, in fact, the church hierarchs were moving away from autocracy towards a reassertion of *sobornost'* as the basic structural principle of their believing community.

There was division, though, among the reformers about how the Synod should be replaced. Broadly speaking, they split into 'episcopal authoritarians' and 'parish-centred liberals'. Both wanted greater freedom from the state, but the former saw the bishops, with a Patriarch at their head, forming the backbone of the future church, while the latter felt that religious revival could best be nourished from below, by giving the parishes much greater powers, including that of electing representatives to the church's governing council.[47]

At lower levels of administration, bishops complained of the overwhelming weight of secular business with which they were loaded in their diocesan consistories, much of which was alien to the church's pastoral functions and even damaging to them. They objected to the fact that the consistory staff was appointed by the Holy Synod, wanting to see them instead brought under the control of diocesan congresses elected by the clergy and laity.

There was general agreement that the moribund condition of the parish was one of the greatest obstacles to the church's health. Some bishops even thought that its ineffectiveness had eased the way for the preaching of a surrogate Christianity among the peasants in the form of agrarian socialism. Reviving the parish would mean restoring *sobornost'* from below, and thus preparing the way to revive true Christianity and defeat socialism. To do this, the parish should be granted the standing of a juridical person, able to acquire property, manage its own finances, build and run schools, organize charitable work and perhaps provide cheap credit for peasants and artisans. Reformers were divided over whether priests should continue to be appointed by bishops or should be elected by parish assemblies.[48]

The person appointed to succeed Pobedonostsev in October 1905 as Procurator of the Holy Synod, Alexander Obolenskii, was a convinced supporter of the idea of a Local Council. He summoned a Pre-Conciliar Commission, consisting mostly of bishops and theologians, to discuss the various ideas for reform and to submit draft proposals to a future council. This Commission sat for several months in 1906 and recommended convening a Local Council, to be elected by clergy and laity, which would itself elect a Patriarch. Obolenskii warned that parish reform was also urgent, in view of the threats from sectarianism and socialism, and the Commission proposed that parishes should become self-governing, should influence the appointment of their own priests, and should have the right to manage their own funds.[49]

In the end, however, Nicholas II decided against summoning a Council. It would have been the first since the seventeenth century, and, having only just survived the revolutionary upheavals and the confrontation with the first two Dumas, he did not want to provide another forum for possibly hostile opinions, especially since the result might be an elected Patriarch who could rival him in the eyes of ordinary people. In this attitude he was supported by Stolypin, who wanted instead to institutionalize religious diversity within the empire by replacing the Holy Synod with a Ministry for Religious Denominations, which would bear responsibility for all faiths.[50]

The irremediable weakness of the Orthodox Church was the most fateful of the deficiencies of Tsarist Russia. Even at their most secular, the Tsars claimed to rule by divine right, so that the very legitimacy of their authority was indissolubly connected with the church's ability to inspire a strong and lasting faith among ordinary people. Yet they persistently humiliated and impoverished the church in the interests of pursuing secular goals, leaving it in a condition where it was incapable either of reforming itself from the inside or of being manipulated from outside. In part, this was a sign of the latent *strength* of the church: it was potentially so powerful that the Tsars held back from unleashing that potential for fear of creating a rival.

The peasants' Orthodox faith was strong, and it was a vital part of their sense of community, but it was primitive and relatively inflexible. The church in its unreformed state was unable to help them by building bridges from low to high culture or to respond adequately to the challenges to faith posed by increasing social mobility and mass literacy. A pious young man from the village, as he moved into town, was more likely to become a sectarian or an atheist than a renewed Orthodox believer.

Structurally too, the church was vulnerable to the intrigues of someone like the debased *starets* Rasputin: the spectacle of a corrupt and semi-educated sectarian picking candidates for the Holy Synod did more than perhaps anything else in the final years of empire to discredit the idea of autocracy.

Towns and the Missing Bourgeoisie

Many nineteenth century Russian towns were so laid out that their history presented itself in layers to the approaching traveller. In the 1840s, Baron August von Haxthausen described the unfolding scene:

> On arriving in a Russian town . . . [the traveller] comes first to a Russian village, the remnant of the old one converted into a town. Here dwell the old peasants, who generally cultivate kitchen-gardens for the supply of vegetables to the town, carrying on their cultivation, not in enclosed grounds, but in the open fields. Passing through the village, he enters the town of Catherine II, built like one of the outer suburbs of Moscow: it is composed of long, broad, unpaved streets, running between two rows of log houses one storey high, with their gable ends turned to the street: here is concentrated the industrial life of the population: here dwell the smiths, the cartwrights, the corn-dealers: here are the inns, the alehouses, the shops etc. Issuing from this second quarter, he enters the modern European town, with its straight and sometimes paved streets, and its spacious squares: we see on all hands buildings like palaces; but this part of the town has generally a deserted appearance: the streets present little bustle or animation, with the exception of the droshkies stationed in the squares and at the corners of the streets, with which no provincial capital, or even large district village, is ever unprovided. The oldest buildings of this quarter are the public ones: the greater number of the private houses date from after 1815.[1]

Haxthausen was talking of Khar'kov, but his remarks would apply to many medium-sized and larger Russian towns of the period. The geography of these places was also their history. They were at one and the same time peasant village, artisan precinct and residence of the powers that be. Symbolically, the latter function occupied the centre of the town and rendered it lifeless: for in the eyes of the authorities, the town was a place where authority was exercised, and also where dignity, grandeur, hygiene and public order were on display for all to see.[2] It both exemplified and practised the peculiar virtues of the empire as a whole. It was an imperial institution imperfectly grafted on to a peasant society.

In most of Europe towns have had a crucial role to play in the formation of nations. They have been the places where, in the terminology of Karl Deutsch, 'assimilation' and 'mobilization' most frequently take place, where a language is fixed, patterns of culture, social intercourse and economic exchange are forged, and where civic associations are formed. In France, as Eugen Weber has shown, 'peasants became Frenchmen' as urban customs and organizations disseminated themselves in the countryside: railways, schools, manufactures, newspapers, literacy in the national language.[3]

However, for towns to play this role, they have to be distinguished in some way other than mere size from the villages which surround them, either through wealth, culture, independent institutions or through charters and immunities granting them self-government or a special legal status. In Russia, right up to the nineteenth century, this distinction was minimal. In this respect Russian towns continued to play the role which, according to Max Weber and Otto Brunner, traditional cities exercised in Europe until the early middle ages and in Asia right up to the twentieth century. In such societies there were two distinct and mutually exclusive commercial milieux: on the one hand 'a peasant-agrarian world with local markets and often well-developed domestic and village crafts', and on the other a cosmopolitan centre of exchange, 'the seat of the elites, of a long-distance commerce in which those elites or the traders in their service play the decisive role, and of certain luxury crafts, such as gold- and silversmithery'.[4]

In such economic surroundings, which characterized Russia till the early nineteenth century, commercial elites were either servitors or dependent clients of the ruling powers, while the great majority of plebeian traders and craftsmen were indistinguishable from peasants. One and the same person would often combine several skills, and until the eighteenth century no craft was organized in a guild, with its own programme of training and qualification. There was thus no basis on which municipal corporations could be built, of the kind which emerged in much of Europe from the eleventh century onwards. 'City air' did not 'liberate', and towns were usually administered as part of the rural district in which they lay. If a serf came to the city and practised a trade or craft, then he remained a serf, still tied by personal bondage to his lord and sending him regular quit-rent. If a fugitive, he could at any time be reclaimed.[5]

In Russia international trade actually weakened in the late middle ages. After the fall of Byzantium and the fragmentation of the Golden Horde, Russia stood aside from the great trade routes of the world, and its own immense extent and relatively infertile soil made it difficult to generate more than local commerce. The manufacture of articles in everyday use was carried out mainly by peasant, themselves or by modest artisans, for the needs of perhaps a small town and a few surrounding villages.

This meant that from the sixteenth to the eighteenth centuries probably a greater proportion of the population was engaged in trade than in most European countries, but that trade was nearly all on a tiny scale and conducted by people who did not specialize in trade or manufacture, but simultaneously practised small-scale agriculture as well, or perhaps hunting and fishing. The amount of money in circulation was small, and coinage was heavy and inconvenient, so that merchants were driven to considerable expenditure merely to convey it or store it in security. Paper money, when it came in the 1760s, proved to be unstable. Devices such as bills of exchange and letters of credit, let alone joint stock companies, were non-existent, while the law and customs of contract were in their infancy. As late as the 1770s the English clergyman William Coxe remarked that 'Russian merchants and tradesmen seldom keep any book of accounts, as few of them can either read or write, and they are unacquainted with the knowledge of figures. Their manner of reckoning is by a kind of machine with several rows of wires, upon which beads are strung . . . By means of this machine they subtract, multiply and divide with great exactness.'[6]

The absence of elementary commercial practices meant that all transactions carried a higher element of risk than in more settled and prosperous economies, where a businessman's word was his bond and might if necessary be enforced in the law-courts. To cover this risk, profits had to be high and the enforcement of contract sometimes brutal. Bankruptcies were frequent, and creditors were unprotected. Most foreigners considered the Russian commercial world to be a jungle of sharp practice and downright fraud.[7]

For these reasons, Russia remained largely a country of small-scale manufacture, local trade and cottage industry. Even the largest cities, with the possible exception of St Petersburg, had a rural air about them. As Coxe observed, 'The merchants and peasants still universally retain their beards, their national dress, their original manners; and, what is most remarkable, the greatest part of the merchants and burghers of the large towns, even the citizens of St Petersburg and Moscow, resemble, in their external appearance and general mode of living, the inhabitants of the smallest village.'[8]

Commerce which exceeded purely local significance was usually conducted by itinerant merchants, or from the mid-seventeenth century at urban trade fairs. The largest of these was in Nizhnii Novgorod, whose location gave it easy access to rivers leading all the way from the Baltic to Central Asia. Originally established in 1624, this fair met annually in July and August, and by the early nineteenth century had an annual turnover estimated at 140 million rubles, three-quarters of which was Russian, especially clothing and metal goods.[9]

Not until the mid-nineteenth century were fairs being replaced as the main purveyor of commodities by settled shops trading permanently. Only in Moscow had such retail trade developed on a large scale before then, in the *gostinyi dvor* (merchants' courtyard) on the east side of Red Square, in effect a huge oriental bazaar, where under glass arcades traders offered their wares in rows of stalls, each row specializing in a particular type of product. According to Haxthausen, 'It would be difficult to find in the whole world, under the same roof, a stock of goods surpassing this one in the variety and richness of the different articles.' All the same, even there, merchants declined to patronize the splendid new commercial exchange building which was opened in 1839, preferring their traditional stalls.[10]

St Petersburg (founded 1703) and Odessa (1794) were partial exceptions to the general pattern of the hesitant growth of urban institutions. Odessa grew especially fast, thanks to its key situation as the port handling Russia's buoyant grain export trade, and to the policies of the early nineteenth-century governor of New Russia, the Duc de Richelieu (a French émigré), who planned from the outset for a large city, with a modern port, grand public buildings, open squares and streets and good public hygiene. It became a great cosmopolitan city, populated by Germans, Jews, Poles and most of the nationalities of the Middle East, as well as Russians and Ukrainians.[11]

Right up to the late eighteenth century, branches of trade and manufacture which exceeded a modest local scope were usually declared to be royal monopolies, and those who conducted them thus became administrators as well as entrepreneurs, delivering up a fixed amount in cash or kind to the treasury, and making a profit only out of the surplus which remained. Such was the case with the fur trade, cereals, dyes, leather, vodka and salt, as the trade in these items became more widespread and specialized. Commerce was indistiguishable in principle from tax-farming, and many merchants did both.

The operation of such monopolies offered the best prospects of making a fortune in Russia, as one can see from the career of Vasilii Zlobin, a state peasant from Saratov guberniia, who in Catherine II's reign won the favour of Procurator-General Viazemskii and was entrusted with the running first of a distillery, then of a whole tax-farming operation. He used his wealth to acquire licences for the sale of salt in several provinces and of playing-cards for the entire empire. Soon he was making half a million rubles a year and riding around 'in a magnificent coach, in fine clothes, with a diamond medallion at his throat, the title of an honorary citizen, and millions in his purse'. True, his fortune proved as vulnerable as his acquisition of it had been sensational: when he suddenly lost imperial favour, he was accused of irregularities, had to mortgage his possessions, and died in 1814 a bankrupt.[12] These abrupt changes of fortune were typical of the unstable and factional Russian business milieu.

Industry thus came abruptly and selectively to Russia. In the eighteenth century, branches of industry connected with the needs of war – metallurgy, ordnance, shipbuilding and clothing – flourished under state control or licence. The iron industry was the largest in Europe, and right up to the end of the eighteenth century was exporting its products to other European countries, including Britain; thereafter it declined, since it failed to develop new technologies and suffered from backward communications and from British competition.[13] Between 1721 and 1762 merchants were permitted to purchase serfs as labourers for these factories, the only time any estate other than nobles and monastic clergy possessed this right. A few private entrepreneurs made their fortunes during the upsurge, nobably the Demidov family, who by the late eighteenth century were pulling in an annual income estimated at more than half a million rubles. But no coherent class of industrialists developed, with their own organizations, to influence government policy. Indeed, successful entrepreneurs would often seek and obtain admission to the nobility, buy a landed estate and thereafter downgrade their commercial and manufacturing activity. The rewards for nobles were potentially greater and certainly far more secure.

During the first half of the nineteenth century, private enterprise contributed a greater proportion of industrial growth, but a good many of the entrepreneurs were foreign, as one can see if one glances at a list of some of the largest mid-century factories in St Petersburg: Baird, Stieglitz, Thornton, Ellis & Butts, Hubbard, Carr & McPherson, the Duke of Lichtenberg. Even firms which were run by Russians depended to a great extent on foreign capital and technology.[14] However, during this period a class of native Russian industrial entrepreneurs did at last emerge. Few of them were nobles, despite the immense wealth in serfs, buildings and land at the disposal of some noble families. Most were either merchants or, more surprisingly, former serfs.

Many Russian towns were military in nature, especially in the east and south, where they housed troops stationed to keep an eye on the open frontiers. Smaller ones would have a blockhouse or fortress, larger ones a kremlin, or fortified area, inside which would be found the residence of the voevoda (military governor), the customs house and the liquor monopoly outlet. Between the kremlin and the city walls was the *posad*: the term originally denoted a suburb or quarter of the city, but increasingly came to indicate a category of the population, the people whose names were entered in the census books as discharging particular kinds of state obligations. Originally membership of the *posad* was conditional on owning a certain amount of commercial or industrial capital. But membership was hereditary and departure was difficult; since economic conditions were unstable, and obligations onerous, this meant that the *posad* contained many members who had long ago ceased regular commercial activity, yet continued to bear their share of obligations.[15]

Fundamentally, the town, with its inhabitants and institutions, fulfilled the same function as the village: it was a provider of recruits, taxes and other services to the state. Those services might be administrative, military, commercial or industrial, according to circumstance, but the people who discharged them were registered and fixed in the same way as state serfs. The duties of the *posad* folk involved conducting trade and manufacture, acting as accountants, surveyors and quantity controllers, building and maintaining roads and bridges, collecting taxes and customs dues, and acting as policemen, watchmen or firefighters. These were all tasks which needed to be done, and the state had no money to pay anyone to do them, so they became part of the *tiaglo*, the service obligation incumbent on certain urban dwellers, who in return were freed from recruitment and some other taxes, and were permitted to engage in certain kinds of economic activity. Fulfilling their obligations might involve *posad* people in long journeys, extended absences from home and considerable expense, usually uncompensated. In that sense a member of a *posad* was like a soldier, whose time, person and property were at the disposal of the state.

There was no institution which represented all the inhabitants of a given town. The *posad* people had their own assembly, the *posadskii skhod*, until the late eighteenth century, but in form it closely resembled the village assembly, and it performed similar functions. For the discharge of their obligations, its members were bound by 'mutual responsibility', just like villagers, and were similarly fixed at their dwelling place, entitled to leave only if the elected elder gave permission and handed over a passport. Fugitives could be hunted down and reclaimed, just like serfs, and the community had a strong interest in doing so, for otherwise it had to make up collectively the undischarged dues of absconded colleagues. The departure of a wealthy merchant could be a disaster for those who remained behind. For that reason, it was made very difficult, and the economically most successful therefore lacked the mobility to build on their success.[16]

The *posadskii skhod* made the vital decisions regarding urban welfare, the election and supervision of municipal officials, the presentation of grievances and petitions to higher authorities and distribution of obligations among the population. All its members were entitled to attend its meetings, indeed theoretically were obliged to: those who failed to show up were sometimes dragged bodily to sessions. All the same, the evidence suggests that participation rates were low, except perhaps when the distribution of obligations was under discussion. In practice, it was the wealthiest and most influential members who attended. They dominated the election of the leading city officials, since they bore the greatest responsibility for the fate of the community, being best able to make up potential shortfalls in the budget. The leadership of the *posad* was thus typically a tight self-perpetuating oligarchy.[17]

Peter I, conscious of the weakness of urban institutions, established commercial guilds, in the hope that they would provide a certain backbone both for economic activity and for municipal government; but he failed to imbue them with the requisite enterprise or corporate spirit. They enjoyed no monopoly over their branch of trade and until the late eighteenth century had no provisions regarding training or the quality of their products and services. Their main function was administrative: to provide a convenient subdivision of the *posad* commune, ensure the readier collection of taxes and, in the words of Kizevetter, 'to guarantee [to the state] the availability of craftsmen whom it would be possible at any given moment to call upon to carry out state tasks'.[18]

Meanwhile nobles, the church, peasants and in larger towns foreigners were all able to compete for the market of the *posad* folk without bearing comparable obligations. For this reason merchants and tradesmen continually petitioned the government for monopoly rights and a greater control over their sources of income. Occasionally they received what they sought, as when the *Ulozhenie* of 1649

– following urban rioting – gave accredited townsmen a monopoly over business establishments within the city walls. Typically, however, such monopolies soon crumbled, since the state lacked the capacity to prevent their infringement, and in any case derived benefit from economic activity conducted in competition with them.[19]

In 1775 Catherine II acceded to the persistent request of the wealthier merchants, and extracted them from the undifferentiated mass of the *posad*. Henceforth the title 'merchant' was to be awarded only to those declaring capital totalling more than 500 rubles (later set at 1000 rubles). Those with less were to be referred to as *meshchane* or 'townsfolk'. The merchants proper were freed from the poll tax in recognition of their special service responsibilities and corresponding dignity. In this way for the first time an honourable status was awarded to certain townspeople. But at the same time the principle of 'mutual responsibility' in tax-paying was seriously undermined, since those best able to bear the costs of it had been exempted. This could only lead in due course to the demise of the *posadskii skhod*.[20]

Catherine II's City Charter of 1785 was an attempt to deal with this problem, and also to begin the process of creating a 'middle class', an aim which Catherine explicitly set as part of her attempt to give her country autonomous social institutions. For the first time, the Charter took a straightforwardly territorial view of the city: that is, that it was a community consisting of its entire population, not just of the people subject to certain state-imposed obligations. All citizens received certain rights: for instance, not to be deprived of property or good name without redress in the courts. Merchants were freed from corporal punishment and given the right to substitute payment for military service and other obligations. The Charter divided citizens into six categories, each of which was in theory an independent corporation, enjoying the right to meet to conduct its own affairs and to elect representatives to the municipal council, which was responsible for overseeing the city's affairs as a whole, and for electing a six-man executive, headed by the mayor, to handle day-to-day contingencies.[21]

After the early years, however, in most towns this elaborate structure slid gradually into desuetude. By the 1840s it was discovered that the municipal council scarcely met any more in any town. One reason for this dereliction of duty was that, like her predecessors, Catherine failed to balance the obligations of urban corporate bodies with concomitant economic privileges. Both nobles and peasants retained the right to trade in the cities unencumbered by accompanying obligations: since merchants and other urban estates continued to bear many onerous duties, these outsiders had inbuilt advantages and hence posed formidable competition.

These advantages were of great importance for the development of *kustarnyi* (cottage) industry, which blossomed in the later eighteenth century. In textiles, for example, peasants were learning to adapt the simpler techniques of dyeing and printing for use in small workshops and selling their products to a localized market, often on the streets of towns.[22] It is interesting that in Russia the coming of heavy industry seems actually to have stimulated rather than displaced cottage industry. It generated techniques and produced tools which made small-scale production easier and more convenient. Given poor communications, the small producer then had a palpable advantage over a factory several hundred miles away, since he could sell his wares himself.

However, this was hard on merchants, who had additional responsibilities to discharge at their own expense. Moreover they had no security. Merchants who fell on bad times and saw their capital diminish automatically lost their status and relapsed into the category of *meshchane*, with all the attendant disabilities. In the absence of any security of status, members of urban estates felt over-burdened and threatened, and accordingly did everything they could to avoid municipal office, even bribing their colleagues not to elect them.

To curb the competition from outsiders, in 1824 the government acknowledged 'trading peasants' as a separate category, and decided to issue licences to them in return for a fee. This measure in turn proved exceedingly cumbersome to administer, for it meant catching up with countless humble street traders at their makeshift stalls, and charging them money which most could ill afford. Where it succeeded, it threatened food supplies to the towns, but mostly it failed.[23]

Even more damaging to frail municipal institutions was that the authorities hedged their powers around with petty tutelage and supervision – supervision which was seldom systematic enough to prevent continual abuses, but which could be invoked without warning to further the intrigues of this or that faction in the council chamber. Obtaining permission for unforeseen expenditure – for instance, to repair fire hoses or install new street lighting – could take years. The police, on whom the city authorities depended to maintain law and order, were not under their command but that of the provincial governor, who thereby had a potent means of interference at his disposal. Municipal officials more or less had to resort to bribery to get things done, but then lived permanently in fear of the sudden arrival of Gogol's 'government inspector' (*revizor*).

Attempts to combat the arbitrariness of the state authorities could prove expensive. In 1800 the mayor of Kaluga, I.I. Borisov, 'honorary citizen' and industrialist, complained to the Senate that unwarranted taxes were being extorted from the town. Thereupon the governor and police swiftly launched an investigation into whether Borisov had received official permission to employ the 'possession' serfs in his factory, and whether his honorary title had been properly acquired. He was pronounced guilty, and lost both his title and his factory. Faced with risks of this kind, it is understandable that people of wealth and standing were reluctant to assume public office.[24]

One result of the relative insecurity of urban status was that, although between the mid-eighteenth and mid-nineteenth centuries Russian towns were becoming less agricultural, more commercial and industrial, nevertheless the proportion of the population which lived in towns was actually declining, from 11% in the 1740s to 7% in the 1860s. This was in striking contrary motion to the rest of Europe during the same period. The reason for the decline seems to have been that price relationships made agriculture or cottage industry a safer source of income, while the relative abundance of land ensured that villagers were not pressured to seek alternative employment in towns.[25]

The abolition of serfdom rendered meaningless most of the distinctions which remained between the peasants and the *meshchane*, and the last of the distinctions from the merchantry was eliminated in 1863, when the *meshchane* were exempted from the poll tax. The government did not however go so far as to abolish the *meshchanstvo* as a separate social estate, leaving it with a few functions, mostly police registration and social welfare.[26]

Not until 1870 did most towns receive a statute which at last made it possible to speak of a functioning municipality (only St Petersburg in 1846, and Moscow and Odessa in 1862–3, were reformed earlier). Under legislation passed in that year towns received elected councils responsible for municipal finance, utilities, social welfare, public health and education. The electoral provisions ignored estate categories entirely: they were based purely on property ownership, and were heavily weighted in favour of the wealthy. In St Petersburg, for example, in the first municipal elections, the wealthiest curia consisted of 202 voters, the second of 705, and the third of 15,233: as a result, a deputy from the first curia represented 2.4 voters, one from the third curia 181.3. This system had the unfortunate effect that it excluded from citizenship anyone who merely rented an apartment rather than owned it, a category which included many distinguished scholars and professional people. However, at least it provided a basis for self-government which was free of officially defined categories. Moreover, the governor and the treasury were now able to challenge municipal decisions only where they held them to be illegal, not on other grounds.[27]

In other respects, however, municipal government retained many of the defects it had previously suffered from. Its right to raise revenue was limited, and the police force which had to implement many of its decisions remained as before under the command of the governor. Furthermore, governors and police chiefs did not always observe the restraints on their authority imposed by the 1870 law. On a number of occasions mayors were forced to resign after incurring the displeasure of the authorities, notably Boris Chicherin as mayor of Moscow in 1883, when he made a speech calling for a unification of zemstvo and municipal activists.[28] A new electoral law in 1892 made the electoral system even less democratic and strengthened official supervision of the municipalities.

Only one urban group in the empire generated its own autonomous political life and at the same time projected its own vision of nationhood: that was the Moscow merchants. Their original core lay among communities of Old Believers who had settled in Moscow around the Rogozhskii and Preobrazhenskii cemeteries during the period of relative toleration of their faith under Catherine II. Even more than the Old Believer communities in the far north, they developed a flourishing commercial life, not least because of the strong ties of kinship and trust which bound them and which replaced the missing framework of commercial and contract law. The earlier generations practised strict community of property and denied family inheritance. This made it relatively easier for them to accumulate capital – though it is said that in some communities a horse and cart would hover at the door of a dying person to remove his valuables before his relatives could secure them! They would also take in runaway serfs, orphans and destitute people, protect them from police investigation, inculcate in them their own strict moral code and retrain them in a useful skill.[29]

During the first half of the nineteenth century many wealthier Old Believer families forsook these austere morals and began to accumulate hereditary fortunes. Under pressure from the persecution of Nicholas I many of them also joined the *edinoverie*. Whatever their compromises, however, they never altogether lost their distrust of the imperial state and its bureaucracy. Their patriotism rested not on the official church and the tsarist system but on the religious instincts and the independent economic activity of the ordinary people. It was the closest approximation to 'bourgeois nationalism' that might be found in Imperial Russia.[30]

As a geographical setting, Moscow fitted the aspirations of its leading merchants perfectly. Already by the mid-eighteenth century it was the focus of the largest unified market zone in the empire.[31] It was the centre of an extensive and diverse industrial region in which light industry and textiles played the major role – producing mainly articles for popular consumption, unlike Russia's other industrial regions. It was also the hub of the empire's communications, and specifically of the rapidly growing network of railways, which was the vital instrument in mobilizing Russia's wealth during the second half of the nineteenth century. Culturally, it was a symbol of *Rus'*, of pre-imperial Russia, the 'original capital city' (*pervoprestol'nyi gorod*) where each Emperor was still crowned, and which was therefore still capable of offering a counterweight to the grimly Europeanized capital city on the Neva.[32]

During the 1860s and 1870s Moscow merchants were at the forefront of agitation for an 'organic' and 'national' economic policy, which would promote investment not by seeking finance from abroad but by encouraging the establishment of banks at home, raising protective import tariffs and using targeted state support – tolerating a certain level of inflation and the continued use of the paper ruble if this was necessary. V.A. Kokorev, one of the principal proponents of this point of view, argued that the government should if necessary print extra paper rubles to finance railway-building: the return would justify it, and in any case the people (as distinct from foreign bankers) trusted the *assignaty*.[33]

For similar reasons, Moscow merchants' organizations supported expansion into Central Asia and better exploitation of all the empire's peripheral regions – though they were worried by the competition from the Polish textile industry once tariff barriers with Poland had been abolished in accordance with their own policy.[34]

Overall, one may say that competent internal organization and vigorous, well-targeted lobbying among government officials enabled Moscow merchants to defend their own interests, and to promote some of their political aims. It cannot, however, be said that they ever enabled the commercial middle class to replace the nobility as the principal social base of tsarism – partly because they themselves did not fully represent the interests of industrialists and traders from other regions of the empire. Nor did they ever win control over official economic policy, as distinct from influencing certain aspects of it.

In some ways their greatest influence turned out to be in the field of arts and culture, where they succeeded in leaving their mark in a way which adumbrated a new definition of nationhood. The most remarkable pioneering effort was that of P.M. Tret'iakov, owner of a flourishing textile mill in Kostroma, who founded and directed a picture gallery with the express aim of providing a collection of Russian art for the general public. His aim was not that of the usual art patron, to collect fine artefacts for his appreciation and that of a few chosen friends. On the contrary, as he wrote to his daughter towards the end of his life, 'My idea from my earliest years was to make money so that what had been accumulated by society should be returned to society, to the *narod*, in some sort of beneficial institutions. This thought has never deserted me during my entire life.'

He stipulated in his will, composed at the age of 28, that admission to his gallery should be in the range of ten to fifteen kopecks, so that even the less well-paid could enjoy it. In a sense, what animated him was the same desire to serve the people which inspired both the most selfless state officials and their most dedicated opponents.[35] The gallery in Moscow which still bears his name is a lasting monument to his aspirations.

The most prominent school of painters Tret'iakov patronized – though he always conceived of his collection as being all-embracing – was the *Peredvizhniki* (Travellers). What he shared with them was the desire to escape from the dual grip of the imperial court and the Academy of Arts, with their elitism and cosmopolitan classicism, and to promote an art understandable and available to the ordinary public. The original members of the school had broken away from the Academy in 1863 by collectively refusing the subject set for their graduation examination. They had confirmed their autonomy by setting up a profit-sharing *artel'* on the model of Chernyshevskii (see Part 4, Chapter 2) to paint and sell pictures depicting the life of ordinary people, particularly those which demonstrated the oppression suffered by the lower classes. Some of its members later founded an Association of Travelling Art Exhibits (hence their name), to make Russian art better known in the provinces.[36]

In the end, after two decades of secession, with encouragement from Alexander III, the *Peredvizhniki* rejoined the Academy. By that time it was widely accepted that their style of painting, which included portraits, landscapes and historical scenes as well as realist vignettes of *narodnyi* life, was a viable and distinctive Russian art form. The *Peredvizhniki* defined Russianness in a manner independent both of the imperial court and of the revolutionary movement.[37]

A comparable enterprise was launched in the theatre by the actor-director Konstantin Stanislavskii and his colleague Vladimir Nemirovich-Danchenko, who dreamed of an 'open' theatre performing the best of foreign and Russian drama at prices affordable by the masses. The theatre was to house a troupe run on communal principles, without the 'stars' who customarily monopolized the critics' attention and the investors' funds. Stanislavskii pioneered a style of acting which had analogies with the realist approach in painting, encouraging the actor to impart extra power to his performances by drawing on his own memories, experiences and emotions. With the financial help of Savva Mamontov, one of the wealthiest and most civically conscious of the Moscow entrepreneurs, they succeeded in founding the Moscow Arts Theatre, which soon established itself as perhaps the leading theatre in Russia.[38]

By the end of the nineteenth century, then, the cultural and intellectual life of Russian cities was developed at a far higher level than its civic institutions. Its most robust and enduring achievements were to be found in its universities, theatres, concert halls, publishing houses and art galleries. True, a basis had been laid for municipal corporate self-government, but, because of over-anxious official restrictions, it was still far from being able to function effectively. This stunted development reflected a general characteristic of Russian society at this time: that many of its members were still administratively categorized by functions which they or their forebears had once discharged in the service state. In most respects these categories no longer reflected reality, as the government had acknowledged in the electoral laws to the zemstvos and municipalities, which rested wholly or entirely on categories of wealth and property ownership. But the complete redefinition of subjects along economic divisions was still outstanding. Meanwhile, old border-lines obstructed new forms of solidarity and self-organization.[39]

By the early twentieth century, to integrate the huge new mass of immigrants streaming in, the Russian town had only rudimentary institutions, which excluded the great majority of the population and were vulnerable to government pressure. Yet towns were becoming the critical forum for the fissiparous social processes of a society which, rather than moving towards consciousness of itself as a nation, was on the contrary fragmenting in almost every conceivable way.

Over the previous two centuries the Russian Empire had undergone Peter I's radicalization of the service state, Catherine II's attempt to create the elements of civil society and local government, Alexander II's emancipation of the serfs and accompanying reforms, then an abrupt programme of heavy industrialization. Throughout this time it had continued to absorb new territories and new ethnic groups, finding different solutions for each of them, integrating them and not integrating them into the empire. Each of these changes had left its trace on the social structure, creating new social or legal forms without obliterating those created by its predecessors. The result was the segmented city observed by Haxthausen. Russia, in the felicitous phrase of Alfred Rieber, was a 'sedimentary society': 'throughout modern Russian history a successive series of social forms accumulated, each constituting a layer that covered all or most of society without altering the older forms lying under the surface.'[40]

In this condition Russian towns were becoming the incubators of new kinds of social, economic and ethnic conflict, with only the feeblest instruments of mediation to alleviate their severity. In their rudimentarily developed form, they were to be the arena of the critical political collisions of the early twentieth century.

6

The Birth of the Intelligentsia

The term 'intelligentsia' is one of the vaguest and most difficult to define in the whole social science vocabulary. There is widespread consensus that, if not a specifically Russian phenomenon, it made its first and defining appearance in nineteenth-century Russia. It would also be generally agreed that it cannot be captured in purely socio-economic categories, that it does not just designate people who have completed higher education or are employed in one of the professions, but carries a connotation of ideological attitude. Given this essential ideological ingredient, it is natural that the use of the term, historically speaking, has varied considerably with the political outlook of the user.[1]

The key to understanding the Russian 'intelligentsia' is that it arose from a discrepancy between social status and social function generated by the imperial state in its relationship to society, especially after the failure of the nobles' attempt to create civil society in their own image. As we saw in the preceding chapter, by the mid-nineteenth century, Russia's social structure was bursting out of the confines of the categories defined by the service state. The mismatch was especially marked in the towns, where taxable status was often only distantly related to economic function, and where education and culture plucked many individuals out of one social category without necessarily placing them in another. These were the *raznochintsy* or 'people of sundry ranks'. We have seen that as early as the 1760s Catherine II was sufficiently worried by their dislocation to try to create a new 'third estate' to offer them a home: however, nothing came of her attempt.

The term *raznochintsy* at least had some relation to official categories, if only by negation. The term 'intelligentsia', increasingly used in literature and the press from the 1860s onwards, did not even have that tenuous link. It originally designated a class of people rendered distinctive by their degree of education, but during the final decades of the nineteenth century the term gradually lost any fixed socio-economic meaning and changed its tonality so that it became largely subjective, an indicator of socio-ethical attitudes, a badge of honour or of disgrace, worn with pride or execrated with contempt according to the outlook of the writer.

The core of the intelligentsia was to be found among the *raznochintsy*, and especially among the professional people employed in increasing numbers by state, zemstvos, municipalities, law courts, universities and other institutions during the later decades of the nineteenth century. Since these employees had little or no opportunity to organize themselves in distinct professional associations, the vague and inclusive term 'intelligentsia' offered them a way of designating themselves and boosting their self-esteem. Lacking institutional markers, these people defined themselves in moral and increasingly ideological terms, as those who were educated, intelligent (in the normal sense of the word), independent and critical of mind, far-sighted, selfless and committed to a cause.[2]

That cause was dedication to the *narod*. The *intelligent* (member of the intelligentsia) was someone critical of the existing regime, concerned about the condition of society, and especially about the gulf which separated the elite (including himself) from the mass of the people. The *intelligent* was someone committed to closing that gulf by raising the people to the level of a humane and cultured existence. That attempt might be made from either a Slavophile or a socialist perspective, and the term was used in both senses for a long time. Ivan Aksakov, for example, argued that a 'Russian intelligentsia' was needed in the western provinces to mobilize the 'moral and spiritual strength of the people' there against domination by Polish culture. This intelligentsia would represent the people 'conscious of itself' and help integrate them into a worthy national life.[3]

But by the end of the nineteenth century one use of the term was beginning to crowd out all others: the view of the intelligentsia as the bearers of a radical or socialist outlook. From Dmitrii Pisarev's 'thinking realist' of the 1860s (the nihilist rejecting all traditional values) to Petr Lavrov's 'critically thinking personality' of the early

1870s (rejecting old social and ethical values in order to create new ones) the baton passed to N. V. Shel'gunov's progressive and socially committed *intelligent*, ready both to bring enlightenment to the people and to be enlightened by them. 'We, the intelligentsia, are the representatives of individualism; the people are the representatives of collectivism. We represent the *personal I*; the people represent the *social I*.' By going to the people and learning from them, but also by bringing to that encounter its own distinctive contribution, the intelligentsia would enable Russia to merge the two principles and thus to 'say her own word' in world history.[4]

The key task of the intelligentsia, in its own eyes, was thus to reknit the torn ethnic and civic fabric of Russia, to reunite elite and people and thereby to create a new society which was both more humane and more authentically Russian. The individuals who took it upon themselves to attempt that task had perforce come from a background capable of affording them education and culture, but had detached themselves spiritually from that background sufficiently to feel discontent and dismay at their isolation from the plight of the mass of the people. As the radical publicist N.K. Mikhailovskii put it in a much-quoted article of 1881, 'We feel a painful sense of responsibility before the people, of an undischargeable debt to them for their ox-like labour and bloody sweat, thanks to which we have gained the opportunity to reach these logical conclusions. We can say with a clear conscience: "We are the intelligentsia" . . . Through a blind historical process we are cut off from the *narod*, we are foreign to them, like all so-called civilised people, but we are not hostile to them, for our hearts and minds are with them.'[5]

In that sense the spiritual predecessors of the intelligentsia were Novikov, Radishchev and the generation of young nobles and army officers round the Decembrists. They had attempted to create the framework of a nation as that had been accomplished by elites in the countries from which they had drawn their culture, in France, Britain, the United States, and in post-Napoleonic Germany, by the creation of institutions of culture, philanthropy and social intercourse which had the potential gradually to broaden privilege downwards to the mass of the people. Frustrated by the autocracy and precipitated into a rushed uprising, they had failed, and with their failure the dilemma which was the intelligentsia's defining problem was starkly posed. As a result, the formative years of the intelligentsia lay in the reign of Nicholas I.

Most of those who sympathized with the Decembrists' aims had wanted to pursue them in alliance with the autocracy, not in defiance of it. After all, as Pushkin is said once to have remarked, 'the government is our only real European'. Such people were shocked both by the rebellion and by the subsequent execution of five of the principal conspirators. Nicholas I's regime, with its paradomania and its narrow-minded censorship, degraded social and intellectual life. Where a measure of boldness and free-thinking had once been *de rigueur*, under Nicholas a timid conformity became the rule. As Herzen observed, 'the aristocratic independence, the cavalier elan of Alexander's time vanished after 1826 . . . The dross of Alexander's generation moved into the top jobs; gradually turning into servile and mercenary creatures, they forsook the wild panache of aristocratic revelry and lost every trace of individual dignity.'[6]

It was now far more often the case that young nobles of talent and vigour felt alienated from the regime they had been trained to serve. Encouraged by that regime to believe that Russia needed change and that they were the best people to bring it about, they no longer took it for granted that a post in the state service was the best way to achieve that change. As Boris Chicherin, a student at Moscow University in the 1840s, wrote, 'How could I be attracted by state service in the political conditions then prevailing? To become the direct instrument of a government which was ruthlessly suppressing all thought and all enlightenment, and which for that reason I loathed with all my heart, to crawl abjectly up the service ladder, fawning on my superiors and never expressing my convictions, often doing what seemed to me great evil, that was the prospect which the civil service offered me.' Or, as Chatskii, the hero of the dramatist Alexander Griboedov, put it more pithily in *Woe from Wit*, 'I'd be glad to serve, but I'm sick of being servile' (*Sluzhit' by rad, prisluzhivat'sia toshno*).[7]

KRUZHKI This situation dictated new social forms and provoked new ways of thinking. Hitherto the dilemmas of reforming Russia had been discussed in officers' messes or in polite society salons, where elite and counter-elite – not really distinct yet anyway – could meet in natural and unembarrassed intimacy. After 1825 that could no longer be the case: army officers were carefully vetted for political loyalty, and agents of Nicholas's new Third Department, descendants of Peter's *fiskaly*, were ubiquitous in the salons, observing and reporting to their superiors. Young people of critical spirit sought more secluded forms of intercourse.

The natural place for them to meet was in the universities. That of Moscow was particularly suitable, since its successive curators, Prince S.M. Golitsyn and Count S.G. Stroganov, managed to attract good professors and to maintain a relatively tolerant regime even after 1825 in the more relaxed atmosphere of the second city. Some of those professors were also editors of journals, which kept up a modicum of independent intellectual life in the new conditions: Nadezhdin of *Teleskop*, Kachenovskii of *Vestnik Evropy*, Pogodin of *Moskvitianin*.[8]

With a few exceptions, however, it was not so much the official course of studies which attracted intelligent young members of the elite: it was more the opportunity the university offered them for gathering in cosy, informal discussion circles, or *kruzhki*. They did so not only to find congenial company or to avoid the eyes of the authorities, important though these motives were: they also subscribed to a philosophy which attributed cardinal importance to friendship, to the cultivation of intimate relationships in which complete openness and honesty were practised as a matter of principle. Its adepts shared not only their thoughts but their private experience with one another, and endeavoured to live up to the highest moral standards.

In this heady atmosphere, 'nobility' was defined by character, culture and behaviour rather than by birth, rank or wealth. It followed that it need not be confined to the *dvorianstvo*. The *kruzhok* was a miniature republic, in which differences of wealth and lineage were ignored in the interests of friendship and truth. P.V. Annenkov, a young intellectual who became the Boswell of the *kruzhki*, went so far as to claim an affinity with the village commune.

> The distinctive feature of the *kruzhok*... is to be found in the ardour of its philosophical inspiration, which not only eliminated the disparity in people's social position, but also

the difference in their education, their mental habits, their unconscious urges and dispositions, and transformed the circle into a commune (*obshchina*) of thinkers, prepared to subordinate their own tastes and passions to principles discussed and acknowledged.[9]

Unlike the *obshchina*, however, these young people mostly came from privileged social strata, chose their associates for conscious reasons, and were at liberty to disavow their choice at any time. As so often happens, ardent attachment to all those within the magic circle was reinforced by vehement detestation of those outside it who did not share their views, something which was to become a lasting feature of Russian intellectual life. As Herzen said of the circle of his great friend Nikolai Ogarev,

> They were bound by a common religion, common language and even more – by a common hatred. Those for whom that religion was not a matter of life and death gradually fell away, while others appeared in their place, and both our thought and our circle were strengthened by this free play of selective affinities and of binding shared conviction.[10]

For its members the *kruzhok* replaced all other social processes, becoming family, college, church and society drawingroom all in one. As one of them, Vissarion Belinskii, reflected, 'Our education deprived us of religion, the circumstances of life (the cause of which was the structure of society) did not give us a solid education and made it impossible for us really to master knowledge. With reality we are at loggerheads, and justifiably hate and despise it in the same way it hates and despises us. Where then is our refuge? On a desert island which is our *kruzhok*.'[11]

Herzen thus describes the routine of the *kruzhok* he led along with Ogarev: 'Our little *kruzhok* would meet at the home of one or another member, and most often at my place. Together with gossip, banter, supper and wine went a very active and lively exchange of thoughts, news and knowledge; each of us would communicate what he had read or found out, our discussions broadened our views, and what each one had worked out became the common property of all. In no branch of learning, literature or art was there a significant phenomenon which one of us would not notice and pass on to all.'[12]

The content of their discussions was shaped by the post-Decembrist situation, by the yawning gap between thought and deed, between noble moral intention and abject practical failure. The French Enlightenment thought on which the Decembrists had been nurtured did not offer an explanation of either the gap or the failure. But the new German idealist philosophy, just beginning to penetrate to Russia in the 1820s, did suggest some insights and some hope. Kant's postulate that our understanding of reality is shaped by the categories of the human mind, such as space, time and causality, was developed – or distorted – in later German thinkers into the view that the human mind in some sense 'creates' understandable reality. Fichte, Schelling, and later on Hegel, all of whom became popular in Russia during the 1830s, blurred the distinction between things-in-themselves and things-as-perceived, asserting that the human mind not only interprets reality but also forms it. In this view, mind and ultimate reality were fundamentally of the same essence: any change in thought was a change in reality, and vice versa. Hegel held that mind and thought were both part of the Absolute, which came to fulfilment only through their interaction.

This exalted concept of the human mind was extremely attractive to young men highly educated in preparation for state service, but in practice either repelled by it or barred from it as a result of some misdemeanour. It reassured them that even such apparently useless activities as thought and conversation had an impact on reality. This was the existential situation which created the 'intelligentsia'. Taking over the enlightenment belief in progress, they persuaded themselves that, in some inscrutable way, their intellectual speculations were helping to bring about a better future for mankind.

Confidence in themselves was a necessary condition for action, but certainly not a sufficient one. In order to know what they should do after the baffling fiasco of 1825, they had to attempt to understand themselves and their place in the social organism of Russia. The question also arose of what Russia was, what was its place in the world? 1825 had demonstrated that Russia was not what the optimists of 1812 had imagined and would not follow the path to nationhood of France or England. Thereafter patriotism, if possible at all, had to assume a different form. Educated people had become uncomfortably aware that they were estranged not only from the government, but also from the ordinary people whom they had aspired to help. So the question 'What is Russia?' became all-consuming.

Again German philosophy offered the hope of an answer. Herder had proposed the theory that each nation has an enduring essence, unchanging over the centuries and manifested in the language and culture of the people, in their folktales, songs, dances, their dress, food, customs and rituals. It was the task of modern writers, artists and thinkers to embody this essence in compelling forms and integrate them into world culture. Hegel assimilated this idea into his concept of the progress of world history, teaching that in mankind's path to self-realization in the Absolute, each nation has its own contribution to make, and therefore each stage in world history is marked by the spirit of a particular nation. He believed that the dominance of Romano-French civilization was nearing its end, and that the Germanic spirit would inspire the next period of human evolution.

It was but a short step from this assertion to the hypothesis that Slavic civilization, led by Russia, would succeed it in that calling, and would lead Europe on to a new and higher stage of civilization. In this way, intellectuals travelled by a circuitous route from the secular rationalism and social activism inspired by Peter, via the French and German Enlightenments and romanticism, to arrive at a version of history not altogether dissimilar to the old Third Rome theory.

CHAADAEV'S CHALLENGE   The immediate precipitant of the great debate about Russia was an article published in the form of a letter (significantly written not in Russian but French) in *Teleskop* in 1836 by a retired Guards officer, Peter Chaadaev. He was of the older generation which had experienced the 1812 war: he had abandoned his studies at Moscow University in order to volunteer for the army. Later he became associated with the Decembrists, but drifted away from them before the rebellion. Associated with no particular group or circle, he was generally respected for his sharp intelligence, integrity and independence of mind.

Russia, he charged, was a kind of void in the history of nations, a vacuous and footloose people who had accomplished nothing of real cultural substance. Poised between the civilizations of Asia and those of Europe, it had borrowed nothing fruitful from either. 'In our houses we are like squatters; in our families we are like strangers; in our cities we are like nomads ... Alone in the world, we have given nothing to the world, learnt nothing from the world, and bestowed not a single idea upon the fund of human ideas. We have not contributed in any way to the progress of the human spirit, and whatever has come to us from that progress we have disfigured.'[13]

According to Herzen, the effect of this letter was that of a gun-shot on a dark night: 'Whether it was a distress signal, a cry for help, an announcement of morning or an announcement that there would be no morning – whatever it was, we had to sit up and take notice.'[14] If Chaadaev's opinion could have been dismissed as the ramblings of an ageing eccentric, it would not have had the impact it did. Nicholas I, in a sense, did try to treat it that way: he had Chaadaev declared insane, and ordered him to report for a regular psychiatric examination. But he also showed that he took his ideas seriously by closing down *Teleskop* for publishing them.

The fact was that Chaadaev had touched a raw nerve. His indictment conveyed effectively the hollowness of Russia's imperial culture, its lack of organic development and of ethnic substance. This was something which most intellectuals sensed. Indeed, others had articulated it earlier. The poet Prince P.A. Viazemskii, for example, had written in 1823: 'Literature should be the expression of the character and opinions of a people. Judging by the books which are printed in our country, one might conclude either that we have no literature or that we have neither character nor opinion.'[15]

One could not, then, ignore Chaadaev's diagnosis, but on the other hand no one could simply accept it either – not even Chaadaev himself, who in his later writings suggested that Russia's lack of historical experience bestowed on her a youthful freshness which might prove in the future to be a strength.[16] Serious thinkers felt bound to take up his challenge: one way and another, the questions he raised haunted Russian thinking for several decades.

THE SLAVOPHILES   One response was to declare that Chaadaev was mistaken. Russia did have its own history, its own culture, its own valuable contribution to make to the world. Chaadaev had simply overlooked them, blinded, like most of his generation, by the superficial and seductive culture of the West. In the course of this debate, the 'west' became a determining concept in Russian intellectual life, representing everything Russia had imperfectly borrowed while becoming a European great power, and which it should now, according to one's viewpoint, either embrace more firmly or resolutely reject. In the course of the debate, the real and diverse countries of western Europe were distorted beyond recognition, homogenized in a convenient package to be either worshipped or abhorred.

The adherents of the first point of view became known as Slavophiles. They originated in the *beau monde* of Moscow, and their characteristic milieu was the salon rather than the *kruzhok*. This befitted their position as relatively wealthy landowners. Avdot'ia Petrovna Elagina would systematically invite promising young writers, scholars and society figures to her drawingroom, and took pleasure in introducing them to one another, as well as in listening to their readings and offering friendly but perceptive advice. At first she received people of differing opinions and currents, but by the kind of self-selection Herzen described Slavophiles came to predominate.[17]

It may be said that Slavophilism was born in 1834, when Ivan Kireevskii, a convinced disciple of Schelling and Hegel, married a young woman who had been brought up in the traditional piety of the Orthodox Church. When he read Schelling to his bride, she remarked that the German philosopher's thoughts were already familiar to her from the Greek church fathers, on whose writings she had been nurtured. Amazed by this discovery, Kireevskii set about studying and translating patristic literature. In the course of his work, he took theological advice and spiritual guidance from Father Makarii at Optyna Pustyn', renewing the link with the ascetic, contemplative tradition in Orthodoxy which eighteenth-century elites had almost completely lost.

Kireevskii felt his studies equipped him to rebut Chaadaev's strictures on the emptiness of Russian culture. In reality, he asserted, Russia had a rich heritage, derived ultimately from Byzantium and transmitted by the Orthodox Church. Russia, in fact, had preserved what the West had lost, the integrity of the Christian faith, manifested in its church and in its social institutions, especially the peasant commune. Now, however, this heritage was under threat, as a result of the way Russia's elite had been disfigured by alien influences since the early eighteenth century.

In the eyes of Kireevskii and his colleagues, what was valuable about Russian culture and social arrangements was their *sobornost'*, their 'conciliarity' or 'congregationalism'. In their eyes, the Roman Church had violated *sobornost'* in the ninth century, when it added the word *filioque* to the Creed without obtaining the authorization of an Ecumenical Council. Thereafter Rome had been a schismatic church, able to maintain the integrity of its doctrine only by the imposition of worldly authority. Aleksei Khomiakov, who became the major theorist of *sobornost'*, defined the concept as 'unity in multiplicity', a faculty whereby individuals are able to join with others in decision and action, each making his own distinctive contribution but gaining strength from the diverse contributions of others. Only through this principle could the individual fulfil himself as a person, 'not in the impotence of spiritual solitude, but in the might of his sincere spiritual union with his brothers, with his Saviour'.[18]

Without *sobornost'*, Khomiakov asserted, man was doomed to a spiritual poverty which manifested itself in egoism, mercenariness, factionalism and abstract rationalism, all of which the Slavophiles held to be characteristic of the West. Luther and the Protestants had been right to rebel against the false authority of Rome, but, imprisoned by western traditions, had found nothing better than individual judgement with which to replace this authority. Even the scriptures, to which Protestants liked to appeal, were interpreted in the light of individual judgement undisciplined by the *sobornyi* church. 'Protestantism retained the idea of freedom and sacrificed to it the idea of unity.'[19]

This unmitigated individualism was the fundamental reason for the spiritual crisis of the West, which the Slavophiles maintained was leading to its inner decay. Russia, by contrast, was young and unencumbered by false ideas: it was inexperienced, but still illuminated by the full light of the Christian faith. The Russian people had no external brilliance: they were a humble and simple people, alien to luxury, generous, outgoing and trusting, imbued with sympathy for the unfortunate, staunch in defence of their land, but otherwise peaceful and unpolitical. They were capable of supreme efforts, but also liable to bouts of idleness and passivity. Their innate *sobornost'* was best exemplified by the peasant commune, which Konstantin Aksakov considered 'a union of the people, who have renounced their egoism, their individuality, and who express their common accord; this is an act of love and a noble Christian deed ... A commune thus represents a moral choir, and, just as in a choir one voice is not lost but is heard in the harmony of all voices, so in the commune the individual is not lost, but renounces his exclusivity in favour of the common accord.'[20]

The Slavophiles contrasted these qualities with those of the Germans, who as always were the emblematic foreigners: proud, disciplined, organized, industrious, law-abiding, but without the inwardness and simplicity of true humanity. Unfortunately, since Peter the Great, it was precisely these features which were becoming dominant in Russian society too, inculcated by an oppressive and alien Germanizing bureaucracy. The Slavophiles held that Peter had created a fateful split in Russian society between the 'people of the land' (*zemskie liudi*) and the 'state servitors' (*sluzhilye liudi*). In the words of Aksakov, 'There arose a rift between the Tsar and his people, and the ancient union of land and state was destroyed. In its place the state imposed its yoke on the land. The Russian land was, as it were, conquered, and the state was the conqueror. Thus the Russian monarch became a despot, and the people who had been his free subjects became slaves and prisoners in their own land.'[21]

The political ideal of the Slavophiles was a return to what they took to have been the organic, truly Russian monarchy of pre-Petrine days. The monarch should restore *sobornyi* government by reconvening the *zemskii sobor* as a regular institution representing the various strata of the population. As a father caring for his people, he would not need to be bound by any juridical guarantees such as were laid down in Western constitutions, but he did need the regular contact with them which a *zemskii sobor* would ensure. The church had also become bureaucratized and needed to return to its own basic principles by abolishing the Holy Synod and restoring the *pomestnyi sobor* (local council) as its governing body, properly elected to give due weight to the voices of prelates, monks, priests and laity. At the lowest level, the parish council must also be reinstated, as an autonomous body empowered to elect its own priest and tend the material life of the congregation.

Serfdom was abhorrent to the Slavophiles, since it did not allow the application of *sobornye* principles in economic life or in the conduct of village affairs. Censorship they also rejected: true harmony depended on each voice in the choir actually being heard and not stifled by crude external interference.

The Slavophiles represented a major turning-point in the search for a Russian national identity. They were the first thinkers to draw systematic conclusions from the huge gulf which had opened up between the imperial elite and the ordinary Russian people and make it the cardinal element in their thinking. Their historical analysis of that rift was deficient in several respects. To take only the most obvious examples: serfdom long pre-dated the supposedly Germanizing reforms of Peter the Great, while *sobornye* principles in the church had been crudely violated by his predecessors. How far Russians had ever exemplified the qualities the Slavophiles praised is debatable. But they had correctly identified the main obstacle to Russian nationhood.

Their views had some similarity with the old Third Rome theory, based as it was on the idea that the Roman Church was suffering from an original sin which Russia had rejected, preserving Christianity in its original form. But they suffered from the familiar confusion between the national and the universal: their insistence on the peculiar Russianness of the human qualities they admired rendered their ideas liable to degenerate into xenophobic chauvinism.

WESTERNERS   The Slavophiles' adversaries are often referred to as 'Westerners', but the term is misleading if it implies an idealization of the West or an intention to imitate it. The fact is that most Westerners disapproved of the contemporary West almost as much as did the Slavophiles. If they admired the past of western Europe, then so did many Slavophiles. The Slavophiles' thinking, moreover, derived as much from Western philosophy as did that of the Westerners. Herzen, an ambivalent member of the 'western' camp, felt this similarity of background and outlook keenly, which is why he jokingly called the Slavophiles *nos amis les ennemis*.[22]

Liah Greenfeld has rightly pointed out that both Slavophiles and Westerners were 'steeped in *ressentiment*', the resentful reaction against a neighbouring civilization perceived as superior. 'Both were

Westernisms, for ... both defined the West as the anti-model. And both were Slavophilisms, for the model for them was Russia, which they idealised each in its own fashion, and whose triumph over the West both predicted.'[23]

This general dependence on Western models was scarcely surprising, since the state had been fostering it for well over a century, to the extent that, as one historian has remarked, 'many of the country's lecture halls were in effect located in Berlin, Munich and Paris.'[24] By the early nineteenth century, when educated Russians studied French, German or English culture and thought, they were delving into their own heritage. They were even rediscovering a kind of homeland, which had been theirs in the most sensitive years of youth, and the rediscovery was tinged with all the pain and yearning of exile or of unrequited love. That is why the word 'West' has from that day to this evoked such a powerful reaction among Russians, whether positive or negative – a reaction which long ago lost contact with the 'really existing' countries that make up western Europe and North America.

Symptomatic of this emotional condition was the lively public reaction to the lectures of Timofei Granovskii on medieval European history, delivered at Moscow University in 1843. There is no doubting Granovskii's devotion to Russia, yet he laid special emphasis on those European traditions which had never come to Russia, or had affected her only weakly: the classical heritage of the city-state, republicanism and Roman law; the intellectual tradition derived from medieval scholasticism and nurtured in the universities; the political independence of the Roman Catholic Church; feudalism resting on fealty and contract between lord and vassal; the immunities of cities and corporations; the rights of parliaments and law-courts. According to Annenkov, at the end of his lecture on Charlemagne, 'when the professor turned to the public to remind them what an immeasurable debt of gratitude we owe to Europe, from which we have received the benefits of civilisation and a humane way of life, which she had earned by blood, toil and bitter experience, his words were lost in a surge of applause from every corner of the auditorium.'[25]

Westernism always provided this vivid sense of what was missing in Russia, together with the desire to begin making up the deficit. But a spiritual orientation towards what one lacks carries with it its own debilities: a tendency to sweeping and categorical argument, to dismiss unheedingly the benefits one actually possesses, to hate and reject, focusing on the unattainable, rather than to cooperate, seeking compromise and practical possibilities. Those tendencies were to become characteristic of Russian thinkers. The 'West' was for them not a real set of countries, very different from one another, and each with its own difficulties, but an adventure playground of the imagination in which they could disport themselves, innocent of the self-discipline required by real institutions and actual problems.

This was especially the case in a country where a medium for serious public debate on fundamental political issues was lacking up to the late 1850s, and even thereafter was liable to unpredictable curtailment at the hands of a capricious censorship. This meant that intellectual life never really escaped from the *kruzhki*, each of which had its master thinker, to whom other members deferred rather than enter into debate. Disputation over ideas took place not in open discussion but in underground pamphlets and leaflets, the intellectual equivalent of salvoes fired broadside from a battleship: the only effective response was an equal and opposite salvo. Disagreements within a *kruzhok* usually led not to the evolution of ideas but to a split, over personalities as much as issues, and to the creation of a break-away group.

The material from which these master thinkers borrowed came first of all from German idealism, as we have seen, then during the 1840s from French socialism. The former led to some kind of reassertion of national identity, the latter to the rediscovery of the virtues of community. Put together, they generated the distinctive Russian variety of socialism.

BELINSKII   The man who summed up the peripeteia of Russian thought in this period was Vissarion Belinskii, archetypal habitué of the *kruzhki*, but also one of the first *raznochintsy* to pursue the path of independent thought. Son of a poverty-stricken naval doctor, he went to Moscow University on an official stipend, but was expelled for writing a play demonstrating the evils of serfdom. Nikolai Nadezhdin was one of his teachers, and was sufficiently impressed to rescue him by offering him reviews and articles. After *Teleskop* was closed, Belinskii passed on to *Sovremennik*, where his trenchant personality and style soon made him the leading figure.

A thin, consumptive, haggard young man, he was by all accounts transformed when expounding some idea which gripped him. Then his eyes would sparkle, his cheeks would flush red, and he would hold forth with passionate intensity. Ideas were for him an all-consuming obsession, and he was completely at home in the overheated milieu where 'every minor pamphlet of German philosophy ... would be sent for and in a few days devoured till it was in holes and stains and pages were falling out. People who loved each other would separate for weeks because they disagreed on the definition of the "all-embracing spirit", and would take mortal offence at an opinion about "absolute personality and its existence *an sich*".'[26]

For Belinskii the paramount question was how to reconcile the life of the mind with social reality in Russia. For a time he was gripped by the view that the only way to do so was by supporting the regime for the same reason that Pushkin had done, because it alone could bring enlightenment and material progress to his backward and benighted country. 'Russia', he asserted in a letter to a friend in 1837, 'will not develop her liberty and her civil structure out of her own resources, but will obtain it at the hands of her tsars like so much else.'[27]

Belinsky however did not have the irony or lightness of touch which characterized Pushkin. He espoused his idea of 'reconciliation with reality' with his habitual passionate intensity, and as a result broke with all his friends for a time: they were shocked to see their usually radical comrade crawling subserviently to the regime of 'Nicholas the Stick'. But equally characteristically, he soon abandoned his position, proclaiming 'I abominate my contemptible desire to reconcile myself with a contemptible reality!'[28]

Later on Belinskii placed his hopes in literature as a way in which Russian reality might be transformed and the rifts in Russian society healed [See the following chapter]. In political terms he moved towards what he called *sotsial'nost'*, which might be translated as 'social commitment' or even as a euphemism for the S-word which the censor forbade, 'socialism'. 'For me', he said, 'it has swallowed up history, religion and philosophy ... What does it profit me that *I* understand the idea, that the world of ideas in art, religion and history is open to me, if I cannot share them with those who should be my brothers in humanity, my dearly beloved in Christ, but who are alien and hostile to me because of their ignorance?'[29]

Belinskii's language betrays his debt to Christianity as much as to German idealism, but Russian socialism was to be largely atheist and wholly anti-clerical in its religious outlook, treating the church and its teachings as a component part of a repressive order.

BAKUNIN There were a number of strands to this socialism. The first originated with Mikhail Bakunin, who came from a family of wealthy landowners in Tver' guberniia. He was a leading figure in the Westerner *kruzhok* of Nikolai Stankevich, partly thanks to his flamboyant and dominating personality, partly because of his good knowledge of German, which enabled him to act as mentor towards those of his colleagues, including Belinskii, who could not read Fichte and Hegel in the original.

Bakunin came to socialism without ever having more than the most superficial contact with ordinary Russian peasants. His route to it lay not through knowledge of the people but through German philosophy. He saw the Hegelian dialectic as a struggle between those who upheld the existing order of things, both in Germany and Russia, and those who wished to destroy it to create a more humane society. It was in this spirit that he first conceived his famous dictum: 'The urge to destroy is a creative urge!'[30]

In his characteristic maximalist style, he identified the coming social revolution with the moment when the contradictions hitherto inherent in human existence are finally resolved in one great purgative conflict, after which humanity – and with it the Absolute Spirit – will come to full self-knowledge and be reconciled with itself. He believed the Russian people would be the bearers of this beneficent upheaval, because in Russia the alienation of the masses from the elite was at its most glaring.

> Any honest thinking Russian is bound to realise that our empire cannot change its attitude to the people. By its very existence it is doomed to be its blood-sucker and tormentor. The people instinctively hate it, and it cannot help but oppress the people, since its whole being and strength are founded on the people's misery ... The only worthwhile

constitution from the people's point of view, is the destruction of the empire.[31]

Bakunin believed that the Slavs as a whole had retained forms of human solidarity which the rationalizing, Germanized state bureaucracies of the modern era – including the Russian one – had undermined or were undermining. The imperial state he considered not Russian at all, but a kind of sinister mongrel, 'an original combination of Mongol cruelty and Prussian pedantry', or, as he pithily dubbed it in the title of one of his articles, 'Knutogermaniia'.[32]

This kind of state was totally alien to the Slavs. 'By their very nature and in their very being the Slavs are absolutely not a political, that is, state-minded people ... The Slavs are predominantly peaceable and agricultural ... Living in their separate and independent communes, governed according to patriarchal custom by elders, but on an elective basis, and all making equal use of the commune's land, they ... put into practice the idea of human brotherhood.'[33]

He regarded the spread of German power in Europe, and the domination of 'the German principle' in the bureaucracy of Russia as a form of creeping enslavement, from which Europe could be emancipated only by the Slav principle of cooperation and mutual aid. In his Appeal to the Slavs of 1848 he prophesied that 'Russian democracy, with its tongues of fire, will swallow up state power and light up all Europe in a bloody glow ...'[34]

Bakunin's imagery marks the return of full-blooded messianism, repudiated since Tsar Alexei, to Russian politics. Only now it took the form of a revolutionary belief, that a Russian popular insurrection would bring liberation to the whole of Europe. Bakunin always saw his revolution as all-European, and devoted much of his life to working among the oppressed of other European countries. He founded an International which had its main support in Italy and Spain.

Isaiah Berlin remarked that Bakunin 'has not bequeathed a single idea worth considering for its own sake'.[35] From a strictly intellectual point of view, that is correct. He never seriously argued out the contradictions in his propositions; he had little to say about the means or even the practical aims of the uprising he envisaged. He remained an overgrown adolescent enacting his fantasies on a universal stage of his own imagining. All the same, such self-confident, sparkling personalities often radiate a conviction beyond the importance of their ideas, and Bakunin was the first to articulate in such fiery and infectious terms the vision of the Russian people as the bearers of a revolution of world-historical significance, and to locate the motivation for that revolution in the split between the mass of the people and the state.

The heritage of this vision was to prove enormously influential, not least because it corresponded to a real social gulf and because it bore echoes of the original national myth which the imperial state had repudiated. Bakunin projected a flaming and persuasive idea, while leaving the details of its implementation to become the battleground on which the internal conflicts of the Russian revolutionary movement would be fought out in the coming decades.

HERZEN If Bakunin was the fiery prophet of revolutionary socialism, Alexander Herzen was its hesitant sage. He was born in Moscow, the illegitimate son of a wealthy and cultured nobleman, in the fateful year of 1812, just before his native city fell into the hands of Napoleon. He remained all his life an aristocrat by taste and temperament, brilliant, with a broad culture, attached to individual freedom as an ideal, impatient at the restrictions imposed on him by Nicholas's regime and concerned to do something to emancipate the people from their sufferings. At the age of fourteen, with his beloved friend Nikolai Ogarev, he stood on the hills outside Moscow, and took an oath to avenge the recently executed Decembrists by continuing their cause and if necessary sacrificing his life for it.[36]

He was true to his word: this underlying preoccupation remained with him through his endless discussions in the *kruzhki* and his frequent changes of opinion. He went through a fascination with German idealism and then with French socialism. Twice arrested and exiled, he saw the underside of Nicholas's Russia, though from the relatively secure position of a minor post in the provincial bureaucracy.

In 1847 he inherited his father's fortune, and decided to leave Russia, having tired both of the narrow-mindedness of the official world and of the incurable dissensions of the unofficial one. Once abroad, in France, Italy and finally England, he created almost single-handedly that enduring institution, the Russian emigration as a refuge where Russian intellectual life could carry on, projecting its image of an ideal Russian nationhood, out of the reach of censors and secret policemen. He was both the ambassador of a 'free Russia' abroad, and the purveyor of information to his colleagues back at home – not only information about foreign events but about conditions in Russia itself. During the 1850s and early 1860s his journal *Kolokol* (The Bell), published from a cramped and dingy office in Paternoster Row, London, became essential reading for high officials in the Russian government who wished to find out what their subordinates were concealing from them.

Herzen's reaction to France was characteristic of Russian intellectuals faced with the reality of life in one of the countries which collectively they dubbed 'the West'. He was irritated by the condescending – even if benevolent – manner he felt French intellectuals adopted towards him and towards Russia in general. He reacted against the high stone walls of Provence, encrusted with broken glass to defend private property against allcomers, whether needy or not. He felt they 'affronted the Slavic soul': contrasting with them the open fields of home, he wrote as early as December 1847, 'Long live the Russian village. Its future is great!'.[37] As for the bourgeoisie, supposed bearers of the ideal of liberty for which he had sworn to die: 'It is impossible to replace the dogmas of patriotism, the tradition of courage, the shrine of honour by the rules of political economy ... The heir of the brilliant nobility and of the coarse plebs, the bourgeoisie has united in itself the most glaring deficiencies of both after having exhausted their good qualities. It is rich, like a *grand seigneur*, and miserly, like a shopkeeper.'[38]

Herzen was an incurable scion of the enlightened, cosmopolitan, humane Russian aristocracy. That was true even before he witnessed the crushing of the workers' rising in Paris by the troops of General Cavaignac in June 1848, an event which finally convinced him, if he still needed convincing, that the bourgeois ideal of liberty was ruthlessly egoistic and mercenary, the natural ally of repressive government. The election of Louis Napoleon as President persuaded him that a republic based on universal suffrage could erect a tyranny no less oppressive than monarchs. There was no space here for the free unfolding of the individual personality within the supportive community, which had always been his ideal.

In these circumstances, his thought – always inclined to idealize conditions he did not have before his eyes – turned naturally to Russia, the homeland he had left for good. There, he hypothesized, for all that the state was ineluctably corrupt and overbearing, the people had been left untouched by its vices; estranged from the regime, 'people obey because they are afraid; but they do not believe'.[39] They continued, as far as they were able, with their old and preferred style of life, based on their self-governing communes and shared property. 'The commune saved the Russian people from Mongolian barbarism and from imperial civilisation, from the gentry with its European veneer and from the German bureaucracy. Communal organisation, though strongly shaken, withstood the interference of the state; it has survived, fortunately, until the development of socialism in Europe.'[40]

Once he had upbraided the Slavophiles for idealizing the commune, in which he had then seen only slavery and institutionalized poverty. Now he was prepared to see its potentiality as yet untapped, but at least unharmed by European mercenariness and ready to be developed by contact with European socialism. 'To return to the village, to the working man's artel, to the *mir* assembly, to Cossackdom, but not in order to freeze them in lifeless Asiatic crystallisations, but to develop them, to set free the principles on which they are based, to cleanse them from all the distorting artificiality, the unwanted flesh deposited on them – that is our mission.'[41]

Herzen ended, then, by believing that Russia, precisely because it was young and undeveloped, had the capacity to synthesize its experience with ideas imported from the West and thus to create new social forms, in fact an original style of socialism, which would revive Europe itself. It would do so on the basis of the village commune, which rested on the free cooperation of equals, and thus obviated the need for private property, a legal system and police, of the kind fetishized by western nations. To make this cooperation possible, though, Herzen believed the peasants need two things: 'land and freedom'. Thus he launched the slogan of the first generation of Russian socialists.

A more developed and consistent thinker than Bakunin, Herzen expounded for the first time what was to become the kernel of the Russian form of socialism. But he had little to say about the means by which his vision might be brought to fruition, and in truth he wavered a good deal on that point. He dreaded violent revolution, which he knew would probably destroy much of what he held dear in the civilization of Russia. He was also capable of hoping that the essentials might be accomplished by the autocracy. When he heard that Alexander II was planning to emancipate the serfs, he wrote a welcoming article entitled 'Oh Galilean, Thou hast triumphed!'. After the emancipation showed that such hopes were futile, Herzen was elbowed aside by younger, more determined thinkers without aristocratic scruples. He had set the terms of the debate, but he could not resolve the practical problems which flowed from it.

The intelligentsia was not limited to socialist thinkers. Some *intelligenty*, such as the Slavophiles and later the Panslavs [see Part 4, Chapter 3], envisaged other ways of bridging the gap between elites and masses. The importance of the *kruzhki* in generating images of Russian nationhood can scarcely be overstated. Out of them came (i) the distinctive Russian form of socialism; (ii) some of the major writers of Russian literature; (iii) some of the leading reformers of Alexander II's reign; and (iv) some of the main protagonists of Russification. It is no exaggeration to say that most of the rest of this book will be concerned to trace their heritage in the projects of Russian thought and Russian statecraft. But it was the socialists who in the long run were to prove most successful in bridging that gap, in reaching out to the people and galvanizing them for political action in 1905 and 1917.

Fruitful though they were, however, the *kruzhki* had serious defects which left their indelible mark on later developments. In the terminology of Miroslav Hroch, the activity of the *kruzhki* represented Phase A of the development of the Russian national movement, the period of 'scholarly interest', unduly prolonged by the conditions in which it evolved. The interaction between intelligentsia and people, when it came, took place belatedly, on a small scale and under conditions of great pressure. By then the intelligentsia had formed its collective personality in ways which were to vitiate its contacts with the people. Its members were marked by an arrogant gnosticism, the dogmatic and uncompromising worship of manifest truths, a manipulative view of organizations, a corrosive underestimation of both law and property, and a condescending attitude towards the masses paradoxically combined with high expectations of them. The intelligentsia mainstream had become socialist and split into two main tendencies, one of which (the Populists) took an ethnic and introverted view of the masses, emphasizing their peculiarly Russian traits, while the other (the Marxists) took an imperial and cosmopolitan line, stressing the integration of Russian peasants and workers into an international community. Socialism too was thus to be split by the two forms of Russian national identity.

7

Literature as 'Nation-Builder'

'The Tsar of all the Russias, he is strong, with so many bayonets, Cossacks, cannons, and does a great feat in keeping such a tract of earth politically together; but he cannot yet speak. He is a great dumb monster hitherto. His Cossacks and cannons will all have rusted into nonentity while that Dante's voice is still audible. The Nation that has a Dante is bound together as no dumb Russia can be.'[1] Thus Thomas Carlyle in 1840, and his bleak vision of a mighty empire without national identity because it lacked a defining narrative haunted many thinking Russians at the time.

The first version of Russia as 'imagined community' was based on a religious mission at its most elaborate in the compilations of Metropolitan Makarii and his scribes. It was thrust aside by the seventeenth-century schism and by Peter's reforms. It continued to exist, though, in rudimentary form in the cultural sub-conscious, cultivated in particular by the Old Believers. However it was so disconnected from the power structure that it could not serve as the foundation for a national myth, especially in an empire in which there were now so many faiths and so many nationalities.

Peter and his successors tried to create a secular myth to supplant it, to be nourished by Russia's size and diversity, her armed forces, the strength of her industry, her high culture and learning, and her position as European great power, demonstrated by numerous battle honours. This new myth necessarily entailed fostering a secular and Europeanized culture, together with the education system to sustain it among the empire's elites. As we have seen, Tsars from Peter to Alexander I strove to do this. Peter had initiated some of the necessary social and educational institutions: balls, soirées, newspapers, schools, an Academy of Sciences. His successors, especially Elizabeth and Catherine II had added to them theatre, ballet, opera, and given permission for private printing presses and journals of some social and intellectual substance.

By the late eighteenth century, in spite of the underdevelopment of the empire's civic institutions, the potential was present for a cultural and educational system which at its highest levels would equal the best in Europe. A major role in creating it was already being taken by persons and associations independent of the state which, after a difficult period at the end of Catherine's reign and under Paul, had again been given free rein by Alexander I.

During the same period a new Russian language had been taking shape, though in a chaotic and controversial manner. Peter's reforms had generated a veritable Babel's tower of linguistic confusion. Words and expressions were imported wholesale from Swedish, Dutch and German, especially in the fields of public administration, technology and war. Grammar and syntax were dislocated without any systematization of the innovations. To compound the problem, many educated Russians were beginning to adopt foreign languages, especially French, as their normal mode of communication, particularly in social life but increasingly in the home as well.

Russia was also adopting forms of social intercourse from France. There from the mid-seventeenth century salons made a major contribution towards the creation of a sense of civic nationhood distinct from the monarchy and potentially detachable from it, what Simon Schama calls 'the cultural construction of a citizen'.[2] An analogous process was going on in Russia from the late eighteenth century, but with certain peculiarities. The prototypes on which the conventions of cultured society were modelled were foreign, mostly French and English. The language of urbane conversation was usually French, or a form of Russian heavily influenced by French diction, very different from the language of church, chancellery or village assembly. To lapse into any of these inherited forms of Russian was considered bad taste.

Russian was not, however, altogether pushed into the background: it remained the official language of a great power, with the capacity for development and modernization. A Russian Academy (on the model of the Académie Française) was established in 1783, in order, among other things, to systematize Russian vocabulary and syntax.

It issued an authoritative dictionary in 1789–94, and a grammar in 1802.[3]

Their appearance did not end the disputes over the language appropriate to polite society and artistic literature: rather it provided ammunition for them. One party, led by the historian and fiction writer Nikolai Karamzin, argued that the Russian literary language should be purged of both bureaucratic and ecclesiastical influences and become more like the conversational language of polite society, that is, based on the simple and elegant syntax of French. In this form he maintained it would be better adapted both to intellectual discourse and to the analysis of feelings than the old Russian language, with its stiff Church Slavonic and Muscovite chancery roots adulterated by Petrine imports. His principal opponent, Admiral Shishkov, objected that his Frenchified style lacked both weight and dignity, and was cut off from tradition. Religious truths, he believed, could be expressed only in Slavonic, which had been a scriptural and liturgical language alongside Latin long before French had even existed.

Perhaps the language Shishkov championed might have become the vehicle for a Russian high culture had it not been for the sharp breaks in linguistic continuity brought about by the imperial state. As it was, after the end of the eighteenth century, that language remained peculiar to the clergy, whose unmodernized educational system still transmitted it together with Latin. It gradually became a symptom of their isolation from the imperial culture, and eventually even they moved away from it: too slowly, however, to participate in serious intellectual debate till the final decades of the nineteenth century.

The renewed Russian language opened up untried worlds of expression and systematic discourse, brought educated Russians yet closer to the major European cultures, and made possible the flowering of Russian literature in the nineteenth and twentieth centuries. But it achieved these benefits at the cost of deepening yet further the rift between the elite imperial culture and that of the mass of the people, a rift which, as we have seen, the church was unable to bridge.

Benedict Anderson has suggested that the creation of vernacular print-languages taken from the region centred around a monarchical court or capital city is a vital stage in the creation of nationhood. 'The convergence of capitalism and print technology . . . created the possibility of a new form of imagined community which, in its basic morphology, set the scene for the modern nation.'[4] Something like this happened in Russia in the late eighteenth and early nineteenth centuries. For most of Catherine's reign and again from Alexander I onwards, printing and publishing were in the hands of private enterprise, anxious to create and capture an audience, and able to distribute its products with considerable success in the larger towns and especially in the two capitals.[5]

Not that they necessarily provided a propitious milieu for the authors of *belles lettres*. In the later decades of the eighteenth century the liveliest market was in devotional and practical works, romances, adventure stories and children's books.[6] High-quality literature was still largely written for the court or for great patrons and was couched in the genres appropriate to such addressees: chronicles, odes, tragedies, epics, increasingly satires – genres heavily influenced by the European models which these patrons expected.

Once again, it was Karamzin who broke the split mould of literary genres by employing his new 'sentimental' language to write romantic stories, involving ordinary people, which had literary distinction yet also appealed to the intimate feelings of his readers. Later he transferred this style to the narration of history. His multi-volume *History of the Russian State* (1804–1826) was the first to rise above the dryness and fragmentation of the chronicles, and to provide an intelligible and appealing narrative thread for the non-specialist reader. In the words of his biographer, 'It became a rich source of "national subjects" for Decembrist and conservative writers alike.' His adulation of autocracy also opened up one of the major themes of intellectual debate for the next century.[7]

In the early nineteenth century there was a gradual transition towards a more specialist and egalitarian setting for literature in what one might term 'family circles' of writers, critics, editors and publishers, often located within an aristocratic salon or soirée, but becoming more autonomous and sometimes finding humbler venues. The conversation in such gatherings was informal, but serious and well-informed. One of the most successful salons was that of Karamzin himself, and it was continued long after his death by his widow. The later Slavophile and social reformer, A.I. Koshelev, was a habitué, and recalled it later with warm affection. 'The subject of conversation was not philosophical matters, but nor was it hollow Petersburg gossip and old wives' tales. Literature, Russian and foreign, important events in Europe – especially the activities of the then great statesmen of England, Canning and Huskisson – comprised most frequently the content of our lively talks. Those soirées ... refreshed and nourished our souls and minds, which was especially healthful for us in the stifling atmosphere of St Petersburg.'[8]

The model was French, and so it was natural that these salons should try, like eighteenth-century French ones, to shape public opinion. They also tended over time to become less exclusive and more democratic. As one of the most assiduous frequenters of them, Prince P.A. Viazemskii, noted: 'Parisian society was a republic then, ruled by an oligarchy of a new sort, consisting of intelligent people and *littérateurs*.'[9] In Russia too one can see in these salons the embryo of a 'republic of letters', to which one gained admittance by being good at the accomplishments polite society expected: entertaining conversation and literary improvisation in the form of epigrams, *bouts-rimés*, and verses penned in the albums of young ladies and society hostesses.

This meant that the 'cultural construction' of Russian citizenship had largely foreign underpinnings. To put it another way, citizenship in the Russian 'republic of letters' presupposed a cosmopolitan upbringing, the sense that one's roots were as much in Paris, London or Göttingen (the romantic poet Lenskii in Pushkin's *Evgenii Onegin* is said to have a 'Göttingen soul') as they were in Moscow or St Petersburg. To be fully Russian, one had to be a citizen of the world. Now on the one hand this meant that Russian intellectuals of the nineteenth century – some Russian aristocrats too – had the broadest and most universal culture to be found in any European nation. But it also meant that Russian elite culture and learning were more cut off from both the church and the ordinary people than elsewhere in Europe. In the opinion of Anthony Smith, 'lateral' ties, that is, ties with neighbouring elites, far outweighed, indeed almost smothered 'vertical' ones, that is, ties with the masses in one's native land.[10]

Another peculiarity of the Russian development was that, especially after the Decembrist rising, the authorities regarded with deep suspicion any manifestation of civil society – philanthropy, educational initiatives, the formation of interest groups and voluntary associations – seeing in them the progenitors of subversion. They regarded literature askance too, but in the duel with official bloodhounds literature had certain inbuilt advantages. Unlike music or painting, it dealt in words and hence could comment directly on political or social matters; but at the same time its use of words was ambiguous and multi-layered. Compared with other varieties of text, it posed the censor far trickier problems: it was difficult for him, without appearing foolish before the educated public (and censors were members of the educated public too), to assign a single unambiguous meaning to a text and then in good conscience declare it unacceptable.

Besides, literature already possessed a network of printing presses and bookshops independent of the government, and a good many eager customers, even if their taste might not always be what the aspiring writer wished. The 'convergence of capitalism and print technology' had already taken place, and was beginning to generate an 'imagined community' whose cohesion was to be sustained neither by the scriptures nor by the ordinances of chanceries but by the creations of gifted writers.

The thinker who put all this into perspective was Vissarion Belinskii. For him ideas were not just an intellectual pastime: they were to be put into practice. For that they needed to be disseminated, made available and comprehensible to ordinary people, and Belinskii believed that was best done through literature. Not that his devotion to literature was purely utilitarian. The truth, he believed, was beautiful and should therefore be communicated in a form that was itself beautiful: to do anything else would be to betray its essential nature. 'I am a *littérateur*,' he wrote. 'I say this with a painful, yet proud and happy feeling. Russian literature is my life and my blood.'[11]

There was another reason why literature was paramount to him: like Carlyle, he believed it could generate a sense of community transcending the narrow interests of individual social classes and estates. He complained to Konstantin Aksakov in 1840: 'We are so many individuals outside a society, because Russia is not a society.

We possess neither a political nor a religious nor a scientific nor a literary life.'[12] Belinsky approached the task of literary criticism in the same spirit as did Luther his Biblical exegeses: he was revealing the truth latent in a text, making it more widely available and indicating its links to other cardinal texts, thereby helping to form a tradition. As his language betrays, Belinskii viewed literature in a Hegelian framework, as a manifestation of the Absolute Spirit coming to self-awareness. In his vision, it played a vital role in the onward advance of history, a process in which different nations at different times took the lead in pointing the way forward. He was haunted by Chaadaev's castigation of Russian cultural emptiness, and he despised the vacuous chauvinism of the official nationalists; rejecting both, he saw in literature the potential for a way forward which was authentically Russian.

He hoped that literature would weave together the torn social and cultural fabric of Russian society, indeed create a society where none yet existed. It would, he hoped, 'pave the way for an inner rapprochement of the estates, forming a species of public opinion and generating a sort of special class of society which differs from the middle estate in that it consists not of the merchantry and commoners alone, but of people of all estates who have been drawn together through education, which, with us, has centred exclusively in the love of literature.'[13] Literature would be the means by which the Spirit would come to self-expression in Russia, the form wherein the Russian people would make their original contribution to world culture and the evolution of world history.

Before it could do this, however, Russian literature had to outgrow its infancy. Belinskii held that a nation's culture moves through three phases. The first is what he called 'natural immediacy', essentially folklore, the direct cultural expression of the people's ethnic traditions. Spirited and valid though it may be in its own terms, it is largely incomprehensible to foreigners and certainly contributes nothing to world culture. It is succeeded by 'abstract universalism', when writers borrow from foreign models, assimilating the best of world culture: works produced then, though worthy, are often pallid and lifeless, because they lack the robust earthiness which comes from folk culture. This is nevertheless a constructive phase – here Belinksii parted company with the Slavophiles – marked in Russia by Peter the Great. 'Russia before Peter the Great was only a people (*narod*): she became a nation (*natsiia*) thanks to the impetus supplied by the reformer.'[14]

Finally comes the phase of 'rational consciousness', when the culture is capable of synthesizing world-historical elements with its own ethnic traditions: this is the period of true greatness, when a nation contributes something distinctive and valuable to world culture.[15] This is the phase which Belinskii believed Russian culture was entering in his own lifetime. The first work which in his view embodied the new achievement was Pushkin's *Evgenii Onegin*, because of the way it absorbed folk elements into a higher synthesis. Belinskii called it the first 'Russian national narrative poem', and saw Pushkin as 'not only a poet, but also a representative of the newly awakened public consciousness'. 'A great national poet', he asserted, 'is able to make both the master and the peasant speak, each in his own language . . .'[16]

If we follow Belinskii's logic, the natural direction for Russian literature to take was to heal the ethnic rift by moving towards the common people, giving a detailed and authentic account of their life, and beginning to assimilate their language, not for ethnographic or documentary reasons but for moral ones, and to communicate the distinctive Russian national essence.[17] Such a literature would be critical of the conditions in which the people lived: it would have to be if it were to be honest. But it would also, at least by implication, project the ideal of a better life: since what was true was also beautiful, a genuine work of art could do no less.

Thus was born the theory of the distinctive Russian style in literature: realist, identifying with the *narod*, informed by deeply held social and political convictions, and haunted by the question 'What is Russia?'. Belinskii's insight was to prove extremely influential, not to say prophetic. This kind of literature, and the language in which it was couched, was to do far more during the next half-century than the output of state or church to lay the foundations for a Russian national identity which could embrace both elite and people. Russia's 'imagined community' was fashioned by literature more than by any other factor, and along the lines foreseen by Belinskii. Yet the very magnitude of the mission devolved upon literature put constant pressure on writers to move outside their profession and take on themselves roles to which they were by nature less well-suited: those of political commentator, public tribune, even religious prophet. Also, literature had to face the question of the Russian empire and what it meant, especially in the face of the original messianic national myth returning to the surface.

PUSHKIN   The first work which aroused Belinksii's full-hearted admiration as embodying his vision was Pushkin's *Evgenii Onegin*, which he called an 'encyclopedia of Russian life'. It was characteristic of him that he should praise it for the knowledge it afforded, and it is true that it offers a broad picture of Russian life at the period, in town and country, among the elite and the people. But what has sent Russians back to read it again and again is its depiction of the spiritual consequences of living in a society which regulates itself by foreign models, models which have been deeply absorbed by educated people without penetrating to the people.

Each of the main characters sees him- or herself in a distorting mirror of European origin and seeks a fate in accordance with the false reflection. Onegin has his dandified, disillusioned way of life borrowed from the poetry of Byron and from the drawing-rooms of Paris and London; Lenskii, with his 'Göttingen soul', declaims his beloved romantic verses, and misunderstands his bride in their light; Tat'iana goes into raptures over English love novels and recasts Onegin as a character from them; and the narrator weaves his way in and out among them, leading the same way of life, yet always just a little wiser and a little sadder, injecting occasional touches of common sense derived from experience.

The counterposition of elite European and popular Russian culture is at its starkest when Tat'iana tries to tell her old nurse that she is in love. This a concept utterly alien to the nurse, for whom marriage was a loveless and painful experience, meaning separation from her family and subjection to a strange one.[18]

Pushkin engaged directly with the problem of Peter the Great's heritage in his verse narrative *The Bronze Horseman*. This is a paean of praise to St Petersburg, but also a dramatization of the human cost inflicted on its inhabitants by building it on such an unsuitable site. Evgenii, the minor civil servant who is its 'hero', loses his sweetheart, drowned in one of the floods to which the imperial city is susceptible because of its low-lying marshy location. Wandering the city crazed by his grief, he comes up against the famous Falconet statue of Peter rearing up on his horse in a gesture of enlightenment and domination. Raising his fist, Evgenii fiercely but impotently curses the 'wonder-working builder' and then, struck with terror at his sacrilege, rushes off, thinking he hears the tyrant pursue him through the streets, and eventually goes mad. In *The Bronze Horseman* Peter is creator of a great city, but also ruthless destroyer of lives, a ruler heedless of moral and natural laws in his pursuit of imperial greatness.

Brought up to the tradition of the French Enlightenment (his father was an admirer of Voltaire), with its materialism and hedonism, Pushkin reassessed it in the light of his own experience and of those comrades who had participated in the Decembrists' rising (where, as he later confessed to Nicholas I, he might have been himself, had he not been in exile). In his later life he came to feel that such a philosophy, with its claim to special knowledge, could generate selfish and cynical immoralism just as easily as altruistic commitment.

In his *Queen of Spades* Hermann (note the German name) is a young officer desperate for money and willing to violate every moral precept to obtain it. Hearing that an eighty-year-old countess has the secret of three magic cards which will enable him to gamble with the certainty of success, he manipulates the affections of her young confidante to gain access to the Countess's boudoir and intimidate her into yielding her magic knowledge. The Countess is herself a product of the masonic French Enlightenment, having learnt her secret in a Parisian drawing-room from one Count Saint-Germain, who made himself out to be 'the eternal Jew, inventor of the elixir of life and the philosopher's stone'.[19] Here is an early example of the Russian conviction that amoral doctrines penetrate their country from cosmopolitan western influences, especially from Jews and Freemasons.

In his later years Pushkin turned away from poetry, as if feeling that verse could no longer explore the issues he wished to fathom, and began to write prose fiction and history. What concerned him was the question, opened up by the Decembrists' failure, of what was peculiar about Russia's development, and what made her different from most European countries. He wrote both a novel and a historical chronicle of the Pugachev revolt, and at his death was engaged on a history of the reign of Peter the Great. He also founded the journal *Sovremennik*, as if conscious that, as the acknowledged leading writer of his generation, he had a duty to provide a way for literature to gain greater resonance in society.

His journal was indeed a pioneering venture. Although he himself did not have the business acumen to conduct a successful enterprise and soon got into financial difficulties, as well as having conflicts with the censorship, *Sovremennik* in the long run contributed a rich vein to nineteenth-century literary and intellectual life. It became the prototype of the 'thick journal', publishing not only fiction, poetry and drama but contemporary social and political comment, as well as works of scholarship in history, ethnography, economics and even the natural sciences. The epithet 'thick' came to have its own significance: it referred to the custom that longer publications were less rigorously censored – after 1865 explicitly those of more than ten 'author's sheets', or 160 pages – on the assumption that sheer quantity of pages would put off the less educated reader.

Throughout the century, and especially in periods of tight censorship, the protection afforded by 'thickness', together with that usually accorded to 'artistic literature', meant that such journals could risk comment, veiled perhaps in circumlocutions but still unmistakable, on a range of issues closed to other publications. They became in themselves centres of intellectual life, each with its coterie of writers, critics, reviewers and publicists, and each with its political tendency, whether Slavophile, official nationalist, liberal or radical. The monthly salvos fired in the 'thick journals' were the nearest thing Russia had to a political life for most of the nineteenth century.

GOGOL   Nikolai Gogol offers a striking example of the tendency of writers to outgrow the bounds of 'artistic literature' to fulfil a higher mission, in the process losing their rapturous supporters. At the beginning of his career he was proclaimed by Belinskii as the exemplar of what Russian literature should be, yet later was excoriated by him as a 'preacher of the knut'.

He was a provincial, a Little Russian (as Ukranians were officially termed) from Poltava province. His early works were provincial sketches, celebrating a warm and humane but narrow and banal way of life in the small towns and villages of his homeland. His first novel, *Taras Bul'ba*, was a romantic portrait of the alternative Russian ethnos, the Cossacks of the Ukrainian frontier, in their unceasing struggle against the Tatars and Poles.

He soon abandoned Ukraine, however, going to St Petersburg after a successful school career with dreams both of service to the state and of personal advancement. In many ways he was a typical product of Imperial Russia's meritocratic educational system. What he found in the capital city soon appalled him: a world of cold and pretentious facades which contrasted with the modest but reassuring warmth of his home town. He discovered that people were judged not by their personalities but by their status: humanity was defined by position on the Table of Ranks, and persons had dissolved in administrative hierarchies. Even intimate matters like love and marriage were decided on this basis. The hero of his *Notes of a Madman*, on finding that he cannot compete with a *kamer-iunker* (gentleman of the bedchamber) for the hand of the daughter of his department head, rails to himself: 'How do you mean, there can't be a marriage? What if he is a *kamer-iunker*? . . . A *kamer-iunker* doesn't have a third eye on his brow. His nose isn't made of gold.'

Such collisions of dream and reality spark off bravura passages in which the vulgar, banal and trivial – the more incongruous because of their magnificent setting – are interwoven with the bizarre and fantastic. The 'madman's' protests take him into a realm of self-questioning and of fairy tale, both of which seem a natural response to the phantasmagoric milieu of St Petersburg. 'Why am I a titular counsellor? For what reason? Maybe I'm really a count or a general and just seem to be a titular counsellor . . . After all, there are plenty of examples in history: a simple person, not even a nobleman, but a simple townsman or peasant – and suddenly it's discovered that he is a great lord, or even the emperor himself.' He is well on the way to madness and the delusion that he is King of Spain.[20]

Gogol's imagination is peopled by many similar heroes, such as the humble-ranked Akakii Akakievich, office copyist in *The Greatcoat*, who becomes his own King of Spain by the simple device of purchasing a good-quality overcoat. Again externals define identity, and

Akakii's coat seduces him into a mood of self-respect unbecoming one of humble rank, and so destroys him.

Then there is the egregious Khlestakov, of *The Government Inspector*, who abuses his assumed status as *revizor* to demand every honour and material blessing from the intimidated provincials he claims to have been sent to monitor. Most luxuriantly developed of all is the personality of Chichikov, in *Dead Souls*, who exploits the characteristic coexistence of law and lawlessness to aggrandize himself by buying up serfs who have died since the last census. Here Gogol plays on the administrative fiction that all peasants counted in the last census are still alive, and on the incongruous official terminology – which the Old Believers had found offensive – that designates a tax-paying adult a 'soul'.

In all these works the imperial state, with its uniforms, ranks and hierarchies, takes on a nightmarish quality as it consumes and destroys people's lives, both spiritually and physically, and becomes the embodiment of everything immoral and anti-human. Was there a redemption from this perverted universe? Gogol hoped there was, and that he was the person to reveal it to the world. Returning to Russia in 1839 for the first time since Pushkin's death two years earlier, he discovered that he was in demand everywhere as the figure for whom polite society thirsted in the parched territory of Nicholas I's Russia: the great writer who discloses the Truth. This was a role he was only too predisposed by personality to assume – but not in the way that either the critics or the public expected. He aspired to the role of prophet, in the Old Testament sense. He declared the first part of *Dead Souls* to be merely the 'grubby vestibule' leading to the temple which would be the second part. There, he gave his public to understand, he would explain the image, at the end of the first part, of the troika 'speeding past everything on earth, while other peoples and states stand aside dazzled and make way for it'.[21]

Alas, it was not to be. Gogol's struggle over the second part of *Dead Souls* was emblematic of the situation of the Russian writer in his epoch: wanting to discover through his works a worthy national identity, but coming up against the hard reality that Russia under the present regime could not fulfil its historical mission as he understood it. And so he burnt the manuscript of the second part, secretly and without ever referring directly to his decision even to his closest friends. The nearest he came to an explanation was that 'One should not write about a holy shrine without first having consecrated one's soul.'[22] But the question he posed at the end of the first part, '*Rus*', whither art thou speeding?' remained unanswered.

Instead, feeling himself close to death, Gogol composed a work which was half confession and half sermon, with the austere title *Selected Excerpts from Correspondence with Friends*. Addressed to 'fellow-countrymen', it was a meditation on death and God, on the function of literature in Russia and on the need to overcome pride, the sin of the nineteenth century. Gogol envisaged himself as prophet, called upon to preach repentance, submission and acceptance of the existing order of things as willed by God. Why he should recommend acceptance of an order he had so vividly impeached in the first part of *Dead Souls* he did not explain.

Just as Gogol had been acclaimed from all sides earlier, now everyone turned against him. Most savage of all was the broadside from Belinskii, who felt personally betrayed and now castigated Gogol as 'preacher of the knut, apostle of ignorance, champion of superstition and obscurantism'. Russia, he thundered, 'needs not sermons (she has had her fill of them!) nor prayers (she knows them by heart), but the awakening in people of the feeling of human dignity, for so many centuries buried in mud and dung; she needs laws and rights compatible not with the doctrines of the church, but with justice and common sense.'[23]

A contemporary wrote of Gogol that he 'broke under the weight of his own calling, which in his eyes had taken on enormous dimensions'.[24] He was not the only writer to feel both tempted and awestruck by the expectations placed on Russian authors by the middle of the nineteenth century. Sucked in by the failure of both church and state to protect an image of Russia's national identity which could be convincing to elites and people, its major writers, and a good many of its minor ones, were drawn into prophetic and oracular roles for which they were by temperament or talent ill-fitted.

TOLSTOY Nationhood is often best defined in opposition to an enemy, and the most satisfying anti-hero to define Russian nationhood was Napoleon. Just as he provoked conscious patriotism in Russian society in 1812, so too in later years he appeared as a formative negative influence in a number of key works of Russian literature. In Pushkin's *Queen of Spades* the amoral and ruthless dreamer Hermann is said to have a 'Napoleonic profile'. In Gogol's *Dead Souls* rumours circulate that Chichikov is 'Napoleon in disguise' and even perhaps the Antichrist bearing the mystic number 666. In Dostoevskii's *Crime and Punishment* Raskol'nikov is inspired by Napoleon to believe that a great man may permit himself any act, no matter how immoral it may seem to received opinion, and he murders an old moneylender. In all these works Napoleon appears as the embodiment of the principle that the end justifies any means, especially if they are rationally calculated to satisfy egoistic and power-seeking ambitions.

The writer who entered into the most extended polemic against Napoleon was Tolstoy, who made him the negative hero of his great patriotic novel *War and Peace*. The original germ of the novel was the anxious but expectant patriotism of the late 1850s, after the Crimean War. Tolstoy intended his hero to be a former Decembrist returning to the family estate after decades in exile; the novel would show the reform movement of Tolstoy's time as continuation of the social ferment of Alexander I's reign. As he worked on the text, however, he became more and more absorbed in the pre-history of the Decembrist movement, finding its roots in the victory over Napoleon, and then tracing the patriotic mood of 1812 back to the defeats of 1805–7. In the course of this revision, the nature of Tolstoy's own patriotism underwent a transformation, and what was intended to be a prelude became a huge novel in itself: perhaps the work which did more than any other to fix the Russians' sense of their national greatness.[25]

It is strange, but indicative, that this most patriotic of Russian novels should open in French. The subject is Napoleon, and a society hostess, Anna Sherer, is execrating him as the Antichrist. The Old Believers would have agreed, but here the setting and the social ambiance is about as far removed from them as can be imagined. Although her views were widely held among the peasants, Sherer articulates them in the language of Napoleon himself, which nobles used when they wanted their peasants *not* to understand them. She also partly misunderstands why Napoleon is such a threat to Russia:

assuming that he merely wants Genoa and Lucca as family appanages overlooks the whole legacy of the French revolution and the new-style nationalism which underlies Napoleon's strength.

The opening thus deploys, in garbled and trivialized form, the major themes of the novel: the rise of mass patriotism, which takes very different forms in France and Russia; the role of leaders and their relationship to the people they lead; the morality of war and peace, of the individual and the family.

Tolstoy's renewed patriotism takes the form of a polemic against historians, who in his view have exaggerated the role of leaders and of conscious planning in shaping events. In his conception, it is rather the accumulation of chance occurrences, and above all the morale of hundreds of thousands of ordinary people, which is con-clusive. He sees the battle of Borodino as a Russian success, because 'This was a victory determined not by the quantity of pieces of cloth called banners picked up on the battlefield, and not by the amount of space occupied by the armies: this was a moral victory, of the kind which convinces the opponent that they are helpless in the face of the moral superiority of their enemy. That was the victory which the Russians won at Borodino.'[26]

This patriotism distances itself from the generals and even to some extent the nobility and the imperial court, and focuses instead on all Russian people, peasants and ordinary soldiers as much as their leaders. Not that Tolstoy's understanding is without contradictions: he sees quite clearly the enormous role played by both Alexander I and Napoleon in attracting the loyalty and enthusiasm of their troops, but this is a leadership expressed through moral factors, not through planning.

The mutual solidarity of the small group of soldiers becomes the decisive factor, such as the battery under the command of Captain Tushin which, forgotten by the command, swings the battle of Schöngraben just as it seems to be going to the French, or the improvised charge of Nikolai Rostov's cavalry squadron in the engagement at Ostrovnoe.[27] This 'family spirit' is fostered by the regimental structure: when Rostov returns to his regiment, he 'experienced the same feeling as when his mother, father and sisters embraced him . . . The regiment was also a home, permanently cher-ished and close to his heart, like his parents' home.'[28]

In this conception, the task of the historian in explaining a major battle like Borodino becomes like that of the mathematician who through the technique of integration is able to aggregate very large quantities of infinitesimally small numbers.[29]

Kutuzov is a wise commander because he accepts the limitations of his role, and by and large merely confirms what is going on around him, not trying to interfere in what he cannot control. Napoleon is the complete opposite, a kind of super-German – Tolstoy hates the Germans far more than the French, for whom, like most Russian aristocrats, he entertains considerable affection even when they are enemies. Napoleon believes a battlefield is a chessboard, and that his orders have a decisive effect on the progress of the battle.[30]

Tolstoy's conception inevitably pushes the centre of gravity in explaining historical processes towards the common people, not only the peasants but the townsfolk, and even those nobles who have retained some feeling of closeness to the people. In his view their multiple personal decisions generate the collective act of abandoning Moscow and letting it burn. This collective acceptance of inevitable sacrifice and suffering is what constitutes genuine patriotism, not the hysterical and falsely demotic rhetoric of the Governor of Moscow, Count Rostopchin.[31]

Tolstoy is far from starry-eyed about the patriotism of peasants. Those at Bogucharovo, on Princess Mary's estate, are shown as given to 'mysterious talk about their enrolment as Cossacks or their conversion to a new religion . . . or their oath to the Emperor Pavel Petrovich in 1797 from whom it is said they expected freedom, but the landlords had taken it away'. The coming of Napoleon awakens new expectations in them of 'the Antichrist, the end of the world and pure freedom', and they refuse to evacuate Princess Mary from the approaching French army. Her encounter with them is an object lesson in the mutual incomprehension of peasants and landlords, even the best-disposed among them.[32]

For all his patriotism, Tolstoy saw that the peasant concept of property was dangerously alien to that held by the nobility. While he was composing *War and Peace* he wrote in his notebook that the Russian peasants 'deny the most tangible form of property, that which is least dependent upon work, that which creates most obstacles to the acquisition of property by others – namely land . . .

The Russian revolution will be directed not against the Tsar and despotism, but against the ownership of land.'[33]

Tolstoy manages to combine the depiction of the movements and conflicts of masses of people with meticulous attention to the psychology and spiritual evolution of individuals. The characters to whom he devotes the greatest attention, and above all Pierre Bezukhov and Prince Andrei Bolkonskii, are by nature seekers, alienated and bewildered by the world in which they find themselves – even when outwardly they appear successful in it – and looking for a fuller understanding and an integration. They reflect two emblematic temptations of the Russian spirit. Andrei is drawn towards rationalism, the belief that social problems can be solved by calculated administrative action, and at one stage he enters the circle of reformers around Speranskii. Pierre by contrast is the mystic, attracted by Freemasonry, and convinced at one point that he is destined to become the saviour of Russia by assassinating Napoleon. It is he who finds a resolution in the end, through the homespun teaching of the peasant Platon Karataev, which emphasizes serene acceptance of God's will.

Pierre's spiritual pilgrimage to the *narod* was to be recapitulated on a grander scale by Tolstoy himself. Like Gogol, he came to believe that literature was a vacuous pastime, the plaything of the idle, and that his true mission lay in preaching the word of God. Unlike Gogol, he actually founded a religious movement, whose message was a reformulation of the gospels intended to be comprehensible to elites and masses.

His faith was a kind of spiritualized Populism, a rejection of the whole imperial heritage – especially government and armed force – in favour of an ethic of peaceful mutual cooperation, which he held to be the central message of the Gospels. The works in which he expounded it were declared heretical by the Holy Synod, and he was excommunicated. In the later years of his life he became in a sense a *starets* himself, rejected by the official church but visited by intellectuals and peasants alike in search of wisdom and spiritual comfort. Alexander Solzhenitsyn later wrote of him that he constituted an 'alternative government'; perhaps it would be truer to say that he offered an alternative religious morality, acceptable to a secular age. Certainly, the denial to him of a church burial after his death in

1910 provoked a heartfelt public reaction, and sparked off student disorders, accompanied by widespread resignations among the professors of Moscow university.

DOSTOEVSKII The circumstances of Fedor Dostoevskii's life faced him starkly with the gulf between educated strata and people. While he was a student, his father died in circumstances which suggested that he had been murdered by the serfs on his estate. Recent research has shown that there is some doubt whether this was the case, but the young Dostoevskii undoubtedly thought it was. He was left with a strong sense of guilt, for his profligate lifestyle had led him frequently to pester his father for money, and now it seemed that extortion from the peasants might have been the motive for the murder. His early fiction, which impressed Belinskii, was full of sympathy for the 'humiliated and insulted' (as one of his early novels is called), and of insight into the psychological and spiritual burdens borne by the poor.

His guilt over serfdom may have motivated him to enter a discussion group of young intellectuals, led by a junior Foreign Office official, M.V. Petrashevskii, who, inspired by the theories of the French socialist, Charles Fourier, dreamed of reorganizing society as a network of producers' cooperatives. Although the group never got beyond talk, they were arrested and condemned to death. At the last minute, already on the execution ground, they were reprieved and sent to convict camp (*katorga*) instead. The experience of being delivered from death to life remained with Dostoevskii permanently. As he wrote to his brother, 'Never till now have such rich and healthy stores of spiritual life throbbed within me . . . I am being born again in a new form.' This was also the time when his epileptic fits started, with their moments of terror and of visionary radiance, which imparted a distinctive intensity, and morbidity, to his writing.[34]

The convict camp afforded Dostoevskii a prolonged and personal view of what life was like for the unprivileged classes in an autocratic state which claimed unlimited authority over its subjects, unconstrained by any law, human or divine. What tormented him there was the knowledge that he was in the absolute power of the camp commandant, a certain Major Krivtsov, who used to boast that for the slightest misdemeanour he would order a birching. The power of such men over their fellow human beings, fostered by the imperial state, Dostoevskii regarded as limitlessly corrupting.

> Whoever has experienced . . . unlimited domination over the body, blood and spirit of a fellow human being . . . and the full licence to inflict the greatest conceivable humiliation on another human being, bearing the image of God, such a person loses control over his own feelings. Tyranny is a habit which has its own inherent development: in the end it becomes a disease.

In Dostoevskii's view the spiritual perversion of sadism endangers not only the individual but the whole of society.

> The human being and the citizen evaporate for ever within the tyrant . . .
> Besides, the very possibility of such arbitrariness is contagious for the whole of society, for such power is tempting. In short, the right of corporal punishment, given to one human being over another, is a social ulcer, one of the most efficient means of crushing any rudiments of civic spirit.[35]

Katorga also sharpened Dostoevskii's awareness of the gulf separating him from the common people. Even though he now lived among them and shared their sufferings, they did not accept him as one of their own. His theoretical desire as a socialist, an Orthodox Christian and a Russian patriot, to understand them and bring benefit to them did not ease this alienation. They rejected him even when he tried to join in their protest over conditions in the camp kitchen. Solidarity across social class meant nothing to them. He was also repelled by their casual brutality, which affronted his belief that the people bore within them the seeds of a harmonious social life.

The ceaseless tension, disillusionment and fear generated by the camp environment provoked epileptic fits in Dostoevskii and led to a conversion experience, triggered by a sickening scene of cruelty, in which several convicts beat a drunken Tatar senseless. Lying in the barracks afterwards, he recalled a moment from childhood when one of his father's serfs had saved and comforted him when he was frightened that he was being chased by a wolf. 'Only God, perhaps, saw from above what deep and enlightened human feeling, what delicate, almost womanly tenderness could fill the heart of a coarse, bestially ignorant Russian serf.'[36]

Even in the convict camp he had witnessed scenes which showed that Russian peasants were capable of finer feelings: the Easter celebrations and the amateur theatricals put on for Christmas, when, as he recalled, 'some strange glow of childlike joy, of pure, sweet pleasure lit up those wrinkled and branded foreheads and shone in those eyes hitherto so gloomy and sullen'.[37]

These memories of collective celebration, coupled with Dostoevskii's growing experience of the irrational side of human nature, led him finally to abandon any idea of intellectuals imposing their conception of a rational and humane society on the people. On the contrary, his later novels became an extended polemic against the project of Russian socialism, starting with *Notes from the Underground*, where he caricatures the idea of the perfect society in the crystal palace, set out in Chernyshevskii's *What is to be Done?* He came to believe that the peasants' capacity to transcend sinfulness, even if temporarily and precariously, in the common celebration of their inherited Christian faith, would reach upwards to redeem and reintegrate the intellectuals into a society from which they, with their ratiocination, had alienated themselves. That became the core message which he preached, both in his novels and in his journalism, which he regarded as indissolubly connected, for the rest of his life.[38]

Dostoevskii believed he had rediscovered the true Orthodox and popular Russia, overlaid by the apparent Russia of rationalism, socialism and materialism, and his aim was to project an image – if you like, an icon – of this true Russia as a means of reorienting the outlook of the public. This true Russia he saw as a beacon to other nations: it would 'utter the definitive word of great universal harmony', which would reconcile the warring and unhappy nations of Europe. This is the theme of the *Diary of a Writer*, of *The Brothers Karamazov* and of his speech at the Pushkin celebrations of June 1880.

To articulate his ideas in *The Brothers Karamazov*, he drew upon the semi-buried Russian tradition of the *startsy* or 'holy men' [see pp. 239–42]. The autobiography and spiritual reflections of Father Zosima form a discrete section of the text. Zosima's early life has about it something of another characteristic Russian figure, the *iurodivyi*, or 'holy fool', who assumes folly or madness as a feat of ascetic self-abnegation, in order to challenge the conventions and common assumptions of 'sane' humanity. The young Zosima is inspired by the example of his elder brother, who was an atheist but underwent a conversion at the end of his brief life and preached a message of universal love and forgiveness: 'We are all guilty for one another and for everything.' Therewith Dostoevskii elevated the peasant custom and administrative category of 'mutual responsibility' to a redemptive spiritual conception.

Zosima began his adult life like many other young elite males in Imperial Russia: he attended a Cadet Corps, learnt elegant manners and perfect French, became a favourite with his regimental comrades. But suddenly he broke away from it in the manner of a *iurodivyi*, by breaking off a duel without firing a shot and seeking the forgiveness of his adversary – an act which so outraged regimental mores that he resigned from the army and entered a monastery. This experience and his long years of ascetic discipline give him the right to advise his disciples that 'The salvation of Russia (*Rus*') will come from its people ... The people will take on the atheist and defeat him, and a united Orthodox Russia will arise. Take care of the people and cherish their souls. Unobtrusively enlighten them. That is your monastic mission. For this people is the bearer of God.'[39]

Dostoevskii never wrote the intended continuation of *The Brothers Karamazov*. In particular, he never developed the character of Alesha, the 'holy sinner', as he had conceived it. Alesha would have replicated the experience of Zosima, only laid out much more fully, going through the temptation of atheist socialism before becoming a 'holy man' himself. But even without the later volumes, we may surmise that Dostoevskii accomplished in some measure the task that Gogol had set himself in the second part of *Dead Souls*, the imaginative redemption of Imperial Russia. He did it by more or less ignoring the empire's official structures and concentrating on Orthodox Christianity and the peasantry as the sources of salvation.

With *The Brothers Karamazov* Dostoevskii became the central figure in what we may call the 'literary construction of Russia'. More than any other writer, he exemplified in his life and writings the contradictory hopes and fears which beset thinking Russians when they tried to understand what their country was and to set out their hopes for what it should become. What he offered in the end was an image of a 'God-bearing people', marked out for exceptional suffering but also, by virtue of that suffering, endowed with an exclusive mission to bear witness before other peoples to the truths of Orthodox Christianity.

This was the messianic Russian national myth, the idea of 'holy Russia' reformulated for the late nineteenth century, for the Europe of science, material progress and the nation-state. Dostoevskii combined it with the post-Petrine imperial myth: he hoped that his vision might be transmuted into practical great-power politics. During the Balkan war of 1877–8, he prophesied the conquest of the Second Rome, Constantinople, and the inauguration of a reign of 'eternal peace' in the Slav spirit. 'Our war . . . is the first step to the attainment of that eternal peace in which we are fortunate enough to believe, to the achievement of a *genuinely* caring prosperity for humanity.'[40] In this way Dostoevskii came closer than anyone else to combining the two incompatible Russian myths into a synthetic image: the empire which paradoxically is great because its people are passive, humble and suffering, able to take on themselves the imprint of the culture of other peoples. In his vision the multi-ethnic empire and the village commune came together.

THE PUSHKIN CELEBRATIONS OF 1880   The event which did more than any other to crystallize literature as the bearer of Russian national identity was the unveiling of the Pushkin memorial in Moscow in 1880. Pushkin had long been a writer who could be admired on both sides of the great political divide, by official Russia as well as by those bitterly opposed to it, and he was therefore a figure appropriate to an attempt to bridge those divisions.

During the hopeful years of the early sixties, alumni of the Alexander Lyceum had attempted to raise a subscription for a Pushkin memorial, and they had been supported by the Ministry of the Interior. But the initiative ran into the sands, perhaps because of the deteriorating political atmosphere of the later sixties. It was revived during the seventies, with the significant innovation that the site proposed for the memorial was no longer Tsarskoe Selo, but Moscow, not only Pushkin's birthplace but Russia's ancient capital and the symbol of the country's revival since the Napoleonic War. Money was raised from all strata of literate society, including schoolteachers, journalists, government officials, the imperial family and a variety of provincial clubs and societies. Organization of the occasion was taken over by the Society of Lovers of Russian Literature, which since the late fifties had been trying to create a forum for freedom of speech and the autonomy of literature by arranging banquets – the only form of large public gathering routinely authorized by the authorities – in memory of every conceivable writer.

The commemoration took place during what might be described as a truce, shortlived though it proved, between the terrorists and the regime: Loris-Melikov's 'dictatorship of the heart' [see pp. 337–8]. The Society made a real effort to bring together writers and journalists of widely differing political persuasions and aesthetic views, for instance the liberal, westernized Turgenev, and the imperial nationalist Katkov. In a sense this was the last attempt to reunite the old *kruzhki* of the forties, whose members had dispersed in so many different directions.

It was only partly successful. Turgenev pointedly snubbed Katkov at the banquet. Moreover, Tolstoy refused to come: he was increasingly isolating himself from society and the literary world, convinced that the literature of the past half-century was superficial and immoral because it did not address itself to the *narod*.

Two speeches, however, made the occasion memorable, and one of them had a resonance which was to prove enduring. In the first of them, Turgenev implicitly answered Tolstoy by taking up Belinskii's distinction between *narodnyi* and *natsional'nyi*. Pushkin, he argued, was read, 'not by the *narod* but by the nation'; but the *narod* would learn to read him, and since art was 'the elevation of life into an ideal', would both ennoble itself and discover its true national identity in doing so.[41]

The speech which left the strongest impression, though, was Dostoevskii's. He composed it at the same time as he was writing *The Brothers Karamazov*, and he expounded the same vision of Russia saved by Orthodox Christianity and by the peasants' spirit of community. He took up Chaadaev's image of the Russian as 'wanderer', eternally in search of the truth, and urged him to humble himself before the *narod* in order to find it.

Like Belinskii, Dostoevskii asserted that literature could express the essential substance of a nation and embody its contribution to the evolution of history as a whole. Pushkin had a special role in this process because 'he alone among world poets possessed the capacity to reincarnate himself completely in another nationality', to become a Faust, a Don Juan, or a 'blunt, gloomy northern Protestant'. He spoke, as it were, in tongues, thus reversing the sundering of humanity at the Tower of Babel. 'Yes, the mission of the Russian is unquestionably an all-European and a universal one. One can only become completely Russian, a genuine Russian ... by becoming a brother of all people, if you like, a universal human being ... To become a genuine Russian means to attempt to bring reconciliation to the contradictions of Europe and to offer relief for Europe's anguish in the all-human and all-embracing Russian soul.'[42]

Dostoevskii's image of Russia was that of a super-nation whose mission is to provide the conditions in which other nations can develop and resolve their conflicts, so long as they acknowledge Russia's leading role. The Russian people were uniquely marked by Christ: they had endured suffering on a scale far greater than any European people. This suffering had brought them a distinctive and humble wisdom which fitted them supremely well to bring the light of Christ's salvation to other peoples.

This image is the one which has convinced educated Russians themselves more than any other what the identity and mission of their nation is. Here was the spiritual correlate of Russia's geo-strategic situation: the immense extension, the uncertain frontiers, the signal ethnic diversity. Its influence was strongly felt not only in the late nineteenth century but even more under a communist regime hostile to Dostoevskii. His message was repudiated by the Soviet ideologists, but it survived strongly in the major libraries and in the cultural underground, and now in the 1990s resurfaces as a guideline to people as diverse as Alexander Solzhenitsyn and Alexander Rutskoi.

THE EMERGENCE OF THE CANON   Of course, for all the enthusiasm over Dostoevskii's speech, it was always possible to argue, as Tolstoy did, that most peasants had never heard of Pushkin, and that therefore he could not serve as the symbol of a unified Russian nation. In the new era of expanding primary education, however, that was beginning to change, and *obshchestvennost'* was beginning to disseminate good literature widely among the people.

By 1899 the Tsar himself ordered another celebration, this time of the centenary of Pushkin's birth, and the event was marked by liturgies, requiems, public readings and distribution of his portrait. The Metropolitan of St Petersburg called Pushkin a 'glorious son of the Russian land' and, despite his stormy life, a Christian.[43]

Already Russian publishers, educators and philanthropists were disseminating the major nineteenth-century writers, either for commercial profit or in the interests of popular enlightenment. The St Petersburg Literacy Committee published nearly two million copies of *belles lettres* between 1880 and 1895, including Pushkin, Lermontov, Gogol and Korolenko. Similar committees operated in Moscow and Khar'kov. In partnership with Tolstoy and his disciple, V. Chertkov, Sytin, publisher of *Russkoe Slovo*, founded the *Posrednik* (Mediator) series, intended at first to bring out didactic works for peasants, but later switching to literary classics. The popular weekly illustrated journal *Niva* issued cheap editions of Dostoevskii, Chekhov, Gor'kii and others as a supplement to attract subscribers. Schoolteachers would sometimes buy such editions, even out of their own meagre savings, to pass on to children in their schools.[44]

Newly literate peasants, it is true, were on the whole not reading this kind of literature, but rather paperback romances, adventure stories, horoscopes and the like.[45] All the same, a reading public was emerging which, at least in the towns, extended far beyond social elites and those with completed secondary education to those who read weekly illustrated magazines like *Niva* and their literary supplements. Publishers existed to guide their tastes and to direct them to works which would improve them and imbue them with a more vivid sense of what it meant to be Russian.

By the end of the nineteenth century, a genuine Russian nation was beginning to take shape, though only as yet in the form of a reading public, an 'imagined community' whose precarious survival through the Soviet period has kept alive the possibility – not the certainty – that Russia may yet become a nation-state.

PART FOUR

Imperial Russia under pressure

1

The Reforms of Alexander II

THE POST CRIMEAN CRISIS   Defeat in the Crimean War was a profound shock to Russians, and one which compelled a complete reappraisal of the empire and of its place in the world. It revealed what many had long suspected, that profound disorder was undermining the empire's capacity to sustain its role as a European great power. It demonstrated that the army, reputedly the strongest in Europe, could not defend a fortified base in its homeland against troops despatched from thousands of miles away. It is said that Nicholas I on his deathbed acknowledged the tacit condemnation of his system, enjoining his son to take action to remedy the 'disorder in the command'. [On defects in the army, see Part 3, Chapter 2]

The shortcomings of Russia's military performance were due not least to the backward state of her industry and communications, and the precarious condition of her finances. She was unable either to manufacture new rifles to match those her adversaries possessed or to purchase them abroad. Much of what was available, including food and weapons, never reached the battlefield over the muddy tracks and dusty post-roads which connected the southern extremity with the heartlands of the empire.

No less alarming for the authorities was the evidence of peasant discontent disclosed by the war. When appeals went out for volunteers to enlist in the militia, far more serfs offered themselves than the military was capable of absorbing. As in 1812, they clearly hoped that after their service they would be freed. Peasants rejected by the recruiting sergeant were indignant, and sometimes caused trouble, especially in Ukraine and the south. When gendarmes were sent in to deal with the situation, they usually found the peasants loyal and

315

patriotic in mood, anxious to serve the Tsar (whether simulating or not), but often aggrieved over some recent new obligation their landlord had imposed on them. Even after the war was over, peasants continued to make for the Crimea where, they stoutly maintained, 'on Perekop, in a golden chamber, sits the Tsar, who gives freedom to all who come, but those who do not come or are too late will remain as before, serfs to the lords.'

It was not simply Russia's internal condition which was threatening. The Treaty of Paris deprived of any claim to special rights inside the Ottoman Empire and forbade her to maintain any naval installations on the Black Sea. She was thus deprived of much of her influence in the Middle East and barred from rebuilding her Black Sea Fleet or offering protection to the merchant vessels in which much of her vital export trade was carried.

Russia's whole external strength and standing were profoundly weakened by these provisions. She had been the key figure first of all in the Congress system, then in the loose balance of power which had succeeded it; now she had become a weak and dissatisfied component of an unstable, anarchic European constellation of powers. She was merely one among a number of European states, the most successful of which were nation-states with a fast-developing industrial base; and during the next two decades Germany and Italy were added to their number. The industrialized nation-state was becoming the norm in the European network: those which did not fit the pattern, the Habsburg, Ottoman and Russian Empires, were becoming relatively weaker, threatened with disruption and possible dissolution.

The much-needed reappraisal had long been maturing inside the *kruzhki* and the salons, which had represented the only forum for serious intellectual discussion in the Russia of Nicholas I. With the easing of censorship, the contents of that discussion now burst out into the open, and it turned out that Slavophiles and Westerners had far more in common than might initially have been expected. Both were prepared in the national emergency to curtail the extremes of their positions, and to agree on the necessity for the abolition of serfdom and the creation of institutions which would enable the educated and politically conscious public to support the regime.[2]

The change began during the war itself, which plunged Russian intellectuals into a mood of chastened patriotism. The Slavophile Aleksandr Koshelev, a former member of the 'Lovers of Wisdom' literary group could say that 'we were convinced that even defeats were more tolerable and perhaps more beneficial for Russia than the condition in which it had existed in recent years.'[3] The official historian Mikhail Pogodin used the occasion to appeal to Nicholas I in the tones of traditional patriotism for a more open political system: 'Dispel with gracious and blessed rays the impenetrable atmosphere of fear which has built up over so many years, enter into contact with the people, summon to work all the talents – there is no shortage of them in Holy Russia – free the press from the needless restraint, which forbids it even to use the term "general welfare", open wide the gates to all the universities, colleges and schools ... It is not light which is dangerous, but darkness.'[4]

Petr Valuev, Governor of Kurland, was a Westerner who had long moved in fashionable literary circles, been acquainted with Pushkin and Lermontov, and married the daughter of the poet Viazemskii. Yet his diagnosis was couched in terms similar to those of the Slavophiles. In 1855 he also warned the Tsar in a personal letter that the greatest danger lay in the way the regime had lost touch with the people. 'Everyone sees the antagonism of the government and the people, of the official and the personal, instead of the cultivation of their natural and indissoluble links. Contempt for each of us individually and for human personality in general has taken root in the laws.'[5]

In similar vein the Slavophile Iurii Samarin, a former member of the Elagin salon, wrote 'We were defeated not by the external forces of the Western alliance, but by our own internal weakness ... Stagnation of thought, depression of productive forces, the rift between government and people, disunity between social classes and the enslavement of one of them to another ... prevent the government from deploying all the means available to it and, in emergency, from being able to count on mobilising the strength of the nation.'[6]

Slavophiles and Westerners concurred that, if there was a single problem undermining Russia's strength, productivity and international standing, it was serfdom. As the Westerner and close friend of Granovskii, B.N. Chicherin put it, 'Someone bound hand and foot cannot compete with someone free to use all his limbs. Serfdom is a shackle which we drag around with us, and which holds us back just when other peoples are racing ahead unimpeded. Without the abolition of serfdom none of our problems, political, administrative or social, can be solved.' He gave as an example the way in which the Tsar had had to revoke the decree creating a militia because it aroused among serfs the false hope that they would be freed.[7]

Konstantin Kavelin, member of the Granovskii circle and pupil of Belinskii, enumerated the obstacles which serfdom posed to rational schemes of reform. 'The reform of the conscription system is imposs-ible, because it would lead to the abolition of serfdom; it is impossible to change the present tax system, because its roots lie in serfdom; for the same reason we cannot introduce a different and more rational passport system; it is impossible to extend education to the lower classes of society, to reform the legal system, civil and criminal pro-ceedings, the police, the administration in general or the existing censorship system, which is fatal for science and literature – all because these reforms would directly or indirectly lead to the weak-ening of serfdom, and the landowners do not want this on any account.'[8]

Not least serious, the existence of serfdom obstructed moderniz-ation of the army and thereby burdened the treasury with huge and unproductive military expenditure. As the military reformer R.A. Fadeev pointed, 'Under serfdom, anyone becoming a soldier is freed; hence one cannot, without shaking the whole social order, admit many people to military service. Therefore we have to maintain on the army establishment in peacetime all the soldiers we need in war.'[9]

Iurii Samarin summed up serfdom as a moral and legal split run-ning right down the middle of Russian society. 'Why should twenty-two million subjects who pay poll tax to the state be placed outside the law and outside any direct relationship with the supreme power, appearing on official lists merely as the lifeless chattels of another social estate?'[10]

Altogether, it was clear that the political, economic and military system which had enabled Russia to build and defend a huge empire, and to become and remain a European great power, was now not only inadequate to sustain that status but an actual threat to it. The Crimean War had made that manifest and thereby removed the taboos on the discussion of radical change which had for several decades inhibited statesmen who could see the fragility of the existing order. For the first time since the early eighteenth century, radical reform seemed less dangerous than doing nothing.[11]

There were two alternative strategies which the regime might adopt in order to bridge the gap between itself and the people, and to move Russia closer to becoming a nation-state. The first was a civic strategy: to create institutions which would enable the various social and ethnic groups to articulate and defend their interests and to participate in the political process. With reservations and backslidings, that was the policy pursued for most of his reign by Alexander II. The second was an ethnic strategy: to try to bring people and empire closer together by making Russians more conscious of their national identity and non-Russians more like Russians. That was the policy pursued intermittently by Alexander II and more consciously by his two successors, Alexander III and Nicholas II.

Proponents of both strategies could be found in the *kruzhki* and salons. In the late 1850s and early 1860s most supported the civic strategy, but many of them, when its difficulties and drawbacks revealed themselves, transferred their allegiance to the other approach.

Many leading advocates of the civic strategy were members either of the Imperial Geographic Society or of the salon of the Grand Duchess Elena Pavlovna, Nicholas I's sister-in-law. Nikolai Miliutin, who was to be one of the most influential figures in elaborating the emancipation decree, was at the heart of a circle of young officials from the Ministries of Justice, Interior and State Domains, who were in regular contact with leading journals such as *Sovremennik* (The Contemporary) and *Otechestvennye Zapiski* (Fatherland Notes) and with writers like Herzen, Nekrasov and Turgenev. All of these coteries were imbued with a spirit of irreverent youthful criticism towards their superiors. The Imperial Geographical Society also continued the work of the eighteenth-century Academy by collecting data about Russia's natural and human resources as a preparation for the work of reform in which its members hoped one day to participate. Some of them were able to do so in the Chief Editorial Commission which put together the final draft of the edict emancipating the serfs.[12]

Something of the Hegelian confidence in progress remained with these young – or not so young – reformers. They were convinced that under their expert guidance Russian society would move towards the rule of law, a more productive economy, and a greater equality of rights and obligations for all subjects. This did not mean they wanted to end the autocracy: on the contrary, most believed that it was needed, at least for the time being, to guide society through upheavals in which a strong and unbiased hand from above would be indispensable. However, they did want to curtail its arbitrariness and personal whimsicality and bring it under the rule of law, for which the basis had been laid by the Law Code of 1833. This implied abolishing serfdom, guaranteeing subjects the protection of the law, instituting more openness (*glasnost'*) in the conduct of public affairs, and bringing all subjects into closer contact with the state, both in its authoritative and its welfare roles.

However, *glasnost'* did not mean freedom of speech, and the rule of law did not mean an elected legislative assembly. Alexander's reforming officials believed that they, and they alone, possessed broad enough mental horizons and sufficient impartiality to guide the reform process without causing destructive conflict. To that extent they perpetuated Nicholas I's distrust of social initiative. In the elaboration of the numerous reforms, only once were members of a particular social estate consulted: that was when the nobility was brought into the drafting of the emancipation of the serfs. Nobles' associations were involved in preliminary discussions, first of all at provincial level, then through delegates sent to the Editorial Commissions in St Petersburg which digested local reactions and made proposals for the final form of the law.

At all these stages, the landowners were expected to do no more than make detailed observations. When some of them tried to raise matters of principle and to put forward a programme of political reforms to supplement the emancipation, they were officially rebuked – even though some of the suggestions were later adopted.[13] All the crucial drafting work went on far from the eyes of the public in the seclusion of St Petersburg offices.

THE EMANCIPATION OF THE SERFS The keystone of the reforms was the emancipation of the serfs, which, by releasing roughly half the peasants from personal bondage while guaranteeing them land, cleared the way – in principle – for them to become small property owners and full citizens, able to participate without handicap in political life and in the market economy. In practice the emancipation edict stopped well short of doing that. We have seen that the provisions regarding land disappointed most peasants, leaving them with an abiding grievance. Furthermore, though no longer enserfed, they remained segregated in so-called 'village societies', usually the old village commune, which contained only peasants as members; priests, schoolteachers, medical orderlies and other people who happened to live in the village were excluded from membership.

Peasants were bound to these 'village societies', which held their pass books, until they had paid in full for the land they were allotted, in a redemption operation scheduled to take forty-nine years; during that time they could not mobilize their resources by selling their allotments or using them as collateral to raise loans. They were subject to a legal system distinct from that introduced for the rest of the population, they were tried in segregated volost courts, and they were still liable to corporal punishment and to 'mutual responsibility'. In effect, they suffered a form of social (though not racial) apartheid. The *volosti* or 'cantons', the higher-level administrative unit encompassing several villages and perhaps a small town, likewise admitted peasants only to its assembly and its courts.

Even in the administrative and judicial sense, they were poorly integrated into the imperial structures. It is true that they had some new rights: they could participate in the elections to the uezd zemstvo, and their village and volost officials could serve in the new juries for criminal cases [on zemstvos, see p. 322]. But in return the zemstvos had no jurisdiction over the volosti which were the highest-level peasant institutions. In the absence of the landlord, the only official supervision over them was the so-called 'peace arbitrator' (*mirovoi posrednik*), who was usually a local noble appointed by the government. But his main function was to oversee the conclusion of contracts for the transfer of land to the peasants, on the completion of which his authority lapsed. In 1874 his post was in any case abolished, and thereafter there was minimal coordination between government, zemstvos and peasant societies: what there was went through the police – as so often in Russia when other institutions failed.

Worried by this lack of control over the majority of the population, the government introduced in 1889 the post of 'land commandant' (*zemskii nachal'nik*). He was a kind of 'district commissioner', drawn wherever possible from among local nobles, and empowered to revoke or amend the verdicts of volost courts and the decisions of village and volost assemblies.[14] His appointment may have improved coordination, but certainly did not enhance the civil rights of peasants or increase their participation in politics.

Apart from giving the peasants potentially explosive grievances, then, the emancipation fell well short of integrating peasants into the political community by giving them civil rights, secure property or institutions which meshed with those of the rest of the empire. In some respects, indeed, it reinforced their segregation. This was especially dangerous in that social and economic change over the coming decades was destined to bring peasants into much closer contact with urban culture and the all-empire economy. They entered such contact without any feeling of belonging to the political nation, and without much respect for imperial law or institutions, or even for property itself.

LOCAL GOVERNMENT The creation of zemstvos in 1864 and municipal councils in 1870 gave Russia for the first time a proper network of elective local government assemblies. The zemstvos were elected by landowners, urban dwellers and peasants under a voting system which was based partly on *soslovie*, partly on property qualification. This system itself reflected official ambivalence about whether Russia was still a hierarchical society, based on state service, or a more open civil society.

The distribution of seats favoured the landowners and wealthier urban voters, but all the same the peasants, thanks to their sheer numbers, had a plurality in many areas: in uezd zemstvos the proportion of representatives from each curia was peasants 42%, landowners 38%, townsfolk 17%. The municipalities were markedly more elitist in their composition: a stiff tax qualification ensured that a tiny group of the wealthy dominated the assemblies. In St Petersburg, for example, the top tax bracket contained 202 voters, the second 705 and the third 15,233: each category sent an equal number of deputies to the municipal assembly. Significantly, zemstvos were introduced only in regions where both the mass of the population and the elites of town and country were predominantly Russian. The government did not want to risk putting local institutions in the hands of ethnic groups who might exploit them for separatist purposes.[15]

The zemstvos gave nobles, other property owners and to some extent peasants a way of participating in local affairs, especially in the development of education, public health, communications and the economy. Nobles and their former serfs had to learn to work together, and at least in some regions managed to do so. Koshelev reported in 1865 from the first sessions of an uezd zemstvo in Riazan': 'The peasant deputies, our former serfs, took their seats among us as simply and unostentatiously as if they had sat there a lifetime. They listened to us with great attention, requested explanations of what they did not understand and, having understood, agreed with us.'[16] They were perhaps overawed, but the evidence suggests that, once brought into local government, they contributed something of their own to it.

Perhaps even more important, the zemstvos brought non-noble professional people for the first time in considerable numbers into the smaller towns and villages. To a lesser degree, the same was true of the municipalities. If one looks at the guberniia of Tver', for example, the number of professional people employed by the zemstvos rose from 17 in 1866 to 669 in 1881, 773 in 1882, 941 in 1891 and more than 2,000 in 1910. Teachers made up about half the number, and the remainder were *fel'dshera* (medical orderlies), doctors, veterinary surgeons, statisticians, bookkeepers, secretaries and clerks. Overall, the number of doctors employed by uezd zemstvos rose from 613 in 1870 to 1,069 in 1880, 1,558 in 1890, 2,398 in 1900 and 3,082 in 1910.[17]

This was the so-called 'third element' (the first two were the official bureaucracy and the zemstvo deputies). It consisted mostly of people outside the official *soslovie* structure – *raznochintsy*, as they were known. [See above, p. 263] Animated by a lively service ethic and professional self-esteem, they were proud of being pioneers in bringing the fruits of professional skill to the small towns and villages. In a more modest but perhaps more effective way, they continued the 'going to the people' of the 1870s [see below, p. 349], establishing both businesslike and humane contact with the peasants. Most of them were probably ambivalent about the state: it was their most promising source of assistance yet the greatest obstacle to the success of their work.[18] The attempts of professional people, many of them from the zemstvos, to organize themselves in order to combat these obstacles, provided a strong impetus towards political reform by the early twentieth century.

The Volga famine of 1891–2, and the accompanying cholera epidemic, for example, dramatized the isolation of the doctors and the difficulties under which they were labouring. On the one hand the government failed to provide the resources they needed to deal with hunger and disease; on the other, the peasants suspected the anti-cholera precautions of being the cause of the illness, and sometimes physically assaulted doctors who tried to apply them. Thereafter medical congresses, especially those of the N.I. Pirogov Society (set up in 1885 to commemorate a famous surgeon), took on an increasingly political colouring. When one delegate asked 'What use are all our medical efforts when people have not the basic necessities – food, clothing and a warm home?', the congress passed a resolution calling for more active community work in famine relief. At its 1904 congress the Pirogov Society took a directly political stance, calling for freedom of speech and assembly and an end to corporal punishment. Those present began to sing the Marseillaise and shout 'Down with autocracy' before the meeting was broken up by the police. Thereafter the Pirogov Society became part of the liberal mainstream which campaigned with the Union of Liberation and many of its members joined the Kadet Party.[19]

Local government bodies were never given the powers they needed to do their job properly: their taxes were determined by decisions of the Ministry of Finance, while for the maintenance of law and order they depended on the police force appointed and paid for by the Ministry of the Interior. Even the limited degree of autonomy they did possess, combined with the non-conformist views of the 'third element', disquieted the government to such an extent that in 1890 it subjected all their decisions to a suspensive veto by the provincial governor (appointed by the Minister of the Interior), who also gained the right to countermand personnel appointments and to make his own choice of peasant deputies from those elected in the volost assemblies. Congresses of zemstvo deputies or employees from different gubernii were frequently prohibited, even when they were needed for purposes such as the coordination of public health measures.[20]

Zemstvo deputies and employees were restive under these official restrictions, and at times tried to propose a more relaxed and open-minded model for Russia's development, which would give them greater freedom to run local affairs. In Chernigov zemstvo, activists began a study circle to discuss ways of 'turning the zemstvo institutions into a school for self-government and thus preparing the country for a constitutional system.'[21] The Turkish war of 1877–8 stimulated a wave of patriotic resolutions promising help and support for the government, but also appealing for greater political rights in return. One Khar'kov delegate entreated the Emperor: 'Most Gracious Sovereign! Give your loyal people the right to self-government which is natural to them. Give them graciously what you gave the Bulgarians.'[22] This aspiration for a constitution and an elective assembly at the centre, a kind of all-Russian zemstvo, was expressed by a number of zemstvos at this time: it was known as 'crowning the edifice', but it was always censored out of published zemstvo documents.

In the zemstvos we see for the first time a new social force emerging: *obshchestvennost'*. This term is difficult to translate, but might be rendered as 'educated society', 'politically aware society' or even 'public opinion'. It implied an educated and informed public engaging or wishing to engage in political affairs. In their own eyes its members represented a kind of 'alternative establishment', more truly representative of the Russian nation than the regime was. It was not a revolutionary intelligentsia, dreaming of total transformation, but a more practical and moderate opposition, anxious to work independently of the government to bring about gradual social improvement. All the same, many of them were proud of the intelligentsia heritage. They were the heirs of the peacefully inclined majority of the Decembrists. Their radical opponents accused them dismissively of being content with 'small deeds' which would never generate real change. The government remained, all the same, intensely suspicious of them.

Overall, elective local government resembled a new building

erected among ruins – ruins which were then not dismantled but actually renovated by a regime which knew that change was necessary, but could not stomach its consequences. The zemstvos and municipalities offered new scope for service to society and thereby aroused the aspiration for autonomous political activity without being able to satisfy it.

EDUCATION   The field where the zemstvos enjoyed greatest success was in primary education. They were the prime (though not the only) movers in a remarkable expansion which began in the 1870s and lasted right through to the end of the empire. It was especially conspicuous in the countryside. The number of rural primary schools rose from around 23,000 (9,100) in 1880 to 54,416 (13,129) in 1890, 89,718 (27,944) in 1911 and 108,280 (44,879) in 1914 (figures for zemstvo schools shown in brackets). The church also expanded its school network greatly during the same period, provoked not least by the challenge of secular schools.[23] This expansion generated a rapid growth in popular literacy, in the course of a few decades bringing peasants, and especially young male peasants, potentially much closer to urban and educated society. By 1910 the Ministry of Education was speaking of universal primary education as a practical objective in a decade or so.

The schoolteachers offer perhaps the clearest example of a profession driven to political action by the experiences of their professional life, in spite of the enormous handicap of being so dispersed. The village primary teachers worked in very difficult conditions, earning minimal salaries and depending on the *mir* for board, lodging and somewhere to teach. Zemstvos were far away and seldom able to intervene effectively if conditions were unsatisfactory. The peasants' attitude to education was on the whole practical: they wanted their children taught what would enable them to hold their own in agriculture and commerce and in dealing with the authorities. At busy periods of the agricultural cycle they would withhold their children from school, and teachers had no redress.[24]

To grapple with their practical difficulties, primary teachers would organize mutual aid societies at local level, often with the support of the zemstvo. As well as providing material aid in emergency, the societies organized summer courses and libraries to help teachers.

From 1902 Teachers' Societies existed in some gubernii to press for salary rises, security against arbitrary dismissal, greater autonomy in running schools and representation on zemstvo education committees. In this way teachers were drawn by their professional concerns into making demands which had political relevance.[25]

In secondary education, the government was in a familiar cleft stick: it could not limit the intake of pupils without depriving itself of educated personnel the country badly needed in an epoch of accelerating economic change (though it did make a feeble and unsuccessful attempt to restrict the entry of the offspring of 'cooks and coachmen'). Instead Minister of Education D.A. Tolstoi did his best to restrict what students might learn, insisting on an enriched diet of mathematics, Greek and Latin – with plenty of grammar and not too much about citizenship and republics – at the expense of history, social studies and Russian literature, all of which were thought to be potentially more subversive. He also raised admission fees, insisted on school uniforms and increased the powers of inspectors to determine the syllabus and examine pupils' work.[26] To judge by accounts which have come down to us, these efforts stimulated little but ridicule among the more talented students, and the determination to find out more about forbidden subjects.

As with all other professions, the government discouraged teachers from gathering in congresses to discuss their common concerns. It was not till 1905 that they managed to convene a national congress, by which time their outlook was thoroughly politicized, as the congress's resolutions showed. Like those of other professional associations at this stage, they covered such matters as a constituent assembly, the abolition of the death penalty and the emancipation of the Jews. Among its specifically educational demands were the introduction of universal primary education free of charge; the creation of a single educational ladder (so that talented children would not be debarred from social mobility by having attended the wrong kind of school); the elimination of religion in schools; guarantee of the teacher's freedom to teach (and in the local language); local control of education; and the right of individuals and organizations to set up new schools.[27] In other words, their outlook was secular, egalitarian and emphasized professional and intellectual freedom.

Universities and colleges of higher education were as always the government's greatest headache. It needed them to train the empire's elites, both for the professions and for state service, since by the second half of the nineteenth century few noble families were arranging private education at home for their offspring. But higher education inculcated a spirit of independent and critical thinking which the authorities found distasteful and at times downright dangerous. By the 1860s the best Russian universities maintained standings of learning and research comparable to the best anywhere in the world, and the ethos of free scientific enquiry had become a component of the national myth second only to literature. As V.V. Markovnikov, Professor of Chemistry at St Petersburg University later recalled, 'Everyone who had the opportunity strove to learn. On all sides we heard the cry "We are backward!" . . . Everyone tried to make up for lost time. These were the years of ecstatic enthusiasm for science and learning.'[28] The Zeitgeist was impatiently anti-authoritarian, anti-mystical, striving to build a new life on the basis of utility and equality. Science, progress and rejection of the past became a token of personal enlightenment, a mood which communicated itself readily to students, and which Turgenev depicted with a mixture of affection and reserve in *Fathers and Sons*, in the person of Bazarov.

When Nicholas I's restrictions were withdrawn in 1856 and intellectual life perked up with the new reign and the prospect of reform, students proved to be the most discontented and vociferous stratum of society. What they were agitating for was the right of corporate citizenship as they understood it: that is, the right to hold meetings or to set up self-governing associations, whether for intellectual enrichment, mutual aid or recreation. They created mutual funds for needy colleagues and libraries for collective use. They began to protest against expulsions, searches and arrests, and to boycott the lectures of professors who were unpopular, whether for their political views or because of incompetent teaching. A climax was reached in April 1861, when 400 students at Kazan University held a memorial service for the peasants recently killed by troops at Bezdna [see p. 221]. Ten of them were expelled, whilst Professor Shchapov, who had made a fiery speech at the requiem, was dismissed, arrested and sent into exile.[29]

The government issued temporary regulations banning student

meetings and placing all student associations under the control of university councils. Students responded with massive and in some places destructive demonstrations, invading lecture theatres and damaging furniture where they could not get satisfaction of their demands. Professors struggled to keep control of the situation while losing as little of their self-government as possible.[30]

The University Statute of 1863 showed that the government, in spite of everything, still wanted to retain many of the traditional freedoms of universities. It made them into largely self-governing corporations. It doubled finance and provided for faculty election of rectors, deans and new professors, subject to ultimate ministerial control. Faculty gained control over student admittance and discipline and over programmes of teaching and research. All higher education colleges won the right to admit students from a broader variety of backgrounds, notably from ecclesiastical seminaries. The only serious restrictions imposed were that they were not permitted to admit women, and students were not allowed to form their own corporations.[31]

As a result of the Statute the numbers of students at universities grew sharply, from a total of 4125 in 1865 to 8045 in 1880, 12,804 in 1885 and 16,294 in 1899. The social origin of these students was as follows (percentages):[32]

	1880	1895
Nobles and officials	46.6	45.5
Clergy	24.1	5.0
Merchants and honorary citizens	9.0	7.7
Meschchane and other urban dwellers	12.0	33.2
Peasants	2.9	6.8
Foreigners and others	5.4	2.0

One can see that the nobles were by now sending their sons to universities in large numbers. Clergy sons were strikingly successful at getting into university: because they were prominent among the radical activists, the government curbed entry from seminaries in 1879. Students from the humbler urban estates then took the places they might have occupied. Overall, compared with other European countries, Russian universities continued to have a relatively democratic intake, and many students were poverty-stricken, struggling to keep themselves alive with tiny stipends, tutoring and menial jobs.[33] These were the circumstances in which mutual aid groups, joint libraries and kitchens flourished, encouraging a self-reliant and collectivist student culture, as we shall see in Chapter 2, despite the continuing official ban on student corporate organizations.

Student disorders, together with the evidence that terrorists and revolutionaries were being recruited in the universities, worried the authorities greatly. There was especial concern when a student named Karakozov attempted to shoot the Emperor in 1866. There was, however, no easy way out of the problem, for the government needed universities enjoying a good deal of intellectual freedom to provide high-quality recruits for future official posts. It was compelled to go on fostering qualities of mind dysfunctional to itself: concern for the truth, independence of thought, a capacity to criticize and to question established authority. But in 1884 it passed a new University Statute which handed the appointment of rectors, deans and professors back to the Ministry of Education, and increased the powers of inspectors over students and teachers. It also raised student fees to restrict entry and required students to wear uniforms so that they could be easily identified in public places. In this way the regime hedged the most successful institutions of civil society about with supervisors and spies.

In spite of all difficulties, Russian universities continued to foster both an ethic of service and devotion to learning at the highest international levels, which inevitably also meant the fierce defence of intellectual liberty. It was because they did this that their standards continued to be high – but for the same reasons student disorders remained endemic. Universities were microcosms where the freedom, equality and cosmopolitanism of learning induced a kind of spontaneous republicanism or an idealistic socialism. Many alumni found the transfer from this congenial atmosphere to the closed hierarchical world of bureaucracy extremely repugnant.

Besides, especially in the scientific and technological faculties, many students and not a few professors were convinced that scientific progress made it possible both to convert Russia into a highly productive and wealthy society and to extend effective help to the poor and disadvantaged.[34] In the light of this idealism, the government's restrictive attitude to student self-organization and intellectual enquiry appeared not just unimaginative but actively malevolent.

CENSORSHIP AND THE PERIODICAL PRESS   The easing of censorship flowed naturally from the drive for *glasnost'* launched by Alexander's reformers. In the late fifties they wished to stimulate public discussion of the momentous issues facing the empire, and for that purpose refrained from implementing the draconian censorship laws still theoretically in force. Thereafter in practice newspapers and journals enjoyed a measure of real freedom for some years.

Ironically, therefore, the new 'temporary rules' of 1865 looked like a tightening of the censorship when they appeared, even though they considerably relaxed the statutory controls over publication. Preliminary censorship was ended for daily newspapers, for periodicals and books of more than ten 'signatures' (160 pages) and for academic works. But any publication could still be withdrawn from circulation if the Chief Censorship Committee of the Ministry of the Interior discerned in it a 'dangerous orientation'. The Minister could also warn or fine a periodical, with three warnings leading to suspension or closure. In addition publishers could be charged before the courts for offences such as 'justification of acts forbidden by law', 'insulting an official person or establishment', 'inciting one section of the population against another', or 'calling into question the principles of property or the family unit'.[35]

The new regulations were certainly an improvement from the viewpoint of the circulation of information and ideas. All the same, they created a situation which was much more hazardous for publishers and editors, who could no longer shelter behind the censor. For a bold editor with ample financial backing the situation was rich in possibilities: he could probe at the ill-defined frontiers of the permissible, publishing risky material of public interest and often selling a good many lucrative copies before the censors reacted. The way was opened for a potentially thriving newspaper press – which, however, could thrive only if it had either official support or abundant financial resources, preferably both. Mikhail Katkov, for example, by gaining the support of the Tsar, managed to keep his *Moskovskie vedomosti* afloat and earning good money even after it had received three warnings.[36] Those with more limited means or less prestigious contacts sometimes preferred to remain under preliminary censorship rather than risk responsibility for what they published.

Popular journals could be and were closed down under the new regime. Pushkin's offspring, *Sovremennik*, suffered this fate in 1866 for its thinly concealed socialist orientation. Its editor, the popular poet, Nikolai Nekrasov, arranged with the publisher A.A. Kraevskii to lease his journal, *Otechestvennye zapiski*, under an agreement that he would pay all its fines and would step down if the journal received two warnings. He took many of his contributors with him, and *Otechestvennye zapiski* remained for nearly two more decades a bastion of critical and radical thought, specializing in the use of Aesopian language. The government closed it in 1884, commenting that it could not permit 'an organ of the press which not only opens its pages to the spread of dangerous ideas, but even has as its closest collaborators people who belong to secret societies'. Even then, many of its contributors found themselves homes in other monthly journals, such as the legal populist *Russkoe bogatstvo* or the liberal *Vestnik Evropy*.[37]

The restrictions were irksome and inconvenient, but they could not wholly suppress inconvenient opinions. The regime surrendered its day-to-day control of print communication because it thought it still had the ultimate weapons of suspension and closure. What it did not foresee was how the ever denser web of information, ideas, comment and discussion would gradually create a new kind of public. Indeed, the very use of the word 'public' suggests that a new social entity was coming into being, able to discover information independently of the regime, absorb it, evaluate it and remould it as part of a view of the world. This was *obshchestvennost'*, largely an offspring of the great reforms.

The later decades of the nineteenth century saw the creation of Russia's first mass-circulation newspapers. This was an important development, for it signalled the moment when *obshchestvennost'* became an autonomous factor in public life, when information and ideas about issues of domestic and international politics began to spread beyond a relatively narrow circle of officials and oppositional intellectuals and to reach a broader segment of the public: at first professional people, then increasingly literate shopkeepers, employees and workers. In Hroch's terminology, this was Phase B of the development of national awareness: 'the period of patriotic agitation'. Only, because of the restricted nature of politics in Russia, it was not politicians but still a relatively small coterie of writers, editors and journalists who projected a picture of what it meant to be Russian.[38]

Benefiting from telegraph, improved print technology and railways, newspapers issued in St Petersburg (with a 55–60% literacy rate by the 1860s) and Moscow (40%) were able to disseminate their information to provincial towns as well, and increasingly from there to small towns and even among the literate in the village (who would frequently pass on their ideas or even directly read from the paper in the local tavern). The first major crisis which tested their new role the massacres in the Balkans followed by the Turkish war of 1877–8. Graphic descriptions of the atrocities visited on the Bulgarians aroused strong feelings among readers and certainly intensified pressure on the Russian government to react effectively. General Cherniaev's action in resigning his Russian commission so as to lead the Serb army against the Ottoman forces was a dramatic gesture perfectly designed to appeal to newspaper readers, and he showed his public relations flair by appointing a journalist to his staff.[39]

Many newspapers were more or less Pan-Slav at this point, impatient at official Russia's vacillation and in favour of intervention on behalf of fellow Slavs and Orthodox believers. Their pressure was not the only force moving the government towards a declaration of war on the Ottoman Empire – for other reasons too Russia could not afford to lose influence in the Balkans – but it was certainly one of the most important, especially since ministers were divided and uncertain what to do for the best. Similarly, the diplomatic humiliation of Russia at the subsequent Congress of Berlin generated vehement denunciations in the press, led by the redoutable Katkov. The Pan-Slav General Skobelev identified the press as one of the 'Great Powers', an echo of its status as the Fourth Estate in France.[40]

Broadly speaking, there were two trends among newspapers in

their attitude to Russian nationhood. *Moskovskie vedomosti*, edited by Katkov and, less stridently, *Novoe vremia*, edited by A.S. Suvorin, took the view that as a European great power Russia needed the cement of a strong national consciousness, which was so evident in Germany. Suvorin argued that common devotion to the Tsar shared by its numerous tribes and nationalities was the raw material out of which this consciousness was being fashioned. On the other hand, *Golos*, edited by Kraevskii, and later *Russkoe slovo*, edited by V.M. Doroshevich and owned by I.D. Sytin, a supporter of Lev Tolstoi, took a more eclectic and socially radical view, closer to that of the reformist zemstvo 'third element'. But all newspapers took a close interest in social problems, often manifesting understanding and sympathy for the victims of oppression and exploitation, and they evinced a pride in Russia's civilizing mission among its Asiatic peoples – for which they felt their country was not given sufficient credit in the West.[41]

One may say that by the end of the century, with the aid of newspapers, educated Russians were beginning to conceive of their country as distinctive, which differed from other European powers in its multi-ethnic and semi-Asiatic character, and in its tendency to seek collective rather than individualist solutions for its social problems. Neither of these two distinctive marks was seen as cause for shame.[42] In that sense a positive image of the national identity of Russia was taking shape in *obshchestvennost'*.

LAW COURTS   The new judicial institutions established in 1864 were intended to end closed legal procedures in socially segregated courts, making the despatch of justice public and available to all. The reformed courts were conceived according to the most advanced models: Alexander instructed the commission charged with drafting the necessary legislation to proceed according to 'those fundamental principles, the undoubted merit of which is at present recognised by science and experience of Europe'.[43] All criminal cases were to be tried in public before a jury and a judge who was appointed with life tenure; each party was to have a qualified representative. Lower-level courts were to be presided over by justices of the peace elected by the local uezd zemstvo. The investigation of suspected criminal offences was to be removed from the police and entrusted to special investigating magistrates. These were principles whose enunciation during the reign of Nicholas I would, as the censor A. V. Nikitenko noted in his diary (29 Sept 1862), have branded one as 'a madman or political criminal'.[44]

The radical nature of the judicial reforms bore witness to the significance Alexander's reformers attributed to the rule of law. But the new low-level courts had one grave defect from the start: as we have seen, they did not hear cases involving peasants, which went to the segregated volost courts. The exclusion of eighty per cent of the population from the operation of judicial reform severely dented its claim to underpin the rule of law.

Even as they were, the new courts fitted badly into the autocratic political framework. In the 1870s cases with any political element were withdrawn from the investigating magistrates and handed back to the police. This did not prevent a remarkable case in 1878, involving the attempted murder of the Governor of St Petersburg, General Trepov, in retribution for his ordering the flogging of a political prisoner. The law stated that corporal punishment could only be applied to members of the lower, tax-paying estates. Bogoliubov was a *meshchanin* by origin, so that Trepov was legally justified in ordering the punishment. But in the eyes of the radicals, Bogoliubov had by his membership of their movement promoted himself to a kind of aristocracy of the spirit, so that Trepov's act was an unforgivable breach of elementary decency.

On 24 January 1878, a young radical, Vera Zasulich, requested an audience with Trepov. Waiting till she was summoned, she went into his office, took a revolver out of her muff and, in the sight of several witnesses, shot at him, wounding him. The government sought to make an example of Zasulich, as it had of Nechaev, by trying her before a normal jury and having her case reported in the newspapers. Minister of Justice Count Palen asked the presiding judge. A.F. Koni, whether he could guarantee a verdict of 'guilty' in such a clear-cut case: 'In this damned case the government has the right to expect special services from the court'. Koni replied, 'Your Excellency, the court gives verdicts, not services'.[45] These were two concepts of justice which it was difficult to reconcile. The press supported Koni's view and backed it up with human-interest stories about Zasulich; even the staunch monarchist Dostoevskii wrote that 'to punish this young woman would be inappropriate and superfluous'.[46]

In the event, the defence counsel, falling in with this mood, did not argue about the evidence of the crime, but evoked Zasulich's unhappy youth in exile under police supervision, and praised her as a 'woman who had no personal interest in her crime, a woman who bound up her crime with the fight for an idea', and appealed to the jury as a 'court of the people's conscience'. They duly acquitted her, to the deafening applause of the public.[47] The outcome of this case was a remarkable revelation of the rift between the government and public opinion, and moved the government to transfer all further cases involving violence against officials to military courts.

All the same, the reformed law courts created a whole new profession which was to prove very important to Russia's future: among its future members were Kerenskii and Lenin. This was the *advokatura*, the corporation of defence counsels, or sworn attorneys. The *advokaty* had their own Bar Council, which admitted members on grounds of professional competence alone, and was supposed to uphold the standards of the profession. It was to prove a fruitful nursery, not only for legally trained individuals but for Russia's future politicians, many of whom came from its ranks.

Here too the government soon imposed restrictions which distorted the character of the profession. In 1874, when only three branches of the Council had been set up, in St Petersburg, Moscow and Khar'kov, the government forbade the opening of any more, so that the profession remained inadequately institutionalized. In 1889, furthermore, the Council was forbidden to admit Jews to membership, though – or maybe because – Jews had proved to be among the most effective lawyers. The government also permitted unqualified attorneys to plead before courts, thus creating a two-tier system of justice rather than subsidize access to properly qualified advice for the poor.[48] In 1889, furthermore, the judicial functions which justices of the peace exercised in rural areas were abolished and transferred to the land commandant.

Both as a corporate profession, and as upholders of the law, *advokaty* were to be of the greatest importance. They were the only professional group in Russian society with a clear interest in the rule of law and thus, for example, the defence of private property. Courtrooms were moreover the only places in Russia where freedom of speech was consistently upheld. As one prominent lawyer, V.D. Spasovich, liked to say: 'we are knights of the living word, more free today than the press'.[49]

Taken as a whole, the reforms of Alexander II went a long way towards erecting the framework for a civil society. From the outset, however, the government was uneasy about what it was letting loose, worried that the new or freer institutions it was creating were fostering an oppositional and seditious frame of mind. The student disorders of the early sixties, the Polish rebellion, the formation of terrorist groups and the Karakozov attempt on the Tsar's life [see p. 347], the Zasulich court hearing – all these occurrences served the government notice that creating a civil society was dangerous, since it afforded niches where seditious activity could safely be planned and executed, and gave political power, at least in local government and law courts, to people who were not prepared simply to act as transmission belts in an administrative hierarchy.

Having taken the risk, therefore, the government then held back, preventing the new institutions from fulfilling their potential and frustrating the expectations it had aroused. The social basis was created for a civil society, but not permitted to develop organically. People of moderate and liberal opinion were consequently thrown into the embrace of socialists and even terrorists. 'No enemies to the left!' was a slogan born of the tergiversations of Alexander II himself.

Only at the very end of the reign, reacting to the crisis occasioned by terrorist assassinations, did Alexander return to the prospect of serious reform, in the face of evidence that the regime did not have the convinced support even of moderate members of the public. He invited General M.T. Loris-Melikov, an Armenian and a hero of the Turkish war of 1877–8, to coordinate anti-terrorist measures. Loris-Melikov soon reported that 'police and punitive methods are insufficient' and proposed that repression should be accompanied by measures which 'indicate the government's attentive and positive response to the needs of the people, of the social estates and of public institutions, and which could strengthen society's trust in the government and would induce social forces to support the administration more actively than they do now in the struggle against false political doctrines.'[50]

Loris-Melikov began to work out practical reform measures to this end, by enhancing the civic status of peasants, and revivifying local government. He recommended, for example, abolishing the salt tax and poll tax, replacing them with an income tax, and making it easier for peasants to acquire their allotments as private property. He wanted to ease official restriction over zemstvos and allow them to increase their tax base.[51]

To institutionalize the contribution of *obshchestvennost'* to legislation he proposed to admit two elected representatives from each guberniia zemstvo and certain larger towns (together with representatives from non-Russian areas and Siberia to be appointed by the Tsar) to a preliminary committee of the State Council, where they would examine draft bills. Ten or fifteen of these public representatives would also participate in the legislative work of the State Council itself. These proposals were watered down by a special conference of senior officials: in particular, the notion of public representatives in the State Council was rejected. But the idea of having elected representatives in a preliminary committee was approved, and was initialled by Alexander II on the very morning of his assassination on 1 March 1881.[52]

When his successor, Alexander III, summoned his ministers to decide whether or not to proceed with the idea, his former tutor, now Procurator of the Holy Synod, K.P. Pobedonostsev, denounced it passionately. This was 'foreign falsehood', the formation of a 'talking-shop', the first step to a Western-style constitution – in short *finis Rossiae*. 'Russia has been strong thanks to autocracy, thanks to the limitless mutual trust and the close tie between the people and its Tsar . . . We suffer quite enough from talking-shops, which, under the influence of worthless journals, simply stoke up popular passions.'[53]

The obsession with autocracy won the day. In the end, after some hesitation, Alexander III decided to reject Loris-Melikov's scheme, and the latter resigned, taking with him most of his colleagues. The attempt to reinforce Russia's civic institutions was abandoned for quarter of a century.

THE ECONOMY Raising the productivity of the Russian economy was one of the main motives for embarking on the emancipation of the serfs. Yet the economic results of the measure have always been the subject of fierce debate. There have been two main Western interpretations, both focusing on the fate of the peasants. The traditional one holds that they were emancipated on terms – shortage of land, excessive payment for it and fixation to the commune – which made it difficult or impossible for them to develop their economies. Taxation intended to generate capital for industrial growth and export forced them to part with their grain on the commercial market on unfavourable terms. Progressive impoverishment then generated an agrarian crisis which found its outlet in the peasant revolution of 1905–6. Since the peasant economy could provide neither surplus funds nor a reliable internal market, the capital for industrialization had to come from the government and from foreign investors.[54]

An alternative and more recent interpretation holds that the fate of the peasant economy was much more diverse than was previously thought: some at least were able to buy land on a large scale, diversifying and specializing their production, successfully seeking employment outside agriculture, and contributing something to economic growth. On this view, the state was less dominant in economic development than had earlier been assumed, and a greater role is assigned to internal capital generation through mechanisms such as joint-stock banks.[55]

What is clear is that at the beginning of the period the needs of empire had skewed the economy to the point where the failure to exploit human and natural resources was undermining Russia's military might and therewith its claim to be considered a great European power. Peasants were burdened with heavy taxes and many of them with personal bondage and dues as well. Available supplies of capital were being dissipated to prop up an under-productive and heavily indebted nobility. The state budget, dependent on mass drunkenness for much of its revenue, was in chronic deficit, in so far as it could be determined at all by the loose and unaudited methods of accounting then practised. The paper money which dominated circulation was subject to marked fluctuations and discouraged investment, especially from abroad. The Crimean War accentuated all these problems, and made a further large issue of unbacked *assignaty* necessary.

More far-sighted financial administrators could see that the basic problem was to find ways of raising the overall prosperity of the population and of mobilizing the resultant wealth to enable Russia to bear the costs of great-power status. Thus Iu.A. Gagemeister, a senior official of the Ministry of Finance, wrote in a report of early 1856 that 'the first duty of financial management is to enrich the people.'[56]

From current reality to that 'first duty' was, however a long and uncharted path. Most financial advisers considered that the key measure would be to build railways, which would not only improve communications in wartime but help to mobilize the rich resources lying untapped in remote regions of the empire. M.Kh. Reitern, who became Finance Minister in 1862, reported to the Tsar that 'without railways and mechanical industry Russia cannot be considered safe even within its own borders.' But how to build them? There was little or no capital available for investment internally, since 'for many years the government and the upper classes have been living beyond their means.' Therefore finance could only be raised from abroad, and this could not be done unless the ruble were stabilized. This in turn required balancing the budget, which could only be achieved by cutting expenditure and raising taxes – mainly on the peasants.[57]

This was in essentials the policy actually pursued, and it helps to explain the fiscally stingy provisions of the emancipation act: the peasants' redemption payments were required to raise revenue. The founding of a State Bank in 1860 also helped to raise confidence in Russian credit-worthiness: as a bank of last resort it demanded certain disciplines of the fairly numerous joint-stock banks which then arose, often with decisive foreign participation.

The immediate result was a railway boom, partly financed by banks in London, Paris and Amsterdam. The track mileage rose nearly sevenfold during the 1860s, and doubled again in the following decade. This remarkable growth (admittedly from modest beginnings) was only accomplished after the government underwrote the debts of the new railway companies, while leaving them their profits to dispose of at their discretion. Only by these means could it entice enough capital to make a breakthrough possible. Even then, construction proceeded by fits and starts, and a number of firms went bankrupt, leaving their debts to the treasury. Nevertheless, as a result, the grain-growing regions began to be linked by rail to the capital cities and to the Black Sea ports, which could despatch grain for sale around the world.[58] These new facilities made possible a rise in grain exports from 60.3 million rubles worth in 1861–5 to 305.9 million rubles in 1876–9. Thereafter a levelling off took place owing to competition from Canada and the USA, but growth resumed after 1900, to 568.3 million rubles in 1905 and 749.4 million in 1909 (the highest figure ever reached).[59]

These figures represent in part produce from the estates of those landlords, especially in the steppes of the south, who had adjusted to the new commercial conditions, importing machinery and hiring wage-labour to replace *barshchina*. But to a considerable degree grain exports came from the peasants themselves. When one considers the minute size and far-flung geographical dispersion of their holdings, that fact is remarkable. Some would sell grain in desperation, some-times months in advance of the crop and at ruinous rates of interest; others would turn their strips of land into small businesses. Either way the grain purchased would be bought by a middleman (*skupsh-chik*), transported to the nearest town, and from there to a river or sea-port for storage, possibly grinding, and then transferred to a ship for export.[60]

The rapid extension of the railways helped to open up remote and hitherto unexploited regions, as well as drawing all parts of the empire into a single and expanding market. The Trans-Siberian, in particular, whose construction was embarked on only after great hesitation because of the enormous expense, made it possible to begin exploiting the greatest single under-used geographical area in the world. It opened the way to Manchuria, Korea and China, while railways into the Transcaucasus and the Transcaspian boosted Rus-sian trade with Persia and the Ottoman Empire. These were all countries where Russia could assume the role of the more advanced power, seeking outlets for its manufactures, as distinct from its raw materials and agricultural products.[61]

The railways were the basis for an impressive expansion of indus-trial output in the late 1880s and 1890s, continuing from 1907–14. Not only did they make it possible to transport materials, fuel and finished products much more easily: they provided a market for industrial goods, such as iron, steel and coal. Between 1883 and 1913 total industrial output rose by an annual average of as much as 4.5 or 5%, a rate comparable with the USA, Germany or Japan at their peak periods of economic expansion.[62]

This growth was promoted by the policy adopted by Finance Ministers I.Ia. Vyshnegradskii (1887–1892) and S.Iu. Witte (1892–1903): protecting infant Russian industries with a high import tariff and stabilizing the ruble with large gold and foreign currency reserves so as to put it on the gold standard, a conversion which was achieved in 1897. Both policies were highly controversial: the ruble stabilization programme was actually rejected in the State Council, and could be pursued only because Nicholas II gave Witte his autocratic authority. Opponents – both modernizing landowners and (though unrepresented in the State Council) Populist intellectuals – urged that this kind of economic growth was artifical and 'un-Russian', creating goods for which Russians had no need, requiring Western individualism and contract law for its operation, and violating the native principle of collectivism. They further asserted that tariffs both obstructed the import of much-needed foreign machinery and provoked retaliatory tariffs in Russia's trading partners, impeding her otherwise promising agricultural exports to them.[63] Witte's more flamboyant and unscrupulous adversaries charged that he was the puppet of an international conspiracy financed by Jewish capital to sap the might of 'Holy Russia'. [see pp. 391–3]

Some countenance was given to these allegations by the degree to which Russian industry was dependent on foreign investment. Foreign capital represented about one-quarter of all joint-stock capital in 1890 and rose sharply in the 1890s to reach 45% in 1900 and 47% in 1914.[64] This gave some plausibility to the assertion that Russia was becoming a colony of more advanced European countries – though it is difficult to demonstrate that this status imposed economic strategies which Russia would not have accepted anyway. The French government, major supporters of investment in Russia, requested that railways should be built with military mobilization on the Western frontier in mind, but that was a priority which the Russian military argued for no less fiercely.

It used to be believed that heavy industry squeezed out the small peasant artisan, the *kustarnik*, who turned out items like clothes, footwear, furniture, tools and cooking utensils. It now seems more likely that, at least in the early decades, manufactured products made *kustar* industry simpler and more profitable to conduct, for example by providing it with nails, rope or good quality cheap cloth. Industry also offered a market for some peasant products and helped to diffuse mechanical skills more widely among small manufacturers in their workshops.[65]

All this evidence of growth is not to deny that substantial pockets of helpless poverty and under-development remained. Most unfortunate of all were the central agricultural provinces south of Moscow. Here the dense population, the shortage of large towns offering a market for produce, and the predominance of very small allotment holdings trapped the majority of rural households in a vicious circle of under-production, under-investment and over-taxation which stimulated the most energetic and able to leave and find employment elsewhere. Here it was possible to write of 'the dying village'. In the mid-Volga region similar, if somewhat less extreme conditions persisted: it was here that in 1891–2 famine and disease took their severest toll, exacerbated by still primitive communications to the outside world.[66]

By contrast, areas near towns, major communications arteries, ports or foreign borders were likely to be more prosperous, and to offer greater opportunities for the enterprising, able or well-qualified peasant households to make a go of it. This was true of much of the central industrial area, the Baltic, Poland, the western provinces, the steppes of the Don, the Kuban' and the north shore of the Black Sea. A striking consequence of this geographical spread of differentiated opportunity was that nearly all the poorest regions were Russian in population, while many of the prosperous ones had a considerable non-Russian population.

Overall, the growth of industry and the patchy but unmistakable improvement of agriculture were creating a more prosperous, mobile and confident population. They were also stimulating the large-scale migration of Russians into their largest cities and into the fastest growing, often non-Russian, regions.[67] This change in their condition was not matched by any improvement in their civic status. By the early twentieth century, the mismatch of economic effervescence and political stagnation was becoming acute, while many of the victims of economic growth were the Russians, supposedly the leading people of the empire.

2

Russian Socialism

The long, isolated apprenticeship of Russia's intellectuals in *kruzhki* came to a welcome but incomplete end in the discussions which preceded Alexander II's reform programme. As we have seen, some of them were drawn into practical statecraft; others, for reasons of personality or outlook, remained on the fringes, while a younger generation, nurtured on their ideas, prepared to take over.

The emancipation act itself brought disillusionment for many, the realization that the regime was incapable of bridging the fatal gap between elites and people, which its advisers had diagnosed as the principal cause of Russia's weakness. The natural inference seemed to be that intellectuals should take the initiative in bridging that gap, should come out of their quarantine, make contact with ordinary people and launch political action. The regime, however, offered them no legitimate way of doing this, even during its relative tolerance of the late fifties and early sixties. Without experience or precedent to draw upon, the first generation of political activists thrashed about, improvising in grotesque and helpless ways.

Some of their inspiration in doing so was provided by Nikolai Chernyshevskii, who occupied a key position as an editor of *Sovremennik*. He was the son of a priest, and he brought to his political convictions the asceticism, single-mindedness and self-abnegation worthy of the clerical calling he had trained for but abandoned. In him the ideal of the pastoral service which a clergyman renders to his parishioners had been transferred to the sphere of social and political service to the people as a whole. Yet he was also a sober utilitarian, a believer in rational egoism and in the calculus of pleasure and pain. These two elements, the religious and the secular, the ascetic and the calculating, remained in unresolved tension in his

345

personality, but on the level of theory he sought a resolution in the idea of a social revolution to be promoted by the best people on the basis of personal example. Disillusioned with the emancipation of the serfs, and also with the vacillating aristocratic socialism of Herzen, he became convinced that only a revolution from below could bring about lasting improvement, and that in the meantime it was the duty of educated people both to spread socialist ideas among the people and show what a future society should look like by living in cooperatives engaged in productive work.[1]

Although he wrote long philosophical, aesthetic and political tracts, Chernyshevskii's most celebrated work was a novel, *What is to be Done?*, published legally in 1862, in which he portrayed an artel of seamstresses, who live together and pool their resources to make clothes which they sell and live on the revenues. In the background, somewhat veiled because of the censorship but nevertheless unmistakeable, is a circle of political activists, preparing for revolution by means of theoretical study, conspiratorial organization and the steeling of the will. Rakhmetov, their leader, consciously trains himself for the coming struggle by an ascetic, body-building regime of sleeping on hard floors, staying away from women, and eating only food which ordinary people can afford – except for best-quality steak to strengthen his muscles.

In Rakhmetov, Peter the Great's ideal of the commanding government official, ruthless, self-denying and devoted to change was transmuted into a revolutionary ideal. It was to have enormous influence on two generations of revolutionaries, including Lenin.[2]

One young man inspired by Chernyshevskii was a former official, N.A. Serno-Solovevich: he had himself once handed the Tsar a note urging reform in the spirit of Christianity, but had later abandoned hope of the regime transforming society, and had resigned from the service. He opened a bookshop and library in St Petersburg to make political writings available to the masses. Round it he gathered a small group of like-minded young people, named after Herzen's slogan 'Land and Freedom' (*Zemlia i Volia*), with the intention of making contact with workers and peasants. But the whole group was broken up by the police before it could get anywhere.[3]

In Moscow a nineteen-year old student, P.G. Zaichnevskii, circulated a pamphlet entitled *Young Russia*, urging the reconstruction of

Russia as a federation of village communes and communally run factories. If there was resistance from the regime to this idea, then 'with full faith in ourselves and our strength, in the people's sympathy with us, in the glorious future of Russia, to whose lot it has fallen to be the first country to achieve the glorious work of socialism, we will utter a single cry: "Seize your axes!" '[4]

Another young radical, N.A. Ishutin, did not even entertain the notion that the Tsar might introduce socialism. He set up an enigmatic 'Organization', which claimed to have an inner conclave, luridly named 'Hell', an artel of students whose single-minded aim was to assassinate senior state officials, culminating with the Tsar himself. His circle was recruited from a group of Saratov seminarists whose regular reading included the New Testament and histories of Russian sectarianism. Ishutin said at his trial that he acknowledged only three masters: Christ, St Paul and Chernyshevskii.[5]

A fringe member of this group, D.V. Karakozov, did actually fire a shot at Alexander in 1866. Before his attempt he wrote a Manifesto which throws light on the mentality of this strange and tormented generation. 'Brother, I have long been tortured by the thought and given no rest by my doubts why my beloved simple Russian people has to suffer so much! ... Why next to the eternal simple peasant and labourer in his factory and workshop are there people who do nothing – idle nobles, a horde of officials and other wealthy people, all living in shining houses? ... I have looked for the reason for all this in books, and I have found it. The man really responsible is the Tsar ... Think carefully about it, brothers, and you will see that the Tsar is the first of the nobles. He never holds out his hand to the people because he is himself the people's worst enemy.'[6] The guilt feelings, the crass over-simplification, the Manicheanism, the naive faith in books, the pathetic appeal to popular approval: all this was characteristic of an elite cut off from its people, deprived of practical experience, nourished on religious sectarianism and harbouring alternating visions of omnipotence and helplessness.

A figure even more contemptuous of the existing system, and imbued with an even firmer conviction that the end justified the means was Sergei Nechaev, who composed a 'Catechism of the Revolutionary' to act as a guide for his associates in conspiracy. 'The revolutionary', he proclaimed, 'is a lost man; he has no interest of his own, no cause of his own, no feelings, no habits, no belongings; he does not even have a name. Everything in him is absorbed by a single, exclusive interest, a single thought, a single passion – the revolution. In the very depths of his being, not just in words, but in deed, he has broken every tie with the civil order, with the educated world, with all laws, conventions and generally accepted conditions, and with the ethics of this world. He will be an implacable enemy of this world, and if he continues to live in this world, that will be only so as to destroy it the more effectively.' The ascetic self-abnegation, the wilful hermit-like isolation, the anticipation of an approaching last judgement are reminiscent of those extreme Old Believers who refused to have anything to do with the state of the Antichrist; but in Nechaev they were combined with a cynicism symptomatic of a generation brought up on a pseudo-scientific materialism.

Nechaev set up a secret society, persuading its other members that it was but one cell of a vast organization, whose sole representative among them was himself. Visiting Switzerland, he persuaded the ageing Bakunin to part with a good deal of money on the strength of his fabrications. Back at home, he tested his followers by accusing one of them of being a police spy and ordering the others to murder him, which they did. When the regime brought him to trial, it did so publicly in the conviction that his example would be sufficiently repugnant to shock the public into condemnation of all secret insurrectionists.[7]

The intellectuals' renewed messianic expectations interacted with the repressiveness of the regime, its censorship and its hostility to voluntary social organizations to generate an apocalyptic and polarized view of the world. The intellectuals felt that a beneficent transformation was within their grasp, thwarted only by a malevolent regime. They were left in a kind of limbo, unable directly to communicate their message in the media or among the mass of the people. None of the eccentric and evanescent groups of the 1860s solved the problem.

The thinker who suggest how communication might be accomplished was Petr Lavrov, former military engineer and member of Serno-Solovevich's *Zemlia i volia*. Compared with Chernyshevskii's downright 'rational egoism', his philosophy gave greater weight to subjective and ethical motives in human conduct. By the late 1860s Lavrov had come to the conviction that it was the duty of intellectuals to 'go to the people' and spread the knowledge and insight which they had acquired as a result of their education. That was the conviction which he advanced in his *Historical Letters (Istoricheskie Pis'ma*, 1869–70), which enjoyèd an immediate and widespread success among young people.

Lavrov viewed this obligation in both a moral and an instrumental manner. Intellectuals had acquired their education at the cost of the people, who had laboured to keep them alive while they studied, and they therefore had a debt to pay. Moreover, as a result of their studies intellectuals were in a unique position to criticize existing society, to understand the underlying laws of social evolution and therefore to work out what had to be done and to spread that knowledge among those who lacked their advantages. These 'critically thinking individuals must be determined not only to fight but to win ... they must seek each other out, must unite, stand at the head of the party and direct others. Then the force will be organised; its action can be focused on a given point, concentrated for a given purpose.'[8]

Lavrov, then, envisaged intellectuals forming a political organization – a party – in order to promote the work of propaganda among the workers and peasants and to prepare for the 'given purpose', which, though he did not state it openly, was the overthrow of the existing regime. The schemata of a hierarchy of persons with superior knowledge carrying out radical and ruthless social change was borrowed directly from the Tsarist regime. At the same time, the ethical qualifications required for membership were intended to prevent the movement falling into the hands of crude manipulators like Nechaev.

Nearly sixty per cent of those who tried during the 1870s and 1880s to put Lavrov's vision into practice were children of the nobility or the clergy: the two social estates which in Imperial Russia were consciously trained for a life of service to either state or church. Moreover, more than half of them had attended an institution of higher education.[9] The name they gave to their movement, 'going to the people' (*khozhdenie v narod*), speaks volumes about the distance which they felt existed between themselves and the peasants: it was almost as if they were missionaries on an expedition to darkest Africa. As Dmitrii Klements put it, when asked why he had given up everything to engage in the enterprise, 'We speak so much of the people, but we do not know them. I want to live the life of the people and suffer for them.'[10]

In this way a small detachment of young offspring of Imperial Russia broke with their fellows and tried to reknit the torn ethnic fabric by getting in touch with peasant Russia, living among the *narod*, learning about their way of life and reinterpreting their customary notions in the light of the latest European political doctrines.

They indicated their longing for restored ethnic unity first of all by the clothes they wore. Eschewing the starched collar and frock coat of civil servants, the young men went about in red shirts, baggy trousers and overalls, and kept their hair long, while the women avoided the frills of society ladies and kept their hair short, wore plain white blouses, black skirts and male boots.[11]

Although many of the students came from noble families, few of them were really well off, and they practised their ideals by sharing a life of cautious parsimony, if not downright poverty. Class and estate distinctions melted away in the face of the common aspiration for learning and social service. Science enjoyed a high reputation as a practical basis for generating social change, but all learning was valued as part of a culture which ought to be the heritage of all humanity. Students of different origins would help one another out by establishing common libraries, cafeterias and mutual aid funds, sometimes associated with a self-organized seminar or *kruzhok*.[12]

The first systematic *kruzhok* of this type was the one set up by Mark Natanson in 1869 at the Medical-Surgical Academy in St Petersburg, and after his arrest in 1871 it was continued by Nikolai Chaikovskii. The ideals of this circle were primarily cultural and ethical, at least to begin with: its members consciously rejected the 'Jesuitism and Machiavellianism' of Nechaev. Their qualification for admitting new recruits was a moral one: they expected them to take their education seriously and if possible to complete their course of study before paying back their debt to the people. Chaikovskii used to say 'We must be as clean and clear as a mirror. We must know each other so well that, should there arise difficult times of persecution and struggle, we are in a position to know a priori how each of us will behave.' For this reason, he called his circle 'an Order of Knights'. He himself frequently visited sectarians and became a member of a sect whose declared aim was 'Godmanhood'.[13]

As this term suggests, the new movement could be regarded as a militant religion. Bervi-Flerovskii, a social scientist whose works were popular among the radicals, realized that 'success could only be assured when the explosion of enthusiasm among these young people was changed into a permanent and ineradicable feeling. Constantly thinking about this, I grew certain that success was possible only if one path was followed: that of founding a new religion. I wanted to create a religion of equality.' The statement of his creed began: 'Go to the people and tell them the truth to the very last word.' The 'truth' was that all men are equal, that in particular the land has been provided for all equally, and that it was the right and duty of the people to seize their proper share for themselves from the landowners and exploiters.[14] In the same spirit, Aleksandr Dolgushin, one of the first to leave for the villages, kept at his dacha, along with a printing press, a cross, on the head of which was inscribed 'In the name of Christ', and on the crossbar 'Liberty, Equality, Fraternity'.[15]

Some of the early attempts to contact the ordinary people were targeted at Old Believers and sectarians, because of their history of alienation from the regime. Already in the early sixties Herzen and Ogarev had tried from exile in London to get in touch with them through a young impoverished nobleman who was fascinated by the 'schismatics', V.I. Kel'siev. He found his Old Believer contacts well-disposed to him and inclined to share many of his views. They were also very anxious to have their books published abroad to replenish their own meagre stocks. They were reluctant, however, to engage in any political activities, particularly in alliance with émigrés. Not only did they find the atheism of their radical contacts repugnant but they were worn down by nearly two centuries of persecution and discrimination: they were pessimistic, passive and inclined to be content with the concessions Alexander II had recently made to them.[16] The old rebellious spirit, it seemed, had finally evaporated among the Old Believers.

The Chaikovskii circle began by collecting and distributing books and pamphlets, at first for their members, then for wider dissemination. Among them were Marx's *Das Kapital*, Lavrov's *Historical Letters*, Bervi-Flerovskii's *The Situation of the Working Class in Russia* and his *ABC of Social Sciences*, Louis Blanc's *History of the French Revolution* and works by Herzen, Chernyshevskii and Shchapov. The first attempt at wider distribution was made among the workers of St Petersburg and other cities, supplemented by discussion and instruction groups organized clandestinely.[17]

By 1873 the feeling was catching on that the time had come to venture outside the towns, to the heartlands of the *narod*, the villages. This was a much more radical decision than to agitate among workers, for going to the village meant abandoning one's studies, breaking with family and friends and probably relinquishing any prospect of an official career. The Chaikovskii group provided a minimal organizational framework, but often counselled restraint to the more impetuous.

The movement was a largely spontaneous one, borne aloft by what Aptekman described as the 'Hannibal's oath' of contemporary youth. 'They vowed to serve the people. They would wash its wounds, cure its griefs, and bearing aloft the torch of learning and freedom would lead it forth on to the broad expanses of a cultured existence!' And so 'these revolutionary young folk, full of belief in the people and in their own strength, gripped by a kind of ecstasy, set out on the long journey into the unknown. They left behind cherished images of their nearest and dearest . . . and the higher educational establishments, with their "rights and privileges". All their boats were burnt. There was no return.'[18]

To supplement their book-learning, many of them first learned skills that they thought would be useful to people. They flocked to workshops, where under the guidance of a sympathetic artisan they could learn cobblery, joinery, metalwork – whatever they felt able to cope with. Others set out without a clear idea of how they were going to be able to make a living or create village contacts. Iakov Stefanovich and Vladimir Debagorii-Mokrievich, for example, left Kiev with three companions and a bag of cobbler's implements, though they did not all know how to use them. In the event, they first of all worked at loading sleepers into railway wagons, then they decided to become dyers, but found few customers, since most villagers already had contacts for that kind of work. They discovered, moreover, that if they were poorly dressed few peasants would risk offering them an overnight stay, being afraid of robbers.[19] Some, like Aleksandr Ivanchin-Pisarev, thought it would be more sensible to take a job requiring literacy, like that of volost clerk, in which they could exercise a skill in real demand, since it was possessed by few peasants, and also influence the conduct of village business.[20]

How did the peasants respond to contact with the radicals? Historians' traditional view has been that they regarded the propagandists with incomprehension and suspicion, and sometimes turned them over to the authorities. Recent research suggests however that the situation is not quite so clear-cut. As Daniel Field has pointed out, much of the evidence for the usual interpretation comes from the documents of the investigation and trial of those radicals who had been arrested: in answering the authorities' questions everyone – the accused, peasant witnesses, village officials – had an interest in minimizing the success of the propaganda, as otherwise they could expect either a longer sentence or further tiresome inquiries.[21] If one reads the memoirs of the propagandists, they paint a more varied picture; though here one must make allowance for a natural tendency to exaggerate positive achievements in hindsight.

There can be no doubting the initial difficulties in communication. Most radicals felt baffled and discouraged when they first faced the villagers, who, after all, revered the Tsar and held religious beliefs which most students regarded as either superstitious or sentimental. As Aptekman later recalled his misgivings on settling in a village in Pskov guberniia: 'How can I approach the people with my ideas? My outlook on the world is completely different from theirs. We have two categories of ideas, two mentalities, not only opposite to, but contradicting one another.'[22] Vera Figner, working as a medical orderly in a Samara rural zemstvo hospital, was overwhelmed by a feeling of hopelessness when she contemplated peasant poverty. 'Each day, when work was done, I would flop down on the heap of straw laid on the floor as a bed, and despair overcame me. Would there ever be an end to this ghastly poverty? Wasn't it hypocrisy to hand out all those medicines in such surroundings? Wasn't it a mockery to talk about resistance and struggle to people overwhelmed by physical afflictions?'[23]

All the same, there were appropriate techniques for establishing human contact. When he became a medical orderly, Aptekman found he could win the peasants' confidence by asking them attentively about their lives while he treated them; he even set up a kind of club in the convalescent ward, where they would come and chat about their lives and listen to his ideas about how to improve things.[24] Figner discovered a similar approach: 'The people were not used to getting attention, to being questioned in detail, to receiving sensible instructions on how to take their medicines.'[25] When her sister Evgeniia opened a school, offering tuition free of charge, she encountered a ready response: not only children, but adults as well, came to learn arithmetic, which was useful to them in their personal and community affairs. 'Every moment we felt that we were needed, that we were not superfluous. That awareness of being useful was the force which attracted our young people to the villages; only there was it possible to have a pure heart and a peaceful conscience.'[26]

Peasants did in fact share some of the radicals' ideas, even if they saw them in a completely different context. Stefanovich and Debagorii-Mokrievich discovered, for example, that peasants in Kiev guberniia thought the land should be redivided and awarded equitably to all who needed it, 'to the muzhik, the lord, the priest, the Jew and the gipsy, all equally'. But they were convinced that such a boon could come only from the Tsar, perhaps when they had completed their short period of military service recently introduced under the Miliutin reform.[27] In the late 1870s, Stefanovich and Debagorii-Mokrievich actually succeeded in attracting several hundred peasants in Kiev guberniia into a *druzhina* (armed band) by the device of circulating a forged manifesto purporting to come from the Tsar and calling on the peasants to rise and seize the land from the landowners who were thwarting his will.[28] This episode, unique of its kind, suggests that peasants were willing to become politically active in order to take the land, provided they thought the Tsar supported them. Most radicals felt, however, that practising deceit to gain peasant support contravened the moral principles which were inherent in their beliefs.

It was not so much the rank-and-file peasants as the village authorities who regarded these strange outsiders with suspicion and resentment. Vera Figner suggests why: 'If I was summoned to the bedside of a dying person at the same time as the priest, then he could not very well haggle over the fee for the last rites. If we were present at volost court hearings, then the clerk would count up every 25- and 50-kopeck piece, every bribe in kind, of which we were depriving him. And there remained the fear that, in case of abuse, violence or extortion, we might write a complaint for the victim and, through acquaintances in town, bring it to the notice of judicial or ecclesiastical officials.' The Figners, unusually, were working as bona fide zemstvo employees. Even so, they were vulnerable: rumours began to spread that they were going from hut to hut reading proclamations, and that in their school the peasant children were learning that 'There is no God, and we don't need the Tsar.' One day the local police chief came to interrogate them, and he closed down their school as an establishment unauthorized by the local education committee.[29]

When, as very often happened, the village activists were arrested, their situation became grim and demoralizing. The investigation of their case took a very long time, as there were so many accused, the collection of evidence was cumbersome, and it was not always obvious what they should be charged with. It was a shock to be suddenly plucked out of a life of commitment and activity and plunged into solitary confinement, with no one but warders and interrogators for company. A life of energy and hope, even if mixed with frustration, was replaced by one of pointless idleness, often under-nourished and in repellent physical conditions.

Even worse were the pressures of the investigation, as prisoners began to feel that their cause was hopeless and to discover that not all their colleagues were the irreprochable 'knights' they had seemed. Some detainees began to inform on their colleagues, beginning a chain reaction of clandestine collaboration between the political police and individual revolutionaries which was to poison the whole movement. Nikolai Charushin, who had propagandized in the St Petersburg factories, recalled the impact the discovery of betrayal produced on him. 'Everything I had lived for, everything I had believed in, was destroyed. My friends and comrades in the great work had failed, and I did not know if any of them were still alive. The cause itself had failed too, and the workers, even if only three of them, to whose affairs I had devoted myself heart and soul, had turned out to be traitors!'[30] Not surprisingly, some prisoners reacted by going insane or committing suicide.

As a whole, the experience of 'going to the people' suggested that propaganda among the peasants might be fruitful in the long term, but that it required a more patient approach and a better organized network, with for example 'centres' in nearby towns to which propagandists could repair to pick up more material, discuss their work with comrades and perhaps relax for a while from the strains and discomforts of rural existence. It was for this reason that some of those who had survived the campaign set up the nucleus of a centralized organization in St Petersburg in 1876, and began to try to establish contact with those still carrying out propaganda in the towns and villages. This was the first attempt to create an empire-wide political party in Russia. It took the already familiar name of *Zemlia i volia*.

Almost from the outset, *Zemlia i volia* was plagued by a division which soon grew into a permanent split. The rural experience of 1873–4 led many to the conclusion that propaganda among the peasants could not be successful in the existing structure of society, and that first of all political activity was necessary to destroy the existing state and replace it with a new one, as a *prerequisite*, not a result, of successful propaganda. In a word, as they put it at the time, the 'economic' struggle must be preceded by a 'political' one. Since there was no way to bring about change peacefully, a political struggle could only be violent.

In spite of the original peaceful ideals of the movement, and the revulsion against Nechaev, this impetus towards violence proved to be extremely vigorous and persistent. It was born of frustration, as a defence against the possibility of arrest, from a desire for heroic and conspicuous action, and as a product of rational political calculations. As Alexander Mikhailov, a leading proponent of violence, wrote to a friend, 'You know, I loved work among the people. I was ready to make any sacrifice within my powers, but we were a mere handful, we were powerless to achieve anything under the autocracy; all our best efforts were expended in vain. There was only one alternative for our modest strength: either completely to abandon revolutionary activity, or to enter into single combat with the government. For the latter we had enough strength, heroism and capacity for self-sacrifice.'[31]

From the beginning the party had a 'disorganization' section, charged at first with defending comrades against search or arrest, or with rescuing them once in detention. Its occasional successes bred a certain self-confidence and the sense that at least something was being accomplished. The pressure towards systematic rather than sporadic violence intensified in 1878, as a result of the Zasulich affair [see pp. 335–6]. The wave of public sympathy for Zasulich induced even Dostoevskii to confess to the conservative newspaper editor Suvorin that, were he fortuitously to hear of a terrorist outrage being prepared, he would not report it to the authorities for fear of public exposure and ridicule.[32] Petr Valuev, heading a commission of investigation into terrorism, felt bound to report that 'specially worthy of attention is the almost complete failure of the educated classes to support the government in its fight against a relatively small band of evil-doers . . . Indeed, they almost always react disapprovingly to the authorities' measures.'[33]

To prepare for a possible violent political struggle, *Zemlia i volia* became a conspiratorial organization: members' right to know other members was restricted and a lifelong oath of secrecy was imposed, breach of which was punishable by death. Finally, in 1879, at a secret congress, a majority of delegates came out in favour of a systematic policy of terror, with the aim first of disorganizing the government by assassinating its leading members, then of overthrowing it and installing a new regime charged with convening a constituent assembly and paving the way to popular rule. There was some dissension, but the only prominent activist who refused to accept this decision was Georgii Plekhanov, who broke away and tried unsuccessfully to found an alternative organization. The remainder reconstituted themselves as *Narodnaia volia*, or the 'people's will', so called to indicate the intention to allow the people the decisive say in the formation of a new political system.[34] The use of the word *volia* also evoked the old Cossack ideal of freedom.

Within a few months, the Executive Committee of *Narodnaia volia* had established in a number of towns a network of cells among workers and students, and even a few in the army and navy. But its main drive was towards terror rather than propaganda. *Zemlia i volia* had already embarked on the assassination of high police and government officials, and *Narodnaia volia* from the outset aimed even higher. On 26 August 1879 the Executive Committee condemned Alexander II to death 'for crimes against the people', and from then on its members' priority was to organize and carry out that sentence.[35] After a number of failures, they succeeded, on 1 March 1881, in blowing him up as he drove in his carriage along a St Petersburg embankment.

The murder of Alexander II marks the greatest success of Russian socialism up to that time, yet also its greatest failure. For the Executive Committee was powerless to make good its promise and convene a constituent assembly, or even to influence the policy of the new Tsar, Alexander III, in any but a negative manner. One immediate result was the declaration of a 'state of emergency' or 'reinforced protection' in many provinces: under these regimes police and local authorities could detain suspects without trial, impose administrative exile, search premises without warrant, dismiss officials, suspend or close periodicals, and otherwise curtail even the meagre civil rights which were normally observed. In a few provinces these provisions remained in force right through to 1917.[36]

The mass of the people remained indifferent: in fact the most active popular response was a series of anti-Jewish pogroms in the towns of the south and west. Far from being advanced, everything *Narodnaia volia* claimed to believe in – whether socialism, democracy or civil liberties – had been set back by their deed.

Police investigation of the assassination soon severely weakened the Executive Committee. Even more damaging, however, were the intrigues of the editor of its Odessa newspaper, Sergei Degaev. Degaev was recruited in December 1882 by a secret police inspector, G.D. Sudeikin, who lured him by feigning approval of many of the aims of *Narodnaia volia* and giving him money 'in the interests of the common cause'. Degaev gave the police enough information to destroy the party's military wing and its southern organization while at the same time becoming a leading figure in its St Petersburg branch and recruiting many new members.

The motivation of both these men is difficult to fathom. Perhaps they were using each other to rise in their respective hierarchies. At one stage they were planning a fake assassination attempt on Sudeikin, which was calculated to enhance Degaev's reputation with his colleagues and to have Sudeikin promoted and awarded a medal by the Tsar. However, they called it off. Later, under pressure from suspicious colleagues to prove his loyalty, Degaev did actually bring about Sudeikin's murder.[37]

This was the first major example of a grotesque phenomenon which was to become endemic in the final decades of the empire: the double agent or, as he was often known, the *agent provocateur*. Opposition parties deprived of regular contact with the public, together with a secret police not importuned by effective supervision from any authority, offered enticing opportunities for men attracted by the exercise of power for its own sake. The police needed information about what the terrorists were planning, information which was almost impossible to obtain and verify without secret agents; and once those agents were ensconced inside the terrorist league, they had to keep up their credibility by taking part in terrorist activities. The logic of the situation was inescapable and provided unlimited scope for abuse. The agent working for both sides was extremely difficult to detect and could orchestrate alternating betrayals and assassinations as required to keep his reputation with both parties clean. Here the *fiskal* and the revolutionary, both direct descendants of Peter the Great, amalgamated in one sinister figure.

When the surviving members of *Narodnaia volia* began to reconstitute themselves during the 1890s to form the Union of Socialist Revolutionaries (later the Socialist Revolutionary Party), they were faced with the same dilemmas as their predecessors of twenty years earlier. While attempts to work among the peasants were somewhat more hopeful than in the 1870s,[38] it still seemed impossible to get anywhere without systematic terrorism to protect the revolutionaries, disorganize the government and inspire the masses with the sense that the regime was not invincible.

This time, however, the party did try not to be taken over by the technicians of assassination. It put them in a separate Fighting Detachment (*boevoi otriad*), leaving members of the Central Committee free to concentrate on tasks of organization and peaceful propaganda. Ironically, though, the very isolation of the terrorists had the effect of emancipating them from considerations of ideology or morality. The Fighting Detachment generated among its members an intense and battle-hardened group loyalty and a suicidal capacity for self-sacrifice which could not always be constrained by their soberer comrades in the Central Committee.[39]

Between 1902 and 1905 the Fighting Detachment succeeded in assassinating two Ministers of the Interior (Sipiagin and Pleve) and the Governor-General of Moscow, Grand Duke Sergei Aleksandrovich, as well as a number of lesser officials. This was merely part of a campaign of terror conducted by various revolutionary groups and individuals against the regime and its officials, which killed or wounded more than 4,000 of them during the years 1905–7.[40] Rarely if ever can any regime have sustained such an onslaught of terror, and it was not till Prime Minister Stolypin instituted special field courts-martial in August 1906, with curtailed procedures and instant sentences (usually death), that the tide began to be reversed.

Many of these outrages were committed by individuals who had lost – or never had – any ideological commitment, but were moved by the need for excitement, status or belonging, or by the desire for material gain. They did much to discredit both the revolutionary parties (especially the SRs) and the regime. The nadir was reached in 1908, when it was revealed that the principal figure in the Fighting Detachment had been all along an agent of the Department of Police. Evno Azef had played a vital role in amalgamating local groups to form the Socialist Revolutionary Party; he had later led its Fighting Detachment and provided its liaison with the Central Committee. Yet all along he had been reporting to the police and had been responsible for the arrest of many of his colleagues. Such a revelation could not but undermine the whole moral and political standing of the SRs. Indeed the party scarcely survived it, despite its relative success in mobilizing workers and peasants during 1905–7 [see Chapter 4].[41]

The one man in the Populist movement who had stood out against the adoption of terror was Georgii Plekhanov. Despairing of achieving anything useful in Russia, he had gone into exile in Switzerland, where he undertook a thorough study of the European tradition of socialism and especially of Marx. Before long he became convinced that he had found in Marx the key to understanding why all the various tactics employed by Russian socialists had proved abortive. The essence of the matter was that none of them had made a scientific study of the evolution of human societies, so that their efforts were grounded on passionately held but unrealistic appreciations of the possibilities before them.

He expounded his views in two key works, *Socialism and the Political Struggle* (1883) and *Our Differences* (1885), published in 1883–5. Their conclusions became the foundation of a new variety of Russian socialism, the first which consciously denied that Russia had a special, unique path, but asserted that it must follow the universally applicable laws of social development, like other European countries, as described by Marx (a view not necessarily shared by Marx). In progressing from its current condition of feudalism, Plekhanov asserted, Russia could not avoid capitalism on its way to the ultimate destination of socialism. The peasant commune held no hopes for the future: it was merely the remnant of a dying mode of economic life, and was already succumbing to erosion by advancing capitalism. Peasants were moving inexorably towards private property and a petty bourgeois consciousness. The leading revolutionary class would therefore be the workers, who were quite distinct from the peasantry in their outlook. Since capitalism was still only modestly developed in Russia, and the proletariat was as yet a comparatively small social class, the conditions for socialist revolution were far from being mature, which explained why all attempts to carry out such a revolution had failed, and why they had ended up in fruitless violence and the moral degradation spread around by *agents provocateurs*.[42]

Plekhanov believed that only this version of history had the right to be called 'scientific socialism'. He contemptuously dismissed all existing Russian socialists, except his few colleagues, as *narodniki*, which, coming from his disdainful pen, sounded like 'people-nuts', but can more properly be translated as 'Populists', the name by which all pre-Marxist Russian socialists are now generally known. The effect of this polemical technique has been to exaggerate in retrospect the clear-cut nature of the distinction between the two revolutionary traditions. Although there was a lively intellectual debate between the two in the 1880s and 1890s, in the Russian cities there was also much practical cooperation between them, and most Russian Marxists began their lives as 'Populists' without going through any great conversion experience before reaching their ultimate position.[43]

Like the Populists before them, the Marxists, calling themselves

Social Democrats in deference to the contemporary German movement, began to make contact with factory workers, at first holding evening classes and self-education groups, teaching the illiterate to read, discussing texts not only by Marx and Engels but by John Stuart Mill, Herbert Spencer, Chernyshevskii and Lavrov. Then came the stage of 'agitation': picking on grievances which were widely shared, whether over pay, conditions, hours of work, or a hated foreman, and encouraging the workers to protest over them. If they were not successful, Social Democrats hoped they would still gain insight into the way the whole system was loaded against them, and would become sensitive to the possibility of direct political action in solidarity with their fellows.

Although this strategy was aimed first at 'conscious' workers, in effect it lumped all together in the same boat. There was a certain disequilibrium here: the workers mostly wanted to improve their conditions, the intellectuals wanted to transform society. In spite of this discrepancy, however, the young agitators had a certain success: in the late 1890s there were a number of strikes in major cities – St Petersburg, Kiev, Ekaterinoslav, Khar'kov. They were usually organized by the workers themselves, but drew on the repertoire of techniques the activists had taught them.[44]

With the revival of hopes for political change in the early years of the twentieth century, two distinct socialist parties did emerge: the Russian Social Democratic Workers' Party, which held its first congress at Minsk in 1898, and the Socialist Revolutionary Party, established in Paris in 1901. The first represented the Marxist tradition, the second the Populist.

Almost before it was properly founded, however, the Social Democratic Party underwent a split, spawning a fraction which in some ways represented a return to the Populist tradition. Vladimir Il'ich Ul'ianov, or Lenin, who headed this wing, had experienced during his teenage years the trauma of losing his beloved elder brother, Aleksandr, executed for his participation in the terrorist wing of *Narodnaia volia*, plotting to assassinate the Tsar. Going through his brother's books, the young Lenin came across Chernyshevskii's novel *What is to be Done?* He had already read it once without real understanding, but now, as he later told a comrade, 'after the execution of my brother, knowing that Chernyshevskii's novel was one of his favourite works, I began what was a real reading and pored over the book, not for several days but for several weeks. Only then did I understand its full depth. It is a work which gives one impetus for a whole lifetime.'[45] What impressed him about Chernyshevskii was that he 'not only demonstrated the necessity for every correctly thinking and really honest man to become a revolutionary, but also ... [showed] what the revolutionary must be like, what his rules must be, how he must go about attaining his goals, and by what methods and means he can bring about their realisation.'[46]

Presumably, then, it was the portrait of Rakhmetov, his asceticism, his dedication, his goal-directed studies, his careful preparation of the mind and steeling of the body, which impressed Lenin, as well as the implication – not fully developed in the novel, because of censorship – that revolutionaries are a small, elite group of disciplined and selfless people who sacrifice everything for their supreme aim.

In studying Marx closely, Lenin was not breaking with Chernyshevskii or with what had become known as the Populist tradition. Chernyshevskii had admired Marx and had helped to make him better known in Russia, while a leading Populist, German Lopatin, had published the first translation of *Das Kapital* in Russia – or indeed anywhere in the world – in 1872. Yet in his early days Lenin did align himself decisively with Plekhanov and those who rejected the Populists' alleged sentimentalism, their obsession with peasants, their narrow Russocentric horizons, their lack of scientific rigour. What Lenin sought from Marx was certainty, the certainty which he thought was characteristic of science. He wanted to ensure that he would not repeat his brother's mistake of sacrificing himself, however heroically, in a cause not properly grounded in an understanding of objective social circumstances.

Reading *Das Kapital* was a revelation to him. He regarded it as the incontestable truth about social and economic evolution, though he recognized that, since it did not touch directly on Russia, adaptation of its ideas would be necessary to reach valid conclusions about the correct revolutionary path there. He accepted Plekhanov's interpretation that Russia, being more backward than most European countries, had to go through two stages before reaching socialism: (i) a 'bourgeois democratic' revolution, when the feudal system would be finally overthrown by an alliance of the workers' party with the bourgeois liberals, and (ii) a later socialist revolution, which would come in the fullness of time, when capitalism was fully developed and the working class had reached maturity.

Among Russian Marxists, however, Lenin distinguished himself by his advocacy of the notion of a small, conspiratorial band of 'professional revolutionaries'. He expounded the idea in a pamphlet which, significantly, he gave the same name as Chernyshevskii's novel, *What is to be Done?* What he proposed was actually the only practical way to organize a political party of any kind in Russia at the time, let alone a revolutionary one. But on the other hand Lenin was recommending this structure for universal rather than specifically Russian reasons. Workers on their own, he argued, cannot generate socialist ideas: they 'did not have, nor was it possible for them to have, an awareness of the irreconcilable contradiction of their interests with the whole modern political and social system'. On the contrary, 'The history of all countries shows that by itself the working-class can only develop a trade union consciousness,' that is, they would merely struggle for material improvements within the existing system rather than fight to transform the whole structure of society, which was the fundamental cause of their misery. Only the 'educated representatives of the propertied classes – the intelligentsia' could really understand the long-term interests of the workers and lead them properly. Without them the 'spontaneous development of the working-class movement leads to its subordination to bourgeois ideology'. It followed that a revolutionary party should 'consist chiefly of people professionally engaged in revolutionary activity', that is 'professional revolutionaries'.[47]

At the Second Congress, in effect the founding congress, of the Social Democratic Party, held in Brussels and London in 1903, Lenin pushed his obduracy to the extent of breaking with some of his most-valued colleagues and causing an enduring split in the party they had worked together to create. He insisted that 'personal participation in one of the party's organisations' was to be the key qualification for party membership, while his opponents, led by Martov, favoured a slightly looser definition: 'regular personal assistance under the direction of the one of the party's organisations'. Martov wanted to maximize the recruitment of ordinary workers, even in conditions of clandestinity, while Lenin's priority was to prevent the infiltration of the party by people who did not sufficiently understand its policies and practices. Lenin lost that vote, but, because of a walk-out by some of his opponents on an unconnected issue, was able to emerge from the congress claiming a majority.[48] Henceforth he called his faction the 'Bolsheviks' or 'men of the majority', while his opponents had to content themselves with the unimpressive sobriquet 'Menshevik', or 'men of the minority'.

That split, to all appearance over a minor verbal quibble, not only proved to be lasting but became wider and more bitter with the passing years. That was because Lenin's concept of the interaction of Marxism and revolution was fundamentally different from that of the Mensheviks. The Mensheviks laid great store by the establishment of a parliamentary 'bourgeois' republic, in which the guarantee of civil liberties would enable the working-class party to act as a legal opposition until they were strong enough to take over power. Lenin, by contrast, regarded civil liberties as a sham, and became increasingly impatient at the protracted timetable entailed by this version of the future. Although he did not clarify his change of heart fully till 1917, it was apparent earlier that he hankered after a telescoping of the whole process, running the two revolutions into one. His experience of 1905–7 convinced him that this could be done, since the peasants were also a revolutionary class, albeit an 'auxiliary' one, and would help the workers to turn the 'bourgeois' revolution into a socialist one straight away.[49]

If one regards Populism and Marxism as two separate traditions, Bolshevism must be seen as a synthesis of the two, Marxist in its original impulse, but borrowing from the Populists the ideas of the peasants as a revolutionary class, of leadership by a small group of intellectuals and of overstriding the bourgeois phase of social evolution to reach the socialist revolution directly. Actually, it would be more sensible to regard Bolshevism as the form of revolutionary socialism best adapted to Russian conditions, where it was impossible in the long term to form a mass working-class party without strong leadership, where the peasants were extremely discontented with the existing state of affairs, and where the bourgeoisie was very weak. Marx himself had indicated the possibility of just such a revolution in Russia.

As Robert Service has remarked, where Populism and Marxism are concerned, 'there was no butcher's blow which severed the two traditions neatly and irreparably. Rather there was a messy, complex fracture.'[50] Most Marxists began as Populists, and Bolshevism did no more than reassemble certain elements of their past experience which for a time had been unfashionable among them.

There was certainly, however, a difference of emphasis between Populism and Marxism. Populism stressed the uniqueness of Russian experience and the ancient democratic institutions of the peasantry, while Marxism stressed universality and modernity, wishing to see Russia rejoin the European mainstream. In a sense, then, Populism was Russian ethnic socialism, while Marxism was Russian imperial or Europeanized socialism. By trying to synthesize the two visions in 1917, Bolshevism created an unstable amalgam of Russian nationalism and internationalism, coloured with the messianic expectations of the revolution which would put an end to exploitation.

It was in this divided state that in 1905 Russia's socialists faced the sudden leap from highly restricted and artificial contact with the people to an open style of mass politics, the sudden legalization of parties and associations, the introduction of a legislative assembly based on a broad franchise. Having been long delayed in the anteroom of Hroch's Stage B, 'the period of patriotic agitation', trying vainly to make contact with the mass of the people, they were suddenly and unprepared plunged into the middle of Stage C, 'the rise of the mass national movement'. By that time, their protracted isolation, their cliquishness and their disposition towards extreme solutions unfitted them for creative political work in situations which demanded compromise.

3

Russification

Alexander II's policy of trying to bind regime and elites closer through the creation of a civil society had failed – or at the very most had been only partly successful, and in the process it had thrown up new dangers to internal order. The obvious alternative was to replace a civic by an ethnic policy, to bolster political cohesion by promoting identification with the nationality whose name the empire bore, the Russians.

It cannot be said that civic reforms were cleanly abandoned and replaced by Russification. Gradual disillusionment with the reforms set in almost as soon as they were launched, with the result that, as we have seen, most of them never spread to non-Russian regions; from the outset they were reined back by legislative and administrative acts, without being altogether abandoned. By the same token, the alternative policy of Russification was introduced at the first sign of crisis, during the Polish rebellion of 1863–4, and was thereafter never wholly relinquished, though it was not consistently applied until the 1880s.

Russification was in part a continuation of policies which Nicholas I had pursued: administrative centralization, the elimination of local privileges and other anomalies. Now, however, there was a major new element: the attempt to inspire among all peoples of the empire a subjective sense of *belonging* to Russia, whether through the habit of using the Russian language, through reverence for Russia's past, its culture and traditions, or through conversion to the Orthodox faith. This kind of Russian-ness did not necessarily imply abandoning altogether a localized non-Russian identity. Most practitioners of Russification saw Russian identity as overarching, not destroying other ethnic (or 'tribal', as they called them) loyalties. Some, like Pobedonostsev or Katkov, were admirers of the British political system, where a compound national loyalty existed, the sense of being British complementing English, Scottish or Welsh ethnic affiliation. Others looked more to the Habsburg system, where overarching loyalty was to the person of the Emperor and to the dynasty rather than to 'Austria'. Many combined the two models: hence the obsession both with Russian-ness and with autocracy.

PANSLAVISM There were different versions, then, of what the 'unity of Tsar and people' might mean. During the 1860s and 1870s, an influential public pressure group arose proposing its own reading of the Russian empire, envisaging that it should renew its national identity by sponsoring nation-building among the Slav and Orthodox peoples of Central and Eastern Europe, and by leading a crusade on their behalf against the Ottoman and Habsburg Empires.

Panslavism was a response to Russia's post-Crimean dilemma. When the maps laid down at the Congress of Vienna were being redrawn, and nations hitherto divided by political boundaries were being united, it began to seem advisable that Russia should compensate for its recent reverses by cultivating its relations with the other Slavic and Orthodox peoples of Europe, and perhaps move towards some sort of political alliance or even union with them. There was an unspoken premise to this proposal: that if the other Slavs were absorbed into the empire, they would strengthen Slavic numerical dominance within it and make it possible to move more easily to some form of democratic state, perhaps with a national assembly, or *zemskii sobor*, which would be dominated by Slavs.

One reason for the appeal of Panslavism was that, even before it was formulated as a doctrine of *Realpolitik*, it contained a messianic element. Fedor Tiutchev's poem 'Russian Geography', written as early as 1849, exemplifies the characteristic exalted ambition, the portentous vagueness about frontiers, the sense of historical and religious mission:

Moscow and Peter's city and the city of the Constantines –
These are the secret capitals of Russia's realm . . .
But where are her bounds and where her frontiers?
To north and east and south and towards the evening light?
Fate will reveal them to coming generations.

Seven internal seas and seven great rivers . . .
From Nile to Neva, from the Elbe to China,
From Volga to Euphrates, from the Ganges to the Danube . . .
That is the Russian realm . . . and it will never fade,
As the Spirit foresaw and Daniel prophesied.[1]

The messianic mood was transmuted into cultural-historical prophecy by Nikolai Danilevskii, in his *Russia and Europe* (1869). He believed that the period of Romano-Germanic dominance in Europe, sunk now in corruption, materialism and factionalism, was approaching its end and would be replaced by the dominance of Slavic-Orthodox culture, which 'represented a close organic unity held together not through a more or less artificial political mechanism, but through deep-rooted popular confidence in the Tsar'. In Danilevskii's view, the new Slavic civilization, with its capital at Constantinople, would synthesize the highest achievements of its predecessors in religion (Israel), culture (Greece), political order (Rome) and socio-economic progress (modern Europe), and would supplement them with the Slavic genius for social and economic justice. 'These four rivers will unite on the wide plains of Slavdom into a mighty sea.'[2] This was visionary geopolitics, and its evocation of a culminating earthly empire with its capital at the Second Rome revived memories of the original Russian myth.

An ethnographic exhibition in Moscow in 1867 provided the first forum for Panslavism as practical power politics. Mikhail Katkov urged that Russia should play the role of Prussia within Germany, bringing the Slavs together as a single polity. Such a campaign, he asserted, 'would complete the triumph of the principle of nationality and provide a solid foundation for the contemporary equilibrium of Europe'. The rector of Moscow University proclaimed 'Let us unite as Italy and Germany have been united in one whole, and the name of the united nation will be: Giant!' He also called for a common Panslav language: 'May one literary language alone cover all the lands from the Adriatic Sea and Prague to Arkhangel'sk and the Pacific Ocean, and may every Slav nation irrespective of its religion adopt this language as its means of communication with the others.'[3] There cannot be any doubt that he had Russian in mind.

Not all the other Slavs present were content to accept unquestioningly Russian hegemony over their national life. The principal Czech spokesmen, Palacky and Rieger, called for a reconciliation between Russia and Poland, one moreover in which Russians as well as Poles would make concessions. The Russians, however, were adamant that they had made every possible attempt, since 1815, to give Poland its own state and its own national life, but had encountered ingratitude, rebellion and attempts to annex Russian territory and population.[4] These exchanges highlighted one of the ineluctable dilemmas of Panslavism: that those whom it purported to serve rejected cardinal elements of its programme and did not wish to become part of a Russian state where there was no guarantee that democracy would prevail. The Poles in particular, thoroughly Roman Catholic and Westernized in outlook, were unwilling to accept continued Russian domination, of which they had already had more than enough direct experience.

With the formation of the German Empire in 1871, Panslavism became unequivocally a doctrine of *Realpolitik*, a means of containing the expansion of German influence in Central and Eastern Europe. General Rostislav Fadeev believed that the stage was set for a show-down between the Germans and the Slavs, and he urged that Russia must either counter-attack, making use of its Slav ties to undermine Germany's ally, Austria, or retreat behind the Dnieper and become a predominantly Asiatic power. With the support of the Slav peoples, furthermore, the way would lie open to Constantinople, which he proposed should be declared an open Slav city. For him, Panslavism was a pre-condition for remaining a European great power: 'Slavdom or Asia' he loved to repeat to Russian diplomats.

They, however, were reluctant to accept the logic of his position, and he was dismissed from active service for propagating his ideas. The official Foreign Office view was that Russia should cooperate with Germany and Austria to reaffirm the legitimist monarchical principle in Eastern Europe, to counteract revolutionary movements there, whether nationalist or not, and to promote a stable balance of power.[5] Panslavism could never be consistently espoused by the Russian government, for it was a policy which would inevitably lead to war against the Ottomans and Habsburgs, if not against the European powers in general. Besides, it was in essence a revolutionary strategy, directed against legitimate sovereign states. For the Russian empire to promote the principle of insurrectionary nationalism was, to say the least, double-edged.

However, the Serb and Bulgarian revolts of 1875–6 against Ottoman rule provided the ideal soil for Panslav agitation and caused the Russian government considerable embarrassment. Army officers, society ladies and merchants formed Slavic Benevolent Committees which called meetings, collected money, and began to send volunteers to fight for the Serbian army. Dostoevskii, as we have seen, preached war against the Turks as a means of achieving 'eternal peace'. The authorities decided they could not condemn these efforts out of hand, and allowed Russian officers and men to take leave and volunteer for the Serbian army: among them was Fadeev's friend, General Mikhail Cherniaev, who soon became an emblematic hero for the Panslavs.[6]

The defeat of the Serbs faced the Russian government with a dilemma. It was engaged with other European powers in trying to impose on the Ottoman Empire a programme of reforms eliminate grievances of the kind which had caused the revolt. The Ottomans were resisting the proposals, which left Russia in the position of having either to to the aid of the Serbs and Bulgarians or see her influence in the Balkans sharply downgraded.

Thus in the end Russia officially espoused the Panslav cause, and declared war on Turkey, but more to preserve Russia's position in the European balance of power than with Panslav aims in mind. At a Slavic Benevolent Society meeting Ivan Aksakov called the Russo-Turkish war a 'historical necessity' and added that 'the people had never viewed any war with such conscious sympathy'.[7] There was indeed considerable support for the war among peasants, who regarded it as a struggle on behalf of suffering Orthodox brethren against the cruel and rapacious infidel. A peasant elder from Smolensk province told many years later how the people of his village had been puzzled as to 'Why our Father-Tsar lets his people suffer from the infidel Turks?', and had viewed Russia's entry into the war with relief and satisfaction.[8] Others had a more confused picture: in his letters from the same province, the landowner Aleksandr Engel'gardt showed that the peasants of his village were extremely curious about the war to which menfolk and horses were being called up, but had no conception of the issues involved: 'The Turks are hard up, so they rebel. We have to quieten them down.'[9] Either way, peasants provided the bulk of the volunteers and even of the voluntary contributions, in money, food and labour.

Panslavism launched the man who was perhaps the first mass-media star of modern Russia: General M.D. Skobelev (1843–1882). The hero of Shipka Pass (1877, a turning-point in the war against Turkey) and of Geok Tepe (1881, the decisive victory over the Turkmens in Central Asia), he had a reputation for winning brilliant victories by disobeying orders from above – a reputation which he would polish by regularly denouncing creeping German influence at court. Lionized as the 'Slavonic Garibaldi', he wore a white uniform, rode a white charger, and took care to ensure that there was always a journalist or two accompanying him. His portrait was sold by peddlers and displayed in magic lantern shows. His death in suspicious circumstances in 1882 completed his elevation to martyrdom, gratefully written up by the newspapers. In a confused way, as Hans Rogger has remarked, he represented 'a groping for a non-dynastic nationalism', a national consciousness with roots among peasants, workers and merchants. Such Russian-ness needed among other things to articulate a degree of protest against existing elites.[10]

Whatever the popular mood, the government was not inclined to push the fruits of victory in the war to the point where they jeopardized the European balance of power. At the Treaty of San Stefano, signed with Turkey in March 1878, Russia won acceptance of its claims to act as guarantor of reforms in the Ottoman Empire, and secured the creation of an enlarged Bulgarian client state, with access to the Aegean and including nearly all of Macedonia. However, when the other European powers objected to such an extension of Russian influence in the Balkans, the Foreign Ministry backed down and consented to the holding of an international congress in Berlin (a mini-Vienna, one might say) to redraw the frontiers there. As a result of the congress, Bulgaria was slimmed down and split into two states, while Macedonia was left under Ottoman rule, and the European powers in general took over from Russia the 'guarantee' of Ottoman reform.

At a Slavic Benevolent Society banquet in June 1878 Ivan Aksakov furiously denounced the Berlin Congress as 'an open conspiracy against the Russian people, [conducted] with the participation of the representatives of Russia herself!'.[11] Yet in fact, as a result of the war and the subsequent diplomatic manoeuvrings, Russia had regained its foothold at the mouth of the Danube (with the re-annexation of southern Bessarabia, lost in the Crimean War), and acquired important territory in the Caucasus, including the port of Batum, which was to be vital to the expanding oil industry. It had also restored some kind of relative equilibrium among the European powers. Compared with the brilliant but evanescent achievements of San Stefano, these gains seemed insignificant in the eyes of the Panslavs.

Panslavism represented, then, an attempt to bring empire and people closer together through an aggressive, nationally oriented and semi-democratic foreign policy in the image of German unification. But, although it had considerable support in educated society and the press, it was only partly comprehensible to most ordinary Russians, and in any case bore overtones of social protest for them. Overall then, it was poorly suited to a multi-national empire which feared democracy, war and ethnic conflict, and for that reason it never became official policy.

Nor was the democratic aspect of Panslavism acceptable as practical politics inside Russia itself. The closest it came to being implemented was in 1882, when Count N.P. Ignat'ev, former ambassador in Constantinople and now Minister of the Interior, put forward a scheme for the revival of the seventeenth-century *zemskii sobor*. His idea was that the Tsar should be crowned at Easter 1883 at the new Cathedral of Christ the Saviour in Moscow in the presence of an assembly to consist of senior officials and clergymen and of elected representatives of peasants, merchants and noblemen from every uezd. The peasants were to outnumber all other delegates and were to be chosen directly by householders. Delegates were to be sent from non-Russian regions, but they would sit apart, 'to maintain order and to forestall any undesirable behaviour by Poles, Finns or our liberals'.

The assembly was to make known to the monarch the mood of the 'representatives of the land' and would enable him to 'communicate his sovereign word to the whole land, the whole people and society'. Ignat'ev envisaged that its first business would be local government (volost) reform to bind peasant institutions more closely into the imperial administrative structure. Its findings would be advisory only, and would go before the State Council. Although in purely procedural terms these proposals resemble those of Loris-Melikov, they far outdid them in the extent of public participation envisaged, and their decorative and symbolic aspects were quite distinct. Looking back on it later, Ignat'ev expressed the view that this arrangement would have constituted 'a unique Russian kind of constitution, for which Europe would envy us and which would silence our pseudo-liberals and nihilists'.[12]

Pobedonostsev was certainly inclined to view the proposal as some kind of constitution, but in his eyes that condemned it out of hand. He warned the Tsar that 'If will and decision-making are transferred from the government to any kind of popular assembly, that will be a revolution, the downfall of the government and the downfall of Russia.'[13] In the same spirit Katkov wrote a leading article damning the idea as 'the triumph of subversion'.[14] On 27 May 1882 Alexander turned the proposal down at a meeting of ministers, and requested Ignat'ev's resignation.

MIKHAIL KATKOV AND IMPERIAL NATIONALISM   The career of Mikhail Katkov, Russia's leading newspaper editor from the 1860s to the 1880s, exemplifies the way in which belief in civil society as a way of healing Russia's internal splits transmuted itself under the pressure of events into the advocacy of autocracy plus Russification. In his youth Katkov had been a member of the Westernising circle of Nikolai Stankevich and for a time a close friend of Belinskii. He had begun his career as an admirer of the British political system: what particularly impressed him at that stage was the way in which a strong state was combined with the rule of law, upheld by a wealthy and therefore independent landed gentry. He hoped that something similar would emerge from Alexander II's reforms.[15]

Two events shook his faith in this outcome: the student unrest of 1861–3 and the Polish rebellion of 1863–4. The latter revealed in dramatic form that in a multi-national empire the local gentry, far from upholding law and order, might lead the forces of sedition and separatism. 'Freedom of conscience and religious freedom are good words,' he said in August 1863, but added: 'Freedom – religious or any other – does not mean freedom to arm the enemy.'[16] His watchword became 'It must be one thing or the other: either Poland or

Russia.'[17] By this he meant that Poland and Russia could not both be sovereign states: 'In the ethnographic sense there is no antagonism between Russians and Poles, indeed there is not even an essential difference. But Poland as a political term is Russia's natural and irreconcilable enemy.'[18]

This view of Poland helped to determine his view of Russia in an age when the nation-state was becoming the most successful form among the European great powers. 'There is in Russia one dominant nationality, one dominant language, developed by centuries of historical life. However, there are also in Russia a multitude of tribes, each speaking in its own language and having its own customs; there are whole countries, with their separate characters and traditions. But all these diverse tribes and regions, lying on the borders of the Great Russian world, constitute its living parts and feel their oneness with it, in the union of state and supreme power in the person of the Tsar.'[19]

He was not looking for ethnic homogenization of the empire's various nationalities, but he considered political unity vital. He regarded the Russians as a kind of political super-nation, with the right to impose its will and its system of rule on others. In a sense his model continued to be Britain, with its compound national identity binding English, Scots, Welsh and at least some Irish in a shared civic consciousness without destroying their ethnic distinctiveness. The problem was that Russia had only the feeblest of civic institutions to offer, so that this approach would work only if the non-Russians remained under-developed and infinitely malleable. Such thinking was close to that of Dostoevskii, and is reminiscent of the confusion between national and universal values in the idea of 'Moscow the Third Rome'. It was seriously misleading when applied to the more Westernized and culturally advanced nationalities, such as the Poles, the Finns, the Germans or the Jews.

Katkov attacked these unassimilable peoples forthrightly: 'In the Russian state there are forces at work which are hostile to the Russian people, parasites which have insinuated themselves into its lifeblood, various privileged political nationalities, and so the Russian government has taken on a non-Russian character in its policies.'[20] In effect, this was a disparagement of the government's traditional policy of balance between the empire's diverse ethnic elites.

Katkov became a power in Russia partly because he caught the mood of officialdom and much of educated society after the Polish rebellion, when the pro-Polish views of Herzen and the radical democracy of the journal *Sovremennik* seemed to betoken sedition. He also knew how to profit by the opportunities open to an outspoken, skilful and hard-working editor in the era of 'responsible freedom' opened up by the new censorship laws and practices of the 1860s. His attempt in his daily *Moskovskie vedomosti* to fuse imperial and ethnic Russian patriotism seemed realistic and was sufficiently independent of official policies to bestow on him the seductive status of frondeur. Once, in March 1866, his newspaper was suspended and placed under new editorship for Katkov's attacks on government officials, but only a few months later the Karakozov assassination attempt seemed to vindicate his judgement, and the tables were turned: Alexander II personally ordered that Katkov be reinstated.

It was in the reign of Alexander III, however, that Katkov really came into his own. The new Tsar pursued more or less consistently a national policy which his father had applied only sporadically. Its aim was to draw the non-Russian regions and peoples more securely into the framework of the empire, first of all by administrative integration, then by inculcating in each of them the language, religion, culture, history and political traditions of Russia, leaving their own languages and native traditions to occupy a subsidiary niche, as ethnographic remnants rather than active social forces. It was accompanied by an economic policy which emphasized the development of transport and heavy industry, and the assimilation of outlying regions into a single imperial economy.

POLAND   The policy was first applied in full force to Poland after the rebellion of 1863–4. This was the first part of the empire where the Russian authorities abandoned their policy of cooperating with local elites: many nobles were exiled and had their estates confiscated, in order to weaken the *pany* (landlords) as bearers of the Polish national ideal. The same aim dictated a relatively generous emancipation of the Polish serfs, giving them more land on more favourable terms, in an attempt to encourage Polish, Ukrainian and Belorussian peasants to see the Russian government as their patron. The Catholic Church was forbidden to communicate with Rome, and those bishops who disobeyed were dismissed, while in the eastern provinces (Russia's western ones) there were mass forced conversions from the Uniate Church to Orthodoxy. In the western provinces, M.N. Murav'ev, formerly a Decembrist but now known as the 'hangman of Vil'na', was given special powers to investigate, arrest and sentence those suspected of involvement in the insurrection.

The remnants of Poland's separate identity were abolished, and the former Congress Kingdom became known in official parlance as 'the Vistula region' of Russia. Most Polish officials were replaced by Russian ones, and the Russian language was imposed for official business. The University of Warsaw was converted into a wholly Russian institution, whilst it was stipulated that Polish schools, even at primary level, should teach all subjects in Russian, save the Polish language itself. In practice, the government had no means to impose these provisions, and Polish-language schooling continued, albeit semi-clandestinely.[21]

Poland did derive economic benefits from being included within the empire's tariff enclosure: it was able to sell its industrial products in a huge market that needed them. With some 8% of the population, Poland produced about a quarter of the empire's industrial output, notably in textiles, metallurgy and machine tools. Its manufacturers did so, however, by ruthlessly exploiting a workforce which was without rights, as in Russia proper, and largely illiterate because of the educational laws.

As a result, Polish elites were divided about the place of their country in the empire. The political parties which emerged from the underground in 1905 split three ways. The Polish Socialist Party (PPS), led by Josef Pilsudski, favoured an insurrection leading to complete secession and national independence: Pilsudski sought help from the enemy, the Japanese, in 1904 to help finance his planned rising. The Social Democratic Party of the Kingdom of Poland and Lithuania (SDKPiL), whose most prominent personality was Rosa Luxemburg, took an impeccable Marxist line: Poland should remain within the international proletarian state which the Russian Empire would become after a forthcoming socialist revolution. The National Democrats, led by Roman Dmowski, wanted to stay within the existing empire, but with political autonomy and an end to discriminatory laws: they represented the industrial and commercial bourgeoisie, who profited from the imperial market and regarded Germany as the main danger.

In 1905–6 Poland was perhaps the most violent part of the empire. Immediately after Bloody Sunday, in January 1905, workers in the textile centre of Lodz went on strike and demonstrated with placards proclaiming 'Down with the autocracy! Down with the war!'. They also had economic demands: an eight-hour day and huge wage rises. The police intervened, and in the resultant fighting perhaps one hundred people were killed. That scene was repeated several times during 1905. At times Poland was in a state of virtual civil war, in which students, schoolchildren and often criminal bands were involved as well as workers. Only the peasants remained relatively quiescent: they had neither the grievances nor the communal solidarity of those in Russia.

Altogether the armed struggle in Poland during 1905–6 lasted longer than the guerrilla war of 1863–4 and claimed more lives. It was also a grave strain on the Russian armed forces: at the height of the troubles some 300,000 men were stationed there, as compared with 1,000,000 on the Japanese front.[22] No clearer example could be imagined of the high cost of trying to Russify a people with a well-developed national identity and sense of culture, religion and citizenship quite different from those of Russia.

UKRAINE   Associated with this anti-Polish policy was the government's determination to impose a Russian identity on Ukraine, which was now officially known as 'Little Russia'. By the second half of the nineteenth century the Ukrainian sense of separate identity was in any case rather weak, being borne mainly by intellectuals and professional people in the smaller towns. Large numbers of peasants spoke variants of Ukrainian, but they had no wider national consciousness, and their colloquial tongue was viewed by most Russians as a farmyard dialect Russian. However, the survival of Ukrainian culture was quite strong, thanks to the heritage of the poet Taras Shevchenko, the writings of historians such as Mykhaylo Drahomaniw, and the possibility of smuggling materials across the frontier from Habsburg Galicia, where Ukrainian identity was officially fostered as a counterweight to Polish influence.

In 1863 P.A. Valuev, Minister of the Interior, issued a circular prohibiting the publication of books in Ukrainian, other than *belles-lettres* and folklore. He commented that 'there never has been a distinct Little Russian language, and there never will be one. The dialect which the common people use is Russian contaminated by Polish influence.'[23] In 1876 a further decree prohibited the import of Ukrainian-language books from abroad and the use of Ukrainian in the theatre.

This almost complete suppression of a language was unique in nineteenth-century Russia. The reason for it appears to have been that the national identity of Ukrainian peasants was an unusually sensitive matter for officials. Ukrainians were the second largest ethnic group in the empire: 22.4 million according to the census of 1897, or nearly 18% of the entire population. If they were assimilated to Russian culture and language, Russians would constitute a secure majority, some 62%, of the empire's population. If, on the other hand, Ukrainians became literate and adopted their own 'dialect' as a distinct language, Russians would be a minority in their own empire.

This concern was reflected in the preparation of the Ukrainian language law. Valuev noted in a memorandum for the Tsar that 'proponents of the little Russian nationality have turned their attention to the uneducated mass, and under the pretence of disseminating literacy and enlightenment, those of them who are striving to realise their political designs have set about publishing elementary readers, primers, grammars, geography books and so on.' Similarly in 1876 a senior official warned that 'permitting the creation of a special literature for the common people in the Ukrainian dialect would signify collaborating in the alienation of Ukraine from the rest of Russia ... To permit the separation of thirteen million Little Russians would be the utmost political irresponsibility, especially in view of the unifying movement which is going on alongside us among the German tribe.'[24]

During the later decades of the nineteenth century, industrialization was rapidly changing the ethnic composition of Ukraine. The incoming workers were mostly Russian: Ukrainian peasants, since they had a relatively more fertile soil and a better climate, did not feel the same need to gain off-farm income by going into the towns, even their own towns. As for merchants, industrialists and professional people, they were mainly Russian, Jewish, German or Polish. Industrialization, then, worked in favour of official national policy, while the Ukrainian intelligentsia was shorn of its potential elites and confined to small-town employment, typically as in the zemstvos and municipalities.[25]

All the same, the authorities reacted allergically to the slightest symptom of separate Ukrainianism. In the 1870s they closed down the south-western section of the Imperial Geographical Society, which was suspected of Ukrainophile leanings. Drahomaniw was dismissed from his chair at Kiev University; he took himself off to L'wiw, capital of Austrian Galicia, where he helped to develop Ukrainian cultural societies which would never have been tolerated inside the Russian empire. In spite of the import ban, Galicia became a kind of 'Ukrainian Piedmont', without which Ukraine might not have become a distinct nation in the twentieth century.

FINLAND   During the second half of the nineteenth century, Finland was beginning to take advantage of the relatively favourable constitutional position it had enjoyed under the provisions of the Diet of Poorvoo (1809). Its parliament, the Diet, began to meet regularly after 1863, and passed a number of measures which underlined Finland's distinctive status within the empire: the spread of education, consolidation of freedom of worship, the issue of a separate currency and the establishment of a Finnish army. At the same time, backed by the high level of literacy among the peasants, the proponents of the Finnish language gained the Emperor's support for their cause in challenging the previous dominance of Swedish.[26]

The Emperor's support for the Finns could be seen as an example of applying the policy of 'divide and rule' – setting the Finns against the Swedes to dominate both. What was undoubtedly also weighed in the minds of successive emperors was that the Finns behaved with restraint – quite unlike the ostentatious nation-building of the Poles. It was not until the final decades of the nineteenth century that Russian publicists began to warn that a separate and semi-sovereign nation state, with its own army, was taking shape a few miles from their capital city. Russian jurists began to argue that, although Alexander I had, by virtue of his autocratic power, granted certain privileges to the Grand Duchy of Finland, his successors could at any time withdraw them, by virtue of the same power.[27]

In 1899 Nicholas II acted on this advice by issuing a manifesto submitting Finnish legislation to Russian supervision. 'We have found it necessary to reserve to Ourselves the final decision as to which laws come within the scope of general imperial legislation': in such matters, he announced, the Diet would henceforth have only a consultative voice. The previous year Nicholas had appointed as Governor-General Nikolai Bobrikov, who proposed a programme for the full integration of Finland into the empire by ending the separate status of its army and making Finns liable for conscription into the Russian army, by introducing the Russian language into Finnish administrative offices, increasing the tuition of Russian in Finnish secondary schools and abolishing the Finnish State Secretariat, which was the head of the autonomous Finnish executive. Nicholas's manifesto gave Bobrikov carte blanche to proceed with his programme, which he did in the teeth of protests by Finns that their constitution, confirmed by Nicholas on his accession, was being crudely violated.

The Finns responded first of all with a petition for which they collected the signatures of no less than one-fifth of their population, and then with a boycott of all Russian institutions. This affected especially the army: in 1902 less than half the young men called up for service reported for duty, and they had to run the gauntlet of hostile crowds of their compatriots around the draft boards. In time, this passive resistance began to crumble or to degenerate into violence: in July 1904 Bobrikov was assassinated by a Finnish terrorist.[28]

Finland is an outstanding example of the difficulty the empire experienced in dealing with its more advanced peoples once national awareness had spread from a small elite to a wider educated stratum and was beginning to reach the masses.[29] To leave them a substantial degree of home rule implied that they would develop in their own direction, with scant respect for the needs of the empire as a whole. This was by and large the policy pursued by the Habsburg Monarchy, especially in the Austrian half of their realm, and one cannot say that it solved the national question there. On the other hand, any attempt to try to make them conform to imperial models risked calling forth the very resolution and national unity it was designed to thwart. Pursuing the latter policy converted Finland's people into a highly disaffected and conscious nation. As a result, when the empire was at war with Japan in 1904–5, it was not difficult for Japan to supply arms to Russian revolutionaries through Finland.[30] The Russians responded with conciliation, hastily restoring Finland's constitution.

THE BALTIC The Baltic region resembled Finland in so far as the Russian authorities supported, up to a point, the claims of the subordinate nationalities, the Estonians and Latvians, against the dominant Germans. But they pursued this policy with much greater caution than in Finland, since the Baltic Germans were far more important to them than the Swedes. Indeed, it could be argued that, of all ethnic groups in the whole empire, the Baltic Germans were the most loyal. However, their loyalty was to the Tsar personally, and to the empire as a multi-national entity, not to Russia as a nation. As Alexander Graf Keyserling, former rector of Dorpat University, wrote in 1889, 'As long as the Emperor dominates the nation, we shall be able to survive and develop further.'[31] It was not only the Russian nation he had in mind. The growth of German nationalism was equally ominous for the Baltic landowners, since it threatened to swamp the *Ritterschaften* (aristocratic corporations) with Germans from the towns and Estonians or Latvians from the countryside, both more numerous than themselves. In the long run they would all become the mere pawns of European great-power politics.

The first Russian statesman to attack the German domination in the Baltic was Iurii Samarin, who was sent to Riga as a senatorial inspector in 1849. He regarded the German urban guilds and the *Ritterschaften* as corrupt relics of an antiquated system which prevented the monarch from acting as the protector of ordinary people and obstructed Russians from exercising their legitimate authority in the Russian Empire. 'We Russians claim the right to be in Russia what the French are in France and the English throughout the British dominions.' At this stage, before the drive to national homogenization had gripped the authorities, such views were unwelcome to the Tsar: Nicholas ordered that Samarin be detained in the Peter-Paul Fortress for twelve days and personally rebuked him. 'Your attack is aimed directly at the government: what you really meant was that since the reign of the Emperor Peter we have been surrounded by Germans and have ourselves become Germanised.'[32]

By the 1870s, however, different views prevailed in St Petersburg. Reform had come to Russia, rendering Tsars more reluctant to acknowledge intermediate authorities between themselves and their subjects. Besides, the unification of Germany naturally reinforced the ethnic identification of Baltic Germans, especially those in the towns. Ivan Aksakov had warned of this danger in 1862, when he complained that the Baltic Germans, 'though devoted to the Russian throne, preach war to the death against the Russian nationality; faithful servants of the Russian state, they care not a fig for the Russian Land'.[33] Alexander III took a symbolically important decision when, on his accession to the throne in 1881, he declined to confirm the privileges of the *Ritterschaften*, as all his successors had done since Peter the Great.

Administrative integration began with the introduction of the new municipal institutions in the Baltic in 1877, but the authorities shrank from undermining the Ritterschaften in the countryside by introducing Russian-style zemstvos there. To that extent, the old policy of accommodating local elites continued: the *Ritterschaften* remained as the ultimate repositories of local authority right through to 1917, though their practical power was gradually being chipped away both by social change and by governmental measures. In the 1880s they lost judicial powers with the introduction of the new Russian courts, along with the use of Russian in all administrative and judicial procedures. Their supervision of schools was weakened by the opening of numerous 'ministerial schools' run from St Petersburg and offering tuition in Russian only: it was here that many Estonians and Latvians received their basic education and began to move into professional and administrative positions, becoming what St Petersburg hoped would be the agents of future Russian domination. At the same time an attempt was made to make Russian compulsory in all but the lowest forms of primary schools. In 1893 Dorpat University was closed and reopened as Iur'ev University, a Russian institution: professors and lecturers (with the revealing exception of theology) who were not prepared to teach in Russian had to resign.

In religious matters there was a return to the policy of forbidding Estonians and Latvians who had converted – usually under threat – to Orthodoxy to return to the Lutheran faith. Those who had done so now found that their marriages were declared invalid, while pastors who had celebrated them were suspended pending investigation. Some 120 suffered this fate before the policy was abandoned in 1894. Meanwhile, bulky Orthodox cathedrals with conspicuous golden cupolas were erected incongruously in the midst of the austere Hanseatic architecture of Riga and Reval.

In the Baltic, then, Russification was pursued at times with small-minded zeal, but a complex balance of forces was in play, and Russification had sometimes to be muted if social stability was being undermined or if it seemed that the policy was working not in favour of Russians, but rather of Estonians and Latvians.[34]

The unstable mixture generated a major explosion in 1905–6. The fundamental misfit was the high economic development of the Baltic combined with primitive political arrangements. Riga produced a second Bloody Sunday in January 1905, when workers protested over the first one: General Meller-Zakomel'skii's troops turned out in force to block the procession and killed 22 and wounded some 60 of them.[35] Thereafter workers and peasants often acted together, especially in the regions populated by Latvians. Peasants went on strike, refused to pay rents and boycotted courts and administrative institutions run by Russians or Germans. In the end they physically attacked and burned down many of the manor houses of the barons, who improvised vigilante armies to defend them. In Kurland and south Livland some 38% of manors were damaged during the unrest; 19% in north Livland and Estland. Later, when the Russian army returned from the Far East, punitive expeditions were sent in to impose summary justice.[36]

The mutual slaughter left an uneasy legacy, in which the Russian government decided to return to its earlier policy of conciliating the Baltic barons and defending their interests as synonymous with those of the state. Some Baltic Germans, however, started to wonder how long the Russian government could, or would, defend them. German associations began to spring up in the towns of the Baltic, with the aim of defending German economic interests, promoting German-language education, and of trying to resettle German farmers from other parts of the empire in the Baltic – an aim in which they were not especially successful, since most German landowners were not prepared to give up land to them. The important point about these associations, though, is that they embraced Germans of all social classes and cultivated ties with the Reich, casting off the exclusivism of the old Ritterschaften.[37] The Germans of the empire, including the most 'Tsartreu', the Baltic barons, were beginning to realign along ethnic lines.

THE CAUCASUS   In the Caucasus no less than the Baltic the local Christian elites, the Georgians and Armenians, had solid reasons for cooperating with the imperial authorities, in view of the threat from the Turks across the border and the continued disaffection of the recently conquered mountain Islamic peoples. Nor should the task of retaining their loyalty have been especially difficult, since they were so dependent on Russian protection. However, the authorities were disconcerted by the way in which Georgian and Armenian national feeling was taking shape during the second half of the nineteenth century.

In Georgia the relative stability brought by the Russians, the accompanying upswing in their economy, the increased communications with the outside world, and the consolidation of a nobility with a Europeanized education all combined to create the nucleus of a modern Georgian nation. The way the emancipation of the serfs was implemented left many Georgian nobles impoverished (not unlike the Russian ones) and compelled them to take up professional careers in the towns. There they discovered that administration and police were run by Russians, while Armenians dominated banks and commerce.

To assert themselves against both, the Georgians developed their own variety of nationalism, based paradoxically on Marxism. Their nationalism had an anti-capitalist colouring, owing to the competition with the Armenians. They also considered that, as a small nation, their interests were best protected by internationalism, or more specifically, by membership of a democratic multi-national federation formed on the framework of the Russian Empire. Two of the leading Georgian radicals, Noa Zhordania and Filip Makharadze, studied in Warsaw, where they became convinced that Poles and Georgians, for all their differences, were conducting a common struggle against the autocratic empire, and must work together. Marxism fulfilled both the internationalist and the anti-capitalist requirements. The Georgians became perhaps the most sophisticated Marxists in the empire, taking over from the Austrian Marxists the notion of individual cultural autonomy as the best way of making possible inter-ethnic cooperation in a multi-national state. They also adapted their original agrarian programme so that it met the demands of peasants, and in that way were able to make themselves the leading political force in the countryside as well as the towns.[38]

The Armenians' sense of nationhood sharpened markedly during the second half of the nineteenth century in mutual interaction with the Russian and Ottoman Empires. In both states the leading, ostensibly 'imperial' peoples, the Russians and the Turks, had for long been oppressed by their 'own' empires, but were now beginning to assert themselves. In the Ottoman Empire the Armenians were the direct victims of this process, in the massacres of the mid-1890s, and in the growth of anti-Armenian feeling among the Azeri people, most of whom considered themselves Turks. But in Russia, too, anti-Armenian feeling was growing during the 1880s.

The Armenians were capable of enthusiastic support for Russia, as in 1878, when the triumph of Russian arms held out the prospect of Armenians gaining more territory from the Ottoman Empire, or at least of having Ottoman reforms in their favour guaranteed by the Russians. But after the diplomatic defeat at the Congress of Berlin, where she had to give up any exclusive right to speak for the Armenians, Russia became more inward-looking and defensive on the problem. Armenians reacted with disappointment and embitterment.

Anti-Armenian stereotypes had always existed in the Russian official mind. According to an official report of 1836, 'Armenians, like the people of Moses, have been dispersed about the face of the earth, gathering wealth under the weight of their rulers, unable to enjoy their own land. This is the cause of the Armenian's lack of character: he has become a cosmopolitan. His fatherland becomes that land where he can with the greatest advantage and security and through the resourcefulness of his mind make a profit for himself . . .'[39] All the same, up to the 1880s, the view of the Armenians as a fellow Christian people, allies against Islam, predominated. In 1836 Nicholas I had issued a charter to the Armenian Church, guaranteeing it institutional autonomy, freedom of worship and the right to run its own schools. In 1885, however, this charter was suddenly abrogated by the closure of all parish schools and their replacement with Russian schools. Although the measure was rescinded a year later, it left a bitter deposit of resentment and suspicion among Armenians.[40]

This was the atmosphere in which the first Armenian revolutionary parties were created. The principal one, the *Dashnaktsiutiun* (The Federation, close to the Russian Populists in outlook) initially directed its hostility mainly against the Ottoman Empire, but all the same the Russian authorities were intensely wary of them. The suspicion that Armenian parish schools and seminaries were turning out terrorists was instrumental in the decision in 1896 to subordinate all of them to the Ministry of Education in St Petersburg. In 1903 the Viceroy of the Caucasus, Prince Grigorii Golitsyn, took over direct administration of all the church's properties, in the words of one observer, 'placing the church under tutelage, like an infant or a lunatic'. To enforce this decree Russian police had to occupy the residence of the Catholicos at Echmiadzin, break open his safe and seize the title deeds.[41]

This offensive procedure, coming on top of two decades of insensitive and overbearing administration, finally persuaded the terrorists to turn their weapons against Russia and converted nearly all Armenians into their allies. A number of Russian officials were assassinated, and in October 1903 Golitsyn was seriously wounded by a terrorist. Armenians boycotted official schools, law-courts and administrative offices, and set up their own underground equivalents to take over their functions. The Dashnaks were the main political inspiration behind this movement of peaceful protest, which they conducted parallel to their terror campaign.[42] Gross and tactless measures of imperial integration had provoked the Armenians into creating national institutions, directed against Russia, where none had existed before.

Helpless against this wave of passive and active resistance, the Russian authorities reacted as they had in earlier imperial crises: by dividing in order to rule. In Baku, as in Tiflis, the Armenians formed a conspicuous and relatively successful middle class, easy targets for resentful Azeris, many of whom were poverty-stricken workers in the oil fields. In February 1905, unhindered by the police, Azeris swarmed into the Armenian quarter to take revenge for a recent incident, and in several days of fighting about 1,500 people were killed, including probably 1,000 Armenians. The Armenians responded by creating their own armed militias, many of whose soldiers were refugees from the Ottoman Empire.[43]

Although the mutual butchery was symbolically ended by a joint procession headed by the Armenian bishop and the Chief Sayyid of the Shia Muslim community, ethnic solidarity had been thoroughly awakened on both sides, and Armenians and Azeris continued to define themselves by opposition to each other.

Alarmed by a breakdown in public order which they themselves had helped to precipitate, the Russian authorities hastened to restore to the Armenian church its lands and schools. The incoming Viceroy, Count I.I. Vorontsov-Dashkov, argued that Russian policy should aim at restoring and maintaining an alliance with the Armenians which was inherently valuable in view of the menace of external invasion and internal Muslim rebellion. At times, under pressure, he was forced to cooperate with the Dashnaks to restore order, a policy for which Stolypin later reproached him.[44]

The communal clashes cemented not only Armenian solidarity, but also that of the Azeris, who hitherto had been politically relatively unorganized. An Azerbaidjani literary language had already been created, based on colloquial speech and distinct from both Persian and Turkish (though close to the latter), a process which at first had enjoyed the support of the Russian authorities. It had become the language of a growing periodical press concerned with problems of Muslim education and the place of Muslims within the empire. 1905–6 was the time when consciousness of a separate Azeri identity crystallized among ordinary Muslim peasants and workers, as they joined guerrilla bands to defend villages and to exact revenge. The emblem under which they assembled was the green banner of the Prophet: the enemy was the Armenians.[45]

In the Caucasus, then, Russian policy alienated loyal subjects, inflamed ethnic passions and stoked up conflict which seriously jeopardized internal order in a strategically sensitive area.

CENTRAL ASIA In Central Asia, the thrust of imperial policy was economic rather than assimilationist. Uniquely in the Russian empire, one may consider this region a genuine colony. Its status differed from that of other parts of the empire in several ways. Its inhabitants were known as *inorodtsy*, a category common enough in other contemporary empires, but not applied elsewhere in the Russian one: it implied an alien and inferior political status. The whole territory was not even fully incorporated into the empire: the Khanate of Khiva and the Emirate of Bukhara remained nominally sovereign, as protectorates bound to Russia by one-sided treaties which included them in the Russian customs union.

In the regions incorporated into the empire, the Russian authorities did not interfere in religion, education, local administration or law courts. These were Muslim and so far removed from Russian practice that any attempt to adapt them would have had scant chance of success and would have provoked intense resistance, which might have been exploited by the British to bolster their position in Central Asia. In this way a largely military supreme power in the region overlay a traditional and unchanged medium- and lower-level hierarchy.

The only aspect of local life which the Russians seriously disrupted was economic, with the introduction of irrigated cotton farming for the imperial market as a whole. In addition, Russian peasants were beginning to settle in quite large numbers on potentially fertile nomadic pasture land, a policy increasingly promoted and financed by the imperial authorities, especially by Stolypin after 1906. These settlements provoked intense resentment, but it was difficult for the nomads to resist them. They were mostly poor and unarmed, they were scattered over thousands of square miles of territory, and they were often divided among themselves by tribal feuds. The only force which could bring them together was Islam.

It was natural, therefore, that the focus of resistance to Russian rule lay in the Fergana valley, the most fertile and densely populated region of Central Asia, and one where Islam already had a long history. The first rising there, in Andizhan in 1898, was led by a Sufi holy man, Dukchi Ishan.

Not until 1916 did the sporadic unrest in the Fergana valley coalesce with the resentment felt by the steppe dwellers to generate a large-scale insurrection. The precipitant was the ending of the Muslims' exemption from military service: they became liable for labour service in rear units. As lists of draftees were drawn up, rumours spread among the local people, many of whom regarded manual labour as unworthy of horsemen, and crowds began to attack police stations and administrative buildings. There were riots in most of the chief towns of the Fergana district, and unrest spread from there to cover most of Turkestan. Fighting was extremely ruthless on both sides. Gradually order was restored by the army under General A.N. Kuropatkin, but then a further disaster ensued: hundreds of thousands of Muslims fled across the border into China. It has been estimated that about 17% of the population of Turkestan was lost, either through death or emigration, as a result of the disorders, and in the worst affected regions the loss was as high as two-thirds.[46]

THE JEWS Nowhere did 'Russification' reveal its destructive potential so unambiguously as in the authorities' policy towards the Jews. Actually, 'Russification' in this case is a misnomer, for the policy was abandoning hope of assimilation and rejecting the Jews as aliens: from the 1880s they, like the nomads, were classified as *inorodtsy*.

The crisis of 1878–82 had suggested that both Panslavism and revolutionary Populism had failed as strategies for reknitting the torn ethnic fabric, for bringing state and people closer together. The wave of anti-Jewish pogroms which followed the assassination of Alexander II encouraged the idea that a more successful way of generating patriotism among the masses might be to play upon anti-Jewish prejudice. Since in the Pale of Settlement the Jews were confined to jobs such as that of steward, publican, shopkeeper and moneylender, they tended to appear to the peasants and workers as extortioners, for ever demanding high prices and exorbitant interest rates. During the period of their relative emancipation under Alexander II, moreover, they had been successful in gaining entry to the urban professions, so that some educated Russians also resented their competition.

Ivan Aksakov, having failed in his Panslav prescriptions, played the decisive role in converting anti-Semitism into a political doctrine which became almost respectable in Russia during the last two decades of the nineteenth century. He based his ideas on a work which had been published about fifteen years earlier by a Jewish convert, professor of Hebrew at the Orthodox seminary in Minsk,

Jakob Brafman, the *Book of the Kahal*.[47] The *kahal* had been the Jews' self-governing corporation in independent Poland, but the Russian government had curtailed its powers on absorbing Polish territories, and had finally abolished it in 1844. According to Brafman, however, now supported by Aksakov, the *kahal* not only continued to exist but enjoyed powers of self-rule unparalleled among any other people of the empire and gave the Jews a charter to exploit with impunity the Orthodox believers among whom they lived.[48]

They had moreover, according to Aksakov, powerful foreign backers with an interest in weakening Russia. 'The Jews in the Pale of Settlement constitute a "state within a state", with its own administrative and judicial organs, and with a local national government – a state whose centre lies outside Russia, abroad, whose highest authority is the "Universal Jewish Alliance" in Paris.' This embryonic international authority enabled them to continue to strive for the universal rule which they had not achieved in the person of Jesus Christ and which they were therefore now pursuing in the form of 'anti-Christian world domination, Jewish world domination'.[49]

The reason for the Jews' insidious power over Russia was thus, in Aksakov's view, that they had formed an international conspiracy which had been able to carve out for itself a sphere of self-government within Russia itself. We may see this as a projection on to the Jews of an impression that many Russian intellectuals did have, especially at such a time of crisis: that they were unable to bring their nationhood to full flowering because they were being internally undermined by some mysterious alien force strengthened by international links. In a way they were right, but the real culprit was the imperial state, which had imported an alien culture and outlawed the Russians' original national myth.

Anti-Semitism was a kind of frustrated Slavophilism, conceived in awareness of the ways in which Russians had failed to fulfil their potential nationhood. In the interests of great-power status, the Russians had spurned their myth of the chosen people and the empire of truth and justice. The Jews, by contrast, continued to believe they were a chosen people and to hold to their messianic prophecies. Where Slavophiles dreamed of a peasant commune based on Orthodox principles, the Jews seemed still to have successful communities ruled over by their religious leaders.[50] They had succeeded where the Russians had failed: in making a messianic religion the essence of their national identity.

In 1881 N.P. Ignat'ev, on taking up his post as Minister of the Interior, sent the Tsar a memorandum outlining his fears about domination by 'alien forces'. In it he linked the whole Westernizing trend with the Jews and the Poles, the two peoples who by now were uppermost in the demonology of the new-style Russian patriots. 'In Petersburg there exists a powerful Polish-Jewish group in whose hands are directly concentrated, the stock exchange, the *advokatura*, a good part of the press and other public affairs. In many legal and illegal ways they enjoy immense influence on officialdom and on the course of affairs in general.' They used this influence to mould public opinion in the interests of their favourite schemes: 'the broadest possible rights for Poles and Jews, and representative institutions on the western model. Every honest voice from the Russian land is drowned out by Polish-Jewish clamours that one must only listen to the "intelligentsia" and that Russian demands should be rejected as old-fashioned and unenlightened.'[51]

These assertions amounted to a claim that the professions, modern business and finance, and most of the recently reformed institutions of the empire were in the grasp of an alien international conspiracy striving to bring Russia to her knees. This was a convenient explanation why Alexander II's reforms, far from strengthening Russia, seemed to have weakened her. All the same, it was not generally accepted among Russia's high officials. When Ignat'ev's memorandum was discussed in the government, for example, Finance Minister N.Kh. Bunge objected that the Jews played a productive role in commerce, and that they were very useful in attracting much-needed foreign capital to Russia.[52] But this in a sense was to confirm Ignat'ev's fears: he saw foreign capital as the weapon of an international conspiracy aiming to undermine Russia's true economic strength, its agriculture and cottage industry.

In the alarmist mood predominant after the assassination of Alexander II, Ignat'ev's paranoid vision prevailed. The 'temporary rules' of May 1882 forbade Jews to resettle or acquire property in rural areas, even within the Pale, while outside it the police were instructed to enforce restrictions on Jewish residence which had previously been widely flouted. In the following years Jews were barred from entering the *advokatura* and the military-medical professions, while a *numerus clausus* was imposed on their admission to secondary and higher education in general. They were also denied the vote in *zemstvo* and municipal elections. In 1891, at Passover, there was a mass expulsion of illegal resident Jews from Moscow, which deprived the city of two-thirds of its Jewish population.[53]

The identification of Jews with finance and commerce meant that they became a pawn in the feud between the Finance and Interior Ministries, which symbolized the clash between the imperatives of economic growth and internal security. Significantly, the commercial and technical colleges promoted by Witte as Finance Minister did not restrict the entry of Jews or that of any other social or ethnic category. Successive Ministers of the Interior, especially V.K. Pleve (1902–4), warned that Witte's measures were encouraging Jews, as a naturally gifted and energetic people, to tighten their grip on the country's economy, to gain control of the professions and the media, and to exploit the peasants, who would be helpless without the protection of the village commune. Witte's opponents persistently characterized him as a 'state socialist' and 'friend of the Jews'.[54]

The anti-Witte campaign reached its climax in a document forged inside the Police Department of the Minister of the Interior. The so-called *Protocols of the Elders of Zion* purported to be the verbatim record of a meeting of leaders of international Jewry, planning the final stage in their campaign to take over the world, a stage in which the Russian autocracy would be the chief target as the most serious obstacle remaining in their path after Western Europe and North America had fallen to them. It recorded how the slogans of liberalism and of the French revolution had been launched by Jews to undermine legitimate monarchy all over Europe, how they had used industry and finance to destroy the landed aristocracy, had exploited schools and universities to weaken morality, and had preached atheism to turn people away from the church. The discussions in the text laid out the supposed Jewish strategy of utilizing financial institutions, the media and the educational system to subvert the existing regime and to seize power, after which the successful Jewish world government would set up a ruthless and efficient police state, exploiting both propaganda and espionage to defend its power permanently.[55]

This was the old vision of the Antichrist from abroad, revived in a new version more appropriate to the era of its conception. It appeared too late to have much effect on the fortunes of Witte, but it was to play a sinister role in constitutional politics after 1905, and later on in the fate of Jews all over Europe. Ironically, its nightmare vision anticipated features of the Soviet Communist state far more accurately than it described Imperial Russia or the actual organization of the Jews.

Anti-Semitism did produce a mass nationalist politics of a kind, in the form of pogroms against Jews, the most destructive of which swept Russia during 1903–6. They followed a period of rapid economic growth and population migration, which had heightened fears and resentments directed against those who seemed to disrupt a traditional way of life. They reached a culmination during the autumn and winter of 1905–6, when the grant of the October Manifesto [see p. 398] left local officials disoriented, while non-Jews inside the Pale worried that, if Jews were to be granted full civil rights, then they would probably prove even more effective competitors than previously. A station-master in Kherson guberniia remarked, on hearing of the Manifesto, 'It is time to beat the Jews, or we shall all have to clean their boots.'[56]

Popular response to the Manifesto and to the perceived weakness of the imperial government has to be seen in the context of violent disorder taking place all over Russia: peasant unrest, strikes, demonstrations and armed insurrections among the workers, communal fighting between ethnic groups. In the Pale such violence was far more likely to be directed against the Jews, as conspicuous targets known to be disapproved of by many people in power. In a period of disorder, traditions of popular *samosud* [see Part 3 Chapter 3] naturally reasserted themselves vigorously, usually against those who seemed the most obvious culprits. As for local policemen and officials, they were often at their wits' end, not certain any longer where authority lay and having insufficient coercive force at their disposal to deal with large-scale disorders. Some officials directly encouraged anti-Semitic violence, but this was never the agreed policy of the government.

The first pogrom of the period took place in 1903 in Kishinev, the principal city of Bessarabia. It happened at Easter, which even in more peaceful conditions was a time of inflamed religious and ethnic tensions. It followed the murder of an adolescent boy, which revived rumours that the Jews were killing Christian children as part of a ritual which involved using their blood to prepare the Passover *matzoh*. By the end of two days of rioting, 47 Jews had been murdered and more than 400 wounded, 700 houses had been burnt down and 600 shops destroyed.

This bloody riot enormously aggravated ethnic tension throughout the Pale. The principal Bessarabian newspaper, edited by P.A. Krushevan, persistently denigrated Jews for disloyalty and subversion, and for exploiting other nationalities economically. The official report and the court cases arising out of the pogrom demonstrated that prosecutors were lenient to anti-Jewish protesters, and that many officials believed the Jews had brought violence on themselves by their provocative behaviour. No charges were preferred against Kishinev officials, despite evidence that some of them had taken the side of the rioters.[57]

The series of pogroms which took place during 1905–6 was incomparably more bloody. More than 3,000 Jews were killed, mostly in the period October 1905 to January 1906: in Odessa alone 800 were killed and 5,000 wounded in those three months. By this time it was not just a question of a threat to law and order: the monarchy itself was in danger from the revolutionary movement. Officials who had earlier tried to suppress disorders, including those directed against the Jews, were swamped, not knowing where to turn for support, and were therefore tempted to condone violence which was at least nominally being applied in defence of the monarchy. Police, Cossacks and troops were poorly trained, or wholly untrained, in crowd control. Under pressure, they could easily panic or unleash their own gut prejudices, as they frequently did, against students, strikers and demonstrators of all kinds, not only against Jews. It was at this stage that the so-called Black Hundred groups were formed from among workers, peasants, shopkeepers, clerks and the unemployed, and their umbrella organization, the Union of the Russian People, which claimed to defend 'Tsar, faith and fatherland' against 'the enemy within', which meant especially the Jews.[58]

At this time also official complicity in the crimes against Jews was at its most stark and unequivocal. A printing-press at police headquarters in St Petersburg turned out thousands of pamphlets saying, among other things:

> Do you know, brethren, workmen and peasants, who is the chief author of all our misfortunes? Do you know that the Jews of the whole world ... have entered into an alliance and decided to destroy Russia completely? Whenever those betrayers of Christ come near you, tear them to pieces, kill them.[59]

D.F. Trepov, Governor-General of St Petersburg and Assistant Minister of the Interior, did not necessarily authorize the dissemination of such inflammatory proclamations, but he did not hasten to prevent it either. Besides, the Tsar himself supported the formation of the Union of the Russian People, accepted the insignia of the movement and ordered that it be publicly subsidized. He liked to persuade himself that, in spite of bureaucrats and politicians, the Russian people were deeply loyal to him and that now, in a real crisis, they were giving vent to their true feelings, however crudely. Soon after the October Manifesto he wrote to his mother:

> In the first days after the Manifesto, evil elements boldly raised their heads, but then a strong reaction set in and the whole mass of loyal people took heart. The result, as is natural and usual with us, was that the *narod* became enraged by the insolence and audacity of the revolutionaries and socialists; and because nine-tenths of them are Yids, the people's whole wrath has turned against them. That is how the pogroms happened.[60]

In many ways the Russian pogroms of 1905–6 can be compared with the urban violence against blacks in the cities of the USA in the early years of the twentieth century. When economic difficulties or political discord aggravated the insecurity and frustration of ordinary people, they took it out on the most visible and recently arrived alien group.[61]

But there is an important difference. In Russia officials who had to deal with the violence usually knew well what the Tsar's prejudices were, and surmised that, in case of doubt, their superiors were less likely to disapprove of their actions if they did not strive too zealously to thwart those who were attacking Jews. In that sense, official anti-Semitism was a grotesque attempt to mobilize support among ordinary people at a time of bewilderment and disorder, and to induce Russians to show solidarity with the imperial government from which they were otherwise alienated.

CONCLUSION   Probably the Russian government had no alternative but to pursue some kind of Russification policy in an era when economic growth required greater administrative unity and coordination, and when national solidarity was establishing itself as a paramount factor in international relations and in military strength. The aim of the policy was to cement relations between Russian elites and masses, and to bring non-Russians closer to the empire. But the policy did little to attract greater loyalty among Russians: many landowners and professional people, on the contrary, were repelled by it as crude and chauvinist, while the masses remained largely indifferent, having different political imperatives altogether. The effect of Russification on the non-Russians, however, was very marked, and in a manner destructive to the empire. It stimulated non-Russians, in different ways, to discover or rediscover their ethnic solidarity, even across class divisions, and to begin to seek a solution to their problems in a national rather than an imperial framework.

The example of Austria-Hungary suggests, however, that the alternative policy, of allowing subordinate nationalities greater freedom to develop their own ethnic and even civic life, was not a panacea either. Although historians today argue that the Habsburg Monarchy was not destroyed by the national problem, the fact remains that in 1914 it launched an ultimately suicidal war in order to thwart irredentist South Slav nationalism. The dilemma of the multi-national empires in an age of nationalism was fundamental and perhaps insoluble.

4

The Revolution of 1905–7

Obshchestvennost' and Liberalism   The revolution of 1905–7 completely changed the context of Russian politics. Hitherto confined to timid and artificially restricted contacts among themselves and occasionally with a few workers and peasants, members of the intelligentsia and *obshchestvennost'* were abruptly thrust into mass electoral politics. In a few short months they had to create political parties, draw up programmes and project them to a population even less accustomed to politics than they were themselves.

The decisive change came with the Manifesto of 17 October 1905, in which the Tsar guaranteed his subjects a broad repertoire of civil rights and announced the establishment of a legislative assembly, the State Duma, to be elected on a wide suffrage, including workers, peasants and non-Russian nationalities. This was a triumph for the majority of political activists among *obshchestvennost'* who had long called for an end to the autocracy.

The origins of the liberal movement went back to the early 1890s, in the upsurge of public opinion which resulted from the famine of 1891–2. The spectacle of rural poverty and official incompetence which the famine disclosed moved many young intellectuals and professional people first of all to offer their services in the provision of supplies and the treatment of disease, then to start trying to do something to change the conditions which had caused the famine in the first place. The natural arena for such activity was the zemstvos, which had responsibilities for economic aspects of local life. Another was autonomous scientific associations like the Moscow Law Society, and the St Petersburg Free Economic Society (see Part 2, Chapter 3) and its offshoot, the St Petersburg Literacy Committee.

During the 1890s consultative meetings of professional associations took on an increasingly political colouring. Delegates were especially concerned by the barriers which segregated peasants from the rest of society: the administrative isolation in volosti, the tutelage of the land commandant, the stigma of corporal punishment. Many called for the introduction of universal primary education. The zemstvos too were trying to coordinate their activities. In 1896 D.N. Shipov, chairman of the Moscow provincial zemstvo board, convened a meeting of his colleagues at the Nizhnii Novgorod Fair, to discuss common concerns, but when he tried to repeat the exercise the following year, the police refused him permission.[1]

Real unrest began, however, where it always lay closest to the surface, in the universities. In February 1899 the students of St Petersburg University were forbidden by the police to celebrate Foundation Day in their usual exuberant manner on the streets of the city. They ignored the prohibition, citing their 'rights', and clashed with the police, who dispersed them forcibly. The students went on strike in protest, and sent emissaries to other universities: within a few days Moscow and Kiev students were boycotting lectures too, calling for an end to arbitrary discipline and police brutality. The authorities arrested the strike leaders, but later released them as their colleagues drifted back to their classes.

The whole incident was typical of the tense relations which existed between the authorities and the students. As Richard Pipes has commented, 'The government chose to treat a harmless manifestation of youthful spirits as a seditious act. In response radical intellectuals escalated student complaints of mistreatment at the hands of the police into a wholesale rejection of the "system".'[2] This proved to be merely the beginning of chronic unrest in higher educational institutions during the following years.

In the zemstvos discontent was also mounting, though it was less exuberantly expressed. By the early years of the twentieth century, faced with blank immobilism from the regime, the participants at 'third element' consultations were beginning privately to discuss forming clandestine political movements to bring about change.[3] In 1901 a liberal newspaper, *Osvobozhdenie* (Liberation) began to appear abroad, in Stuttgart: its editor, P.B. Struve, was a former Marxist (he had in fact written the initial programme of the Social

Democratic Party). The following year, in Switzerland, twenty representatives met, from the zemstvos and the radical intelligentsia, and formed the Union of Liberation, whose aim was the abolition of the autocracy and the establishment of a constitutional monarchy, with a parliament elected by universal, direct, equal and secret suffrage (the 'four-tail formula', as it became known).[4]

Following the reverses in the Japanese war during the summer and autumn of 1904, the Union began to campaign ever more openly inside Russia, distributing its newspaper and holding 'liberation banquets', at which oppositional speeches were made and money was contributed for the cause. At some of these banquets, demands were heard for a Constituent Assembly – a more radical demand, since it left open the question of whether Russia should continue to be a monarchy, or should become a republic.

Although the Union of Liberation was a liberal movement, and opposed violence as a means of changing the regime, the circumstances in which it had to operate willy-nilly threw it together with the revolutionary socialist parties. In October 1904 it held a joint consultation with them in Paris. All those present agreed to cooperate to achieve the goals they had in common, which included at this stage ending the autocracy and establishing a democratically elected legislative assembly responsible for appointing the government.[5]

Liberals were thus thrown together with revolutionaries, *obshchestvennost'* with workers and peasants, and, perhaps most important, moderates with terrorists. This indiscriminate mingling of political views and methods continued for much of 1905. Whatever their other opinions, everyone agreed that the first priority was to get rid of the autocracy. Zemstvo activists began to demand a democratically elected parliament, then some of them a Constitutional Assembly and the 'four-tail formula', and together with Liberationists proclaimed 'No enemies to the left!' The Union of Unions, set up in May 1905, to coordinate the political campaigns of the professional associations, typified this polymorphism. Largely professional in composition, it also included one workers' union and two single-issue campaigning groups. Its member unions were those of the professors, schoolteachers, *advokaty*, doctors, engineers, journalists, pharmacists, veterinary surgeons, accountants, railwaymen and zemstvo employees, the Association for the Emancipation of Women and the Association for the Emancipation of the Jews.[6]

The circumstances of its formation thus imparted to the Russian liberal movement a radicalism, even a revolutionary tendency which was to colour its subsequent political activity and to prevent it achieving a fruitful working relationship even with a reforming government committed to cooperation with the Duma. This tendency was later reinforced by the radical nature of the liberals' electorate in the elections to the First Duma.

The standard-bearer of Russian liberalism and of *obshchestvennost'* was the Constitutional Democratic Party, set up at the height of the revolution, in October 1905, under the leadership of the Professor of Russian History at Moscow University, P.N. Miliukov. Its rather stodgy name reflected the fact that professors and lawyers set the tone, but it was handily shortened in popular parlance to 'Kadets'. From the outset this was a real party, with a network of branches in the provinces, whose members agitated among the public and elected delegates to regular policy-making congresses. In spite of this, it was never formally legalized by the regime, even at the height of official tolerance, because it refused to condemn revolutionary terrorism.

At its first two congresses the new party rejected the October Manifesto as inadequate and called for the establishment of a full 'constitutional and parliamentary monarchy', based on universal suffrage. Its programme included compulsory expropriation of landowners (with compensation) for the benefit of land-hungry peasants; the replacement of indirect taxes by a graduated income tax; guarantees of civil rights; the introduction of an eight-hour day and workers' insurance; the introduction of universal, free and compulsory primary education; and self-determination for the nationalities of the empire.[7]

Having experienced little political responsibility, *obshchestvennost'* had always tended to be radical in its outlook. All the same, there was a substantial minority, especially among the zemstvo landowners and the commercial bourgeoisie, which found the Kadets' programme subversive, likely to undermine social order rather than to guarantee it. These more conservative liberals founded the Union of 17 October, whose leader was A.I. Guchkov, a Moscow businessman from a family of Old Believers. The Octobrists shared much of the Kadets' programme, but they saw themselves as moderate reformers, gave greater weight to the state and to private property. As their name implies, they did not regard themselves as a party, but as a union of political groups with similar concerns. Unlike the Kadets, they denounced revolutionary terror and accepted the political order springing from the October Manifesto, and they opposed compulsory expropriation of private property, including land. They also gave greater priority to maintaining the unity of the empire than to granting ethnic rights to non-Russians.[8]

Divided though its political representatives were, *obshchestvennost'* was largely united in the view that after the October Manifesto further violent attempts to overthrow the regime were unjustified and should not be supported. The regime had thus achieved the aim of splitting its opponents. Most workers and peasants, and of course the socialist parties remained dissatisfied with the concessions made by the government, and were ready to support further violence. Even the self-avowedly liberal and peaceful Kadet Party felt unable openly to condemn this violence: they continued to feel pressure from below, and did not renounce the slogan 'No enemies to the left!'.

WORKERS AND PEASANTS IN THE CITY   Eugen Weber has shown how in France in the late nineteenth century peasants were gradually being drawn into a national civic culture as a result of the spread of markets, the building of roads and railways, the spread of primary education, universal military service, the growth of the mass media, and so on.[9] Many of these processes were visible in Russia, too, especially from the 1880s onwards. The short-term call-up of young men meant that an increasing proportion of village males had seen the wider empire and met non-Russians in the course of their military service. Primary education was expanding rapidly, especially in the villages, and by the first decade of the twentieth century was turning out a generation of young village men of whom many were literate. It has been estimated that the literacy rate among the rural population rose from just under ten per cent in the early 1880s to about a quarter by 1910–13, while literacy among army recruits rose from 21.4% in 1874 to 67.8% in 1913.[10]

Above all, more peasants were gaining experience of urban life through work in industry and transport. Urban and rural culture were beginning to come together, but not in such a way as to generate a secure urban identity among the newcomers, or to contribute to the consolidation of a civil society. So many migrant workers were coming to the city that in 1881, 42% of St Petersburg's inhabitants were peasants, in 1900 63% and in 1910 69%. In 1902 the similar figure for Moscow was 67%.[11] Some of these were 'peasants' only in the administrative sense that they were classified as such in their passports: actually they had long ago left the village and broken their ties with it. But that was true of surprisingly few. A survey of the Tsindel' cotton-printing mill in Moscow in 1899 showed that, although the workers interviewed had spent an average of ten years in industrial labour, 90% of them still possessed a land allotment in the village (though they left relatives to cultivate it) and had to have their passports renewed annually by the elder of their commune.

A high proportion of migrant workers, then, came to the towns without fully losing their rural identity. Even those who did were not in a position to join urban institutions or integrate into urban society. The factory and its housing was often a semi-closed world, especially if, as was usually the case, it was situated in the outer suburbs, or even outside the town in an industrial settlement close to a railway station. Besides, the regime prevented the establishment of associations of any kind to represent workers' interests. A worker might join an artel or *zemliachestvo* (an association of migrants from the same region), or he could become a member of a cooperative or mutual credit association run by the employer.[12] In other words, the only societies he could participate in were either those with their roots in the village or those dominated by the employer. He had not been able to break out of the village and semi-serfdom, though he *had* lost the relative degree of protection, participation and self-government afforded by the rural community.

It is natural, then, that workers who stayed for more than a short time in the city often itched to gain some degree of control over their living and working environment – such as a peasant normally expects to have – and to reassert some sense of their dignity as human beings. The harsh industrial environment offered them precious little of this, and the regime permitted them no institutions through which they could advance their own interests in the framework of a class struggle regulated by legal boundaries. The response of workers to this situation differed according to many individual factors: the length of time they had worked in the town, the strength of their links to the village, their education, skills and qualifications, whether they had a family with them or not. Most historians, and some contemporary observers as well, divided them into two main categories, 'conscious' workers and the rest, the 'grey' mass.

If this classification corresponds even roughly to the truth, it shows how the absence of civil society simplified and, as it were, flattened the workers' movement. There was in Russia just as great a variety of industrial employments, skills and qualifications as in advanced European countries, but they did not each generate guilds and unions, associations and hierarchies, for these were prohibited. Workers were excluded from access to culture, society and the political process. All reacted to this basic situation with bitterness and often despair. But while the mass of workers probably resigned themselves to their fate, perhaps seeking solace either in drink or in some form of religious belief, perhaps hoping that the Tsar might one day come to their aid, 'conscious' workers tried to understand their plight and even, when it seemed possible, to change it.

Such workers were attracted to the study groups or libraries set up by young radical intellectuals from the 1870s onwards. Here, in the congenial company of the like-minded, they could take a basic course in social sciences, read the classics of European socialism and learn about the labour movement in other countries. In the course of their studies and discussions, they would usually abandon the vestiges of the faith they had inherited or brought with them from the village, in the Orthodox religion and the Tsar, seeing them as linked indissolubly to the capitalist system to which they attributed their sufferings. Marxist circles were especially popular, for they claimed to offer a science and inculcated a special pride in the status of worker, but Populist ones persisted too, for they spoke to the consciousness of many workers that they were close to the peasantry, and they taught that Russia had a special mission, was not fated simply to imitate advanced European countries.[13]

As for the mass of workers, their resignation or apathy was punctuated by outbursts of primitive lawlessness and casual violence, directed against foremen, officials or police, or against the property of the employers.[14] At root, they had not abandoned the peasant belief that property is legitimate only when it is earned by the sweat of one's brow; hence they regarded the capitalist's property as basically theirs, as fair game to be pilfered in difficult times or openly attacked if opportunity offered. They resented the casual and brutal treatment they often received from employers and foremen, and the way they were addressed with the pronoun *ty*, which implied that they were children or serfs. As with peasants, their apparent indifference would at times become moods of violent defiance, surging into rebelliousness which would astonish not only the authorities but the intelligentsia leaders who were normally in despair over their apathy.[15]

To oversimplify what all this meant was that workers and radical intelligentsia were thrown into mutual dependency. Workers, like peasants, needed outside leadership if they were to become politically effective. In the study circles they were taken seriously as individuals, they learnt a good deal about their wider environment, and some of them assimilated techniques of 'agitation' which were useful to them in conflicts with their employers. But there remained a distance between the intellectuals and the workers: workers wanted political change because there was no other way to improve their condition and achieve some degree of human dignity, while intellectuals wanted a transformation of society. As Allan Wildman has commented, the primary commitment of the Social Democratic intellectual was 'to the mystique of revolution itself, to the vision of a faultless society purged of the anomalies of the existing order in which the "intelligentsia" had no place. The workers' movement had always served him as a vehicle through which the world of values he rejected could be overthrown.'[16]

WORKERS AND POLITICS   For that reason workers were always willing to try out other methods of making an input into the political system. A much larger number of workers than had ever entered study circles were willing to join labour unions run by the police from 1901 by Sergei Zubatov, head of the Moscow Okhrana. This was not necessarily because police unions were inherently more attractive but because they were legal, and offered the worker a sanctioned mode of economic self-defence. Zubatov believed that the great advantage of autocracy, compared with the bourgeois state, was that it was above social class, and need not take sides in the class struggle. It could and should defend the economic interests of the workers, since otherwise they would be compelled to do so by political means, and thus would be delivered free of charge into the camp of the revolutionaries.[17]

Zubatov wanted to integrate workers into patriotic, Orthodox and monarchical Russia. This was not hopeless, as was shown by a demonstration of February 1902, commemorating the emancipation of the serfs, when some 50,000 workers took part in a peaceful procession, led by clergy bearing icons, to the statue of Alexander II, where they celebrated a requiem mass, laid wreaths and said prayers.[18] The trouble was that Zubatov's support among his colleagues was not strong enough for him to deliver what he promised. The Ministry of Finance openly encouraged industrialists to stand out against the demands of the Zubatovite unions. Many of Zubatov's workers lost patience and deserted to the Social Democrats. He was finally discredited when a general strike in Odessa in the summer of 1903, launched by his union, fell into the hands of the Social Democrats. He was dismissed and his union disbanded.

His indirect successor was a priest, Father Gapon, who admired Zubatov but felt that the church was a far more appropriate agency for helping workers than the police, since it could attend to the workers' spiritual as well as political needs. He suggested to the authorities that it would 'be better to allow workers to satisfy their natural desire to organise for self-help and mutual aid and to engage in independent activity explicitly and openly, rather than leave them to organise (as they surely will) and manifest their independence *secretly and guilefully, harming themselves and perhaps the entire nation.* We particularly underscore the *danger of exploitation by others, enemies of Russia.*' Instead he proposed to 'build a nest among the factory and mill workers where *Rus'*, a truly Russian spirit, would prevail'.[19] For this purpose he set up his Assembly of Russian Factory and Mill Workers.

Patriotism, however, proved to be insufficient because by this time it did not attract the conscious workers, who were vital to the success of the movement. Realizing that he was politically inexperienced, Gapon turned for advice to the Union of Liberation and to a group of Social Democrats, led by Aleksei Karelin, who were dissatisfied with their party's narrowness and secrecy, and wanted to appeal to a wider working-class constituency. Together with them Gapon drafted a programme, radical but not revolutionary in nature, which drew upon constitutional and moderate socialist thinking. Since we shall see elements of this programme cropping up again and again in 1905-7 and in 1917, among both workers and peasants, it is worth describing.

One of the early drafts put the main problem succinctly. 'The present position of the working class in Russia is totally unsecured by law or by those free personal rights which would enable workers to defend their interests independently. Workers, like all Russian citizens, are deprived of freedom of speech, conscience, press and assembly ... No improvements coming from a bureaucratic government can achieve their aim. Therefore workers must strive to acquire civil rights and participation in the administration of the state.'[20]

This was the sentiment which underlay the Gapon petition. Workers had learnt by experience that to obtain improvements in their desperate material circumstances they required political rights, and that the best way to fight for them was by class solidarity. The two main evils they faced were 'bureaucratic lawlessness' and 'capitalist exploitation', hence their petition was both political and economic in its demands. It called for the working day to be limited to eight hours, for 'normal' wage rates, and for state insurance of workers, as well as the freedom to form unions and associations and to elect workers to factory committees responsible for settling grievances. Significantly, it took account of peasant concerns, recommending the abolition of redemption payments, the transfer of land to those who worked it and the provision of cheap credit to them. Its political demands were for popular representation to be guaranteed through a constituent assembly elected by the four-tail formula; the replacement of indirect taxes by income tax; equality before the law and freedom of speech, press, association and worship; free universal and compulsory primary education; an amnesty for political prisoners; a law-abiding government answerable to the people's representatives; separation of church and state.[21]

By the autumn of 1904, in view of the war with Japan, and the mounting wave of agitation from professional groups and constitutional associations, Gapon considered it essential for the workers to register their aspirations publicly. After much hesitation, he decided that the most appropriate form would be a loyal petition to the Tsar, presented after a peaceful march through the capital city.

Workers received the idea enthusiastically, especially since the discussion coincided with the fall of Port Arthur to the Japanese and with the outbreak of a strike at the huge Putilov works. In workshop meetings which were held to discuss the situation, observers spoke of a 'kind of mystical, religious ecstasy'. 'People listened reverentially, as if in church. On Vasil'ev Island the branch president asked "And what, comrades, if the Ruler will not receive us and does not want to read our petition . . . ?" Then, as if from a single breast, a mighty shattering cry exploded: "Then we have no Tsar!" and like an echo repeated from all corners: "No Tsar! No Tsar!" '[22]

This was a climactic moment when workers dared to hope that at last they might become citizens by laying their grievances and aspirations at the feet of their sovereign: this was the age-old *chelobit-naia* (loyal petition) in a new form. Such was the feeling that pervaded the procession held on 9 January 1905. Thousands of workers, dressed in their best as for a religious festival, marched solemnly from the various industrial suburbs towards the city centre, carrying their petitions together with icons and portraits of the Tsar. The government tried at the last moment to ban the procession, failed and brought in troops without proper instructions: they panicked, opened fire and killed two hundred people.

Bloody Sunday, as it immediately became known, was a crisis in the long confrontation of empire and people. It was the moment when the workers, on behalf of the peasants as well as themselves, tried to break out of the semi-rural ghetto and into the modern urban world of citizenship and interest representation. Gapon's Assembly was appropriate to the occasion: a cross between a trade union and a traditional Russian *soslovnyi* delegation presenting its humble requests to its sovereign lord. The massacre was the moment when both types of representative association, the ancient and the modern, failed, and the image of the just and merciful Tsar, hitherto almost universal among the people, was fatally besmirched. The church – admittedly in the person of a maverick priest – had made a last attempt at mediation, and it had miscarried. The workers and the peasants were thrown back on systematic opposition, if necessary violent, and on the radical liberal and revolutionary parties. As one St Petersburg worker later recalled: 'On this day I was born a second time, but now not as an all-forgiving and all-forgetting child, but as an embittered man, prepared to struggle and to triumph.'[23]

The memory of Gapon's Assembly and its demands remained vivid with the workers throughout the tumultuous year which followed. Bloody Sunday ignited a series of strikes and protests all over the empire. The government yielded so far as to appoint a special commission, with working-class representatives, under Senator Shidlovskii, to consider the labour question. Such was the standing of Gapon's Assembly that many workers submitted petitions that its 'locals' (branches) be revived, to be used as a framework for the elections to the commission. When elections were held, a good number of Assembly members were chosen. The representatives were suspicious of the government and wanted to be sure that their participation would have a palpable impact, and so they put forward a number of conditions. They wanted the 'locals' reopened, and worker representatives to have the right to appear en bloc before the committee, not just be invited to appear separately. They also demanded immunity from arrest and complete freedom of speech, together with a guarantee that their views would be published in full. The government refused to grant these conditions, and as a result the Shidlovskii Commission never met. Another attempt at mediation had broken down.[24]

The impact of Bloody Sunday was such that strikes broke out in towns and industrial settlements all over the empire. They swiftly became massive and political in the non-Russian regions [see previous chapter], where ethnic sentiment helped to impart an immediacy and solidarity. In Russia they arose more sporadically, and at first with mainly socio-economic demands. Those involved included railway, river and port workers, coalminers, textile and machine-tool workers, printers and bakers. Some of them protested about Bloody Sunday or the closure of the Shidlovskii Commission; most made demands about pay, hours and conditions of work, compensation for injury and representation on conflict commissions at the workplace.[25]

In the early part of the year, the socialist parties were still poorly prepared for involvement in the workers' movement. Their leaders were in emigration, engaged in heated polemics with one another and isolated from the rank and file inside Russia. The local activists, students and young professional people, living from hand to mouth, kept in touch with workers as they could, convening the occasional *letuchka* – an improvised gathering at the factory gate or in a corner of one of the shops – and composing appeals and leaflets for handing out. Their influence on the workers was already strong – they had suggested the whole tactic of 'agitation', and they inspired the thinking behind the slogans and demands – but it was not yet organized or consistent. For the most part workers improvised their own organizations to cope with the demands of strikes and demonstrations: workshop and factory committees, strike committees to negotiate with employers and police.[26]

In September the government, anxious to conciliate liberal opinion, granted autonomy to the institutions of higher education, which meant that the police were no longer authorized to break up meetings held in them. This concession transformed the prospects of the socialist parties, which were henceforth able to call mass meetings and enrol large numbers of members. SRs, Mensheviks and Bolsheviks hastened to take advantage of the situation.

The new freedom augmented workers' self-confidence and their readiness to react in organized fashion to any incident. In St Petersburg towards the end of September a meeting of railway employees took place to discuss a pension scheme: it was soon infiltrated by the new Railwaymen's Union and turned itself into the 'first delegates' conference of railway representatives'. When rumours – false, as it transpired – reached Moscow that some of these delegates had been arrested, workers on the Kazan' railway went on strike, demanding their release. They were soon joined by the staff on other lines. Since Moscow was the centre of the railway network of the entire empire, the movement spread to other towns and sparked off stoppages there. By rapid osmosis the strikes became general and assumed a radical political colouring, with demands for an amnesty, civil liberties and a constituent assembly elected on the four-tail formula. By the middle of October many towns were paralysed. In Moscow, a newspaper reported, 'Neither gas nor electric lights work . . . A majority of the shops are closed, and the entrances and windows are boarded up with grilles and shutters . . . In various parts of the city, water is available [only] at certain times.'[27] This was the situation which compelled the Emperor to concede the October Manifesto.

Such widespread action demanded a new form of workers' solidarity. Some precedents were to hand. From the early summer onwards, workers began to improvise a novel kind of organization, not anticipated by the government, the liberals or even the socialists. Known as soviets (councils) of Workers' Deputies, they were joined when a general strike broke out in a particular town and workers' representatives were needed to lead the strike, to keep order and to negotiate with employers, government and police. Shidlovskii delegates often played a key role in their creation, as the only halfway legitimate spokesmen for their colleagues. Social Democrats were at first hesitant to endorse them, since they seemed disorganized and lacking in political direction, but the Mensheviks and Socialist Revolutionaries soon gave their support. The largest soviet of all, St Petersburg, was launched following an appeal issued by the Mensheviks to form a 'strike committee' at the Technological Institute.[28]

In any given town soviets were elected from all the major factories and workshops, usually one per 500 workers in larger towns, fewer in smaller ones. They met in a large building, or even on a river bank, where not only deputies but their constituents were permitted to attend and contribute to debates, although only deputies could vote. In principle, a deputy could be recalled at any time by those who had elected him and replaced by someone else. Each soviet elected an executive committee to deal with day-to-day business. Although at first soviets declared themselves non-partisan, in practice executives were composed more or less equal numbers of Mensheviks, Bolsheviks and Socialist Revolutionaries, as a tacit expression of the workers' perceived need to have an undogmatic socialist leadership.[29]

The soviets enabled the intelligentsia, the conscious workers and the mass workers to cooperate in political action better than any other organizations, certainly better than the socialist parties, which were hierarchical, liable to splits, and dominated by intellectuals. The soviets saw themselves as embodying direct democracy, where the people, their representatives and their 'government' (executive committee) were brought as closely together as possible, cutting out formality and bureaucracy. In that respect they resembled the village assemblies more than any other form of workers' organization, and it may be that the worker-peasant experience of rural politics explains the readiness and spontaneity with which the workers improvised them, and the high reputation which they enjoyed. Certainly the soviets were very different from workers' organizations seen else-where in Europe at this time, even in revolutionary situations.

Of course it was impossible for anything like a village assembly to function effectively in twentieth-century urban politics. The strengths of the soviets were also their weaknesses. They did not organize the general strike of October 1905, but came into being as a result of it, to take charge of it, to negotiate with employers, police and government, and to keep minimal public services operating dur-ing its course. However, their very spontaneity, the impetus which gave them birth, prevented them from becoming stable institutions. They could not sustain the routine business of daily administration without contradicting their own nature. Either they kept up their revolutionary elan, or they collapsed. As Trotskii commented of the St Petersburg Soviet: 'From the hour it came into being till the hour it perished, it stood under the mighty elemental pressure of the revolution, which most unceremoniously outpaced the work of politi-cal consciousness.'[30] However, pace Trotskii, it was also true that they were too disorganized to launch an armed uprising to end the autocracy, though their delegates daily deployed the rhetoric appropriate to one and openly encouraged workers to arm themselves with weapons for it.

The greatest moment for the St Petersburg Soviet came on the day after the October Manifesto, 18 October, when huge crowds from all strata of society thronged the streets and squares to celebrate Russia's liberation from autocracy. For a brief moment the workers enjoyed the enthusiastic support of propertied society. From the balcony of the university building Trotskii, who was gaining a repu-tation as the soviet's most brilliant orator, harangued the assembled multitudes, urging decisive action to complete the victory over Tsar-ism. Political demands were approved by acclamation: an amnesty for all political prisoners, abolition of the death penalty, the dismissal of Trepov (Governor-General of St Petersburg), the removal of the army from the city and its replacement by a people's militia. For a short time, St Petersburg became a huge and rebellious village assembly, euphoric and carried away by the collective mood. But by evening fighting had broken out, involving Cossacks or the newly formed Black Hundred gangs. The crowds dispersed, having achieved little beyond sonorous declarations of principle.[31]

The soviet's tactics reflected this turning point. The October Manifesto had split the support the soviet had enjoyed among all strata of society. The general strike began to subside, some participants feeling that its main aims had been achieved, others that in any case it no longer had solid public backing. The soviet switched its focus to a demand voiced by all workers: the eight-hour working day. This campaign had the advantage that it could be implemented by workers themselves, by simply putting down their tools and going home each day after eight hours' work. By the same token, however, the initiative shifted from the soviet to each factory floor and its workers' meeting: the sense of collective, unanimous action was diluted.[32]

Eventually the government plucked up courage to exploit the Petersburg Soviet's political weakness. At the end of November the police arrested its chairman and a week later closed it down by sealing its building and arresting the entire Executive Committee and some two hundred delegates.

The resulting explosion came not in St Petersburg but in Moscow, where the largest surviving soviet decided to launch an armed rising despite considerable misgivings among its leaders about whether this was wise. They were impelled by the feeling that the alternative was a passive and inglorious defeat. As one activist said, 'It was better to perish in a struggle than to be bound hand and foot without fighting. The honour of the revolution was at stake.'[33]

Without the support of most Muscovites and facing government artillery, the rising was doomed. On 15-17 December the Presnia textile district, its centre, was mercilessly bombarded. The soviet acknowledged the inevitable and surrendered, after more than a thousand citizens, many neither soldiers nor workers, had been killed in the fighting.

In the course of 1905, workers had moved from being respectful petitioners to being deputies negotiating from a position of weakness, then deputies negotiating from strength, to a brief heady moment when they seemed able to dictate to both employers and government.

413

Then came the collapse. But at no stage had they been able to create functioning representative institutions which could advance their interests in competition with other social groups. Trade unions had appeared semi-legally during 1905, but were not given legal standing till March 1906, and even thereafter found it difficult to enforce their rights.

THE ARMED FORCES   Almost nowhere during 1905–6 were the workers able to gain support from soldiers or sailors. In June 1905 sailors in the Black Sea seized control of the battleship *Potemkin*, one of the most powerful ships in the Russian fleet, and took it into Odessa harbour, where its appearance sparked off rioting in the city. There was however no serious attempt to coordinate mutiny and insurrection: troops massacred the crowds near the harbour while the ship's guns remained silent, and the crew later put to sea in an unsuccessful attempt to arouse solidarity elsewhere in the fleet.[34] Only once did soldiers and workers act together. This was in November at Chita and Krasnoiarsk, on the Trans-Siberian railway, where discontented troops being ferried home from the war mutinied and seized local stations and garrisons, and then joined workers' strike meetings. In Krasnoiarsk a railway battalion became the mainstay of a 'workers' and soldiers' soviet', which held power locally for a couple of months. Special troops had to be despatched along the line to restore order.[35]

Elsewhere, as John Bushnell has shown, soldiers' mutinies were self-contained, directed against the officers in their own regiments, and they did not link up with workers' or peasants' movements. Indeed, on occasions the authorities managed to use mutinous units to suppress disorder: 'peasants as soldiers repressed themselves'.[36] If one compares 1905 with 1917, the isolation of the soldiers and sailors within the revolutionary movement becomes especially conspicuous. It underlines the extent to which the 1905 revolution took place in a society whose strata were still divided from one another, deprived of a civic focus and incapable of common action.

PEASANT POLITICAL ACTION   The spectacle of the autocracy undergoing crisis affected the peasants almost as much as the workers. As we have seen, peasants had often responded in an excitable and rebellious way to the authorities' perceived weakness; and in 1905 the regime was closer to breakdown than ever before. As the year advanced, the peasants tried out a variety of different tactics, according to circumstance, for gaining a purchase on the system and remoulding the rural world to their vision. Sometimes they petitioned the authorities or elected delegates to officially sanctioned assemblies; sometimes they tried to take the law into their own hands, if necessary violently, in a kind of extension of *samosud*, to impose their own conception of what land tenure, law and order should be.

Like the workers, the peasants began by presenting petitions, not in one big demonstration but piecemeal in their village assemblies. The Tsar in his manifesto of 18 February 1905 had called on 'well-intentioned people of every estate and calling to join together to bring succour to Us by word and deed', and had instructed the Committee of Ministers to 'examine and consider the ideas and suggestions presented to Us by private persons and institutions concerning improvements in the state structure and the improvement of the people's existence'.[37] It was ironic that he should do this so soon after refusing to receive a workers' petition of precisely such a nature, but the peasants responded enthusiastically, often encouraged and helped by schoolteachers, zemstvo employees or representatives of political parties.

The resulting *prigovory* (petitions or *cahiers*, to use the French revolutionary term) came in three waves: one after the Tsar's February appeal, another after the October Manifesto, and a third during the elections to the First Duma. They must be viewed as joint efforts of the peasants and the rural intelligentsia, especially the village schoolteachers, who were regularly drafted in to help the peasants as ' "decoders" of the political terminology and concepts in the newspapers now flooding the villages'.[38] There is little doubt, however, that in essentials the petitions reflected strongly-held peasant views. Petr Maslov, a Menshevik who attended a volost meeting in Krivoi Rog heard two agitators address the meeting: the peasants, 'amazed that they were now allowed to make demands of which they had long dreamed, shouted "we all agree", some crossing themselves'.[39] According to Bernard Pares, who witnessed a village meeting in Tver' guberniia, the peasants evinced 'a lively interest' in every paragraph of the draft petition and demanded lengthy explanations of the less familiar terms. Nor were the points of the motion approved indiscriminately: they were sometimes amended and voted on paragraph by paragraph, before being passed more or less unanimously after a discussion which lasted well into the night.[40]

Overwhelmingly the most popular demand expressed in the *prigovory* was for the land to be given to those who cultivated it. Virtually every village and volost assembly wanted private ownership of land abolished, and land no longer to be the object of commercial transactions, and in one form or another they wanted pomeshchik land to be redistributed to peasant households on an egalitarian basis. 'It is essential to abolish private property in land and to transfer all privately owned, state, appanage, monastery and church land to the disposal of all the people. Land should only be used by those who cultivate it, in their families or in mutual associations (*tovarishchestva*) but without hiring labour, and in such quantity as they are able to cultivate.' This resolution, from peasants in the Volokolamsk uezd of Moscow guberniia, reflected an almost universally-held view. Most meetings refused any thought of compensation for those expropriated, but a few did envisage it, perhaps because among them enough peasants already owned private land to appreciate its benefits.[41]

The next commonest grievance was over indirect taxation and redemption payments, both of which were felt to be inequitable and oppressive. Many petitions called for an income tax, to be levied fairly, so that it fell most heavily on those most able to pay, and/or for taxes on commercial and industrial capital.[42]

Another very widespread demand was for universal, free primary education, evidently because increasing contact with the outside world and with government officials 'numerous as stars in the sky' (as one petition put it) had persuaded peasants that they were at a permanent disadvantage without being able to read, write and add up. 'One of the main reasons we have no rights is our ignorance and lack of education, which result from the lack of schools and the poor teaching in them; therefore it is essential to introduce universal education at the state's expense.' Thus a village in Kursk province.[43]

Peasants were less concerned than workers about civil rights and the political structure of the empire as a whole, but when they mentioned the subject they envisaged an assembly elected by all the people, to which the government should be answerable. 'Let all the officials, from the lowest to the highest, be elected by the people and answer to the peoples' delegates. The officials we have now receive money collected from us, but do us nothing but harm.'[44] For some village societies this meant a demand for a Constituent Assembly, to be elected on the four-tail formula; others were less definite and still seemed to envisage some kind of monarchy. Many specifically mentioned that peasants should no longer be segregated, but should enjoy the same civil rights as the rest of the population.[45]

In essence, what the peasants were demanding was that the business of the 1861 emancipation be completed, both by awarding them all the land they cultivated, and by elevating them into full citizenship on equal terms with the rest of the population. The tone and nature of their petitions was on the whole very close to that of Gapon. Despite Bloody Sunday – which was much talked about in the countryside as well as in the towns – the peasants mostly still revered the Tsar.[46]

Village assemblies drew up their *prigovory* when there seemed some prospect that they would be listened to. When that was not the case peasants tried other methods, but always with the same aim in view: gaining control over the land and over their own affairs, and ensuring that their grievances were listened to 'higher up'. Differences between wealthier and poorer households, which had undoubtedly widened over the preceding decades, lost much of their significance at this time of crisis and opportunity. Much more important was the conflict between the whole of the village community and external authorities, including pomeshchiki, police, tax-collectors and army. Within the community itself, it was usually not the rich or the poor who took the initiative and exercised leadership, but those whom sociologists refer to as 'middle peasants': that is to say, traditional householders, heart and soul of the community, those neither impoverished nor much enriched by recent commercial opportunities. Following their lead, communities tended to act where possible as a whole, taking their risks together, in accordance with the familiar pattern of 'mutual responsibility'.[47]

During the spring and summer of 1905 peasants gradually took the law into their own hands in many areas. There was a kind of demonstration effect at work, as news spread from village to village, so that disorder was regionally concentrated. It might start like this:

'A bale of straw or a bonfire would be set alight. At that signal a crowd would swiftly gather from the surrounding villages. Sometimes 500–700 carts would arrive. The crowd would make for the estate buildings, would break open the padlocks on the grain stores, would load up grain in their carts and peacefully trundle it back to their homes.'[48] Methods of action varied according to local economic conditions and work relationships. In some places peasants would go with axes into the woods owned by the pomeshchik and fell his timber; or they would graze their cattle on his meadows; or they would plough his pasture land and sow it with grain for themselves; or, if wage labourers, they would go on strike. Increasingly, especially if the police showed up to discouraging lawbreaking, they would raid the manor house and outbuildings, seizing whatever they could for themselves, and then set fire to them all, driving the pomeshchik out and ensuring that he would find it very difficult to return.[49]

After a lull during the haymaking and harvesting period, disorders resumed in October. The publication of the October Manifesto seemed to show the government in a hesitant and yielding mood, and the peasants reacted by redoubling their efforts to secure political and economic power in the village. A wave of burnings of manor houses began in Saratov guberniia in the east and Chernigov in the west and spread to cover much of the central black-earth and mid-Volga regions, where poverty and land shortages were greatest. Decisions to burn were usually taken in the village assembly and followed by immediate action, in which as many villagers as possible would be involved. Over large areas of rural Russia the night sky was red with the glow of flaming buildings, the 'red cockerel', as the spectacle was known. The peasants were 'smoking them out', getting rid of the gentry, so as to take over both the land and the fullness of authority in the countryside.[50]

According to a Soviet historian's estimate, some three thousand manor houses were burnt down at this time, and more than forty million rubles' worth of damage inflicted.[51] Then the flow of destruction abated as suddenly as it had arisen. Part of the explanation is determined repression by police and army. When systematic official coercion was applied, it became clear that the peasants had not the material or organizational resources to sustain a full-scale armed uprising, as many of the Socialist Revolutionaries would have liked.

They had not mastered the art of coordinating their activities at a level higher than the volost, and they had little or no military equipment. Besides, many peasants were naturally ambivalent about the prospect of taking on even a weakened imperial state. The government exploited their hesitation, sending in punitive expeditions. Where, as was usually the case, the community refused to name any 'ringleaders', they would flog all the men; where, however, they could identify the militants, they would deport them individually.[52]

Then in the summer of 1906 the disorders broke out again in the form of a further wave of arson, almost as intense as the previous year, and accompanied more frequently by personal violence against landowners. This time the precipitant was the Duma's failure to persuade the government to expropriate the gentry in favour of the peasants. The troops had finally all returned from the Japanese war, and the government was in a stronger position to restore order. The result was a heightened level of repressive violence, which probably explains the peasants' more sanguinary response.[53] In some areas disorders continued well into 1907.

Peasants often made great efforts, not always successful, to preserve some order during the seizure of land and goods, not to allow violence to get out of hand and become anarchy. After all, they wanted to establish a new kind of social order, not to unleash mutual destruction. In the autumn of 1905, for instance, during disturbances in Saratov guberniia, 'everywhere the liquor shops would be closed. The money seized from the landowner would become public property. The landowners were peacefully conveyed to the nearest railway stations and despatched to the town. Grain, cattle and produce was distributed according to strict rules. Advance wages were paid from the common treasury to the labourers and servants. Then the estate's manor house and outbuildings were set alight.' This effort did not always succeed, and probably was not even made in all cases, and in some places peasants looted indiscriminately or broke into liquor shops and drank themselves stupid – simplifying the authorities' task of dealing with them.[54]

One serious attempt was made to organize peasants above the level of the volost, and thus to enable them to feed their aspirations and grievances into the imperial political system. This was the All-Russian Peasant Union. Characteristically its formation resulted partly from an initiative by the authorities, and was helped on from outside, by non-peasants. In the spring of 1905, the Moscow marshal of the nobility called a meeting of several village assemblies to persuade them to pass a patriotic resolution in favour of the war. The meeting expressed its patriotism in a manner different from the one intended, and issued a statement condemning officials who 'from the local policeman upwards to the ministers themselves . . . conduct the state business of Russia wrongly and waste money collected from the poor'. On 5 May a congress of peasants from various parts of Moscow guberniia met, prompted by their example, and called for the establishment of a Peasant Union on the model of the professional unions already coming into existence in the towns. Their resolution was widely published in the liberal newspapers.[55]

The Union underwent ups and downs in keeping with the turbulent events of 1905–6. Its documentation is haphazard, but it has been estimated that by the late months of 1905 it had perhaps as many as four to five thousand branches, and twelve guberniia centres, with some 200,000 members. The Union held two congresses, in July–August and in November 1905, much of the organizational work for which was carried out by a 'Support Bureau' of professional people from the Union of Unions. At the first of the congresses about one hundred peasants represented twenty-two gubernii, and there were some twenty-five non-peasant delegates: teachers, agronomists and zemstvo officials, some of whom were members of the Socialist Revolutionary Party. The second congress was nearly twice as large, two thirds of its members having been elected by village and volost assemblies, and as well as Russians they included Ukrainians, Belorussians, Estonians, Latvians and Mordvins.[56]

These congresses were the closest approximation to an all-Russian peasant assembly yet seen. The choice of the delegates reflected Socialist Revolutionary influence, as the SRs were much the most popular party in the countryside. The debate on the land question at the first congress showed clearly where peasant sentiment lay. One popular view was that, in the words of a delegate, 'It is necessary to abolish private property in land and to transfer the land to those who will work it with their own family labour.' Other speakers expressed the same thought in religious terms: 'God gave the land to all alike. The land provides us with food and drink . . . [It] should be handed over to all who can work it.' 'The land is the true mother of us all. It was made not by human hands, but by the Holy Spirit, and therefore ought not to be bought and sold.' The final resolution was not quite so categorical: 'Land should be confiscated from private owners partly for compensation, partly without compensation.' This was a compromise between those who insisted that land should only be collectively owned, and those who held that small-scale private property for subsistence was justified.[57]

On other matters, the Union was close in spirit to the majority of peasant *prigovory*. The first congress unanimously passed a resolution demanding full civil liberties and the convocation of a constituent assembly elected by the four-tail formula. There were also demands for more democratic and autonomous local government, and for universal, secular primary education free of charge. The second congress, in November, in more robust political mood, condemned government repression, demanded democratic freedoms and an amnesty for political prisoners, and the immediate transfer of land into peasant hands. It called for a national strike and boycott of landowners, but rejected the idea of an armed uprising.[58]

Thereafter, unexpectedly and precipitately, the Peasant Union fell apart as a national organization. This was in part the result of government repression. After the November congress orders went out to arrest all its participants. In Sumy uezd alone 1100 peasants and rural intellectuals were arrested or exiled.[59] But this was probably not the only reason for the Union's collapse: elections to the First Duma had been announced, and peasants saw in them a new opportunity to put their case where it mattered. Without the constancy of purpose to concentrate on more than one tactic at a time, they let the Peasant Union slide. This happened even though the Socialist Revolutionary party tried to keep it going, and urged peasants to boycott the elections. Here the split between the masses and the intellectuals came into play again, with the peasants ignoring intellectuals' advice in order to use every opportunity presented to them to achieve their paramount goal of obtaining the land.

The attraction of the Duma elections was perhaps enhanced by the fact that their first stages took place in the familiar village and volost assemblies. In most regions, though not all, peasant participation was high. As in the previous year, many assemblies took the chance to draw up a *prigovor*, which their delegate would be expected to present at the next stage of the electoral process and ultimately if possible to the Duma. One Menshevik observer reported that the peasants 'took the nomination of electors to the uezd electoral conventions very seriously, often nominating them after public prayers and giving them detailed instructions'.[60]

The land issue, as before, overwhelmed all others in salience, and assemblies of otherwise differing political views would agree on this one point. A typical motion was the following, from Nizhnii Novgorod guberniia: 'Land should belong to the entire people so that anyone who needs it can have use of it. Therefore the lands of the state, appanages, monasteries and church are transferred to the use of the labouring masses without compensation; private lands are transferred compulsorily, in part for compensation by the state, in part without compensation.'

In nearly all cases, peasant electors avoided party labels: they were chosen for their literacy, their social status, their proven political competence, or merely as 'worthy people'. In some cases, local professional people were elected, for the same reasons. Sometimes village officials were chosen for similar considerations, and sometimes rejected because of them. Much depended on the circumstances in individual villages. Peasants who voted in the landowners' curia by virtue of holding a private plot as well as an allotment expressed the same views on the land question as their counterparts in the village curia.[61]

On the other hand, when peasants were disappointed by the work of the First Duma, they returned to direct action in their villages, as we have seen above.

The experience of revolution in 1905–7 showed that the disparate elements of Russian society – workers, peasants, soldiers and sailors, professional people, non-Russians – were each capable of articulating their grievances and taking action on them. But they were not capable of cooperating with each other or of projecting a vision of nation or empire which could appeal over boundaries of *soslovie* and ethnos. Nor could their disparate grievances be reformulated within the framework of a class struggle conducted under the rule of law. There was a brief moment when all the discontented elements seemed to work together, but the promulgation of the October Manifesto punctured what unity there had been, and the revolution subsequently dissipated its impetus in futile and uncoordinated violence.

The new political framework which emerged from the unrest offered some prospect of a civic forum, centred on the Duma, where diverse social and ethnic groups could minimize their differences and work together. The attempt to achieve such cooperation forms the subject of the next chapter.

5

The Duma Monarchy

On 27 April 1906 a strange ceremony took place in the Grand Hall of the Winter Palace. The Tsar received all the deputies to the newly elected First State Duma, the 'best people', as he hopefully called them in his address from the throne. The American ambassador filed a graphic description of the scene:

> On the left of the throne, taking up the entire left side of the hall, were the members of the Duma, in every conceivable costume, peasants in rough clothes and long boots, merchants and tradespeople in frock coats, lawyers in dress suits, priests in long garb and almost equally long hair, and even a Catholic bishop in violet robes.
>
> On the opposite side of the hall were officers in braided uniforms, courtiers covered with decorations, generals, members of the Staff and members of the State Council . . .
>
> In watching the deputies I was surprised to note that many of them did not even return the bows of His Majesty, some giving an awkward nod, others staring him coldly in the face, showing no enthusiasm and even almost sullen indifference.[1]

This was the first time since the seventeenth century that the Tsar and representatives of all his people had met and gazed on each other. For a brief moment, the population of the empire in all its coarse and uncouth diversity confronted the stiffness and pomposity of official Russia. It was not a happy encounter. The Tsar was offended by the coolness of his reception, while the deputies, many of them peasants who had never ventured beyond their local small town, were disconcerted and bewildered by the affectation and splendour of the court.

At the beginning of the twentieth century, Russia had abruptly embarked on a remarkable experiment. Its rulers were trying, half-accidentally, half-deliberately, to transform a multi-national empire into a nation-state, and an autocracy into a constitutional monarchy. Russia was taking the first steps towards creating both an ethnic and a civic nation out of the diverse and scattered materials of the old empire. The attempt was unsuccessful: that was scarcely surprising. What is remarkable is that it was made at all. And, having been started, it plunged Russia into a political turmoil from which it has not re-emerged even today.

This attempt to redefine Russia's political identity was not under-taken willingly, but was precipitated by the revolution of 1905, at the height of which the regime was in such straits and the danger of disintegration so great that it conceded to the population, in the October Manifesto, a guarantee of civil rights and a broadly elected legislative assembly. Both innovations went entirely contrary to Russia's previous political traditions; both attempted to create in a few months what in most European nations had taken centuries to evolve.

The powers accorded to the Duma, the new legislative assembly, were roughly equivalent to those held by the Reichstag in Germany, or the legislatures of Austria and Japan. It was part of a bicameral system, the upper house being a reformed State Council. Both chambers had the right to initiate bills, to amend them and to veto bills of which they disapproved. The government, for its part, had the right to issue emergency provisions, under article 87 of the Fundamental Laws, but they had to be approved subsequently by both houses.

The government continued to be appointed by the Emperor, and he normally chose senior civil servants, so that neither house had direct influence on the selection of a ministerial team. One major change had, however, taken place. In 1905, Witte had been appointed Chairman of the Council of Ministers, in effect prime minister, with responsibility for coordinating government policy. Therewith the Emperor's own haphazard regulation of his ministers' disparate fiefs came to an end – a gain for the consistency of government policy, but a palpable curtailment of his own prerogatives. Witte tried to strengthen his own independence of the court by inviting representatives from the zemstvo congresses to join his government, but found them reluctant to diminish their own moral authority by making common cause with the 'oppressors' unless they had cast-iron guarantees of reform. Some of them demanded a Constituent Assembly and the four-tail formula.[2]

Nicholas II continued, however, to insist that the system he presided over was an 'autocracy'. During the drafting of the constitution, the Minister of Justice, M.G. Akimov, who disapproved of the October Manifesto, nevertheless told Nicholas, 'Your Majesty voluntarily placed limits on your legislative authority; it remains in your power only to veto resolutions of the Duma and State Council of which you disapprove. Where legislative authority does not belong fully to the Emperor, the monarchy is limited.'[3] Nicholas was unmoved. The word 'autocracy' remained in the Fundamental Laws, though without the accompanying adjective 'unlimited', causing confusion to all who tried to interpret the new constitution.

The Emperor's power within the reformed system was embodied in the upper house, the State Council, which, unlike its analogues in other countries, was not entirely elected by regions or established institutions. Half its membership was renewed annually by the Emperor's personal appointment. Thus he was always assured of a blocking agency, should he wish to obstruct legislation without conspicuously using his veto. The other half of the State Council was to be elected by the zemstvos (34 deputies), noble associations (40), the Orthodox Church (6), the Academy of Sciences and universities (6) and the chambers of commerce (12). Overall, the landowning nobility were guaranteed an overwhelming dominance: on top of their own vote, they would dominate those of the zemstvos, and also figure prominently among the senior officials appointed by the Emperor.

The landowning nobility was in a bruised and anxious mood. Condemned, like all other estates, to political impotence in St Petersburg before 1905, they now found themselves brusquely outpaced by intellectuals, workers and peasants. Having lost 40% of their landholdings between 1861 and 1905, they then became victims of the 'red cockerel' and surrendered a good deal more. In the early months of 1906, in an effort to stop the rot, provincial nobles' associations got together to formed a pressure group, the United

Nobility, whose standing council remained permanently on hand in St Petersburg to lobby ministers and make use of their privileged access to the court.[4]

The Duma's electoral system was broad without being all-embracing. It excluded, for example, women, domestic servants, agricultural labourers and workers in small establishments. It was also a highly complex system, with multiple voting stages, which discriminated in favour of landowners and urban householders as compared with peasants and workers. Even so, factory workers and communal peasants *were* represented. A Special Conference of senior statesmen had decided that universal suffrage would not be appropriate, but that all peasant households holding allotment land in village communes should have the vote. Witte, who argued for this outcome, took the view that the new political system should not develop out of estate-*soslovnyi* privilege, as in the west, but out of the distinctively Russian heritage of 'Tsar and *narod*'.[5]

It is not clear from Witte's remarks whether he still anticipated that the peasants would vote in a traditional monarchical spirit, or whether, on the contrary, he reckoned their discontent so great that only giving them the vote would assuage it. Nicholas was similarly ambivalent about the prospect of a Duma with so many peasant deputies. As he told Witte, 'I understand very well that I am creating not a helper but an enemy, but I console myself with the thought that I will succeed in reinforcing the political strength that will help guarantee Russia's peaceful development in the future, without a sharp breach of those foundations on which she has existed for so long.' Actually, the creation of the Duma was such a sharp breach that this last remark can be understood only if the Tsar meant that giving the vote to peasant communities would ensure a link with Russia's past.

If that is what Nicholas and Witte thought, then they were to be sharply disabused. Peasant participation in the elections to the First Duma was high, as we have seen, despite the boycott recommended by the Socialist Revolutionary Party: their votes went to candidates who, whatever their general political views (often none), agreed that land should be transferred to the peasants.[6] Peasant deputies were sent off to the capital city bearing greetings and petitions from village assemblies all over the country. Some of these reflected purely local concerns: the building of a bridge, the right to timber in a particular forest, the dismissal of a hated policeman.[7] Others conceived matters much more broadly, affirming their support for the deputies in the 'present and future struggle with the government'. As one gathering in Voronezh guberniia put it: 'The people are sending you, not to exchange compliments, but to obtain land and freedom, and to impose on the authorities the curb of the people's supervision [*kontrol'*].'[8]

As they assembled in St Petersburg for the opening of the Duma sessions, many of these peasant deputies gravitated to the Trudovik (Labour) fraction, improvised by rural intellectuals and a few veterans of the Peasant Union. Others avoided any party labels, but generally voted with the Trudoviki.[9] The presence of this large army of peasants, with their staunchly-held views on the land question, exercised appreciable pressure on the largest party in the First Duma, the Kadets, most of whose deputies were professional people, but many of whom had benefited from peasant votes. The Kadets were aware that they owed their electoral success to the mood of radicalism among the mass of people, and felt obliged to keep up the pressure on the government.

They accordingly agreed a programme with the Trudoviki which mixed traditional liberal aspirations with the kind of demands which peasants had been making in their *prigovory*: a government answerable to the Duma rather than to the Tsar; full guarantee of civil rights; universal suffrage; universal and free primary education; abolition of capital punishment; an amnesty for political prisoners; and, above all, the expropriation of large landholdings of the pomeshchiki, church and state for the benefit of land-hungry peasants. 'The greater part of the population of the country, the toiling peasantry, awaits with impatience the satisfaction of its urgent need for land, and the First Russian State Duma would not be fulfilling its duty if it did not draw up a law for the satisfaction of that vital need by requisitioning to that end state, appanage and monastery lands, and by the compulsory expropriation of privately owned lands.'[10] Here *obshchestvennost'* and *narod* spoke, if fleetingly, with one voice.

Their main demand offered an opportunity for an imaginative initiative on the part of Nicholas to win the confidence of the peasants' representatives. As one of his most perceptive biographers has remarked, 'For a monarch committed to the view that the crown's most loyal ally was the peasantry, here perhaps was the moment to make a dramatic gesture to bring tsar and peasant together at the expense of a sometimes disloyal section of the educated class.'[11] An offer of land reform in favour of the peasants would have been thoroughly in the spirit of the traditional union of 'Tsar and *narod*', which he had extolled.

The government had moreover been pondering just such a solution to the land question. During the winter of 1905–6, Agriculture Minister Kutler, with the support of Witte, had drafted a proposal which would have effected the compulsory purchase of land from private owners to transfer to land-hungry peasants. Nicholas, however, decisively rejected the proposal, noting in the margin 'Private property *must* remain inviolable'.[12]

This was an important turning-point. No Russian Tsar had ever offered such a sweeping guarantee of private property. Catherine II had guaranteed private landed property to the nobility in her Charter of 1785, but that guarantee had been breached by Alexander II when he awarded some *pomeshchik* land to the peasants in 1861. The ultimate intention of the emancipation had been to ensure both landlords and peasants of private landed property, but that intention was so long postponed in respect of the peasants that it lost its force. Now Nicholas was going much further than Catherine or Alexander had done and offering a general guarantee of private property to *all* his subjects. Prime Minister I.L. Goremykin made that clear in his speech to the Duma on 13 May 1906, when he asserted that 'the state cannot recognise the right to property in land for some while denying others that right . . . The principle of the inalienability and inviolability of private property is throughout the world and at all stages of the development of civil life the keystone of people's welfare and of social development, the foundation of the state's being.'[13] Hereby the government finally disavowed the patrimonial state, whose shadow had so long hung over Russia.

As in the reign of Catherine II, however, this enunciation of a principle vital to civil society carried a cost: it meant denying the already deprived, and thus intensifying socio-economic polarization and conflict. In the short term, too, it meant a damaging confrontation with the newly created legislative assembly and thus a weakening of the scarcely established constitutional order. The government was actually propounding an innovative doctrine, while the Kadets and Trudoviki were defending the traditional Russian outlook, transmitted through the radical intelligentsia, that land was a communal resource which should be available to those who needed it. Neither side would budge. Here empire and people faced each other head-on, and *obshchestvennost'*, albeit uneasily, cast in its lot with the people.

There were other points at issue between the government and the Duma. Some deputies imagined themselves as French deputies in the Tennis Court of 1789 and demanded that the government surrender supreme executive authority to them. But the land question was paramount. Both sides were in entrenched positions and the failure to find a compromise between them prompted the government prematurely to dissolve the First Duma in July 1906.

The Kadets and some of the Trudoviki decided to appeal to the people from whom they had received their mandate only a few months earlier. They slipped across the border into Finland (whose home rule had been restored in 1905) and from the small town of Vyborg issued an appeal 'To the People from the People's Representatives', calling on them to refuse to pay taxes or to provide recruits for the army. 'Do not give a kopeck to the treasury or a soldier to the army. Be firm in your refusal, stand up for your rights, all as one man. No force can withstand the united and unwavering will of the people.'

The popular response was feeble. There were a few protest demonstrations, but there is little evidence that tax receipts or recruitment suffered. The most conspicuous response was that peasants, frustrated in their expectations of the Duma, set about burning manor houses as never before. The truth is that the Kadets had acted out of shock and frustration, in the anticipation that the support for them evident in the recent elections could be mobilized for a campaign of civil disobedience. However, such campaigns require a high level of both organization and of civic awareness, such as the Finns had displayed in recent years, but neither of which were present at this juncture in the Empire as a whole. As if fearing that they were losing their appeal to the masses, the Kadets stuck rigidly during the following period to their refusal to condemn revolutionary terror.[14]

STOLYPIN   The Prime Minister who took over at this juncture, Petr Stolypin, was the most remarkable statesman of the Duma period. Unlike most of his colleagues, he accepted the constitutional innovations of 1905–6, not just because they were on the statute book, but because they offered a basis on which the empire could be modernized. In effect, he wanted to make Russia an imperial nation by combining two policies which had hitherto been tried only separately, Russification and the construction of civil society. This meant also standing up for the newly proclaimed principle of private property.

The keystone of his strategy was to use the Duma to broaden the 'political nation', both by carrying out social reform and by bringing new social classes into sharing responsibility for the exercise of power. In his concept, this did not mean limiting the monarchy, but rather broadening the monarch's social base. He backed up his concept by devoting a good deal of attention to public relations, cultivating the press instead of manipulating personal connections at court and in the bureaucracy, and prefacing new laws with explanatory preambles which he drafted himself.[15]

In the economic sense, the key to his plans was the agrarian reform which he promulgated on 9 November 1906. Since the Duma had already rejected it, he issued it as a decree under Article 87. This was a blatant abuse of a clause intended only for emergencies, but he justified his action on the grounds that Russia was in a critical situation and reform was needed urgently. His decree gave the heads of peasant households the right to claim as private property the land they held under communal tenure. In communes practising regular repartition, households which held more land than they were currently entitled to (for example, if the family had got smaller since the last redistribution) would be permitted to retain the notional surplus if they paid for it at the price laid down in the emancipation settlement. Since land prices had risen steeply since 1861, this provision offered a palpable incentive for those in such a fortunate position to leave the commune and set up on their own.[16] The terms under which the Peasant Land Bank extended credit to peasants were eased by reducing its interest rates and making it possible to mortgage allotment land. Land Settlement Commissions were set up in each uezd and guberniia to help with the complex process of consolidating strips of land so that they became enclosed smallholdings.

These measures were framed by others whose aim was to end the peasant's segregated status and make him a full legal person. A start had been made even before Stolypin's accession, with the abolition of 'mutual responsibility' and of corporal punishment in 1903–4, while outstanding redemption payments had been abolished in 1905. Now peasants were to be entitled to renounce membership of the village commune, and thus free themselves from the supervision of the volost elder, becoming full legal persons and gaining freedom of movement under passport regulations no more restrictive than those which affected the rest of the population.[17]

Since the political complexion of the Second Duma meant a lot to him, Stolypin put pressure on the electoral process to try and weaken the left-wing vote. If anything, his efforts were counter-productive, though this was probably mainly due to the decision by the Social Democrats to lift their boycott of the elections. Both the right and left wings of the house were strengthened, especially the left, with 65 SDs and 37 SRs, as well as 104 Trudoviki. It was a foregone conclusion that the deputies should once again reject any agrarian reform not based on compulsory expropriation.[18]

Stolypin therefore dissolved the Second Duma, but he resisted pressure to abolish the Duma altogether, or to reduce it to purely advisory status. He was determined to continue the experiment of working with a legislative assembly, though he now considered it should represent disproportionately those social classes disposed to cooperate with his reform programme. In this decision he was supported by the United Nobility, which realized that, with an electoral law more skewed in their favour, they could dominate the legislature. Count D.A. Olsuf'ev declared that the Russian nobility should play throughout the empire the same role that it was already playing in Poland, as 'bearers of the religious, national and political idea'.

The United Nobility also called for greater discrimination in favour of Russians. Prince N.F. Kasatkin-Rostovskii from Kursk put starkly the implications of democracy for a multi-national empire when he argued that, if the British adopted the present Duma electoral law for their parliament, then a hundred or so English deputies 'would be swamped by 350 Indians, 150 Somalis and Canadians'. His statistics were shaky, but in substance he was right: his assertion shows up the difference between the British and Russian Empires, and helps to explain why the Russian one was so much more difficult to combine with democracy and civil society.[19]

Stolypin's vision of the Russian nation was close to that suggested by Olsuf'ev. He was an unusual figure among St Petersburg officials, a man who in his own person foreshadowed what a Russian 'political nation' might have looked like. Scion of a long-established family of landed nobles, he had broken kinship traditions by entering university (St Petersburg) and taking a science degree. He spent a number of years as Marshal of Nobility in Kovno guberniia, where he gained experience both of estate management – at which he was more successful than many of his colleagues – and also of official duties, including the supervision of village and volost institutions. He saw at first hand there the difficult ethnic relationships between Russians, Poles, Jews and Lithuanians. As governor of Saratov province during 1905, he had displayed skill and determination in dealing with the revolutionary movement.

His combined experience as provincial landowner and as government official fitted him well to try to bring the two worlds of *obshchestvennost'* and bureaucracy closer together. To a journalist who reproached him with not having included members of *obshchestvennost'* in his cabinet, he remarked: 'Well, what am I myself? . . . I am an outsider in the bureaucratic world of St Petersburg. Here I have no past or any court connections. I consider myself an *obshchestvennyi deiatel'*.[20] Here he was being somewhat disingenuous: he came from an ancient pedigree, and he had friends and relatives at court. But he was anxious to project an image of representing *obshchestvennost'*, to help broaden the basis of support for the government.

His reforms were designed to strengthen and broaden *obshchestvennost'*, and thus fill out the gap between regime and people. He wanted to dissolve *soslovnye* and ethnic barriers within the empire, starting with the systems of local government and justice. His programme envisaged spreading zemstvos throughout the empire, including non-Russian regions, democratizing the elections to them at all levels (basing them on tax brackets rather than social estate) and eliminating the gap between peasant and other institutions by creating an all-estate volost zemstvo. He also wanted to reform local justice by abolishing the segregated volost courts, and the tutelage over them of the land commandant, and replacing them with normal local courts presided over by Justices of the Peace.[21]

His agrarian reforms were designed, as we have seen, to increase the number of property owners enormously by enabling peasant households to leave the commune and set up on their own as smallholders. Village assemblies would then cease to be segregated peasant institutions and would be properly integrated into the imperial administrative hierarchy. At the same time he wanted to provide for the prosperity of the new peasant smallholders by lifting the burden of redemption payments, by making the provision of cheap credit through the Peasant Bank easier, and by creating local land-settlement commissions to assist in the complicated and always controversial work of enclosing strips, demarcating fields and defining access to water-courses, timber and so on. He also offered incentives to households to migrate from over-populated areas to the almost deserted steppe lands of Siberia and northern Turkestan.

It was to create a majority in favour of these reforms that Stolypin, on dissolving the Second Duma on 3 June 1907, changed the electoral law so as to bolster the position of Russians as opposed to non-Russians, and landowners as opposed to peasants and townsfolk.[22] He succeeded in gaining the majority he wanted: a solid core of Russian landowners belonging to the Octobrist and Moderate Right fractions, prepared to vote for the kinds of reform he had in mind.[23] With their help he succeeded, third time lucky, in passing the agrarian reform in an acceptable form.

In some ways his agrarian reform was remarkably successful during the relatively short time in which it was able to operate. By 1916 some 2.5 million households (out of 12.3 million, though that had risen to 15.3 million by 1916, as a result of population growth and family divisions) had received title deeds to land they previously held under communal tenure. Of these some 1.3 million had completed the further step of enclosing their land in one plot. On the other hand, much of this privatization took place in the early years of the reform and then tailed off, which suggests that it was carried out by former villagers who had actually already left the land and were merely tidying up their affairs. In most areas, besides, households were too poor to set up independently on farmsteads (*khutora*): only in the south, the Baltic and one or two north-western provinces did they establish themselves in significant numbers.[24]

So the progress of the Stolypin land reform did not necessarily indicate a decisive movement in favour of private peasant land-ownership. In 1916 61% of all households still held their land in communal tenure (down from 77% in 1905), and some 70% of allotment land was still held in such tenure. Those who left the commune tended to be at the two extremes of the economic scale: the wealthy, who wanted to maximize their opportunities, and the poor who wanted to sell up and leave the village altogether. Their departure still left a solid group of 'middle peasants' to act as the core of continuing communal arrangements.[25]

Interestingly enough, of the land which changed hands through the Peasant Land Bank during the period, more than half was purchased by collectives – village communes and cooperatives. This may reflect the remarkable growth in cooperatives which took place in the decade after 1905: including consumers', producers', credit and agricultural associations, they rose from 5,080 in 1905 to 35,600 in 1915, involving by then about ten million households.[26]

Furthermore, general redistributions of land within the commune were becoming more frequent between the 1890s and 1910s, attesting to the vitality of the communal principle. Even the smallholders who withdrew their land from the commune did not necessarily want to quit communal institutions altogether. The village assembly was not just about land. The withdrawers' holdings might not be involved in future repartitions, but in other respects the decisions of their village assembly were still of direct interest to them, and normally they continued to participate in its meetings. Even where land was concerned, they often had a say, since they depended as before on common pasture land, access to timber and water.[27] It is known, too, that some of the departures were bitterly contested by the households remaining in the commune, and that a proportion of rural disturbances, perhaps a third, during 1907–14 involved conflict over departures. Perhaps for this reason, land settlement commissions and land commandants increasingly encouraged villagers to dissolve the land tenure aspect of the commune by joint action rather than individually.[28]

As with other aspects of creating civil society in this period, the Stolypin agrarian reforms opened the way for peasants to become full citizens and to play a full part in an empire-wide market, but at a cost: that of intensifying polarization and conflict *within* the village, which had previously been less significant than conflict between the villagers and outsiders.

NATIONALISM   Politically, Stolypin promoted the integration of the empire by abrogating once again the special status of Finland, reducing its Sejm (parliament) to a status roughly equivalent to guberniia zemstvo assembly. He did this with the full support of the Octobrists, who saw the occasion as one which they could use to strengthen the powers of the Duma. One of their deputies, von Anrep (himself a Baltic German) stated: 'In my view, inside the Russian Empire there has never been, is not and never will be a "Finnish state". Between Finland and Russia there is no plaintiff and no defendant, and the Duma is not a law-court: it is an institution charged with the interests and needs of the state, and it will carry out its duty.'[29]

One of the keys to Stolypin's programme was the introduction of zemstvos in the western provinces, the region from which he himself came. These were provinces absorbed from Poland in the First Partition of 1772, inhabited by Ukrainian, Belorussian and Lithuanian peasants, by Polish landowners, and with a mixed urban population including many Jews. Their ethnic mix, and especially the rural dominance of Poles, had inhibited the reformers of the 1860s from introducing elective local government there. Now, with a more democratic electoral system, Stolypin intended to give the peasants greater weight and to curb Polish influence. Even so, his proposed electoral law provided for a complicated system of gerrymandered ethnic curiae, designed to ensure that Poles would not gain the upper hand.

The Octobrists and Moderate Rights supported Stolypin, and his bill passed the Duma. But in the State Council it ran into a solid bloc of landowners determined to defend the traditional local hegemony of the *dvorianstvo* – even if in this case the beneficiaries were

Poles. They rightly saw the western zemstvos as the thin end of a wedge, a trial run for the introduction of similar more democratized local government in the rest of the empire. Some Councillors also considered that the whole concept of ethnic curiae was pernicious, as Prince A.D. Obolenskii put it, a 'violation of the principle of a unified imperial nationality'. The main reason, though, that the State Council rejected the bill was that the Emperor had indicated to his appointees there that he would have no objection to their voting against it. Their principal motive was not the nature of the bill, but their desire to cut down to size Stolypin, the united cabinet and the Duma and restore some of the recently forfeited dominance of the court and the autocracy.[30]

Thereupon Stolypin suspended both chambers for three days, a ruse to enable him to pass his law under article 87. This blatant breach of the spirit – if not the letter – of the Fundamental Laws lost him most of his allies in the Duma, and he remained thereafter an isolated figure, shorn of reliable support from almost any quarter. His fate suggested that a determined reformer was bound to create so many enemies as to make his own position untenable. As his erstwhile ally, Guchkov, said, 'He died politically long before his physical death.' His assassination shortly thereafter was however unrelated to the political constellation around the Duma: he was killed by a former revolutionary turned police agent who was anxious to rehabilitate himself in the eyes of his former comrades. Stolypin was victim of a poison in the body politic which long preceded his premiership.[31]

By 1911, though Nicholas was grateful to him for suppressing the revolution, he had become convinced that Stolypin was the most serious threat to his autocratic powers. For his part, Stolypin consistently defended the monarchy, contending that it alone could 'save Russia in times of peril and upheaval for the state and guide her on the path of order'.[32] Nicholas viewed his relationship with the peoples of his empire in a manner which was actually incompatible with Stolypin's vision, even though it started out from the same perception: that state and people had become dangerously alien to one another. Nicholas attributed this alienation to the growth of an unresponsive and self-seeking bureaucracy which obstructed his direct contact with his own subjects. He was, in other words, at root an

437

old-fashioned Slavophile. He called his son and heir Alexei, after the greatest Tsar of the seventeenth century, the supposed golden age of monarchical solidarity; and he endeavoured throughout his reign to recreate a personal and religious link with the *narod*.

Like earlier Tsars, he believed he could best achieve this through the church and the army. He felt happiest when inspecting regimental parades, and, as one biographer has remarked, 'The tsar's ethics were those of an honourable if naive Guards officer. His conception of patriotism and duty was a high one. The intrigue, ambition, jealousy and frequent pettiness of the political world revolted him.'[33]

To recreate for himself the world he yearned for he initiated religious ceremonies, such as the canonization of St Serafim of Sarov. St Serafim had been an ascetic *starets* of the early nineteenth century who had dispensed spiritual counsel and worked miraculous cures. Some 300,000 people converged on a remote monastery in Tambov guberniia in 1903 to see the Tsar bear his coffin into the church. One celebrant described the scene: 'People standing in reverent silence filled the grounds of the monastery; every hand held a candle ... Here, literally, was a pilgrims' encampment – masses of people, carts and carriages of every description ... Chanting voices rose from various places, but the singers could not be seen, and the voices seemed to come from heaven itself.'[34] This was the atmosphere which Nicholas loved, and it convinced him, at least for a time, that he was at one with the 'real' people.

But there was another side to the canonization of Serafim. It was carried through hastily, at Nicholas's express insistence, without the lengthy enquiries which the Holy Synod normally required to ensure that sainthood was conferred on a worthy candidate. The church thus felt itself overruled and humiliated in a matter peculiarly its own. Besides, the arrangements for the ceremony were poorly handled, so that many pilgrims from among the ordinary people were excluded from it while nobles and courtiers arrived in luxurious carriages to occupy their reserved places. Altogether, for all its reassuring splendour, the canonization underlined both the subjugation of the church and the depth of social divisions.[35]

To stress their identification with the religious pre-Petrine heritage, the imperial couple would spend every Easter in Moscow, at the Kremlin. Nicholas believed that the peasants and ordinary people of the provinces, away from the evil influences of St Petersburg, supported him and had faith in him, and it was to renew his links with them that he undertook journeys through provincial Russia. After the celebrations of the 300th anniversary of the battle of Poltava, Nicholas told the French military attaché about the enthusiasm of the crowds present at the ceremony, and remarked: 'We were no longer at St Petersburg, and no one could say that the Russian people do not love their Emperor.'[36]

It was partly for this reason that the imperial couple became so attached to the *soi-disant* 'holy man', Grigorii Rasputin. He was an ordinary Siberian peasant, who had gained access to them in spite of obstruction by courtiers and officials, and so Nicholas regarded him as his direct line to simple Russian believers. As he told the Palace Commandant, who expressed doubts about Rasputin's character, 'He is just a good, religious, simple-minded Russian. When in trouble or assailed by doubts, I like to have a talk with him, and invariably feel at peace with myself afterwards.'[37]

In Nicholas's eyes, the advent of the Duma and of the Council of Ministers aggravated his alienation from the common people, since they offered further forums for intrigue and constituted alternative centres of power which diminished his own grip on affairs. In a more subtle sense, they were beginning to embody the state and the nation as entities separate from the person of the monarch. All this saddened and embittered him, making him prone to support political forces which wanted the Duma and the cabinet cut down to size. Hence his support of intriguers in the State Council.

It was symptomatic of the monarchy's isolation that it was unable to sponsor the formation of a real conservative party for the Duma. The largest of the monarchist organizations, the Union of the Russian People, took pride in not being a party at all, but simply a 'union', dedicated to the defence of the monarchy, the Orthodox Church and the Russian people. Its core lay in the volunteer militias, the so-called Black Hundreds, which had sprung up in the autumn of 1905 to fulfil this mission of 'defence' by attacking socialists, students and Jews. Its ideal was 'Russia one and indivisible', or 'Orthodoxy, autocracy, nationality' in the spirit of Nicholas I. It accepted the Duma as a 'direct link between the sovereign will of the monarch and the legal consciousness of the people', but repudiated its legislative power as deleterious to autocracy.[38]

It must be doubted whether a political organization of such vehement ethnic exclusiveness could have been a conservative force in a multi-national empire. Far from being a bulwark of law and order, the Union of the Russian People was a threat to it. Its agitation provoked some of the most violent and destructive episodes of the 1905 revolution, including the huge Kiev and Odessa pogroms [see Part 3, Chapter 3]. The attitude of *obshchestvennost'* was summed up in the caustic phrase used to rebuke anyone for boorish and uncivilized behaviour: 'You're not in a tea-room of the Union of Russian People!'[39]

Nor could they claim much in the way of popular electoral success. In the elections to the Second Duma they did well in the western provinces, where Russians were in frequent conflict with Jews and Poles, and the Orthodox Church with Catholics. They also gained some successes among peasants and landowners in the central agricultural provinces, where agrarian disorders had been especially severe and law and order slogans had considerable appeal. Otherwise they could poll few votes among peasants and workers. In the Third Duma elections, where the situation should have been more favourable to them, they blurred their identity in loose local alliances of non-party and right-wing electors.[40]

The Union might have been able to sustain its self-appointed role more successfully if it could have claimed the allegiance of a substantial proportion of peasants. But this it was unable to do. This became clear at its fourth congress in April 1907, when peasant delegates insistently demanded the compulsory expropriation of pomeshchik land. The party leaders were extremely embarrassed by the whole issue, for they were anxious not to be thought to have anything in common with socialists. In the end, they succeeded in stitching together a compromise, which acknowledged the peasants' need for more land, but left its satisfaction to a future *zemskii sobor*, in which peasants would be well represented.[41]

The well-known monk Iliodor proposed a delegation to the Tsar to put the request for compulsory land reform. Iliodor was a strange mixture of *starets* and demagogue, in tune with the times. He would write letters to the Tsar advising him to banish all non-Orthodox believers from his court, and to renew the sacred union of Tsar and people by expropriating the landlords in favour of the peasants. Based in Tsaritsyn, he would travel up and down the Volga on a steamer, disembarking from time to time to preach his message to enthusiastic crowds. His progress was chronicled in loving detail by the newspapers. But his message as well as his flamboyant behaviour displeased the Tsar, and he was defrocked on the orders of the Holy Synod.[42]

OTHER REFORMS   Stolypin had great difficulty with the rest of his reform programme too, even though he had the support of the Duma. The United Nobility opposed the weakening of the *dvorianstvo* in local government and justice, and ending of its tutelage, through the land commandant, over peasant institutions. Their resistance was reflected in votes in the State Council. P.N. Durnovo, for example, denounced the proposed all-estate volost zemstvo as the brainchild of 'liberal discussion circles'. 'What they want is . . . the eradication of all traditional beliefs among the people and the inculcation of denial and criticism. The bill hands over all local administration and local economic affairs to the peasants – those same peasants who only eight years ago were robbing and burning the landowners and who to this day still covet their land.'[43]

Other potentially fruitful legislation foundered on the embittered ethnic and religious conflicts within the empire. Duma and State Council could not agree on the principles to underlie the introduction of universal primary education: the State Council wanted the Holy Synod to have greater influence over the administration of schools, and for Russian to be the universal language of tuition. Similarly, the principle of religious toleration, proclaimed in a manifesto of April 1905, was never enshrined in law, since the State Council insisted on continued severe restrictions on sectarians and Old Believers.[44]

Another category of subjects to whom Stolypin intended to extend full civil rights was the Jews. It was consistent with his inclusive imperial Russian nationalism that he should wish to remove the disabilities which prevented Jews from acquiring full civic status and identifying with the Russian empire as their homeland. This idea, however, did not even get as far as the Duma. Nicholas II vetoed it in advance, following the dictates of an 'inner voice', supplemented by telegrams from the Union of Russian People.[45]

PEASANTS AND WORKERS   Although peasants and workers participated strongly in the Duma elections of 1906–7, they soon lost interest in the Duma, since it failed to fulfil their aspirations, and since in any case the electoral law was deliberately amended to weaken their influence. Fewer villages took part in the elections to the Third Duma, and, with few exceptions, peasant electors at the later stages of the electoral process followed the lead of the landowners in their district.

All the more striking, then, is the fact that the peasant deputies in the Third Duma, even those in the centre and right, were far from enthusiastic in their support for Stolypin's agrarian reform law. At the very least they thought it inadequate. No fewer than fifty-one of them – two-thirds of the peasants in the house – tabled two separate proposals to supplement it by forming a state land fund in each district, made up of state, appanage, church and (where necessary) expropriated private land: out of this fund land would be provided for peasant households which could not make a living from their present holdings. S. Nikitiuk, a right-wing peasant from Volynia, welcomed the Stolypin law, but added that 'I would welcome it even more if we had justice, if at the same time land were redistributed to landless and poor peasants.' G.F. Fedorov, an Octobrist peasant from Smolensk, went even further: 'We cannot vote for the law [of 9 November 1906] because in it nothing is said about the landless and land-hungry who, if it is passed, will be left completely without land and will be cast on the mercy of fate.' The peasant proposals were 'buried' at committee stage and never reached the floor of the house.[46] Peasants, then, even loyalist ones, had little reason to feel that the Duma had adequately dealt with their concerns.

Workers were granted the right to strike, over economic matters only, in December 1905, and in March 1906 the right to form trade unions to represent their interests in negotiating with employers over pay and conditions of labour. The numerous unions which had sprung up over the previous autumn and winter were thus retrospectively legalized. For a short time they became the focus of working-class life, setting up mutual assistance funds, running libraries, tea rooms and some of them even issuing news-sheets. They also played an appreciable political role: during the Second Duma, worker deputies would address meetings organized by unions to report on their activities in the legislature.[47]

However, following the coup of 3 June 1907, the government took a much more restrictive line towards trade unions. The Ministry of the Interior warned that they were 'already acquiring the fully defined character of Social Democratic organisations and are therefore highly dangerous for the state'. Police kept a closer watch on their activities, and did not hesitate to break up meetings or even close down whole union branches at the slightest whiff of sedition. Emergency laws operative in many provinces made it especially easy to destroy union branches there. Employers too became more reluctant to consult seriously with them. Membership dwindled from inactivity and discouragement. Ironically, the unions which survived best were those with a solid core of Social Democrats, usually Mensheviks, who could inject motivation and organization.[48]

The semi-outlawing of the labour movement after 1907 explains why, after a massacre of workers demonstrating at the Lena gold fields in April 1912 prompted its revival, it took such turbulent and unpredictable forms. Strikes and demonstrations, often with ambitious political aims, would flare up and die away, led by young, skilled and impatient workers reluctant to recognize any outside leadership. During 1913–14 the Bolsheviks, more in tune with this mood, were able to challenge the Mensheviks successfully for dominant influence in a number of unions. Even they, however, were sometimes taken aback at the volatility of the workers' moods. On the eve of war, in July 1914, there were barricades in some of the industrial quarters of St Petersburg.[49]

Overall, the government's treatment of the workers' movement explains why workers felt they had little stake in the existing order. As those at the Old Lessner plant in Petrograd declared after a year of war, in September 1915: 'We will stand up for our fatherland when we are given complete freedom to form labour organisations, complete freedom of speech and the press, freedom to strike, full equal rights for all nations of Russia, an eight-hour day, and when the landlords' lands are handed over to the poor peasants.'[50]

443

THE PRESS   One area in which civil society made a remarkable advance after 1905 was in the mass media, which meant mostly the press. According to official statistics, the number of periodicals published in Russia trebled between 1900 and 1914, while the number of newspapers (appearing weekly or more often) actually increased tenfold. Most of the increase came after 1905 and went along with the easing of the censorship and the explosive growth of political consciousness attendant on the creation of the Duma and the political parties. The number of readers is more difficult to estimate, but it seems likely that by 1914 every second or third adult in Russia had regular contact with a newspaper, including a substantial proportion of peasants. In the towns this can be said of most adults, including ordinary employees and workers. Newspapers specifically aimed at a poorly educated audience of workers and employees were beginning to appear, like *Gazeta kopeika* (The Kopeck Newspaper), which attained a circulation of 250,000 in only its second year of publication.[51]

It was not only the expansion of the press which was striking, but also the sheer quantity of information newspapers contained and the diversity of opinions expressed. The government abandoned preliminary censorship in 1905, even for publications of less than 160 pages, but still maintained the right to fine, suspend and close press organs which 'published false information', 'fostered disorder' or 'provoked the population's hostility to officials, soldiers or government institutions'. In the provinces, the continued existence of emergency rule and the relative financial vulnerability of papers and journals often enabled officials to repress unwelcome information. But in the larger cities, and especially in St Petersburg and Moscow, editors were prepared to risk fines in the interests of publicity and increased sales. Journals that were closed often reappeared after a brief interval under another name.[52]

The Duma's existence enormously eased the task of enterprising editors. They could report anything, no matter how subversive, which was spoken during a session of the house, since in effect they were merely passing on what was contained in the official stenographic reports. In January 1912, for example, the Octobrist newspaper *Golos Moskvy* tried to publish a letter from a theological expert alleging that Rasputin was a member of the heretical sect of *Khlysty*

444

(Flagellators) and therefore not a fit person to be attending regularly at court and influencing the policies of the church. The number of the newspaper was confiscated, but Guchkov submitted an interpellation in the Duma containing the entire text of the letter, which thus became available to every newspaper in the country and received far more publicity than it would if it had never been suppressed.[53]

In this sense, Russia abruptly became part of the twentieth-century world, with all its problems over sensationalism, press freedom and press responsibility. Newspapers would delight in reporting the lurid details of crime and scandal. The wave of terrorism which was still running high in 1907 and abated only slowly thereafter gave them ample scope for talented journalists to horrify the public and arouse their appetite for more news. The intriguing and sordid details of the Azef affair (see above, p. 360) were trailed through the papers day after day. So too were the rumours and innuendos about Rasputin's religious and sexual activities.[54]

The considerable degree of *de facto* press freedom undoubtedly helped both to discredit the authorities (including the Emperor himself) in the eyes of the population and to intensify political conflict springing from socio-economic and ethnic motives. On the other hand, newspapers also adumbrated a new image of Russian nationhood. Aiming their product at workers, and treating them as no different from other social classes carried its own message. So did the increasing attention given to Russian arts and culture, and the commemoration of writers and intellectuals, which reached its greatest intensity in 1910 at the time of the eminently newsworthy death of Lev Tolstoi. The frequent reporting from non-Russian regions aroused interest and pride among readers, as well as the sense of belonging to an imperial community which was not just defined by the Tsar and the Orthodox Church.[55]

RE-EVALUATION OF THE INTELLIGENTSIA TRADITION All the new and unaccustomed opportunities for contact with the people moved *obschestvennost'*, and the intelligentsia as its radical wing, to attempt a reassessment of the attitudes which had sustained it during the long decades of only intermittent contacts with the *narod*. The failure of the 1905 revolution placed question marks over an outlook which assumed that the educated were automatically at one with the

445

people and had an overriding duty to serve them. Experience at closer quarters suggested that the mass of the people had their own interests, and were not necessarily content to be guided by their betters. It also suggested that there were serious dangers in an outlook which assigned a low value to property, law and culture. These values were essential to the life of professional people, and without them they had little to offer to the people or even to themselves: they certainly could not create a civil society. The other-worldly asceticism of an earlier generation of intellectuals now began to seem out of place.

The man who more than any other personified this re-examination of the intelligentsia's role was Petr Struve, the economist and former Marxist who had become a leading member of the Union of Liberation and had edited its journal. As a member of the Kadet Party he had been a deputy in the Second Duma, and had witnessed at first hand the extremely fractious and divisive nature of Russian politics in action. He never wavered from his view that the government, through its contempt for legality and its tendency to stoke up popular prejudice, was a prime cause of Russia's plight. The new element in his indictment was that after 1905 he blamed the intelligentsia equally for the debacle: they had despised legality as much as had the government, and their encouragement of class warfare was morally no better than the authorities' pandering to anti-Semitic violence. They were 'the spiritual heirs of the Cossacks' in their dedication to apparently noble ideals which implied the destruction of the state. In contrast to them Struve lauded the 'conservative forces' which in the early seventeenth century had pushed aside the Cossacks to rebuild Russia on the 'state and national principle'.[56]

Struve's writings after 1906 betokened the first clear awareness among left-wing intellectuals that the state might have a value in itself, overarching the battleground of political parties and social interests, and regardless of who at any moment formed the government. He was the leading spirit in a collection of articles called *Vekhi* (Landmarks), which appeared in 1909, denouncing the heritage of the intelligentsia for its contribution to the political bankruptcy of the country. Nearly all its authors had, like Struve, once been Marxists, had abandoned Marxism for philosophical reasons, and had joined the Union of Liberation and then the Kadets, only to become disillusioned with the Kadets' tactic of 'no enemies to the left'.

The *Vekhi* contributors accused the intelligentsia of giving excessive priority to politics, a priority which had revealed itself to be self-destructive, since it accorded no autonomous value to law, to culture and creativity, to ethics, or even to religion. Bogdan Kistiakovskii, professor of law at Kiev University, charged that left-wing activists had proved incapable of observing elementary civil liberties: 'In our meetings freedom of speech was enjoyed only by speakers acceptable to the majority . . . The legal consciousness of our intelligentsia is at a stage of development corresponding to the forms of a police state.'[57]

The intelligentsia, they charged, had allowed service to the people to become a jealous and exclusive superstition. Sergei Bulgakov, an economist later ordained as an Orthodox priest, remarked on the intelligentsia's guilt feelings towards the people, its 'social repentance not . . . in the sight of God but in the sight of the "people" or the "proletariat"'. This had become a form of idol-worship, the divinization of human beings (*cheloveko-bozhestvo*).[58]

Struve concluded that 'The intelligentsia's dedication to the people did not impose any obligations on the people and did not expect from them any attempt at self-improvement (*vospitatel'nye zadachi*). And since the people is made up of individuals each with their own interests and instincts, the intelligentsia ideology, when spread among them, produced a very unideal fruit. The preaching of Populism and even more of Marxism was transformed in historical actuality into debauchery and demoralisation.'[59]

Struve's recipe for improving the situation was to cultivate among people and intelligentsia a greater consciousness of the value both of the state and the nation. No state could survive in the modern age, let alone pursue a successful foreign policy, without the support of national awareness. 'The national idea of contemporary Russia is the reconciliation between the authorities and the people, which is awakening to its own identity . . . State and nation must organically coalesce.'[60]

He felt that this coalescence would take place most naturally in the Balkans in struggling for the national self-determination of Slav and Orthodox peoples in the Habsburg and Ottoman Empires.

Therewith he arrived back at the Pan-slav prescription for democratizing Russian nationalism. This gave him much in common with the Octobrists, who also advocated Panslavism at this stage, and made foreign and military policy the focus of their campaign to win greater influence for the Duma in the empire's affairs.[61] His espousal of the unification of Germany as a model, though, shows that Struve had not appreciated how difficult the multi-national nature of Russia's empire made the inculcation of a state-based nationalism, nor how little the peasants had yet grown beyond a localized consciousness.

Struve's vision of Russian nationhood was also close to that being espoused with increasing self-assurance by the commercial and industrial bourgeoisie, especially that of Moscow. They had initially tended towards the Octobrist Union, but found that in it their concerns were crowded out by those of the landowners: for example, that no tax reform or democratization of local government, which they supported, could be pushed through while the landowners opposed it. Two Moscow families, the Riabushinskiis and the Konovalovs, both of Old Believer stock, took the initiative in founding a new political party, the Progressists, and a newspaper, *Utro Rossii* (Russia's Morning), to act as the mouthpiece of the 'Lopakhins who buy up cherry orchards'.[62]

At a speech celebrating the centenary of his family firm, A.I. Konovalov summarized the credo of the new party. 'For industry what is as vital as air is a peaceful and smooth political life, the guarantee of property and personal interests against arbitrary interference, a firm sense of justice and law and a widespread education system. So, gentlemen, the immediate interests of Russian industry coincide with the deeply held aspirations of all of Russian society . . .'[63]

By 1914 the attempt to use the Duma as a focus for creating a new, more democratic imperial Russian nationalism had largely failed. Ethnic conflict, though temporarily dormant, had certainly not gone away. Socio-economic divisions, which in 1905 had temporarily healed in the common struggle against autocracy, had re-emerged. Neither peasants nor workers felt involved in the Duma or in any way satisfied by its activities. The upsurge in worker militancy in 1912–14 suggested, on the contrary, that it was precisely the younger, more skilled and urbanized workers who felt most alienated from the system and were most liable to anomic outbursts of discontent.

For its part, *obshchestvennost'* regarded the monarchy with weary distaste, repelled by its rigidity, but also by the corruption and demoralization revealed, in different ways, by Azef and Rasputin. As a result of nearly a decade of the Duma, and of serious newspapers, it was better informed than ever before and had largely – not entirely – lost the identification with the *narod* which had grown out of the intelligentsia's earlier isolation. The St Petersburg worker rebels of 1914 manned the barricades on their own.[64]

THE FIRST WORLD WAR   There was one last chance to bring regime and *obshchestvennost'* closer together. The First World War, as in all the combatant nations, raised the stakes of politics enormously, and made it more important than ever to induce cooperation among the various socio-economic strata. Military needs required industrial mobilization on an unprecedented scale, and also caused the most massive incursion of the outside world into peasant life that had ever occurred. It offered, therefore, a new opportunity – also an urgent need – to integrate both workers and peasants better into society.

In the days of heady patriotism in August 1914 the Duma agreed to its own indefinite prorogation, on the grounds that its members would be better employed contributing directly to the war effort than making speeches in the chamber. At that stage, patriotism meant supporting Emperor and government, not obstructing them or even critically monitoring their performance. All social classes were drawn into a more acute awareness of 'Russia' as their shared community which they were called upon to defend together. The salience of this mood is indicated by the decision to alter the German-sounding name of the capital to the impeccably Russian Petrograd, by the mass expulsion of people with German-sounding surnames (often actually Jewish) from Moscow in 1915, and by the popular hysteria concerning enemy spies and the spiteful allusions to the Empress as 'that German woman'.

By the spring of 1915, however, cooperation between elites and the regime had soured. Grave defeats on the western front, caused at least partly by a catastrophic shortage of munitions, and the consequent retreat from Poland, cast doubt on the government's competence, and hence on its right to continue leading the country unchallenged.

A potential ally, or rival, was waiting in the wings. Since the beginning of the war, on the initiative of the Moscow zemstvo, the zemstvos and municipalities had formed unions to take over evacuation of the sick and wounded from the front and the provision of medical care for them. During the munitions crisis the two unions united to form *Zemgor* (the Union of Zemstvos and Municipalities), under the chairmanship of a non-party liberal, Prince Georgii L'vov. It offered to help in the recruitment of labour and in the placing of orders for military materials. In this it was supplemented by new War Industry Committees, set up to oversee the conversion of factories hitherto used for other purposes and bring them into military production. This too was a Moscow initiative, and it was launched by Riabushinskii not only in order to increase output but also to challenge the monopoly of the state ordnance factories and the Petrograd-dominated cartels. The real importance of the Committees was that they represented all interested parties: the government, the zemstvos and municipalities, the employers and the workers. This was the first time workers had been represented on public bodies with any official standing, other than the Duma.[65]

If these associations had been complemented at the centre by the formation of a government ready to cooperate with them, then the lynchpin for a new civic patriotism would have been in place, anchored in *obshchestvennost'*, but with institutional links to the workers. To advance this aim, in August 1915 the centre parties in Duma and State Council (reconvened to deal with the munitions crisis) formed a so-called Progressive Bloc, which commanded a majority of votes in the Duma and about a third of those in the Council. It demanded the formation of a 'government enjoying public confidence' (*ministerstvo obshchestvennogo doveriia*), including members from the Duma. The Bloc published a reform programme which was a kind of minimal manifesto for a civil society: full citizenship for peasants, an end to all discrimination on ethnic or religious grounds (including measures aimed at the eventual emancipation of the Jews), an amnesty for political and religious prisoners, and a guarantee of workers' rights, including the legalization of trade unions. It had some support among ministers, and for a time it looked as if a 'government of public confidence' might be formed.[66]

Nicholas II, however, decided otherwise. In September he adjourned the Duma, dismissed the ministers who supported the Progressive Bloc and announced that he would henceforth take personal command of the army. For a modern civic concept of nationhood he substituted his own medieval version, in which he would personally lead his troops to victory. This was characteristic of his view of monarchy, but the decision was disastrous for the existing order. Not only did he miss the opportunity of strengthening the civilian side of government, but he removed even his own coordinating influence (essential in a real autocracy) by taking himself off to Stavka (army headquarters), from where he could not keep in close touch with his ministers.

Thereafter the affairs of state drifted. Nicholas frequently changed the composition of his government, partly on the advice of his wife, in an undignified series of moves which became known as 'ministerial leapfrog'. Even staunch supporters of the monarchy began to despair and to talk of the possibility of forcing him to abdicate. Rumours abounded, hinted at in the newspapers, that Rasputin was having a liaison with the Empress, or that, even worse, the pair of them headed a court party trying to take Russia out of the war by concluding a treacherous peace with Germany. In December 1916 Rasputin was sensationally murdered by a group of conspirators whose political views had little in common save their desire to rescue the monarchy from the monarch.

Meanwhile Zemgor was broadening its responsibilities, taking a hand in the organization of food supplies on top of its other commitments. At a speech to zemstvo delegates in 1916, L'vov identified his organization as representing *le pays réel*, displaying both real competence and genuine patriotism. 'The Fatherland is in danger ... The regime is not guiding the ship of state ... [All the same] the ship is holding steady to its course, and work aboard has not ceased. The ship's crew is preserving order and self-control. We shall not stop, and we shall not fall into confusion. In our possession is a trusty guide – love for the homeland.'[67]

There is disagreement over how effective the voluntary associations were in actually aiding wartime mobilization, but however that may be the politicians involved in them or active in the Progress-ive Bloc were positioning themselves to claim a monopoly of genuine patriotism and to isolate the regime as detrimental to the war effort. In a widely reported session of the Duma in November 1916 Miliu-kov lined up a series of grave accusations against the government, punctuating each one with the question 'Is this incompetence or is it treason?' He had an answer to his own question: 'Does it matter practically speaking whether we are dealing with incompetence or with treason? . . . The government persists in claiming that organis-ing the country means organising a revolution and deliberately pre-fers chaos and disorganisation.'[68]

This was the atmosphere in which demonstrations among food queues in Petrograd could lead to the downfall of the dynasty. Mutual suspicion between elites and regime had once again generated a revolution and created a temporary alliance of *obshchestvennost'* and *narod*.

6

The Revolution of 1917

1917 was the great simplifier. It stripped away all the multi-layered accretions of the 'sedimentary society', sweeping aside estate, class and ethnos, and leaving a stark confrontation: Whites versus Reds. Neutrality between them was impossible. Even though neither was fighting to restore the old autocratic empire, their visions of Russia were incompatible. The Whites took the policies of the Russifiers to their logical conclusion, envisaging a state dominated by ethnic Russians: 'Russia for the Russians!' 'Russia one and indivisible!' The Reds' crusade was for a socialist order, a workers' and peasants' state which would be the harbinger of 'proletarian internationalism'.

When the Tsarist regime collapsed in March 1917, it was replaced not by one regime, but by two, 'dual power', as it became known. This was a natural result of the pre-1914 political configuration, in which the Tsar had faced not one opponent, but two, *obshchestvennost'* and *narod*. The duality greatly hampered the search for legitimacy. The new Provisional Government drew its members mostly from the Duma and from the voluntary organizations. Its head, Prince Georgii L'vov, had been chairman of Zemgor, while Pavel Miliukov, the Foreign Minister, and Aleksandr Guchkov, the War Minister, had been leaders of the Kadets and the Octobrists, the two principal liberal parties in the Duma. All the same, the new government felt unable to evoke the Duma as the sole source of its authority, for the workers and peasants recognized no allegiance to it.

Instead the Provisional Government claimed a revolutionary heritage, and a dual one at that, resting on the approval of both *obshchestvennost'* and *narod*: 'The unanimous revolutionary enthusiasm of the people . . . and the determination of the State Duma has created the Provisional Government.' It undertook to overcome the duality

by convening a Constituent Assembly, elected on the four-tail formula. It also declared a political amnesty, promised the full range
of civil liberties, abolished the police force and the death penalty,
even within the armed forces. It thus at a stroke left itself without
coercive power, dependent on the continuation of the harmonious
alliance of *narod* and *obshchestvennost'* to which it attributed its
birth.[1]

For the next few months, the Provisional Government tried to
give substance to the vision of Russia which it had inherited from
generations of intelligentsia and *obshchestvennost'*, that was, Russia as
a unified and patriotic nation in which workers, peasants and soldiers
enjoyed the full range of civil freedoms and as far as possible could
run their own lives in their own self-governing communities. All
discrimination based on *soslovie*, religion or ethnic origin was abolished, and thereby a vital pre-condition for modern nationhood was
created.

The middle of a great international war both was and was not the
best time to attempt this task. If it was to be achieved at all, everything
depended on persuading *obshchestvennost'* and *narod* that they both
had a vital stake in the war. Thus throughout its career the paramount
questions for the Provisional Government were: what kind of war
are we fighting, and what means are we entitled to use to fight it?
In practice, the Provisional Government had, however reluctantly,
to assume the heritage of the empire, without the coercive means
the empire had had at its disposal.

The other side of 'dual power' was the network of soviets. As soon
as food queues in Petrograd turned into rebellious crowds workers,
recalling their short-lived dreams of 1905, began to swarm towards
the Tauride Palace, the home of the Duma, to set up a representative
assembly which should be truly their own. The initiative came from
the worker members of the War Industries Committee and was given
organizational form by the Petrograd Mensheviks. On 28 February
factories and army units stationed in the capital started carrying out
hurried elections, which went on at different workplace sites over
several days: by the second half of March there were some three
thousand elected delegates to the Petrograd Soviet, of whom about
two thousand were soldiers, in spite of the fact that workers in the
city outnumbered soldiers several times over.[2]

There is no mistaking the enthusiasm these ragged assemblies aroused among the people: they embodied in some real way the peasants' and workers' vision of running their own affairs. For that reason alone the Provisional Government had to take them seriously. But in addition the government had renounced the coercive power to restrain the soviets, even had it wanted to do so. The soviets had no desire actually to assume governmental authority at this time: it was an accepted part of socialist theory that what was beginning was a bourgeois epoch, during which the representatives of the people should be in vigilant opposition, not in power.

In relations between Provisional Government and soviets the war was the vital issue: it circumscribed the conditions in which any reform was possible. Besides, one's attitude towards the war defined one's attitude towards the identity of the new Russia. For a time a compromise between *obshchestvennost'* and *narod* seemed to be possible on the basis that the new democratic Russia was struggling for ideals different from those of the old regime: Tsarist Russia had been fighting for the straits and the Panslav promised city of Constantinople, but the new regime had renounced imperialist war aims, and was committed to fighting a purely defensive war while trying to bring about a negotiated peace 'without annexations or indemnities'. That compromise, known as 'revolutionary defencism', was crucial, since without it there could be no alliance between *obshchestvennost'* and *narod*.

The alliance was first tested when Miliukov delivered a note to the allies in April, which suggested that the Provisional Government had not after all renounced annexationist war aims. It was tested even more severely in June by an offensive launched at the front line, which most soldiers considered incompatible with the concept of a purely defensive war. The third test, the Kornilov coup of August, finally blew the compromise apart: it raised in the most intractable form the problem of the authority and discipline required within the army in order to continue fighting. Here the great simplifier was at work: in order to conduct the war at all, the Provisional Government could not help but take on the heritage of the empire, even against its will.

While the compromise lasted, however, the Provisional Government permitted the establishment of a whole range of popular institutions representing workers, peasants and soldiers. It had little choice in the matter, since it could not prevent their formation, but it also tried to make them work, as a pledge of the creation of a new democratic Russia. It granted the workers the eight-hour day and the prospect of greater influence over the life of their factories: 'workers' control'. It promised the peasants a thorough land reform and the right to run their own villages. The soldiers were to receive the right to administer their own regiments outside combat conditions. The non-Russian nationalities were to enjoy self-determination. All these promises were to be redeemed and given legal form by the Constituent Assembly.

However, the Provisional Government constantly postponed the convocation of the Constituent Assembly, and this delay was in the long run fatal to the founding alliance of the new Russia. The prevarications indicated that the mutual distrust between *obshchestvennost'* and *narod*, intensified by the events of 1905–6, had not been healed. With the Tsarist regime out of the way, indeed, it was even more nakedly exposed. The Provisional Government felt itself obliged to assume the full responsibility for the empire, that is, in effect, to replace the Tsarist regime. The Kadet party, which the Tsarist government had regarded as an ally of terrorists, undermining Russia, now saw itself as the principal guarantor of the integrity of Russia as a state.[3] As the Kadets were squeezed out of government by popular hostility, the logic of events pulled even the leaders of the Soviets, SRs and Mensheviks, into compromises with this neo-imperialism, at the cost of causing splits in their own parties, which were to prove fatal.

Meanwhile the aspirations of the people, channelled through their own institutions and encouraged by the Bolsheviks, were proving incompatible with carrying on any kind of war, or indeed with the continued existence of a central authority in any form. The empire, briefly inherited by the Provisional Government, disintegrated, plunging Russia into civil war, from which it only re-emerged with the appearance of a new and more ruthless imperial authority.

SOLDIERS   The soldiers' situation in 1917 was quite different from what it had been in 1905. They were far more numerous, and three and a half years of war had overcome their separation from the rest of the population. They were now part of the people as a whole, a part which happened to be at the front line. That was even more true of the troops manning the city garrisons: many of them were recent conscripts, undergoing training and not yet fully socialized into the separate disciplines of military life.

It is difficult to gauge the feelings of ordinary peasants about the country for which they went to war in 1914. There was an excellent response to the mobilization order, but General Danilov, the Quartermaster-General, put this down to habitual obedience rather than conscious patriotism. 'The Russian people turned out to be psychologically inadequately prepared for war. The great majority of them, the peasants, scarcely had any definite idea of why they were being called up for the front. The aims of the war were unclear to them.' Huge distances, ethnic diversity and poor communications made it impossible, in his view, for most peasants to appreciate the unity of their homeland. 'We are from Viatka, or Tula, or Perm: the Germans won't get as far as us!' – that he felt summed up their attitude.[4]

General Golovin, on the other hand, surmised that Danilov was reading back to 1914 anti-patriotic attitudes which had only become widespread among peasant soldiers during the upheavals of 1917. In his view, the enthusiastic response to mobilization indicated that peasant patriotism, though primitive and unformed, was genuine and indeed profound. 'The political outlook of the multi-million mass of soldiers in the first years of the war is well summed up in the dictum "For Faith, Tsar and Fatherland!"'[5]

A contemporary ethnographer has reached the conclusion that, although some peasants were becoming nationally conscious by 1914, for the great majority of them 'homeland' remained synonymous with the locality of which they had personal experience, which might not reach further than the nearest small town.[6]

All the same, peasant patriotism was beginning to evolve away from Faith, Tsar and Fatherland, and fixation on the locality, towards a more inclusive view of the Russian nation, its ethnic and religious diversity and its institutions. That evolution must have been greatly accelerated by the war. Younger male peasants, now often literate, formed the bulk of the army: they fought alongside regimental comrades from distant parts of the empire, and grew accustomed to the counter-position of 'Russia' and 'Germany'. During the war, the experience of fighting against the enemy focussed their national feeling further, and coloured it with the comradeship of the trenches as well as with resentment of overbearing officers, war profiteers and perhaps of everyone leading a 'cushy' life in the rear. As for their traditional loyalty to the Tsar, that had been affected by 1905, and then further undermined by the wartime rumours of misdeeds and even treachery in high places. During a mutiny in the 20th Siberian Rifle Regiment in December 1916, the rebellious soldiers yelled at their commanding officer: 'The commanders are all traitors . . . The Tsar has surrounded himself with Germans and is destroying Russia.'[7]

This emerging patriotism explains why the collapse of the monarchy did not lead directly to the disintegration of the army. On the contrary, research by Allan Wildman has shown that the formation of soldiers' committees in the spring of 1917 was not a symptom of the breakdown of authority, but rather an attempt by the supporters of the new soviets to regain a grip over quite a small number of mutinous troops, especially from the large garrison cities, and to reconstitute the army on the basis of a new kind of patriotism.[8] Order no. 1, drawn up in the Petrograd Soviet on 1 March, was an attempt to reconcile military discipline with grass-roots democracy: it instructed soldiers to set up their own elected committees to take charge of all regimental affairs except during actual combat, when the officers' authority was recognized.

This was a compromise between mutinous troops in Petrograd and the new authorities, but it straightaway proved overwhelmingly popular. Rumours of Order no. 1 spread like wildfire, and as soon the men of a unit heard about it they would insist on its immediate implementation. In many units they exceeded the rights granted by it, and actually elected their officers, which was not envisaged. Even in such units, however, the new order soon settled down and a routine was established. In the Izmailovskii Regiment, for example, a new commanding officer was speedily elected and explicitly conferred with the 'full power of his office', which meant responsibility for military training and the assignment of duties. The regular meetings of the soldiers' committee showed a lively interest in the economic life of the regiment: the cash box always had to be opened in the presence of committee representatives and recent expenditures had to be accounted for.[9] The powers conferred by Order no. 1 could, then, be construed as an extension of the powers of the traditional soldiers' artel.

The ordinary soldier's patriotism was certainly ambivalent in the spring of 1917. Some regimental committees passed resolutions promising to 'settle Wilhelm's hash' better than the old 'army of slaves' could have done. On the other hand, many soldiers obviously hoped that the fall of the Tsar and the renunciation of imperialist war aims would bring immediate peace. Fedor Stepun, a democratically inclined officer, talked in confidence to some infantrymen, calling them 'my comrades in battle', but they told him 'We have freedom now, your Honour. In Piter [Petrograd] supposedly an order came out making peace, since we don't need anything that belongs to anyone else. Peace – that means going home to our wives and kids.' To others the fall of the Tsar meant the satisfaction of the demand for land, which was another reason for wanting peace: 'What's the use of turning up our toes in Galicia, when back at home they're going to divide up the land?'[10]

An officer of the Pavlovskii Regiment reflected ruefully in his diary on the rift dividing the two Russias which the disappearance of the Tsar had made manifest in the relations between officers and men. 'Between us and them it is an impassable gulf. No matter how well they get on with individual officers, in their eyes we are all *barins*. When we talk about the *narod*, we mean the nation; when they talk about it, they understand it as meaning only the democratic lower classes. In their eyes, what has occurred is not a political but a social revolution, which in their opinion they have won and we have lost ... We can find no common language: that is the accursed heritage of the old regime.'[11]

As Minister of War, and later as Prime Minister, Aleksandr Kerenskii tried to revive the army's fighting spirit by creating 'shock battalions' as new-style democratic Guards, and by mounting a fresh offensive. He had a vision of a revolutionary nation in arms, its patriotism the more effective with the collapse of the old regime, *obshchestvennost'* and *narod* now allied and unencumbered by the divisions which the old society had perpetuated. He made a whirlwind tour of the front line, visiting many units and inspiring them with his vision, though it is not clear how long the impression lasted once his staff car had departed.

His vision of the new national unity was not borne out in practice. When the offensive was launched in June, it enjoyed success for a few days on some sectors of the front. But elsewhere regimental committees debated whether to obey the order to advance; some even rejected it out of hand. In one battalion committee a soldier exclaimed 'Comrades! Whose land are we on anyhow? We're no annexationists, and our government says "No annexations or indemnities". Let's give the Austrians back their land and return to our own borders. But then, if they try to go further, over our dead bodies!' The committee resolved 'What's ours we won't yield, what belongs to others we don't want.' (*Svoego ne dadim, chuzhogo ne khotim.*)[12] Inevitably, in a few days the offensive collapsed, leaving officers to deal with a wave of insubordination.

Kerenskii's attempt to weld together *obshchestvennost'* and *narod* in a surge of aggressive patriotism failed. Instead it precipitated a crisis which severely tested the army and prepared the way for its ultimate collapse. The 'Kornilov affair' deepened the crisis, showing up as it did all the contradictions of 'revolutionary defencism'.

Appointed Commander-in-Chief in early July, General Lavr Kornilov was prepared to tolerate the bare existence of the soldiers' committees, but he wanted them emasculated by the abolition of all meetings at the front and by the restoration of officers' full disciplinary powers, including the death penalty. Kerenskii strung him along, though he must have realized that the full implementation of his programme would tear apart the delicate compromise which he had hitherto precariously maintained between the demands of war and the pressure from below. He was now straddling two stools which were moving further and further apart. In August, Kornilov exploited Kerenskii's dilemma to move elite troops towards Petrograd, with the intention of declaring martial law and installing a military government. His troops were halted on the way by railway workers, and Kerenskii had finally to decide which stool to sit on. He dismissed Kornilov and ordered his arrest for treason.[13]

The ambiguities finally crumbled away: the Provisional Government and the Soviet leadership were caught between generals who wanted unrestricted pursuit of the war, and a popular mood which increasingly identified the war as a pretext for perpetuating the exploitative and repressive apparatus of the old empire. The confrontation was no longer between *obshchestvennost'* and *narod*, but between empire and *narod*. As a group of soldiers asked on the Romanian front, 'For what purpose did our brothers overthrow Nicholas II, and why did the soldiers put in Kerenskii if not to get the war over as soon as possible?'[14]

Since the Bolsheviks promised an end to the war, more and more army committees during the autumn were either electing Bolsheviks, or were being brushed aside, to be replaced by mass meetings led by Bolshevik agitators or by Military Revolutionary Committees which were committed to overthrowing the Provisional Government and ending the war. These owed their success to the widespread suspicion that the Provisional Government and the high-level soviets were merely the old regime in a new guise and that the only way to secure the things the peasant-soldier really cared about was to declare peace unilaterally, leave the front and return to the countryside to take over the land. The revolutionary situation was replacing hard-won national consciousness with a new crisis-stricken localism. The army was breaking up into a loose conglomeration of *skhodki*, each ready to go its own way.

The Bolshevik seizure of power in October legitimized these aspirations. By declaring a ceasefire and passing a law handing over all land to the village communities, the new Soviet government set the seal on the reversion to localism and allowed soldiers to do *en masse* what they had already begun to do individually, desert the front and make their way back to the village to participate in the redistribution of land. It launched 'proletarian internationalism' on the precarious basis of a new parochialism.

WORKERS   The experience of 1905–6, the Duma and the world war had convinced most workers that they had little to gain from channelling their demands through established institutions. They saw capitalism and autocracy as part of the same implacable power structure, and felt little or no attachment to law, private property or parliamentary procedures. Where they had been successful in the past, it had been through setting up their own institutions on the basis of universal working-class solidarity against employers and government alike. They had accepted the socialist intelligentsia as useful and dedicated leaders, but remained sceptical about their genuine commitment to the workers, and resentful over their irresponsible fractionalism, which constantly threatened to undermine solidarity.

As soon as the February revolution took hold, the workers, whatever their political allegiances, first in Petrograd and then elsewhere, hastened to restore the institutions which, in their own eyes, had been most successful in 1905, the soviets. They did this even though no socialist party envisaged soviets as the spearhead of the workers' struggle.

All the same, socialist intellectuals, especially the Mensheviks, took a lead in their formation, sensing how popular they were among the workers. Together with worker members of the War Industry Committee, just released from prison, they moved into the Tauride Palace on 27 February, next door to the Provisional Government being formed on the same day, and formed a 'Provisional Executive Committee of the Soviet of Workers' Deputies'. The new Committee issued a general appeal for elections of one deputy per one thousand workers, and one per army company, and declared that 'The Soviet of Workers' Deputies . . . considers its basic function to be: organisation of the people's forces in the struggle for political freedom and people's rule in Russia . . . Let us all together . . . fight for the annihilation of the old regime and the convocation of a constituent national assembly, to be elected by universal, equal, direct and secret ballot.'[15]

The new soviet differed from that of 1905 in that it emerged in a situation where the revolution had already triumphed. It was thus from the outset partly an organ of government as well as one of revolution. It did not presume to take over complete governmental responsibility, but concluded an agreement with the Provisional Government to support it as long as it declared a political amnesty and civil freedoms, pursued a purely defensive war and prepared the way for a Constituent Assembly.[16] Unlike in 1905, moreover, the soviets had something to defend. That share in responsibility put a new kind of pressure on the soviets' leaders, that of striving to uphold the institutions created by the February revolution, and not let them be swept away, either by counter-revolution or by irresponsible mass action.

As a result of these new pressures, there was from the outset a tendency for the Executive Committee to become a new kind of bureaucracy. From the beginning the assembly had agreed that the main socialist parties could appoint their own nominees to the Executive Committee, and that practice was followed in other towns.[17] The tendency towards bureaucracy was reinforced by the chaotic nature of the debates on the floor of the soviet, where workers and soldiers could come and go without any restriction. 'The crowd of those standing became so dense that it was difficult to make one's way through, and those sitting in chairs abandoned them, so that the whole hall, apart from the front rows, stood in one huge throng, everyone craning their necks ... The "presidium" was also standing on a table, while around the shoulders of the chairman was a whole swarm of energetic people who had clambered on to the table and were hindering him from conducting the session.' With semi-official responsibilities to fulfil, the Executive Committee did its work, in the words of one of its members, 'almost without heeding what was going on in the chamber next door'.[18]

This was political education of a kind – receiving information on events, learning to distinguish different political opinions, formulating resolutions and voting on them – but it was scarcely possible to keep a grip on a fast-changing revolutionary situation by relying on such mass meetings for decision-making. So the Executive Committees had to take decisions on their own initiative.[19] Through their grip on these committees, the socialist parties dominated the soviets from the outset: at first the Mensheviks and Socialist Revolutionaries, later, as popular discontent swelled, the Bolsheviks.

Within the first few weeks, soviets were set up in all the large towns in Russia, and in most small towns and some villages too. Sometimes they were combined workers' and soldiers' assemblies, as in Petrograd; sometimes workers and soldiers created separate ones, as in Moscow. Most workers at this stage aspired to universal working-class solidarity, but the various socialist groups present in a particular town would usually devise their own arrangements for the executive committees, and then get the assemblies to approve them.[20]

The soviets rested on lower-level organizations, the factory committees, which organized elections in individual factories and

463

workshops. They often emerged from informal strike committees active during February and March 1917, and continued in being to handle affairs at the workplace, and to keep up pressure on employers, soviets and government to satisfy the workers' demands. In Petrograd they were legitimized by an agreement of 10 March between the city soviet and the employers, under which they were (i) to represent the workers in their dealings with the employers, (ii) to articulate the workers' opinions on questions of public life, and (iii) to resolve problems arising from relations among the workers themselves.[21] As the soviets fell under the dominance of political parties, workers would look to the factory committees to represent them more directly, so that those committees tended to become repositories of working-class radicalism.

In some cases workers did not even wait for the establishment of elected factory committees, but took action in mass meetings. Foremen would be called to account for their behaviour towards their charges. At the Thornton textile mill in Petrograd they were hoisted up on to a table, where they had to answer questions shouted from the floor. At the Putilov Works, and elsewhere, an unpopular foreman would have a sack tossed over his head, he would be shoved into a wheelbarrow and trundled out of the works to be dumped on the street or even in a nearby river.[22] This procedure was reminiscent of village *samosud*, with its ritual humiliations.

The factory committees took the lead in the campaign for the eight-hour working day, which they would simply declare instituted in their workplace. The employers, under pressure to conciliate the workers, conceded this early on. Then the stage was set for a more serious conflict: over the running of individual factories. The economic crisis intensified in the course of the summer: inflation rose sharply, deliveries of fuel, raw materials and spare parts became more uncertain, and worker discipline weakened. Employers began cutting output and trying to lay off workers, or even closing their plants altogether. The workers, suspicious that the employers were simply trying to increase their profits, demanded the right to inspect the books and generally to supervise the running of the workplace. This was termed 'workers' control' (*rabochii kontrol'*).

In June 1917, for example, the director of the Langezipen Machine-Building Works in Petrograd announced imminent closure because of a decline in labour productivity, lack of funds and shortage of fuel and raw materials. The factory committee responded by resolving that 'no goods or raw materials may be shipped out of the factory without the permission of the factory committee', and that 'no order from the administration is valid without the sanction of the factory committee'.[23]

This radical breakdown in trust between workers and employers reflected the way in which autocracy and capitalism had been superimposed one on top of the other, so that questions of class struggle automatically became enmeshed in the political battle. In most combatant countries questions of war profiteering were dealt with (not necessarily successfully) by the state, but in Russia the employers categorically rejected the notion of state intervention in 1917, believing the die was already cast against them by the fact that, as they saw it, the government was already under the control of the soviets.[24]

The factory committees proved to be the most radical of the workers' associations of 1917, in the sense that they came out earliest and most consistently against the compromises proposed in the name of national unity by the Provisional Government and partly supported by the soviet leaders. Maybe this radicalism sprang from the fact that the factory committees were the closest to the workplace and so reflected most keenly workers' rapidly growing alarm at the deterioration of their working conditions and the threat to their jobs. Some of the committees had a syndicalist vision of Russian industry as a federation of self-governing factories run by workers for workers. But where they attempted to put it into practice it was often not for theoretical reasons, but by necessity – the imminence of closure or mass lay-offs.

The Mensheviks in the Provisional Government found themselves in a cruel dilemma over these industrial conflicts. Committed to mass working-class action and to the soviets, many of their leaders nevertheless felt that for the moment the workers' primary loyalty must be to the new civil order which had emerged in Russia and which was being jeopardized by further class struggle. In June Minister of Labour, M.I. Skobelev, appealed to workers not to disrupt production by striking and by using threats against employers in order to gain wage rises which, if granted, would 'disorganise industry and deplete the Treasury'. In August he followed this exhortation up with a tougher circular reaffirming that enterprise management must have the right to settle questions of employment and giving them the right to fine workers for meetings held during working hours.[25] Most workers regarded such admonitions as a betrayal of their struggle, and became more sensitive to Bolshevik appeals to take power in the factories for themselves.

A Petrograd conference of factory committees in June was the first mass organization to adopt an unambiguously Bolshevik resolution and summon the soviets to take power on their own. It called for regulation by workers of the production and distribution of goods, 'transfer into the hands of the people of a large part of the profits, income and property' of merchants, bankers, and so on, direct exchange of produce between town and country, and the establishment of a workers' militia.[26]

It was not only industrial conflict but also the issue of the war which fuelled distrust between workers and *obshchestvennost'* during the summer and autumn of 1917. Already in April the factory committee of the Petrograd Optical Works passed a resolution proclaiming that 'we do not want to shed blood for the sake of Miliukov and Co in cooperation with the capitalist oppressors of all countries'.[27]

Much more serious, at the beginning of July, the First Machine-Gun Regiment, ordered to transfer from Petrograd to the front, refused to go. From the Putilov Works, the Vyborg district and Vasilevskii Island, some of the most militant parts of the capital, workers swarmed into the centre of the city and demanded that the soviets should now take full power into their hands, renounce the discredited coalition with the Provisional Government and declare an end to the war. When Chernov, the Socialist Revolutionary leader, urged restraint, someone from the crowd shouted at him, 'Take power when it's offered to you, you son of a bitch!' The government brought in regular troops to disperse the demonstrators, with the loss of some three hundred lives, a massacre which outstripped Bloody Sunday. This was a vivid demonstration of the workers' faith in the soviets and their paradoxical but simultaneous loss of faith in those soviets' leaders.[28]

The most militant workers' organizations of 1917 were the militias or, as they later became known, the Red Guards. Like the factory committees, they originated in the events of February, when the soldiers' rebellion enabled workers to acquire thousands of weapons. At the 1886 Electric Power Company in Petrograd a squad of forty-five volunteers appeared already on 2 March, and appointed a chief whom they called a *sotnik* (literally 'centurion': originally a term used by peasants for the headman of part of a large village). They wore red arm bands, carried permits issued by the factory committee and were paid for their patrolling work by the enterprise.[29]

Their example was widely followed and, since the Provisional Government never managed to create an effective citizens' militia to replace the old police, the workers' militias soon became the only serious coercive force on the streets of the towns. All the same, the socialist parties were slow to strike up an effective relationship with them. Even the Bolsheviks remained suspicious of home-made militias not directly under their own control. It was during and after the Kornilov affair that they came into their own. Soviets, now increasingly under Bolshevik control, set about creating a network of paramilitary organizations, Military Revolutionary Committees, which could defend them against possible further attempts at counter-revolution. During October itself, the Red Guards in Petrograd and elsewhere played a crucial role in securing and defending vital strategic points.[30]

Militant low-level workers' organizations thus played a crucial part in mobilizing mass indignation against the Provisional Government and the soviet leaders increasingly aligned with it. They also provided a large part of the relatively small-scale forces which actually seized power in October.

PEASANTS   The abdication of the Tsar offered the peasants an opportunity which had for centuries been little more than a dream: to get the authorities off their backs and run their affairs themselves for their own benefit. When news of the February revolution filtered out into the countryside, most villages held open assemblies to discuss what they should do. Often, in keeping with the novelty of the situation, these were not the traditional assemblies, confined to peasant householders: instead, all inhabitants were allowed to attend, including women, schoolteachers, medical orderlies and priests.

The war had already broadened the peasants' horizons considerably. Not only were many of the menfolk at the front, but those who stayed behind now had to sell food at fixed prices to the state, or provide horses for the cavalry, or billet refugees and prisoners of war. So they had plenty to discuss: the progress of the war, the position of the gentry, the price of food. And they moved quite rapidly on to exercising influence on these issues, beginning at the volost level, where many of the existing elders, land commandants and police officials were dismissed and replaced by ad hoc peasant nominees.[31]

In the course of the next few months a peasant tide from below, its impulse coming from the village assemblies, gradually swamped the new institutions the Provisional Government was trying to establish in the countryside to deal with local government, the land and supply problems. A law of 1916 had at last set up volost zemstvos, but peasants now either obstructed them or took them over. Thus, in the Simbirsk village of Beklemishevo, the landowner Sergei Rudnev discovered that the volost zemstvo peasant deputies deferred to the elders from its constituent villages. 'The deputies would hold forth, but whenever it was time to take decisions, then the chairman would always ask 'Well, elders, what do you think?' The elders would discuss the matter sedately and, if they could reach a common decision, would announce it; if not, then they were invited to consult their various village assemblies and bring back their findings to the next meeting.'[32]

Even at uezd and guberniia level, with the disappearance of the governor and the police institutions, elected peasant committees or 'committees of people's power' (*komitety narodnoi vlasti*) began to exercise real influence, articulating peasant grievances at a level previously always dominated by the state. They ignored the zemstvos and rivalled or even took over the uezd and guberniia land committees set up by the Provisional Government to prepare land reform proposals for the Constituent Assembly.[33] Because peasant institutions had hitherto always been segregated, these committees tended to express only narrowly conceived peasant interests, ignoring those of other rural inhabitants. A few of them began to act as autonomous local government bodies for agrarian and supply questions. The one in Samara, for instance, would acknowledge the Provisional Government's commissar 'only on condition that he is elected to the executive of the "committee of people's power", to which he will be completely subordinate'.[34]

As the spring and summer wore on the new peasant bodies became increasingly impatient with the Provisional Government's hesitant and piecemeal approach to all agrarian problems. Some peasant committees began to take control of all private land in their area, forbidding sales, laying down tight rules on renting and taking over the allocation of seeds, tools, livestock and prisoners of war. Prince Sergei Trubetskoi discovered on his Begichevo estate in Moscow guberniia that 'a local "land committee", regarding Begichevo as already its own property, prevented me from selling anything, even from the harvest or newborn livestock, and yet demanded that agricultural activity should continue at its usual high level. Wages were rising but labour productivity was falling disastrously. The land committees insisted that expenses on the estate should be covered not from the revenues but from elsewhere: "Withdraw money from your bank!" Of course, with the best will in the world, it was impossible to run an estate in these conditions.'[35]

As Trubetskoi perceived, many land committees were not merely trying to improve food supplies: they were consciously preparing the way for the confiscation and redistribution of all private land to peasant communities on their own terms. Some peasant assemblies had made no secret of their intention of doing this from the outset. Already before the end of March the Samara guberniia peasant assembly had resolved that 'Private property in should be abolished. All land . . . should be handed over to the toiling people. Only those who cultivate the land can claim a right to it.[36] One delegate said: 'I believe that land means freedom. It is wrong to pay the landowners for the land. Will we be any better off if we wait for the Constituent Assembly to resolve the land question? In the past the government decided the land question for us, but their efforts only led us into bondage . . . The land question should be resolved now, and we should not put our trust blindly in the political parties.'[37]

Similarly on 14 May a village assembly in Voronezh guberniia passed a resolution that 'All land should immediately be handed over to the toiling people without any compensation. This transfer should take place now, without waiting for the Constituent Assembly. The people, who have suffered from the war, should enjoy the fruits of the revolution.' The resolution added cautiously that 'the final settlement of the land question should be reserved for the Constituent Assembly', but if the transfer were to take place first, then possession would become nine points of the law.[38]

It had always been the policy of the Socialist Revolutionary Party to encourage seizure of private land by the village communes for immediate redistribution. The newly revived All-Russian Peasant Union also supported this position and at its first congress in May called for 'the transfer, without compensation, of all lands now belonging to the state, monasteries, churches and private persons to the possession of the people, for equitable and free use'.[39] By a terrible irony the SR leader, Viktor Chernov, was now not only in the Provisional Government but, as its Minister of Agriculture, responsible for this very issue. Like his colleague Skobelev at the Ministry of Labour, he was placed in an agonizing dilemma by the opportunity to carry out his own programme. However desirable the satisfaction of peasant land hunger might be, he feared that the upheavals associated with it would disrupt food production and marketing, endanger supplies to the towns and the army and strain beyond endurance the fragile alliance of *obshchestvennost'* and *narod*. In July he attempted a compromise by authorizing local land committees to take over land which was 'poorly used', but underwent the humiliation of having his circular countermanded forthwith by the Minister of the Interior, Tseretelli, who instructed guberniia commissars to penalize 'calls for seizures of land with all the force of the law'.[40]

Thus discouraged by the Provisional Government, the peasants gradually turned to unilateral action. In the early months of the new regime they largely confined themselves to withdrawing labour, felling timber belonging to the landlord, pasturing cattle on private land and limiting rents paid for the use of land. These actions were nearly always mandated by village or volost assemblies, for solidarity was vital to their success. During the summer and autumn, however, peasants increasingly took more direct and sometimes violent action to secure the rights they believed they were entitled to. They would mow private meadows, harvest the lord's crops, confiscate his tools and livestock and then proceed to the formal expropriation of his land and perhaps his expulsion from the village. Seldom was the landowner able to obtain any kind of official coercive force to protect his property or person.[41]

Such direct action was especially common in the central black-earth region and the mid-Volga, both areas where peasants were particularly dependent on agriculture for their survival. Belorussia and Right-Bank Ukraine were also turbulent, perhaps because they were near the front, and unrest was often prompted by the return of deserting soldiers.[42] Direct action was almost invariably initiated by a general meeting of peasants, and many communities insisted that all adult males should participate in any action decided upon, partly in order to spread the 'mutual responsibility' as widely as possible in case of reprisals, partly to ensure that the ensuing redistribution of property should be equitable. 'If anyone is responsible, then everyone is' (*otvechat'* – *tak vsem*) was a common saying.[43]

Then 'at a selected time, the peasants assembled their carts in front of the church and moved off towards the manor, armed with guns, pitchforks, axes and whatever came to hand. The squire and his stewards, if they had not already fled, were arrested and forced to sign a resolution placing the property of the estate under the control of a village committee. The peasants loaded on to their carts the contents of the barns and led away the cattle, except the property which had been left for the use of the landowners and his family. Pieces of large agricultural machinery, such as harvesters and winnowing machines, which the peasants could not move or could not use on their small farms, were usually abandoned or destroyed.'[44]

This account makes the important point that the peasants had their own procedure for expropriation, which they considered legal. In some villages even landlords, priests and others previously considered 'alien' were drawn into the egalitarian arrangements and allotted land, provided they cultivated it without hired labour.[45] However, much depended on local circumstances. In some areas, especially the central black-earth and mid-Volga regions, the landlord's house, barns and outbuildings were often deliberately demolished as their movable property was removed. The squire and his family might be peacefully transported to the nearest railway station, but if they resisted or attempted to call in reinforcements, they might easily be murdered. In Penza guberniia it was reported that one-fifth of all manor houses had been destroyed during September and October alone. In the face of such pressures, many landowners naturally abandoned their estates, sometimes seen off or even accompanied by tearful domestic servants.[46]

After the expropriations, a partial or general redistribution took place. This happened even in communes which had never, or not for half a century, redistributed land at all. In that way, the revolution actually strengthened communal practices. 'Stolypin peasants' and those who had bought land in addition to their allotments had their private property expropriated and re-integrated into the communal holdings. In that way, the polarization into rich and poor which had been proceeding for decades was halted and even reversed.[47] In some areas, especially in the Volga basin, a so-called 'black repartition' took place: all categories of land, including peasant allotments, were amalgamated into a common pool for redistribution. The amount each household should receive was calculated either 'by eaters', that is, according to the number of mouths each household had to feed or 'by labour', that is, according to the number of working hands available to cultivate the newly obtained soil.[48]

In general, the upheavals of 1917 had given the peasants roughly what they wanted. Their communal institutions had thrown off the supervision of police and bureaucracy, and had taken over and redistributed the land. Whether under the name of 'village soviet' or 'land committee', or simply as the mir, those communal assemblies had taken over power in the countryside. This was not at all what the Bolsheviks had originally intended, but they endorsed it in October [see p. 474] and until the civil war was over, there was little they could do about it.

Overall, then, in the army, the towns and the countryside, we see the attempts to establish a new civic patriotism, based on an alliance between the masses and *obshchestvennost'*, breaking down rapidly under pressure from below, from soldiers, workers and peasants impatient to secure real benefits and to impose their own political will on institutions which had always been unresponsive to them in the past. The process went fastest in the army, where the soldiers swiftly imposed their will on the new committees, and often moved on to mutiny or desertion. In the towns, it was the grass-roots organizations, factory committees and Red Guards, which proved most effective, and they radicalized the soviets from below. In the country-side, peasants first of all obstructed or hi-jacked the Provisional Government's innovations, then proceeded to direct action man-dated by village assemblies. In all cases, the superimposition of politi-cal and economic grievances on deep-seated cultural estrangement created a polarization which was quite insurmountable. By attempting to bridge this gap, the moderate socialists weakened their own morale and split among themselves, leaving the way open for the extreme socialists to capture the people's allegiance.

In taking advantage of this situation, though, the Bolsheviks had to jettison quite a few sacred cows of their own. The notion of lean and disciplined ranks led by 'professional revolutionaries', which Lenin had expounded in *What is to be Done?*, now had to be aban-doned in face of the Bolsheviks' sheer popularity. During the summer and autumn, new members flooded into their organizations, mostly young, working-class and Russian, all impatient at the prevarications or outright betrayal of the other political parties. The slogans of 'Peace, Land and Bread', together with 'All Power to the Soviets', summed up well what attracted their support.

The Bolsheviks had been the first and till October the only party to adopt the slogan 'All Power to the Soviets', which naturally appealed to these eager newcomers. But they differed greatly about how it should be implemented – and for a time even about whether it should be. Party meetings and congresses at all levels, far from simply obeying directives handed down by their intelligentsia leaders, resounded to lively, spontaneous and often fractious debate, degener-ating at times into noisy disagreement. The Bolsheviks were the most successful party in 1917, not because they were tightly disciplined or well led (though it is true they were more skilfully led than their rivals), but rather because they were the most sensitive to the mood of the masses, above all of the workers and soldiers, and their local activists enjoyed high morale and were tactically adroit at directing this mass energy to political ends.[49]

In the factory committees from June onwards, and in the soviets after the Kornilov coup, the Bolsheviks steadily won more and more majorities; they made similar progress in the soldiers' committees, especially among the infantry regiments at the front and in the urban

473

garrisons. As a result, they were able to present their seizure of power as having been conducted in the name of the masses. The instrument of the seizure in Petrograd, the Military Revolutionary Committee, was not a Bolshevik organization, but was created by the Petrograd Soviet as a whole on 16 October, with the support of the soviets of the Northern Region, to organize the defence of the capital against the dual threat of another military coup or of a German attack. Its leadership bureau consisted of three Bolsheviks and two Left Socialist Revolutionaries.[50]

Starting from about 20 October, the MRC took control of the strategic points in the city as a defensive operation, designed to secure the right of the Second All-Russian Congress of Soviets to meet. The final operation began when Kerenskii closed down two Bolshevik newspapers and put out warrants for the re-arrest of some Bolsheviks released on bail after the Kornilov affair. Most participants were under the impression that they were fighting for 'All Power to the Soviets' in the form of a coalition socialist government. However, Lenin was able at the Congress to set up a purely Bolshevik government (or Council of People's Commissars) and gain a mandate for it thanks to support from left-wing SRs, and to a walk-out by most Mensheviks and the remaining SRs.[51] The SRs finally split in two on this occasion, the Left SRs breaking away because they thought support of the Bolsheviks was the best way to promote an immediate peace, the institution of workers' and peasants' democracy through the soviets and the immediate transfer of land to the peasants.[52]

Of the laws which Lenin proposed to the Congress, the most difficult was the Decree on Land. This was the point at which the Marxist tradition was most markedly at odds with the aspirations of the peasants. The Bolsheviks' programme had originally envisaged reorganizing agriculture on an industrial model by nationalizing all land and setting up large collective farms. They abandoned it now in favour of the programme passed by the peasant congress in June, and supported by the Left SRs. Peasant support was absolutely crucial to Lenin at this stage, and to obtain it he was prepared to sponsor what he had previously regarded as a 'petty-bourgeois' revolution in the countryside handing over power and material resources to the village assemblies. 'As a democratic government,' he declared, 'we cannot ignore the decision of the popular masses.'[53]

474

The Bolsheviks thus came to power by promising the people through 'soviet power' what they wanted but had been unable to obtain from the Provisional Government: peace, land, bread, workers' control in the factories, self-determination for the nationalities. More than that, the Bolsheviks seemed to be fulfilling a dream which peasants and workers had harboured for centuries: control over the land and over their own lives. The tragedy was that that dream could only be fulfilled at a time of the total breakdown of authority. In peacetime, under a normal state, it would have been impossible.

But those very conditions also made it impossible for the people to retain the benefits they had gained. The Bolsheviks, in order to consolidate their power, inevitably had to deprive the people of the rewards of their fleeting victory. They promised the people peace, but plunged them into a new and terrible civil war. They promised them bread, but instead generated hunger on a scale not seen for three centuries. They promised them land, but deprived them by force of the fruits of that land. They promised workers' control, but then aggravated the economic breakdown, causing mass unemployment and almost destroying the working-class. They promised soviet power but established a single-party dictatorship, closing down the Constituent Assembly which might have been a counter-weight to it. The soviets proved to be organizations too labile and chaotic to administer a twentieth-century state, especially in such adverse conditions, and fell easily into the hands of the most determined and self-confident political party.

During the civil war, most peasants and workers still on the whole supported the Bolsheviks, if with waning enthusiasm and growing misgivings, simply because they rather than their opponents had actually given them the land. By 1919 and 1920, when mass discontent at the new regime's policies had mounted, some peasants reflected the ambivalence of their own feelings and the confusion aroused by the bewildering succession of events in the despairing and meaningless slogan 'Down with the Communists! Long live the Bolsheviks!'[54]

But either way, the mass of the people did not want the restoration of any kind of old regime. And as for *obshchestvennost'* and the moderate political parties, in these terrible times they scarcely existed any more, crushed and dispersed in the crude struggle between Reds and Whites. Their cherished dream, the Constituent Assembly, had been rudely shut down by the Bolsheviks almost without popular protest: not that workers and peasants exactly supported the closure, but in the fatal narrowing of horizons generated by chaotic conditions their own local assemblies had become far more important to them. The modern state capitulated to primitive communal self-rule.

THE TWILIGHT OF THE POPULAR UTOPIA After the end of the civil war there was a brief final flicker of the ancient popular dream. In the winter of 1920–21 there was a general strike in Petrograd and serious disturbances in Moscow; there were peasant risings in a number of regions, the most serious in Tambov guberniia; and then, most dangerous of all, an armed mutiny among the sailors of the Baltic Fleet stationed on the island garrison of Kronstadt, just outside Petrograd.

Workers, peasants and sailors shared many aspirations in common. First of all, there were economic demands: for the restoration of free trade, an end to grain requisitions and a lifting of the road blocks which had been stationed on the approaches to large towns to prevent peasants bringing in their produce to sell in the market. Then there were political demands: for an 'end to commissarocracy', the restoration of civil rights and of genuine and freely elected soviets, and an amnesty for socialist political prisoners. The workers in addition demanded equal rations for all, and the sailors demanded the abolition of the commissars and political departments which had replaced their elected sailors' committees in the fleet.[55]

These rebels remained hostile to *obshchestvennost'*. For the most part, they were not interested in the Constituent Assembly or in amnesties for liberals. They certainly did not want to see the restoration of private property in the means of production. What they advanced, for the last time, was the age-old vision of an egalitarian democracy of peasants and small producers, free from exploiters and oppressors, and using the land as a common resource.

Lenin quite rightly regarded these risings as a fundamental challenge to his regime. After all, the workers of Petrograd and the Kronstadt sailors had been what Trotskii once called 'the pride and joy of the revolution'. Lenin estimated their rebellion as

476

'undoubtedly more dangerous than Denikin, Iudenich and Kolchak combined'. While making economic concessions to them, he took the opportunity at the Tenth Party Congress to frighten his colleagues into banning freedom of speech within the party and giving the Central Committee complete control over party discipline. Thereafter serious political opposition, even of a peaceful nature, soon became impossible even inside the party, let alone outside it.

The people's last challenge thus impelled the party to put the final struts of the totalitarian framework into place. The Communist Party, now becoming a new kind of imperial regime of even greater ruthlessness than its predecessor, rested on nothing more substantial than its own internal discipline and the remains of a peasant tradition of local democracy which it would soon destroy. As before, between the people and the empire there was no room for the nation.

Conclusions

The Russian Empire fell apart in 1917 along fault-lines which were inherent in its situation as an empire with extensive vulnerable borders straddling Europe and Asia. For more than three centuries its structures had been those of a multi-ethnic service state, not those of an emerging nation. Social hierarchy and status were shaped by the need to provide the sinews of that empire, through taxation, recruitment, administration and military command. The economy was deflected from productive purposes to sustain the army and the administrative apparatus. A nobility was maintained in expensive non-productivity, absorbing an alien culture to guarantee Russia's status as European great power.

Most damaging of all, perhaps, Russia's church was compelled to renounce its function as guarantor of the national myth to become the marginalized prop of an activist secular state. A messianic national myth which had demonstrated its viability in the crises of the sixteenth and seventeenth centuries was spurned in favour of a cosmopolitan Enlightenment project which required all the refinements of the 'well-ordered police state'.

All these structural changes, long in preparation, were given their final form by Peter the Great. He consolidated the cardinal divide between the 'service people' and the 'taxed people', a divide which touched all aspects of life, from language, culture and outlook to concepts of law, property and authority. Russians and non-Russians were to be found on both sides of the divide, especially at the very top and very base of the hierarchy.

For much of the eighteenth and nineteenth centuries the army was the cement which held this society together. It took serfs, emancipated them and remoulded them into citizens of a kind, with a consciousness of fighting for Tsar, faith and fatherland. That is why nearly all Tsars identified so strongly with the army. But that achievement could be sustained only at the terrible cost of separating the former serfs from their home villages, in other words of tearing the social fabric apart.

The nobility were the principal stakeholders in the cosmopolitan imperial project, as military commanders, diplomats and officials of central and local administration. They found it expedient to acquire a Europeanized culture and way of life, and in time came to appreciate it for its own sake, not just as a mark of status. But when some nobles tried to take its ideals seriously they came into collision with the imperial state which still fundamentally required Asiatic satraps rather than European gentlemen. To the rift between elites and people was added the rift between elites and regime.

After the Crimean defeat, Russia's rulers realized the need to turn the empire into something more like the nation-states which were proving so successful in Europe. They attempted two approaches to this problem, which we may characterize as civic and ethnic, but they never solved it because they felt unable to relinquish the authority structures which had held the empire together in earlier days. For the *sosloviia* (social estates defined by their relationship to the service state) to have redefined themselves as classes (defined by their relationship to the means of production) and as members of a civic nation would have required a re-conceptualization of the purposes of the state which was never undertaken, and perhaps could not be undertaken in Russia's geo-political situation. Sergei Witte, who as Minister of Finance was in the best position to discern the economic destruction wrought by empire, lamented that 'the mistake we have been making for many decades is that we have still not admitted to ourselves that since the time of Peter the Great and Catherine the Great there has been no such thing as Russia: there has been only the Russian Empire.'[1]

The authorities tried for a time to transform the empire into 'Russia' by the process of Russification: compelling ethnic non-Russians to accept the Russian language, the Russian religion, Russian laws and administrative structures, and/or an influx of Russian immigrants. None of these processes started in the late nineteenth century, but they were then reformulated into a more or less consistent government policy, pursued with the conscious aim of imparting to a jeopardized empire the adhesive of a single ethnic identity.

As the development of the economy brought the social estates into closer association with each other during the later decades of the nineteenth century, their juridical distance from one another and the failure to create institutions which would have enabled them to interact became more and more damaging. The urban workers were at the sharp end of this incongruity. Still defined by the state as peasants or *meshchane*, fixed for taxation and recruitment purposes, and without rights to participate in politics or even in the settlement of industrial disputes, they made their inputs instead by illegal strikes, demonstrations or acts of violence. The peasants, brought closer to urban culture both by their own 'outworkers' and by professional people working in the countryside, strove to appropriate the benefits of urban politics for themselves, to create a space at least within their own villages where they could both govern themselves and regulate their own land tenure in accordance with their view of authority, law and tradition. They too were prepared to use violence to attain their ends when peaceful means led nowhere.

If in the seventeenth and eighteenth centuries peasants and workers had looked for leadership to the Cossacks, with their free-booting way of life, their *vol'nitsa* and their self-governing military communities, by the early twentieth century it was increasingly the 'intelligentsia', the disaffected professional people, to whom they turned, especially those who had reforged the messianic vision of the nation's destiny in the form of Populist or Marxist socialism.

Meanwhile professional people tried to assert what they saw as their political rights, some nobles tried (but failed) to redefine themselves as commercial landowners, and merchants and industrialists chafed at what they regarded as a political impotence grotesquely at odds with their fast growing economic significance. The Duma, especially after the electoral law was changed in 1907, offered a forum which partly satisfied the nobility, but no other social estate or class as a means of feeding their aspirations into the system.

Ironically, it was the during the first world war, at the time of greatest danger to Russia, that the best opportunity arose to forge a closer ethnic and civic unity. The very process of war drew people of all social classes into a more acute awareness of 'Russia' as their community whose survival needed to be defended. The failure then to give institutional form to the outline of a civic nation taking shape in Zemgor and the War Industry Committees doomed the monarchy to alienation from even its normally most loyal supporters, the largest landowners and the senior officer corps. In the critical days of late-February/early March 1917 it found almost no supporters.

The regime which replaced it in March 1917 also reflected the age-old fault-lines in the empire's social structure. There was not just one revolutionary authority, but two, one representing *obshchestvennost'*, the professional strata, the other the *narod*, the workers, peasants and soldiers – still a distant reminder of the old dichotomy between 'service people' and 'taxable people'. Neither authority could claim undivided support on its own, and the attempt of the two to work together left the *narod* dissatisfied, opening up a political vacuum which the Bolsheviks, with their own vision of 'soviet power', could occupy.

Afterthoughts
on the Soviet Experience

It may help to understand the evolution of Russian national identity in the twentieth century if one contrasts it with the experience of a neighbour. After the first world war the Turks disengaged themselves from the Ottoman Empire, where they had ostensibly but not actually been the principal nationality, turned their backs on the universalist doctrine of Islam (at least in its political expression), and set up their own nation-state under the leadership of Kemal Ataturk. Russians did precisely the opposite: after the collapse of the Russian Empire, they did not create a nation-state, but, under the leadership of Lenin, reconstituted their empire under the banner of an even more all-embracing universalist doctrine. In 1922, the year of the establishment of the new Turkey, Russia became part of the Union of Soviet Socialist Republics, perhaps still in some sense a Russian Empire, but one which did not even bear the name of Russia.

From then until 1991 the Russian Soviet Federated Socialist Republic was much the largest one within the Soviet Union, but in certain respects it was actually disadvantaged: it did not have its own capital city, its own radio and television, its own national encyclopedia or Academy of Sciences, nor until the very end its own Communist Party – attributes enjoyed by all other republics. Russian national institutions were dissolved in imperial Soviet ones. Furthermore, unlike the Tsars, the Communists encouraged, at least initially, the emergence of non-Russian national consciousness, as a counterbalance to Russian chauvinism, and as a necessary stage on the way to proletarian internationalism. They created ethnically-named territorial administrative units – the Ukrainian Soviet Socialist Republic, the Bashkir Autonomous Soviet Socialist Republic, and so on – something which the Tsars had always avoided doing. They consciously trained and promoted indigenous cadres to run those republics – a policy known as *korenizatsiia*. From 1932 every Soviet citizen's nationality was entered in his passbook, as an unchangeable and essentially racist category.

Russian national identity seemed even more deeply buried than under the Tsars. Yet this appearance was partly deceptive. As early as the Treaty of Brest-Litovsk in March 1918 Lenin tacitly abandoned the goal of immediate world revolution and fell back on the policy of protecting fortress Russia as the headquarters of the international proletarian movement. Thereafter internationalism became unmistakably Russian-tinged. As Karl Radek, secretary of the Communist International, said in 1920, 'Since Russia is the only country where the working-class has taken power, the workers of the whole world ought now to become Russian patriots.' Nationalism and internationalism were inextricably intertwined as much as in the days of 'Moscow the Third Rome'.

Stalin pushed the scales heavily in favour of Russian nationalism. 'Socialism in one country' came to mean primarily Russian socialism. Under Stalin the leadership of the Soviet Communist Party, the armed forces and the secret police was largely Russianized. In the course of the first Five Year Plans Russians, both as specialists and as manual workers, were resettled in large numbers in the non-Russian republics. Indigenous non-Russian cadres would be accused of 'bourgeois nationalism', purged and replaced by appointees more obedient to Moscow. The symbols of Russia's historical identity were revived, and the victories of the Tsarist army were once again glorified in the schools.

The glories and disasters of Stalinism lay bare the paradoxes of Russian national identity. Stalin was indisputably in some sense a Russian nationalist, arguably the most successful ever. Yet in another sense, as Alexander Solzhenitsyn has persuasively argued, he did his best to destroy everything that was most quintessentially Russian. Under him the neo-Russian *Empire* attained its apogee as one of the world's two superpowers, while simultaneously the Russian *nation* was reduced to its most abject prostration. The peasant community (*mir*) was destroyed, the Russian Orthodox Church was devastated, the best of Russian literature, art and music was suppressed, and millions of Russians were uprooted and relocated in raw new 'melting-pot' industrial towns, where different ethnic groups lived elbow to elbow. And that is to say nothing of the Gulag Archipelago, where, according to Solzhenitsyn, a whole new 'nation' of *zeks* (inmates) was created, a kind of caricature of proletarian internationalism. The whole Stalinist experience reaffirms in hobnailed boots what has been the thesis of this book: that for Russians imperial greatness can be achieved only at the cost of stunted nationhood.

After Stalin the Russian-tinged internationalism of the Soviet Union began to unravel. *Korenizatsiia* got stuck halfway on the road to proletarian internationalism: once the threat of Stalin's purges was removed, the indigenous cadres began gradually and unostentatiously to build little embryo nations in the non-Russian republics. Russians living among them started to feel increasingly out of place in what they had thought of as their own homeland: some even began to leave, especially the Central Asian republics.

The post-Stalin decades witnessed some degree of ethnic disentanglement: peoples who had been jumbled together in army barracks, building sites and labour camps began to dissociate themselves, gradually but unmistakably. The number of Soviet citizens speaking Russian as their main language began to fall, the number of mixed marriages declined, the incidence of ethnic conflicts within the Soviet Army increased. Russians and non-Russians alike set about exploring their own history, religion and folklore.

National dissent made its appearance, directed against the Soviet state and the Soviet Communist Party, now seen as imperial exploiters of a familiar kind. This was true even of Russians who, underground and sometimes discreetly in the official media too, began to assert Russian-ness *against* the Soviet state or at least the Soviet Communist Party. The fashion for 'village prose' bore witness to a nostalgia for traditional Russian values implicitly at odds with the official ethos of internationalism and modernization.

Contrary to its professed aims, the Soviet state thus ended by preparing the way in the 1990s for the emergence of new nation-states where none had previously existed, except in the most primitive and fleeting of forms. This was true at least of the non-Russians. But what of the Russians? One cannot say that, as it stands, the post-1991 Russian Federation is really a nation-state. It is more a bleeding hulk of empire: what happened to be left over when the other republics broke away.

The problem is not so much that it contains a large number of non-Russians. The figure is about 17%, and many nation-states function perfectly well with ethnic minorities on that scale. Rather the problem is that some twenty-five million Russians (and several million more Russian-speakers, not necessarily the same thing) remain outside its framework, suddenly transformed into 'foreigners' in what they were accustomed to regard as their homeland. Besides, nearly all Russians are used to the borders of the USSR: they find it especially difficult to take Ukraine, Belorussia and much of Kazakhstan seriously as foreign countries. If, as Ernest Renan used to say, a nation is a 'daily plebiscite', that is a tacit day-to-day agreement to live together in community, then most Russians would wish to exercise their putative voting rights within borders different from those of the current Russian Federation.

Yet, in spite of everything, the Soviet state did do something to prepare the way for the creation of a Russian nation. Its education system generated the pre-conditions for healing the rift between Russian elites and Russian masses by inculcating universal literacy on the basis of a Leninized version of the old imperial culture. (The attempt to create a special 'proletarian culture' was abandoned quite early on.) More brutally, the Soviet state dismantled social barriers in other ways too: by destroying the segregated peasant community and with it much of the old popular culture, and by mixing people of all strata together in the armed forces, the labour camps and the communal apartments. As a result, Russians have today a more or less homogeneous culture, though one which still has about it the whiff of scorched earth and barbed wire. Without an accompanying civic awareness it can only go a certain way towards giving them the feeling of belonging to one nation.

The rift which remains is that between the political elites, joined now by a nouveau-riche business elite, and the masses. Between the two sides there is little or no sense of common citizenship only mutual suspicion and, from below, a bewildered and cynical resentment. The 1993 constitution, imperfect though it is, does at least provide a framework within which a civic culture might be created, and restrains – up to the time of writing – the various political factions from settling their differences in a naked power struggle.

Russians are closer today to nationhood than they have ever been, but the question still remains open whether they can decide who should belong to that nation and what its boundaries should be, and whether a political system can be created which gives all or most of them a feeling of having some stake in it.

Is it even wise for them to become a nation in an age when many commentators feel we are moving 'beyond the nation-state'? I believe, however, that the nation-state will be with us for a long time yet, partly as a counter-weight to the globalization of our economies. In any case, most Russians feel a strong yearning for legitimate authority and greater social cohesion. A strong national identity still provides the simplest way to achieve both. It will not be created in Russia, however, without turbulence which will affect neighbouring countries. Minimizing this turbulence without insulting and belittling the Russians remains one of the major problems facing the international community today.

Chronology

Ivan IV 1533–1584

1549	Council of Reconciliation
1550	Publication of the 'Thousand Book'
1551	Stoglav Church Council
1552	Conquest of Kazan'
1556	Conquest of Astrakhan'
1557–1582	Livonian War
1564	Flight of Kurbskii; establishment of *oprichnina*
1570	Sacking of Novgorod
1571	Crimean Tatars sack Moscow
1581–2	Ermak conquers Khanate of Siberia

Fedor I 1584–1598

1589	Establishment of Moscow Patriarchate

Boris Godunov 1598–1605

Time of Troubles 1604–1613

1611	Formation of a popular militia under Pozharskii
1612	The militia relieves Moscow and drives out the Poles
1613	A *zemskii sobor* elects Mikhail Romanov as Tsar

Mikhail Fedorovich 1613–1645

1639	The first Cossacks reach the Pacific coast

Aleksei Mikhailovich 1645–1676

1649	A *zemskii sobor* adopts a Law Code (*Ulozhenie*)
1652	Nikon becomes Patriarch
1653	He begins the first reforms of the liturgy and scriptures
1654–1667	War with Poland for suzerainty of Ukraine, ending in Treaty of Andrusovo, in which Muscovy gained the eastern Ukraine, Kiev and Smolensk
1658	Nikon lays down the Patriarchate
1666–7	A Church Council anathematizes those who refuse to accept the reforms
1670–1	Major peasant rebellion in the south-east, led by Stepan Razin

Fedor Alekseevich 1676–1682

Peter I 1682–1725 (Until 1689 jointly with Ivan V)

1689	Treaty of Nerchinsk marks the border between Russia and China
1695–6	Two campaigns against Azov, the second successful
1697–8	Peter's European journey – revolt of *strel'tsy*
1700	Great Northern War against Sweden:
1700	Defeat at Narva
1709	Victory at Poltava
1721	Treaty of Nystadt, by which Russia acquired the Baltic provinces
1703	Foundation of St Petersburg
1711	Establishment of Senate
1718	Establishment of Colleges
1721	Establishment of Holy Synod
1722	Institution of Table of Ranks
1723	Introduction of poll tax

Catherine I 1725–1727

1726	Opening of Academy of Sciences

Peter II 1727–1730

Anna 1730–1740

Ivan VI 1740–1741

Elizabeth 1741–1762

1753	Abolition of internal customs duties
1755	Establishment of Moscow University

Peter III 1762–1763

1762	Emancipation of nobility from compulsory service

Catherine II 1762–1796

1764	Secularization of church lands
1767–8	Law Code Commission
1768–1774	War with the Ottoman Empire, ending with the Treaty of Kuchuk Kainardji
1769	Introduction of paper money (*assignaty*)
1772, 1793, 1795	The three partitions of Poland
1773–5	Pugachev revolt
1775	Reform of provincial administration: creation of *gubernii* and *uezdy*
1783	Russia incorporates the Crimea
1785	Charter of the Nobility; Charter of the Cities
1786	Statute of Popular Schools
1787–92	War with the Ottoman Empire, ending with the Treaty of Jassy, which brought the Russian frontier up to the River Dniester
1792	Foundation of city of Odessa

Paul I 1796–1801

Alexander I 1801–1825

1801	Russia annexes Georgia (which had been under Russian protection since 1783)
1803	'Preliminary Regulation for Public Education'

1804–13　War with Persia; annexation of Georgia confirmed and other territory acquired in the Transcaucasus

1805–7　War of the Third Coalition against France, concluding with the Treaty of Tilsit, by which Russia and France became allies

1806–9　War against the Ottoman Empire, ending with the Treaty of Bucharest, by which Russian acquired Bessarabia

1808–9　War against Sweden, ending with the acquisition of Finland

1810　Establishment of State Council and Ministries

1812　Invasion of Russia by Napoleon

1815　Congress of Vienna and creation of the Holy Alliance; establishment of Congress Kingdom of Poland under Russian rule

1816　Creation of combined Ministry of Spiritual Affairs under Prince Golitsyn; founder of the first secret societies

1818　Appearance of New Testament in Russian

1821　Alexander bans Freemasonry

1824　Dismissal of Golitsyn

1825　Death of Alexander and Decembrist rising

Nicholas I 1825–1855

1826–8　War with Persia, ending with Treaty of Turkmanchai: Russia secures parts of Armenia, including Erevan'

1828–9　War with Ottoman Empire, ending with Treaty of Adrianople, under which Russia received the coast of the Black Sea as far as the mouth of the Danube

1830–1　Polish revolt

1832　Publication of a new Law Code

1836　Chaadaev's 'First Philosophical Letter' appears in *Teleskop*

1848　Revolutions in Central Europe; establishment of Buturlin Committee to tighten censorship

1849　Arrest of Petrashevskii circle; the Russian army suppresses the revolution in Hungary

1853–6　Crimean War, ending with Treaty of Paris, under which Russia had to accept neutralization of the Black Sea

Alexander II 1855–1881

1858　Treaty of Aigun settled the Russian-Chinese border along the Amur River

1861　Emancipation of the serfs

1863	University Statute
1863–4	Polish revolt
1864	Establishment of zemstvos; judicial reform
1865	New censorship regulations
1865–76	Russian advance in Central Asia: conquest of the Khanates of Kokand and Khiva and Emirate of Bukhara
1866	Attempt by Karakozov on the life of the Tsar
1870	Reform of municipal government
1871	Abrogation of the Black Sea clauses of the Treaty of Paris
1873–4	The climax of the 'going to the people' movement
1874	Army reform: introduction of universal military service
1876	Formation of *Zemlia i volia*
1877–8	War against Ottoman Empire, ending with the Treaty of San Stefano, revised at the Congress of Berlin
1879	Formation of *Narodnaia volia*
1880	Establishment of a Supreme Commission under General Loris-Melikov, to coordinate the struggle against terrorism
1881	Assassination of Alexander II

Alexander III 1881–1894

1882	The May Laws, discriminating further against Jews
1884	New, more restrictive University Statute
1889	Introduction of *zemskie nachal'niki* (land commandants)
1890	More restrictive legislation on zemstvos
1891–2	Famine in the Volga basin
1891–4	Negotiation of the Franco-Russian Alliance

Nicholas II 1894–1917

1898	Formation of Social Democratic Party, which split into Bolsheviks and Mensheviks at its second congress (1903)
1901	Formation of Socialist Revolutionary Party
1903	Formation of Union of Liberation Completion of single-track Trans-Siberian Railway
1904	Assassination of Pleve (Minister of the Interior) by the Fighting Detachment of the SRs
1904–5	War with Japan
1905	January Bloody Sunday in St Petersburg

August   Peace with Japan

October   General strike; establishment of St Petersburg Soviet (and others); Tsar issues a 'manifesto establishing an elective legislative assembly (Duma) and granting civil rights

December   Workers' insurrection in Moscow

1906   April   Convening of First Duma

July   Dissolution of First Duma; Vyborg Appeal

November   Stolypin issues main agrarian decree under Article 87

1907   February-June   Second Duma, also dissolved prematurely

June   New electoral law

November   Convening of Third Duma

1908   Austrian annexation of Bosnia-Herzegovina

1911   Assassination of Stolypin

1914   August   Outbreak of First World War

Loss of the Battle of Tannenberg

1915   May   Defeat in Galicia; loss of Poland

Summer   Attempt to set up a Progressive Bloc government fails

1916   December   Murder of Rasputin

1917   Feb–February–March   Revolution in Petrograd; abdication of Nicholas II; establishment of Provincial Government and soviets

Notes

Introduction

1 M. N. Tikhomirov, 'O proiskhozhdenii nazvaniia "Rossii"', *Voprosy Istorii*, 1953, no. 11, 93–96.

2 Georgii Gachev, *Russkaia duma: portrety russkikh myslitelei*, Moscow: Novosti, 1991, 150–151.

3 The best of them is Andreas Kappeler, *Russland als Vielvölkerreich: Entstehung, Geschichte, Zerfall*, Munich: Verlag C.H. Beck, 1992. This present book may be seen as an attempt to continue Kappeler's work in tracing the development of the Russian empire, but reversing his priorities, that is giving more attention to the Russians than to the non-Russians.

4 E.J. Hobsbawm, *Nations and Nationalism since 1780: programme, myth and reality*, 2nd edition, Cambridge University Press, 1992, 18–23; Liah Greenfeld, *Nationalism: five roads to modernity*, Harvard University Press, 1993, 9–12; Edward Shils, 'Nation, nationality, nationalism and civil society', *Nations and Nationalism*, vol. 1 (1995), 93–118.

5 Charles Tilly, *Coercion, Capital and European States, AD 990–1992*, Oxford: Blackwell, 1992, 160. See also Michael Mann, *The Sources of Social Power, vol. 2, The rise of classes and nation-states, 1760–1914*, Cambridge University Press, 1993, especially chapter 7.

6 Karl Deutsch, *Nationalism and Social Communication: an enquiry into the foundations of nationality*, 2nd edition, Cambridge: Massachusetts, MIT Press, 1966; Ernest Gellner, *Nations and Nationalism*, Oxford: Blackwell, 1983; John Breuilly, *Nationalism and the State*, Manchester University Press, 1982; Benedict Anderson, *Imagined Communities: reflections on the origin and spread of nationalism*, London: Verso, 1983; W.H. McNeill, *Polyethnicity and National Unity in World History*, Toronto University Press, 1986.

7 Ernest Gellner, *Nations and Nationalism*, 48, 55.

8 Anthony D. Smith, *The Ethnic Origins of Nations*, Oxford: Blackwell, 1986, and *National Identity*, Harmondsworth: Penguin Books, 1991; John Armstrong, *Nations before Nationalism*, Chapel Hill: University of North Carolina Press, 1982. On the role of warfare, see especially Anthony D. Smith, 'war and ethnicity: the role of warfare in the formation, self-images and cohesion of ethnic communities', *Ethnic and Racial Studies*, vol. 4 (1981), 375–397. The debate is well summarized in John Hutchinson, *Modern Nationalism*, London: Fontana Press, 1994, chapter 1.

9 Benedict Anderson, *Imagined Communities: reflections on the origin and spread of nationalism*, London: Verso, 1983, especially 47–49; Michael Mann offers an interesting commentary on this idea in *The rise of classes and nation-states*, 35–39.

10 Eric Hobsbawm, 'Introduction: inventing traditions', in Eric Hobsbawm & Terence Ranger (eds), *The Invention of Tradition*, Cambridge University Press, 1983, 1–14.

11 Miroslav Hroch, *Social Preconditions of National Revival in Europe*, Cambridge University Press, 1985.

12 Charles Tilly, 'Reflections on the history of European state-making' in Charles Tilly (ed.), *The Formation of National States in Western Europe*, Princeton University Press, 1975, 3–83; John Breuilly, *Nationalism and the State*, Manchester University Press, 1982, shows how dependent national movements are on the state and existing political structures, even when they are in ostensible opposition to them.

13 V.O. Kliuchevskii, 'Kurs russkoi istorii', *Sochineniia*, Moscow, 1957, vol. 3.

14 Smith, *National Identity*, 54–68: see also his article 'State-making and nation building', in John A. Hall (ed.), *States in History*, Oxford: Blackwell, 1986, 228–263.

15 See for example Mathew Horsman and Andrew Marshall, *After the Nation-State: citizens, tribalism and the new world disorder*, London: HarperCollins, 1994.

PART ONE The Russian Empire: How and Why?

1 *Polnoe sobranie russkikh letopisei*, vol. 29, Moscow, 1965, 108.

2 The Mongols briefly had a larger one, but it fell apart very swiftly compared with its Russian successor.

3 *Polnoe sobranie*, 108.

4 Quoted from Cyril Toumanoff, 'Moscow the Third Rome: genesis and significance of a politico-religious idea', *Catholic Historical Review*, vol. 40, no. 4 (January 1955), 438; for the dating and purpose of Filofei's epistle, see N. Andreyev, 'Filofei and his epistle to Ivan Vasilievich', *Slavonic & East European Review*, vol. 38 (1959–60), 1–31.

5 A.V. Kartashev, *Ocherki po istorii russkoi tserkvi*, Moscow: Terra, 1993, vol. 1, 431–433.

6 David B. Miller, 'The velikie minei chetii and the stepennaia kniga of Metropolitan Makarii and the origins of Russian national consciousness', *Forschungen zur osteuropäischen Geschichte*, vol. 26 (1979), 263–382.

7 Jaroslaw Pelenski, *Russia and Kazan: conquest and imperial ideology (1438–1560s)*, The Hague-Paris: Mouton, 1974.

8 Michael Cherniavsky, 'Khan or basileus: an aspect of Russian medieval political theory', *Journal of the History of Ideas*, vol.20, no.4 (Oct.–Dec. 1959), 455–476; quotation on 476.

9 John H. Kautsky, *The Politics of Aristocratic Empires*, Chapel Hill: University of North Carolina Press, 1982, 72–75.

10 Andreas Kappeler, *Russlands erste Nationalitäten: das Zarenreich und die Völker der mittleren Volga vom 16 bis zum 19ten Jahrhundert*, Köln-Wien: Böhlau Verlag, 1982, sections E and F.

11 Valerii Chalidze, *Ugolovnaia Rossiia*, New York: Khronika, 1977, Part 1; Stephen Handelman, *Comrade Criminal: the theft of the*

second Russian Revolution, London: Michael Joseph, 1994, chapter 2.

12 David Collins, 'Russia's conquest of Siberia: evolving Russian and Soviet historical interpretations', *European Studies Review*, vol.12, no. 1 (Jan. 1982), 17–44; Henry Huttenbach, 'Muscovy's penetration of Siberia: the colonisation process, 1555–1689', in Michael Rywkin (ed.), *Russian Colonial Expansion to 1917*, London: Mansell, 1988, 70–102.

13 Andreas Kappeler, *Russland als Vielvölkerreich: Entstehung, Geschichte, Zerfall*, Munich: Verlag C. H. Beck, 1992, 40.

14 David Collins, 'Subjugation and settlement in 17th and 18th century Siberia', in Alan Wood (ed.), *The History of Siberia: from Russian conquest to revolution*, London: Routledge, 1991, 41–46.

15 Collins, in Wood, *History of Siberia*, 47–49.

16 Kappeler, 43–45: Alton Donnelly, 'The mobile steppe frontier: the Russian conquest and colonization of Bashkiria and Kazakhstan to 1850', in Rywkin, 189–207.

17 Alan Fisher, *The Crimean Tatars*, Stanford, California: Hoover Institution Press, 1978, chapters 3–5.

18 William C. Fuller, Jr., *Strategy and Power in Russia, 1600–1914*, New York: The Free Press, 1992, 31–33, 110–111.

19 Fuller, 94–6; Richard Hellie, *Enserfment and Military Change in Muscovy*, Chicago University Press, 1971.

20 Fisher, chapters 6–8.

21 General Rostislav Fadeev, *Shestdesiat let kavkazkoi voiny*, Tiflis, 1860, 8–9.

22 Rywkin, 145.

23 R.G. Suny, 'The emergence of political society in Georgia', in Suny (ed.), *Transcaucasia: nationalism and social change*, Ann Arbor: University of Michigan Press, 1983, 109–140.

24 R.G. Suny, *The Making of the Georgian Nation*, 2nd edition, Bloomington: Indiana University Press, 1994, 114.

25 R. G. Hovannisian, 'Russian Armenia: a century of Tsarist rule', *Jahrbücher fur Geschichte Osteuropas*, vol.19 (1971), 31–48; Christopher J. Walker, *Armenia: the survival of a nation*, London: Croom Helm, 1980, chapter 2; R. G. Suny, *Looking to Ararat*, chapter 1.

26 F. Kazemzadeh, 'Russian penetration of the Caucasus', in T. Hunczak (ed.), *Russian Imperialism from Ivan the Great to the Revolution*, New Brunswick, NJ: Rutgers University Press, 1974, 247–8; Uwe Halbach, '"Heiliger Krieg" gegen den Zarismus', in A. Kappeler, G. Simon, G. Brunner (eds), *Die Muslime in der Sowjetunion und in Jugoslavien*, Cologne: Markus Verlag, 1989, 213–234.

27 Kazemzadeh, 256–7.

28 E. Willis Brooks, 'Nicholas I as reformer: Russian attempts to conquer the Caucasus, 1825–1855', in Ivo Banac (ed.), *Nation and Ideology: essays in honor of Wayne S. Vucinich*, Boulder, Colorado: East European Monographs, 1981, 227–263: Paul B. Henze, 'Fire and sword in the Caucasus: the 19th century resistance of the North Caucasian mountaineers', *Central Asian Survey*, vol.2, no.1 (July 1983), 5–44.

29 Fuller, 275; Moshe Gammer, 'Russian strategies in the conquest of Chechnia and Daghestan', in Marie Bennigsen Broxup. *The North Caucasus Barrier: the Russian advance*

towards the Muslim world, London: Hurst, 1992, 45–61.

30 Kappeler, 153.

31 William McNeill, *Europe's Steppe Frontier, 1500–1800*, Chicago University Press, 1964.

32 The early history of Ukraine is well treated in Orest Subtelny, *A History of Ukraine*, University of Toronto Press, 1988.

33 Subtelny, chapter 8; 'left-bank Ukraine' is the area west of the Dnieper.

34 Zenon E. Kohut, 'Ukraine: from autonomy to integration (1654–1830s)', in Mark Greengrass (ed.), *Conquest and Coalescence: the shaping of the state in early modern Europe*, London: Edward Arnold, 1991, 184–5.

35 Orest Subtelny, *The Mazepists: Ukrainian separatism in the early eighteenth century*, Columbia University Press, (East European Monographs, no. 87), 1981, 25–47.

36 Zenon E. Kohut, *Russian Centralism and Ukrainian Autonomy: imperial absorption of the Hetmanate, 1760s–1830s*, Harvard University Press, 1988.

37 George F. Jewsbury, *The Russian Annexation of Bessarabia, 1774–1828: a study of imperial expansion*, Boulder: East European Quarterly, 1976.

38 Norman Davies, *God's Playground*, Oxford: Clarendon Press, 1982, vol. 1, chapter 10.

39 *Polnoe sobranie zakonov Rossiiskoi Imperii*, vol. 23, 410, no.17108.

40 Piotr. S. Wandycz, *The Lands of Partitioned Poland, 1795–1918*, Seattle: University of Washington Press, 1974, 11, 17.

41 Norman Davies, *Heart of Europe: a short history of Poland*, Oxford: Clarendon Press, 1984, 202.

42 M. Kukiel, *Czartoryski and European Unity, 1770–1861*, Princeton University Press, 1955, 44–50.

43 Wandycz, 74–5; Janet Hartley, *Alexander I*, London: Longman, 1994, 166.

44 Wandycz, 74–79, 87–91.

45 R.F. Leslie, *Polish Politics and the Revolution of 1830*, London: Athlone Press, 1956.

46 Wandycz, 122–125.

47 R.F. Leslie, *Reform and Insurrection in Poland, 1856–1865*, London: Athlone Press, 1963.

48 John Doyle Klier, *Russia Gathers her Jews: the origins of the 'Jewish question' in Russia, 1772–1825*, Dekalb: Northern Illinois University Press, 1986, 56. This section is based on Klier's book, plus Louis Greenberg, *The Jews in Russia: the struggle for emancipation*, 2 vols, New York: Schocken Books, 1976, and Heinz-Dietrich Löwe, *The Tsars and the Jews: reform, reaction and anti-Semitism in Imperial Russia*, Chur: Harwood Academic Publishers, 1993.

49 *PSZ*, I, vol. 28, 731–737, no 21547.

50 Klier, 145.

51 The Estonians, for example, called themselves simply *maarahvas*, or 'country people', while the word *saks*, meaning German, they normally used in the sense of 'lord' or 'master': see E.J. Hobsbawm, *Nations and Nationalism since 1780: programme, myth, reality*, Cambridge University Press, 1990, 48–49.

52 Reinhard Wittram, *Baltische Geschichte: die Ostseelande Livland, Estland, Kurland, 1180–1918*, Munich: Verlag R. Oldenburg, 1954, 128.

53 Erik Amburger, *Geschichte der Behördenorganisation Russlands von Peter dem Grossen bis 1917*, Leiden: E.J. Brill, 1966, 502, 510, 516–519;

see Walter Laqueur, *Russia and Germany*, London: Weidenfeld & Nicolson, 1965, 40–41, for their percentage in high officialdom by the early nineteenth century.

54 Eino Jutikkala, *A history of Finland*, London: Thames & Hudson, 1962, chapters 7–8.

55 S.S. Tatishchev, *Imperator Aleksandr II: ego zhizn' i tsarstvovanie*, St Petersburg, 1903, vol. 2, 115–116.

56 Dietrich Geyer, *Russian Imperialism: the interaction of domestic and foreign policy, 1860–1914*, London: Berg, 1987, 86–100.

57 In my conclusions, as well as in everything I have written about the empire, I owe a great deal to Andreas Kappeler, *Russland als Vielvölkerreich: Entstehung, Geschichte, Zerfall*, München: C.H. Beck Verlag, 1992, and to two articles, Marc Raeff, 'Patterns of Russian imperial policy towards the nationalities', in E. Allworth (ed.), *Soviet Nationality Problems*, New York: Columbia University Press, 1971, 22–42, and S.F. Starr, 'Tsarist government: the imperial dimension', in J.R. Azrael, (ed.), *Soviet Nationality Policies and Practices*, New York: Praeger, 1978, 3–38.

58 N.M. Karamzin, *Istoriia gosudarstva rossiiskogo*, Moscow: Nauka, 1989, vol.1, 14–15.

PART TWO State-Building

1 *The First Crises of Empire*

1 S. M. Solov'ev, 'Vzgliad na istoriiu ustanovleniia gosudarstvennogo poriadka v Rossii do Petra Velikogo', in his *Izbrannye trudy. Zapiski*, Moscow: Izdatel'stvo moskovskogo universiteta, 1983, 5–34.

2 Robert O. Crummey, *The Formation of Muscovy, 1304–1613*, London: Longman, 1987, 101–110.

3 Nancy Shields Kollman, *Kinship and Politics: the making of the Muscovite political system, 1345–1547*, Stanford University Press, 1987, especially pp. 146–161.

4 Werner Philipp, *Ivan Peresvetov und seine Schriften zur Erneuerung des Moskauer Reiches (Osteuropäische Forschungen*, neue Folge, Band 20), Königsberg, 1935, 1–10.

5 A.A. Kizevetter, *Mestnoe samoupravlenie v Rossii IX-XIX stoletii*, Petrograd, 1917 (reprinted The Hague/Paris: Mouton, 1974), 40–69. Kizevetter comments that by the seventeenth century 'the *mir* had ceased to be a freely self-governing association, and had become an auxiliary administrative apparatus subordinated to the voevoda':[69].

6 R.G. Skrynnikov, *Tretii Rim*, St Petersburg: Izdanie Dmitriia Bulanina, 1994, 101.

7 V.O. Kliuchevskii, 'Sostav predstavitel'stva na zemskikh soborakh drevnei Rusi', *Sochineniia*, vol. 8, Moscow, 1959, 5–112; L.V. Cherepnin, *Zemskie sobory russkogo gosudarstva v xvi-xvii vv.*, Moscow: Nauka, 1978, 55–115. J. Pelenski suggests that the model for these assemblies may have been the Mongol-Turkic *qurultai*, gatherings where the Khan consulted with his military chiefs and service nobles: see his 'State and society in Muscovite Russia and the Mongol-Turkic system in the sixteenth century', *Forschungen zur osteuropäischen Geschichte*, Band 27 (1980), 156–167.

8 A.A. Zimin, A.L. Khoroshevich, *Rossiia vremeni Ivana Groznogo*, Moscow: Nauka, 1982, 46–58;

R.G. Skrynnikov, *Ivan Groznyi*, Moscow: Nauka, 1975, 56–64.

9 A.V. Kartashev, *Ocherki po istorii Russkoi tserkvi*, Moscow: Terra, 1993, vol. 1, 433–442; R.G. Skrynnikov, *Sviatiteli i vlasti*, Leningrad: Lenizdat, 1990, 175–184.

10 This view is well expounded by James Billington in *The Icon and the Axe: an interpretive history of Russian culture*, London: Weidenfeld & Nicolson, 1966, 66–69.

11 *Perepiska Ivana Groznogo s Andreem Kurbskim*, Moscow: Nauka, 1993; see especially the interpretive article by A.S. Lur'e, 'Perepiska Ivana Groznogo s Kurbskim v obshchestvennoi mysli drevnei Rusi', on pp. 214–249.

12 A.A. Zimin, *Oprichnina Ivana Groznogo*, Moscow: Mysl', 1964, 342–3.

13 Zimin, *Oprichnina*, 249–257.

14 Kartashev, vol. 2, 10–47.

15 V.O. Kliuchevskii, *Sochineniia*, Moscow, 1957, vol.3, 29–30. However, the standard biography of Godunov, by S.F. Platonov (Petrograd, 1921), contains no mention of an intended charter: see pp. 116–132.

16 R.G. Skrynnikov, 'The civil war in Russia at the beginning of the seventeenth century (1603–7): its character and motive forces', in Lindsey Hughes (ed.), *New Perspectives on Muscovite History*, London: St Martin's Press, 1993, 61–78.

17 Kliuchevskii, vol 3, 41–3.

18 S.F. Platonov, *Smutnoe vremia*, Prague, 1924. The whole declaration, with commentary, can be found in *Rossiiskoe zakonodatel'stvo X–XX vekov*, vol. 3: *akty zemskikh soborov*, Moscow:

Iuridicheskaia Literatura, 1985, 43–62.

19 P.G. Liubomirov, *Ocherki istorii nizhegorodskogo opolcheniia, 1611–13gg.*, Moscow, 1939, 72–77.

20 Platonov, 203–8: quotation on 206; R.G. Skrynnikov, *The Time of Troubles: Russia in crisis, 1604–1618*, Gulf Breeze, Florida: Academic International Press, 1988, 183–199.

21 Maureen Perrie, 'Popular socio-utopian legends in the Time of Troubles', *Slavonic & East European Review*, vol, 60 (1982), 221–243.

22 *Smutnoe vremia*, 238.

23 Sergei Zen'kovskii, *Russkoe staroobriadchestvo: dukhovnye dvizheniia 17-ogo veka*, Munich: Wilhelm Fink Verlag, 1970, chapter 7.

24 Zen'kovskii, chapters 18–20; N.F. Kapterev, *Patriarkh Nikon i Tsar' Aleksei Mikhailovich*, Sergiev Posad, 1909, vol. 1, 60–69.

25 Kapterev, vol. 1, 394–409.

26 Zen'kovskii, *Staroobriadchestvo*, chapter 28, especially pp. 300–304.

27 V.V. Andreev, *Raskol i ego znachenie v narodnoi russkoi istorii*, St Petersburg, 1870, 68; P.N. Miliukov, *Ocherki po istorii russkoi kul'tury*, Paris, 1931, vol. 2, part 1, 48.

28 Pierre Pascal, *Avvakum et les Débuts du Raskol: la crise religieuse du XVIIème siècle en Russie*, Paris, 1938, 407–8, 411, 511.

29 Robert O. Crummey, *The Old Believers and the World of Antichrist: the Vyg community and the Russian state, 1694–1855*, Madison: University of Wisconsin Press, 1970, 13.

30 Crummey, 16.

31 Crummey, 19.

32 Serge A. Zenkovsky, 'The

ideological world of the Denisov brothers', *Harvard Slavic Studies*, vol. 3 (1957), 49-66, especially 57-8.

33 ibid., 60.

34 A.S. Prugavin, *Staroobriadchestvo vo vtoroi polovine XIX veka*, Moscow, 1904, 7-23.

35 Frederick C. Conybeare, *Russian Dissenters*, Cambridge, Massachusetts, 1921, 245.

36 'Ispoved' V.I. Kel'sieva', *Literaturnoe nasledstvo*, vol. 41-42 (1941), 319.

37 Miliukov, *Ocherki*, vol. 2, part 1, 50.

2 *The Secular State of Peter the Great*

1 V.O. Kliuchevskii, 'Kurs russkoi istorii', in *Sochineniia*, vol. 4, Moscow 1958, 10-15, 20-21; Reinhard Wittram, *Peter I: Czar und Kaiser*, Gottingen: Vandenhoek und Ruprecht, 1964, vol. 1, 90.

2 Wittram, vol. 1, 129-167.

3 Geoffrey Parker, *The military Revolution: military innovation and the rise of the West, 1500-1800*, Cambridge University Press, 1988; but see the reservations expressed in Jeremy Black, *A Military Revolution? Military change and European society, 1550-1800*, London: Macmillan, 1991.

4 Brian M. Downing, *The Military Revolution and Political Change: origins of democracy and autocracy in early modern Europe*, Princeton University Press, 1992.

5 John Keep, *Soldiers of the Tsar: army and society in Russia, 1462-1874*, Oxford: Clarendon Press, 1985, chapter 4.

6 Evgenii Anisimov, *Vremia petrovskikh reform*, Leningrad: Lenizdat, 1989.

7 Richard S. Wortman, *Scenarios of Power: myth and ceremony in Russian monarchy*, vol. 1 (from Peter the Great to the death of Nicholas I), Princeton University Press, 1995, chapter 2.

8 Wortman, vol. 1, 49-50; further on Peter's ecclesiastical reforms, see Part 3, Chapter 4.

9 Anisimov, 121-143; E.I. Zaozerskaia, *Manufaktura pri Petre I*, Moscow-Leningrad, 1947, 129-146, 150.

10 *Polnoe sobranie zakonov Rossiiskoi Imperii*, vol. 6, no. 3534, 28 Feb. 1720, chapter XLV.

11 *Polnoe sobranie zakonov*, loc.cit; chapter LV.

12 This dichotomy is explored in Marc Raeff, *The Well-Ordered Police State: social and institutional change through law in the Germanies and Russia, 1600-1800*, New Haven, Connecticut: Yale University Press, 1983.

13 Anisimov, 308. Peter used the term *shliakhetstvo*, on the Polish model, but the word *dvorianstvo* (literally 'courtiers') became generally used by the mid-eighteenth century.

14 See the decree of 28 February 1714 in Basil Dmytryshyn (ed.), *Modernisation of Russia under Peter I and Catherine II*, New York: Wiley & Sons, 1974, 10-11.

15 *Polnoe sobranie zakonov*, vol. 6, 491, no. 3890, article 11.

16 Anisimov, 311-313.

17 Joseph Brodsky, *Less than One: selected essays*, New York: Farrar Straus Giroux, 1986, 76.

18 Quoted in L. Jay Oliva, *Russia in the Era of Peter the Great*, Englewood Cliffs, NJ: Prentice-Hall, 1969, 154.

19 Anisimov, 385-93.

20 Marquis de Custine, *Letters from Russia*, London: Penguin Books, 1991, 50.

21 'The Sylphide', quoted in Yuri M. Lotman, *Universe of the Mind: a semiotic theory of culture*, London: Tauris, 1990, 196.

22 Custine, 52.

23 Anisimov, 357–361.

24 Alexander Vucinich, *Science in Russian Culture*, vol. 1, London: Peter Owen, 1963, chapter 2.

25 Ilya Z. Serman, *Mikhail Lomonosov: life and poetry*, Jerusalem: Centre of Slavic and Russian Studies of the Hebrew University, 1988, chapter 1.

26 'Reglament glavnogo magistrata', 1724: *Polnoe sobranie zakonov*, vol. 6, 297, no. 3708.

27 Wittram, vol. 1, 106–111.

28 Michael Cherniavsky, 'The Old Believers and the new religion', *Slavic Review*, vol.25 (1966), 27–33.

29 Anisimov, 139–43; Oliva, 158–9.

30 Marquis de Custine, *Letters from Russia*, London, 1854, 455.

3   Assimilating Peter's Heritage

1 On the nature of the eighteenth-century Russian state, see John P. LeDonne, *Absolutism and Ruling Class: the formation of the Russian political order, 1700–1825*, New York: Oxford University Press, 1991, especially p. 300.

2 The essential documents on the events of 1730 are translated in Marc Raeff (ed.), *Plans for Political Reform in Russia*, Englewood Cliffs, New Jersey: Prentice-Hall, 1966, 41–52. See also Brenda Meehan-Waters, *Autocracy and Aristocracy: the Russian service elite of 1730*, New Brunswick, New Jersey: Rutgers University Press, 1982.

3 O.A. Omel'chenko, '*Zakonnaia monarkhiia' Ekateriny II: prosveshchennyi absoliutizm v Rossii*, Moscow: Iurist, 1993, 39–45; Kerry Morrison, 'Catherine II's Legislative Commission: an administrative interpretation', *Canadian Slavic Studies*, vol.4 (1970), 464–484.

4 P. Dukes (ed.), *Russia under Catherine the Great*, vol.2 (Catherine the Great's Instruction (Nakaz) to the Legislative Commission), Newtonville, Massachusetts: Oriental Research Partners, 1977, 43.

5 Article 37: ibid, 46.

6 This is the view of Marc Raeff, *The Well-Ordered Police State*: and also of the most recent Russian student of Catherine's legislation: Omel'chenko, 86–102.

7 Paul Dukes, *Catherine the Great and the Russian Nobility: a study based on the materials of the Legislative Commission of 1767*, Cambridge University Press, 1967; Omel'chenko, 112–126.

8 Omel'chenko, 195–6.

9 Omel'chenko, 341–3; M. Raeff, 'The Empress and the Vinerian Professor' in his *Political Ideas and Institutions in Imperial Russia*, Boulder, Colorado: Westview, 1994, 213–233.

10 Isabel de Madariaga, *Russia in the age of Catherine the Great*, London: Weidenfield and Nicolson, 1991, chapters 29–30.

11 Omel'chenko, 236–8; R.P. Bartlett, 'Catherine II's draft charter to the state peasants', *Canadian-American Slavic Studies*, vol. 23 (1989), 36–57.

12 S.M. Troitskii, *Finansovaia politika russkogo absoliutizma v xviii veke*, Moscow: Nauka, 1966, 221–224.

13 S. M. Troitskii, 115–118, 125–129.

14 Troitskii, 214; A. P. Pogrebinskii, *Ocherki istorii finansov dorevoliutsionnoi Rossii*, Moscow, 1954, 99; David Christian, *Living Water: vodka and Russian society on*

the eve of emancipation, Oxford: Clarendon Press, 1990, 42–43.

15 Christian, 142–151.

16 *Kolokol*, 1 November 1859, ii, 454–5, quoted in Christian, 153–4.

17 'Koe-chto ob otkupakh', *Kolokol*, 1 March 1858, i, 79–81, quoted in Christian, 131.

18 Charles Tilly, *Coercion, Capital and European States, AD 990–1992*, Oxford: Blackwell, 1992, 87–91.

19 Pogrebinskii, 18, 35–37, 68–69.

20 Roger P. Bartlett, *Human Capital: the settlement of foreigners in Russia, 1762–1804*, Cambridge University Press, 1979; an English translation of Catherine's Manifesto of 1763 inviting foreign settlers is on pp. 237–242.

21 This is the conclusion of William H. McNeill, who compared Russia's policies in this region with those of Poland, the Habsburg Monarchy and the Ottoman Empire: *Europe's Steppe Frontier, 1500–1800*, University of Chicago Press, 1964.

22 R. E. Jones, 'Opposition to war and expansion in late eighteenth century Russia', *Jahrbücher für Geschichte Osteuropas* vol. 32 (1984), 34–51.

23 Arcadius Kahan, *The Plow, the Hammer and the Knout: an economic history of 18th century Russia*, University of Chicago Press, 1985, 50–51.

24 For general remarks on the significance of pretenders in Russia, see B.A. Uspenskii, 'Tsar and Pretender: *Samozvanchestvo* or royal imposture in Russia as a cultural-historical phenomenon' in I.M. Lotman & B.A. Uspenskii, *The Semiotics of Russian Culture*, Ann Arbor: *Michigan Slavic Contributions*, no. 11 (1984), 259–277.

25 *Pugachevshchina*, vol. 1 (Iz arkhiva Pugacheva), Moscow-Leningrad, 1926, 25.

26 *Pugachevshchina*, vol. 2, 113.

27 *Pugachevshchina*, vol. 1, 40–42; the shaky syntax is in the original.

28 Dorothea Peter, 'Politische und gesellschaftliche Vorstellungen in der Aufstandsbewegung unter Pugačev (1773–5)', *Forschungen zur osteuropäischen Geschichte*, Band 17, Berlin, 1973, 156–163.

29 S.I. Tkhorzhevskii, *Pugachevschina v pomeshchich'ei Rossii*, Moscow, 1930, quoted in J. T. Alexander, *Emperor of the Cossacks: Pugachev and the frontier jacquerie of 1773–1775*, Lawrence, Kansas: Coronado, 1973. 169.

30 Alexander, 83.

31 A.L. Lozanova, *Pesni i skazaniia o Razine i Pugacheve*, Leningrad, 1935.

32 Marc Raeff, 'Pugachev's rebellion', in Robert Forster and Jack P. Greene, *Preconditions of Revolution in Early Modern Europe*, Baltimore & London: Johns Hopkins Press, 1970, 161–201; quotation on 190.

33 John T. Alexander, *Autocratic Politics in a National Crisis: the Imperial Russian government and Pugachev's revolt, 1773–1775*, Bloomington & London: Indiana University Press, 1969, 72–74.

34 On the Pugachev rising, in addition to the sources quoted above, see the excellent general account by Philip Longworth, 'The Pugachev revolt: the last great Cossack-peasant rising', in H.A. Landsberger (ed.), *Rural Protest: peasant movements and social change*, London: Macmillan, 1974, 194–256.

35 de Madariaga, 337–342.

36 ibid., 497–498; William H.E. Johnson, *Russia's Educational Heritage*, New York: Octagon Books, 1969, 49–57.

37 The best summary of Catherine's educational policy is Isabel de Madariaga, 'The foundation of the Russian educational system by Catherine II', *Slavonic & East European Review*, vol. 57 (1979), 369–395.

38 Alexander Vucinich, *Science in Russian Culture*, vol. 1, 163–4.

39 ibid., 150–154.

40 Quoted in de Madariaga, 537.

4   *The Apogee of the Secular State*

1 Richard S. Wortman, *Scenarios Of Power: myth and ceremony in Russian monarchy*, vol. 1, Princeton University Press, 1995, 171–192.

2 Roderick McGrew, 'Paul I and the Knights of Malta', in Hugh Ragsdale (ed.), *Paul I: a reassessment of his life and reign*, Pittsburgh: University Center for International Studies, 1979, 44–75.

3 The best of study of Paul is Roderick McGrew, *Emperor Paul I of Russia, 1754–1801*, Oxford: Clarendon Press, 1992.

4 *Correspondance de Frédéric-César de la Harpe et Alexandre Ier*, Neuchâtel, 1978, vol. 1, 216; N. Berdiaev, *Russkaia ideia*, Paris: YMCA, 1946, 23.

5 Marc Raeff, *Plans for Political Reform in Imperial Russia, 1730–1905*, Englewood Cliffs, NJ: Prentice-Hall, 1966, 75–84.

6 *Memoirs of Prince Adam Czartoryski and his Correspondence with Alexander I*, London, 1888, vol. 1, 111; M.M. Safonov, *Problema reform v pravitel'stvennoi politike Rossii na rubezhe 18-ogo i 19-ogo vekov*, Leningrad: Nauka, 1988; for a summary of the views of the Secret Committee, see Raeff, *Plans*, 85–91.

7 For a good discussion of Alexander's early reforming dilemmas, see Janet Hartley, *Alexander I*, London: Longman, 1994, 30–49.

8 James T. Flynn, 'Tuition and social class in Russian universities: S.S. Uvarov and "reaction" in the Russia of Nicholas I', *Slavic Review*, vol.35 (1976), 236.

9 William H.E. Johnson, *Russia's Educational Heritage*, 70.

10 Cynthia H. Whittaker, *The Origins of Modern Russian Education: an intellectual biography of Count Sergei Uvarov, 1786–1855*. De Kalb: Northern Illinois University Press, 1984, 59–61; James T. Flynn, *The University Reform of Alexander I, 1802–1835*, Washington, D.C: Catholic University of America Press, 1988, 20–25.

11 Flynn, Part 2.

12 Whittaker, especially 156–172.

13 N.A. Troitskii, *Aleksandr I i Napoleon*, Moscow: Vysshaia shkola, 1994, especially 120–128, 178–183; see also F.M.H. Markham, *Napoleon and the Awakening of Europe*, London: English Universities Press, 1954, and Stuart Woolf, *Napoleon's Integration of Europe*, London: Routledge, 1991.

14 Marc Raeff, *Michael Speransky, statesman of Imperial Russia, 1772–1839*, 2nd edition, The Hague: Nijhoff, 1969, 64–5.

15 John Gooding, 'The liberalism of Michael Speransky', *Slavonic & East European Review*, vol.64, no. 3 (July 1986), 401–424.

16 Raeff, *Speransky*, 147–8; excerpts from Speranskii's draft are in Raeff, *Plans*, 92–109.

17 A.P. Pogrebinskii, *Ocherki istorii finansov dorevoliutsionnoi Rossii (xix–xx vekov)*, Moscow, 1954, 19–21, 25–28.

18 Pogrebinskii, 58–61.

19 Raeff, *Speransky*, 90–101.
20 Richard Pipes, 'Karamzin's conception of the monarchy', *Harvard Slavic Studies*, vol. 4 (1957), 35–58; see also his edition of *Karamzin's Memoir on Ancient and Modern Russia*, Harvard University Press, 1959.
21 E.V. Tarle, *1812 god*, Moscow, 1959, 585.
22 Tarle, 613; William C. Fuller, Jr., *Strategy and Power in Russia, 1600–1914*, New York: Free Press, 1992, 204–6, quoting *1812 god*, Moscow, 1962, 34.
23 V.I. Semevskii, 'Volneniia krest'ian v 1812g i sviazannye s otechestvennoi voinoi', in A.K. Dzhivelegov, S.P. Mel'gunov, V.I. Pichet (eds), *Otechestvennaia voina i russkoe obshchestvo*, Moscow, 1912, vol.5, 76–7, 81.
24 ibid., 89–92; Tarle, 599–601.
25 ibid., 92–3.
26 A.V. Buganov, *Russkaia istoriia v pamiati krest'ian XIX veka i natsional'noe samosoznanie*, Moscow: Institut Etnologii i Antropologii imeni N.N. Miklukho-Maklaia, 1992, 153.
27 Tarle, 593.
28 Tarle, 670–1.
29 Tarle, 674–5.
30 A.K. Kabanov, 'Opolcheniia 1812-ogo goda', in Dzhivelegov et al, vol.5, 49.
31 Kabanov, 50–54; General Sir Robert Wilson, *Narrative of Events during the Invasion of Russia in 1812 by Napoleon Bonaparte*, London, 1860, 156.
32 Kabanov, 98–100.
33 Kabanov, 103–4, 111.
34 Further on the military settlements, see Part 3, chapter 2, on the army. For a good summary of their organization, see Richard Pipes, 'The Russian military colonies, 1810–31', *Journal of Modern History*, vol. 22 (1950), 205–219; also Keep, *Soldiers of the Tsar* 283.
35 M. Florinsky, *Russia: a history and an interpretation*, New York: Macmillan, 1960, vol. 2, 644.
36 Georgii Florovskii, *Puti russkogo bogosloviia*, Paris, 1937, 132.
37 A.N. Pypin, 'Rossiiskoe bibleiskoe obshchestvo', *Vestnik Evropy*, 1868, no. 8, 665–667.
38 Pypin, 672–3.
39 Pypin, *Vestnik Evropy*, 1868, no. 11, 262–4; for the Bible Society's innovative use of printing presses, see Stephen K. Batalden, 'Printing the Bible in the reign of Alexander I: towards a reinterpretation of the Imperial Russian Bible Society', in G.A. Hosking (ed.), *Church, Nation and State in Russia and Ukraine*, London: Macmillan, 1991, 65–78.
40 Pypin, *Vestnik Evropy*, 1868, no. 11, 224.
41 Ibid., 228.
42 Igor Smolitsch, 'Geschichte der russischen Kirche', part 2, *Forschungen zur osteuropäischen Geschichte*, Band 45 (1991), 19.
43 H. Seton-Watson, *The Russian Empire, 1801–1917*, Oxford: Clarendon Press, 1967, 185.
44 M. Polievktov, *Nikolai I: biografiia i obzor tsarstvovaniia*, Moscow, 1918, 54–58, 76–78.
45 'Aleksandr Dmitrievich Borovkov i ego avtobiograficheskie zapiski', *Russkaia starina*, vol.29 (Nov.1898), 353–362.
46 Nicholas Riasanovsky, *Nicholas I and Official Nationality*, Berkeley: University of California Press, 1959, 74.
47 Riasanovsky, 137–138.
48 N. K. Shil'der, *Imperator Nikolai I: ego zhizn' i tsarstvovanie*, SPB, 1903, vol 1, p 147.
49 Polievktov, 312.

50 Olga Crisp, 'The state peasants under Nicholas I', in her *Studies in the Russian Economy before 1914*, London: Macmillan, 1976, 84–95; N. M. Druzhinin, *Gosudarstvennye krest'iane i reforma P. D. Kiseleva*, Moscow, 1958, vol.2, 465–498.

51 Polievktov, 348–363.

PART THREE Social classes, religion and culture in Imperial Russia

1 *The Nobility*

1 A. Romanovich-Slavatinskii, *Dvorianstvo v Rossii ot nachala xviii veka do otmeny krepostnogo prava*, St Petersburg, 1870, 11–14.

2 *Polnoe sobranie zakonov*, vol. 6, no.3890, 24 January 1722, arts 11, 14, 19; Romanovich-Slavatinskii, 14–22.

3 *Zhizn' i prikliucheniia Andreia Bolotova, opisannye samim im dlia svoikh potomkov*, Moscow: Sovremennik, 1986, 42–3; Brenda Meehan-Waters, *Autocracy and Aristocracy: the Russian service of 1830*, New Brunswick, NJ: Rutgers University Press, 1982.

4 S.M. Troitskii, *Russkii absoliutizm i dvorianstvo v xviii veke*, Moscow: Nauka, 1974, 213–215.

5 Walter Pintner, 'The evolution of civil officialdom, 1755–1855' in W.M. Pintner and D.K. Rowney, *Russian Officialdom: the bureaucratization of Russian society from the seventeenth to the twentieth century*, London: Macmillan Press, 1980, 199.

6 Romanovich-Slavatinskii, 82–3; Troitskii, 269–271; *Modern Encyclopedia of Russian and Soviet History*, vol.6, 86–89.

7 PSZ, vol. 22, no.16187, 21 April 1785.

8 R.E. Jones, *The Emancipation of the Russian Nobility, 1762–1785*, Princeton University Press, 1973, 267–283.

9 Jerome Blum, *Lord and Peasant in Russia from the ninth to the nineteenth century*, New York: Atheneum, 1964, 380–386.

10 Romanovich-Slavatinskii, 66–7, 84–6.

11 See the comparative survey of education and culture among European aristocracies by Dominic Lieven in his *The Aristocracy in Europe, 1815–1914*, London: Macmillan, 1992, 161–180.

12 Raeff, *Origins*, 75; V. O. Kliuchevskii, 'Kurs russkoi istorii', *Sochineniia*, Moscow, 1958, vol. 5, 183.

13 Michael Confino, 'Histoire et psychologie: à propos de la noblesse russe au dix-huitième siècle', in his *Société et Mentalités, Collectives en Russie sous l'Ancien Régime*, Paris: Institut d'Études Slaves, 1991, 345–387.

14 P.A. Kropotkin, *Zapiski revoliutsionera*, Moscow: Moskovskii rabochii, 1988, 218.

15 R. Wittram, *Baltische Geschichte: die Ostseelande, Livland, Estland, Kurland, 1180–1918*, Munich, 1954, 128–134.

16 Erik Amburger, *Geschichte der Behördenorganisation in Russland*, Leiden: E.J. Brill, 1966, 517.

17 Walter Laqueur, *Russia and Germany*, London: Weidenfeld & Nicolson, 1965, 16.

18 Brenda Meehan-Waters, 'Social and career characteristics of the administrative elite, 1689–1761', in Pintner and Rowney, 83–4; the top 179 officials are listed in her *Autocracy and Aristocracy*, 170–203.

19 Hans Rogger, *National Consciousness in Eighteenth Century Russia*, Harvard University Press, 1960, 30–32.

20 For an account of the coup and of Elizabeth's policies, see E. V. Anisimov, *Rossiia v seredine XVIII veka: bor'ba za nasledie Petra*, Moscow: Mysl', 1986, chapters 1–2.

21 Arcadius Kahan, *The Plow, the Hammer and the Knout* 49–65; Blum, 394–398.

22 M. Confino, *Domaines et Seigneurs en Russie vers la fin du 18ème siècle: étude de structures agraires et de mentalités économiques*, Paris: Institut d'Études Slaves, 1963, 113–115.

23 Confino, 51–62, 80–86, 117–126; V.A. Aleksandrov, *Sel'skaia obshchina v Rossii (xvii-nachalo xix v.)*, Moscow: Nauka, 1976.

24 Confino, 143–150.

25 Arcadius Kahan, 'The costs of "westernisation" in Russia: the gentry and the economy in the eighteenth century', *Slavic Review*, vol. 25, (1966), 40–66.

26 Blum, 380–385.

27 Pypin, chapter 4; see the figures in G. Vernadskii, *Russkoe masonstvo v tsarstvovanie Ekateriny II*, Petrograd, 1917, 83–90.

28 Vernadskii, 109.

29 Gareth W. Jones, *Nikday Novikov, Enlightener of Russia*, Cambridge University Press, 1984, 145; *Modern Encyclopedia of Russian and Soviet History*, vol. 25, 102.

30 Jones, 183–92; Gary Marker, *Publishing, Printing and the Origins of Intellectual Life in Russia, 1700–1800*, Princeton University Press, 1985, 122–133.

31 Jones, 206–215; de Madariaga, 524–531; K.A. Papmehl, 'The Empress and "un fanatique": a review of the circumstances leading to the government action against Novikov in 1792', *Slavonic & East European Review*, vol. 68 (1990), 665–691.

32 Allen McConnell, *A Russian Philosophe: Alexander Radishchev, 1749–1802*, The Hague: Martinus Nijhoff, 1964, 15–16.

33 A.N. Radishchev, 'Beseda o tom, chto est' syn otechestva', *Polnoe sobranie sochinenii*, Moscow-Leningrad, 1938, vol. 1, 215–223.

34 McConnell, 106–122.

35 M.V. Nechkina, *Dvizhenie dekabristov*, vol. 1, Moscow, 1955, 90–102.

36 ibid., 100.

37 ibid., 113.

38 I.D. Iakushkin, *Zapiski*, Moscow, 1951, 7.

39 Nechkina, vol. 1, 110.

40 Nechkina, 142; Iakushkin, 11.

41 Nechkina, 152–7.

42 A. Murav'ev, 'Moi zhurnal', in V.A. Fedorov (ed.), *Memuary dekabristov: severnoe obshchestvo*, Moscow: Izdatel'stvo moskovskogo universiteta, 1981, 124.

43 Nechkina, vol. 1, 149; Iakushkin, 16–17.

44 'Zakonopolozhenie Soiuza Blagodenstviia', in Iu.G. Oksman (ed.) *Dekabristy: otryvki iz istochnikov*, Moscow-Leningrad, 1926, 84–85.

45 Oksman, 84–102.

46 Iakushkin, 28–31.

47 Iurii Lotman, 'The Decembrist in everyday life: everyday behaviour as a historical-psychological category', in Iu.M. Lotman & B.A. Uspenskii, *The Semiotics of Russian Culture*, 71–123; see also Franklin A. Walker, 'Christianity, the service ethic and Decembrist thought', in Geoffrey A. Hosking (ed.), *Church, Nation and State in Russia and Ukraine*, Basingstoke: Macmillan, 1991, 79–95.

48 Franklin A. Walker, 'K.F. Ryleev: self-sacrifice for revolution?' *Slavonic & East European Review*,

vol. 47 (1969), 446; Iakushkin, 20, 44.

49 Substantial excerpts from the two main drafts of *Russkaia pravda* can be found in Marc Raeff (ed.), *The Decembrist Movement*, Englewood Cliffs, NJ: Prentice-Hall, 1966, 124–156; quotation on 130.

50 Raeff, 140–1.

51 ibid., 147.

52 ibid., 146.

53 ibid., 135–6.

54 ibid., 136–8.

55 The term designates the popular assemblies of the towns of Kievan Rus'. It was used in Pestel's constitutional draft, which appears in Oksman, 179–181.

56 Raeff, 153–6.

57 The point is made in the excellent analysis of Pestel's programme by Hans Lemberg, *Die nationale Gedankenwelt der Dekabristen*, Cologne/Graz: Bohlau Verlag, 1963, 133–8; for an outline of the views of Katkov and Pleve, see Part 4, Chapter 3.

58 Extensive excerpts are in Raeff, 100–118; the full text is in Oksman, 236–249.

59 Raeff, 120–1.

2   *The Army*

1 Vladimir Voinovich, *The Life and Extraordinary Adventures of Private Ivan Chonkin*, London: Jonathan Cape, 1977.

2 John Keep, *Soldiers of the Tsar*, 102–107; in 1734 the size of the army seems to have been about 205,000 men, a figure reached by adding together the data given in L.G. Beskrovnyi, *Russkaia armiia i flot v XVIII veke*, Moscow: 1958, 29.

3 Christopher Duffy, *Russia's Military Way to the West: origins and nature of Russian military power, 1700–1800*, London: Routledge

& Kegan Paul, 1981, 128; Walter Pintner, 'The burden of defense in Imperial Russia', *Russian Review*, vol. 43 (1984), 246–247.

4 William C. Fuller, Jr., *Strategy and Power in Russia, 1600–1914*, 100–101.

5 Keep, 178 n.

6 Beskrovnyi, 29–30.

7 Beskrovnyi, 38–9.

8 Keep, 167–8.

9 Graf Lanzheron, 'Russkaia armiia v god smerti Ekateriny II', *Russkaia starina*, vol 26 (1895), no 3, 148.

10 Beskrovnyi, 300; André Corvisier, *Armies and Societies in Europe, 1494–1789*, Bloomington & London: Indiana University Press, 1979, chapter 3; William H. McNeill, *The Pursuit of Power: technology, armed force and society since AD 1000*, Oxford: Blackwell, 1983, chapters 4–5.

11 Duffy, 129.

12 Fuller, 172.

13 Quoted in Duffy, 134; see also John Bushnell, 'Peasants in uniform: the Tsarist army as a peasant society', *Journal of Social History*, vol. 13 (1979–80), 567; Lanzheron, *Russkaia starina*, 147–149.

14 A.I. Denikin, *Staraia armiia*, Paris, 1929, vol. 1, 93; Elise Kimerling Wirtschafter, *From Serf to Russian Soldier*, Princeton University Press, 1990, 87–88.

15 John Keegan & Richard Holmes, *Soldiers: a History of Men in Battle*, London: Hamish Hamilton, 1985, chapter 2: 'Fighting spirit'. They conclude that 'In the last analysis, fighting spirit centres upon the morale of the individual soldier and the small group of comrades with whom he fights.' [56]

16 Keep, chapter 5; Duffy, 133–135.

17 Wirtschafter, chapter 5.

18 Duffy, 135.

19 Fuller, 274: Paul Kennedy, *The Rise*

and Fall of the Great Powers, London: Unwin Hyman, 1988, 173.

20 Pintner, 'The burden of defense', 248.

21 Keep, 283.

22 A good summary of the organization of the settlements can be found in Richard Pipes, 'The Russian military colonies, 1810–31', *Journal of Modern History*, vol. 22 (1950), 205–219.

23 Michael Jenkins, *Arakcheev, Grand Vizier of the Russian Empire: a biography*, London: Faber and Faber, 1969, 188–9.

24 Keep, 296–8.

25 *La Russie et les Russes*, Paris, 1847, vol. 2, 466.

26 R.A. Fadeev, *Vooruzhennye sily Rossii*, Moscow, 1868, 26; William C. Fuller, *Strategy and Power in Russia, 1600–1914*, New York: Free Press, 1992, 260; see also the report of January 1856 on the military situation by D. A. Miliutin, then a Major-General in the General Staff, in 'Iz istorii krymskoi voiny, 1853–1856gg', *Istoricheskii arkhiv*, 1959, no. 1, 204–208.

27 John S. Curtiss, *The Russian Army under Nicholas I, 1825–1855*, Durham, N.C., Duke University Press, 1965, 126–130, 367–370.

28 Dietrich Beyrau, *Militär und Gesellschaft im vorrevolutionären Russland*, Köln-Wien: Böhlau Verlag, 1984, 222, 269–270.

29 Peter Kenez, 'A profile of the prerevolutionary officer corps', *California Slavic Studies*, vol.7 (1973), 121–158.

30 Kenez, 'Profile'; Bruce W. Menning, *Bayonets before Bullets: the Imperial Russian Army, 1861–1914*, Bloomington: Indiana University Press, 100–103.

31 John Bushnell, 'Miliutin and the Balkan War: military reform versus military performance', in Ben Eklof, John Bushnell & Larissa Zakharova (eds), *Russia's Great Reforms, 1855–1881*, Bloomington & Indianapolis: Indiana University Press, 1994, 139–158; Menning, chapters 2 & 5.

32 P.A. Zaionchkovskii, *Samoderzhavie i russkaia armiia na rubezhe XIX i XX stoletii*, Moscow: Mysl', 1973, 273.

33 John Bushnell, *Mutiny amid Repression: Russian soldiers in the revolution of 1905–6*, Bloomington: Indiana University Press, 1985, 226.

3   The Peasantry

1 Quoted in E.V. Anisimov, *Rossiia v seredine XVIII veka: bor'ba za nasledie Petra*, Moscow: Mysl', 1986, 54.

2 Ben Eklof, 'Mir', *Modern Encyclopedia of Russian and Soviet History*, vol.22, 208–223; S.G. Pushkarev, *Krest'ianskaia pozemel'no-peredel'naia obshchina v Rossii*, Newtonville, Massachusetts: Oriental Research Partners, 1976; Horace Dewey, 'Russia's debt to the Mongols in suretyship and collective responsibility', *Comparative Studies in Society and History*, vol.30 (1988), 249–270.

3 Jerome Blum, *Lord and Peasant in Russia*, chapters 8–14, and pp. 420–422.

4 Quoted in Peter Kolchin, *Unfree Labour: American slavery and Russian serfdom*, Cambridge, Massachusetts: Harvard University Press, 1987, 42.

5 John Locke, *Second Treatise on Government*, Book 2, section 27.

6 V.A. Aleksandrov, *Sel'skaia obshchina v Rossii (xviii-nachalo xix veka)*, Moscow: Nauka, 1976, chapters 2–3.

7 A.I. Novikov, *Zapiski zemskogo nachal'nika*, St Petersburg, 1899, 39–42; see also the accounts of village assembly meetings in Vladimir *guberniia* in the 1890s drawn up by the ethnographic researchers of Prince V.N. Tenishev, in *Byt velikorusskikh krest'ian-zemlepashtsev*, St Petersburg: Izdatel'stvo Evropeiskogo Doma, 1993, 45–50.

8 Novikov, 28–9.

9 Aleksandrov, chapter 4; Dorothy Atkinson, 'Egalitarianism and the commune', in Roger Bartlett (ed.), *Land Commune and Peasant Community in Russia*, London: Macmillan, 1990, 7–20; Michel Confino, *Systèmes Agraires et Progrès Agricole: l'assolement triennal en Russie aux 18–19ème siècles*, Paris-The Hague: Mouton, 1969.

10 Beatrice Farnsworth and Lynne Viola, 'Peasant women before the revolution', in their *Russian Peasant Women*, New York: Oxford University Press, 1992, 6; Christine D. Worobec, *Peasant Russia: family and community in the post-emancipation period*, Princeton University Press, 1991, chapter 2.

11 Stepniak, *The Russian Peasantry*, 2nd edition, London: Routledge, 1905, 635–6; *Entsiklopedicheskii slovar' Brokgauz i Efron*, SPB, 1890–1907, vol 3, 184.

12 Georg Staehr, *Über Ursprung, Geschichte, wesen und Bedeutung des russischen Artels*, Dorpat, 1890–1, vol.1, 12–14.

13 N. Kalachov, *Arteli v drevnei i nyneshnei Rossii*, St Petersburg, 1864, 85–6.

14 R.E. Zelnik (ed.), *A Radical Worker in Tsarist Russia: the autobiography of Semen Ivanovich Kanatchikov*, Stanford University Press, 1986, 91.

15 Jerome Blum, 'The internal structure and polity of the European village community from the fifteenth to the nineteenth century', *Journal of Modern History*, vol.43 (1971), 543–576.

16 M.M. Gromyko, *Mir russkoi derevni*, Moscow: Molodaia Gvardiia, 1991, 74–76.

17 A.N. Engel'gardt, *Iz derevni: 12 pisem, 1872–1887*, Moscow, 1960, 78.

18 ibid., 42–3.

19 ibid., 81.

20 Peter Czap, 'Peasant-class courts and peasant customary justice in Russia, 1861–1912', *Journal of Social History*, vol.1, (1967), 149–178.

21 See the opinions quoted in Cathy Frierson, 'Rural justice in public opinion: the volost court debate, 1861–1912', *Slavonic & East European Review*, vol.64 (1986), 526–545.

22 Czap, 'Peasant-class courts'.

23 Stephen P. Frank, 'Popular justice, community and culture among the Russian peasantry', *Russian Review*, vol. 46 (1987), 239–265.

24 Frank; Cathy Frierson, 'Crime and punishment in the Russian village: rural concepts of criminality at the end of the nineteenth century', *Slavic Review*, vol. 46 (1987) 55–69.

25 A.V. Buganov, *Russkaia istoriia v pamiati krest'ian xix veka i natsional'noe samosoznanie*, Moscow: Institut etnologii i antropologii imeni N.A. Miklukho-Maklaia, 1992, 83–94, 115–120.

26 Buganov, 99–110.

27 On the peasant's changing sense of 'homeland', see Robert J. Kaiser, *The Geography of Nationalism in Russia and the USSR*, Princeton University Press, 1994, 83–93.

28 P. Znamenskii, *Prikhodskoe dukhovenstvo v Rossii so vremeni*

reformy Petra, Kazan', 1873, chapter 1. Further on this subject, see Part 3, Chapter 4.

29 I.S. Belliustin, *Description of the Clergy in Rural Russia: the memoir of a nineteenth century parish priest* (translated and edited by Gregory Freeze), Ithaca, New York: Cornell University Press, 1985; further on village priests, see the next chapter, pp. 234–6.

30 Linda J. Ivanits, *Russian Folk Belief*, Armonk, NY: M.E. Sharpe, 1989, 51–57.

31 Ivanits, 59–60.

32 Ivanits, chapter 7.

33 Eve Levin, '*Dvoeverie* and popular religion', in Stephen K. Batalden (ed.), *Seeking God: the recovering of religious identity in Orthodox Russia, Ukraine and Georgia*, De Kalb, Illinois: Northern Illinois University Press, 1993, 31–52.

34 F.M. Dostoevskii, *Zapiski iz mertvogo doma*, in *Polnoe sobranie sochinenii*, Leningrad: Nauka, 1972, vol. 4, 33–34; Robert O. Crummey, 'Old Belief as popular religion: new approaches', *Slavic Review*, vol. 52 (1993), 700–712.

35 Donald Treadgold, 'The peasant and religion', in W.S. Vucinich (ed.), *The Peasant in Nineteenth Century Russia*, Stanford University Press, 1968, 93–6; A.I. Klibanov, *Istoriia religioznogo sektanstva v Rossii (60-ye gody xix veka-1917g)*, Moscow: Nauka, 1965, 39–49.

36 Treadgold, 89–91; Conybeare, 267–287.

37 Treadgold, 91–3; Conybeare, 289–326. Miliukov classifies them as an evangelical rather than a spiritual sect, because of their use of the scriptures: *Ocherki*, vol. 2, part 1, 130.

39 P.Ia. Miroshnichenko, 'Narodnye istoki utopicheskogo sotsializma v Rossii', in *Istoriia obshchestvennoi mysli: sovremennye problemy*, Moscow: Nauka, 1972, 480.

40 A.I. Klibanov, *Narodnaia sotsial'naia utopiia*, Moscow: Nauka, 1978, 9–10.

41 P.Ia. Miroshnichenko, 475–506, quotation on p. 484.

42 Dorothea Peter, 'Politische und gesellschaftliche Vorstellungen in der Aufstandsbewegung unter Pugačev (1773–5)', *Forschungen zur osteuropäischen Geschichte*, Band 17, Berlin, 1973, 156–163.

43 V.A. Fedorov, 'Krest'ianskoe dvizhenie v tsentral'nopromyshlennykh guberniiakh Rossii v 1800–1860–kh godakh', *Ezhegodnik po agrarnoi istorii vostochnoi Evropy, 1965*, Moscow: Izdatel'stvo MGU, 1970, 308–320; see also his 'Noveishaia sovetskaia literatura o krest'ianskom dvizhenii v Rossii pervoi poloviny XIX veka', *Voprosy Istorii*, 1977, no. 1, 140–148. The definition of 'unrest' used by Soviet historians is quite restrictive, since it does not include murder or attempted murder of the landlord, or the burning down of his manor house, unless these incidents led on to collective activity which had to be countered by the forces of repression.

44 Russian peasant unrest in the first six decades of the nineteenth century is well summed up in Peter Kolchin, *Unfree Labour*, chapter 5.

45 S.N. Valk (ed.), *Krest'ianskoe dvizhenie v Rossii v 1796–1825 gg. (sbornik dokumentov)*, Moscow, 1961, 739–745, 816n; Kolchin, 260–1.

46 Kolchin, 320–326.

47 David Moon, *Russian Peasants and Tsarist Legislation on the Eve of Reform*, Basingstoke: Macmillan, 1992, especially p. 181; see also

Rodney Bohac, 'Everyday forms of resistance: serf opposition to gentry extractions, 1800–1861', in Esther Kingston-Mann and Timothy Mixter (eds.), *Peasant Economy, Culture and the Politics of European Russia, 1820–1921*, Princeton University Press, 1991, 236–259.

48 Daniel Field, *Rebels in the Name of the Tsar*, Boston: Houghton Mifflin, 1976, 42.

49 The most thorough and discriminating account of the Bezdna affair is in Field, 31–112.

50 Sylvain Bensidoun, *L'agitation paysanne en Russie de 1881 à 1902*, Paris: Fondation Nationale des Sciences Politiques, 1975.

51 On one side of the argument is A. Gerschenkron, *Europe in the Russian Mirror: four lectures in economic history*, Cambridge University Press, 1970, and T. Shanin, *Russia as Developing Society*, Basingstoke: Macmillan, 1985; on the other are Paul R. Gregory, *Russian National Income, 1885–1913*, Cambridge University Press, 1982, and Heinz-Dietrich Löwe, *Die Lage der Bauern in Russland, 1880–1905*, St Katharinen: Scripta Mercaturae, 1987. On the growth of an empire-wide agricultural market, see I. Koval'chenko and L. Milov, *Vserossiiskii agrarnyi rynok*, Moscow: AN SSSR, 1974, and A. Nifontov, *Zernovoe proizvodstvo Rossii vo vtoroi polovine XIX-ogo veka*, Moscow: AN SSSR, 1974.

52 Bensidoun, 424.

53 Jeffrey Brooks, *When Russia Learned to Read: literacy and popular literature, 1861–1917*, Princeton University Press, 1985, especially 214–245.

4 The Orthodox Church

1 James Cracraft, *The Church Reform of Peter the Great*, London: Macmillan, 1971, 33.

2 Quoted in Cracraft, 35.

3 Cracraft, 107–111.

4 Igor Smolitsch, *Geschichte der russischen Kirche, 1700–1917*, Leiden: E.J. Brill, 1964, 99–120.

5 Cracraft, 49–50.

6 A.V. Muller (ed.), *The Spiritual Regulation of Peter the Great*, Seattle: University of Washington Press, 1972, 10.

7 Muller, 6.

8 Evgenii Anisimov, *Vremia petrovskikh reform*, Leningrad: Lenizdat, 1989, 333.

9 *Polnoe sobranie zakonov*, vol. 6, no.4012, 685–9; Muller, 22–27, 60–62; Gregory Freeze, *The Russian Levites: parish clergy in the eighteenth century*, Harvard University Press, 1977, 29–30.

10 P.V. Znamenskii, *Prikhodskoe dukhovenstvo v Rossii so vremeni reformy Petra*, Kazan', 1873, chapter 1; Igor Smolitsch, *Die Geschichte der russischen Kirche, 1700–1917*, vol. 2, in *Forschungen zur Osteuropäischen Geschichte*, Band 45, 1991, 96–100; Gregory Freeze, 'The disintegration of traditional communities: the parish in eighteenth century Russia', *Journal of Modern History*, vol. 48 (1976), 32–50.

11 From a leading article in his newspaper, *Moskva*, 3 September 1868: *Sochineniia I.S. Aksakova*, vol. 4, Moscow, 1886, 144.

12 Cracraft, 86–7, 251–261; Igor Smolitsch, *Russisches Mönchtum: Entstehung, Entwicklung and Wesen, 988–1917*, Amsterdam: Verlag Adolf M. Hakkert, 1978, 390–395.

13 G.V. Florovskii, *Puti russkogo bogosloviia*, Paris, 1937, 84: A.V.

Kartashev, *Ocherki po istorii russkoi tserkvi*, Moscow: Terra, 1992, vol. 2, 323–330.

14 Aleksandr Shmeman, *Istoricheskii put' pravoslaviia*, New York, 1954, 380–381; Florovskii, *Puti*, 82–83.

15 Isabel de Madariaga, *Russia in the Age of Catherine the Great*, London: Weidenfeld & Nicolson, 1981, 114–119; Smolitsch, *Geschichte*, vol. 1, 342–356.

16 Smolitsch, vol. 1, Leiden, 570–573.

17 Freeze, *Levites*, 148–156, 175–179.

18 Freeze, *Levites*, 90–96; Smolitsch, vol. 1, 570–573.

19 Freeze, *The Parish Clergy in Nineteenth-Century Russia: crisis, reform, counter-reform*, Princeton University Press, 1983, 113–119.

20 A.Ia. Panaeva, *Vospominaniia*, Moscow, 1972, 263–264. In Turgenev's *Fathers and Sons*, Pavel Petrovich refers to the hero, Bazarov, as 'a seminary rat', and this is a literary commonplace. See also Nabokov's novel about Chernyshevskii, *The Gift*.

21 P.V. Znamenskii, *Osnovnye nachala dukhno-uchilishchnoi reformy v tsarstvovanie Imperatora Aleksandra I-ogo*, Kazan', 1878.

22 Quoted in *Dictionnaire de Théologie Catholique*, Paris, 1932–4, vol. 12, col. 1386.

23 Smolitsch, vol. 2, 21, 29.

24 Smolitsch, vol. 2, 21–23.

25 S.N. Val'k (ed.), *Krest'ianskoe dvizhenie v Rossii v 1796–1825gg*, Moscow, 1961, 33–34, 77–79.

26 I.S. Belliustin, *Description of the Clergy in Rural Russia: the memoir of a nineteenth century parish priest* (translated and edited by Gregory Freeze), Ithaca, New York: Cornell University Press, 1985, 122; further

on village priests, see Part 3, Chapter 3.

27 Freeze, *Levites*, 194–210; *Parish Clergy*, 146–155.

28 Freeze, *Parish Clergy*, 188.

29 Freeze, *Parish Clergy*, 81–101; 311–319; 363–372.

30 Quoted in V.S. Solov'ev, 'Russkaia ideia', in his *O khristianskom edinstve*, Moscow: Rudomino, 1994, 171.

31 Smolitsch, *Geschichte*, vol. 2, 180–182.

32 Smolitsch, vol. 2, 169–180.

33 Smolitsch, vol. 2, 182–184.

34 Smolitsch, vol. 2, 185–6.

35 Smolitsch, vol. 2, 190–200.

36 Smolitsch, vol. 2, 199–200.

37 Smolitsch, vol. 2, 240.

38 Vladimir Lossky, *The Mystical Theology of the Eastern Church*, London: James Clarke, 1957, 101, 180.

39 John Dunlop, *Starets Amvrosy: model for Dostoevsky's Starets Zosima*, Belmont, Massachusetts: Nordland, 1972, 17–28.

40 Father John Meyendorff, *The Byzantine Legacy in the Orthodox Church*, Belmont, Massachusetts: Nordland, 1982, 167–194.

41 Smolitsch, *Mönchtum*, 482–490.

42 Father Sergii Chetverikov, *Starets Paisii Velichkovskii: his life, teachings and influence on Orthodox Monasticism*, Belmont, Massachusetts: Nordland, 1980, 301–314.

43 K. Mochul'skii, *Dukhovnyi put' Gogolia*, Paris: YMCA Press, 1976, 131; see also D.P. Bogdanov, 'Optina pustyn' i palomnichestvo v nee russkikh pisatelei', *Istoricheskii vestnik*, 1910, no. 10, 327–339.

44 A.G. Dostoevskaia, *Vospominaniia*, Moscow: Pravda, 1987, 347. Further on Gogol, Tolstoy and Dostoevskii, see Part 3, Chapter 7.

45 F.M. Dostoevskii, *Brat'ia*

Karamazovy, in *Polnoe sobranie sochinenii*, vol. 14, Leningrad: Nauka, 1976, 26–29.

46 N.A. Pavlovich, 'Optina pustyn'. Pochemu tuda ezdili velikie?' *Prometei*, vol. 12 (1980), 84–92.

47 Freeze, 'Handmaiden of the state? The Church in Imperial Russia reconsidered', *Journal of Ecclesiastical History*, vol. 36 (1985), 100–101; N.S. Gordienko, P.K. Kurochkin, 'Liberal'no-obnovlencheskoe dvizhenie v russkom pravoslavii nachala XX veka', *Voprosy nauchnogo ateizma*, vol. 7 (1969), 313–340; J.Y. Cunningham, *A Vanquished Hope: the movement for church renewal in Russia, 1905–1906*, Guestwood New York: St Vladimir's Seminary Press, 1981, 133–162.

48 Details of the bishops' views are given in Cunningham, *A Vanquished Hope*, chapter 4.

49 Cunningham, chapters 6–7.

50 Episkop Nikon (Rklitskii), *Zhizneopisanie Blazhennogo Antoniia, Mitropolita Kievskogo i Galitskogo*, New York, 1957, vol. 3, 159–160; A.V. Zen'kovskii, *Pravda o Stolypine*, New York, 1956, 81–84.

5   Towns and the Missing Bourgeoisie

1 Baron August von Haxthausen, *The Russian Empire: its people, institutions and resources*, London, 1856, vol. 1, 393–4.

2 See Daniel R. Brower, who specifically mentions Khar'kov, showing how the city governor demolished wooden shanties in the centre without providing alternative dwellings for their inhabitants: *The Russian City between Tradition and Modernity, 1850–1900*, Berkeley: University of California Press, 1990, 12–13.

3 Eugen Weber, *Peasants into Frenchmen: the modernisation of rural France, 1870–1914*, London: Chatto & Windus, 1979.

4 Otto Brunner, 'Stadt und Bürgertum in der europäischen Geschichte', in his *Neue Wege der Verfassungs- und Sozialgeschichte*, 2nd edition, Gottingen: Vandenhoek und Ruprecht, 1968, 214.

5 Brunner, 225–241.

6 William Coxe, *Travels into Poland, Russia, Sweden and Denmark*, London, 1784, vol.2, 109. One may add that the device Coxe mentioned, the abacus, remained firmly in place right up to the recent advent of calculators and computers towards the end of the twentieth century.

7 J. Michael Hittle, *The Service City: state and townsmen in Russia, 1600–1800*, Harvard University Press, 1979, 109–111.

8 Coxe, vol. 2, 95.

9 William L. Blackwell, *The Beginnings of Russian Industrialisation, 1800–1860*, Princeton University Press, 1968, 73–5; Anne Lincoln Fitzpatrick, *The Great Russian Fair: Nizhnii Novgorod, 1840–1890*, London: Macmillan, 1990, chapter 1.

10 Haxthausen, vol. 1, 43; Blackwell, 76–8.

11 Patricia Herlihy, *Odessa: a history, 1794–1914*, Harvard University Press, 1986, especially chapters 1 and 10.

12 Manfred Hildermeier, *Bürgertum und Stadt in Russland, 1760–1870: rechtliche Lage und soziale Struktur*, Köln-Wien: Böhlau Verlag, 1986, 120–1.

13 Blackwell, 19–20, 56–58; I.M. Kulisher, *Ocherk istorii russkoi torgovli*, Petrograd, 1923, 216–221.

14 Blackwell, 44, 62–5, 114–115;

15 A.A. Kizevetter, 'Posadskaia obshchina v 18-om veke', in his *Istoricheskie ocherki*, Moscow, 1912, 244–7.

16 Kizevetter, 242–263; Hittle, chapter 6; P.G. Ryndziundskii, *Gorodskoe grazhdanstvo doreformennoi Rossii*, Moscow, 1958, 40–51.

17 Hittle, 129–131; Kizevetter, 256–263.

18 A.A. Kizevetter, *Posadskaia obshchina v Rossii 18-ogo veka*, Moscow, 1903, 145; Hittle, 126–9.

19 David H. Miller, 'State and society in seventeenth-century Muscovy', in M.F. Hamm, *The City in Russian History*, Lexington: University of Kentucky Press, 1976, 40–1.

20 Hittle, 198–212; Hildermeier, 73–81.

21 Hittle, chapter 10; Hildermeier, 81–90.

22 Hildermeier, 139–140.

23 ibid., 193–206.

24 ibid., 254–270.

25 B.N. Mironov, *Russkii gorod v 1740–1860-ye gody: demograficheskoe, sotsial'noe i ekonomicheskoe razvitie*, Leningrad: Nauka, 1990.

26 Hildermeier, 319–321.

27 Valeriia A. Nardova, 'Municipal self-government after the 1870 reform', in Eklof, Bushnell and Zakharova (eds), *Russia's Great Reforms, 1855–1881*, 183–5.

28 Nardova, 188–196.

29 William L. Blackwell, 'The Old Believers and the rise of private industrial enterprise in early nineteenth century Moscow', in Blackwell (ed.), *Russian Economic Development from Peter the Great to Stalin*, New York: New Viewpoints, 1974, 139–158.

30 Alfred J. Rieber, *Merchants and Entrepreneurs in Imperial Russia*, Chapel Hill: University of North Carolina Press, 1982, 139–148.

31 Mironov, 235.

32 The political symbolism of the two cities is well discussed in Richard Wortman, 'Moscow and Petersburg: the problem of political center in Tsarist Russia, 1881–1914', in Sean Wilentz (ed.), *Rites of Power: symbolism, ritual and politics since the middle ages*, Philadelphia: University of Pennsylvania Press, 1985, 244–271.

33 Rieber, 191–198.

34 Rieber, 203, 206–213.

35 John O. Norman, 'Pavel Tretiakov and merchant art patronage, 1850–1900', in E.W. Clowes, S.D. Kassow and J.L. West (eds), *Between Tsar and People: educated society and the quest for public identity in late Imperial Russia*, Princeton University Press, 1991, 93–101 quotation on p. 97.

36 Elizabeth Valkenier, *Russian Realist Art: the Peredvizhniki and their tradition*, Ann Arbor: Ardis, 1977, 33–43.

37 Valkenier, chapter 5.

38 Marc Slonim, *Russian Theater from Empire to Soviets*, Cleveland, Ohio: World Publishing Co., 1961, 102–118.

39 Gregory Freeze, 'The *soslovie* (estate) paradigm and Russian social history', *American Historical Review*, vol. 91 (1986), 11–36.

40 Alfred J. Rieber, 'The sedimentary society', in Clowes *et al.*, 343–366.

6 *The Birth of the Intelligentsia*

1 For a discussion of the ways in which the term has been used, see Martin Malia, 'What is the intelligentsia?', in Richard Pipes (ed.), *The Russian Intelligentsia*, New York: Columbia University Press, 1961, 1–18; Vladimir C.

Nahirny, *The Russian Intelligentsia: from torment to silence*, New Brunswick: Transaction Books, 1983, chapter 1.

2 The most thorough attempt to trace the usage of the word is Otto Wilhelm Müller, *Intelligencija: Untersuchungen zur Geschichte eines politischen Schlagwortes*, Frankfurt: Athenäum Verlag, 1971: see especially the summary on pp. 246–251. For the link of the term with *raznochintsy* see Elise Kimerling Wirtschafter, *Structures of Society: Imperial Russia's 'People of Various Ranks'*, De Kalb: North Illinois University Press, 1994, especially chapter 6.

3 Müller, 141–150, 253–269; Alan Pollard, 'The Russian intelligentsia: the mind of Russia', *California Slavic Studies*, vol. 3, 1964, 13–15.

4 Pollard, 15–16; Müller, 287–8.

5 Müller, 295–304; N.K. Mikhailovskii, *Sochineniia*, SPB, 1896–7, vol. 5, 538.

6 Aleksandr Gertsen, *Byloe i dumy*, Moscow, 1963, vol. 1, 366, 455.

7 B.N. Chicherin, *Moskva 40-kh godov*, Moscow, 1929, 114.

8 Martin Malia, *Alexander Herzen and the Origins of Russian Socialism, 1812–1855*, Harvard University Press, 1961, 58–60.

9 P. V. Annenkov, *Literaturnye vospominaniia*, Leningrad, 1928, 306.

10 *Byloe i dumy*, vol. 1, 347.

11 Letter of Belinskii to Botkin, 13 June 1840, in V. G. Belinskii, *Polnoe sobranie sochinenii*, Moscow, 1953–9, vol. 12, 527.

12 *Byloe i dumy*, vol. 1, 428.

13 Raymond T. McNally (ed.), *The Major Works of Peter Chaadaev*, University of Notre Dame Press, 1969, 28, 37.

14 *Byloe i dumy*, vol. 1, 449.

15 P. A. Viazemskii, *Polnoe sobranie sochinenii*, St Petersburg, 1878, vol. 1, 103.

16 Chaadaev, 'Apology of a madman', in McNally (ed.), 199–218.

17 N.L. Brodskii (ed.), *Literaturnye kruzhki i salony*, Moscow-Leningrad, 1930, 326–331.

18 N. Riasanovsky, 'Khomiakov on *sobornost*', in E.J. Simmons (ed.), *Continuity and Change in Russian and Soviet Thought*, Harvard University Press, 1955, 183–4.

19 N. Riasanovsky, *Russia and the West in the Teachings of the Slavophiles: a study of Romantic ideology*, Harvard University Press, 1952, 93.

20 Riasanovsky, *Russia and the West*, 135.

21 N.L. Brodskii (ed.), *Rannie slavianofily*, Moscow, 1910, 85–6.

22 *Byloe i dumy*, vol. 1, 445.

23 Liah Greenfeld, *Nationalism: five roads to modernity*, Harvard University Press, 1992, 265.

24 N.V. Riasanovsky, *A Parting of the Ways: government and educated public in Russia, 1801–1855*, Oxford: Clarendon Press, 1976, 275.

25 Annenkov, 309–310; Derek Offord, *Portraits of Early Russian Liberals*, Cambridge University Press, 1985, 56–62.

26 Gertsen, *Byloe i Dumy*, vol. 1, 350.

27 Quoted in Isaiah Berlin, *Russian Thinkers*, Harmondsworth: Penguin Books, 1978, 165.

28 Berlin, 169.

29 Letter to Botkin of 8 September 1841, in V.G. Belinskii, *Polnoe sobranie sochinenii*, Moscow, 1956, vol. 12, 66, 69.

30 Aileen Kelly, *Mikhail Bakunin: a study in the psychology and politics of utopianism*, Oxford: Clarendon Press, 1982, especially 52–60; Bakunin, *Sobranie sochinenii i pisem*,

1828–76 (edited by Iu.M. Steklov), vol. 3, Moscow, 1935, 148.

31 'Gosudarstvennost' i anarkhiia', *Archives Bakounine*, Leiden: E.J. Brill, 1967, vol. 3, 50.

32 Kelly, 121; 'L'empire knouto-germanique et la révolution sociale', *Archives Bakounine, vol.7*.

33 M. Bakunin, *Statism and Anarchy* (translated and edited by Marshall S. Shatz), Cambridge University Press, 1990, 38–39.

34 M.A. Bakunin, *Sobranie sochinenii i pisem, 1828–1876* vol.3, 360; Kelly, 131–132.

35 Berlin, 113.

36 *Byloe i Dumy*, vol.1, 87.

37 A.I. Gertsen, 'Pis'ma iz Frantsii i Italii', no.5, in his *Polnoe sobranie sochinenii i pisem*, vol.6, Petrograd, 1919, 6–7.

38 'Pis'ma iz Frantsii i Italii', no.2, *loc.cit.*, vol.5, 133.

39 Malia, 398.

40 'Russkii narod i sotsializm' (letter to Jules Michelet) *Polnoe sobranie sochinenii i pisem*, vol.6, 447.

41 *Byloe i dumy*, vol.1, 458.

7   Literature as 'Nation Builder'

1 'The Hero as Poet', in 'On Heroes, Hero-Worship and the Heroic in History', *Works of Thomas Carlyle*, vol. 5, London, 1898, 114.

2 Simon Schama, *Citizens: a chronicle of the French Revolution*, London: Penguin Books, 1989, chapter 4.

3 Hans Rogger, *National Consciousness in Eighteenth Century Russia*, Harvard University Press, 1960, 117–119.

4 Benedict Anderson, *Imagined Communities: reflections on the origin and spread of nationalism*, London: Verso, 1983, 49.

5 On its origins see Gary Marker, *Publishing, Printing and the Origins of Intellectual Life in Russia,*

1700–1800, Princeton University Press, 1985.

6 Marker, 235.

7 A.G. Cross, *N.M. Karamzin: a study of his literary career, 1783–1803*, Carbondale: Southern Illinois University Press, 1971, 225.

8 William Mills Todd, *Fiction and Society in the Age of Pushkin*, Harvard University Press, 1986, 59.

9 *Polnoe sobranie sochinenii*, SPB, 1878, vol. 1, 268.

10 Anthony D. Smith, *National Identity*, Harmondsworth: Penguin Books, 1991, 52–54.

11 Isaiah Berlin, 157.

12 Berlin, 169.

13 V.G.Belinksii, 'Thought and remarks on Russian literature, 1846', *Selected Philosophical Works*, Moscow, 1948, 37.

14 *PSS*, vol. 5, 124.

15 He outlined this theory in a review of an anthology of Russian folklore in 1841: *PSS*, Moscow, 1956, vol.5, 308–310.

16 *PSS*, vol.7, 435–440; S.S. Hoisington (ed.), *Russian Views of Pushkin's Evgenii Onegin*, Bloomington & London: Indiana University Press, 1988, 21.

17 This point is explored in Herbert Bowman, *Vissarion Belinski, 1811–1848: a study in the origins of social criticism in Russia*, Harvard University Press, 1954, 63–69.

18 *Evgenii Onegin*, III, 18–19.

19 A.S. Pushkin, *Polnoe sobranie sochinenii v desiati tomakh*, Vol. 6, Leningrad: Nauka, 1978, 211.

20 *Sochineniia v dvukh tomakh*, Moscow, 1962, vol. 1, 599.

21 Igor' Zolotusskii, *Gogol'*, 2nd edition, Moscow: Molodaia Gvardiia, 1984, 353.

22 ibid, 378.

23 V.G. Belinskii, vol. 10, Moscow, 1956, 213–214.

24 Count Sologub, quoted in Donald Fanger, *The Creation of Nikolai Gogol*, Harvard University Press, 1979, 225.

25 R.F. Christian, *Tolstoy's 'War and Peace': a study*, Oxford: Clarendon Press, 1962, chapter 1.

26 *War and Peace*, vol. III, part 2, chapter 39.

27 I, 2, 16–17; III, 1, 15.

28 II, 1, 15; see my remarks on the importance of small-group solidarity within the Russian army: p. 188.

29 III, 3, 1.

30 See his reflections on the eve of Borodino: III, 1, 26–29.

31 III, 3, 5.

32 III, part 2, chapters 9, 11.

33 Henri Troyat, *Tolstoy*, New York: Dell, 1969, 350.

34 Joseph Frank, *Dostoevsky: the seeds of revolt, 1821–1849*, London: Robson Books, 1977, chapters 17–19; *Dostoevsky: the years of ordeal, 1850–1859*, London: Robson Books, 1983, chapter 5.

35 'Zapiski iz mertvogo doma', in F.M. Dostoevskii, *PSS*, vol. 4, Leningrad, 1972, 154–155.

36 Frank, *Dostoevsky: years of ordeal*, 116–127.

37 *PSS*, vol. 4, 122–123.

38 Andrew Baruch Wachtel, *An Obsession with History: Russian writers confront the past*, Stanford University Press, 1994; Gary Saul Morson, *The Boundaries of Genre: Dostoevsky's Diary of a Writer and the traditions of literary Utopia*, Austin: University of Texas Press, 1981.

39 *PSS*, vol.14, 285; II, 6, 3. For the significance of the image of the 'holy fool' in Dostoevskii, see Harriet Murav, *Holy Foolishness: Dostoevskii's novels and the poetics of cultural critique*, Stanford University Press, 1992.

40 'Dnevnik pisatelia', April 1877, *PSS*, vol.25, 100.

41 I.S. Turgenev, *Polnoe sobranie sochinenii i pisem*, Moscow-Leningrad: Nauka, 1968, vol.15, 68.

42 Dostoevskii, *PSS*, vol.26, Leningrad: Nauka, 1984, 136–149. My account of the Pushkin celebrations is based on Marcus C. Levitt, *Russian Literary Politics and the Pushkin Celebration of 1880*, Ithaca: Cornell University Press, 1989.

43 Jeffrey Brooks, 'Russian nationalism and Russian literature: the canonisation of the classics', in Ivo Banac et al. (eds), *Nation and Ideology: essays in honor of Wayne S. Vucinich*, Boulder, Colorado: East European Monographs, 1981, 322.

44 Jeffrey Brooks *When Russia learnt to read: literary and popular culture*, Princeton University Press, 1985, 324–327.

45 Brooks, Chapters 4, 5, 9.

PART FOUR Imperial Russia under pressure

1 *The Reforms of Alexander II*

1 J.S. Curtiss, *Russia's Crimean War*, Durham, N.C: Duke University Press, 1979, 538–46.

2 I.N. Kovaleva, 'Slavianofily i zapadniki v period krymskoi voiny, 1853–6gg', *Istoricheskie zapiski*, no. 80 (1967), 181–206.

3 A. Kizevetter, 'Russkoe obshchestvo i reforma 1861g', in his *Istoricheskie otkliki*, Moscow, 1915, 192.

4 Kizevetter, 194.

5 P.A. Valuev, 'Duma russkogo vo vtoroi polovine 1855g', *Russkaia Starina*, vol. 79 (1893), 512–513.

6 Iu. Samarin, 'O krepostnom sostoianii i o perekhode iz nego k

grazhdanskoi svobode', *Sochineniia*, vol. 2, Moscow, 1878, 17–20.

7 B.N. Chicherin, 'O krepostnom sostoianii', *Golosa iz Rossii*, 1 vypusk, 2 chast', London, 1856, reprinted Moscow: Nauka, 1974, 131, 170.

8 K.D. Kavelin, *Sobrannye sochineniia*, vol. 2, St Petersburg, 1989, 33–4. It should be mentioned that Kavelin lost his tutorship of the Tsarevich as a result of submitting this memorandum.

9 Fadeev, *Vooruzhennye sily*, 27, *Rossii*, Moscow, 1868; for the connection between military reform and wider policy, see Dietrich Beyrau, 'Von der Niederlage zur Agrarreform: Leibeigenschaft und Militärverfassung in Russland nach 1855', *Jahrbücher fur Geschichte Osteuropas*, vol. 23 (1975), 191–212.

10 Baron E. Nol'de, *Iurii Samarin i ego vremia*, Paris, 1926, 70.

11 Daniel Field, *The End of Serfdom: nobility and bureaucracy in Russia, 1855–61*, Harvard University Press, 1976, especially 359–360.

12 W. Bruce Lincoln, *In the Vanguard of Reform: Russia's enlightened bureaucrats, 1825–61*, De Kalb, Illinois: Northern Illinois University Press, 1982, 84–9, 194–6; Prince D.A. Obolenskii, 'Moi vospominaniia o Velikoi Kniagine Elene Pavlovne', *Russkaia Starina*, vol.40, no. 3 (March 1909), 504–7.

13 Terence Emmons, *The Russian Landed Gentry and the Peasant Emancipation of 1861*, Cambridge University Press, 1968, Parts 2 and 3, especially pp. 234–242; the text of the proposed reform programme is in A.I. Koshelev, *Zapiski*, Newtonville, Massachusetts: Oriental Research Partners, 1976, 171–206.

14 The voluminous official discussions on this issue are well summarized in Frank W. Wcislo, *Reforming Rural Russia: state, local society and national politics, 1855–1914*, Princeton University Press, 1990, chapters 2–3.

15 Valeriia A. Nardova, 'Municipal self-government after the 1870 reform', in Ben Eklof, John Bushnell and Larissa Zakharova (eds), *Russia's Great Reforms, 1855–1881*, Bloomington: Indiana University Press, 184–185; Robert Philippot, *Société civile et état bureaucratique dans la Russie Tsariste: Les Zemstvos*, Paris: Institut d'études Slaves, 1991, 45–49.

16 Koshelev, *Zapiski*, 167–168.

17 Charles E. Timberlake, 'The zemstvo and the development of a Russian middle class', in Edith W. Clowes, Samuel D. Kassow and James L. West (eds), *Between Tsar and People: educated society and the quest for public identity in late Imperial Russia*, Princeton University Press, 1991, 164–179; Samuel C. Ramer, 'The zemstvo and public health', in Terence Emmons & Wayne S. Vucinich (eds), *The Zemstvo in Russia: an experiment in local self-government*, Cambridge University Press, 1982, 292.

18 Harvey Balzer, 'The problem of professions in Imperial Russia', in Clowes et al., *Between Tsar and People*, 183–198.

19 Nancy M. Frieden, *Russian Physicians in an Era of Reform and Revolution, 1856–1905*, Princeton University Press, 1981, 192–195, 242–261.

20 Kermit E. McKenzie, 'Zemstvo organisation and role within the administrative structure, in Emmons & Vucinich, 31–78.

21 I.I. Petrunkevich, 'Iz zapisok

obshchestvennogo deiatelia', *Arkhiv russkoi revoliutsii*, vol. 21 (1934), 41–2.

22 A reference to the Bulgarian constitution of 1878, which the Russian government had pressed for at the Congress of Berlin. Fedor A. Petrov, 'Crowning the edifice: the zemstvo, local self-government and the constitutional movement, 1864–1881', in Eklof et al., 203.

23 Jeffrey Brooks, 'The zemstvo and the education of the people', in Vucinich and Emmons, 243–278: statistics on 249.

24 Brooks, 255–263.

25 Scott J. Seregny, *Russian Teachers and Peasant Revolution*, Bloomington: Indiana University Press, 1989, 55–67.

26 Allen Sinel, *The Classroom and the Chancellery: state educational reform in Russia under Count Dmitrii Tolstoi*, Harvard University Press, 1973, chapters 5–6.

27 Christine Ruane and Ben Eklof, 'Culture pioneers and professionals: the teacher in society', in Clowes et al., 199–211.

28 Alexander Vucinich, *Science in Russian Culture, 1861–1917*, Stanford University Press, 1970, 4–5; the regime's dilemma over higher education is examined in James C. McClelland, *Autocracy and Academics: education, society and culture in Tsarist Russia*, University of Chicago Press, 1979.

29 William L. Mathes, 'The origins of confrontation politics in Russian universities: student activism, 1855–1861, *Canadian Slavic Studies*, vol. 2 (1968), 28–37.

30 Mathes, 37–45

31 Samuel D. Kassow, 'The University Statute of 1863: a reconsideration', in Eklof et al., 247–263.

32 V.R. Leikina–Svirskaia, *Intelligentsia v Rossii vo vtoroi polovine XIX veka*, Moscow: Mysl', 1971, 56, 62–3.

33 Leikina-Svirskaia, 26–30.

34 See, for example, the views of D.I. Mendeleev, V.V. Dokuchaev and later V.I. Vernadskii, as presented in Kendall Bailes, *Science and Russian Culture in an Age of Revolutions: V.I. Vernadsky and his scientific school, 1863–1945*, Bloomington: Indiana University Press, 1990, 17–19, 51–52.

35 The text of the rules is in Charles Ruud, *Fighting Words: imperial censorship and the Russian press, 1804–1906*, Toronto University Press, 1982, 237–252.

36 Ruud, 156–7; further on Katkov, see Part 4, Chapter 3.

37 Ruud, 176–7, 198–9.

38 M. Hroch, *Social Preconditions of National Revival in Europe*, Cambridge University Press, 1985, 23.

39 Louise McReynolds, *The News under Russia's Old Regime: the development of a mass-circulation press*, Princeton University Press, 1991, 81–87.

40 Dietrich Geyer, *Russian Imperialism: the interaction of domestic and foreign policy, 1860–1914*, Leamington Spa: Berg, 1987, 110–112, 118–121.

41 These trends are analysed in details in McReynolds, *News*.

42 McReynolds, 281–289.

43 G. Dzhanshiev, *Epokha velikikh reform*, 6th edition, Moscow, 1895, 387.

44 Aleksandr Nikitenko, *The Diary of a Russian Censor*, Amherst: University of Massachusetts Press, 1975, 254.

45 Samuel Kucherov, *Courts, Lawyers and Trials under the Last Three Tsars*, New York, 1953, 215.

46 McReynolds, 92–93.

47 Kucherov, 217–225.

48 Kucherov, 130, 269, 274–5; William E. Pomeranz, 'Justice from below: the history of the underground *advokatura*', *Russian Review*, vol.52 (1993), 321–340.

49 Quoted in Pomeranz, 326.

50 P.A. Zaionchkovskii, *Krizis samoderzhaviia na rubezhe 1870–1880-kh godov*, Moscow: Izdatel'stvo moskovskogo universiteta, 1964, 217.

51 Daniel Orlovsky, *The Limits of Reform: the Ministry of Internal Affairs in Imperial Russia, 1802–1881*, Harvard University Press, 1981, chapter 6.

52 Zaionchkovskii, 287–290.

53 E.A. Peretts, *Dnevnik gosudarstvennogo sekretaria, 1880–1882*, Moscow, 1937, 38–39.

54 This traditional interpretation, best expounded in the writings of Alexander Gerschenkron, especially his *Economic Backwardness in Historical Perspective*, Harvard University Press, 1962, has recently been well restated by Theodor Shanin in *Russia as a 'Developing Society'*, London: Macmillan, 1985, and by Dietrich Geyer, in *Russian Imperialism*.

55 See for example Olga Crisp, *Studies in the Russian Economy before 1914*, London: Macmillan, 1976; Heinz-Dietrich Löwe, *Die Lage der Bauern in Russland, 1880–1905*, St. Katharinen: Scripta Mercaturae Verlag, 1987; Paul Gregory, *Russian National Income, 1885–1913*, Cambridge University Press, 1982. The controversy is well summed up in Peter Gatrell, *The Tsarist Economy, 1850–1917*, London: Batsford, 1986, chapter 1.

56 'Gosudarstvennye finansy Rossii nakanune reformy 1861g', *Istoricheskii arkhiv*, 1956, no.2, 103.

57 I.F. Gindin, *Gosudarstvennyi bank i ekonomicheskaia politika tsarskogo pravitel'stva (1861–1892gg)*, Moscow, 1960, 30–32.

58 A.M. Solov'eva, *Zheleznodorozhnyi transport Rossii vo vtoroi polovine XIXv*, Moscow: Nauka, 1975, chapter 2; J. Metzer, 'Railroad development and market integration: the case of Tsarist Russia', *Journal of Economic History*, vol.34 (1974), 529–549.

59 Figures tabulated in Geyer, 44, 164.

60 T.M. Kitanina, *Khlebnaia torgovlia Rossii v 1875–1914gg*, Leningrad: Nauka, 1978, chapter 2.

61 A.M. Solov'eva, chapters 2–4; Stephen Marks, *Road to Power: the Trans-Siberian Railroad and the colonisation of Asian Russia, 1850–1917*, London: Tauris, 1991.

62 Gatrell, chapter 5.

63 T.H. von Laue, *Sergei Witte and the Industrialisation of Russia*, New York: Columbia University Press, 1963, 129–138.

64 J.P. McKay, *Pioneers for Profit: foreign entrepreneurship and Russian industrialisation, 1885–1913*, University of Chicago Press, 1970, 28–31. McKay indicates that, for methodological reasons, these estimates may be slightly too high, but not grossly so.

65 Gatrell, 154–157.

66 'The dying village' is the title of a study of rural conditions in Voronezh guberniia by the Kadet agrarian expert, A.I. Shingarev: *Vymiraiushchaia derevnia*, St Petersburg, 1907.

67 Robert J. Kaiser, *The Geography of Nationalism in Russia and the USSR*, Princeton University Press, 1994, 43–83.

2   *Russian Socialism*

1 William F. Woehrlin,
   *Chernyshevskii: the man and the
   journalist*, Harvard University
   Press, 1971, chapters 7–9.
2 For Chernyshevskii's influence on
   Lenin, see below, p. 362–3.
3 Franco Venturi, *Roots of Revolution:
   a history of the populist and socialist
   movements in nineteenth-century
   Russia*, New York: Universal
   Library, 1966, chapter 10.
4 M. Lemke, *Politicheskie protsessy v
   Rossii 1860-kh godov*, Moscow, 1923,
   518.
5 James H. Billington, *Mikhailovsky
   and Russian Populism*, Oxford:
   Clarendon Press, 1958, 123.
6 Venturi, 345–346.
7 Venturi, chapter 15; quotation on
   p. 365.
8 P. Lavrov, *Historical Letters* (edited
   by James P. Scanlan), Berkeley:
   University of California Press,
   1967, 172–3.
9 Andreas Kappeler, 'Zur
   Charakteristik russischer
   Terroristen (1878–87)', *Jahrbücher
   für Geschichte Osteuropas*, vol. 27
   (1979), 534–541.
10 Venturi, *Roots of Revolution*, 476.
11 Daniel R. Brower, *Training the
   Nihilists: education and radicalism in
   Tsarist Russia*, Cornell University
   Press, 1975, 15–16.
12 Abbott Gleason, *Young Russia: the
   genesis of Russian radicalism in the
   1860s*, University of Chicago Press,
   1980, chapter 4; Brower, 123–126.
13 Billington, 126–127; A.A. Titov
   (ed.), *Nikolai Vasil'evich Chaikovskii:
   religioznye i obshchestvennye iskaniia*,
   Paris, 1929, 53–55.
14 Venturi, 498–9; B.P. Koz'min
   (ed.), *Dolgushintsy*, Moscow, 1931,
   205ff.; N. Flerovskii, *Tri
   politicheskie sistemy*, London, 1897,
   297–298.

15 O.V. Aptekman, *Obshchestvo
   'Zemlia i Volia' 70-kh godov po
   lichnym vospominaniiam*, Petrograd,
   1924, 90.
16 ' "Ispoved" ' V.I. Kel'sieva',
   Literaturnoe nasledstvo, vol. 41–42
   (1941), 297–335.
17 Venturi, chapter 19.
18 Aptekman, 73–4, 133.
19 V. Debagorii-Mokrievich,
   Vospominaniia, SPB, 1904, 132–3,
   139–40.
20 A.I. Ivanchin-Pisarev, *Khozhdenie v
   narod*, Moscow-Leningrad, 1929,
   22–29.
21 Daniel Field, 'Peasants and
   propagandists in the Russian
   movement to the people of 1874',
   Journal of Modern History, vol. 59
   (1987), 415–438.
22 Aptekman, 152.
23 Vera Figner, *Zapechatlennyi trud*,
   Moscow: Mysl', 1964, vol.1, 154–5.
24 Aptekman, 168–177.
25 Figner, 162.
26 ibid., 164–5.
27 Debagorii-Mokrievich, 136–9;
   Figner, 169.
28 Debagorii-Mokrievich, 277–282.
29 Figner, 165–8.
30 N.A. Charushin, *O dalekom
   proshlom: iz vospominanii o
   revoliutsionnom dvizhenii 70-kh
   godov 19-ogo veka*, Moscow: Mysl',
   1973, 232.
31 Deborah Hardy, *Land and Freedom:
   the origins of Russian terrorism,
   1876–1879*, Westport,
   Connecticut: Greenwood Press,
   1987, 116.
32 A.S. Suvorin, *Dnevnik*, Moscow-
   Petrograd, 1923, 15–16.
33 S.S. Tatishchev, *Imperator
   Aleksandr II: ego zhizn' i
   tsarstvovanie*, SPB, 1903, vol.2, 606.
34 S.S. Volk, *Narodnaia volia,
   1879–1882*, Moscow: Nauka, 1966,
   85–99; S.S. Volk (ed.),
   Revoliutsionnoe narodnichestvo 70-

kh godov XIX veka, Moscow-Leningrad: Nauka, 1965, vol.2, 42, 170 174.

35 Venturi, 656.

36 P.A. Zaionchkovskii, *Krizis samoderzhaviia*, 400–410.

37 Norman M. Naimark, *Terrorists and Social Democrats: the Russian revolutionary movement under Alexander III*, Harvard University Press, 1983, 53–59.

38 Viktor Chernov, *Zapiski sotsialista-revoliutsionera*, vol. 1, Berlin, 1922, chapter 8.

39 Manfred Hildermeier, *Die Sozialrevolutionäre Partei Russlands: Agrarsozialismus und Modernisierung im Zarenreich (1900–1914)*, Köln/Wien: Böhlau Verlag, 1978, 58–68; Anna Geifman, *Thou Shalt Kill: revolutionary terrorism in Russia, 1894–1917*, Princeton University Press, 1993, 46–50.

40 Figures in Geifman, 20–21.

41 Geifman, 232–236; Nurit Schleifman, *Undercover Agents in the Russian Revolutionary Movement: the SR Party, 1902–1914*, London: Macmillan, 1988, ix-xi, 82–87, 107–111.

42 J.L.H. Keep, *The Rise of Social Democracy in Russia*, Oxford: Clarendon Press, 1963, 15–24.

43 Richard Pipes, '*Narodnichestvo*: a semantic enquiry', *Slavic Review*, vol. 23(1964), 441–458; Robert Service, 'Russian Populism and Russian Marxism: two skeins entangled', in Roger Bartlett (ed.), *Russian Thought and Society, 1800–1917: essays in honour of Eugene Lampert*, Keele, 1984, 220–246.

44 Richard Pipes, *Social Democracy and the St Petersburg Labour Movement, 1885–1897*, Harvard University Press, 1963; Allan Wildman, *The Making of a Workers' Revolution:*

Russian Social Democracy, 1891–1903, University of Chicago Press, 1967. These two books have different emphases, Pipes maintaining that 'agitation' and strike activity wrecked a viable workers' education movement and budding trade unions, while Wildman holds that the workers profited by Social Democratic techniques even while not sharing the intellectuals' ultimate aims.

45 Nikolai Valentinov, *The Early Years of Lenin*, Ann Arbor: University of Michigan Press, 1969, 135–6.

46 Valentinov, 194–6.

47 V.I. Lenin, *What is to be Done?* (edited by Robert Service), Harmondsworth: Penguin Books, 1988, 98, 107, 185–186.

48 Robert Service, *Lenin: a political life*, vol.1, London: Macmillan, 1985, 100–105.

49 This view of Lenin is most fully expounded in Rolf H.W. Theen, *Lenin: genesis and development of a revolutionary*, London: Quartet Books, 1974.

50 *Russian Thought and Society*, 221.

3   *Russification*

1 F.I. Tiutchev, *Lirika*, Moscow: Nauka, 1965, vol. 2, 118.

2 N.Ia. Danilevskii, *Rossiia i Evropa*, New York: Johnson Reprint, 1966, 537, 556–557.

3 Hans Kohn, *Panslavism: its history and ideology*, New York: Vintage Books, 1960, 179–180; see also I.S. Aksakov's leading article in *Moskva*, 18 November 1867, in his *Sochineniia*, vol. 5, Moscow, 1887, 163–5, 173–8.

4 Kohn, 178–9.

5 Kohn, 184–6.

6 B.H. Sumner, *Russia and the Balkans, 1870–1880*, Oxford, 1937, 183–195; Alfred J. Rieber,

Merchants and Entrepreneurs in Imperial Russia, Chapel Hill: University of North Carolina Press, 1982, 171–177, 210–213.

7 I.S. Aksakov, *Sochineniia*, vol. 1, Moscow 1886, 271.

8 A.V. Buganov, *Russkaia istoriia . . .* 179.

9 A.I. Engel'gardt, *Iz derevni: 12 pisem, 1872–1887*, Moscow, 1960, 231–236.

10 Hans Rogger, 'The Skobelev phenomenon', *Oxford Slavonic Papers*, no.9 (1976), 46–78.

11 *Sochineniia*, vol. 1, Moscow, 1886, 303.

12 Zaionchkovskii, 451–460.

13 *Pis'ma K.P. Pobedonostseva k Aleksandru III*, vol. 1, 381, quoted in Zaionchkovskii, 465.

14 Zaionchkovskii, 469.

15 V.A. Tvardovskaia, *Ideologiia poreformennogo samoderzhaviia*, Moscow: Nauka, 1978, 16–19.

16 Martin Katz, *Mikhail N. Katkov: a political biography, 1818–1887*, The Hague: Mouton, 1966, 83.

17 *Russkii vestnik*, 2/1863, quoted in Tvardovskaia, 26.

18 M.N. Katkov, *Sobranie peredovykh statei Moskovskikh Vedomostei 1867g*, Moscow, 1897, 265.

19 M.N. Katkov, *1863 god: sobranie statei po pol'skomu voprosu*, Moscow, 1887, vol. 1, 100–101.

20 Katkov, *Sobranie. . . 1867g*, 266–7.

21 Norman Davies, *God's Playground: a history of Poland*, Oxford: Clarendon Press, 1981, vol.2, 364–365. Not all Russian statesmen thought it advisable to humiliate the Polish nobility: see Adam Michnik, '1863: Poland in Russian eyes', in his *Letters from Prison and other essays*, Berkeley: University of California Press, 1985, 249–274.

22 M.K. Dziewanowski, 'The Polish revolutionary movement and Russia, 1904–7', *Harvard Slavic Studies*, vol.4 (1957), 375–394.

23 Lemke, *Epokha tsenzurnykh reform, 1859–1865*, SPB, 1904, 303.

24 David Saunders, 'Russia and Ukraine under Alexander II: the Valuev edict of 1863', *International History Review*, vol.57 (1995), 31; see also David Saunders, 'Russia's Ukrainian policy (1847–1905): a demographic approach', *European History Quarterly*, vol.25 (1995), 181–208, quotation on p. 187.

25 Bohdan Krawchenko, *Social Change and National Consciousness in Twentieth Century Ukraine*, London: Macmillan, 1985, chapter 1.

26 John H. Wuorinen, *A History of Finland*, New York & London: Columbia University Press, 1965, chapter 6; Edward C. Thaden, *Russification in the Baltic Provinces and Finland*, Princeton University Press, 1981, 30–32.

27 D.G. Kirby (ed.), *Russia and Finland, 1808–1920: from autonomy to independence*, London: Macmillan, 1975, 70–74.

28 Thaden, 76–83; Kirby, 76–81; Fred Singleton, *A Short History of Finland*, Cambridge University Press, 1989, 96–99.

29 M. Hroch, *Social Pre-conditions of National Revival in Europe*, Cambridge University Press, 1985, chapter 10, shows how an elite nationalist movement, consisting mainly of officials, clergy and professional people, was ready by the 1890s to carry its message to the rural masses.

30 Michael Futrell, *Northern Underground: episodes of Russian revolutionary transport and communications through Scandinavia and Finland, 1863–1917*, London: Faber & Faber, 1963, chapter 4.

31 Gert von Pistohlkors, *Deutsche*

*Geschichte im Osten Europas:
Baltische Länder*, Siedler Verlag,
1994, 382.

32 B.E. Nol'de, *Iurii Samarin i ego
vremia*, Paris, 1926, 48.

33 Leading article in *Den'*, 2 June
1862, *Sochineniia I.S. Aksakova*, vol.
6, Moscow, 1887, 6. (He asserts
something very similar about the
Jews on p 8.)

34 Thaden, 67–69; Pistohlkors,
397–416.

35 A. Ascher, *The Revolution of 1905:
Russia in disarray*, Stanford
University Press, 1988, 94.

36 Ascher, 159–160; Toivo U. Raun,
'The revolution of 1905 in the
Baltic provinces and Finland',
Slavic Review, 1984, no. 3,
453–467.

37 C. Leonard Lundin, 'The road
from Tsar to Kaiser: changing
loyalties of the Baltic Germans,
1905–1914', *Journal of Central
European Affairs*, vol. 10 (1950),
222–254.

38 Ronald Grigor Suny, *The Making
of the Georgian Nation*, London:
I.B. Tauris, 1988, chapters 5–7.

39 Ronald Grigor Suny, *Looking
toward Ararat: Armenia in modern
history*, Bloomington &
Indianapolis: Indiana University
Press, 1993, 39.

40 Suny, Ararat, 40, 45.

41 Christopher J. Walker, *Armenia:
the survival of a nation*, London:
Croom Helm, 1980, 67–71,
126–131; R.G. Suny, 'Populism,
nationalism and Marxism: the
origins of revolutionary parties
among the Armenians of the
Caucasus', *Armenian Review*, vol. 32,
no. 2 (June 1979), 134–151.

42 See the report of Count
Vorontsov-Dashkov to Stolypin in
Krasnyi Arkhiv, vol. 34 (1929),
202–218.

43 'Bor'ba s revoliutsionnym

dvizheniem na Kavkaze', *Krasnyi
Arkhiv*, vol. 34 (1929), 208–9.

44 Ibid., 187–202.

45 Tadeusz Swietochowski, *Russian
Azerbaijan, 1905–1920: the shaping
of national identity in a Muslim
community*, Cambridge University
Press, 1985, chapters 1–2.

46 Richard A. Pierce, *Russian Central
Asia, 1867–1917: a study in colonial
rule*, Berkeley: University of
California Press, 1960, chapters 7,
14.

47 On Brafman and his book, see
Louis Greenberg, *The Jews in
Russia: the struggle for emancipation*,
New York: Schocken Books, 1976,
vol. 1, 93–6.

48 Leading article in *Rus'*, 10 October
1881, *Sochineniia*, vol. 3, Moscow,
1886, 749–750.

49 ibid, 751–2.

50 See the remarks of Aksakov's
biographer: Stephen Lukashevich,
Ivan Aksakov, 1823–1886, Harvard
University Press, 1965, 167–8.

51 Zaionchkovskii, *Krizis
samoderzhaviia*, 338. In this
memorandum Ignat'ev persistently
uses the colloquial and derogatory
word *zhid* for Jew.

52 E.A. Peretts, *Dnevnik
gosudarstvennogo sekretaria,
1880–1882*, Moscow, 1937,
130–133.

53 Greenberg, vol. 2, 30–47.

54 Heinz-Dietrich Löwe, *The Tsars
and the Jews: reform, reaction, and
anti-Semitism in Imperial Russia,
1772–1917*, Chur: Harwood
Academic Publishers, 1993,
chapter 6.

55 S. Nilus, *Bliz griadushchii
Antikhrist*, Moscow, 1911; Norman
Cohn, *Warrant for Genocide: the
myth of the Jewish world conspiracy and
the 'Protocols of the Elders of Zion'*,
London: Eyre & Spottiswoode,
1967.

56 Hans Rogger, 'Conclusion and overview', in John Klier & Shlomo Lambroza (eds), *Pogroms: anti-Jewish violence in modern Russian history*, Cambridge University Press, 1992, 344.

57 Shlomo Lambroza, 'The pogroms of 1903–6', in Klier & Lambroza, 195–207.

58 Don C. Rawson, *Russian Rightists and the Revolution of 1905*, Cambridge University Press, 1995, chapter 5.

59 Lambroza, 205.

60 'Perepiska Nikolaia II i Marii Fedorovny (1905–6)', *Krasnyi arkhiv*, vol.22 (1927), 169.

61 The comparison is made by Hans Rogger in Klier & Lambroza, 361.

4   The Revolution of 1905–7

1 N.M. Pirumova, *Zemskaia intelligentsiia i ee rol' v obshchestvennoi bor'be*, Moscow: Nauka, 1986, 174–176.

2 Richard Pipes, *The Russian Revolution, 1899–1919*, London: Collins Harvill, 1990, 5–8; Samuel Kassow, *Students, Professors and The State in Tsarist Russia*, Berkeley: University of California Press, 1989, 88–104.

3 For example, the 10th congress of scientists and doctors in St Petersburg 1901: I.P. Belokonskii, *Zemstvo i konstitutsiia*, Moscow, 1910, 74.

4 George Fischer, *Russian Liberalism from Gentry to Intelligentsia*, Harvard University Press, 1958, 139–148.

5 P.N. Miliukov, *Vospominaniia*, New York: Chekhov Press, 1955, vol. 1, 241–247.

6 L. Martov, P. Maslov, A. Potresov (eds), *Obshchestvennoe dvizhenie v Rossii v nachale XX veka*, SPB, 1909, vol. 2, part 2, 170–183.

7 Terence Emmons, *The Formation of Political Parties and the First National Elections in Russia*, Harvard University Press, 1983, 41–44, 55–58.

8 Ernst Birth, *Die Oktobristen (1905–1913): Zielvorstellungen und Struktur*, Stuttgart: Ernst Klett Verlag, 1974, 93–106.

9 Eugen Weber, *Peasants into Frenchmen: the modernisation of rural France, 1870–1914*, London: Chatto & Windus, 1979.

10 A.G. Rashin, 'Gramotnost' i narodnoe obrazovanie v Rossii v XIX i nachale XX vekov', *Istoricheskie zapiski*, no.37 (1951), 34, 45, 49.

11 Gerald Surh, *1905 in St Petersburg: labour, society and revolution*, Stanford University Press, 1989, 11–12; R.E. Johnson, *Peasant and Proletarian: the working-class of Moscow in the late nineteenth century*, Leicester University Press, 1979, 31.

12 Johnson, 87–92.

13 Tim McDaniel, *Autocracy, Capitalism and Revolution in Russia*, Berkeley: University of California Press, 1988, chapter 8.

14 Daniel Brower, 'Labor violence in Russia in the late nineteenth century', *Slavic Review*, vol.41 (1982), 417–431.

15 McDaniel, chapter 7.

16 Allan Wildman, *The Making of a Workers' Revolution: Russian Social Democracy, 1891–1903*, University of Chicago Press, 1967, 252; the same point is made more forcefully in Richard Pipes, *Social Democracy and the St Petersburg Labour Movement, 1885–1897*, Harvard University Press, 1963.

17 Jeremiah Schneiderman, *Sergei Zubatov and Revolutionary Marxism,*

Ithaca, New York: Cornell University Press, 1976, 95–8.

18 Schneiderman, 128–135.

19 Italics in original: Walter Sablinsky, *The Road to Bloody Sunday: Father Gapon and the St Petersburg massacre of 1905*, Princeton University Press, 1976, 85, 89–90.

20 *Nachalo pervoi russkoi revoliutsii: ianvar'-mart 1905g*, Moscow, 1955, 16–18.

21 Sablinsky, 344–9.

22 Surh, 161–2.

23 Aleksei Buzinov, *Za nevskoi zastavoi*, Moscow-Leningrad, 1930, 41.

24 Victoria Bonnell, *Roots of Rebellion: workers' politics and organisations in St Petersburg and Moscow, 1900–1914*, Berkeley: University of California Press, 1983, 110–117.

25 *Obshchestvennoe dvizhenie*, vol.2, part 1, 200–226.

26 Keep, *Rise of Social Democracy*, 165–177; Bonnell, 116–117.

27 Ascher, vol. 1, 211–217.

28 Keep, 228–230.

29 Oskar Anweiler, *The Soviets: the Russian workers, peasants and soldiers councils, 1905–1921*, New York: Pantheon Books, 1974, 40–43, 51–55; the formation of the St Petersburg Soviet is described in W.S. Woytinsky, *Stormy Passage*, New York: Vanguard Press, 1961, 36–7.

30 Leon Trotsky, *1905*, Harmondsworth: Penguin Books, 1973, 124.

31 Surh, 337–341.

32 Surh, 348; Woytinsky, 44–5.

33 V. Zenzinov, *Perezhitoe*, New York, 1953, 225.

34 Ascher, vol. 1, 170–174.

35 *Obshchestvennoe dvizhenie*, vol. 2, part 1, 166–174; John Bushnell, *Mutiny amid Repression: Russian soldiers in the revolution of 1905–6*, Bloomington: Indiana University Press, 1985, 88–89.

36 Bushnell, 230.

37 G.G. Savich, *Novyi gosudarstvennyi stroi*, St Petersburg, 1907, 12.

38 Ben Eklof, *Russian Peasant Schools: officialdom, village culture and popular pedagogy, 1861–1914*, Berkeley: University of California Press, 1986, 245–247.

39 P.P. Maslov, *Agrarnyi vopros v Rossii*, vol. 2, St Petersburg, 1908, 206–7.

40 François-Xavier Coquin, 'Un aspect méconnu de la révolution de 1905: les "motions paysannes"', in F-X. Coquin & C. Gervais-Francelle (eds), *1905: la première révolution russe*, Paris: Publications de la Sorbonne et de l'Institut d'études Slaves, 1986, 193–194.

41 L.T. Senchakova, *Prigovory i nakazy rossiiskogo krest'ianstva 1905–1907gg: po materialam tsentral'nykh gubernii*, Moscow: Institut rossiiskoi istorii, 1994, vol.1, 132–138.

42 Senchakova, vol.1, 153–156.

43 ibid., vol.1, 196.

44 Senchakov, vol. 2, 243.

45 ibid., 250–256.

46 Coquin, 181–202.

47 Maureen Perrie, 'The Russian peasant movement of 1905–7', *Past and Present*, vol. 57 (1972), 123–155.

48 A. Shestakov, *Krest'ianskaia revoliutsiia 1905–7gg*, Moscow-Leningrad, 1926, 26–7.

49 Shestakov, 26–32; Theodor Shanin, *Russia, 1905–7: revolution as a moment of truth*, London: Macmillan, 1986, 83–4.

50 Shanin, 94–98.

51 M. Simonova, 'Krest'ianskoe dvizhenie 1905–7gg v sovetskoi istoriografii', *Istoricheskie zapiski*, no. 95 (1975), 214–215.

52 *Obshchestvennoe dvizhenie*, vol 2, part 1, 119–120.

53 Shanin, 96–8.

54 Shestakov, 38–9; Shanin, 101.

55 Shanin, vol. 2, 92; E.I. Kiriukhina, 'Vserossiiskii krest'ianskii soiuz v 1905g' *Istoricheskie zapiski*, no.50 (1955), 97–8.

56 Kiriukhina, 103, 134; P. Maslov, 'Krest'ianskoe dvizhenie v 1905–7gg', in Martov *Obshchestvennoe dvizhenie*, vol.2, et al, part 2, 236–7.

57 Maureen Perrie, *The Agrarian Policy of the Russian Socialist Revolutionary Party from its Origins to the Revolution of 1905–7*, Cambridge University Press, 1976, 108–110.

58 Perrie, loc. cit.; Shanin, vol.2, 94.

59 Shanin, vol. 2, 117.

60 Woytinsky, 99.

61 Emmons, 241–265.

5   The Duma Monarchy

1 Quoted in Abraham Ascher, *The Revolution of 1905*, vol. 2, *Authority restored*, Stanford University Press, 1992, 83.

2 Miliukov, *Vospominaniia*, 320–323.

3 G.A. Hosking, *The Russian Constitutional Experiment: Government and Duma, 1907–1914*, Cambridge University Press, 1973, 10.

4 Hosking and Manning, 'What was the United Nobility?' in L. Haimson (ed.), *Politics of Rural Russia*, Bloomington: Indiana University Press, 1979, 142–183.

5 Andrew M. Verner, *The Crisis of Russian Autocracy: Nicholas II and the 1905 revolution*, Princeton University Press, 1990, 286.

6 Peasant voting is described in Emmons, 241–253.

7 Woytinsky, 98ff.

8 L.T. Senchakova, vol. 2, 245.

9 Emmons, 356–357; S. M. Sidel'nikov, *Obrazovanie i deiatel'nost' pervoi gosudarstvennoi dumy*, Moscow: 1962, 191–199.

10 *Gosudarstvennaia Duma: stenograficheskie otchety* (henceforth GDSO), I, i, 74–76, 239–241.

11 Dominic Lieven, *Nicholas II: Emperor of all the Russias*, London: John Murray, 1993, 153.

12 Hosking, 59–62.

13 GDSO, I, i, 321–4.

14 Ascher, vol.2, 201–209; Miliukov recalls in his memoirs that during the Second Duma he was prepared at Stolypin's request to write a newspaper article condemning terror, in return for a promise to legalize the party. However, Petrunkevich, the party chairman, dissuaded him: 'Better to sacrifice the party than destroy it morally!' Miliukov, *Vospominaniia*, 430–431.

15 See the excellent portrait of Stolypin in Roberta Thompson Manning, *The Crisis of the Old Order in Russia: gentry and government*, Princeton University Press, 1982, 260–272.

16 Dorothy Atkinson, *The End of the Russian Land Commune, 1905–1930*, Stanford University Press, 1983, 57–59.

17 Atkinson, 61–70.

18 Alfred Levin, *The Second Duma*, New Haven: Yale University Press, 1940, 67.

19 Hosking, 33.

20 P.A. Tverskoi, 'K istoricheskim materialam o pokoinom P.A. Stolypine', *Vestnik Evropy*, vol.47 (1912), no.4, 186.

21 Hosking, chapter 6.

22 For an analysis of the new electoral law, see Alfred Levin, *The Third Duma: election and profile*, Hamden, Connecticut: Archon Books, 1973, 3–6. Whole areas of Muslim

Central Asia were excluded from the franchise altogether.

23 Levin, loc. cit., chapters 10 11.

24 W.E. Mosse, 'Stolypin's villages', *Slavonic and East European Review*, vol.23 (1965), 257–274; Judith Pallot, 'Open fields and individual farms: land reforms in pre-revolutionary Russia', *Tijdschrift voor economische en sociale geografie*, vol. 75 (1984), 46–60.

25 Atkinson, 89–91.

26 Atkinson, 75–84; E.M. Kayden & A.N. Antsiferov, *The Cooperative Movement in Russia during the War*, New Haven: Yale University Press, 1929, 14.

27 Atkinson, 74–5; Judith Pallot, 'Did the Stolypin land reform destroy the peasant commune?', in R.B. McKean (ed.), *New Perspectives in Modern Russian History*, London: Macmillan, 1992, 117–132.

28 George L. Yaney, 'The concept of the Stolypin land reform', *Slavic Review*, vol.23 (1964), 275–293.

29 GDSO, III, 3, part 4, cols 1957–8.

30 Hosking, 116–134.

31 For a careful examination of Stolypin's murder, see Pipes, *The Russian Revolution, 187–191*.

32 GDSO, III, 1, part 1, cols 311–312.

33 Lieven, 107.

34 S.S. Oldenburg, *The Last Tsar*, vol. 2, *Years of Change, 1900–1907*, Gulf Breeze, Florida: Academic International Press, 1977, 49–50.

35 G. Freeze, 'Tserkov', religiia i politicheskaia kul'tura na zakate starogo rezhima', *Reforma ili revoliutsiia? Rossiia, 1861–1917*, SPB: Nauka, 1992, 32–35.

36 Lieven, 167.

37 V.I. Rodzianko, 'Krushenie imperii: zapiski predsedatelia Russkoi Gosudarstvennoi Dumy', *Arkiv Russkoi Revoliutsii*, vol. 17, Berlin, 1926, 37–8.

38 See its statutes in A. Chernovskii (ed.), *Soiuz russkogo naroda*, Moscow-Leningrad, 1929, 411–412.

39 S.A. Stepanov, *Chernaia sotnia v Rossii, 1905–1907*, Moscow: Rosvuznauka, 1992, 95–101.

40 Don C. Rawson, *Russian Rightists and the Revolution of 1905*, Cambridge University Press, 1995, chapter 11.

41 Hans Rogger, *Jewish Policies and Right-Wing Politics in Imperial Russia*, Berkeley: University of California Press, 1986, 225–228.

42 Rogger, 225–226; *Modern Encyclopedia of Russian and Soviet History*, vol. 14, 146–149; see one of Iliodor's letters in *The Mad Monk of Russia: Iliodor*, New York, 1918, 38–40.

43 GDSO, Sessiia 9 (1913–14), cols 2297–2302.

44 Hosking, 177–179.

45 Heinz-Dietrich Löwe, *The Tsars and the Jews*.

46 Hosking, 69–71; Joachim von Puttkamer, 'Die Vertretung der Bauernschaft in der dritten Duma and ihr Beitrag zur Debatte über die Stolypinschen Agrarreformen', *Jahrbücher für Geschichte Osteuropas*, vol. 41 (1993), 63–67.

47 Bonnell, 195–209; 260–262; 312–315.

48 Bonnell, chapter 8.

49 Bonnell, chapter 10; Leopold H. Haimson, 'Labor unrest in Imperial Russia on the eve of the first world war', in Leopold Haimson & Charles Tilly (eds), *Strikes, Wars and Revolutions in International Perspective*, Cambridge University Press, 1989, 500–511.

50 Quoted in S.A. Smith, 'Workers and civil rights, 1899–1917', in Olga Crisp & Linda Edmondson (eds), *Civil Rights in Imperial Russia*,

Oxford: Clarendon Press, 1989, 163.

51 Manfred Hagen, *Die Entfaltung politischer Öffentlichkeit in Russland, 1906–1914*, Wiesbaden: Steiner Verlag, 1982, 144–149; Louise McReynolds, *The News under Russia's Old Regime: the development of a mass-circulation press*, Princeton University Press, 1991, 225–6.

52 Hagen, 102–122; Benjamin Rigberg, 'The efficacy of tsarist censorship operations, 1894–1917', *Jahrbücher für Geschichte Osteuropas*, vol.14 (1966), 327–346; Caspar Ferenczi, 'Freedom of the press under the old regime, 1905–1914', in Crisp & Edmondson, 191–214.

53 Hosking, 211–212.

54 Having spent many months in Russian libraries reading the newspapers of 1907–14, I can personally testify to this.

55 McReynolds, chapter 10.

56 Richard Pipes, *Struve: Liberal on the Right, 1905–1944*, Harvard University Press, 1980, especially 81–5; *Vekhi: sbornik statei o russkoi intelligentsii*, Moscow, 1909 (reprinted Frankfurt-am-Main: Posev, 1967), 157–158.

57 *Vekhi*, 141, 144.

58 *Vekhi*, 30, 36.

59 *Vekhi*, 169.

60 P.B. Struve, 'Velikaia Rossiia', *Patriotica: sbornik statei za piat' let, 1905–10gg*, St Petersburg, 1911, 93–94.

61 J.F. Hutchinson, 'The Octobrists and the future of Imperial Russia as a great power', *Slavonic and East European Review*, vol.50 (1972), 220–237.

62 The reference, of coure, os to Chekhov's play *The Cherry Orchard*. P.A. Berlin, *Russkaia burzhuaziia v staroe i novoe vremia*, Moscow, 1922, 286–293; V.Ia. Laverychev, *Po tu storonu barrikad: iz istorii bor'by moskovskoi burzhuazii s revoliutsiei*, Moscow: Mysl', 1967, 78–95.

63 Berlin, 295.

64 Leopold Haimson, 'The problem of social stability in urban Russia, 1905–1917', *Slavic Review*, vol.23 (1964), 619–642; vol.24 (1965), 1–22.

65 Lewis Siegelbaum, *The Politics of Industrial Mobilization in Russia, 1914–1917: a study of the War Industries Committees*, London: Macmillan, 1983, chapter 3.

66 Frank A. Golder, *Documents of Russian History, 1914–1917*, Gloucester, Massachusetts: P. Smith, 1964, 134–136; Michael F. Hamm, 'Liberal politics in wartime Russia: an analysis of the Progressive Bloc', *Slavic Review*, vol.33 (1974), 453–456.

67 Thomas Fallows, 'Politics and the war effort in Russia: the Union of Zemstvos and the organisation of the food supply, 1914–1916', *Slavic Review*, vol.37 (1978), 70–90: quotation on p. 82.

68 R. Pearson, *Russian Moderates and the Crisis of Tsarism, 1914–1917*, London: Macmillan, 1977, 115.

6 The Revolution of 1917

1 R.P. Browder & A.F. Kerenskii, *The Russian Provisional Government, 1917: documents*, Stanford University Press, 1961, vol.2, 722, 731–2; the consequences of this outlook are well exposed in Leonard Schapiro, 'The political thought of the first Provisional Government', in Richard Pipes (ed.), *Revolutionary Russia*, Harvard University Press, 1968, 97–113.

2 A.G. Shliapnikov, *Semnadtsatyi god*, Moscow: Respublika, 1994, vol.3, 176–177.

3 William Rosenberg, *Liberals in the*

Russian Revolution: the Constitutional Democratic Party, 1917–1921, Princeton University Press, 1974.

4 Quoted in N.N. Golovin, *Voennye usiliia Rossii v mirovoi voine*, Paris, 1939, 120–1.

5 ibid., 124.

6 Robert J. Kaiser, *The Geography of Nationalism in Russia and the USSR*, Princeton University Press, 1994, especially pp. 83–87.

7 Allan Wildman, *The End of the Russian Imperial Army: the old army and the soldiers' revolt, March–April 1917*, Princeton University Press, 1980, 116–117.

8 ibid., chapter 5.

9 ibid., 197–8.

10 Fedor Stepun, *Byvshee i nesbyvsheesia*, New York: Chekhov Press, 1956, vol.2, 10–11.

11 'Iz ofitserskikh pisem s fronta v 1917g', *Krasnyi Arkhiv*, vol.50, 200.

12 Wildman, vol.2, 92.

13 George Katkov, *The Kornilov Affair: Kerensky and the break-up of the Russian Army*, London: Longman, 1980.

14 Wildman, vol.2, 238.

15 Oskar Anweiler, *The Soviets: the Russian workers', peasants' and soldiers' councils, 1905–1921*, New York: Pantheon Books, 1975, 103–6.

16 P.V. Volobuev, *Petrogradskii sovet rabochikh i soldatskikh deputatov v 1917g*, Leningrad: Nauka, 1991, vol. 1, 59.

17 Marc Ferro, *October 1917: a social history of the Russian revolution*, London: Routledge, 1980, 190–192.

18 N.N. Sukhanov, *Zapiski o revoliutsii*, Moscow: Izdatel'stvo Politicheskoi Literatury, 1991, vol. 1, 116.

19 For a positive view of the soviets, see Israel Getzler, 'Soviets as agents of democratisation', in Edith Rogovin Frankel, Jonathan Frankel and Baruch Knei-Paz (eds), *Revolution in Russia: reassessments of 1917*, Cambridge University Press, 1992, 17–33.

20 Anweiler, 113–116.

21 David Mandel, *The Petrograd Workers and the Fall of the Old Regime*, London: Macmillan, 1983, vol. 1, 100; S.A. Smith, *Red Petrograd: revolution in the factories, 1917–1918*, Cambridge University Press, 1983, 54–65. Factory committees were salient and increasingly radical in other cities too: see Diane Koenker, *Moscow Workers and the 1917 Revolution*, Princeton University Press, 1981, chapter 4.

22 Mandel, vol. 1, 97.

23 Mandel, vol. 1, 149–50.

24 See the views of the relatively moderate industrialist, P.P. Riabushinskii, quoted in Mandel, vol. 1, 139.

25 Browder & Kerenskii, vol. 2, 731–732.

26 John L.H. Keep, *The Russian Revolution: a study in mass mobilization*, London: Weidenfeld & Nicolson, 1976, 83–4.

27 Mandel, vol. 1, 118.

28 Alexander Rabinowitch, *Prelude to Revolution: the Petrograd Bolsheviks and the July uprising*, Bloomington: Indiana University Press, 1968, chapters 5–6.

29 Keep, 93.

30 Rex A. Wade, 'The Red Guards: spontaneity and the October revolution', in Frankel *et al.*, *Reassessments of 1917*, 54–75.

31 V.V. Kabanov, 'Oktiabr'skaia revoliutsiia i krest'ianskaia obshchina', *Istoricheskie zapiski*, no.100 (1984), 106–110; Orlando Figes, *Peasant Russia, Civil War: the*

Volga countryside in revolution,
1917–21, Oxford: Clarendon
Press, 1989, 32–46.

32 S.P. Rudnev, *Pri vechernikh*
ogniakh, Newtonville,
Massachusetts: Oriental Research
Partners, 1978 (reprint of Kharbin
1928 edition), 85; V.I. Kostrikin,
Zemel'nye komitety v 1917g,
Moscow: Nauka, 1975, 19–21.

33 Kostrikin, 144–8.

34 Figes, 42.

35 Prince S.E. Trubetskoi, *Minuvshee,*
Moscow: DEM, 1991, 170.

36 E.A. Lutskii, 'Krest'ianskie nakazy
1917g o zemle', *Istochnikovedenie*
istorii sovetskogo obschestva, vypusk 2,
Moscow, 1968, 124.

37 Figes, 41–2.

38 *Revoliutsionnoe dvizhenie v mae-iiune*
1917g: iiun'skaia demonstratsiia,
Moscow, 1959, 397–398.

39 Browder and Kerenskii, vol.2,
597–598.

40 ibid., 558–563.

41 A.D. Maliavskii, *Krest'ianskoe*
dvizhenie v Rossii v 1917g, mart-
oktiabr, Moscow: Nauka, 1981,
chapters 2–3; Graeme Gill, *Peasants*
and Government in the Russian
Revolution, London: Macmillan,
1979.

42 Maureen Perrie, 'The Peasants', in
Robert Service (ed.), *Society and*
Politics in the Russian Revolution,
London: Macmillan, 1992, 14.

43 Kabanov, 114.

44 Figes' generalizing summary from
the numerous cases he examined in
the mid-Volga region: *Peasant*
Russia, 52–3, 56.

45 Kabanov, 125–126; John
Channon, 'The peasantry in the
revolutions of 1917', in Frankel
et al, Reassessments of 1917, 119.

46 Figes, 53; Maliavskii, 343–6.

47 Kabanov, 126–129.

48 Maliavskii, 315–321; John

Channon, 'The Bolsheviks and the
peasantry: the land question during
the first eight months of Bolshevik
rule', *Slavonic & East European*
Review, vol. 66 (1988), 593–624.

49 Robert Service, *The Bolshevik Party*
in Revolution: a study in organisational
change, 1917–23, London:
Macmillan, 1979, chapter 2; John
Keep, 'October in the Provinces',
in Pipes, *Revolutionary Russia,*
180–223.

50 *Petrogradskii voenno-revoliutsionnyi*
komitet: dokumenty i materialy,
Moscow: Nauka, 1966, vol.1,
39–41.

51 Alexander Rabinowitch, *The*
Bolsheviks Come to Power, London:
NLB Books, 1979, chapters 14–15.

52 Oliver Radkey, *The Sickle under the*
Hammer: the Russian Socialist
Revolutionaries in the early months of
Bolshevik rule, New York: Columbia
University Press, 1963, chapter 3.

53 Harry Willetts, 'Lenin and the
peasants', in Leonard Schapiro &
Peter Reddaway (eds), *Lenin – the*
man, the theorist, the leader: a
reappraisal, London: Pall Mall,
1967, 223–224; Robert Service,
Lenin: a political life, vol. 2,
London: Macmillan, 1991,
235–237.

54 Figes, 209.

55 Paul Avrich, *Kronstadt 1921,*
Princeton University Press, 1970,
36, 43, 73–4; Oliver Radkey, *The*
Unknown Civil War in Soviet Russia:
a study of the green movement in the
Tambov region, 1920–1921,
Stanford: Hoover Institution Press,
1976, chapter 4.

Conclusions

1 S. Iu. Vitte, *Vospominaniia,* Moscow,
1960, vol.3, 274–275 (written in
1910).

Index